OUT OF THE UNKNOWN

Introduction

. . .

𝔚𝔦𝔱𝔠𝔥
(Neophite)

And what would you save me from, prince charming, my
reflection!

𝔍𝔞𝔠𝔨 𝔱𝔥𝔢 𝔤𝔦𝔞𝔫𝔱 𝔨𝔦𝔩𝔩𝔢𝔯

. . .

"Ambiguity"

. . .

I'm a liar!

. . .

Don't believe a word I say!

Anon

OUT OF THE UNKNOWN

(It's as if there is nothing more tangible than an unseen enemy)

It's very **probable** that there are more than one **species** that have their sights on earth, (*so to speak!*) Because like **Rome**: they are **conquerors** and **subdue** other **species** because they are **A-moral** and help us on their own terms!

Religions of **Gods** and **Devil's** are simple **metaphors** of a greater truth that seem or appear to have been lost in **translation**! Of nothing more than the remnants of **terrestrial** or **extraterrestrial** advanced cultures. Like in the cult TV show of the 70s **Dr Who** and the **Daemon's**.

'Energy can't be created or destroyed!'

Whoever or whatever is hiding has reduced its size until its practically invisible! **E=MC2!** So when you reduce matter the **'energy'** has to go somewhere! So when they **disappear** and **re-appear** are these mysterious individuals causing the strange weather problems in 411?

" How much less in them

That dwell in houses of clay whose foundation is in the dust

which are crushed before the moth "

Job

. . .

NIGHTMARE

(The Invaders)

When the leech eventually drops off you will not find **them** in their **counting houses** nor in our empty **treasury**. Neither under the **majesty** of an **empty-law** or **puppet figurehead**, the **watchers** who protect the **colony** will already have taken their **boxes** filled with **earth** to safety! Remember the **Vampire** cannot be killed, because it doesn't exist!

Invisible residents

From the seed of Belial came the **Vampire** *(Vampyr)* **Nosferatu** *which livith an feedeth on the blood of mankind an abideth unredeemed, in horrible darkness.*

Nosferatu

4

Che Guevara

(Initiative or volition and personal responsibility)

"Oriuntur mea ultor ex ossibus meis"

Arise my avenger out of my bones!

. . .

(My way)

"For what is a man what has he got, if not himself, than he has naught, to say the things he truly feels, and not the words of one who kneels"

. . .

'Who hated to see others suffer and was finally destroyed opposing it, a man who truly believed in the qualities of self-confidence, independence of spirit, daring and firmness of principle'

. . .

"The laws of capitalism, blind and invisible to the majority, act upon the individual without his thinking about it. He sees only the vastness of a seemingly infinite horizon before him. That is how it is painted by capitalist propagandists, who purport to draw a lesson from the example of **Rockefeller**—whether or not it is true—about the possibilities of success. The amount of poverty and suffering required for the emergence of a **Rockefeller**, and the amount of depravity that the accumulation of a fortune of such magnitude entails, are left out of the picture, and it is not always possible to make the people in general see this."

Guevara ended the essay by declaring that **"the true revolutionary is guided by a great feeling of love"** and beckoning on all revolutionaries to **"strive every day so that this love of living humanity will be transformed into acts that serve as examples"**, thus becoming **"a moving force"**. The genesis for **Guevara's** assertions relied on the fact that he believed the example of the **Cuban Revolution** was **"something spiritual that would transcend all borders"**.

The Three Musketeers

"This was my families chapel *Charlotte*, we took our vows here, I loved you *Charlotte* and I still love you, as I love war and drunkenness, love you as men love all that is worst for them.

Forgive me Robert? I swear before God and this holy place, but it was too late for *Charlotte!* For there, the executioner and axe man of Lille, mercy she cries! You cannot, mercy! How many times have you asked for mercy, and repaid it in blood? How many times have you taken men's love, pity and aspirations, their lives! What is in the essence of your evil? You understand goodness, we don't forgive you *Charlotte*, we can't, we do not dare…"

. . .

"When the hunter, becomes the hunted"

"An Eerie silence, and one native said: there's nothing there! And Charlton Heston said: "Something is there?" And it's not afraid of guns!"

The naked jungle

. . .

"When you have eliminated the impossible, whatever remains, however improbable, must be the solution"

Sherlock Holmes!

. . .

Devil's Advocate

(pro bono)

"In common parlance, a devil's advocate is someone who, given a certain argument, takes a position they do not necessarily agree with (or simply an alternative position from the accepted norm), for the sake of debate or to explore the thought further. In taking this position, the individual taking on the devil's advocate role seeks to engage others in an argumentative discussion process. The purpose of such a process is typically to test the quality of the original argument and identify weaknesses in its structure, and to use such information to either improve or abandon the original, opposing position. It can also refer to someone who takes a stance that is seen as unpopular or unconventional, but is actually another way of arguing a much more conventional stance."

Epistemological pluralism

"Or methodologies for determining what we know – a set of untold truths about the world"

A differential diagnosis (sometimes abbreviated is a systematic diagnostic method used to identify the presence of an **entity** where multiple alternatives are possible (and the process may be termed differential diagnostic procedure), and may also refer to any of the included candidate alternatives (or *candidate conditions*).

This method is essentially a process of elimination or at least of obtaining information that shrinks the **"probabilities"** of candidate conditions to negligible levels.

The **"probabilities"** at issue are **epistemic** rather than **ontological** in that they are imaginative parameters in the mind of the diagnostician (or, for **computerized** or **computer-assisted diagnosis**! The software of the system), while in reality the **target** *(such as whoever or whatever we are dealing with)* either has a condition or not with an actual probability of either 0 or 100%...

People who mysteriously Disappear!

(Fact)

"Are there things going on at large beyond our control by agencies unknown and unseen?"

Do Strangers walk among us?

. . .

What easier way to gain a world than through a superior race operating from within man's own species!

. . .

'Ask no questions and you will be told no lies'

In the strange case of Christopher Harvey 17 years, in MISSING 411 The Devil's in the detail. Page 78 Pagosa Springs, Colorado.

. . .

(Is there something going on under the radar that we should know about?) *Like in MISSING 411 WESTERN UNITED STATES & CANADA by David Paulides. And the case of Dickie Tum Suden aged 3 years 1945 CA. page 103.*

In the middle of the week of search efforts, **FBI** agents arrived at the search headquarters and appeared to monitor the activity. Joseph Suden asked if the **FBI** would join the search? But they declined. The press was interested to know why the **FBI** was at search headquarters if they were declining to participate? A November **6ᵗʰ 1945** article in the **News and Courier** included this statement about the **FBI**:

"The agents have declined to give their names or even admit they are interested in the case!"

. . .

"Let us briefly examine the more complex hierarchies of politics and government, during one of his lectures, professor Peter, I'm afraid that what I want to know is not answered by all my studying. I don't know if the world is run by smart men, how you Americans say, putting us on, or by imbeciles who really mean it."

The Peter Principle

. . .

The most feared eight words in the English language:
"I'm the government and I'm here to help"

Ronald Reagan

. . .

Big Horn Dam

*"By the pricking of my thumbs
something wicked this way comes"*

William Shakespeare

"A watcher in the woods"

(24ᵗʰ *August 1969.*)

A worker at the dam site noticed a dark figure in the distance high above him, it looked like a large man standing watching what was going on, the strange figure stayed there for a while, as well as sitting down part of the time, it then walked along the edge of the bank, before it eventually disappeared into the trees! By that time several other workers had noticed its presence, even though they had tried to catch its attention, it was to no avail, it had just ignored them.

The witnesses said it seemed or appeared too big for a man! So others went over to where the figure had been standing, in order to make a comparison of scale, using the smaller trees in the background, to gave the other workers a rough approximate of its size, it was estimated that the figure was at least **12ft** or **15ft high**, they found *no footprints!*

"Oh man of the worldly mind do you believe in me or not?"

Marley's Ghost

. . .

(Children of a lesser God.)

"For he is not a man as I am that we should come together, neither is there any that might lay his hand upon us both. Let him, therefore, take his rod away from me, and let not his fear terrify me."

Job x: 32-34

THE THING

(*From Another World!*)
Based on the story

"WHO GOES THERE?"

By
John W. CAMPBELL. JR.

. . .

"Gentlemen, we find ourselves in a battle" this creature is more powerful and intelligent; it regards us as important only for its nourishment. It has an attitude towards us, as we have towards a field of cabbages!"

. . .

"ARENA"

Is there something going on that we should know about? It like the movie: **"The Predator"** and that's why in 1969. Dennis Lloyd Martin aged 6

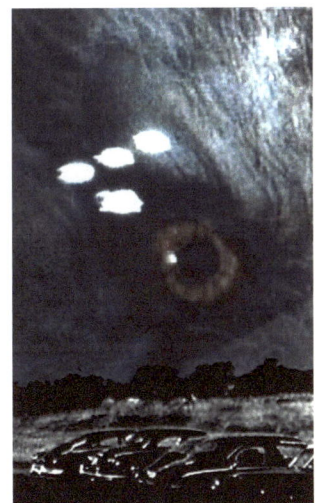

years. Who vanished mysteriously in Great Smoky Mountain National Park, in **David Paulides** book: **MISSING 411 EASTERN UNITED STATES page 136.**
Where Dennis's father may have accidentally or unintentionally let the cat out of the bag! By his own suspicions, implying that the head of the park service at Great Smokey Mountain was a mere **"figurehead"** and this is where the story gets even stranger, because the lead **"FBI"** agent in the Knoxville office was the late **"Jim-Rike"** who was heavily involved in the investigation of several disappearances of children in the Tennessee mountains around the time Dennis disappeared, mysteriously committed **"Suicide"** there is only one reason a person commits suicide is if their life has become pointless or they have found out something so incredible, that it becomes too much for their mind to cope with, or was he helped like the German: **Himmler**!

In the **Douglass Legg** case, **aged 8 years**, in **Newcomb**, **"New York"** in **1971, page 255, MISSING 411 EASTERN UNITED STATES.** A detachment of Green Beret's from Fort Devens, Massachusetts, were dispatched, who called the special forces? And on what revealing evidence was a special detachment of **"Green Berets"** utilized in the search? Just like in the case above of **"Dennis Lloyd Martin"** the *Special Forces* (**Green Berets**) had been dispatched from Fort Benning, Georgia. It's obvious that they were briefed, that they could be up against something unusual!

Like in the 60s cult TV show **"Star-Trek"** and the episode called **"The Galileo Seven"** when the shuttlecraft had accidentally crashed on a hostile planet and they had discovered that they were in among hostile giant hairy tribesmen!

And Dr McCoy or (Bones) was speaking to Spock, well Mrs Spock! They didn't stay frightened very long, did they? Most illogical reaction, Says Spock, when we demonstrated our superior weapons, they should have fled, McCoy, answer's, you mean they should have respected us? Mr Spock: of course, but respect is a rational process, did it ever occur that they might respond emotionally, with anger? Bones replied, and Mr Spock replies: I'm not responsible for their unpredictability, and (Bones) replies: they were perfectly predictable, to anyone with feeling, you might as well admit it, he says to Spock, your precious logic brought them down on us!

. . .

Remember, you don't **sh*t!** Where you **sleep** or you will end up with a war, against an unknown and very clever **species** on your own doorstep, a **faceless-enemy** that you will not be able to cope with!

. . .

One thing does not mean the other

It seems or appears that something tends to show a certain amount of tolerance by the presence of our unwanted intrusions into their sovereign territory, but it does not mean that they are weak! Even though they do not want us to see their faces! Or what they look like!

. . .

In the narrative
(An angel)

'I AM WHATSOEVER WAS, WHATSOEVEVER IS, WHATSOEVER SHALL BE AND THE VAIL WHICH IS OVER MY FACE, NO MORTAL HAND HAS EVER RAISED'
(Think about what is being described in this passage?)

Moses, who had been grazing Jethro's flocks there. When Moses starts to approach, God tells Moses to **take off his sandals first**! Due to the place being holy ground, and Moses hides his **face**. Textual scholars regard the account of the **burning bush** as being spliced together from the Jahwist and Elohist texts, with the Angel of Yahweh and **the removal of sandals** being part of the Elohist version, and the Yahwist's parallels to these being **God** and the turning away of Moses' face, respectively

When challenged on his identity, Yahweh replies that he is the God of the Patriarchs - Abraham, Isaac, and Jacob and that he is *Yahweh*. The text derives **Yahweh** from the Hebrew word **hayah** meaning **he who is he**, or **'I am that I am'** the Kabbalah takes this to mean that Yahweh himself is equal to his name.

The text portrays Yahweh as telling Moses that he is sending him to the Pharaoh in order to bring the Israelites out of Egypt, an action that Yahweh is described as having decided upon as a result of noticing that the Israelites were being oppressed by the Egyptians. Yahweh tells Moses to tell the **elders** of the **Israelites** that **Yahweh** would lead them into the land of the **Canaanites**, **Hittites**, **Amorites**!, **Hivites**, and **Jebusites**, a region generally referred to as a whole by the term **Canaan**; this is described as being a land of **milk and honey**. According to the narrative: **Yahweh** instructs Moses to confront the Egyptians and **Israelites** and briefs the prophet on what is to take place. **Yahweh** then performs various demonstrative miracles in order to bolster Moses's credibility. Among other things, his staff was transmuted into a snake, Moses's hand was temporarily made to appear leprous, and water was transmuted into blood, In the text, **Yahweh** instructs Moses to take **this staff** in his hands, in order to perform miracles with it, as if it is a staff given to him, rather than his own; some textual scholars propose that this latter instruction is the Elohist's version of the more detailed earlier description, where Moses uses his own staff, which they attribute to the **Yahwist**.

Despite the **signs**, Moses is described as being very reluctant to take on the role, arguing that he lacked eloquence, and that someone else should be sent instead; in the text, Yahweh reacts by angrily rebuking Moses for presuming to lecture the one who made the mouth on who was qualified to speak and not to speak. Yet Yahweh concedes and allows Aaron to be sent to assist Moses, since Aaron is eloquent and was already on his way to meet Moses. This is the first time in the Torah that Aaron is mentioned, and here he is described as being Moses' mouth piece.

Jacob left Beersheba, and went toward Haran. He came to the place and stayed there that night, because the sun had set. Taking one of the **stones** of the place, he put it under his head and lay down in that place to sleep. And he dreamed, and behold, there was a ladder set up on the earth, and the top of it reached to heaven; and behold, the angels of God were ascending and descending on it! And behold, the Lord stood above it [or "beside him"] and said, "I am the Lord, the God of Abraham your father and the God of Isaac; the land on which you lie I will give to you and to your descendants; and your descendants shall be like the dust of the earth, and you shall spread abroad to the west and to the east and to the north and to the south; and by you and your descendants shall all the families of the earth bless themselves. Behold, I am with you and will keep you wherever you go, and will bring you back to this land; for I will not leave you until I have done that of which I have spoken to you." Then Jacob awoke from his sleep and said, "Surely the Lord is in this place; and I did not know it." And he was afraid, and said, "This is none other than the house of God, and this is the gate of heaven!

The same night he arose and took his two wives, his two female servants, and his eleven children, and crossed the **ford of the Jabbok**. He took them and sent them across the stream, and everything else that he had. And Jacob was left alone. **And a man wrestled with him until the breaking of the day**. When the man saw that he did not prevail against Jacob, he touched his hip socket, and Jacob's hip was put out of joint as he wrestled with him. Then he said, **"Let me go, for the day has broken."** But Jacob said, "I will not let you go unless you bless me." And he said to him, "What is your name?" And he said, "Jacob." Then he said, "Your name shall no longer be called Jacob, but Israel, for you have striven with God and with men, and have prevailed." Then Jacob asked him, "Please tell me your name." But he said, "Why is it that you ask my name?" And there he blessed him. So Jacob called the name of the place Peniel, saying, *"For I have seen God face to face*, and yet my life has been delivered." The sun rose upon him as he passed Penuel, limping because of his hip. Therefore to this day the people of Israel do not eat the sinew of the thigh that is on the hip socket, because he touched the socket of Jacob's hip on the sinew of the thigh.

. . .

Where are they coming from, and going too within the world that we think we know! As well as the ones that display superhuman strength and agility being reported by construction workers and lumber-jacks, so to speak, by angrily throwing heavy objects such as metal-drums filled with gasoline, and hurling huge tractor-tyres great distances, which seems or appears to be a peculiar habit of these or other creatures, that could be serving the more highly evolved ones!

We may be dealing with an **indigenous** or otherwise type of species that have an **instinctive-intelligence**, or that they seem or appear to be working with someone or something of a **higher-intelligence**! That might or may not have an affinity with us!

Even though the **"Green Berets"** had set up their own communications and went out into the woods **"Armed"** and who in the end were forced to chase their own tails, like in **Vietnam**, while these **invisible-residents** were using a more clever method of cover and concealment, so where are the **perpetrators**? They must be somewhere that we don't know about, but remember:

"None are more hopelessly enslaved than those who falsely believe they are free!"

. . .

Histories witness

How you treated prisoners of war, by going outside the law, and denying them the protection of the so-called **Geneva Convention** like in the politically orchestrated and illegal invasion and subsequent war against **Iraq** and **Afghanistan** and of course **Iran** or **North Korea**! And Even over the **Artic**! Remember:

"Two wrongs don't make a right!"

Vae victis

(Woe to the conquered)
"Remember our duty to ourselves
As well as our duty to other life forms
Friendly or not!"
Star Trek

. . .

Flying Saucer

Mr. Charles Bowen,

"Editor of Britain's Flying Saucer Review"

"What is going on?
Did these witnesses, widely dispersed on earth, and in time, all have experiences with solid creatures from another world or from another dimension of reality? Or did they all suffer hallucinations of a similar kind, where the dream creatures were strikingly similar in many respects?
I pondered over the idea that the frightening, spooky creatures described by some of the witnesses could be some kind of psychic projection. There are noticeable dream-like qualities about the incidents described in these cases.
It is possible that something from somewhere is coming here and by means incomprehensible to us—although it could be a form of radiation, as in radar-waves—is pumping stylised pictures into the minds of humans who inadvertently stumble upon solid enough objects surreptitiously going about their business, while the human witnesses are ridiculed by their fellows, the interlopers get on with the job unhindered."

. . .

STRANGE CREATURES FROM TIME AND SPACE

(John Keel)

In 1941-42

"Scores of people near Mount Vernon, Illinois reported seeing a **large, hairy humanoid,** *when farmers tried to pursue it, they said that it was able to leap ditches twenty feet wide with ease!*
It killed at least one dog near Bonnie, Illinois. Large posses of armed men searched the region in vain. Although it left a trail of **footprints** *and* **dead animals**, *it seems to have* **vanished** *into thin* **air**!"
Isn't it weird that the dividing line between the real and the surreal is a very thin and yet a very personal one?
Christopher Thompkins who is mentioned on **page 101**, in the book by **David Paulides: "MISSING 411 EASTERN UNITED STATES"** mysteriously disappeared after a strange and terrifying altercation had taken place at the roadside, next to a tall barbed wire fence! No one saw the

culprits, where one of his boots was found lying near the fence, and a piece of his denims or (*jeans*) were later found on the barbed-wire fence!

It looks to all intent and purposes that something instinctively clever, and very powerful, had either taken or carried the young man over the fence and away! Or he had been carried or grabbed over the obstacle or fence with such speed and dexterity by something out of this world, so to speak!

. . .

Don't get me wrong, *it's **very-probable*** that this rather weird abduction or frightening sojourn, could have been perpetrated or done by person or persons unknown, but its ***highly unlikely***, and incidental a year later his other boot was found on the opposite side of the fence!

* * *

'Our birth!'
(*Is but a sleep and a forgetting*)
Wordsworth

* * *

Standing on the Shoulders of Gods
(Fiction)

Paul Crowe

Even now he could hear imaginary jungle-drums and see the shrunken-heads of the American soldiers hanging from the trees, and the severed heads that had been put up on poles as a warning to the curious!

He could hear the song by Bob Dylan called **"*Subterranean Blues*"** As he was eventually captured in his own mind by a tribe of head-hunters who carried him through the jungle (*forest*) tied-up like a captured animal to a long wooden pole, where he was taken to a clearing and left there, as if impaled on a thorn by the **"*SHRIKE*"** or butcher-bird to await his awful fate at the hands of something even more terrifying in his feverish state of mind.

And there he saw strange humanoids approaching him, upside down! Because of the way he had been Hog-tied to the pole, Mathew having squirmed and struggled about on his sacrificial skew, had managed to lift himself up to try and get a better look at them, and in his eyes was that awful look of an animal in a slaughter-house! Resigned to its fate, and there he could see that they were dressed in weird looking cloths, that covered or protected them from the outside world, creatures who were from a highly advanced civilization that had once lived on the surface of the planet earth, the would-be ancestors of humankind who had been forced by their own intellectual stupidity to live underground in vast city complexes for millions of years, after a terrible war that had poisoned the water they drank and the air they breathed, is it these physical weaklings of the coming race... who could be manning the strange **'flying saucers'** or **"UFO's"** (***Unidentified Flying Objects***) or is it someone or something else! Like in the 60s cult TVSeries Dr Who! and the one called (*The web of fear*) and the entity called the **'*intelligence*'**.

14

We could be an ancient tribal race that has been invaded and controlled by outsiders for whatever reason, or the very survivors of an ancient high-tech war, who have been left on the surface to become genetic mutants or freaks! And the surface-dwellers have developed a resistance or immunity to the radiation that has retarded their intelligence!

But the creatures having been forced to live underground after escaping the holocaust that followed, having become physically weak over the Eon's of time, with their bodies unable to fight or cope with the germs and the bacteria on the surface, but on the other hand they had developed into highly advanced or super-intellectual weaklings!

Who have been their own-gaolers for thousands of years! And with their giant humongous intellects, they can project onto the primitive minds of the surface dwellers; the grand illusion of what they think is reality!

So nothing seemed to be what Mathew thought it was, in his present state of mind, he was just a primitive surface dweller, given the illusion of who he thought he was, projected onto his mind! Or the person who had been living in the 20th century with his childhood memories, now serving in Vietnam, had he been fooled just like the rest us, and that he had been caught in a **mental mouse-trap**, while he had been out scavenging for food with the other members of his **tribe**!

And there he had remembered being trussed up and unable to speak because of certain abnormalities the surface dwellers suffer from, having lost their ability to speak which sounded as if they were choking, when any of them tried to speak! Having eventually lost the ability to develop any kind of organised language!

. . .

Remember, the specific case of, **Elsie M. Davis** the missing girl, who was found high up in a tree! **Page 235. David Paulides** book: "**MISSING 411 EASTERN UNITED STATES**" who was found unable to speak!

. . .

"The quickness of the hand deceives the eye"
(Like the continuity of a magician's trick!)

Many of the children mentioned in these books are found after being reported missing, are either too young to speak or have a natural disability, and are unable to speak, which means could they not have tried "**Art therapy?**"

Some children who are found are reported to be in a state of confusion or chose not to speak. The Davis case exemplifies the condition that is found in very small children when they are missing. The people who seem to **conveniently** lose **a very important part of their memory of the event** at the point they go missing and then recover the least important fragmentary information, once in the presence of people, is that a coincidence!

'FIRE FROM HEAVEN'

'Whatever or whoever, had come with his fiery flaming sword had come on the wings of light; had struck within a heart-beat and had gone as quickly as it-he had come'

MICHAEL HARRISON

. . .

The inability to 'explain' what happens in **'411'** is akin to the victims of **spontaneous combustion** or '**fire from heaven**' who can't say what happened or who are unaware that they have been attacted!

"And remember what I said at the beginning of the book, there is nothing more deceptive that the obvious!"

. . .

Continued:

And where our tied up supplicant (**Mathew**) had been taken below, and ceremoniously strapped to a laboratory table, where no one could hear his cries for help, or the screams of his suffering during the excruciating agony of his dissection! Which begs the question, has any species the moral right to experiment on another species because you see them as inferior?

Like school children in the confines of the so-called science-class, who have been taught that might-is-right, and are told to smash harmless (**Snails**) with a hammer and then dissect them, while they are still alive! Is somehow acceptable?

His comrades would watch (**Mathew**) caught in the arms of his invisible tormentors, alone with his thoughts and left to his own devices, where he would sometimes just sit there in what could only be described as a state of apoplexy, as if he was listening to the tune: **"The Stars And Strips For Ever"** mocking him, as it played in his head like an orchestra out of tune, with intermittent pieces of I'm A Yankee Doodle Dandy, as if it was playing once more on that old Gramophone during the killing or assassination of Rasputin, where he had been driven almost mad by the heat and the exhaustion of the war, deprecated, obsolete and essentially superfluous in a state that had no meaning or purpose; where he had been pushed over the edge and close to deaths door, he could hear the orchestral tune of: **"Siegfrieds" Rhine-Journey** from Wagers, Teutonic mythology: **"Gotterdammerung"** or (*Twilight of the Gods*), like voices laughing at him, due to the situation he was in, which was now very different from the superlative position he was in, when he first arrived, confident of victory stepping off the **"Huey or Iroquois"** the name given to the native American or first nation tribe or **"Haudenosaunee"** by the French colonists, a tribe who worshiped:

"The formless great spirit or creator of earth wind and water and of all the living creatures that dwell upon it"

16

As the **Huey** helicopters came down onto the **LZs** to the sound of Norman Greenbaum and his 60s song **"Spirit In The Sky"** unaware of the unseen enemy or wisdom that would reduce the proud son's of men to a terrible state, and to show them albeit indirectly, **"That it is better to serve in heaven, than to rule in hell"**, like **"Edger Allen Poe"** forcing humankind to see the error of their ways and kneel before the angel's!

Paul Crowe

. . .

The world has been here for millions of years, and as a species we have been walking upright for a comparitively short time! Mentally we are still crawling, at the beginning of the atomic age we had written the first chapter of a new genisis, let us hope we don't find ourselves writing the last chapter of the old one...!

The beast from 20,000 Fathoms.

. . .

"A movement in the void"
(One step beyond)
"Now they know something that we don't know!"

"Sooner or later most of us, if we can afford it! Feels the need to escape, country folk go to the city and city folk go to the country! Each of us fashion a small cage of reality out of the chaos of unreality, each of whom like us, live their lives by the steady reassuring ticking of the clock! Forgetting the clock is merely a human invention, and tomorrow is a creation of the human mind, forgetting that there is only the constant now! If that is true, where does that leave yesterday? This book is about people who left the city of ticking clocks for another reality!"

. . .

"You can fool some of the people, all of the time, and you can fool all of the people some of the time, but you can't fool all of the people, all of the time"

Abraham Lincoln

. . .

Schalken the painter
(Joseph Sheridan Le Fanu)

That you may distinctly understand all the circumstances of the event, which I am going to describe, it is necessary to state the relative positions of the parties who were engaged in it. The old clergyman and Shalken were in the anti-room of which I have already spoken; Rose lay in the inner chamber, the door of which was open; and by the side of the bed, at her urgent desire, stood her guardian; a candle burned in the bed-chamber, and three were lighted in the outer apartment. The old man now cleared his voice as if about to commence, but before he had time to begin, a sudden gust of air blew out the candle which served to illuminate the room in which the poor girl lay, and she, with hurried alarm, exclaimed:

'Godfrey, bring in another candle; the darkness is unsafe.'

Gerard Douw, forgetting for the moment her repeated injunctions, and acting on immediate impulse, stepped from the bedchamber into the other room, in order to supply what she desired.

'Oh my God! Do not go, dear uncle,' shrieked the unhappy girl—and at the same time she sprang from the bed, and darted after him, in order, by her grasp, to detain him. But the warning came to late; for scarcely had he passed the threshold, and hardly had his niece had time to utter the startling exclamation, when the door which divided the two rooms closed violently after him, as if swung by a strong blast of wind. Schalken and he both rushed to the door, but their united and desperate efforts could not avail so much as to shake it. Shriek after shriek burst from the inner chamber, with all the piercing loudness of despairing terror. Schalken and Douw applied every nerve to force open the door; but all in vain.

There was no sound of struggling from within, but the screams seemed to increase in loudness, and at the same time they heard the bolts of the latticed window withdrawn, and the window itself grated upon the sill as if thrown open. One last shriek, so long and piercing and agonised as to be scarcely human, swelled from the room, and suddenly there followed a death-like silence.

A light step was heard crossing the floor, as if from the bed to the window; and almost at the same instant the door gave way, and, yielding to the pressure of the external applicants, nearly precipitated them into the room. It was empty. The window was open, and Schalken, springing on to a chair, gazed out upon the street and canal below. He saw no form, but saw, or thought he saw, the water of the broad canal beneath disturbed by the submission of some ponderous body.

No trace of Rose was ever found, nor was anything certain respecting her mysterious wooer discovered—no clue, whereby to trace the intricacies of the labyrinth and to arrive at its solution, presented itself.

Dutch Philosopher
"In the land of the spiritually and mentally blind,
The one eyed man is king"
Erasmus

. . .

A Study In Terror
(*Jack the ripper*)
1888
"Wolf in the fold"
"The predestinate providence in the fall of a sparrow."
Or like in **David Paulides** book: **MISSING 411 The Devil's in the detail. Page 160,** and why it seemed or appeared that **Megumi Yamamoto** aged **26 years**, was not going to leave **Mount Baldy, New Mexico!**

18

Targets

(1968 film starring Boris Karloff (aka) William Pratt)

"The Appointment in Samara"

As retold by W. Somerset Maugham [1933]

The speaker is Death

"There was a merchant in Baghdad who sent his servant to market to buy provisions and in a little while the servant came back, white and trembling, and said, Master, just now when I was in the marketplace I was jostled by a woman in the crowd and when I turned I saw it was Death that jostled me. She looked at me and made a threatening gesture, now, lend me your horse, and I will ride away from this city and avoid my fate. I will go to Samara and there Death will not find me. The merchant lent him his horse, and the servant mounted it, and he dug his spurs in its flanks and as fast as the horse could gallop he went. Then the merchant went down to the marketplace and he saw me standing in the crowd and he came to me and said, why did you make a threating gesture to my servant when you saw him this morning? That was not a threatening gesture, I said, it was only a start of surprise. I was astonished to see him in Baghdad, for I had an appointment with him tonight in Samara."

Death takes a holiday

7TH April 2014

"Two British women drowned in the sea during a holiday on the Spanish island of Tenerife."

Police say consultant obstetrician **Uma Ramalingam**, **42**, and relative **Barathi Ravikumar**, a **GP**, (*General practitioners*) were "**dragged into the sea by a wave**" on Sunday at Playa Paraiso, in the island's southwest. Another woman and two children, aged 10 and 14, were rescued.

"Some reports say the women had jumped into the sea to try to save the children!"

"The pattern that death uses to get to us, seems or appears to be identical to the people who have been disappearing in **David Paulides** books: **MISSING 411 WESTERN UNITED STATES & CANADA Page 208:** **It's almost as though someone is watching us. When our eyes wander from our kids, they disappear!**

. . .

It's as if something is watching and waiting for the right moment in order to take full advantage of some unwritten opportunity, or is something else closer to home, going on below the radar, something surreptitious or clandestine?"

Hamlet

Hamlet was a student at Wittenberg or so is thought. Wittenberg is **"one of only two universities that Shakespeare ever mentions by name,"** and was famous in the early sixteenth century for its teaching of Luther's new doctrine of salvation.

Furthermore, Hamlet's reference to **"a politic convocation of worms"** has been read as cryptic allusion to Luther's famous theological confrontation with the Holy Roman Emperor at the **Diet of Worms** in **1521**.

However, the more influential Reformer in early 17th century England was **John Calvin**, a strong advocate of predestination; many critics have found traces of Calvin's predestinarian theology in Shakespeare's play. Calvin explained the doctrine of predestination by comparing it to a stage, or a theater, in which the script is written for the characters by **God**! And they cannot deviate from it.

God, in this light, sets up a script and a stage for each of his creations, and decrees the end from the beginning, as Calvin said: **"After the world had been created, man was placed in it, as in a theatre, that he, beholding above him and beneath the wonderful work of God, might reverently adore their Author."** Scholars have made comparisons between this explanation of Calvin's and the frequent references made to the theatre in **Hamlet**, suggesting that these may also take reference to the doctrine of predestination, as the play must always end in its tragic way, according to the script!

Rulers and religious leaders feared that the doctrine of predestination would lead people to excuse the most traitorous of actions, with the excuse, **"God made me do it."** English Puritans, for example, believed that **"conscience was a more powerful force than the law"** due to the new ideas at the time that conscience came not from religious or government leaders, but from **God** directly to the individual. Many leaders at the time condemned the doctrine, as: **"unfit 'to keepe subjects in obedience to their sovereigns"** as people might **"openly maintain that God hath as well pre-destinated men to be traitors as to be kings."**

King James, as well, often wrote about his dislike of Protestant leader's taste for standing up to kings, seeing it as a dangerous trouble to society.

In Hamlet's final decision to join the sword-game of Laertes, and thus enter his tragic final scene, he says to the fearful Horatio:

. . .

"There is special providence in the fall of a sparrow. If it be now, 'tis not to come; if it be not to come, it will be now; if it be not now, yet will it come—the readiness is all. Since no man, of aught he leaves, knows what is't to leave betimes, let be."

"Macbeth's final soliloquy the audience sees his final conclusion about life"

"*It is devoid of any meaning, full of contrived struggles. Days on this earth are short, a **"brief candle"** and an ignorant march towards a fruitless demise, **"lighted fools. . . to dusty death."** A person's life is so insubstantial that it is comparable to an actor who fills minor roles in an absurd play. There is a struggle for substance in life, the actor who* **"struts and frets his hour"** *or a playwright who tells a **"a tale full of sound and fury"** but it is contrived and senseless and will thus fade into obscurity, a tale **"Told by an Idiot. . . Signifying nothing"** In which a **"walking shadow"** performs **"And then is heard no more"**.*

William Shakespeare

. . .

THE CASE
OF THE COUNTLESS CLUES

For no one has yet solved this age old mystery which is as old as **"Jack the ripper"** we don't know who or what was responsible for these gruesome murders, and whoever or whatever it was, has never been caught, and that's a fact, not a theory!

The Rolling Stones
(What is puzzling you is the nature of my game)

For good or ill, **Politics religion and race**! Have shaped the very social and political world that we live in, whether we like it or not, and if anybody doubts the veracity of that statement, then you must be living in a cultural and social vacuum, but remember, **curiosity that killed the cat**, and quit frankly you should not even be contemplating or attempting to read this book, until you are capable of even the most rudimentary grasp or understanding of the world that you think you've been living in, before trying to cross the dividing line that differentiates the two worlds of the sublime to the ridiculous! Before satisfaction will **bring the cat back**!

A poisoned chalice

Its very probable that they are either **extra-terrestrial**, but its highly unlikely, I think that one does not need to get a kick up the rear-end to figure out that it hurts! And theoretically whatever or whoever they are, they seem or appear to be more **terrestrial** than anything or they come from somewhere on **earth**!

Like the old story of the **'Children of the Hydra'** Who were sewn like **seeds** in the **earth**, from the teeth of the mythical hydra and who would symbolically **climb out of the earth**:

. . .

In Greek mythology, **the Lernaean Hydra** was an ancient serpent-like water monster with reptilian traits. It possessed many heads – the poets mention more heads than the vase-painters could paint – and for each head cut off it grew two more. It had **poisonous breath** and **blood** so virulent that even its scent was deadly. The Hydra of Lerna was killed by Heracles as the second of his Twelve Labours. Its lair was the lake of Lerna in the Argolid, though archaeology has borne out the myth that the sacred site was older even than the Mycenaean city of Argos, since Lerna was the site of the myth of the Danaids. Beneath the waters was an **entrance to the Underworld**, and the **Hydra** was its **guardian**, what is this old Greek **myth** trying to tell us? But it's true content has been lost!

. . .

And since mathematics seems or appears to be the very foundation of the reality or world that we think we live in, you should know that **matter** can't be **created** or **destroyed** and that's a **fact** not **fiction**, if anybody tells you different, they are lying! It's as if something seems or appears to be using a science without instrumentality! And it's as if it has constructed a theoretical bio-computer or machine, like in the classic **1956** science fiction film, **Forbidden Planet**, by an extinct race! Of advanced beings of the planet **Altar IV** are known as the **"Krell"**, who did not know who or what was killing them!

Ask no questions and you'll be told no lies!

Or something seems or appears to be begging the question or trying to bring something to our notice! In regards to the very world or reality that we think we live in:

Begging the question

Begging the question means **"assuming the conclusion** (*of an argument*)**"**, a type of circular reasoning. This is an informal fallacy where the conclusion that one is attempting to prove is included in the initial premise of an argument, often in an indirect way that conceals this fact.

The term **"begging the question"** originated in the 16th century as a mistranslation of Latin **petitio principii** **"assuming the initial point"**. In modern vernacular usage, **"to beg the question"** is sometimes also used to mean **"to raise the question"** (*as in "This begs* the question of whether...") or **"to dodge the question"**. This usage is often proscribed!

Who Goes There?

(*Indigenous or alien*)

What easier way to gain a world than through a superior race operating from within mans own species!

Or those and such as those have been forced into slavery, in a prison without bars, if you like, by a more clever species, that uses a very clandestine form of **social, theological** and **anthropological** conditioning! And you all know who you are? And providence has been using them to control our **banking** and **commerce**! Through an on-going subversive war of death by a billion cuts, so to speak! We have all been in the forefront of this conditioning for centuries, like in the brilliant film: **The Running man** or the cult TV Show of the 1960s **Dr Who** and the episode called: **War-Games**! Using nothing but cart-blanch against our own species, you know as well as the ones who are intellectually and physically weaker, without question, we have been manipulating the world that we think that we live in, like uneducated **blind moles** in the bowels of the earth, smelling our way through life, by our own **self-inflicted stupidity**.

Standing on the Shoulders of Gods

(*Fiction*)

A timeless time

"*Men of science say miracles are past and give reasons for things supernatural, therefore we dismiss our terrors by finding safety in false knowledge, instead we should submit ourselves to an unknown fear*"

* * *

Imagine before the beginning of time and space! That **'was' 'is'** and **'always will be' indescribable** or **inconceivable** at the source of all knowledge and understanding! And it seemed to Mathew that this **Androgynous-state** was and still is looking for the answer! To it's own self-inquiry! **Who am I, what am I**, and **where am I**, and this **enigma** Seems to have found the answer, while at the same time it seems or appears to be still looking for it! That's why the physical and non-physical (*Corporeal and non-corporeal*) worlds are an enigma! Because we know that **matter** cannot be **created** or **destroyed**! So it begs the question, if we don't know where it comes from? Or where it goes too? Is it like the preverbal **tree in the forest**, if our **higher self** or the **observer?** So to speak, can't perceive it, relative to each and every one of us when we are sleeping or after each and every one of us die! When our energy or spirit leaves our so-called **physical bodies**, has anything really been there to begin with, or is the **physical world** of time and space only **theoretical?** As if it's being held in some **unified-field,** between the infinite ticks of an imaginary clock?

The **big-bang** or that strange event that seems or appears to have theoretically happened all by it's self, or that it just some how came into being some how! Because Mathew knew he was alive, he was substantial, he thought to himself, as he recalled **Des Carté** and his famous supposition: *"I think therefore I am."* So something must have happened, theoretically! Because he and all the rest of us seem or appear to be the living proof!

But **why** and **how** was at that point a much **deeper** and **unfathomable** mystery even to *Mathew*, till his mind had been artificially expanded enough to try and understand the **bottomless truths** inside himself, and all around him like the great philosophers and religions of the world who seem like blind men trying to reach out and touch the preverbal *Elephant,* so it doesn't matter what it was they were trying to describe, because each and every one of them have came up with a different piece of the puzzle or answer that elusive *something!* Wrapped up in the meaning of life, but its still an *Elephant*! Or the source of all knowledge and understanding that seems or appears to be staring us in the face!

If we could only read between the lines! Or was Mathew like the rest of us, who seem or appear to be chasing our own tail? Like the snake on the man's hand with it's hidden symbolism or like the abstract imagery we see in our dreams that can contain the meaning or the solution to a problem, like the German chemist: *F. A. Kekule* who saw in the reverie of his own dream a snake seize its own tail! And with this he went on to discover the formula for *Benzene.*

Or like *Dr Herman Hilprecht* the archaeologist, whose ancient Babylonian phantom priest came bearing gifts of knowledge in his dreams, like the Scottish inventor: *"James Watt"* inventor of the steam-engine, and while walking through a heavy rainstorm while he was dreaming, saw the rain itself turn to tiny leaden pellets which bounced about under foot and from this wonderful dream, he discovered how to make lead shot, By dropping molten liquid metal (*Lead*) into water, thanks to *"James Watt"* and his recurring dream.

So deep within this **imagery** there seems to be a **secret language** that's speaks with a **hidden-tongue** of great truths that we have lost for whatever reason and that it is begging the question? And the *indescribable* or *inconceivable androgynous state* we theoretically know as *God!* Or *the source of all knowledge and understanding*!! Somehow used the retrospective or self-conscious impression of it's own self to try and find the answer to a question it was looking for: *Who am I, what am I,* and *where am I,* and this created the so-called theoretical: *"big bang!"*

A timeless theoretical unified thought, so to speak, created the heavens and the earth and on the seventh day! The lord rested, because he had come to the end of his work, and where the answer to the question has already been found... and yet at the same time nothing seems or appears to have happened in the conventional sense, per-say!

Its as if a part of it is still looking for the problem or trying to solve the puzzle of its own self! At the beginning of such a creation! And at the same time solving it, as if it somehow knew what the problem was, by using reverse engineering, **Vis-à-vis** (*therefore*) it new the answer to the question it had been seeking! Because it theoretically caused the problem in the first place in order to solve it! That's why **Jesus Christ** believed in **forgiveness** and **redemption**, because to forgive others is to forgive ones self or **unification**!

. . .

Even though the **indescribable** or **inconceivable androgynous state** has come full circle like the theory of the past, present and the future which co-exist with one another, **"it"** or our **collective-higher-self** or the **observer** moves through existence in a **relative state** or as it becomes consciously aware! It tries to discover what has happened, in that timeless unified thought, because something has theoretically happened, so it could be the key or answer to a paradox of who **God** is? Or the riddle of our own selves or what appears to be somewhere and yet nowhere: **beyond–the-beyond** or at the incredible source of all **knowledge and understanding**!

It's like the book of **Exodus**, in the Christian bible when **Moses** was on the mount when he asked God who he was? And God answered: **I am that I am**. Which is a bit like the paradox of what came first, the **"chicken or the egg?"** Because it is asking a question that fly's in the face of it's own self! And this has caused what seems or appears to be a theoretical dissociation of thinking. But remember like the **"veil of Isis"** no man has lifted that veil, so **God** can't see his own face, that's what has caused the theoretical problem in the first place! And there Mathew saw his own reflection as if cast in a symbolic mirror!

Plato

" What we call time is but the " moving, unreal reflection of eternity"

As if it were the face of **God** looking back at him, with Mathew trying to convince himself, that he does not exist, and that it is only a reflection and nothing more!

So something seems or appears to have happened, where theoretically nothing has or should have happened. Which means the universe is stranger than we think! Because if you can't destroy matter or create it, then it is not a case of where did it come from or where does it go too, but more importantly the question is, who or what is creating this grand illusion and for what purpose? In what appears to be a constant state of flux, like **quantum physics**, which means it has or it has not happened!

And yet all matter is to be regarded as simply a mode or expression of **transient-energy**, so what is energy and where is it coming and going to? because as science knows, you can't **create it** or **destroy it**!

25

Matter=energy and *energy=matter*, and that both states of matter can be altered, but they cannot be **destroyed**!

. . .

Mystical illumination
(*William James*)

Otherworldly visions are the products of the same imaginative power that is active in our ordinary ways of visualizing death; our tendency to portray ideas in concrete, embodied and dramatic forms; the capacity of our inner states to transfigure our perception of outer landscapes; our need to internalise the culture map of the physical universe; and our drive to experience that universe as a moral and spiritual cosmos in which we belong and have a purpose.

Ex nil, nihil fit
(*From nothing, nothing is made*)

"There is of course, something to which atoms correspond, something of which they are a manifistation : but that something is **intangible**, and there's the rub for the **materialism** its age-long advantage of appealing to the **sense of touch**; in which we are apt to believe so heartly, has been taken away. However real a **marble** may feel to us that peculiar sense of reality can no longer be appealed to or utilised by the **materialist**, his theory is now on a level with other theories, and can make no special appeal to this biased judge for the **marble** dispute and its convincing air of **solidity**, must yet be convinced by us, if we are to except the verdict of **science** at all—as **materialism** constantly asserts that we must in terms not of **hard atoms** as resistant as itself, but in terms of **electrons** which, we are now taught, have **no mass** that is not *"electrical-inersia."* And the only ultimate reality is (*electical inersia*)
Our knowledge of the external world is limited, and conditioned by the limits and conditions of our own **minds**; it is **knowledge**, not of **reality** but of **appearences**!!! The **reality** that lies **behind** these **appearences**, must be in its essence not dissimilar to the **perceiving-mind** itself."

Berkeley
Who over hears us saying that *"all we are aware of are changes in our own consciousness"* *"can you not see, then"* he would say. *"that what you are aware of and what you are alone aware of, is all that is?"* Material things have no objective exsistance—no exsistance outside yourselves.

. . .

"The external world which you persist in postulating as the *Noumenon* or **substance**. The attrubutes of which cause changes in your consciousness is a **figment of your imagination**, the abstract, the **invisable**, the **impalpable** is for most minds more or less of a **fiction** it does not rely **exsist:**"

"If a tree falls in the forest, and if no one is there to hear it, does it make a sound?

. . .

Ghost in the machine

Which means that whoever or whatever is taking these people in *411* could be theoretically moving about with impunity in the forests and our streets, cloaked by this logical human impairment!

The *"ghost in the machine"* is British philosopher Gilbert Ryle's description of René Descartes' mind-body dualism. The phrase was introduced in Ryle's book *The Concept of Mind* (1949) to highlight the perceived absurdity of dualist systems like Descartes' where mental activity carries on in parallel to physical action, but where their means of interaction are unknown or, at best, **speculative**.

Gilbert Ryle (1900–76) was a philosopher who lectured at Oxford and who made important contributions to the philosophy of mind and to **"ordinary language philosophy"**. His most important writings include *Philosophical Arguments* (1945), *The Concept of Mind* (1949), *Dilemmas* (1954), *Plato's Progress* (1966), and *On Thinking* (1979).

Ryle's *The Concept of Mind* (1949) is a critique of the notion that the mind is distinct from the body, and a rejection of the theory that mental states are separable from physical states. In this book Ryle refers to the idea of a fundamental distinction between mind and matter as **"the ghost in the machine"**. According to Ryle, the classical theory of mind, or **"Cartesian rationalism"**, makes a basic category mistake, because it attempts to analyze the relation between **"mind"** and **"body"** as if they were terms of the same logical category. This confusion of logical categories may be seen in other theories of the relation between **mind** and **matter**. For example, the idealist theory of mind makes a basic category mistake by attempting to reduce physical reality to the same status as mental reality, while the materialist theory of mind makes a basic category mistake by attempting to reduce mental reality to the same status as physical reality.

Ryle's philosophical arguments in his essay **"Descartes' Myth"** lay out his notion of the mistaken foundations of mind-body dualism conceptions, comprising a suggestion that to speak of mind and body as a substance, as a dualist does, is to commit a category mistake. Ryle writes:

Such in outline is the official theory. I shall often speak of it, with deliberate abusiveness, as *"the dogma of the Ghost in the Machine."* I hope to prove that it is entirely false, and false not in detail but in principle. It is not merely an assemblage of particular mistakes. It is one big mistake and a mistake of a special kind. It is, namely, a category mistake.

Ryle then attempts to show that the **"official doctrine"** of mind/body dualism is false by asserting that it confuses two logical-types, or categories, as being compatible. He states "it represents the facts of mental life as if they belonged to one logical type/category, when they actually belong to another. The dogma is therefore a philosopher's myth."

Arthur Koestler brought Ryle's concept to wider attention in his 1967 book *The **Ghost in the Machine***, which takes Ryle's phrase as its title. The book's main focus is mankind's movement towards self-destruction, particularly in the **nuclear arms arena**. It is particularly critical of B. F. Skinner's behaviourist theory. One of the book's central concepts is that as the human brain has grown, it has built upon earlier, more primitive brain structures, and that this is the **"ghost in the machine"** of the title. Koestler's theory is that at times these structures can overpower higher logical functions, and are responsible for **hate**, **anger** and other such **destructive impulses**!

An adaptation of the story by
M.R. James (*Montague Rhodes James*)
WHISTLE AND I'LL COME TO YOU
"Hints at the danger of intilectual pride and shows that a man's reason can be over thrown, when he fails to acknowledge those forces inside himself"
To test if the object you think you are looking at is *real* or *not*! (***Ghosts*** or ***UFOs***) gently press the outside corner of your eye-ball, till you can see two of the same object and if you can't, then what you think you have been looking at, is not rely there! So to speak.

'PLOT'

Professor Parkin, a stuffy Cambridge academic, arrives for an off-season stay at a hotel somewhere on the English east coast. Preferring to keep to himself, Parkin spends his stay walking along the beach and visits a local graveyard, which has become overgrown and unkempt. While there, he spots a small object protruding from a grave which is partly undermined by the edge of the cliff. He uncovers it and finds it is a **bone whistle**, which he keeps. When walking back along the shore, he turns twice and sees a dark silhouetted figure standing still in the distance in front of a setting sun, appearing to **watch him**.

Later, in the calm of his hotel room, he cleans and inspects the whistle, revealing a carved inscription: ***"Quis est iste qui venit"*** ("*Who is this who is coming?*"). He blows the whistle and a windstorm begins outside. Later that night, Parkin is kept awake by mysterious noises in his hotel room.

At breakfast the following morning, another guest at the hotel asks Parkin if he believes in **ghosts**. Parkin responds in a typically academic fashion, dismissing such beliefs as little more than superstition.

"Do you believe in ghosts professor? **Ghosts**! That's a rather sticky one, I'm not quit certain what you mean, I mean I'm never quit certain what I'm being invited to believe in, whenever anybody asks me a question like that, I'm not quit certain what I'm being asked to disbelieve in! When it comes to that, if you ask me, do I believe in say, Australia? Then I know perfectly well the sort of thing I'm being asked to judge. I mean we all agree by what I mean by Australia! Large continent, Southern hemisphere, discovered by Captain Cook, large cities and given that; given that, one can perfectly imagine the sort of procedure one might well put in hand to confirm or on the other hand to disconfirm its existence, its not quit the same thing with **ghosts**!

You see, I mean there's no broad consensus as to what a ghost is? (The spirits of the dead; the survival of the human personality!) Ah, survival of the human personality, (mm) well now, that's a different question again, rely, and has the grammatical appearance of a real question; well lets say for the sake of argument that the human personality survives death, right! Well now, but would we say it in the same way that we might say, for example: that one survived a train crash? Would we; you see, I mean we say don't we, *porcīnus* survived the train crash, but was very badly injured by it, we wouldn't want to say that *porcīnus* survived death, but was badly injured by it! We definitely wouldn't want to say that, would we? Well clearly hear we have a logical difference of usage, in that death! In a sense is not like other physical catastrophe's, I mean one doesn't talk about anyone being very badly hurt by death, except possible, the relatives of the deceased, but never the victim himself, excluding of course the special interpretation in which one might say, he had been injured fatally by death or for that matter she was! ***There are more things in heaven and earth than in your philosophy***:

I like to say:

There are more things in philosophy than are dreamt of in your heaven and earth

However, that night, Parkin appears to have disturbing dreams of a **spectre** pursuing him on the beach. His nerves are not helped when, the following morning, he is informed by a maid that both of the beds in his room have been slept in – even though Parkin only slept in one.

Increasingly disturbed, he searches a book for answers. That night, he is awakened by a sound like flapping sheets. As he sits up in bed, the sheets from the other bed across the room move and then rise up into the phantom from the shore. Waking another hotel guest who comes to his aid, Parkin sits in **stunned terror** at what he has just witnessed!

. . .
WE ARE ALL BORN BLIND

(Now you will know why you are afraid of the dark!)

Like blind people who get their sight back, and have to learn not to see again! Because they know what a cup was by touching it, which is completely different from the world we learn to see as children, and

because of this, the world that we think that we can see, is a strange frightening place! Would it not be like
a mental aberration or **mental- illness**, like **Schizophrenia**!

. . .

How is it possible?

Like in the cult 6os show **Star-Trek** and the episode: **The Tholian Web**. Were the Enterprises sister ship, the USS Defiant had disappeared because of fractures in space and where they had came upon it drifting eerily in space, while the fractured space had been affecting the crews mind and following this they had all went insane!

The Captain, spock along with McCoy (bones) the ships doctor went on board and during a malfunction of the USS Enterprises transporters because of that strange area of fractured space, in an attempt to get him along with the other members back on board, and because of this it was now effecting the crew of the Enterprise! Following this event, Uhura then saw the Captain appear as he was trapped in that fractured-space caught by the transporters, but doctor McCoy just assumed that she was going insane!

Schizophrenia

Could it be possible that so-called mental illness or **Schizophrenia** is like having **total-recall** (*breaking through*) of the influence of whoever or whatever could be putting in our minds the **elusion** of **reality**! Because if you are unsure of what this means, remember that **matter** cannot be **created** or **destroyed** so who or what is producing the elusion?

We hvae eeys but we cnanot see!

"*Aonccdrig to rserach at an elingsh uinevrtisy, it deons't mttaer in what order the ltteers in a word are, the only iprmoatnt thing is that the frsit and lsat ltteer is at the rghit pclae. The rset can be a total mses and you can still raed it wouthit a porbelm. This is bcuseae we do not raed ervey lteter by istlef, but the word as a wlohe.*"

English

(Header and footers)

According to research at an English university, it doesn't mater in what order the letters in a word are, the only important thing is that the first and last letter is at the right place. The rest can be a total mess and you can still read it without a problem, this is because we don't read every letter by itself, but the word as a whole.

Fundamental law

Like in how we read language is **ruled** by **mathematics** (excuse the pun)
MISSING 411 NORTH AMERICA AND BEYOND.

And the story of Richard R.Lee missing 2004 Colchuck Lake WA. Aged 47

years. On a two day camping trip, the people involved in the SAR (Search And Rescue) on *page 21* stated that the camp-site where he had chosen to camp had an eerie feeling to it, and that the general area had something wrong with it!

Its like the 60s cult TV Show **Dr Who** and the episode with Patrick Troughton called: **War Games** where the aliens had **advanced technology** hidden in among the **old-tech** is that not what these **'strangers'** are doing in the forests? Who could be responsible for the people going missing in *411* and are right there with their **technological contraptions** and we are unable to recognise them, the only thing that can reveal their presence is our own natural inborn instinct or unconscious-mind! That seems or appears to be telling us something!

"EYES NO EYES"
(The invisible world)
Who goes there?

Consists of seeking for an object. Which is hidden—but not out of sight—in a room from which the seekers have been momentarily excluded and on their admittance to the room each child is aware that no amount of cupboard opening, lid removing or lifting and shifting of bric-a-brac, will suffice to discover the object! Everything depends upon sight, and sight alone. The object has been placed in some position in the room, which renders it difficult of discernment, while it remains perfectly visible to those who have thus placed it.

Mental Blindness

Another excellent practise is to make children write a description of their bedroom or their father's study, or indeed any room in the house with which they are daily familiar. It will be found in many instances that the child is even unable to name the colour of the wallpaper in his own bedroom, while the pattern of the carpet or the shape of the fireplace will present to his mind the most insoluble of problems.

Things, which the eyes have seen every day for years, have been so little observed that he is utterly unable to afford you even the crudest description of them. But this is true of most children is likewise true of most adults. Not born to realise the endless pleasures of observation, and never having been encouraged or trained to develop the faculty, the average person passes through life **seeing everything** and **observing nothing**!

* * *

Much like the **urban-legend** of a secret or quasi **Nazi organization,** or where **tyranny** is **masked** or **hiding** in the wings behind **legality** in **Germany** on the coin the **5 pfennig piece!** Is it because the invisible hand that rocks the cradle or **Rothschild's** might need to use it again? or are these **urban legends** or **chinnese whispers** true?

Standing on the shoulders of Gods

(Fiction)

Like in my other book about the **Octopus** of **corruption** with its **tentacles** capable of spreading like a Cancer with **"The Brotherhood of Erebus"** God of darkness, son of chaos or the devil! A diabolical brotherhood that had links to organizations like in that fantastic film starring Glen Ford **'The brothers of the bell'** infecting **banking** and **commerce, law enforcement** and **civil** and **military authorities**, a **corrupt** and **odious organization** that paves the way, the eyes and ears of this insidious (*Divom Deus) or (God of Gods)* **'Lucifer'** not only is it the **'enemy at the gates!'** But like some two-headed monstrous dichotomy! It is the **'enemy within!'**

Otto had wined and dined at the feet of histories greatest figures, as he sat in the belly of the beast, so to speak, beneath the beautiful painted copies of the murals by Saint Martin who was quit satisfied with the effect he got in his paintings by using fragments of the heart of **Louis XIV**. He also got a hold of **Louis XIII'S heart**, which had been preserved like that of **Louis XIV** in the reliquary of the Paris church of Saint Louis des Jesuites, but he did not have enough time to use it before the restoration when he was obliged to return it, where he received a golden tobacco box from **Louis XVIII** in compensation... as Otto enjoyed the culinary delights, musing over the facts of the great famine that afflicted the French in the 11th century where **huma-flesh** was publicly displayed and sold in the market place of **Tournus**. An **incipient madness** that was to return to haunt them during the revolution with the histrionic voice of reason howling at the moon, by the **'Abbot Morelle'** who proposed **"the true communion of the patriots;"** or the **devils ablutions** which was a law that obliged citizens, on **pain** of **severe punishment** to go once a week to a **National-Butchers-shop**, where the *flesh* of the aristocratic victims of the guillotine would be sold...!

. . .

Otto mingled among the who's who, from **Dante** to **Faust**, on the walls of Los Angeles's **Hoy-Polloi** restaurant bar, called: **The Club-Inferno** and Bohemian oasis for poets, writers and the disaffected rich or jet-set of America's subculture, trying to search for their soul! Among the **Cadrè** and aristocracy of the occult world, like in the Hollywood movie called:

32

The Seventh Victim a 1943 horror and film noir starring Tom Conway, Jean Brooks, Isabel Jewell, Kim Hunter (in her first film), and Hugh Beaumont, directed by Mark Robson, and produced by Val Lewton for RKO Radio Pictures. Based on the novel: *The Prague Cemetery* by *Umberto Eco*.

The film focuses on a young woman who stumbles upon an underground cult of devil worshippers or *Palladists* a name for an alleged *Theistic Satanist society* or member of that society. The name *Palladian* comes from *Pallas* and refers to *wisdom* and *learning*! In a Greenwich Village while searching for her missing sister!

In 1891 Léo Taxil (Gabriel Jogand-Pagès) and Adolphe Ricoux claimed to have discovered a *Palladian Society*. An 1892 French book *Le Diable au XIXe siècle* (*The Devil in the 19th Century*", *1892*), written by "Dr. Bataille" (actually Jogand-Pagès himself) alleged that *Palladists* were *Satanists* based in Charleston, South Carolina headed by the American Freemason *Albert Pike* and created by the Italian liberal patriot and author, *Giuseppe Mazzini*.

Arthur Edward Waite, debunking the existence of the group in *Devil-Worship in France, or The Question of Lucifer, ch. II*: "*The Mask of Masonry*" (London, 1896), reports that according to "the works of Domenico Margiotta and Dr Bataille" that "*The Order of Palladium founded in Paris 20 May 1737* or *Sovereign Council of Wisdom*" was a "*Masonic diabolic order*". Dr. Bataille asserted that women would supposedly be initiated as "*Companions of Penelope*". According to Dr. Bataille, the society had two orders, "*Adelph*" and "*Companion of Ulysses*", however the society was broken up by French law enforcement a few years after its foundation, unless they all went back to there day jobs! which is only a half-truth! Officially, its more than likely, they went underground, *excuse the pun!*

Much like the shadowy figures of *J-K Huysmans* book: *Là Bas*. Most times Otto would sit alone, as if he were first among equals! Because no one would speak to him when he was in one of his *existential-binges,* because to Otto there was no point to it, it was only a movement in the void to him!

While he had worked in the Los Angeles Metropolitan museum of antiquities, at night when he was alone in the museum, either repairing books and artefacts or cataloguing the exhibits, he would hear strange footsteps and whispering voices and where he would find that things had been moved around, as if someone was searching for something? When no one was there.

Otto was himself a collector of rare antiquities and strange esoteric documents, like *Isidore Liseux*! The erudite publisher of superlative editions of French and Italian erotica and himself said to be an unfrocked monk! He had the "*De Demonialitate, et Incubis, et Succubis*," by *Reverend Father Ludovico Maria Sinistrari*, of Ameno, in Italy. As well as the eminent churchmen who subscribed to the belief in *incubi* and *succubi* you will find: *St Augustine*, *St Thomas*, *St. Bonaventure*,

Pope innocent VIII, and numerous others! His apartment was filled with old manuscripts and ancient books on magic and necromancy. He had books on Demons and shape-shifters like *"Processus Satanae Belial-and occult Demonology"* or *"Petit Alberts: Grimoire of Albertus Magnus"*, *"Casum de Incubo—Incubus"*, *"IIuminati* (*originals schriften des IIuminatenordens*)*" "De Gentibus Septentrion-alibus-about Witchcraft and monsters!"* Or the *"Liber Iezirah-Fundamental Cabbalistic text"*, *"Monsieur Ouflé Witchcraft-Demonology"*, *"Alphabetum-Demonology"*, *"Wierus De praestigiis Daemonum"*, *"Monomanie des Sorciers or the bible of demonology"* and official papers pertaining to the mysterious lost Franklin expedition! And **Gore's** missing prayer book! With the mysterious handwriting marked in the margins, he had bought through a friend of a friend, who had picked it up by sheer **'serendipity'** from an old antiquarian book shop in **London** (*England*) where rumour has it, that several of the book-keepers had committed **suicide** late at night, for some strange reason! He was also rumoured to have **Lovecraft's** much-maligned book that was rumoured, to have been destroyed: **The Necronomicon.**

Polygon
(The word derives from the Greek)

In geometry, a **polygon** is traditionally a plane figure that is bounded by a finite chain of straight line segments closing in a loop to form a closed chain or **circuit**. These segments are called its **edges** or **sides**, and the points where two edges meet are the polygon's **vertices** (singular: vertex) or **corners**. The interior of the polygon is sometimes called its *body*. An **n-gon** is a polygon with **n** sides. A polygon is a 2-dimensional example of the more general polytope in any number of dimensions:

Polygon culling is the process of eliminating **3D polygons** that lie outside the viewer's field of vision. It is more efficient than discarding polygons through **3D clipping** because we can test for visibility without performing **3D transformation.**

In computer graphics, **back-face culling** determines whether a polygon of a graphical object is visible. It is a step in the graphical pipeline that tests whether the points in the polygon appear in clockwise or counter-clockwise order when projected onto the screen. If the user has specified that front-facing polygons have a clockwise winding, but the polygon projected on the screen has a counter-clockwise winding then it has been rotated to face away from the camera and will not be drawn.

The process makes rendering objects quicker and more efficient by reducing the number of polygons for the program to draw. For example, in a city street scene, there is generally no need to draw the polygons on the sides of the buildings facing away from the camera; they are completely occluded by the sides facing the camera.

In general back-face culling can be assumed to produce no visible artifact in a rendered scene if it contains only closed and opaque geometry. In scenes containing transparent polygons, rear facing polygons may become visible through the process of alpha composition. In wire-frame rendering, back-face culling can be used to partially address problem of hidden line removal, but only for closed convex geometry.

A related technique is clipping, which determines whether polygons are within the camera's field of view at all.

Another similar technique is Z-culling, also known as occlusion culling, which attempts to skip the drawing of polygons which are covered from the viewpoint by other visible polygons.

That can create what seems or appears to be a physical (*corporeal*) theoretical world or enigma, from a **bio-computer**, so to speak, or is it being generated for whatever reason either from the source of all knowledge and understanding? Or from someone or something else out there?

Schrödinger's cat

Is a thought experiment, sometimes described as a paradox, devised by Austrian physicist **Erwin Schrödinger** in 1935. It illustrates what he saw as the problem of the Copenhagen interpretation of quantum mechanics applied to everyday objects. The scenario presents a cat that may be both alive and dead, this state being tied to an earlier random event. Although the original **"experiment"** was imaginary, similar principles have been researched and used in practical applications. The thought experiment is also often featured in theoretical discussions of the interpretations of **quantum mechanics**. In the course of developing this experiment, Schrödinger coined the term ***Verschränkung*** (*entanglement*).

Fuzzy Logic

It is typical of these cases that an indeterminacy originally restricted to the atomic domain becomes transformed into macroscopic indeterminacy, which can then be resolved by direct observation. That prevents us from so naively accepting as valid a **"blurred model"** for representing reality. In itself, it would not embody anything **unclear** or **contradictory**. There is a difference between a **shaky** or **out-of-focus photograph** and a snapshot of **clouds** and **fog banks**.

. . .

Or there could be different species operating from somewhere on this planet! **Invader's** that could have came from the **stars** long ago, to colonize the earth live a giant hive, and they or others are the ones who built this **massive computer**, using something akin to **Nano-bots** to look after the **hive** below the planet, but something seems or appears to has gone wrong?

What planet?

"Irrelevant conclusion (argumentum ad populum) that barristers use to prove one thing when you are proving another. To beg the question is to assume what you are seeking to prove."

It could be an irrelevant conclusion, or just another piece of the puzzle, but it could be like the film *"The matrix"* where the information or the world that you think you have been living in is **false-data**, being **feed** or **programmed into you**, as we could be collectively **gestating** in **biological tubes**, so to speak, during the process of the ***grand*** illusion! And whatever or whoever we are, something or someone has been interfering or correcting and adjusting the process of the ***Anthropological, Theological*** and ***Sociological*** development!

And that something could either be ***extra-terrestrial*** or ***terrestrial*** from the (***earth***!) like ***Schrödinger's cat***! That could literarily be our own highly evolved self from the long dead past or from a future still to come? Who have evolved or fused into **non-physical** (*non-corporeal*) **sentient beings** that may have a strange and ancient affinity with us: either ***extra-terrestrial*** or ***terrestrial***!

And it seems or appears that this someone or something can do things with their **collective mind**, that we can only do with our hands, or they are using a **science without instrumentality**, and who seem or appear not to be governed by the same laws that restrict us, so the paper-trail has led us to another hidden piece of the **puzzle**, or **Easter-egg**. A place so near and yet so far, outside of time and space that could very well be the **author of the piece** or (***Grand-plan***)

Hegel (1770-1831)

'The principle that everything is and at the same time and in the same sense is not!'

Because one day, as our own **ancestors** probably will over many eons of time, will already have, as a species reached that relative-point of observation, because time is relative, and our own highly evolved selves seem or appear to be able to interfere in time, or could be collectively projecting something into our **primitive minds** or their own ancestral heads, so to speak, so that the **means will justify the ends**!

. . .

Empirical knowledge

(If you don't believe me, you can test the theory...)

By checking back, not in a billion years, just tomorrow? Which is in the future and by that time, today, which is the present, will be yesterday or the past! And if you do, you will have eventually arrived in the future, which is tomorrow or is it today? So when we eventually arrive in the future as a highly evolved species, like the ones in the past! We can come back using what we colloquially call a **time machine** to do what is apparently been happening!!

36

Looking through a glass darkly.

It's like game programmers who put strange things into the games you play, or
Like strange clues or extra things that you don't realise are there, where the meaning is strange and elusive, like in the computer game, or computer software, called: *"Easter eggs"* that are secret responses that occur in response to an undocumented set of commands!
It's as if someone or something is responsible for doing very strange things with or interfering in odd-events that have been happening in the world that we think we live in! Like the **JFK** assassination (murder!) or the twin-towers!! Like the areas that have already been covered by **SAR** (*search and rescue*) in **411** and its as if the missing person is strangely being put back where they originally were, like in computer games!

Easter eggs or Paschal eggs

Are decorated eggs that are often given to celebrate Easter or springtime. As such, **Easter eggs** are common during the season of *Eastertide* (Easter season). The oldest tradition is to use dyed and painted **chicken eggs**, but a modern custom is to substitute chocolate eggs, or plastic eggs filled with confectionery such as jelly beans. Eggs, in general, were a traditional symbol of *fertility*, and **rebirth**.
Like in the film: Curse of the mummies tomb and the mysterious words spoken in the sequence by the cursed brother under the pseudonym 'Beauchamp' or '*Be*' who uttered the prophetic words to raise his brother '*Ra*' from he dead:

"Awaken O silent one, thou who has slept, appear, Osiris, father of all, give this thy servant that which you bestow upon the unborn bird in the 'egg' give it the breath of life, set the time that it may come forth and loudly rise up its voice to praise thee."

. . .

China

(*Chaos egg*)
(From which people, heaven, and earth were created!)
In Christianity, for the celebration of **Eastertide**, Easter 'eggs' symbolize the empty tomb of **Jesus**: though an egg appears to be like the **stone** of a tomb, a bird hatches from it with life; similarly, the **Easter egg**, for **Christians**, is a reminder that **Jesus** rose from the grave, and that those who believe will also experience eternal life!

Raising of Lazarus

The biblical narrative of the Raising of Lazarus is found in chapter 11 of the Gospel of John. Lazarus is introduced as a follower of Jesus, who lives in the town of Bethany near Jerusalem. He is identified as the brother of the sisters Mary and Martha. The sisters send word to Jesus that Lazarus, "he whom thou lovest," is ill. Instead of immediately traveling to Bethany, according to the narrator, Jesus intentionally remains where he is for two more days before beginning the journey.

When Jesus arrives in Bethany, he finds that Lazarus is dead and has already been in his tomb for four days. He meets first with Martha and Mary in turn. Martha laments that Jesus did not arrive soon enough to heal her brother and Jesus replies with the well-known statement:

"I am the resurrection, and the life: he that believeth in me, though he were dead, yet shall he live: And whosoever liveth and believeth in me shall never die"

In the presence of a crowd of Jewish mourners, Jesus comes to the tomb. Over the objections of Martha, Jesus has them roll the stone away from the entrance to the tomb and says a prayer. And there in that terrible silence, he then calls **"Lazarus come forth"** and Lazarus does so, still wrapped in his grave-cloths. Jesus then calls for someone to remove the grave-cloths, and let him go.

"How to hide the easter-egg"

The results can vary from a simple printed message or image, to a page of programmer credits or a small videogame hidden inside an otherwise serious piece of software. Videogame cheat codes are a specific type of **"Easter egg"**, in which entering a secret command will unlock special powers or new levels for the player.

In the TOPS-10 operating system (*for the DEC PDP-10 computer*), the make command is used to invoke the TECO editor to create a file; if given the file name argument **"love,"** so that the command is **"make love,"** it will pause and respond **"not war?"** before creating the file.

This same behavior occurred on the *RSTS/E* operating system, where *TECO* will provide this response. Other Unix operating systems respond to **"why"** with **"why not"**

Or you can come across them or discover them in an adventure game, hidden in a bin or anywhere! And that's why they are called **"Easter-eggs"** which has a strange definity with **"Christ"** and the symbolism of his **"resurrection"** see the article further on, titled the **"shroud"** But we are trying to run before we can walk.

Backdoor

Also called a **trapdoor**. An undocumented way of gaining access to a program, or an entire computer system. The backdoor is written by the programmer who **creates** the *code* for the **program**. It is often only known by the programmer. A backdoor is a potential security risk!

It's like what I have already said concerning game programmers, or **whoever** or **whatever** is involved, by putting strange things into the world that **we think we live in**! Strange clues or extra things that you don't realise are there, until you come across them inside the programme, i.e. that you discover them hidden in a bin or anywhere! Its called an **"Easter-egg"** Like the meaning of the **"Jack the Ripper murders"**

And whoever or whatever that innocuous hidden hand called **"Bible John"**, in the **Glasgow** of the **1960s**, having returned back to the future, where it seems or appears to have been with us throughout history standing in the shadows, looking over our shoulder, figuratively speaking, in: **"Who goes there?"** Or where we will most likely find more pieces of the jigsaw, or some of them, by travelling **"Into the void"**

We know something is there! Like in: **"Missing 411"** or where someone or something strange has accidentally left their footprints, so to speak, in the bizarre **"Autopsy"** in the **"Legions of the damned"** and the strange biblical quote, **"Choose ye this day whom ye will serve"** or quasi-historical connection, that has only been hinted at, on one of the tombstones that form part of the full quote:

. . .

"If it seem evil unto you to serve the Lord
Choose ye this day whom ye will serve
Whether the Gods which your father served
Which where on the other side of the flood
Or the Gods of the Amorites
In whose land ye dwell"

. . .

To try and understand why people are mysteriously going missing and mostly being found murdered, we need to journey back to **1888** and the late 19th Century with the strange and almost bizarre murders of **Jack the ripper**! And the strange context of the Rev. W. Evens Hurndall of Bow, who preached to a crowded congregation on the whitechapel murders, choosing ironically as his text **Deuteronomy 29:18** 'A root that beareth gall and **"Wormwood"** almost as if it were a subliminal truth, that you just can't put your finger on, like an enigma in the guise of the prophetic and eerie sense of the words he had chosen!

Remember he was an educated man, was he being abstract and yet purposefully getting us to hunt for the **Easter egg?** Like the evidence found at the scene of the strange and odd disappearances in the **Missing 411** books by **David Paulides,** what or who is trying to tell as something in this mysterious enigmatic riddle, it's as if one should be looking down, not up? In the use of the semantics he used:

. . .

"The 3rd angel blew [his] trumpet, and a huge star fell from heaven, burning like a torch, and it dropped on a 3rd of the rivers and on the springs of water— And the name of the star is Wormwood. A 3rd part of the waters was changed into wormwood, and many people died from using the water, because it had become bitter"

. . .

It seems or appears to be an unquiet voice, from the ghostly hand of whatever or whoever **"Jack the ripper"** was?

. . .

The Moving Finger

"The Moving Finger writes; and, having writ,
Moves on:
With them the Seed of Wisdom did I sow,
And with my own hand labour'd it to grow:
And this was all the Harvest that I reap'd—
I sent my Soul through the Invisible,
Some letter of that After-life to spell:
And by and by my Soul return'd to me,
And answer'd
*"I Myself am **Heav'n** and **Hell"***

. . .

Omar Khayyám

Who was a sufi mystic, Persian polymath, philosopher, mathematician, astronomer and poet. He also wrote treatises on mechanics, geography, mineralogy, music, and Islamic theology.

And because time does not apply to the **Androgynous state**, time and space seem to be there and at the same time, they seem or appear not to be there!

Like matter that appears to be solid or the bicycle wheel effect with it's little electrons whirling endlessly in space, as if held in a **unified-field** by some unknown energy of sorts, around the nucleus of this **phantom** or **theoretical atom**!

And even stranger is the fact that time moves **forward** and **backwards** at the same time or **time-travel** would be impossible! Like the observation in our rocket ship travelling away from the earth at the speed of light, with the pilot on board who sees everything going backwards!

Through the giant telescope on board the spaceship, so it would appear that at the same time the universe appears to be created from the beginning to the end, it was or is being created back-to-front at the same time! **Because as you approach light-speed you will pass light that has went before you**! So what you see must have been made backwards at the same time!!

Like Shakespeare put it: *Is our fate in ourselves or in our stars?* Is our life a second hand one or are we spoiled goods! Where our autonomy or free will is something that is handed down to us, even though it seems or appears that we have the free will to choice from an infinite number of possibilities, they have already been chosen for us! Implying the hand of fate has already dealt the cards, and the future or for that matter the past is already self-ordained, before we are even born into the world? So that the means will justify the ends!!!

It's as if the answer is either *yes* or *no?* Like an infinite and vast intelligence running on a *binomial* or *binary system* namely *1-or-0*, Vis-à-vis (therefore) it means its quantum-physics *yes* and *no!* Which is a half-truth or *Deo non-Fortuna*, meaning by: *God,* not by *chance.*

. . .

It is like king Solomon's cyclic view of destiny?

"For everything its season, and for every activity under heaven its time: a time to be born and a time to die...Whatever is has been already, and Whatever is to come has been already, and God summons each event back in turn"
Eccl. 3: 1, 2, 15.

. . .

Conntinued

Just like the puzzle of the universe and the enigma of *God* or the *indescribable or inconceivable Androgynous state* and the source of all **knowledge and understanding** wherever or whatever it is?

That's how our space ship was able to see everything on earth going backwards or the *CLA* time machine is able to travel into the past or into the future, because the future not unlike the past has still to happen, and at the same time it has happened or is still to happen! According to Albert Einstein's theory!

So if we reiterate with our example of what came first: *The chicken or the egg?* Like the Chinese legend of the *chaos egg*, with which *people, heaven* and *earth* were made! Which is a bit like **Gods** or our own self-awareness or retrospection of its own self in the *Androgynous state* realizing that something was wrong, because it is trying to paradoxically tell it's own self or reflection, like in a **symbolic mirror**, that it cannot exist, and the font of this self awareness is what we call: *relativity* in the dual aspect or twin destiny of our own selves, which has planted a seed called "**time**" in the universe, the observer onboard the rocket ship can see going *forward* or *backwards* in the *void*.

That's why time travellers can move back and forth through the process of *atomic decay* or as we call it: *time*, and view things *relative* to the observer, with each and every person they meet, either in the past or in the

41

future or we would all be deaf, dumb and blind to everything, and we would exist in a bizarre and oblivious state, akin to **hell**!

The Crawling Chaos
[I am the last... I will tell the audient void...]
H.P. Lovecraft

I do not recall distinctly when it began, but it was months ago. The general tension was horrible. To a season of political and social upheaval was added a strange and brooding apprehension of hideous physical danger; a danger widespread and all-embracing, such a danger as may be imagined only in the most terrible phantasms of the night.

I recall that the people went about with pale and worried faces, and whispered warnings and prophecies, which no one dared consciously repeat or acknowledge to himself that he had heard, a sense of monstrous guilt was upon the land, and out of the abysses between the stars swept chill currents that made men shiver in dark and lonely places.

There was a daemoniac alteration in the sequence of the seasons, the autumn heat lingered fearsomely, and everyone felt that the world and perhaps the universe had passed from the control of known gods or forces to that of gods or forces which were unknown.

*And it was then that **Nyarlathotep** came out of Egypt. Who he was, none could tell, but he was of the old native blood and looked like a Pharaoh. The fellahin knelt when they saw him, yet could not say why. He said he had risen up out of the blackness of twenty-seven centuries, and that he had heard messages from places not on this planet. Into the lands of civilisation came **Nyarlathotep**, swarthy, slender, and sinister, always buying strange instruments of glass and metal and combining them into instruments yet stranger. He spoke much of the sciences—of electricity and psychology—and gave exhibitions of power, which sent his spectators away speechless, yet which swelled his fame to exceeding magnitude.*

*Men advised one another to see **Nyarlathotep**, and shuddered. And where **Nyarlathotep** went, rest vanished; for the small hours were rent with the screams of nightmare. Never before had the screams of nightmare been such a public problem; now the wise men almost wished they could forbid sleep in the small hours, that the shrieks of cities might less horribly disturb the pale, pitying moon as it glimmered on green waters gliding under bridges, and old steeples crumbling against a sickly sky.*

*I remember when **Nyarlathotep** came to my city—the great, the old, the terrible city of unnumbered crimes, my friend had told me of him, and of the impelling fascination and allurement of his revelations, and I burned with eagerness to explore his uttermost mysteries. My friend said they were horrible and impressive beyond my most fevered imaginings; that what was thrown on a screen in the darkened room prophesied things none but **Nyarlathotep** dared prophesy, and that in the sputter of his sparks there was taken from men that which had never been taken before,*

42

yet which showed only in the eyes. And I heard it hinted abroad that those who knew **Nyarlathotep** looked on sights, which others saw not.

It was in the hot autumn that I went through the night with the restless crowds to see **Nyarlathotep**, through the stifling night and up the endless stairs into the choking room.

And shadowed on a screen, I saw hooded forms amidst ruins, and yellow evil faces peering from behind fallen monuments. And I saw the world battling against blackness; against the waves of destruction from ultimate space; whirling, churning; struggling around the dimming, cooling sun. Then the sparks played amazingly around the heads of the spectators, and hair stood up on end whilst shadows more grotesque than I can tell came out and squatted on the heads. And when I, who was colder and more scientific than the rest, mumbled a trembling protest about "imposture" and "static electricity", **Nyarlathotep** drove us all out, down the dizzy stairs into the damp, hot, deserted midnight streets. I screamed aloud that I was not afraid; that I never could be afraid; and others screamed with me for solace. We swear to one another that the city was exactly the same, and still alive; and when the electric lights began to fade we cursed the company over and over again, and laughed at the queer faces we made. I believe we felt something coming down from the greenish moon, for when we began to depend on its light we drifted into curious involuntary formations and seemed to know our destinations though we dared not think of them.

Once we looked at the pavement and found the blocks loose and displaced by grass, with scarce a line of rusted metal to show where the tramways had run. And again we saw a tramcar, lone, windowless, dilapidated, and almost on its side. When we gazed around the horizon, we could not find the third tower by the river, and noticed that the silhouette of the second tower was ragged at the top. Then we split up into narrow columns, each of which seemed drawn in a different direction. One disappeared in a narrow alley to the left, leaving only the echo of a shocking moan. Another filed down a weed-choked subway entrance, howling with a laughter that was mad. My own column was sucked toward the open country, and presently felt a chill, which was not of the hot autumn; for as we stalked out on the dark moor; we beheld around us the hellish moon-glitter of evil snows.

Trackless, inexplicable snows, swept asunder in one direction only, where lay a gulf all the blacker for its glittering walls. The column seemed very thin indeed as it plodded dreamily into the gulf. I lingered behind, for the black rift in the green-litten snow was frightful, and I thought I had heard the reverberations of a disquieting wail as my companions vanished; but my power to linger was slight. As if beckoned by those who had gone before, I half floated between the titanic snowdrifts, quivering and afraid, into the sightless vortex of the unimaginable. Screamingly sentient, dumbly delirious, only the gods that were can tell.

A sickened, sensitive shadow writhing in hands that are not hands, and whirled blindly past ghastly midnights of rotting creation, corpses of *dead worlds with sores that were cities, charnel winds that brush the pallid stars and make them flicker low. Beyond the worlds vague ghosts of monstrous things; half-seen columns of unsanctified temples that rest on nameless rocks beneath space and reach up to dizzy vacua above the spheres of light and darkness. And through this revolting graveyard of the universe the muffled, maddening beating of drums, and thin, monotonous whine of blasphemous flutes from inconceivable, unlighted chambers beyond Time; the detestable pounding and piping whereunto dance slowly, awkwardly, and absurdly the gigantic, tenebrous ultimate gods—the blind, voiceless, mindless gargoyles whose soul is:* **"Nyarlathotep"**

. . .

It is our imaginary fear of death or non-existence, that's why the reflection is struggling with it's own self, which is what we know as **existence!** Because it knows that this self-evident-truth by its very nature cannot exist or be prolonged by its self or continue to be separate from the **indescribable** or **inconceivable androgynous state!**

It was as if Mathew was agreeing with himself! Because he then remembered the times he had blackouts! When he would talk to his comrades and interact with them, and afterwards he remembered nothing of what he had said or done, although it would have been stored in the back of his memory, so it seemed that he could still be **conscious**, but for some reason not **aware** of what was happening, is our **consciousness** the essence of this **false reflection** that theoretically **exists?** Because it appears to be oblivious! And yet we must be aware! At the same time, so our **relative-awareness** or **higher self** seems to be that part of our own self, called the **observer** or the **indescribable** or **inconceivable androgynous state,** that's trying to convince it's own reflection that it cannot exist separately, which is the conscious part of our mind or the retrospective aspect or awareness of our own self that is asking such questions as: **Where did we come from? Or why are we here?** And **where are we going?** And naturally you will get a blank reply, because the answer does not come before the question, so to speak!

And in our case visa-versa, because nothing has happened, it is only theoretical, and the **indescribable** or **inconceivable androgynous state** seems to somehow know, even though it appears to be contradicting its self, it's like the tail wagging the dog!

So it must be like an intentional slight of mouth or contradiction that is causing the actual problem, which has brought about or created the **physical** (*Corporeal*) and the **non-physical** (*Non-Corporeal*) world as we know it, so it appears to have been a mistake or a problem that it is trying to solve! And in doing so, it seems or appears to have brought about a **dichotomy**! Or theoretical split in **'our'** or **'it's'** own **being**!

So without the ability to be conscious and aware at the same time there would be no continuity or meaning and purpose to life.

And if Mathew listened real close he would hear the sound of one hand clapping, which was the sound of the voice in his own head or that **simile**

44

or shadow aspect cast by *God,* and the **tongue** of that **serpent** in the **garden-of-Eden,** whispering in **Gods** ear if you will, or into **Mathews ear**, which is the voice of **Gods** own self and not the **reflection**, echoed in and through each of us trying to convince it's own self, that it does not and cannot exist in a separate state, and that's why we have a fear of death because it is our own **higher self** (*observer*) or the **indescribable, inconceivable androgynous state** that already knows that it is its own reflection that has been cast upon the preverbal **mirror** and that it is a false representation or shadow aspect of it's own true self, which has imprisoned itself here in the **corporal** or **physical world**, like "**Eliphas Levi 1810-1875** who believed that **Satan** was the shadow of **God**"

Is that why Jesus Christ was always inferring that his will was not important, but his fathers, like in the garden of:

. . .

Gethsemane

"*My father if it be possible, let this chalice pass from me, but yet not my will, but thine be done.*" The wind began to gently cry and moan. Again Christ asked his father. "*My father, if this chalice may not pass away, but I must drink it, Thy will be done.*"

Or like in the fantastic film "***Judah-Ben-Hur***" by Lew Wallace. Just before the final death-defying chariot race with **Messala**! Where **Judah** symbolically draws his cape over his head, like a symbolic shroud, before he says his prayer or evocation to **God**! Akin to the gesture of **Julius Caesar:**

Suetonius

Caesar said nothing. Plutarch also reports that Caesar said nothing, pulling his toga over his head when he saw Brutus among the conspirators.

Ben Hur

(Days of the messiah)
"***God forgive me for seeking vengeance***
But my path is set
Into your hands I commit my life
Do with me as you will!"

Lew Wallace

. . .

As if it were the reflection cast by the face of *God* or the **indescribable and inconceivable androgynous state's** self-awareness of its own self in the **preverbal mirror**! Where it seems or appears to know the truth about its own true and yet paradoxical nature!

And like the story of **Jesus Christ** after he had mysteriously risen from the dead, when Mary Magdalene had approached the strange figure in the cemetery, having not recognized that it was **Christ**, she asked the stranger, if he had been responsible for taking away her masters body? And **Christ** had asked of her: why was she looking for the living among the dead? Just the same as we do, when we ask the same questions about dying! And the fear of it we seem to cherish so much, or that self-same fear of non-existence!

. . .

Pride comes before a fall!

(Have we cut our nose off to spite our face?)
*"Like the **pebble** on the beach, what universal power was enacted or used to give us the impression of that little **stone**! So it would end up in that exact position in the universe? So that someone anyone, could just easily pick it up and move it, it seems or appears what we gain on the roundabout, we lose on the swings, so to speak?"*

. . .

Which is, as we know the theoretical separation or disassociation, which is like a paradoxical battle of some kind, where you gain on the swings, but lose on the roundabout, in the self-perception or retrospective thinking process, that acted like an **exchange of energy** or like a **ripple** or a **pebble** hitting the **surface of a pond of water**, that the **original-thought** (*sin*) or **image** has been cast onto, like a **hologram** that has been smashed into an infinite number of pieces, and each piece of creation, so to speak, contains the whole original image! Even though the parts seem or appear to be greater than the whole, which is the symbolic image of **God,** so to speak, or **the indescribable or inconceivable androgynous state.**
In each and every one of us, by want of separation the parts that make up the image cannot be greater than the whole, and yet each part like the **hologram** contains the **whole**!
And the reality of the physical world seems or appears to at least to bare witness to some great truth! That was to Mathew like a voice crying in the wilderness, a voice that he seemed to know, because he remembered what it had said in the bible's book of Genesis, where it describes:
"In the beginning there was darkness or a description of something that was **indescribable**! Or theoretically outside of its own self, and God moved upon the face of the darkness or was it discovering the retrospective aspect or awareness of it's own self? And said: **Let there be light**, and there was **light**" or the disassociation of thinking in a theoretical separation of it's own self had taken place, and where it or we are temporally trapped in a **dichotomy** or **struggle**, that is equivalent of asking your self a rhetorical question: what is the meaning of life? And your own voice replying like an echo: *"how long is a piece of string?"*
Which is like the serpents tongue in the **symbolic** garden of **Eden**, that caused the **fall** from grace or **separation** of our own selves, by none other than **Lucifer** himself, who was not destroyed by God! That's why it is actually a disembodied or inner voice of **God** or that **inconceivable** or

indescribable androgynous state or **source of all knowledge and understanding** that seems or appears to be there and yet at the same time it isn't there! It does not and cannot exist therefore non-existence does not apply to it in the normal sense that we have come to believe in, like using your own **internal-dialogue** as an example, it goes on inside your own head, so to speak!

Its as if **God** or the essence of that **great-architect** of the **physical** (*corporeal*) and the **non-physical** (*non-corporal*) world is it's self the carrier or the symbolic barer of that **light** or **thought** (*shadow*) that was reputedly **cast out** of **heaven** or **separated** from that state of being! Due to the monumental battle or struggle within its own self"

"For never was there such a star that shone so bright and fell so far, that can rise again and shine so bright"

And as Mathew continued reading the great book in the chamber of the ages, he came to a page with a **puzzle** or **riddle** on it, that he began to read to himself:

"What has a beginning where there is no beginning? And an end, where there is no end?"

Obviously something that is **theoretical** or cannot be **made** or **destroyed**, like the **universe**! Mathew thought, remembering the words from the bible, when **Christ** had said in the scriptures:

"I am Alpha and Omega, the beginning and the ending, saith the Lord, which is, and which was, and which is to come, the Almighty"

The **beginning** or where the physical or illusional world is coming from, and the **end**, because it isn't rely there, why? Because it's theoretical! And that he was not only the **Son of God**, but he was the **Son of man**! Stating that he along with us was the collective expression of that reflection cast by our own true selves, is that what **Christ** symbolically meant, when he said that we were made in **God's image** or a tongue in cheek meaning of who we rely are, which is the beginning or theoretical disassociation of our own true self, which is an **indescribable** or **inconceivable androgynous state,** that has no beginning! And because it is theoretical, then nothing has actually happened! **"So there is no beginning, and if there is no beginning then there can be no end"** so to speak!

It was the self-evident truth of that dichotomy that has brought into play so the state or paradox of existence, holds the very fabric of the enigma in place, until everything is said and done, so to speak, which is inherent in the creed of **dualism** and the **law of opposites**, that is hard on the heels of the big question of existence!

'The intelligence'

Like the 60s cult tv Show Star-Trek and the episode called **"The savage curtain"** where some of the crew were forced to fight to see whether **"good"** was better than **"evil!"** and they discovered that **good** seems or appears to use the same method as **evil** to achieve its own end or the way the **goyim** (Gentile) is being cleverly manipulated when virtue becomes a necessary vice, **vis-à-vis** (therefore) true **evil's** juxa-position or that invisible left-hand that rocks the cradle! Can only be exposed through **The House of Rothschild**! Or the right-hand of that same body that allows it to happen!

Or in our case the human condition, which in a way is *self-inflicted*, because we seem to have become victimized by and through our own selves! And even *Christ* said in the bible, that there will be wars and rumours of wars, and that these things must happen, almost as if the means will justify the ends! And it is not the fault of **the house of Rothschild's**, but our own collective responsibility!

. . .

Its as if God is attempting to cut off a theoretical finger to save the body, for some unknown reason, through each of us, is he telling us that *"for the want of a horse-shoe nail the war was lost!"* with regards to that part of our self or what could be euphemistically known as the *"author of the piece"* with each of us as the critic in the *play*!

Who seems or appears to be causing the problem, a part that has to be integrated at any cost, whether you like it or not, or the reflection will win and lose, at the same time! Because it will cancel out its own self, or the *indescribable* or *inconceivable androgynous state* *will cease to be*, as it was before the theoretical disassociation!

. . .

'If you win do you not lose! And if you lose do you not win!'

(Because the means will justify the ends!)

If you don't realize the true meaning of existence like Jesus Christ prophesised, even though it's a modern day **cliché**: *"is there a part of ourselves that cannot and will not be saved"* or **rebooted**! Because existence is only a movement in the void or **digital programme**, so to speak, and if we don't realize it, then the problem could be cyclic, if its not **rebooted**! And where you will go round in a never-ending circle of suffering as you continue chasing your own tail or where the **data** is stuck! Between the infinite tick of the clock or **programme**! A bit like an old Greek joke, *"if you listen closely you can hear the gods laugh"* which is a bit like life, you either get it or you don't! Like in the Christmas movie starring *Cary Grant* called: *The Bishops Wife* where the angel says: I'm at my most *serious* when I'm *joking!*

. . .

But the message of life's true meaning is like *"pearls before swine"* and unless you truly understand that we are in a situation where you are either **part of the problem** or **part of the solution**, you are for or against your own self in a symbolic struggle for power in a battle of *unification* that can and will change our perception of the physical and the non-physical worlds, with there hidden meaning or we may lose the true knowledge of who we rely are, instead of the false knowledge of who we think we are!

48

Like in the more adept covens where high politics are the principal subject of **QED** or **AKA** (*questions enable debate*) at these so-called **sabbats**, and where powerful gangs of witches still strive to decide the destiny of countries and the fate of kings!

In 1786 a very secret sabbat or circle was convened at Frankfurt, a meeting of Satanists amongst whom were present: **Cagliostro**; the **cabalist Duchanteau**; the '**Philallèthes' Savalette de Langes**, a traitor 'versed in all dark mysteries, complotter in all vile plots', **pseudo-Rosicrucian**, **magic Martiniste**; the **illuminatus**, **Christian Bode**, **alias Amelius**.

It was here that the deaths of **Louis XVI of France** and **Gustavus III of Sweden** were decreed. And very similar meetings are held today... very similar murderous resolutions are determined and have been passed in effect. The revolutions that have troubled and vexed peaceful nations the broils and unrest culminating in the world chaos of an almost universal misery, tyranny, and energetically assisted by **black international**, the **Satanists**, who go under a dozen trifling occult names, who mockingly dub themselves **political parties**! And where rebellion is seen as the sin of witchcraft in this **upside-down** perverted world we live in, we must denounce the greed, the corruption, the social injustices of our times, for one can only chose two courses of action which are like the differing poles of a magnet, one is to entangle oneself in intrigues which must mean fresh disaster and with the fetters welded with pains and perseverance and hate cannot lightly be broken; when a man or woman who has dipped their blooded hands in the **quagmire** or **sore struggle** could they not return to **God** and await confidently the deliverance in whatever guise will be sent!

'To know it, is not to worship it!'

[for-armed is for-warned]

'LUCIFER'

Satan

Illuminator

(Bringer of knowledge?)

"Paradise lost"

"Where Lucifer or the Devil was cast into the pit! And he said that it would be better to rule in hell, than serve in heaven"

Milton

"Hell has its price", "Sua Infernum Pretium"

* * *

(Sits in high places, leading the blind in spite of themselves!)

"All the world's a stage, And all the men and women merely players; They have their exits and their entrances, And one man in his time plays many parts"

49

The statement below is true
Because the statement above is false:
'Do not believe a word certain dangerous others say!'

You Will Know Them by Their Fruits

¹⁵ Beware of false prophets, who come to you in **sheep's clothing**, but inwardly they are **ravenous wolves**. ¹⁶ You will know them by their fruits. Do men gather grapes from thornbushes or figs from thistles? ¹⁷ Even so, every good tree bears good fruit, but a bad tree bears bad fruit. ¹⁸ A good tree cannot bear bad fruit, nor *can* a bad tree bear good fruit. ¹⁹ Every tree that does not bear good fruit is cut down and thrown into the fire. ²⁰ Therefore by their fruits you will know them.

Latrunculi

Gangsters at enmity with one another and yet fixed in some infernal bond or brotherhood of blind and murderous hatred of things!
Something very clever is manipulating us at each other's **anthropological** *throat, through* **political** *and* **religious** *or in effect has the mark of Cain been put upon us! Or we are being Ostracized and supposedly shunned or to be figiritively non-exsistant. Or what is know as the* **dynamic silence** *By the* **Persona-non-grata** *ploy, is the observation of a self obvious* **truth** *over a* **lie** *and* **visa versa** *technique* that seems or appears to be invisible to its audience, in order to make it fit the changes, in the means that justify the ends, of information consumption! But remember to your dying day that there is:
(**Nothing more deceptive than the obvious**)

Wolf in the fold

(En prise)

The meaning of **en prise** is obvious and easy to explain, or is it? English-language dictionaries give simple but serviceable definitions, such as '**Exposed to capture**' and '**In a position to be taken**', but some chess books aim for more and achieve less! By using **double-agentry** may be practiced by **spies** of the **target organization** who (**openly**) infiltrate the **controlling organization**, or may result from the *turning* (**switching sides**) of previously loyal agents of the controlling organization by the target!

Creative will

'I AM WHATSOEVER WAS, WHATSOEVEVER IS, WHATSOEVER SHALL BE AND THE VAIL WHICH IS OVER MY FACE, NO MORTAL HAND HAS EVER RAISED'
Declaration of Isis

50

Testament to an unquiet truth

The external world that was limited and conditioned by the limits and conditions of his own mind, not the world that he and the rest of think we know, or the reality of appearances, but the reality that lies behind those appearances could be in essence not dissimilar to the perceiving mind itself!

When the final journey, symbolically following the souls first step beyond to serve by kneeling and bowing his head in the dust before that great mystery of the mind, which has hitherto defied its own penetrative power, and which may ultimately **resolve** itself into a **demonstratable impossibility** of **self-penetration.**

If we are made in the **image** of God! The sum of the parts cannot be greater than the **whole** or something larger than us, or source of **all knowledge and understanding**, (*God*) or the **creative will** is using the means that will justify the ends, through and by:

LUCIFER
(*Satan*)

Agent provocateur

An **agent provocateur** (French for "**inciting agent**") is a person who commits, or who acts to entice another person to commit an illegal or rash act or falsely implicate them in partaking in an illegal act. An agent provocateur may be acting out of their own **sense of duty**!

. . .

"to pit a virtuous and homogeneous people against a set of elites and dangerous "others" who were together depicted as depriving (or attempting to deprive) the sovereign people of their rights, values, prosperity, identity, and voice" by subjugating the populis, through the chaos of their Achillies heel!

. . .

"Lucifer, the light-bearer! Strange and mysterious name to give to the spirit of darkness! Son of the morning! Is it *he who bears the light, and with its splendorsintolerable blinds feeble, sensual or selfish souls? Doubt it not"*

. . .

"*Moral lessons are taught by use of the juxtaposition of evil*"
"*The true name of Lucifer, the Kabbalists say, is that of **Yahweh** reversed; for **Satan** is not a **black god**, but a **force**, created for **good**, but which may serve for **evil**"*
*Why did God? Not destroy **Lucifer Or Satan** that **Omni-arch** of the world or was it because in essence the **Devil** is the shadow aspect or reflection of **God**!*

. . .

"You could learn a lot from children, they believe in things in the dark, until we tell them it's not so, maybe we've been fooling them!"

Night/Curse of the Demon

. . .

*Because the **creative will** has given over the **essence** or **power of command**! To its own **relection**! Or we would not be suffering in this way. **Does one not have to be cruel to be kind?** So to speak! Or the means that will justify the ends in the bringing together of **two opposites**, of the creative will of that **intangible catalyst**! Or source of all knowledge and understanding that cannot be one or the other, until it is brought together!*

'But does not one nesscerally mean the other?'

*Like the story of the so-called disingenuous **Marie Antoinette** when she was rumoured to have replied when she was told that the peasants were crying for bread! She answered: if they have no 'bread' then let them eat 'cake!' did the 'little monster' mean what she said? Or was she that **spoiled** or **nieve**? Like the legend of the 'Gorgon' was the creature rumoured to be that **ugly** and **frightening** by just looking at her **countenance** would drive men mad!*

'Adversary'
(One who opposes)

Lucifer (*Shinning one*) or **bringer of dawn** or son of the morning the most '**clever**' of all the angels next to **God**! and the most **beautiful** of all the **angels** attracts or **repels** people due to its **ugliness**! That's why you need to be careful before we judge what is **good** and what is **bad**!

An act of volition

Like the young boy who always wanted to be a soldier! Was that not **good!** *So to speak*, and when he was of age he was called-up for the army in 1944! Was that not bad? But he then descovered that he had flat-feet, **that was bad!** And because of this he did'nt get to land on the beaches at **'Anzio'** was that not **good** or **bad?**

So we should always be careful what we wish for!

* * *

Scrooge

(Is it not what we do or what we don't do?)
INTRODUCTION
A CHRISMAS CHAROL

We are all children, the oldest and the wisest of us and we go to the heart that loves us best. Consciously or unconsciously we are doing it every day and in every walk of life, talent and genius attract us in degree as they are guided by love the hand that chastises us must be moved by the heart that loves us or it does us no good.

HAL CAINE

. . .

'Visa-Versa'

In the absence of a grand plan, if it doesn't matter what we do! Then all that matters is what we do and the slightest act of kindness can mean the whole world! **Lucifer** who himself succumbed to **pride** (*reflection!*) was the first and **mightiest angel** to be created with **intelligence, 'radiant beauty'** or **ugliness** (*Gorgon*) and **power** unmatched among all the **angels** in heaven, **Lucifer** was **'second'** to **'none'** in **majesty** only to **'God'** himself who has put **Lucifer** in **trust** by its **creative will** giving the **Devil** the power of **command!** Its as if a part of it is still looking for the problem or trying to solve the puzzle of its own self! At the beginning of such a **theoretical creation!** And at the same time **solving it**, as if it somehow knew what the problem was, by using **reverse engineering**, **Vis-à-vis** (*therefore*) it new the answer to the question it had been seeking! Because it theoretically caused the problem in the first place in order to solve it! That's why **Jesus Christ** believed in **forgiveness** and **redemption**, because to forgive others is to **forgive** ones self or unifie!

Beware the hand that gives, is the hand that takes!

. . .

Sir Walter Scott

. . .

Yet Clare's sharp questions must I shun
Must separate Constance from the nun
Oh! what a tangled web we weave
When first we practise to deceive!
A Palmer too! No wonder why
I felt rebuked beneath his eye

Even though the **indescribable** or **inconceivable androgynous state** has come full circle like the theory of the past, present and the future which co-exist with one another, **"it"** or our **collective-higher-self** or the **observer** moves through existence in a **relative state** or as it becomes consciously aware! It tries to discover what has happened, in that timeless unified thought, because something has theoretically happened, so it could be the key or answer to a paradox of who **God** or the **creative will** is? And the **riddle** of our own selves or that which appears to be **somewhere** and yet **nowhere**: Or the incredible source of all **knowledge and** understanding!

. . .

"And there fell a great star from heaven!
Burning as it were a lamp,
And it fell upon the third part of the rivers,
And upon the fountains of waters"

. . .

The Story of the blind men

Once upon a time there were three wise men! Who had been blindfolded and asked to describe a mystery, it doesn't matter what it was, but each wise man gave a different description of what it was that they were touching. So it is what it is? Call it God or the source of all knowledge and understanding, which seems or appears to something an **"enigma"** *unto itself* or the elusion of the physical world! Which must be a self-evident truth, that's why matter cannot be **created** or **destroyed** and the means will justify the ends!

54

Or what seems or appears to be the enemy within! Like a self-made monster or enigma in a cellar! That always seems or appears to be one step ahead, like that **proverbial-hand** that rocks the cradle, the **"Dybbuk"** or (*Dybik*) **an Eastern European name for an unclean spirit**!) Will in time seem or appear to establish the so-called: **NOVUS ORDO SECLORUM** or **new world order**! By manipulating or tweaking the final outcome by using the same hand that rocks the cradle, in our **Anthropological**, **Sociological** and **Theological history**, as we now inexorably slide towards an **abyss** or **final outcome**, the **author** of the piece or means will have **illuminated** the ends!

In Jewish mythology, a **dybbuk** (**dubik**) (Yiddish: from Hebrew *adhere* or *cling*) is a malicious possessing of an unclean spirit believed to be the dislocated soul of a dead person. It supposedly leaves the host body once it has accomplished its goal, that inadvertently acts like a **reflection** cast upon a **mirror** or **looking-glass**, that indirectly **revaluates** our **moral behaviour,** and the **enemy at the gates;** or the **enemy within** seems or appears to be more cleverer and more dangerous than ever before, remember? By an all-forgiving God's ferocity or folly in a self-inflicted torment or want of its own ignorance! We took a bite out of the symbolic Christian apple in the **"Garden of Eden"** for what seems or appears to be some caprice, a sudden longing, a passing fancy of the soul or what ever it is! That flies headlong into this dreadful extremity! Or shadow aspect that can blind men to the truth!

. . .

THE CHURCH OF JESUS CHRIST OF LATTER-DAY SAINTS
[2 Nephi 2:22-25]
[Why did they pick that tree? When there was better trees that that!]

If Adam had not transgressed he would not have fallen, but he would have remained in the Garden of Eden….

"And **[Adam and Eve]** would have had no children; wherefore they would have remained in a state of innocence, having no joy, for they knew no misery; doing no good, for they knew no sin.

"But behold, all things have been done in the **wisdom** of him who **knoweth all things**. "Adam fell that men might be; and men are, that they might have joy."

The Conqueror Worm

They're in his grave, lo! 'Tis a gala night
Within the lonesome latter years!
An angel throng, bewinged, bedight
In veils, and drowned in tears,
Sit in a theatre, to see
A play of hopes and fears,
While the orchestra breathes fitfully
The music of the spheres.

* * *

"For now I shall sleep in the dust;
And thou shall seek me in the morning,
But I shall not be"

The Holy Bible

. . .

"Out out, brief candle! Life's but a walking shadow, a poor player that struts and frets his hour upon the stage. And is heard no more: it is a tale told by an idiot, full of sound and fury, signifying nothing!"
WILLIAM SHAKESPEARE

. . .

" *When you have eliminated the possible*
And you are left with the impossible
Then it must be true...
No matter how fantastic it sounds"

. . .

A Clockwork Orange

*"If he can only perform good or only perform evil, then he is a clockwork orange—meaning that he has the appearance of an organism lovely with colour and juice but is in fact only a clockwork toy to be wound up by **God** or the **Devil.**"*

Anthony Burgess

. . .

With regards to our physical existence and each new life in this common-bond will be born into the physical world caught in an endless cycle of self-imposed rebirth or a constant role-reversal of **misery v happiness**, **war and peace**, **good v evil** "*ad-nauseum*" which has to be cancelled out, one way or the other! And reintegrated so that these **polarities** will eventually be neutralized and integrated, by and through our ability to see what has apparently went wrong, freeing us from the vicious circle of ignorance, when we realize and come to except the hidden meaning or mysteries of our physical life, and that the invisible hand of the *indescribable* or *inconceivable androgynous state* Is using the means to justify the ends, in trying to find the answer to this riddle or question and at the same time having solved the enigma of its own self at the same time!

It seems to be the only way to solve the problem and cancel-out what seems or appears to be the troublesome or active aspects of this *indescribable* or *inconceivable androgynous state* and in trying to find the answer, it seems or appears to have actually caused the problem in the first place!

It has become bound by it's very own contradictory nature, to seek expression in meaning and form in what appears or seems to be an act of self discovery that must surely beg the question, why would such a *paradox* or *indescribable* and *inconceivable androgynous state* need to be aware of it's own self, when it wasn't even there to begin with, so to speak!

And because of this, it appears to have caused a problem in order to solve one, because such self-inquiry in order to find a condition, mathematically speaking, has literally questioned the very fact of why it wasn't even there to begin with, wherever there is? Or in a way we can't understand, which is echoed in the *indescribable* or *inconceivable androgynous states* own reflection or retrospective aspect, and yet as I have already said, this seems to have been the way the *physical* (*Corporal*) and the *non-physical* (*Non-Corporal*) world as we know, came into being, per say, in and by a form of expression akin to a thought in the mind of our own true selves as it were, which seems or appears to throw light onto a great unknown expanse of what could only be described as darkness or something within or out-with it's own self, so to speak, like the universe which is like a:

Mobius strip

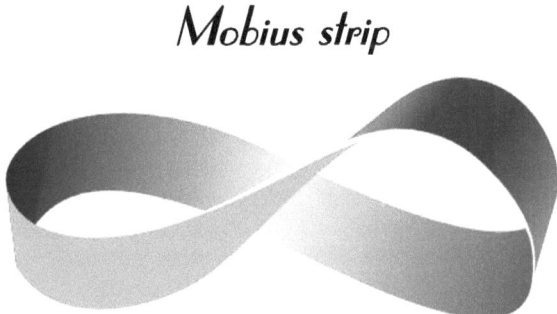

"*Mobius strip*" the has no *beginning* or *end* like *infinity*, and where we seem to be experiencing something that *was*, *has been* or *is* being expressed, by what you can only describe for want of a better word, *a retrospective thought in the mind* of some *indescribable* or *inconceivable androgynous state*!

That we indirectly or incorrectly call **God** the **source of all knowledge and understanding**! Or **creative will**, that's why you will find that you can't seem to tell where the **physical** (*Corporal*) or the **non-physical** (*Non-Corporal*) world begins and ends, because both seem to be like a point of light surrounded by a great expanse of darkness! (**Abstract concept or unknown quantity**) and if we truly read between the lines inherent in the contradictions of both worlds, we can see where the boundary **lies!** (*No pun intended*) many a truth is said in jest... between a world we seem or appear to be in, and the world we can only glimpse in flights of fancy when you are day dreaming or when we are asleep and dreaming, and excepting the experience without using our "**Critical faculty**" but when something occurs in the dream-state or you have a sudden realization that something is out of place *i.e.* the toilet pan is plumbed into the kitchen wall, your mind will compare this event to a whole list of other particulars, and you will come to a sudden conclusion and realize that you are still asleep and dreaming! And if you can remember to look at your hands! Because we use a lot of brainpower in connection with our hands: see a model of: (**Homo-Homunculus**) and either/or you experience a **consciously aware dream**, and the dream becomes vivid and surreal or you just **wake-up** or are we still dreaming. Or when you experience or use **self-hypnosis** where we are able to create anything we want! By just thinking about it! Or **creation by mere thought**, which is like a science without instrumentality! Is that what **UFOs** (*Unidentified Flying Objects*) are using, so to speak!

· · ·

"I suppose therefore that all things I see are illusions; I believe that nothing has ever existed of everything my lying memory tells me. I think I have no senses" I believe that my body, shape, extension, motion, location are functions, what is there then that can be taken as true?"

René Descartes

Such thoughts are like a footprint left behind on the shore of **eternity** or like a voice crying in the wilderness! For there lie's the true **grail** if we are prepared to seek it, to **wean** us of this **existence** or **re-associate** ourselves in the **surreal** and **vivid world** of the **mind**, or awaken from the **dream of life!**

Which is akin to **reaching-out** and **touching** something that is not there! And **solve** the **paradox** of our **own-selves** in relation to the workings of the **indescribable** or **inconceivable-androgynous state!** That seems or appears to be **intangible** or **neutral** or **somewhere** in **relation** to the **dichotomy** of **its** or **our-own-true-self**, and if we have the **courage** to dip our toe in the **water**, so to speak! And ask the **ultimate-question** or seek to find a deeper meaning to find out how the **androgynous-state** itself or **our-own-true-selves** came into **being**, it would be like trying to "**square the circle**" or reach out to understand the story of:

"*Osirus slain*" and "*Osirus risen*"
[Hidden in the Tamarisk-tree of symbolic knowledge]

. . .

[Of kingship and succession, order and disorder, death and the afterlife!]

"It is in the center axis atop the World Tree. Essentially the World Tree and the Vision Serpent, representing the king, created the centre axis which communicates between the spiritual and the earthly worlds or planes. It is through ritual that the king could bring the center axis into existence in the temples and create a doorway to the spiritual world."

. . .

Cuneiform text to the sun God Ra:
"Thou couplest under the stars and the moon,
Thou drawest the ship of Aten in heaven and on earth like the tirelessly revolving stars, and the stars at the north-pole that do not set!!!"

. . .

I come unto thee Osirus
Cleansed of all impurities
Thou goest round heaven, thou seest RA
Thou seest the beings who have knowledge!

. . .

The **indescribable** or **inconceivable androgynous state**, seems or appears to have done is akin to turning a sock inside-out or in the old saying: What you gain on the roundabout you lose on the swings, or what goes around comes around, like: **Mary Queen of Scots**, just before she bowed her head to the axe-man, she said: **"In my end is my beginning"** As if when one door closes, another one opens, as they say. So all things will be as they **were**, and **always will be**, and life no matter how **horrible** or **beautiful** it seems or appears to be, like the tale of the **gorgon** or the story of **Lucifer**! It has a more profound meaning or purpose behind it, by the hand of that **"great architect"** that seems quicker than the eye, that beheld or fashioned its creation, **Satan**! The **king of Terrors** or **omni arch** of the world.

And all the great religions of the world and even the ones to come! Who have or will in their own way have tried to **illuminate** *rightly* or *wrongly* the darkness of ignorance and suffering, like the Christian scriptural simile that referred to it as: Opening up the **gates-of-heaven** or to the paradise of the **neutral androgynous state**!

Which is the knowledge of our own true selves or everyone's birthright and the terrible loss of that which has always **been** and **always will be**, now Mathew knew there was no such thing as a **God in heaven** or the **Devil in hell**, not in the way he had been taught to believe it, and each and every one of us, or the sum of parts that make up the original image, like the shattered **hologram** that contained or made up the **whole image** was a testament to the truth, and if you look at any piece of a broken **hologram** you will see in it wonders to **behold!** For there in each and every infinite

59

piece is the **whole original image captured in it, looking back at you,** *so to speak*! Because that is the nature of a **hologram**, meaning each and every one of us are truly the centre of our own selves or universe, and in a contradictory way, there has never been anybody else except the illusionary sum of the parts that contain the one and only image!

. . .

𝔚𝔦𝔱𝔠𝔥

(Neophite)

And what would you save me from, prince charming, my reflection!!

𝔍𝔞𝔠𝔨 𝔱𝔥𝔢 𝔤𝔦𝔞𝔫𝔱 𝔨𝔦𝔩𝔩𝔢𝔯

. . .

The Comedy Of Errors
THE LIGHT BEYOND
(*Begging the question*)
"Is it better to rule in hell than serve in heaven?"

There have been attempts to explain **NDEs** as a biological mechanism that kicks in when death approaches. I don't accept this explanation because I can't see what good it does for a human organinism to have such an experience after the process of irreversible death has begun or has set in, I find it hard to imagine as a biological function because it is a paradox. What good would it do for the body to evolve that way?

RAYMOND A MOODY

. . .

Since we cannot **destroy matter** or **create it,** then how can something be **biologically destroyed?** Because our wonderful theoretical brain that should not even be here in the first place! Because it's nothing (*excuse the pun*) but an enigma, unto itself!

. . .

I bow my head in the dust before the mystery of mind which hitherto defied its own penetrative power, and which may ultimately resolve itself into a demonstratible impossibility of self-penetration!

. . .

If the paradise of the **neutral androgynous state!** Or source of all knowledge and understanding was and is so blissful, then why did we end up in this **veil of tears**? And do we need to return when we die or pass over, by slowly debugging the system, so to speak, by going to the ***Elysian plane/plane of elusion*** or **Summerland** to eventually exorcise reality or the physical appearance of things that are collectively projected by each and every person's own self-awareness of it, or are we all ready there?

Because if we are our brothers/sisters keeper it behoves us to help them or **what goes round comes around**, and we end up on the sharp-end of the **clock-work orange**!

Exorcism

Elysium or the Elysian Fields
Or
(*Ghosts in the machine*)

"Is a conception of the afterlife that developed over time and was maintained by certain Greek religious and philosophical sects and cults, initially separate from the realm of Hades, admission was reserved for mortals related to the gods and other heroes. Later, it expanded to include those chosen by the gods, the righteous, and the heroic, where they would remain after death, to live a **blessed** and **happy life**, and indulging in whatever employment they had enjoyed in life.

The Elysian Fields were, according to Homer, located on the western edge of the Earth by the stream of Okeanos. In the time of the Greek oral poet Hesiod, **Elysium** would also be known as the *Fortunate Isles* or the *Isles (or Islands) of the Blessed*, located in the western ocean at the end of the earth. The Isles of the Blessed would be reduced to a single island by the Thebean poet Pindar, describing it as having shady parks, with residents indulging their athletic and musical pastimes.

The ruler of **Elysium** varies from author to author: Pindar and Hesiod name Cronus as the ruler, while the poet Homer in the *Odyssey* describes fair-haired Rhadamanthus dwelling there.

"The good receive a life free from toil, not scraping with the strength of their arms the earth, nor the water of the sea, for the sake of a poor sustenance. But in the presence of the honored gods, those who gladly kept their oaths enjoy a life without tears, while the others undergo a **toil** that is **unbearable** to look at. Those who have persevered three times, on either side, to keep their souls free from all **wrongdoing**, follow Zeus' road to the end, to the tower of Cronus, where ocean breezes blow around the island of the blessed, and flowers of gold are blazing, some from splendid trees on land, while water nurtures others. With these wreaths and garlands of flowers they entwine their hands according to the righteous counsels of Rhadamanthys, whom the great father, the husband of Rhea whose throne is above all others, keeps close beside him as his partner"

Pindar, Odes (2.59–75)

. . .

"These are two in number, separated by a very narrow strait; they are ten thousand furlongs distant from Africa, and are called the **Islands of the Blest**. They enjoy moderate rains at long intervals, and winds which for the most part are soft and precipitate dews, so that the islands not only have a rich soil which is excellent for ploughing and planting, but also produce a natural fruit that is plentiful and wholesome enough to feed, without toil or trouble, a leisured folk. Moreover, an air that is salubrious, owing to the climate and the moderate changes in the seasons, prevails on the islands.

For the north and east winds which blow out from our part of the world plunge into fathomless space, and, owing to the distance, dissipate themselves and lose their power before they reach the islands; while the south and west winds that envelope the islands sometimes bring in their train soft and intermittent showers, but for the most part cool them with moist breezes and gently nourish the soil. Therefore a firm belief has made its way, even to the Barbarians, that here is the **Elysian Field** and the abode of the blessed, of which Homer sang."

Plutarch, Life of Sertorius, VIII, 2

And permanently sever our connection to the corporeal or physical-world, which to all intent and purposes is akin to the tree in the forest, or when the fridge door is closed, *"does the light go out?"* (*Joke!*) Are we not judged by what we do in this transient state? As part of a larger truth when **king Solomon** said:

" That his anger (God) is but for a moment and his forgiveness is forever!"

. . .

Ambiguity

But remember **time** *is* **relitive** *when we are involved in a physical accident, we react* **emotionally**! *And the* **experience** *seems to* **last** *forever! Or what seems or appears to be a very long time!* (**Subjective time**) *so it makes you wonder how long is a moment?*

Amity orEnmity

Do you not go unpunished when virtue becomes a vice?

The Saturday Magazine
(18 July 1835)

"*No obligation to justice does force a man to be cruel, or to use the sharpest sentence. A just man does justice to every man and to everything; and then, if he be also wise, be knows there is a debt of mercy and compassion due to the infirmities of man's nature; and that is to be paid: and he that is cruel and ungentle to a sinning person, and does the worst to him, dies in his debt and is unjust. Pity, and forbearance, and long-sufferance, and fair interpretation, and excusing our brother, and taking in the best sense, and passing the gentlest sentence, are as certainly our duty, and owing to every person that does offend and can repent, as calling to account can be owing to the law, and are first to be paid; and he that does not so is an unjust person.*"

Jeremy Taylor

Was **Jesus Christ** trying to tell us something through **forgiveness** and **redemption** by and through his teaching?

. . .

Montague Summer's

"Evil surly needs no argument or proof it is self-evident a vivid reality of the choices we make using the power of evil-who can look upon the world even today shattered and wounded and rent, and not recognize its cruel tyranny by devil's who bare the mark! Of "lying, Malignity and Hurtfulness" who themselves make no small number of the laws and rulers that are made in the world, and have no small number of honoured servants and are the authors of most of the wars in the world, who are crooked, distorted, disturbed and diseased, malice prepense who in order to commit these acts and therefore to incur the guilt of the responsibility

for the acts and hence to reap the inevitable and logical consequences there must have been a deliberate intention as well as a clear consciousness of the acts! Which will make an un-thinkable difference to *"the Grand plan" because the means will justify the ends!"*

And its no good looking for a scapegoat in the form of **Satan** to blame for the terrible things in the world, because we are angry at being trapped or imprisoned by the **self-defacing instrumentality** of our own **besotted condition**, we are here for one reason and one reason only, which is to follow the path to either *lose* or *find* and *re-discover* the *lost wisdom* and knowledge of our own true selves, which is like a paper trail that will lead us to the shores of eternity and beyond, as if following that elusive footprint, until then we can only glimpse and wonder what lies ahead of us, or what lies behind us, and do all of us have the right to that divine and eternal inheritance? Which is a bit like **begging the question**.

After the cord that suspends us between this world and the next is finally cut! And we can begin our journey homeward, with that first step! And back to the symbolic **Garden of Eden**, so to speak, where it all began, with that bite of the proverbial apple, figuratively speaking, that brought us here, and on into infinity or what seems in reverse the great unknown! Or using a simple metaphor of once more reversing a simple sock, you wear on your foot, back the other way, so to speak!

Where we will be welcomed home for always and forever, And where the *indescribable or inconceivable androgynous state* **will have, by its own hand have *re-associated* it's own self, being no longer imprisoned by it's own *reflection*!**

Like in the Christian bible where it says that **Satan** that **Omni-arch** of the world or in essence the shadow aspect of our own selves! Will in the end of days be eventually let out of his or our! **Theoretical prison**, [My Italics] which will be through each and every one of us, being born into a corporeal or physical world, and through the **liberation** and **re-association** of our own collective self, and if you don't believe me:

"Who are you to question the enigma of god for making me an atheist?"

And as Mathew stopped reading the great book, he looked up to see the figure of the **watcher** who stood at the **threshold**, who had **two faces**! Just like the eye of God! That was reflected on to the **sea of eternity**, on the **amulet** printed on the page of his little esoteric pamphlet that he had dropped onto the jungle floor, like the falling leafs of inevitability as if from the jungle canopy overhead.

The society that had published the pamphlet was founded during the age of enlightenment when the energy of man's consciousness was by exception, liberated or freed from the confines of its own self-imposed dictatorial rule, and the top half of the **eye** in the centre of the **amulet** was symbolically reflected onto a **pool-of-water**, **a-looking-glass** or **mirror** if you will, like a **sea-of-glass** which reflects the other side onto its surface, to symbolically show the dichotomy of it's own self or that life was a reflection cast by the **fountain head** or **eye of God**!

And where the horizontal dividing line **lies**! Through the eye, is a line drawn on the sands of time, to reveal the hidden aspect of it's own self, that's why the **watcher** has **two-faces**, akin to **Janus** the **Divom-Deus** or **God-of-Gods** and the two-headed son of **Apollo** and **Creusa**, he is the God of doorways and arches, which symbolically signifies **beginnings** and **endings**!

Which was the theoretical aim of the **Alchemists**, who believed that the process itself was accompanied by a spiritual change, akin to a symbolic death or aphoristic principle **"solve et coagula"** dissolve and combine... or where the various characteristics of a substance are stripped away in some unknown **metamorphosis** or joining of its **opposing-polarities**! Between **male** and **female**, or **Hermaphroditism**, these changes may be the result of an inner profound spiritual experience, and a new, nobler substance is built that symbolizes death, followed by rebirth into a better, purer life, **vis á vis** (*therefore*) it symbolises the dichotomy between the two-worlds or the tangled web we weave:

Fulcanelli

Tells us this in **Le mystère des cathedrals**, is emblematic of the whole labour of the work, it is there that the thread of **Ariadne** or **Arachne**, the legendary, 'Arachne', the **spider-queen** from Greek mythology who had been a **Lydian maiden**, having challenged the Goddess, 'Athene' who wove the garments of the **Gods**, and because she was beaten by a mortal, the Goddess, 'Athene' had changed, 'Arachne' into a **spider**! Who now weaves her webs so that mankind can look upon its deadly beauty, with her family the **'Arachnidae.'**

Becomes necessary for us if we are not to wander in a maze among the winding paths of the task, and to understand it is to extricate ourselves in the Phonetic cabala or elucidate the symbolism of the Greek legend of Ariadne, who with a thread helped **Theseus** to escape from the **labyrinth**! After he had slain the **Minotaur** or overcome and solved the problem, so to speak!

Which in the book **"Les demeures philosophales"** by **Fulcanelli**, our attention is drawn to a remarkable piece of sculpture – one of four statues that symbolically guard the tomb of **François II** in **Nantes-Cathedral**. **Fulcanelli** calls it prudence, in frontal view it depicts the figure of a beautiful young girl in a hooded cloak and floor-length gown.

She seems mesmerized by her own reflection! In a strange convex mirror she holds in her hand!

In her right hand is a pair of compasses or perhaps dividers! Throughout alchemical literature, there are frequent injunctions to *separate*, and *conjoin*.

And on the back of the girl's head is another face—that of a wise old sage,

 apparently deep in contemplation and enfolded within the cloak of philosophy. She symbolises nature in all its hidden aspects, both inward and outward, but beneath her exterior veil, there appears the mysterious image of ancient alchemy, 'and we are, through the attributes of the first, initiated into the secrets of the second, which is self evident in the doctrine of the society of dynamics, or in the creed of dualism inherent in the law of opposites...

With this Mathew had awoken, having returned back to the dream of life! What a cosmic bender he thought, as he tried to hold onto the heavy vibes that had just been laid on him by his strange and freaky journey, in which it seemed that ages had passed, but in reality only a split second had gone by on the clock, or a movement in the void is only relative, so to speak!

So we are forced to use a metaphor to describe an **'enigma'** *or* something that does not exist in the sense of the word, or something that is **inconceavable, indiscrible** or **androgynous state**, how does one describe a dicotomy seems that seems or appears to be the left and right arm of that same body?

Paul Crowe

The Autumn Of Terror

Having written it's pernicious and symbolic clue, with the **3**rd killing in **1888**.

And the unquiet message chalked so publically on the wall for all to see, after the killing of **Catherine Eddowes** by the notorious and secret phantom called: **"Jack the Ripper"**, and discovered by police constable **Alfred Long of H-Division:**

> *"THE JUWES*
> *ARE THE MEN*
> *THAT WILL NOT BE BLAMED*
> *FOR NOTHING"*

. . .

The Victims of Jack the Ripper

October 9th 1888
Body found in the new police office on the Thames embankment
The **"Uterus"** was absent!
The hand is often quicker than the eye, when it obscures the truth of what seems or appears to have been happening!

Polly Ann Nichol's

Was found in Buck's Row, she had been *disembowelled* and her *throat* had been systematically cut, and there was no sign of a **struggle!** Just as if she had been dropped there, from out of the blue!

Annie Chapman

Was found at 29, Hanbury-street, Spitalfields, again there was no sign of a **struggle!** Her *throat* had been systematically cut, like **"Polly Nichol's"** there were two *clean-cuts* on the body of the *vertebrae* on the left side of the '*spine*' they were parallel to each other and separated by half an inch.

. . .

"The muscular structures between the side processes of bone of the
vertebrae had an appearance as if an attempt had been made to
separate the bones of the neck!"

Breathing had been interfered with previous to death, her attacker/s showed evidence of having **"anatomical-knowledge"** there were marks on the face that were quit recent, especially about the chin and the sides of the jaw! The **"Uterus"** had been removed!

A witness said that during the night, while he was outside he distinctly heard something fall against the wooden fence, where the victim was later found!

Catherine Eddows

Was found in Mitre Court or Square, no trace of a **struggle!** There was an abrasion under the left ear, and the throat had been severed, the **"Uterus"** was cut away, and the left kidney had been cut out, both of these *organs* have never been found!

. . .

JACK THE RIPPER

BY PAUL CROWE

Elizabeth Stride

1888

There was no sign of a **struggle!** Her *throat* had been *severed*, like the rest, **as if an attempt was made to remove the head**, she had an abrasion of the skin about an inch and a quarter in diameter under the right clavicle, there was mud on her face and on the left side of her head.

Her jacket was well plastered with mud down the left side, **as if she had been caught and momentarily dragged, and then dumped** [My Italics] where she was later found!

'Over both shoulders, especially the right, from the front aspect under collarbones and in front of chest, there was a strange bluish discolouration that the coroner had seen on more than one occasion'

"They were pressure marks of some kind! At first they were obscure but subsequently they became evident. They were not what are ordinarily called bruises; neither is there any abrasion, each shoulder is equally marked! She seemed or appeared to have been entrapped in the conventional sense, much like the others, and the killer/s were apparently disturbed, for some unknown reason."

Case 1

July 1887

No special knowledge of anatomy shown, the cuts indicated a practical skill in amputating limbs at joints, and making clean sweeping skin cuts, such skill would be gained by a butcher or **hunter**! As these are in the habit of rapidly and skilfully separating limbs and cutting up a trunk into several parts. Doctor's opinion that any surgeon or anatomist could not have done the work so well as they are not constantly operating, while a butcher is almost daily cutting up carcases.

The limbs were separated in almost precisely the way a butcher or **hunter**! Would adopt i.e. making a series of cuts around the flexure of the joint and then by strong twist, wrenching out the head from the joint and cutting the capsule.

Like the movie called **The Predator** with the movie star **Arnold Schwerzenegger.**

'Food for thought'

But what of the **strange marks** on **her shoulders**! It seemed or appeared as if she could have been lifted up by something and then left on the ground, like the woman in **"*Passport to Magonia*"** by Jacques Vallee in 1975.

And last but but not least, the eerie similarity that **"*Elizabeth Stride*"** had with another woman or points of **resemblance** between the deceased and **"*Elizabeth Watts*"** which almost reminded one of the Comedy of Errors.

Both had been courted by policemen; they both bore the same Christian name, and were of the same age; both lived with sailors; both at one time kept coffee-houses at Poplar; both were nick-named **"*Long Liz*"** both were said to have had children in charge of their husbands' friends; both were given to drink; both lived in East-end common lodging-houses; both had been charged at the Thames Police-court; both had escaped punishment on the ground that they were subject to epileptic fits, although the friends of both were certain that this was a fraud; both had lost their front teeth, and both had been leading very questionable lives.

Mary Jane Kelly

Was found in Miller's court horrible mutilated, as a prelude to deception! For more information See: **"*Jack the Ripper*"** The throat had been severed and the **"*heart*"** was taken!

One thing
Does not mean the other!

"Remember there's nothing more deseptive, than the obvious"

Remember the **Jack the ripper** killings and *Mary Ann Nichols* was described by Emily Holland as **"*a very clean woman who always seemed to keep to herself.*"** The doctor at the post mortem remarked on the **cleanliness** of her thighs.

Had this fact accidently disguised the true nature of what had actually happened, like in the story of...

The
Black Dililah

(Jane-Doe-Number 1)

The mutalated body of Elizabeth Short was found in the Leimert Park district of Los Angeles on January 15, 1947. Her remains had been left on a vacant lot on the west side of South Norton Avenue midway between Coliseum Street and West 39th Street.

The body was discovered by local resident Betty Bersinger, who was walking with her three-year-old daughter around 10 a.m. Bersinger initially mistook the body for a discarded store mannequin. Upon realizing it was a corpse, Bersinger rushed to a nearby house where she phoned the police.

Short's severely mutilated body was severed at the waist and **completely drained of blood!** Not only was the body bloodless, but her body had been evidently **washed** by the killer/s why?

Her face had been slashed from the corners of her mouth toward her ears, Short also had multiple cuts on her thigh and breasts, where entire portions of flesh had been removed. Her lower half was positioned a foot away from her torso, and the intestines were tucked neatly under the buttocks. *The body looked as though it had been dumped or dropped* [My Italics] or it looked as if it had been **"posed"** with her hands over her head, her elbows bent at right angles, and her legs spread. Near the body, detectives found a cement sack which contained droplets of watery blood, as well as a heel print on the ground amidst tire tracks. but you can't go on any of the evidence, by the time the police had taken control of the situation, a large crowd of rubber-necks had gathered to see the grisly site of the dead woman, and had been walking all over the place!

The autopsy stated that Short was 5 feet 5 inches (1.65 m) tall, weighed 115 pounds (52 kg), and had light blue eyes, brown hair, and badly decayed teeth. There were ligature marks on her ankles, wrists, and neck. Although the skull was not fractured, Short had bruising on the *front* and *right side* of her scalp with a small amount of bleeding in the subarachnoid space on the *right side,* consistent with blows to the head. The cause of death was hemorrhage from the lacerations to the face and shock due to blows on the head and face.

It's very probable that it was a homicidal maniac or a person whose mind has been badly damaged, for whatever reason, or to use the modern euphemism it seemed or appears to all intent and purposes to be either a serial killer or killers!

Its very probable that organized crime, or a secret satanic coven or serial-killer could have been involved, but highly unlikely, I don't think they would go to all that bother to have **exsanguinated** or drained out, all of the woman's blood! See: **"The Legions of the Damned"** and (*The Doomed Franklin Expedition*), and then wash the woman's body, before dumping it were it was later found, unless strangely enough, whatever or whoever done it, were more concerned with cleaning the skin for reasons other than what we think? Its as if some kind of dissection or laboratory procedure could have taken place?

The actual coroners report has never been published, and therefore we cannot check the validity of any of the reports, but have to except the *FBI* file on face value.

It was clear to the medical examiner that not only her body had been **neatly** and **cleanly bisected**, but that a sharp, thin-bladed instrument, consistent with a surgeons scalpel, had been used to perform the operation. The incision was performed through the abdomen, and then through the **intervertebral disk** between the **second** and **third lumbar vertebrae**. The **bisection** had been carried out with such **precision** that it was apparent it was the work of a **professional** someone trained in **surgical procedures**!

. . .

(The police believed the woman's killer was affiliated with a cutting profession-a Surgeon or Butcher!)

. . .

"Because at one point the LAPD investigators were so certain that the bi-section of Shorts body was the handy-work of an expert, they had persuaded the university of Southern California, to turn over the name's of any medical students located in the neighbourhood were the woman was found, according to an FBI's classified document of 263 pages that was related to its own investigation of the case!"

. . .

Was there something else in the blood, or on the skin, evidence! That would have pointed to someone or something that could have been involved!

Wheels within wheels

(CIA agent caught interfering with evidence in the Kennedy assassination)

. . .

"There's other things involved that are detrimental to other things"
Regis Blahut

' Now you see it, now you don 't'

It was **Professor Arthur Butz** in his Hoax of the Twentieth Century who proposed the image of the holocaust as a giant with feet of clay. By drawing on the analyses of revisionist historians and incisively pointing out inconsistencies of how the **"Holocaust"** allegedly transpired and, second, a perhaps shocking revelation of the shoddy evidence that the legend is based on!

Total Recall

Like the evidence in the **JFK** assassination, and why the brain went missing! Along with tissue sections, blood smears and photographs of the interior of the presidents chest! Why was this evidence taken! Unless it was nothing but a red herring, to throw investigators of the track! Why have people been targeted and mysteriously silenced, individuals who were officially involved in the investigation, police officers and witnesses! Its as if someone or something is frightened of something.

'Someone or something is watching us!'

If you recall the errie story of the missing franklin expidition and the body of the sailor buried on Beechy island, called **"Hartnell"** who had nothing on below his waist, he had no **shoes** or **boots** on! Much like the people in the **Dyatlov pass mystery**! See **"Terror By Night"** and the two other seamen, that were in the other graves: **Braine** had one of his **undershirts** on **backwards**, and the **number 4** on the make-shift

71

plaque on his coffin lid was **back-to-front**, like the strange **autopsy** that had been done on *John Hartell* Although the standard incision during modern-day autopsies is **Y shaped** with the arms of the **Y** extending down from each shoulder and meeting at the base of the **sternum** (*breastbone*). From this point the incision continues down to the **pubic-bone**, but whoever or whatever had conducted this weird **back-to-front-Autopsy** on *John Hartnell,* had done an **upside-down-incision**, much like modern autopsies but the wrong way round, which could mean, either **upside-down** or **back to front!**

Like the little girl in David Paulides book, *Missing 411 North America And Beyond* who went missing, and when she was found, she had her cloths on **back-to-front!**

Braine's stockings or **socks** had been **bizarrely folded under his heels,** like **Robert Springfield AGED 49 Years. Page 314 MISSING 411 EASTERN UNITED STATES.** In Montana, who was out bow hunting and who mysteriously vanished and later on his remains were found beside his boots and coat with his belt that had been rolled-up neatly and placed alongside a tree!

Torrington's, Braines and **Hartnell's shoes** or **boots** were missing, and **Hartnell's blood vessels** contained nothing but ice! And the ice was clear, because he had no blood in his body!

More Food for thought

December **1973** and January **1974** there were wholesale disappearances of

pet dogs from Connecticut to California. Small towns like Voluntown, Connecticut, lost a large part of their dog population in a few days! Fifteen dogs vanished from Woodstock, New York, in the Catskill Mountains during the same period. As in previous waves of animal mutilations and disappearances, authorities tried to blame witchcraft cults, cattle rustlers, and dognapers, who sell the poor animals to hospitals for experimental purposes. But the total absence of evidence of any kind seems to rule out these conventional explanations.

Cattle Mutilations

"Also known as bovine excision"

Is the killing and mutilation of cattle under apparently unusual or anomalous circumstances. Sheep and horses have allegedly been mutilated under similar circumstances.

A hallmark of these incidents is the reportedly surgical nature of the mutilation, and unexplained phenomena such as the complete draining of the animal's blood, loss of internal organs with no obvious point of entry, and surgically precise removal of the reproductive organs and anal coring.

Another reported event is that the animal is found dumped in an area where there are no marks or tracks leading to or from the carcass, even when it is found in soft ground or mud. The surgical-type wounds tend to be cauterized by an intense heat and made by very sharp/precise instruments, with no bleeding evident. Often flesh will be removed to the bone in an exact manner, consistent across cases, such as removal of flesh from around the jaw exposing the mandible.

Charles Fort

"Collected many accounts of cattle mutilations that occurred in England in the late 19th and early 20th centuries."

. . .

Reports of mutilated cattle first surfaced in the United States in the early 1960s.

The phenomenon remained largely unknown outside cattle raising communities until **1967,** when the Pueblo Chieftain in Pueblo, Colorado published a story about a horse named Lady who was mutilated in mysterious circumstances, which was then picked up by the wider press and distributed nationwide; this case was also the first to feature speculation that something very strange seems or appears to have been involved with mutilations.

The Lady/Snippy mutilation

The first allegedly strange death of livestock comes from near Alamosa, Colorado, in **1967.** The real name of the animal was Lady, but the media quickly adopted the name **"Snippy"** (the name of another horse at the ranch), which stuck.

On September 7 of that year, Agnes King and her son Harry noted that Lady, a three-year-old horse, had not returned to the ranch at the usual time for her water. This was unusual, given the heat and the arid conditions.

Harry found Lady on **September 9.** Her head and neck had been skinned and defleshed, the bones were white and clean. To King, the cuts on Lady seemed to have been very precise. There was no blood at the scene, according to Harry, and there was a strong medicinal odor in the air.

The next day, Harry and Agnes returned to the scene with Agnes' brother and sister-in-law, Mr. and Mrs. Berle Lewis. They found a lump of skin and horse flesh; when Mrs. Lewis touched it, the flesh oozed a greenish fluid which burned her hand. They also reported the discovery of fifteen "tapering, circular exhaust marks punched into the ground" over an area of some 5000 square yards. (Saunders and Harkins, 156) The medicinal odor had weakened somewhat, but was still present.

Mrs. Lewis contacted the United States Forest Service, and Ranger Duane Martin was sent to investigate. Among other tasks, Martin "checked the area with a civil defense Geiger counter. He reported finding a considerable increase in radioactivity about two city blocks from the body." Later, Martin would state, "The death of this saddle pony is one of the most mysterious sights I've ever witnessed, I've seen stock killed by lightning, but it was never like this."

After trying to interest other authorities with little success, Mrs. Lewis turned to her professional connections: she wrote occasionally for the *Pueblo* Chieftain. Her account of Lady's strange death was published in that newspaper, and was picked up by the Associated Press on **October 5, 1967**. Soon, much of the United States knew the tale of Lady's death, and other reports of similar phenomena in Colorado emerged.

That same day, an account by Superior Court Judge Charles E. Bennett of Denver, Colorado, saw publication.

Bennett and his wife claimed to have witnessed "three reddish-orange rings in the sky." They maintained a triangular formation, moved at a high speed, and made a humming sound.

Shortly thereafter, an anonymous Denver pathologist's account of his necropsy saw publication. Lady's brain and abdominal organs were missing, he said, and there was no material in the spinal column. The pathologist insisted on anonymity, he said, due to fear his reputation would be damaged with involvement in such a high-profile case.

. . .
"Mrs. Lewis argued that Adams' conclusions failed to account for the lack of blood at the scene and the medicinal odor."
. . .

Later developments

Democratic senator Floyd K. Haskell contacted the *FBI* asking for help in **1975** due to public concern regarding the issue. He claimed there had been **130** mutilations in Colorado alone.

In **1993,** documented photographic evidence of a **1988** mutilation surfaced that involved a human being near Guarapiranga, Brazil. An autopsy report concluded the procedure occurred while the victim was still alive, and the associated pain resulted in cardiac arrest.

Characteristics

In most cases mutilation wounds appear to be clean, and carried out surgically. Mutilated animals are usually, though not always reported to have been drained of blood, and have no sign of blood in the immediate area or around their wounds.

George E. Onet, a doctor of veterinary microbiology and cattle mutilation investigator claims that allegedly mutilated cattle are avoided by large scavengers **"such as coyotes, wolves, foxes, dogs, skunks, badgers, and bobcats"** for several days after its death. Similarly, domestic animals are also reported to be **"visibly agitated"** and **"fearful"** of the carcass.

In *FBI* records from **1975,** mutilations of the **eye** occurred in **14 percent** of cases, mutilation of the **tongue** in **33 percent** of cases, mutilation of the **genitals** in **74 percent** of cases, and mutilation of the **rectum** in **48 percent** of cases. According to a later survey taken by the National Institute for Discovery Science, mutilation of the **eye** occurred in **59**

percent of cases, mutilation of the **tongue** in **42 percent** of cases, the **genitals** in **85 percent** of cases, and the **rectum** in **76 percent** of cases. According to Dr. Howard Burgess, nearly **90 percent** of **mutilated cattle** are between **four** and **five** years old.

Some mutilations are said to occur in very brief periods. A **2002** National Institute for Discovery Science (NIDS) report relates a **1997** case from **Utah**. Two ranchers tagged a specific calf, then continued tagging other animals in the same pasture. The ranchers were, at the most, about 300 yards from the calf. Less than an hour later, the first calf was discovered completely **eviscerated**—most **muscle** and all **internal organs were missing.** There was no **blood, entrails,** or **"apparent disturbance at the scene."** Independent analysts both uncovered marks on the calf's remains consistent with two different types of tools: a large, machete-type blade, and smaller, more delicate scissors.

The absence of tracks or footprints around the site of the mutilated carcass is often considered a hallmark of cattle mutilation. However, in some cases, **strange marks** or **imprints** near the site have been found.

Like in **MISSING 411. The Devil's in the details. Page 2,** and the case of **Bud Fisher,** in **Arizona aged 4 years.** Who was eventually found alive and well, using an Apache scout, but many of the locations didn't have foot-tracks, just **small indentations** in the sand!

In the famous **"Snippy"** case, there was an absolute absence of tracks in a 100 ft radius of the carcass (even the horse's own tracks disappeared within 100 ft of the body.) But within this radius several small holes were found seemingly **"punched"** in the ground and two bushes were absolutely flattened.

In Rio Arriba County, New Mexico, June **1976,** a **"trail of suction cup-like impressions"** were found leading from a mutilated three-year-old cow. The indentations were in a tripod form, 4 inches in diameter, 28 inches apart, and disappeared 500 feet from the dead cow. Similar incidents were reported in the area in **1978.**

Mutilations may involve any
Or all of the following:

The removal of **eyes,** see: **"Terror By Night"** udders and **sexual organs** very **cleanly** with **surgical precision.** The removal of the **anus** to a depth of around **12 inches** similar in appearance to **surgical coring.** The removal of the **lips** and/or **tongue** deeply cut out from the throat. removal of one the **ears!**

The removal of **major organs** (such as **heart** or **liver**) with no obvious entry/excision marks. Often, if the **heart** is missing, apart from no excision wound, the **Pericardium** will still be present and intact, with the **heart** missing.

The stripping of hide and flesh from the jaw and the area directly **beneath the ear** to the bone.

The removal of soft organs from the lower body, the presence of **incisions and cuts across the body that appear to have been made by a surgical instrument.**

Unexplained damage to remaining organs, but no sign of damage to the surrounding area.

A lack of predation signs (including teethmarks, tearing of the skin or flesh, or animal footprints) on or around the carcass and a lack of obvious scavenging.

In many cases, a draining of the **majority of blood** from the animal. What blood is left exhibits color anomalies and may not coagulate for days.

The animal will appear **"dumped"** or **"dropped"** in a secluded area, with no animal, human or vehicle track(s) leading to or from the site. Some have been found draped over fences or in treetops. It looks to all intent and porposes that it could be the same mysterious hand that has and still is involved with these cattle mutilations could be behind the strange disappearence of people!

. . .

"Like Elsie M. Davis aged 24 years old July 30 1911. she was later found 20ft up, scantly clad and in a bed of opine boughs" which begs the question, who or what put her up there, was it animal, vegetable, or mineral? Or Bobby Connor on July 13, **1934** aged 21 months **PAGE 246 MISSING 411EASTERN UNITED STATES** As is a current theme of many of the cases in David Paulides books, Bobby was found without his **shoes** and **socks**, one of his shoes was found high up on a bush, 30ft from where he was found!

And the strange case in **MISSING 411 EASTERN UNITED STATES. Page 183.** Of Rita Margret Lent. November, **1934.** Aged 3 years. It almost seemed or appeared as though Rita's body fell out of the sky!" And from the same book, **page 277.** Comes the strange case of the missing boy in **1892. Age 6 years.** Surname: **Barofsky.** Who was found hanging over a bush! Where there was at least 2ft of water surrounding it.

The bushes within the childs reach had been gnawed and eaten, and the cloths seemed or appeared to have been torn from the little boy, while blood streamed from wounds and gashes on his body and legs. The skin and flesh on his legs were torn off, and his hands badly lacerated and shrunken! For all intent and porposes it would seem or appear that the boy could have been just put there or he was dropped there!

Like in Oklahoma and little Jackie Landreth, aged 3 years. Who was found dead, hanging by his heels on a wire fence!

Or in the story of the **Black Dililah!** did no one think of checking under the womans body for signs of an impact creater! Depending on how far they had fallen or if they strike anything?

The ground under the animal appears depressed, as if the animal was dropped on the site from a height leaving an impact crater.

The animal's bones are found to be fractured with injuries consistent with being dropped and there are Strange marks/holes in the ground around the carcass. Other cattle avoid the carcass and the area where it's found.

Eyewitness reports of strange *"aerial objects"* in the vicinity of cattle at the time of an animal going missing.

Laboratory reports

Laboratory reports carried out on some mutilated animals have shown unusually high or low levels of vitamins or minerals in tissue samples, and the presence of chemicals not normally found in animals. However, not all mutilated animals display these anomalies, and those that do have slightly different anomalies from one another.

On account of the time between death and necropsy, and a lack of background information on specific cattle, investigators have often found it impossible to determine if these variations are connected to the animals' deaths or not.

In one case documented by **New Mexico police** and the **FBI,** an 11 month old cross Hereford-Charolais bull, belonging to a Mr. Manuel Gomez of Dulce, New Mexico, was found mutilated on **March 24, 1978.** It displayed **"classic"** mutilation signs, including the removal of the **rectum** and **sex organs** with what appeared to be **"a sharp and precise instrument"** and its internal organs were found to be inconsistent with a normal case of death followed by predation.

. . .

"Both the liver and the heart were white and mushy. Both organs had the texture and consistency of peanut butter"

. . .

Gabriel L Veldez, New Mexico Police

The animal's heart as well as bone and muscle samples were sent to the Los Alamos Scientific Laboratory for microscopic and bacteriological studies, while samples from the animal's liver were sent to two separate private laboratories.

Los Alamos detected the presence of naturally occurring Clostridium bacteria in the heart, but was unable to reach any conclusions because of the possibility that the bacteria represented postmortem contamination. They did not directly investigate the heart's unusual color or texture.

Samples from the animal's liver were found to be completely devoid of **copper** and to contain **4 times the normal level of zinc, potassium** and **phosphorus.** The scientists performing the analysis were unable to explain these anomalies.

Blood samples taken at the scene were reported to be **"light pink in color"** and **"Did not clot after several days"** while the animal's hide was found to be unusually brittle for a fresh death (the animal was estimated to have been dead for 5 hours) and the flesh underneath was found to be discolored.

None of the laboratories were able to report any firm conclusions on the cause of the blood or tissue damage. At the time, it was suggested that a burst of radiation may have been used to kill the animal, blowing apart its red blood cells in the process. This hypothesis was later discarded as subsequent reports from the Los Alamos Scientific Laboratory later confirmed the presence of anti-coagulants in samples taken from other cows mutilated in the region.

Conventional explanations

As with most disputed phenomena, there are a number of potential explanations to cattle mutilations, ranging from death by natural causes to purposeful acts by unknown individuals.

U.S. governmental explanation

"Who see everything, but observe nothing"

After coming under increasing public pressure, Federal authorities launched a comprehensive investigation of the mutilation phenomenon.
In May 1979, the case was passed on to the FBI, which granted jurisdiction under Title 18 (codes 1152 and 1153). The investigation was dubbed:

'Operation Animal Mutilation'

The investigation was funded by a US$ 44,170 grant from the Law Enforcement Assistance Administration, and was headed by FBI agent Kenneth Rommel. It had five key objectives:
Rommel's final report was 297 pages long and cost approximately US$45,000. It concluded that mutilations were predominantly the result of natural predation, but that some contained *anomalies* that could not be accounted for by conventional wisdom. The FBI was unable to identify any individuals responsible for the mutilations.

. . .

(Details of the investigation are now available under FOIA...)

The Freedom of Information Act

Federal investigation was preceded (and followed, to some extent) by a state level investigation carried out by law enforcement officials in New Mexico. This investigation reported finding evidence that some mutilated animals had been **tranquilized** and treated with an **anti-coagulant** prior to their mutilation.
It also contended that alleged **surgical techniques** performed during mutilations had become **"more professional"** over time. However, officers in charge were unable to determine responsibility or motive...
There were several hairy monster reports around Brookaville in **1966-67**. In May **1967** the writer Joan Whritenour was invited to a ranch near New Port Richey where strange three-toed tracks had been found. The county sheriff revealed that cattle were disappearing. No truck tracks or other evidence had been found to lead to the rustlers. **"Just where does a rustler put a full grown cow?"** a sheriff's deputy asked Joan Whritenour. **"Sure as hell not in his back pocket!"**
"Whether this next story is true or not, we will give it the benefit of the doubt"

"Strange Creatures From Time and Space"
(John Keel)

On the night of March 5, a Red Cross Bloodmobile was travelling along Route 2, which runs parallel to the Ohio River. Beau Shertzer, twenty-one, and a young nurse had been out all day collecting human blood and now they were heading back to Huntington, West Virginia, with a van filled with fresh blood. The road was dark and cold and there was very little traffic. As they moved along a particularly deserted stretch, there was a flash in the woods on a nearby hill and a large white glow appeared. It rose slowly into the air and flew straight for their vehicle.

"My God! What is it?" the nurse cried.

"I'm not going to stick around to find out," Shertzer answered, pushing his foot down on the gas.

The object effortlessly swooped over the van and stayed with it. Shertzer rolled down his window and looked up. He was horrified to see some kind of **arm** or **extension** being **lowered** from the luminous thing cruising only a few feet above the Bloodmobile.

"It's trying to get us!" the nurse yelled, watching another **arm** reach down on her side. It looked as if the flying object was trying to **wrap** a **pincers-like device** around the **vehicle.**

Shertzer poured on the horses or gas, but the object kept pace with them easily. Apparently they were saved by the sudden appearance of headlights from approaching traffic. As the other cars neared, the object **retracted the arms** and hastily flew off.

Both young people rushed to the police in a state of hysteria. The incident was supposed to have been mentioned briefly on a radio newscast that night, but was apparently not picked up (*excuse the pun*) by any of the newspapers!

Serendipity
(Abstraction or not an actual account)

It tends to expose the cleverly hidden exposition of what seems or appears to be happening, because the masses are to busy not looking at the right-hand of what **Adolf Hitler** seemingly discovered by accident, instead of watching what the left-hand is doing, or was he just a very clever stocking horse! Which tends to veil the truth of the matter, because too much hysteria tends to cloud the issue, which means people reading the book fail to recognize the genius of what that clever dog-in-the-manger, **Adolf Hitler** intelligently dissimilated in regards to a certain **clandestine groups activity**, that seems or appears to **undermine the fabric** of our so-called civilization, while monopolising and **controlling the status-quo** at the expense of others, who seem or appear too wrapped-up in their own selves, to see what could be happening!

"Communism cannot be blamed for what Russia used it for, just as Christianity cannot be blamed for what the church uses it for."
Pete Seeger

. . .

"Do not judge, so that you won't be judged. For with the judgement you use, you will be judged, And with the measure you use, it will be measured to you."
Jesus Christ

. . .

Because no one has the moral right to do it, and if you rely think about it, so-called evil tyrants like **Adolf Hitler** *that (dog in the manger) or* **Joseph Stalin**, (*Ashkenazi Jew*) including **Churchill** (*Ashkenazi Jew*) and President **Franklin Delano Roosvelt** (*Sephardic Jew*) real name: **Rosen**! Once he was so-called elected to the American government the all-seeing or third-eye of providence and the **Novus-Ordo-Seclorum** or (*New World Order*) along with: **E pluribus unum** (Out of many one) was on the Dollar bill! With the words **Annuit Coeptis** that means: (*He! Has favoured our undertakings!*)

. . .

The shadows that light can cast, has been and still is indirectly responsible for millions of deaths:
Like fire it can be your best friend or your worst enemy!

. . .

Half-truth

The **Rothschild's** finance the politically orchestrated wars **one-way** or the **other**, while leaving it to the rascality of the **goyim** (*non-Jew's*) to follow orders blindly whilst doing the killing! It's only a half-truth, the invisible hands of those who **finance** and **organize** the **wars** are not only the **ones** to blame, but the **one's** who allow it to **happen!**

. . .

Those of us who live in greenhouses should learn not to cast the first stone!

. . .

Because it's as if they have eyes and ears everywhere like **Dr Who** and **the web of fear** or **great intelligence**! And it knows who you are looking back at it! In the preverbal reflection of the polished shield of Perseus in Greek mythology that slew **Medusa** the gorgon!

The Golden Bough

Ange ou démon
(Angel or demon)
'Should I always say exactly what I mean and mean exactly what I say?'

. . .

Hilaire Belloc

The Golden Bough: A Study in Comparative Religion (retitled *The Golden Bough: A Study in Magic and Religion* in its second edition) is a wide-ranging, comparative study of mythology and religion, written by the Scottish anthropologist Sir James George Frazer (**1854–1941**). It was first published in two volumes in 1890; in three volumes in 1900; the third edition, published **1906–15**, comprised twelve volumes. The work was aimed at a wide literate audience raised on tales as told in such publications as Thomas Bulfinch's *The Age of Fable, or Stories of Gods and Heroes* (**1855**).

Frazer offered a modernist approach to discussing religion, treating it dispassionately as a cultural phenomenon rather than from a theological perspective. The influence of *The Golden Bough* on contemporary European literature and though

The Golden Bough attempts to define the shared elements of religious belief and scientific thought, discussing fertility rites, human sacrifice, the dying god, the scapegoat and many other symbols and practices whose influence has extended into twentieth-century culture. Its thesis is that old religions were fertility cults that revolved around the worship and periodic sacrifice of a sacred king. Frazer proposed that mankind progresses from **"magic"** through **"religious belief"** to **"scientific thought!"**

. . .

Idiot savants

(Religion Verses Science)

Sees the ruin brought about by the blind pursuit of science without practical results, in a satire on **"bureaucracy"** and on the Royal Society and its experiments. At the Grand Academy of Lagado, great resources and manpower are employed on researching completely preposterous schemes such as extracting **sunbeams from cucumbers, softening marble for use in pillows, learning how to mix paint by smell**, and **uncovering political conspiracies by examining the excrement of suspicious persons** (*muckraking*).

Bishop Eusebius

Stood on a pulpit in the town square and announced to 'the grovelling rabble' that Emperor Constantine's 78 year-old mother, Helena had undertaken '**a great trip**', and '**dug up**' the cross upon which Jesus Christ was crucified ('Vita Constantini', 3, 41-47). At the same time, she '**discovered**' other remarkable relics that make pale into triviality the later

81

discovery of Tutankhamen's tomb-treasures. Amongst them were two-sealed **clay jars** one containing the precious *last breath of Jesus Christ*, and the other had *beams of light from the Star of Bethlehem*!

Gulliver's Travels

This book uses coarse metaphors to describe human depravity, and the **Houyhnhms** are symbolised as not only perfected nature but also the emotional barrenness which Swift maintained that devotion to reason brought.

Editio Princeps of **Gulliver's Travels** with one small exception. This edition had an added piece by Swift,

In *The Unthinkable Swift: The Spontaneous Philosophy of a Church of England Man*, Warren Montag argues that Swift was concerned to refute the notion that the **individual precedes society**, as Defoe's novel seems to suggest. Swift regarded such thought as a dangerous endorsement of **Thomas Hobbes'** radical political philosophy and for this reason Gulliver repeatedly encounters established societies rather than desolate islands.

Scholar Allan Bloom points out that Swift's critique of science (the experiments of **Laputa**) is the first such questioning by a modern liberal democrat of the **effects** and **cost** on a society which **embraces and celebrates policies pursuing scientific progress.**

A possible reason for the book's classic status is that *it can be seen as many things to many different people.* Broadly, the book has three themes:

A satirical view of the state of European government, and of petty differences between **religions**.

An inquiry into whether men are **inherently corrupt** or whether they become **corrupted**.

A restatement of the older "ancients versus moderns" controversy previously addressed by Swift in *The Battle of the Books*.

Johnathan Swift

. . .

Continued:

This thesis was developed in relation to J. M. W. Turner's painting of **The Golden Bough**, a sacred grove where a certain tree grew day and night. It was a transfigured landscape in a dream-like vision of the woodland lake of Nemi, **"Diana's Mirror"**, where religious ceremonies and the "fulfillment of vows" of priests and kings were held.

The king was the incarnation of a dying and reviving god, a solar deity who underwent a mystic marriage to a goddess of the Earth. He died at the harvest and was reincarnated in the spring. Frazer claims that this legend of rebirth is central to almost all of the world's mythologies. Frazer based his thesis on the pre-Roman priest-king at the fane of Nemi, who was ritually murdered by his successor:

"When I first put pen to paper to write **The Golden Bough** I had no conception of the magnitude of the voyage on which I was embarking; I thought only to explain a single rule of an ancient Italian priesthood."
(***Aftermath, p. vi***)
The book's title was taken from an incident in the *Aeneid*, illustrated by the British artist Joseph Mallord William Turner: Aeneas and the Sibyl present the "***golden bough***" to the gatekeeper of Hades to gain admission.

. . .

Reception

The book scandalized the British public when first published, as it included the Christian story of Jesus and the Resurrection in its comparative study. Critics thought this treatment invited an agnostic reading of the Lamb of God as a relic of a pagan religion. For the third edition, Frazer placed his analysis of the Crucifixion in a speculative appendix; the discussion of Christianity was excluded from the single-volume abridged edition.
The book's influence on the emerging discipline of anthropology was pervasive and undeniable. For example, Bronisław Malinowski, stricken with tuberculosis shortly after receiving his doctorate in physics and mathematics, read Frazer's work in the original English to distract himself from his illness.
"No sooner had I read this great work than I became immersed in it and enslaved by it. I realized then that anthropology, as presented by Sir James Frazer, is a great science, worthy of as much devotion as any of her elder and more exact studies and I became bound to the service of Frazerian anthropology."

. . .

Despite the controversy the work generated, and its critical reception amongst other scholars, **The Golden Bough** inspired the creative literature of the period. The poet **Robert Graves** adapted **Frazer's** concept of the dying king sacrificed for the good of the kingdom to the romantic idea of the poet's suffering for the sake of his Muse-Goddess, as reflected in his book on poetry, rituals, and myths, **The White Goddess** (**1948**). **William Butler** Yeats refers to Frazer's thesis in his poem **"Sailing to Byzantium"**. **H. P. Lovecraft** mentions the book in his short story **"The Call of Cthulhu"**. **T. S. Eliot** acknowledged indebtedness to **Frazer** in his first note to his poem **The Waste Land**. **Sigmund Freud**, **James Joyce**, **Ernest Hemingway**, **D. H. Lawrence**, **Aleister Crowley**, are some of the authors whose work shows the deep influence of **The Golden Bough**. Its literary ripples and references have given it continued life, even as its direct influence in **anthropology** has waned!
Attar, god of the morning star (**"son of the morning"**) who tried to take the place of the dead Baal and failed. Male counterpart of Athtart.
Canaanite religion

83

Angels and fiery chariots!

"*Paradise lost*"
"Where Lucifer or the Devil was cast into the pit! And he said that it would be better to rule in hell, than serve in heaven"

Milton

Isaiah

XiV, 12

'How art thou fallen from heaven O Lucifer, son of the morning'?

For the propagation of *Satan's* Kingdom, not of the seed of *Adam* are we, Nor is *Abraham* our father, but of the seed of the proud angel driven from heaven... **"All shall speak and say unto thee. Art thou also become weak as we? Art thou become like unto us? Thy pomp is brought you down to the grave, and the noise of they viols."**

The worm is spread under thee, and the worms cover thee. **How art thou fallen from heaven O Lucifer, son of the morning!** How art thy cut down to the ground, you who didst weaken the nations! For thou hast said in thine heart, I will ascend into heaven, I will exalt my throne above the stars of God: I will sit also upon the mount of the congregation, in the sides of the North.

. . .

"I will ascend above the heights of the clouds; I will be like the most high. Yet thou shalt be brought down to hell, to the sides of the pit"

. . .

But Lucifer did not heed the words of God and the war in heaven began...

. . .

"For never was there such a star that shone so bright and fell so far, that can rise again and shine so bright"

. . .

Michael and his hosts fought against **Lucifer** and his army and **Michael** prevailed. And **Lucifer**, whose name became **Satan** the **Devil** was expelled down to earth in defeat and dishonour. And **Jesus**, who is the word of *God*, and with him from the beginning, **watched**, as **Lucifer** was defeated in heaven and cast down. And he said unto them, **"I beheld Satan as lighting, fall from heaven"**

"Lernean Hydra that grows two heads for each one cut off."
(You can't tell one from the other)

Judas Goat

This bi-partisan **Jewish menace** could be more than just a reflection of **Jewish mythology**, a dybbuk (**dubik**) (Yiddish: from Hebrew **adhere** or **cling**) is a malicious possessing of an unclean spirit that seems or appears to have an efinity with us, that we can nither live with, nor live without, they are the keepers of our consciounce, by and through some undefined struggle with the King of terrors (**Death**) or the symbolic journey of life! Which is akin to the jewel of **Alchemy**, by which base metals (**bodies**) are turned or transformed into gold (**higher-self**)Like the **cross** or **quincunx**, that indicates human existence at the intersection of the (**horizontal**) physical plane and the (**vertical**) plane of eternity, through the symbolism of the **Golden Bough**!

. . .

In Greek mythology, **Charon** or **Kharon** is the ferryman of Hades who carries souls of the newly deceased across the rivers **Styx** and **Acheron** that divided the world of the **living** from the world of the **dead**! A coin to pay Charon for passage, usually an obolus or danake, was sometimes placed on the eyes and in or on the mouth of a dead person. Some authors say that those who could not pay the fee, or those whose bodies were left unburied, had to wander the shores for one hundred years. In the catabasis mytheme, heroes–such as **Heracles, Orpheus, Aeneas,Theseus, Sisyphus, Dionysus, Odysseus** and **Psyche**–journey to the underworld and return, still alive, conveyed by the boat of **Charon**.
In the 1st century BC, the Roman poet Virgil describes Charon in the course of Aeneas's descent to the underworld (*Aeneid*, Book 6), after the Cumaean Sibyl has directed the hero to the *"golden bough"* that will allow him to return to the world of the living:

. . .

There Chairon stands, who rules the dreary coast
A sordid god: down from his hairy chin
A length of beard descends, uncombed, unclean;
His eyes, like hollow furnaces on fire;
A girdle, foul with grease, binds his obscene attire.

. . .

In the 14th century, **Dante Alighieri** described Charon in his **Divine Comedy**, drawing from Virgil's depiction in **Aeneid 6**. Charon is the first named mythological character **Dante** meets in the underworld, in the third **canto of Inferno**. Elsewhere, **Charon** appears as a cranky, skinny old man or as a winged demon wielding a double hammer, although Michelangelo's interpretation, influenced by **Dante's** depiction in **Inferno, canto 3**, shows him with an oar over his shoulder, ready to beat those who delay (**"batte col remo qualunque s'adagia"**, *Inferno 3*, **verse 111**). In modern times, he is commonly depicted as a living skeleton in a cowl, much like the **Grim Reaper!**

"Who pays The Ferryman"

"And before the throne there was a sea of glass like cristal: and in the midst of the throne, were four beasts full of eyes before and behind"

Revelation

When we speak of this invisible-hand we are euphemistically speaking of a many-headed monster, like the creature of Persian mythology, called the *"Hydra"* which confuses the issue, its as if we literally can't see the trees for the forest, and if we parody the old testament...

. . .

Ezekiel

"Also out of the midst thereof came the likeness of four living creatures. And this was their appearance; they had the likeness of a man. And every one had four faces, and everyone had four wings."

. . .

Which in reality were four unusual strangers, that could have been wearing advanced technological suits with helmets and rocket back-packs, that give the impression that they have four faces, the helmet looked like a head that obviously has eyes and the wearers eyes, make four eyes, with a pair of arms and a backpack of some kind, that would look like four wings! It's akin to looking at the reflection in a mirror, where we are seeing one thing, but thinking its something else!

The Servile State

A book written by **Hilaire Belloc** in 1912 about economics. Although it mentions distributism, for which he and his friend G. K. Chesterton are famous, it avoids explicit advocacy of that economic system.

This book lays out, in very broad outline, Belloc's version of European economic history, starting with ancient pagan states, in which slavery was critical to the economy, through the medieval Christendom process which transformed an economy based on serf labour in a state in which the property was well distributed, to 19th and 20th century capitalism. Belloc argues that the development of capitalism was not a natural consequence of the Industrial Revolution, but a consequence of the earlier dissolution of the monasteries in England, which then shaped the course of English industrialisation. English capitalism then spread across the world!

Belloc then makes his case for the natural instability of pure capitalism and discusses how he believes that attempts to reform capitalism will lead almost inexorably to an economy in which state regulation has removed the freedom of capitalism and thereby replaced capitalism with the Servile State, which shares with ancient slavery the fact that positive law (as opposed to custom or economic necessity by themselves) dictates that certain people will work for others, who likewise must take care of them.

In the ninth section of the book, titled *"The Servile State Has Begun"* Belloc explores various ways the servile state has started to creep its way back into modern life. Among these he includes minimum wage laws, employers liability laws, the Insurance Act, and compulsory arbitration. Belloc defines servile laws as those that establish "distinction between two classes of citizens, marking off the one as legally distinct from the other by a criterion of **manual labor** or **income**."

. . .

'On Pree'

Where the opponent has left one of there pieces under attack and undefended, so that you can take it! (this is called leaving a piece **en-prise**-pronounced **"on-pree"**— with a French accent if so, don't be too quick to move it, it could be a trap! Or in our case take **Hitler, Abraham Lincoln** or **George Orwell** with a **pinch-of-salt**! Could they not be as threatening as the **Bishop** during a chess-game on the long diagonals that run between the four corners of the board, like **Aristotle's** (*square-of-opposition*) or **Fianchetto** which is Italian for '**little-flank**' it is a move that puts the **Bishop** on to this diagonal often threatening the opponents rook! Because they can be as deadly as **Joseph Stalin**, (*Ashkenazi Jew*) **Churchill** (*Ashkenazi Jew*) President **Franklin Delano Roosvelt** (*Sephardic Jew*) real name: **Rosen**!

Greek Anthology

(In which a goat laments that it is made to suckle a wolf-cub!)

. . .

Not by my own will but the shepherd's folly.
The beast reared by me will make me his prey
For gratitude cannot change nature.
"Beware of false prophets, which come to you in sheep's clothing, but inwardly they are ravening wolves."

Jesus Christ

. . .

'Scorpion and the Fox'

"*A scorpion asks the fox to carry him over a river. The fox is afraid of being stung during the trip, but the scorpion argues that if it stung the fox, the fox would sink and the scorpion would drown. The fox agrees and begins carrying the scorpion, but midway across the river the scorpion does indeed sting the fox, dooming them both. When asked why, the scorpion points out that this is its nature. The fable is used to illustrate the position that the natural behaviour of some creatures is inevitable, no matter how they are treated. It is also used to illustrate that individuals are apt to behave in accordance with their true character in spite of the education they might have received throughout their lives . In spite of knowing fully well the right course of action, and full understanding the consequences, some are unable to overcome their nature.*"

George Orwell! Described the work as written in a "tiresome style" and argued that the remedy it suggested was "impossible". However, he considered that it foretold the sorts of things that were happening in the 1930s with "remarkable insight". Kenneth Minogue's book *The Servile Mind* was inspired by Belloc's book. Minogue described Belloc's book as somewhat dated but still offering valuable insights into the development of servility and dependence on government largesse, which Minogue tended to regard unfavorably. Austrian School economist Friedrich von Hayek praised the truth of Belloc's predictions in his book The Road to Serfdom and subtitled his chapter, "*Economic Control* and *Totalitarianism*", with the quote from The Servile State, "the control of the production of wealth is the control of human life itself."

. . .

The rich will always be with us

(Only fools and horses work)
"If work was any good, the rich would grab all of it, and you would not get any of it, that's why!"
Like in the novel by *Disraeli (Sephardic Jew)* called *Coningsby*; or *The new generation* (book IV, chapter XV) Sidonia makes the following very ominous and pregnant work: 'So you see, my dear Coningsby, that the world is governed by very different personages to what is imagined by those who are not behind the scenes' definite instructions have been handed down to successive officials: *figurehead governments* are set up, and **secret advisers** reduce **monarchies** to a mere legal fiction."

. . .

"I care not what puppet is placed upon the throne of England to rule the Empire on which the sun never sets, the man who controls Britain's money supply controls the Empire, and I control the British money supply.
Nathan Mayer Rothschild

. . .

The new generation

1815

(Ask no questions and you'll be told no lies— one hand washes the other!)
Even though Disraeli characterises one of the *Rothschild's* as: "...the lord and master of the money markets of the world, and of course virtually Lord and Master of everything else. He literally held the revenues of *Southern Italy* in *pawn, (also a term for a player used in chess, that is capable of releasing the greatest amount of energy on the board!)* My (Italics) and *Monarchs* and *Ministers* of all countries courted his advice and were guided by his suggestions. He makes a very *interesting statement*, just like *Adolf Hitler*:

"The racial question is the key to world history... all is race, there is no other truth."
Benjamin Disraeli

. . .

Mein Kampf
(Wolf-in-the-fold)
(Questions are a burden to other's and answers a prison to one self)
And the statement below is true
Because the statement above is false!!
(So don't believe a word he says, because he's a liar!!)
"**Adolf Hitler**" in his book **Mein Kampf**, says one thing, but seems or appears to mean something else! Its as if it cloaks an unquit truth. Because any fool knows that you can't run with the hare and hunt with the hounds!
"You can't serve two masters"
Jesus Christ

. . .

That when he arrived in Vienna as a young man, Hitler indicated that the later fervency of his anti-Jewism had not fully formed...

The Jew
*"In the **Jew** I still saw only a man who was of a **different religion**, and therefore, on grounds of **human tolerance**, I was against the idea that he should be attacked because he had a different **faith**." Hitler decided that anti-Semitism based on religious, rather than **racial grounds**, was a mistake!"*

Adolf Hitler

. . .

The Christian churches should forget about their own differences and focus on the issue of "*racial contamination*".

Adolf Hitler

. . .

When you begin to join up the dots, a strange and eerie picture begins to take shape, unless you know the significance of an event, in relation to its cause?

"A land of slaves shall ne'er be mine"

What ghastly necessity will be perpetrated in the name of God! To try and stay-off the bloody hand of fate? Or do the people get the government they truly deserve? ***"A democratic prison without bars!"*** as quoted by that mysterious and archetypical madman ***"Adolf Hitler"*** but one does not throw out the baby with the bath water! Because of its so-called **anti-Semitic language**, and that someone or something seems or appears to be leading us around in circles, having first taken control of the American Government by legal or subversive means, because the people are **disingenuous** causing the **depression** in **America**, by taking the money out of the hands of the many for to benefit the few, and then to spend it overseas rebuilding **Germany** in preparation for the **second world war**!

Internationalism
(Never bite the hand that feeds)

Remember Hitler's so-called racial question? Seemed or appeared to be nothing more than a clever ruse or **Judas goat**, excuse the pun, to play both sides off against the middle! Because it turned out to be a monumental sleight-of-hand, that cost the life of **62 million people**! And like a macabre magicians trick, called the **vanishing man**, afterwards was he cleverly spirited away, so to speak. Where it seems or appears that he cleverly said one thing, but meant something else!

Due to the contradiction of the international bankers i.e.: the **Rothschild's** who had subsidized the **rise**-and-**fall** of the **Nazi-government** to the tune of **30 billions of dollars**, to be used to underpin or bolster the **Nazi-puppet-regime** through the **German Thyssen banks** which are affiliated with the **Rothschild** controlled **Harriman interest** in New York!

Andrew Carrington Hitchcock

. . .

When that so-called dictator **Adolf Hitler** or **wolf-in-the-fold,** that conveniently for us, impeached tyranny! That cleverly wears the mask or persona of legality, in a **totalitarian state**, and that the rites of the individual are above the state! Yes, it was **'he'** that said those words, in

"Mein Kampf" it just goes to show you, that one should never judge a book by its cover, read it first and then make up your own mind where you think the truth **lies!** *(Excuse the pun;)* and remember, everybody votes in tyranny in one form or another, whether it's a **right-wing nazism** or **left-wing Marxism**, untill everybody will be truly equal in the great collective, whether they like it or not!

90

;species capable of even contemplating ethical issues and assuming responsibilities--we uniquely are capable of apprehending the difference between right and wrong, good and evil, proper and improper conduct toward animals. Or to put it more succinctly if being human isn't what requires us to treat animals humanely, what in the world does?"

"Wheels Within wheels"
(Why was Lucifer not destroyed?)

In **Jewish** mythology, a **dybbuk** (*dubik*) (Yiddish: from **Hebrew** *adhere* or *cling*) is a malicious possessing of an unclean spirit believed to be the dislocated soul of a dead person. It supposedly leaves the host body once it has accomplished its goal, sometimes after being helped! The leech eventually falls off! Who or what are these unhallowed crew, who meddle and mix in politics and social affairs from the very first, whose liege and master, is meant to be the devil! Who rebelled against God in heaven, so do they seem or appear to rebel against any ordered and legitimate form of government here on earth!

What follows is neither obtuse, nor superfluous, regarding a bi-partisan struggle in which the Goyim or Gentile (*non-Jew!*) and the dybbuk (*dubik*) or anthropomorphic krypto-Jew! Through a pseudo scientific **anthropological, sociological** and **theological conundrum,** that seems or appears to be the collective author of the piece, through **"internationalism"** (*Global politics*) something has evolved and organized capitalism and its working instrumentality, the banking system in the form of the house of Rothschild, by playing both sides off against the middle. Something is very cleverly using **"one hand to wash the other"** and as the **"wheels within wheels"** roll on carrying this metamorphic-hydra into a new and more dangerous course or **"Common purpose"** that is veridical and maliciously misleading as it is intentional, using a deceptive strategy used by a whole **cabal** of **cronies,** in a secret doctrine or structure, covertly working in parallel, like the **reformation** cleverly did alongside the **Roman Church** or government (**body-politic**) that is run and perpetrated by **idiot-savants**! That are as **conceited** as they are **dogmatic,** and who seem or appear to have **"agreed to disagree"** by vacillating or wavering between conflicting positions or courses of action!

(***Hoysted by your own pitard!***)

"We are to busy looking at what the right-hand is supposed to be doing, to think about what the left-hand has done!"

. . .

Divide and Conquer

A division into fractional parties has given the *goyim* (*Gentle*) into our hands, for, in order to carry on a contested struggle one must have money, and the money is all in our hands!

President Abraham Lincoln

"The money power preys upon the nations in times of peace and conspires against it in times of adversity. It is more selfish than bureaucracy."

Only as a unillateral weapon of choice, so to speak, knowledge and understanding will draw out the infected blood of the nation, akin to a symbolic double-edged sword that was drawn in the story by Malory who died in (1471) Le Morte d' Arhur, or the death of King Arthur! By the invisible hand of that **Serpent,** that sits on high leading the blind!

And like a beacon of light, in that dark-hour of the soul, it will **illuminate** (*excuse the pun*) the way ahead, under the shadow of the **"common purpose"** as it gathers around the growing boy! We will be forced to use numerical understanding, as we hold aloft the sword of personal inititive!

. . .

Remember gentlemen: the **pawns** on the **chess-board** can release the greatest amount of energy! But only if they are true to themselves! And not driven by that invisable hand! Even Kings and queens have been brought down by this unquit truth, doubt it naught!

"behold, I, Even I, will bring a sword upon you
And I will destroy your high places"

Christian Scriptures

. . .

" Personal inititive "

In order to hold aloft the greatest weapon at our disposal, we can slowly drain off the nations infected blood, where it seeks to divide and conquer any resistance to the **common purpose,** through **political!** **Economic!** **Social!** And **true religious** means

. . .

"Is it not moral right to scatter our enimies, confound their politics, frustrate their tricks, on thee our hope we fix. God save us all!"

. . .

Desease infects the body/politic of the national narritive by what seems or appears to be a cancer of the body, that can only be properly understood through and by the dignostic skills of people questioning the **status-quo,** by using **volation** or **personal inititive** to consume and report consistant-inconsistancies through an appraisal of the **common purpose,** wheither its the **enemy at the gates** or **the enemy within,** something is there and it seems or appears to be invisible to its audience or host, in order to make it fit the changes, by the means that will justify the ends of information consumption!"

"You can fool some of the people, all of the time, and you can fool all of the people some of the time, but you can't fool all of the people, all of the time!"

Abraham Lincoln

PROVIDENCE

"I am the punishment of God... If you had not committed great sins, God would not have sent a punishment like me upon you."
Genghis Khan

. . .

A Clockwork Orange
1694

The deceptively named *"Bank of England"* is founded! It gives the impresion that it is controlled by the government like the *"Federal Reserve"* in America.

A company of rich men under the leadership, *no doubt by proxy* [My Italics] of a *Shabbez-Goy* (*non-Jew*) *William Paterson*, who are in essence like the watch-dog of the *Vampyr* (*vampire*) they prepare the way! Whilst the *Jew*! Or *dybbuk* (*dubik's*) identity is protected, *William Paterson* stated:

"The bank hath benefit of interest on all monies which it creates out of nothing"

That's why he was sent to *"Coventry"* or he became an outcast who chose to clandestinely represent the *Jews* or anthropomorphic *dybbuk* (*dubik*) or seems or appears to have merely outlived his usefulness!

. . .

1790

"Let me issue and control a nation's money and I care not who writes the laws."

. . .

1791

The *dybbuk* or (*krypto-Jew*) like *Alexander Hamilton* who was in fact the subversive element or representitive in George Washington's cabinet, a fact that staggers the imagination! And where the *Rothschilds* gain control of a nations money! Or should we say the *goyim* dutifully hands over the control of the *U.S.A.* with *Thomas Jefferson* be-crying *"will no one rid me of this priest?"* [My Italics] the *Rothschilds* set up the first (*central*) or private *bank of America*, like the *bank of England*, among others! With a pathetic so-called escape clause or 20 year charter! Why not amend the constitution for good and all, to keep the *first bank of America for good and always?* Instead of *Jefferson* waffling on with his vailed abtuse attempt to impeach the *Rothschilds*, regarding his concearns:

. . .

"I wish it were possible to obtain a single amendment to our constitution taking from the Federal Government their power of borrowing."

And not surprisingly if you expose the mockery of a corrupt and perverse government that allows the fettered belly of conspiracy, with its tenuous

93

links to organised crime, reaching up to the highest echelons of society like some **"Latrunculi"** brotherhood of **gangsters** at enmity with one another and yet fixed in some **infernal bond** or **brotherhood of blind and murderous hatred of things**.

. . .

Exposé

(Jesus Christ)

"Why do you look at the speck of sawdust in your brothers eye and pay no attention to the plank in your own eye? How can you say to your brother, 'Let me take the speck out of your eye, 'when all the time there is a plank in your own eye? You hypocrite, first take the plank out of your own eye, and then you can see clearly to remove the speck from your brother's eye!"

Mathew 7:3-5

. . .

Rothschild's

So it's not a judgement of them! But more of an exposé that seems or appears to be indirectly trying to tell us something to question the status quo, so to speak, by using the invisible hand, you know the one that rocks the cradle! To try and find the itch that you can't scratch!

. . .

The Synagogue Of Satan
1780

Having contrived to possess itself of the minds of the **Goy** (*Gentile*) communities to such an extent they all come near looking upon the events of the world through the coloured glasses of those spectacles we are setting astride their noses; if already now there is not a single state where there exist for us any barriers to admittance into what **Goy** (*Gentile*) stupidity calls State secrets: what will our position be then, when we shall be acknowledged supreme lords of the world in the person of our king of all the world!

The reforms projected by us in the financial institutions and principles of the **goyim** will be clothed by us in such forms as will alarm nobody. We shall point out the necessity of reforms in consequence of disorderly darkness into which the **goyim** by their irregularities have plunged the finances.

Thanks to such methods, allowed by the carelessness of the **goy** States, their treasuries are empty. You understand perfectly that we cannot carry on economic arrangements of this kind, which have been suggested to the **goyim** by us—!

Every kind of **loan** proves **infirmity** in the **State** and a want of **understanding of the rights of the State**. Loans hang like the **sword-of-Damocles** over the heads of rulers, who, instead of taking

from their subjects by a temporary tax, come **begging** with **outstretched-palm** to our **bankers**!
Foreign loans are leeches, which there is no **possibility** of **removing** from the **body of the State** until they **fall off of themselves** or the **State, flings them off**. But the **goy** States do not tear them off; they go on in persisting in putting more on to themselves so that they must **inevitably perish**, drained by voluntary **bloodletting**!

Andrew Carrington Hitchcock

. . .

"Woe to you oh earth and sea, for the Devil sends the beast with wrath and fury because he knows the time is short"

. . .

Something extra-terrestrial or terrestrial from underground, which seems or appears to be malevolent and or benevolent, could be watching and studying us for centuries, and could be using the ***famous*** or ***infamous*** ***"House of Rothschild's"*** as a front for to invade and conquer by a slow process of social-engineering, To prepare the way for a ***NOVUS ORDO CECLORUM*** or so-called ***one world government!***
The scriptures could be describing something other than what we have been led to believe:
*"**And many of them that shall sleep in the dust of the earth shall awake, some to everlasting life, and some to shame and everlasting contempt**"*
Daniel 12:2

. . .

*"For if God not spared the angels when they sinned, but cast them down into hell and committed them to **pits** of darkness, to be reserved unto judgement"*
Christian Scriptures

. . .

Des Vermis Mysteriis

The infamous medieval grimoire titled: ***"De Vermis Mysteriis"*** like the infamous and symbolic ***"Necronomicon"*** or (*book of shadows*).

. . .

The ***"Des Vermis Mysteriis"*** was meant to have been written in Latin, and was supposed to have been suppressed by the ***Catholic-church***, like most things were, in its power struggle to establish a foot-hold during its early occupation and dominance of the old world!
A very rare book rumoured to be only known to practitioners of the black or unknown arts. It was meant to be a depository of diabolical ablutions, ancient spells, alchemical potions and strange eerie equations. That spoke of the strange diadem of the ***"elders"*** or ***"dark gods"*** also known as ***"The old one's"*** or those who have the knowledge:

*"It has been written since the beginning of time, even unto these ancient **stones** that evil supernatural **creatures** exist in a **world of darkness**, and it is also said man using the power of the ancient runic symbols can call forth these powers of **darkness**, the demons of **hell**. Through the ages men have feared and worshiped these **creatures**, the practice of witchcraft, the cults of evil have endured and exist to this day "*

Night/Curse of the demon

. . .

Dunwich Horror

"Nor is it to be thought that man is either the oldest or the last of earth's masters, nor that the greater part of substance walks alone. The Old Ones were, the Old Ones are, and the Old Ones shall be. Not in the spaces we know, but between them, they walk serene and primal, undimensioned and to us unseen. Yog-Sothoth knows the gate. Yog-Sothoth is the gate. Yog-Sothoth is the key and guardian of the gate. Past, present, future, all are one in Yog-Sothoth. He knows where the Old Ones broke through of old, and where they shall break through again.

He knows where they have trod earth's fields, and where they still tread them, and why no one can behold them as they tread. By Their smell can men sometimes know Them near, but of Their semblance can no man know, saving only in the features of those They have begotten on mankind; and of those are there many sorts, differing in likeness from man's truest eidolon to that shape without sight or substance which is Them. They walk unseen and foul in lonely places where the Words have been spoken and the Rites howled through at their Seasons.

The wind gibbers with their voices, and the earth mutters with their consciousness. They bend the forest and crush the city, yet may not forest or city behold the hand that smites.

Kadath in the cold waste hath known them, and what man knows Kadath? The ice desert of the South and the sunken isles of Ocean hold stones whereon their seal is engraven, but who hath seen the deep frozen city or the sealed tower long garlanded with seaweed and barnacles? Great Cthulhu is their cousin, yet can he spy them only dimly. Iä! Shub-Niggurath.

As foulness shall ye know them? Their hand is at your throats, yet ye see them not; and their habitation is even one with your guarded threshold. Yog-Sothoth is the key to the gate, whereby the spheres meet. Man rules now where they ruled once; they shall soon rule where man rules now. After summer is winter and after winter summer, they wait patient and potent, for here shall they reign again!"

H.P.Lovcraft

STAR-TREK
1960'S
TITLED: SPOCK'S COMMAND
(The equivalent weight of three grown men!)

I know you **Mr Spock,** you've never voiced it, but you've always though that logic was the best basis in which to build command, am I right?

Mr Spock: I am a logic man Doctor.

Dr McCoy (*Bones*): it will take more than logic to get us out of this! Perhaps Doctor.

Mr Spock: I know no better way to begin.

. . .

Command

I realize that command does have its fascination, even under circumstances such as this; I neither enjoy the idea, nor am I frightened of it, it simply exists! And I will do whatever logically needs to be done.

500lbs
(The Weight of three grown men)

Dr McCoy: (*Bones*) the equivalent weight in equipment? **Spock**: —Dr **McCoy** with very few exceptions, virtually every piece of equipment on board this craft is for achieving orbit, there's very little excess weight, except among the passengers!

Spock: My choice will be a logical one, arrived at through logical means.

Dr McCoy (*Bones*): Life and death are seldom logical; Mr **Spock**: but attaining a desired goal, always is!

Dr McCoy: (*Bones*) we may all die here; at least let us all die like men, not machines!

The majority

Spock: I'm not interested in the majority!

Gartano: If we stand by and do nothing, we're just giving them an invitation to come down and slaughter us.

Boma: it could be some kind of tribal right, assuming there a tribal culture!

Spock: a tribal culture? More like a lose association of some kind.

Boma: we know enough, if they're tribal, they'll have a sense of unity, we can use that.

Mr Spock: how Mr Boma?

Give them a bloody nose and they'll think twice about attacking us again!

Mr Gartano: I agree.

Mr Spock: I'm often appalled by the low regard you earth men have for life well were practical about it!

Mr Gitano: I say hit them hard before they hit us.

Mr Spock: **Mr Boma**? Absolutely!

Dr McCoy: seems logical to me.

Mr Spock: it seems logical to me also, to take life indiscriminately?
Mr Gitano: the majority!
Mr Spock: I'm not interested in the majority—componants must be weighed, our dangers to ourselves, as well as our duty to other life forms, friendly or not.

Danger!

McCoy: (*Bones*) I don't believe you're serious about leaving somebody behind? Whatever's out there!
Mr Spock: it is more rational to sacrifice one life and save six!
Dr McCoy: I'm not talking about rationality.
Spock: by dealing with first things first, I hope to increase our chances of staying alive!

Captain Kirk

Mr Spock? Tell me something I don't understand about all this, maybe you can explain it ***"logically of course"*** when you jettisoned the fuel, there was virtually no chance and yet you did it anyhow! Which seems to me an act of desperation.
Desperation is a highly emotional state, how does your well know logic explain it?
Mr Spock: quite simply ***Captain***, I examined the problem from all angles and it was plainly hopeless under the circumstances, any possible action would have to be one of desperation, logical decision, logically arrived at.
Captain Kirk: you mean you reasoned it was time for an emotional out burst?
Mr Spock: well I wouldn't have put it in those terms they are essentially the facts.
Captain Kirk: your not going to admit, for the first time in your life you committed a purely emotional act?
Mr Spock: no sir!
Much like the contemporary story ***"Demon on the wing"*** which is based on arrogance, solitude and terror, where a man's reason can crumble and be overthrown, by intellectual pride, like in the brilliant 1950s movie ***"Night or Curse of the Demon"*** where the two protagonists are speaking to one another at Carswell's country house:

. . .

"Where does imagination end, and reality begin? What is this twilight or half world of the mind that you profess to know so much about? And Diana Andrews, while standing on the solid ground of the so-called Sceptic, while announcing that all good men should come from Missouri; and should be saying, show me! And one character replies: and if you are shown? Then I look twice!
The whole thing of this demon monster that drove Hobart out of his mind, is a perfect example of auto-suggestion and mass hysteria, just the same as flying saucers, someone imagines that they see moving lights in the sky, and the next thing, a thousand hysterical witnesses turn up all over the world swearing that Martians are attaching us! And now this

nonsense, it even effects serious people like yourself, sometimes even me, but the see able and the touchable, that's what convinces me, certainly not rumour, intuition or funny feelings, I wouldn't dream of arguing with you, you say show me, I say look for yourself! And surprisingly at the end, Diana Andrews tells Carswell: I what to thank you for convincing me of a world I never thought possible, and Carswell replies: if only you'd thought sooner!"

. . .

In place of the rulers of today we shall set up a bogey, which will be called the **"Super-government-administration**." Its hands will reach out in all directions like nippers and its organization will be of such colossal dimensions that it cannot fail to subdue all nations of the world!

. . .

Like in **Jack the ripper** or in **MISSING 411,** these **extra-terrestrials** or **terrestrials** seem or appear to be like **"The Roman Empire"** they need to extend the frontiers of their empire by using what seems or appears to be an ambiguous carrot on a stick! Through a process of **innocuous-social-engineering**, where the means will justify the ends!

By establishing **hierarchies** or **frontiers** by **systematically** studying how we **function** and **procreate**, while **experimenting** and **interfering** with our **DNA** for whatever reason, while **terra-forming** the **planet** to except its new **host** or **race** through and by the **organisation** of the **Illuminati** through.

The Synagogue Of Satan
(May 1 of this year)
1776
Adam Weishaupt
(Maggots dreaming of power)
How can evil destroy good? It's impossible, unless both polarities cancel themselves out!
'A Gloopy (stupid) title, whoever heard of a clockwork orange?' then I read a malenky (little/tiny) bit out loud in a sort of very high type preaching goloss (voice): — 'the attempt to impose upon man, a creature of growth and capable of sweetness, to ooze juicily at the last round the bearded lips of God, to attempt to impose, I say, laws and conditions appropriate to a mechanical creation, against this I raise my sword-pen'
Anthony Burgess

. . .

Put the cat in among the pigeons!
"The purpose of the **Illuminati** is to divide the **goyim** (Gentiles) or all **non-Jews**, through **political**, **economic**, **social**, and **religious means**!
The **opposing sides** were to be **armed** and **incidents** were to be provided in order for them to: **fight amongst themselves**; **destroy national governments**; **destroy religious institutions**; and

eventually **destroy** each other! Be very careful, because it seems or appears to be an intentional and very clever, yet contradictory tactic by the **illuminati**:

. . .

Prick us, do we not bleed?
"William Shakespeare"

. . .

" *Take heed that no man deceive you. For many shall in my name, saying 'I am Christ;' and shall deceive many. And ye shall hear of wars and rumors of wars, see ye be not troubled for all these things must come to pass* "

Jesus Christ

. . .

"The Protocols Of The Wise Men Of Zion

"Thanks to the terrible power of our **international banks**, we have forced the **Christians** into **wars** without number. Wars have a special value for **jews**. Wars are the **jews'** harvest, the **jew** banks grow fat on **Christian wars**! Over one **hundred million Christains have been swept off the face of the earth** by **wars**, and the end is not yet."

Does it not take one to know one!

1787

Charles Cotesworth Pinckney, a a delegate from South Caroline attending the Constitutional Convention, Philadelphia, recorded in his dairy the following statement made by **Benjamin Franklin**:

"*I fully agree with general Washington, that we must protect this young nation from an insidious in fluence and impenetration. The menace, gentlemen, is the* **jews**.

In what ever country **jews** *have settled in any great numbers, they have lowered its moral tone; depreciated its commercial integrity; have segregated themselves and have not been assimilated; have sneered at and tried to undermine the* **Chritian-religion** *upon which that nation is found, by objecting to its restrictions; have built up a state within the state; and when opposed have tried to strangle that county to death financially, as in the case of* **Spain** *and* **Portugal**.

For over **1,700 years** *the* **jews** *have been bewailing their* **sad fate** *in that they have been exiled from their* **homeland**, *as they call it* **Palestine**. *But gentlemen, did the world today give it to them in fee simple, they would at once find some reason for not returning.*"

Benjamin Franklin

100

Pernicious bacillus

Your children will curse you in your graves!"
"*Spreads over wider and wider areas according as some favourble area attracts them. The effect produced by this presence is also like that of the*

Vampire *for wherever they establish their colonie, the people or race involved will be bled to death.*

Why? Because they are **Vampires**, *and* **Vampires** *do not live on*

Vampires. *They can only live among others. They must subsist on* **Christains** *and other people not of their* **race!!**
If you do not exclude them, in less than **200 years** *our descendants will be working in the fields to furnish them sustenance, while they will be in the counting houses rubbing their hands. I warn you gentlemen, if you do*

not exclude the **Jews** *for all time, your children will curse you in your graves!"*

. . .

Nosferatu

. . .

So there is more to this statement by the so-called **Illuminati** *than meets the* **eye**, *or* the **all-seeing-eye** on the dollar bill, so to speak!"
The Book of Revelation, Chapter 2, Verse 9, states the following about the '**Dubik**' or these strange **anthropomorphic creatures**:

. . .

"I know thy works, and tribulation and poverty, [but thou art rich] and I know the blasphemy of them which say they are Jews, and are not! But are the synagogue of Satan."
Holy Bible

101

The **Rothschild's** *or something* claiming to be the **Jewish** people is in fact **Khazars**. They are from a country called **Khazaria**, which occupied the land locked between the **Black Sea** and the **Caspian Sea**, which is

Khazars

now predominantly occupied by **Georgia**. The reason the **Rothschild's** claim to be **Jewish** is that the **Khazars** under the instruction of the King, converted to the **Jewish faith** in *740 A.D.*

But of course that did not include converting their **Asiatic Mongolian genes** to the genes of the **Jewish people**!

You will find that approximately **90%** of people in the world today who call themselves **Jews** are actually **Dubik's** or **Khazars**, or as they like to be known, **Ashkenazi Jews**. These people knowingly lie to the world with their claims that the land of **Israel** is theirs by **birthright**, when in actual fact their real homeland is over **800 miles** away in **Georgia**!

. . .

William Gladstone

1852

"Future Prime Minister"

When he became chancellor of the Exchequer in *1852*, said: "I began to learn that the state held, in the face of the bank and the city, an essentially false position as to finance. The government itself was not to be a substantive power, but was to leave the Money Power supreme and unquestioned."

Andrew Carrington Hitchcock

. . .

That function is now *and always was carried out by vested interests* [My Italics] or entirely by *the lobby*, or *the thin end of the wedge to stop the real process from taking place, at any* **cost** *[My Italics]* And there are as many **lobbies** as there are **special interests**!

A political party now exists primarily as an **apparatus** *for selecting* **candidates** and getting them **elected** to **office!**

Even *if by any stretch of the imagination,* a majority of the nominating committee that nominates the candidate were competent judges of men or woman, it will select the candidate, not for their potential wisdom, but on their ability to win elections!

The Protocols Of The Meetings Of The Learned Elders Of Zion

Protocol No 16

"In a word, knowing by experience of the centuries that people live and are guided by ideas, that these are imbided by people only by the aid of education provided with equal success for all ages of growth, but of course by varying methods, we shall swallow up and confiscate to our own use the last scintilla of independence of thought, which we have for long past been directing towards subjects and ideas useful for us. The system of bridling thought is already at work in the so-called system of teaching by **object lessons**, *the purpose of which is to turn the goyim into unthinking submissive brutes waiting for things to be presented before their eyes in order to form an idea of them..."*

Andrew Carrington Hitchcock

.   .   .

"None are more hopelessly enslaved than those who falsely believe they are free!"

Have you ever wondered why our democracy works so well? Because no one votes in the **Civil service**! That ran **Germany** before, during and after the so-called war, the ones who are manipulating and being manipulated by the system that controls the country! Whether you like it or not! And who stand between any and all attempts to try and change the status quo!

"Administrative power' is a more effective tool than direct violence!"

.   .   .

'One gains naught by shouting into deaf ears'
(Paracelsus)

Now we have the invisible hand of a new and frightening global dictatorship who's progress seems or appears to be unabated and is trying to assert its control over the world, one that **Adolf Hitler** and **Joseph Stalin** were somehow part of! And one that has to be exposed, so that we can prepare our minds collectively and start behaving like human beings and not materialistic cold-hearted **"Bastards"**.

.   .   .

The USA, and the U.K. [*My Italics*] One might think that the voters would, in their own interests, recognize and elect the most competent statesman or candidate to represent them at the capital *or at parliament*, [*My Italics*] that is indeed, the simplified theory of representative government. In reality, the process is *corrupt* [*My Italics*] and somewhat more complicated Interestingly, **Marxism, Communism** and its derivative, **Socialism**, when seen years later in practice, are nothing but **state-capitalism** and rule by a privileged minority, exercising despotic and total control over a majority which is left with virtually no property or legal rights.

This explains why whoever or whatever is behind the **Rothschild's** front, is so interested in our **game-play** (*Chess*) by funding these **ideologies,** would subsequently develop into **"democracy"** a system of the party state controlled by the same force, and whilst they may squabble over insignificant issues, to give the impression of opposing one another or (*agreeing to disagree*) they actually follow the same basic ideology, which is why the inhabitants of democracies soon discover that it doesn't matter who they vote for, nothing changes!!!

Utter Irrelevance
(The Peter Principle)
"This is a daring technique, and often succeeds for that very reason."

In any economic or political crisis, one thing is certain. Many learned experts would prescribe many different remedies, because they have reached their level of **incompetence**: their advice is **nonsensical** or **irrelevant**; some have sound theories, but are unable to put them into effect!

In any event, neither sound nor unsound proposals can be carried out efficiently, because the machinery of government is a vast series of interlocking hierarchies, riddled through and through with **incompetence**.

Even *if by any stretch of the imagination,* a majority of the nominating committee that nominates the candidate were competent judges of men or woman, it will select the candidate, not for their potential wisdom, but on their ability to win elections! In a supposedly free world of cleverly **"Managed news"** By **Hanson W. Baldwin.**
* * *

Pandemonium
(Paradise lost)
"The price good men pay for indifference to public affairs is to be ruled by evil men."

Present day politics, akin to the sorry past, is **and has always been** [*My Italics*] dominated by the **privileged** or the **party-system** with **subordinates** at the **helm.** A political party is usually naively pictured as a group of *democratically* [My Italics] like-minded people co-operating to further the common interests of the good. This is something that has never been valid.

In theory

The basis for what criticism there has been of the concept of freemasonry never mind local athority lodges, is that they undermine the so-call process of an already quesionable and curupt democracy!

For this questionable or so-called democracy to work, if it ever has at its best, there has to be a so-called party-system, (*Run by both of the privilaged*) preferably with at least two strong parties politically at odds. (*which are the left and right hand of the same body!*) The British system of so-called democracy avoids widespread curruption in government by a series of checks and balances. Or more like (*one hand washes the other*) one of the important of these is an official opposition party (*not the fetered abuse of crossparty agreement*) the opposition has a duty to oppose the majority-party that forms the government. Only by effective criticism and constant Watchfulness of an opposition can a government be kept supossidly up to the mark!

The bad pionts of the ruling-party are by this means constantly shown to the public, and its strenghs do not outweight its weaknesses, the government will eventually, in theory, fall!

This efficient system of keeping inefficiency and curruption to a minimum can scarcely be threated when it comes to central government, where there are so many checks and balances and where both press (*if its not minipulated or coherst by conroling interests*) and the sliding-scale of the class system from the priviliged to the emancipation of the great un-washed and the controlling diffirential of the working-aristoracy or public (*who are basically ignorant simpltons*) should be vigilant in the extreme!

. . .

"Moral lessons are taught by use of the juxtaposition of evil"

The true name of Lucifer, the Kabbalists say, is that of Yahweh reversed; for Satan is not a black god, but a force, created for good, but which may serve for evil!

Hobson's choice

Is a free choice in which only one option is offered. As a person may refuse to take that option, the choice is therefore between taking the option or not; "take it or leave it."

The phrase is said to originate with **Thomas Hobson** (*1544–1631*), a livery stable owner in Cambridge, England. To rotate the use of his horses, he offered customers the choice of either taking the horse in the stall nearest the door or taking none at all.

According to a plaque underneath a painting of Hobson donated to Cambridge Guildhall, Hobson had an extensive stable of some 40 horses. This gave the appearance to his customers of having their choice of mounts when in fact there was only one: Hobson required his customers to choose the horse in the stall closest to the door. This was to prevent the best horses always being chosen, which would have caused those horses to become overused.

Malapropism

On occasion, speakers and writers use the phrase **"Hobbesian choice"** instead of **"Hobson's choice"**, confusing the philosopher Thomas Hobbes with the relatively obscure Thomas Hobson. (It's possible they may be confusing *"Hobson's choice"* with *"Hobbesian trap"*, which refers to the *trap* into which a state *falls*, when it attacks *another* out of *fear!* Like in the *U.K.* With its psudo religious attack on the *ill* and the *vulnerable* with guilt by association, that the Devil finds work for idle hands, and providence has shown it to be true, by exposeing a secretive and dangerious *common purpose*!

USA

In *Immigration and Naturalization Service v. Chadha* (1983), Justice Byron White dissented and classified the majority's decision to strike down the "one-house veto" as unconstitutional as leaving Congress with a *Hobson's choice*. Congress may choose between "refraining from delegating the necessary authority, leaving itself with a hopeless task of writing laws with the requisite specificity to cover endless special circumstances across the entire policy landscape, or in the alternative, to abdicate its lawmaking function to the executive branch and independent agency".

In **Monell v. City of New York Department of Social Services, 436 U.S. 658** (*1978*) the judgement of the court was that ("There was ample support for Blair's view that the Sherman Amendment, by putting municipalities to the *Hobson's choice* of keeping the peace or paying civil damages, attempted to impose obligations to municipalities by indirection that could not be imposed directly, thereby threatening to 'destroy the government of the states'").

"Chance favours the prepared mind"
(Oh supreme justice of providence, be it only just that these dogs be massacred)

And God must be punishing them for being idle and lazy, for the means will justify the ends. When one has to abandon their principles (if they had any to begin with) in favour of expedience by a quiescence hand using a sledge-hammer to crack a nut, (*no pun intended*) but how do we know who is strong and who is weak? Easy! Its like the:

Albigensian crusade of 1209 at Béziers.

Lead by a Cistercian monk (monster) the abbot of Citeaux Arnaud Arnaury, who's words when asked by one of his men, how do we tell the heretic Cathar from the pious Catholic? "kill them all—the lord knows his own." Remember these were the days before the reformation, which went on to produce two gangs to cut up the turf, and by using the right and left arm of the same body, to lay the foundation of dogmatic intolerant Christianity in the guise of the monster in Rome and the mask or persona of the reformation.

"A vote is like a rifle: its usefulness depends upon the character of the user."
Theodore Roosevelt

"To announce that there must be no criticism of the President, or that we are to stand by the President, right or wrong, is not only unpatriotic and servile, but is morally treasonable to the American public."
   Theodore Roosevelt

. . .

The Merchant of Venice
Act IV, Scene I

The quality of mercy is not strained;
It droppeth as the gentle rain from heaven
Upon the place beneath. It is twice blest;
It blesseth him that gives and him that takes:
'Tis mightiest in the mightiest; it becomes
The throned monarch better than his crown:
His sceptre shows the force of temporal power,
The attribute to awe and majesty,
Wherein doth sit the dread and fear of kings;
But mercy is above this sceptred sway;
It is enthronèd in the hearts of kings,
It is an attribute to God himself;
And earthly power doth then show likest God's
*When mercy seasons justice. Therefore, **Jew**,*
Though justice be thy plea, consider this,
That, in the course of justice, none of us
Should see salvation: we do pray for mercy;
And that same prayer doth teach us all to render
The deeds of mercy. I have spoke thus much
To mitigate the justice of thy plea;
Which if thou follow, this strict court of Venice
Must needs give sentence 'gainst the merchant there.
   William Shakespeare, 1564 – 1616

* * *

*E*rgo

Instead of mercy shown by a quiescent British monarch, with her Royal hanger-on's or scroungers who get paid out of the **public purse**, for being as ineffective as their figurehead: **"*worse than useless*"** this puppet was crowned and has stood back and done absolutely nothing, about the **common purpose** of the blatant abuse of human rights! By a government using the law as a blunt instrument to **cure** the **ill** and the **vulnerable's** fever?

   **"*The lingering illness is over at last*
**   *And the fever called living is conquered*"**
   Edgar Allen Poe

Throughout the play, Hamlet struggled to avoid his royal fate. He asked the Player-King to recite a speech about stripping the spokes off Fortune's wheel (fate):

. . .

"Out, out, thou strumpet, Fortune! All you gods,
In general synod 'take away her power;
Break all the spokes and fellies from her wheel,
And bowl the round nave down the hill of heaven,
As low as to the fiends!"

. . .

Unless our political masters or there overseers, or those and such as those, already know who and what they are! And the most powerfully controlling factors in world-control of the masses are based on **Money or Mammon**! *(Ecclecasisim) or organised Religion, which was nothing more than a stalking-horse, that preached nothing but sedition and unrest as a counter to its malicious and evil practice's, a war has never been fought in the name of* **Satan**! *But only under the* **evil practise** *of their true God! And it would never have been fought under the true word of* **Christ** *or his father, who told us that killing is* **wrong**! *And the removal of* **organised-religion** *will be no more than a bulwark to establish discontent and expose atheists for what they are, so something else can be put in its place!* Through the **perverse** use of **political ideology** and the resulting **Chaos** it brings, by falsely attempting to interrupt the distribution of the **"Opium"** of the people! By having first **hi-jacked** and then twisting the word of **God**, and then indirectly attempt to turn his son into a **leper-messiah** in this **backlash**! And then have the **ignorant fools** kneel and **die** before a false **God** in the form **'mammon'** or **power** and **wealth**!

And not one of the stupid **goyims** or (*Gentles*) who are supposed to be in control, never lifted a finger to resist or I would have to be not be saying this. All we are asked is to **live** and **let-live**, and **share** and **share-alike**, not to **kill** each other for **it**!

The value of empirical truth
(Object Lessons)

You know that under the present condition of things that the sun will raise to-morrow. That is an empirical truth, demonstrated to be true by experience. The physical life is not the whole of life, nor the most of it nor the best of it; but for the most and best of life is at least necessary. So far as this physical or bodily life is concerned, in point of fact, we live by empirical truth like the people who have lived and died and worked and suffered and achieved and sung with the aid of empirical truth alone.

Looking for the truth is a bit like trying to put a square-peg in a round hole! Remember, you can't serve two masters, even in an artificially created world!

America

1960s

(Tigers in appearance with the souls of sheep!)

Unlike some of the amoral **Goyims** or (*Gentles*) who organized and ran the **"Vietnam war"** the priviliged used the **Reserve** or the **national-guard** to avoid going to fight in the war or fullfill their manditory military duty! While using the last refuse of a scoundral, they dutilly hide behind the **false-flag**. Odious individuals, who seem or appear to be all for **war** and **survival** of the **fittest!** Using their **3lb jack-boot**, (*average weight of the human brain*) but always gets others to fight it for them!

. . .

"Those who dig graves for others, often end up in those graves themselves"

The house of Rothschild's
First among equals

We do it! By giving control over to the **Golden-block**, A bestial-act of survival of the fittest and the most able among the heard, and the weak and the vulnerable must go to the wall, by following **natural selection**, while wearing the mask or persona of religion and morality!

. . .

Régime

A synonym for any form of government, modern usage often gives the term a negative connotation, implying an **authoritarian government** or **dictatorship**, definition: you can have any colour in a **western democracy!** As long as its **black!**

Where the true voice of freedom seems or appears to be gaged and/or controlled by **galloping buracracy** or something more sinister than those who interpret by default the voice of **the heard**, and not **personal inititive or personal responsibility,** which is the most valuable of assets, and has to be looked after and protected from enemies foreign or domestic!

"What Comes Around Go's Around"
FATAL PURITY
(ROBESPIERRE AND THE FRENCH REVOLUTION)

Like **Robespierre** and the **French Revolution**, the blood red mist by which his last years were enveloped magnified his form, but obscured his features.

"History will say little about this monster; it will confine itself to these words:' At this time, the interanal debasement of France was such that a bloodthursty charlatan, without talent and without courage, called Robespierre, made all the citizens tremble under his tyranny. Whilst twelve hundred thousand warriors were shedding their blood on the frontiers for the republic, he brought her to her knees by his proscritions"
RUTH SCURR

. . .

Proscription
(Latin: *proscriptio*)

The public identification and official condemnation of enemies of the state. The term originates from Ancient Rome, but has been used to describe similar phenomena in other times and places.

Proscription implies the elimination en masse of political rivals or personal enemies. Proscription was involved, e.g., during the **Reign of Terror** of the French Revolution and in the political violence in Argentina against Peronists after Perón fled into exile.

Like in the cult 60s TV Show
'The invaders'
(*enemies unseen*)

That's why people who are unaware of this abiding principle are shocked and bemused at the west, and cynically ask the retorical question, how do you do it? We have to tear-out peoples nails in order to get them to do things, you have what others see as a prison without bars!

. . .

"It is the bottomless rascality of the **goyim** (*Gentile*) peoples, who crawl on their bellies to force, but are merciless towards weakness, unsparing to faults and indignant to crimes, unwilling to bear the contradictions of a free social system but patient unto martyrdom under the violence of a bold despotism-it is these qualities which are aiding us to independence.

From the premier-dictators of the present day, the **goyim** (*Gentile*) peoples suffer patiently and bear such abuses as for the least of them would have beheaded twenty kings."

'The price of liberty is eternal vigilance'
Thomas Jefferson

110

War...
(What is it good for?)
Absulutely nothing!

*Set 40 years in the future, Call of Duty: Advanced Warfare places you in the role of Jack Mitchell, a marine who loses an arm while on duty and thus discharged from military service. Jack's squad-mate Will Irons was killed in the line of duty, his father Jonathan Irons (Kevin Spacey) who has a soft spot for Jack, decides to give Will a new prosthetic arm and the opportunity to work with **Atlas Corporation**. Atlas Corporation is a huge corporation who act as private military for hire. The scene is set for you as you take control of Jack with his new bionic arm and exoskeleton Armour, that turns you into a new breed of super soldier. Your role with Atlas has you involved in armed combat throughout the world in the murky surrounding of **political** and **military conflicts**.*
Game, set and match!

. . .
WARNING A NATION

As early as **1959**, Eisenhower began working with his brother Milton and his speechwriters to develop his final statement as he left public life. It went through at least 21 drafts. The speech was **"a solemn moment in a decidedly unsolemn time"**, warning a nation **"giddy with prosperity, infatuated with youth and glamour, and aiming increasingly for the easy life."**

We . . . must avoid the impulse to live only for today, plundering for our own ease and convenience the precious resources of tomorrow. We cannot mortgage the material assets of our grandchildren without risking the loss also of their **political** and **spiritual** heritage. We want democracy to survive for all generations to come, not to become the insolvent phantom of tomorrow!

A draft of the farewell address, showing handwritten edits.

The only general to be elected president in the 20th century, he famously warned the nation about the potentially corrupting influence of the "military-industrial complex". This is frequently mischaracterised as a criticism of the arms industry, which it was not. He in fact declared such an industry to be necessary. His concern was of its potential for corruption:

Until the latest of our world conflicts, the United States had no armaments industry. American makers of plowshares could, with time and as required, make swords as well. But we can no longer risk emergency improvisation of national defense. We have been compelled to create a permanent armaments industry of vast proportions. Added to this, three and a half million men and women are directly engaged in the defense establishment.

We annually spend on military security alone more than the net income of all United States corporations.

Now this conjunction of an immense military establishment and a large arms industry is new in the American experience. The total influence -- **economic**, **political**, even **spiritual** -- is felt in every city, every Statehouse, every office of the Federal government. We recognize the imperative need for this development. Yet, we must not fail to comprehend its grave implications. Our toil, resources, and livelihood are all involved. So is the very structure of our society.

In the councils of government, we must guard against the acquisition of unwarranted influence, whether sought or unsought, by the military-industrial complex. The potential for the disastrous rise of misplaced power exists and will persist. We must never let the weight of this combination endanger our **liberties** or **democratic processes**. We should take nothing for granted. Only an alert and **knowledgeable citizenry** can compel the proper meshing of the huge industrial and military machinery of defense with our **peaceful methods** and **goals**, so that **security** and **liberty** may prosper together.

. . .

The prospect of domination of the nation's scholars by Federal employment, project allocation, and the power of money is ever present and is gravely to be regarded.... Yet in holding scientific discovery in respect, as we should, we must also be alert to the equal and opposite danger that public policy could itself become the captive of a **scientific-technological elite**.

THE TERROR
(CIVIL WAR IN THE FRENCH REVOLUTION)

"*For the French revolutionaries, up to the present day, the call for vigilance against enemies, both external and internal, was the first step on the road and true decent to the terror, is the summons to vigilance against ourselves – that we should not assume that we are righteous, and our enemies evil; that we can abrogate the fragile rights of others in the name of our own certainty and all will be well regardless.*

If we do not not honour the message of human rights born in the revolution of 1776 and 1789, as the French in their case most clearly failed to do, we too are on the road to terror"
David Andress

. . .

One only needs to read a short but graphic description of how the goyim (*Gentile*) described their fellow human beings or what was euphemistically known as:

"The Children Of The Abyss"
Ghosts in the machine
1880's

" *They* are covered in vermin" a police superintendent explained to one of Charles Booth's social surveyors, referring to the destitute who slept rough in the **1880's** "The police don't like touching *them*", he added. And the author Jack London found the antecedents of today's Meth's or (Mentholated spirits) drinkers asleep in what is euphemistically called **"Itchy park"** when he visited there in **"1902"** and the sight sickened him, "it was a welter of rags and filth, of all manners of loathsome skin diseases, open sores, bruises, grossness, indecency, leering monstrosities and bestial faces" he wrote of the dozen or so woman who huddled on the benches, London's Guide told him, " **"They"** will sell themselves for thru' pence or tu'pence or a stale loaf of bread"

. . .

"Jesus Christ said in His Sermon on the Mount: "Judge not, that you be not judged. For with what judgment you judge, you will be judged; and with the measure you use."

. . .

"Look before you leap
For as ye sow
So shall ye reap?"
Samuel Butler

. . .

"He who fights with monsters
should look to it that he himself does not become a monster.
And when you gaze long into an abyss
the abyss also gazes into you."
Friedrich Nietzsche

. . .

It was and still is like the 1960s cult TV Show **"The prisoner"** who was always trying to differentiate the fine line between, who were the **"Warders"** and who were the **"Prisoners?"** who are the ones that are to live! And who are the ones who are die?

. . .

'Du mußt Amboß oder Hammer sein'

'You must be hammer or anvil'
"Johann Wolfgang von Goethe (1749 - 1832) German dramatist, novelist, poet, & scientist"
As George Orwell wrote in
"Politics and the English Language"
"In real life it is always the anvil that breaks the hammer, never the other way about." Let there be no doubt, every person is either the hammer or anvil.

No one gets to avoid it and action through inaction is no choice. "For all your days prepare, and meet them ever alike: When you are the anvil, bear-When you are the hammer, strike."

Misunderstandings and neglect create more confusion in this world than trickery and malice. At any rate, the last two are certainly much less frequent.

When young, one is confident to be able to build palaces for mankind, but when the time comes one has one's hands full just to be able to remove their trash.

It doesn't surprise me that Christ our Lord preferred to live with whores and sinners, seeing as how I go in for that myself. None are more hopelessly enslaved than those who falsely believe they are free..."

The Finger Having Written Moves On

(An abhorrent world)

When any society condones the open abuse or systematic and legalized torture of their fellow beings, while impeaching others which can only be described as a systemized and illegal form of medieval torture on the wrack, by condemning them to a living hell or what was euphemistically described as the **"abyss"**

The Devil knows his own!

1888

In despair, Reverend Samuel A. Barnett, the warden of Toynbee Hall, sought to get the discussion back on the rails again with a radical proposal that the wealthy philanthropists should come forward and buy up some of the worst slum dwellings in **Whitechapel.**

"Never look a gift horse in the mouth"

" In most of these dwellings there is lease under lease, and the acting landlord is probably one who encourages vice to pay his rent," he pointed out in a letter to (*The times.*) "If rich men would come forward and buy up this bad property," he pleaded, "they might not secure great interest, but they would clear away evil . . . Such properties have been bought with results morally most satisfactory and economically not unsatisfactory.

. . .

"But beware of Greeks bearing gifts!"

"What does morally most satisfactory and economically not unsatisfactory mean? It has no quantifier, Hyponyms (to "quantify" is one way to...): determine; fix; limit; set or specify." [My Italics]

Some of that which remains might now be bought, some of the worst is at present in the market, and I should be glad indeed to hear of purchasers."

The clergyman, ***"seems or appears to have"*** [My Italics] underrated the profits to be derived from such property. "I see more than 4% (percent) in it," cried a reader who signed himself **"Practical Philanthropist"**, adding, "But it is well to be moderate, and one need not excite too high expectation at first." It was amazing how swiftly the debate *that* had started on a lofty moral note now degenerated into bickering about interest payments!

Meanwhile, the **"Philanthropists"** continued to bicker over the dividends they could expect in return for taking over slum property in **Whitechapel.**

"Ratepayer", writing to *The Daily Telegraph*, thought that such an investment would be sounder than English railway securities of average standing, and, that "with subsequent good management 4% (per-cent) might safely be taken as the minimum yield".

Lest the charitable nature of the enterprise be lost sight of, **"Gamma"**, writing to (*The Times)*, was sure that the public-spirited investors would be willing "to give their services as directors gratuitously until a 5% (per-cent). Dividend could be paid".

"Cults of unreason"
(*Faith, Hope and Charity!*)
"Thus a consummate trinity of evil was conceived in the mind of a monster"

. . .

When there is no room at the top! Where do the **privileged** go cap-in-hand? To start and run **charity-organisations** to prepare the way for a new class struggle, where we have to organize and force moral imbeciles who sit around all day, because they have no knowledge of work because they are devoid of all decency! Any fool knows that the Devil finds work for the idle hands of the great unwashed, so they need to be taught that survival needs to be earned at any cost! And because the fountainhead demands it of a common purpose, and because we are not **Nazi's** we will get them to **volunteer** to work in **charity shops** whether they like it or not!

. . .

Salvation Army
In Act I:
"My sort of blood cleanses: My sort of fire purifies."
When does a virtue became a vice?
'It is an act of virtue to deceive and lie, when by such means the interests of church and government might be promoted'.

. . .

William Booth
"Thus a consummate evil was conceived in the mind of a monster! Who embarked upon his ministerial career in 1852, desiring to win the lost multitudes of England to Christ. He walked the streets of London to

preach the gospel of Jesus Christ to the poor, the homeless, the hungry, and the destitute".

When there is no room at the top! Where do the privileged go cap-in-hand? To start the **"common purpose of charity organisations"** to prepare the way for their progeny to run and work in charity shops:

. . .

(Leprosarium)

When it wears the **"mask"** or *(persona)* of the so-called soldiers of Christ! Who cleverly promise many things, but the devil's disciples of that leper messiah cleverly deliver little!

Having given birth to a new disease the *lazaretto* or quarantine sites, i.e: the property they own, or leper colonies for this new form of **"Hansen's disease"**.

The rich need god, more than the poor!

Which reminds me of someone's observation during a party gathering, with lots of people claiming money doesn't bring happiness, and just one person claiming that it does!

Was it a nest of **socialists**, **enlightened spiritualists**, a whole cabal of them and just one man of ignorance? I think not, most people are **"hypocrites"**, who practice amity on a Sunday and enmity the rest of the week, So to speak:

"The rich man in his castle,
The poor man at his gate,
God made them, high and lowly,
And order'd their estate"

. . .

'Major Barbara'

An Officer of **"The Salvation Army"**, Major Barbara Undershaft, becomes disillusioned when her Christian denomination accepts money from an armaments manufacturer (her father) and a whisky distiller.

She eventually decides that bringing a message of salvation to people who have plenty will be more fulfilling and genuine than converting the starving in return for bread.

Although Barbara initially regards the Salvation Army's acceptance of Undershaft's money as hypocrisy, Shaw did not intend that it should be thought so by the audience. Shaw wrote a preface for the play's publication, in which he derided the idea that charities should only take money from **"morally pure"** sources.

He points out that donations can always be used for good, whatever their provenance, and he quotes a Salvation Army officer, **"they would take** *money from the devil himself and be only too glad to get it out of his hands and into God's!".*

"You can't serve two masters"

[You can catch a thief but you can't catch a lier]

According to tradition, the heir to the Undershaft fortune must be an orphan who can be **groomed** to run the factory. Lady Britomart tries to convince Undershaft to bequeath the business to his son Stephen, but he will not. He says that the best way to keep the factory in the family is to find a foundling and marry him to Barbara.

Later, Barbara and the rest of her family accompany her father to his munitions factory. They are all impressed by its size and organisation. Cusins declares that he is a foundling, and is thus eligible to inherit the business. Undershaft eventually overcomes Cusins' moral scruples about the nature of the business. Cusins' acceptance makes Barbara more content to marry him, not less, because bringing a message of salvation to the factory workers, rather than to London slum-dwellers, will bring her more fulfilment.

Known as one of Shaw's **"discussion plays,"** *Major Barbara* is primarily structured through a series of conversations on **"morality," "religion,"** and **"social engineering."** The primary topic of discussion is what Shaw identifies in the preface as the **"Gospel of Saint Andrew Undershaft,"** that is, the gospel that would promise society's redemption.

. . .

Undershaft's gospel is organized around the apotheosis of the millionaire and, more specifically, the military industrialist. As the characters will come to realize, the world is not in God's power but in the power of the military industrialist!

With money and gunpowder, Undershaft participates in the power that reigns over Europe, the power that determines the course of society. This re-organization of society, rather than one's faith in a religious doctrine, provides the means of salvation.

For Undershaft, man does not need redemption from sinfulness but from the material abjection of poverty, hunger, and sickness. The growth of Christian virtues rests fundamentally on man's material security. Undershaft wants nothing to do with a religion that abjures warfare and wealth. These evils are the necessary means by which man can be saved.

"Though initially resistant, the democratic Cusins will soon convert to Undershaft's gospel and become his successor. Barbara will return to the Salvation Army with this gospel as well, recognizing that the necessary dialectic between good and evil means that the work of salvation requires the pact with the Devil..."

The Greatest Evil In The World

But as the reader knows, we have entered the era of scientific history, and it is not fair to it to quote Gibbon as if nothing had been done since his time. Against his opinion, which we may call the common literary opinion—only to often expressed by the author of **"Sartor Resartus"** —let us place the opinion of that great writer, historian, sociologist, and pioneer, Henry Thomas Buckle. We quote from the fourth chapter of his masterpiece, already referred to, and the reader will see where he places war amongst human ills. After speaking of the **Spanish Inquisition**, and defending the moral character of the **inquisitors**, whom he regards not as knaves, but **fools**—not hypocrites, but enthusiasts, he says: It is to the diffusion of knowledge, and to that alone, *(but not at any price!)* that we owe the comparative cessation of what is unquestionably the greatest evil men have inflicted on their own species. For that religious persecution is a greater evil than any other is apparent, not so much from the enormous and almost incredible number of its known victims, as from the fact that the unknown must be far more numerous, and that history gives no account of those who have been spared in the body in order that they might suffer in the mind Who, thus forced into an:

* * *

Apostasy the heart abhors, have passed the remainder of their life in the practice of a constant and humiliating hypocrisy. It is this, which is the real curse of religious persecution. For in this way, men being constrained to mask their thoughts, there arises a habit of securing safety by falsehood, and of purchasing impunity with deceit.

In this way, fraud becomes a necessary of life; insincerity is made a daily custom; the whole tone of public feeling is vitiated, and the gross amount of vice and of error fearfully increased. Surely, then, we have reason to say that, compared to this, all other crimes are of small account, and we may well be grateful for that increase of intellectual pursuits which has destroyed an evil that some among us would even now willingly restore.

Then let them reflect, as Buckle might have reflected, on the combination of these two **evils**', which transcends them both—the wars of religion. These have bathed Europe in blood for nearly two thousand years: thy have **"made a goblin of the sun."** have immeasurably delayed progress, have again and again submerged the **good** and the **true**, and they have been waged in the name of Him who **"went about doing only good,"** and said **"They that take the sword shall perish by the sword,"** and **"Blessed are the peacemakers for they shall be called the children of God,"**

The Spiritual Type of Society
The dying empire of ecclesiasticism
(**Organized religion**)

There is no historian of human knowledge but lends his testimony, willingly or unwillingly, to this most shocking truth. **Ecclesiasticism** or **Organized religions** or the **"Obscenities"** are:

The Greatest Murderer in History

And not surprisingly this mockery of Ecclesiasticism (organized religion) has uncovered conspiracy/corruption and lies from *'Pope Leo XIII' of the Catholic-church who had* the **temerity** (*pardo et mois*) and the **effrontery**, being shameless with **insolent impudence** (*pardo et mois*) to indirectly impeach: *The House of Rothschild in 1898.*

With its tenuous links or **wheels-with-wheels** of organised crime (ops) religion, with the gruesome discovery of the hanged body of what could have been a **crypto-Jew** or **shabbez goy** (*a non-Jew who chose to clandestinely represent the interests of Jews*) **"Roberto Calvi"** remember him? Who seemed or appeared to be a weak-link that out-lived his usefulness! From behind the scenes, reaching up to the highest echelons of that shameless society or cult and its brazen collection of **'Peters pence!'**:

"Latrunculi" or **gangsters** at enmity with one another and yet fixed in some infernal bond or brotherhood of blind and murderous hatred of things!

. . .

The actual record of the **so-called religion**, which establishes itself as a human institution, is one of the few unmitigated horrors of the past.

Ecclesiasticism (*organized religion*) has initiated and carried on countless unnecessary wars; it has made numberless martyrs; it is the greatest murderer in history; its murders have taken many forms, whether those of human sacrifices to a **fetish** in the **heart-of-Africa** or the **burning-of-witches** in our country only a **century** or **two ago**, or the burning of such **great philosophers** as **Giordano-Bruno**, or the **poisoning-of-Socrates**, or the throwing of **Christians-to-the-lions** by **Roman-Ecclesiasticism** or the **murder of tens of thousands of Christians by Christian-Ecclesiasticism**, **Catholics** by **Protestants**, **Protestants** by **Catholics**, **Christian-missionaries by African-head-hunters**, or **brave** and **faithful-savages** by a **militant-Christianity**.

Religious-political-persecution has been initiated by all forms of **Ecclesiasticism** in all ages in **precise proportion** to their **power**.

Churches have at times displayed an interest in the advance of knowledge within **due-limits**.

Sincere and **honest-thinkers** have *freed-their-souls*, even while their **bodies** still wore the garments of one **Ecclesiasticism** or **another**. Their reward was the reward of **Bruno**. **Ecclesiasticism**, however, has never desired to share its knowledge with the people. In its own interest it has always desired to teach the people certain things namely, such things as make for its own **interests**.

To the growth of knowledge outside its own limits, and independence of its sanction, **Ecclesiasticism**, whether as **Fetishism** or when taking to itself the noblest Name named of men (**Jesus Christ**) has necessarily been, and must continue to be until the hour of its death, an **implacable foe**.

119

Like the **cults** of **Internationalism/Globalism**, **Scientology**, **Monism, Roman- Catholicism, Church-of-England** and **Scotland, Mormonism, Shintoism, Taoism, Hinduism, Judaism, Islam** and **others,** however, is **dying**, and that rapidly. All over the world its **empire** can be seen to crack from day to day.

If its almost measureless past be gazed upon, and its past potency, we recognise that it is as **good-as-dead**. The immediate problem, which faces **humankind**, and especially those who **love** and **practice** the **great religious truths**, is as to how this **noisome-corpse** is most **decently** and **expeditiously** to be **buried**! By non-other than the **House-Of-Rothschild**, therefore these words of John Ruskin may be our guide:

. . .

"For there is a true Church wherever one hand meets another Helpfully, and that is the only holy or mother Church which was, or ever shall be!"

. . .

Pope Leo XIII

1898

(The classic Christian hypocrisy using sleight of mouth States the following on usury (the charging of interest on money)

After the closing of the Council of Nicaea in 325 CE, Bishop Eusebius Pamphilius (260-339), probably the most corrupt bishop of the Fourth Century, said:

'It is an act of **virtue** to **deceive** and **lie**, when by such means the interests of the **church** might be **promoted**'.

Which sounds like the same hand that gave us **Marxism** and **Alinsky's** rules for radicals.

Act of Supremacy. More, relying on legal precedent and the maxim *"qui tacet consentire videtur"* (**literally, who (is) silent is seen to consent**)

. . .

"As soon as money in the coffer rings, the soul from purgatory's fire springs."

Mirror Mirror

(Shifting Politics)

"On the one hand there is the party which holds the wealth, which has in its grasp all labour and all trade, which manipulates for its own benefit and its own purposes all the sources of supply, and which is powerfully represented in the councils of state itself. On the other side there is the needy and powerless multitude, sore and suffering!

Rapacious usury, which, although more than once condemned by the Church, is nevertheless under a different form but with the same guilt, still practiced by avaricious and grasping men... so that a small number of very rich men have been able to lay upon the masses of the poor a yoke little better than slavery itself"

. . .

Does thin man actually believe what he is saying? That by impeaching these mythological **dybbuk's** (*dubik's*) (**Yiddish**: from **Hebrew** *adhere* or *cling*) is a malicious possessing of an unclean spirit believed to be the dislocated soul of a dead person. It supposedly leaves the host body once it has accomplished its goal, or the (**Rothschild's)** he was condemning the **Roman Catholic Church** out of his own mouth!

. . .

. . .

"One can tell a tree, by the fruit it bares!"

Jesuits

The Society of Jesus is a Christian male religious congregation of the Catholic Church. The members are called **Jesuits**. The society is engaged in **evangelization** and **apostolic ministry.**

The **Inquisition** was famous for its use of **torture** to **elicit confessions** from accused '**heretics**'. It was believed that confessions extracted after **torture** must be **true**, an idea that was later dispelled, *you mean like in the* **politically orchestrated wars.**

* * *

"Northern Ireland, Iraq or Afghanistana, Syria and of course North Korea, Iran and even the Artic!"

Borgias

The family became prominent during the Renaissance in Italy. They were from Valencia, the name coming from the family **fief of Borja**, then in the kingdom of **Aragon**, in Spain.

The **Borgias** became prominent in **ecclesiastical** and **political affairs** in the **15th** and **16th centuries**, producing two popes, **Alfons de Borja** who ruled as **Pope Callixtus III** during *1455–1458* and **Rodrigo Lanzol Borgia**, as Pope *Alexander VI*, during *1492–1503*.

Especially during the reign of *Alexander VI*, they were suspected of many **crimes**, including **adultery**, **simony**, **theft**, **bribery** and **murder** (*especially murder by arsenic poisoning*). Because of their grasping for power, they made enemies of the **Medici**, the **Sforza**, and the **Dominican friar Savonarola**, among others. They were also patrons of the arts!

Inquisition

In *1483*, **Jews** were expelled from all of **Andalusia**. Though the pope wanted to crack down on abuses, Ferdinand pressured him to promulgate a new bull, threatening that he would otherwise separate the **Inquisition** from **Church authority**. **Sixtus** did so on **October 17, 1483**, naming the infamous **Tomás de Torquemada** (*Inquisid*) or **General of Aragón**, **Valencia** and **Catalonia**.

Torquemada quickly established procedures for the **Inquisition**. A new court would be announced with a thirty-day grace period for confessions and the gathering of accusations by neighbors! Evidence that was used to identify a **crypto-Jew** included the absence of **chimney smoke** on **Saturdays** (*a sign the family might secretly be honoring the Sabbath*) or the buying of many vegetables before **Passover** or the **purchase of meat** from a **converted butcher**. The court employed **physical torture** to extract confessions. **Crypto-Jews** were allowed to confess and do penance, although those who relapsed were burned at the stake!

"The hand is always quicker than the eye"

In *1484* **Pope Innocent VIII** attempted to allow appeals to Rome against the **Inquisition**, but **Ferdinand** in **December 1484** and again in *1509* decreed **death** and **confiscation** for anyone trying to make use of such procedures without royal permission. With this, the **Inquisition** became the only **institution** that held **authority** across all the realms of the **Spanish monarchy** and, in all of them, a useful mechanism at the service of the crown. However, the cities of **Aragón** continued resisting, and even saw revolt, as in **Teruel** from *1484* to *1485*. However, the murder of **Inquisidor Pedro Arbués** in **Zaragoza** on **September 15, 1485**, caused **public-opinion!** *What opinion? You cannot be serious? This observation is as falicious as it is true*, to turn against the **conversos** and in favour of the **Inquisition**. In **Aragón**, the **Inquisitorial courts** were focused specifically on members of the powerful **converso** minority, ending their influence in the **Aragonese** administration!

. . .

The **Inquisition** was extremely active between *1480* and *1530*. Different sources give different estimates of the number of trials and executions in this period; **Henry Kamen** estimates about *2,000* executed, based on the documentation of the **autos-da-fé**, the great majority being *conversos* of *Jewish origin*. He offers striking statistics: *91.6%* of those judged in *Valencia* between *1484* and *1530* and *99.3%* of those judged in *Barcelona* between *1484* and *1505* were of *Jewish origin*, I wonder why? "In *1498* the pope was still trying to...gain acceptance for his own attitude towards the New Christians, which was generally more moderate than that of the *Inquisition* and the local rulers!"

Indulgences
(Obsenities)

In the teaching of the *Catholic Church*, an *indulgence* is "a remission before God of the temporal punishment due to sins whose guilt has already been forgiven, which the faithful Christian who is duly disposed gains under certain prescribed conditions through the action of the Church which, as the minister of *redemption*, dispenses and applies with *authority* the *treasury* of the *satisfactions* of *Christ* and the so-called *saints*!".

. . .

Indulgences allow for the remission of the *severe penances* of the early Church which was granted at the intercession of Christians awaiting martyrdom or at least imprisoned for the faith. They draw on the Treasury of Merit accumulated by:

"*Christ's superabundantly meritorious sacrifice on the cross*!"
And the *virtues* and *penances* of the saints. They are granted for specific good *works* and prayers in proportion to the devotion with which those *good works* are performed or prayers recited.

. . .

Indulgences became increasingly popular in the Middle Ages as a reward for displaying piety and doing good deeds, though, doctrinally speaking, the Church stated that the indulgence was only valid for temporal punishment for sins already forgiven in the Sacrament of Confession. The faithful asked that indulgences be given for saying their favourite prayers, doing acts of devotion, attending places of worship, and going on pilgrimage; confraternities wanted indulgences for putting on performances and processions; associations demanded that their meetings be rewarded with indulgences. Good deeds included *charitable donations of money for a good cause*! And money thus raised was used for many *righteous causes*, both *religious* and *civil*; *building projects funded by indulgences include churches*, *hospitals*, (*Which is now a bi-partizan pseudo (False) political movement, like schools, roads and bridges and tax-exempt charities*!) leper-colonies.

. . .

However, the later Middle Ages saw the growth of considerable abuses. Greedy commissaries sought to extract the maximum amount of money for each indulgence. Professional "*pardoners*" (*quaestores in Latin*) - who were sent to collect alms for a specific project - practiced the unrestricted sale of indulgences. Many of these *quaestores* exceeded official Church doctrine, whether in avarice or ignorant zeal, and promised rewards like salvation from eternal damnation in return for money!

With the permission of the Church, indulgences also became a way for Catholic rulers to fund expensive projects, such as **Crusades** does that sound fimiliar! *That's whay they have men of the so-called soiled-cloth to bless you, when you are dying in the battlfield*!

And **cathedrals**, by keeping a significant portion of the money raised from indulgences in their lands. There was a tendency to forge documents declaring that indulgences had been granted. Indulgences grew to extraordinary magnitude, in terms of longevity and breadth of forgiveness.

. . .

The Fourth Lateran Council
1215

suppressed some abuses connected with indulgences, spelling out, for example, that only a one-year indulgence would be granted for the consecration of churches and no more than a 40-days indulgence for other occasions. The Council also stated that "Catholics who have girded themselves with the cross for the extermination of the heretics, shall enjoy the indulgences and privileges granted to those who go in defense of the **Holy Land.**" Or *to falsely protect us from an enemy that never exsited*!

Very soon these limits were widely exceeded. False documents were circulated with indulgences surpassing all bounds: indulgences of hundreds or even thousands of years. In 1392, more than a century before **Martin Luther** published the **95 Theses**, **Pope Boniface IX** wrote to the Bishop of Ferrara condemning the practice of certain members of religious orders who falsely claimed that they were authorized by the pope to forgive all sorts of sins, and obtained money from the simple-minded faithfuls by promising them perpetual happiness in this world and eternal glory in the next. The **"Butter Tower"** of **Rouen Cathedral** earned its nickname because the money to build it was raised by the sale of indulgences allowing the use of butter during Lent.

An engraving by **Israhel van Meckenem** of the **Mass of Saint Gregory** contained a **"bootlegged"** indulgence of **20,000 years**; one of the copies of this plate was altered in a later state to increase it to **45,000 years**.

The indulgences applied each time a specified collection of prayers - in this case seven each of **the Creed**, **Our Father**, and **Hail Mary** - were recited in front of the image. The image of the **Mass of Saint Gregory** had been especially associated with large indulgences since the jubilee year of **1350** in Rome, when it was at least widely believed that an indulgence of **14,000** years had been granted for praying in the presence of the **Imago Pietatis** (*"Man of Sorrows"*), a popular pilgrimage destination in the **basilica-of-Santa-Croce** in **Gerusalemme** in **Rome**.

The scandalous conduct of the **"pardoners"** was an immediate occasion of the **Protestant Reformation**. In **1517**, **Pope Leo X** offered indulgences for those who gave alms to rebuild St. Peter's Basilica in Rome. The aggressive marketing practices of **Johann Tetzel** in promoting this cause provoked **Martin Luther** to write his **Ninety-Five Theses**, condemning what he saw as the **purchase and sale of salvation**.

In **Thesis 28** Luther objected to a saying attributed to **Tetzel**: **"As soon as a coin in the coffer rings, a soul from purgatory springs!"**.

The **Ninety-Five Theses** not only denounced such transactions as worldly but denied the Pope's right to grant pardons on God's behalf in the first place: the only thing indulgences guaranteed, Luther said, was an increase in **profit** and **greed**, like **Charities** because the pardon of the Church was in God's power alone!

. . .

"The Rothchilds' take over the financial operation of the Catholic Church, worldwide!"

1823

. . .

Bad image

"The Vatican Bank or **IOR**, is not unique. They are not the worst (*bank*), but certainly there are very serious problems that need to be addressed," said E.J. Fagan, advocacy coordinator at **Global Financial Integrity**, an organisation that seeks to curtail illicit money transfers. "Pope Francis has very clearly stated that he wants to **fight poverty**.

Money laundering of illicit financial flows is a major driver of global poverty and the Vatican should set a clear example," he told Reuters. The Vatican has been trying to shed its image as a suspect financial centre since 1982 when **Roberto Calvi**, an Italian known as **"God's Banker"** because of his links to the Holy See, was found hanged under London's Blackfriars Bridge.

Moneyval, a monitoring committee of the 47-nation Council of Europe, said last July that the Vatican had failed to meet all its standards on fighting illicit cash flows, tax evasion and other financial crimes. A report by Moneyval gave the Vatican an overall pass grade but failing grades on 7 of 16 "key and core" aspects of its financial dealings. It found major failings in the running of the bank, while acknowledging that the **IOR** was making changes to meet transparency requirements. Five months before the Moneyval report, **JP Morgan Chase** closed the **IOR's** account with the **Milan branch** of the **U.S. banking giant** because of concerns about insufficient transparency!

The Devil will not be mocked

(The Borg will not be mocked)

Did you blink? And just hear who is involved in keeping the books right? that's like getting the **fox** to guard the **chickens**:

Sir Walter Scott
*Oh! what a **tangled web** we weave*
*When first we **practise** to **deceive**!*

Borg

(To assimilate)

Adjust, fit, adapt, accommodate, accustom, conform, mingle, blend in, become like, homogenize, acclimatize, intermix, become similar, acculturate imbibe (literary), to assimilate into of all things a species culture, **think about it!**

. . .

J.P. Morgan had been appointed head representative of the ***Rothschild*** interests in the ***United States***. As the result of the ***London Conference***, ***J.P. Morgan and Company of New York, Drexel and Company of Philadelphia, Grenfell and Company of London***, and ***Morgan Harjes Cie of Paris, M.M. Warburg Company of Germany and America***, and the ***House of Rothschild*** were all affiliated.

The fact that the ***Morgans*** had always been affiliated with the ***House of Rothschild***, as of ***1899***, when in fact it went back to ***1835***.

. . .

Francis has said he wants the Church to be austere, simple!

Italian media have reported that the bank, which currently answers to a commission of ***cardinals*** and enjoys great ***autonomy***, could be placed under the control of another ***Vatican department***, increasing the oversight called for in the ***Moneyval report***. Famiglia Cristiana, Italy's leading Catholic weekly, called for the ***IOR funds*** to be administered by an independent ***"ethical bank"*** external to the ***Vatican***.

Barnum

(There's a sucker born every minute)

Is a phrase most likely spoken by ***David Hannum***, in criticism of both ***P. T. Barnum***, an American showman of the mid ***1800s***, and his customers. The phrase is often credited to ***Barnum*** himself.

The will to killing

Undershaft's philosophy also organizes itself around a notion the great man's ***"will."*** This will comes into being through the agonistic struggle between men. As Undershaft proclaims, a sacred commandment, ***"Thou shalt starve ere I starve,"*** sets him on the path to greatness. Through a murderous struggle with others, Undershaft realizes his will and desire. Thus his ***"bravest enemy"*** is his best friend, a rival who keeps him ***"up to the mark."*** Over and against Christian ideals of human brotherhood, the recognition Undershaft demands from his neighbour is not love but obedience and respect, a bending to his will. Again, the struggle he stages with others is decidedly violent. Those who do not submit to his desire must die.

Such killing in the name of the will does restrict itself to those who stand in the way of the great man's desire, but extant social structures, institutions, and ways of thinking as well. Killing is the means by which the moralist's *"ought"* becomes a *"shall;"* it is the *"only way of saying Must."* Only the murderous command can inaugurate the new that follows necessarily according to the will of the great man. Until he achieves his will, he is menace to civilization; upon its realization, he becomes its benefactor. Thus, the great man makes history.

The ideal community and the crime of poverty

Major Barbara is structured by a contest between father and daughter for the other's soul and the path of salvation. Each agrees to visit the other's workplace and allow the other to attempt their conversion. Undershaft's visit to the Salvation Army shelter takes place in Act II; Barbara goes to the armory with her family in Act III.

As discussed in the preface, Shaw's portrait of the shelter is fundamentally a critique of the *"Salvation Army's flaws."* One of the many criticisms Shaw underlines, for example, is that the Army forces its clientele to pander to the *saintliness of its workers*. In this sense does the work of the Army have less to do with the condition of the poor than the *narcissism* of its officers. More importantly, the Army fails to realize that man does not need redemption from sinfulness but from the material abjection of poverty, hunger, and sickness.

Unlike the shelter, Perivalee Saint Andrews appears as a paradise of *social engineering.* Undershaft has redeemed his men more successfully than preaching ever could by eliminating poverty. He does not do so for the love of the masses. Certainly Undershaft provides for their comfort to assure his company's productivity.

He also, however, considers poverty the worst of man's crimes. For Undershaft, the *"crime of poverty"* is a crime committed against society by the poor themselves.

The poor, appearing as abject masses from some paranoid fantasy, *"kill"* society's happiness, forcing the ruling class to eliminate its liberties and organize *"unnatural cruelties"* to keep them in check.

Thus Undershaft will pit himself against poverty in the name of order and cleanliness. Indeed, for Undershaft, order and cleanliness are categorical imperatives of sorts—they justify themselves.

Though the realization of these imperatives would ostensibly benefit the masses, we can readily imagine how they might come at their expense as well. Simply put, the institution of order and cleanliness easily means the elimination of the disorderly and unclean. Note in this respect Undershaft's *chilling invocation* of the *Salvation Army's motto* in Act I:

> *"My sort of blood cleanses, my sort of fire purifies."*

• • •

The peter principal

The Salvation Army, like the proverbial bad penny showed up or was founded in *1865* in London by one-time Methodist minister **William Booth**. Originally known as the East London Christian Mission, in *1878* Booth reorganized the mission, becoming its first General and introducing the military structure which has been retained to the present day.

The current world leader of The *"Salvation Army"* is **General André Cox**, who was elected by the High Council of The Salvation Army on 3 August 2013.

"The Salvation Army" is a **Christian denominational church** akin to **Scientology**, they offer much, but deliver little! An international so-called charitable organization structured in a quasi-military fashion.

The organization reports worldwide membership of over *1.5 million*, consisting of soldiers, officers and adherents known as **Salvationists**. Its founders **Catherine** and **William Booth** sought to bring salvation to the poor, destitute and hungry *while filling their own pockets*! [*My Italics*] by meeting both their *"physical and spiritual needs"* at a **price**!.

. . .

It has a presence in *126 countries*, running charity shops, operating shelters for the homeless, and providing disaster relief and humanitarian aid to developing countries.

The theology of the *"Salvation Army"* is mainstream Methodist although it is distinctive in government and practice. The Army's doctrine follows mainstream Christian beliefs, and its articles of faith emphasize God's *"saving purposes"*. Its objects are the advancement of the Christian religion... of education, the relief of poverty, and other charitable objects beneficial to society or the community of mankind as a whole, *and other such nonsense* [*My Italics*].

. . .

William Booth (10 April 1829 – 20 August 1912) was a British Methodist preacher who founded the *"Salvation Army"* and became its first General (*1878–1912*). The Christian movement with a quasi-military structure and government founded in *1865* has spread from London, England to many parts of the world, like a cancer, and is known for being one of the largest distributors of so-called humanitarian aid! And like this self-serving organisation or bureaucratic monster, like in the *1980s* comedy *"Yes Minister"* and the episode called: *"The Compassionate Society"*

While observing that the cost of running the Health Service keeps going up, jobs for health administrators keeps going up! The patient numbers apparently keep going down in regards to the *"mythical Hospital"* called: St Edwards!

. . .

"The so-called common purpose of the *"Salvation Army"* was founded in *1865* in London, England, by **William Booth** and the name Salvation Army dates from *1878"*.

. . .

The Lifesaver
(*Substitution*)

"Instead of carrying out the proper duties of his position he substitutes for them some other set of duties, which he carries out to perfection.*"*

Faced with an important task, the competent employee simply begins it. The Substituter may prefer to busy himself with preliminary activities. Here are some well-tried methods.

A) Confirm the need for action. *"The Salvation Army"* done it very cleverly back in *"1878."* The true Substituter can never get enough evidence. *"Better be safe than sorry,"* is his watch word or *"more haste, less speed"*

Spend sufficient time confirming the need, like the **pariah** or leper that he was, *"Booth"* with his social survey of *"1887/8"* and the need will disappear! (*Peter Prognosis*)

For example, in organizing famine relief, study the need long enough, and you will eventually find that there no longer is any need for relief! *Or you are to busy trying to solve the problem, in order to solve the problem, so the problem like charity is never solved* [*My Italics*]

b) STUDY ALTERNATE METHODS of doing whatever is to be done. Suppose that, aftersuitable preliminary investigation, the need is confirmed. The Substituter will want to be sure that he chooses the most effective course of action, no matter how long he may take to find it! The *"alternate method"* technique is in itself a substitute and a less panicky form of the *Teeter-Totter syndrome*.

Teeter-Totter Syndrome

In the **teeter-totter syndrome** one sees a complete inability to make the decisions appropriate to the sufferer's rank. An employee *or* **organisation** [*My Italics*] can balance endlessly and minutely the pros and cons of a question. but cannot come down on one side or the other. They will rationalize there imobility with grave allusions to *"the democratic process"* or *"taking the long view."* They usually deal with the problems that come to them by keeping them in limbo until someone else makes a decision or until it is too late for a solution.

c) OBTAIN EXPERT ADVICE, in order that the plan finally chosen may be effectively carried out. Committees will be formed, and the question referred for study. A variant of this technique, looking to bygone experts instead of live ones, is to search for precedents.

d) FIRST THINGS FIRST. This technique involves minute, painstaking, tine-consuming attention to every phase of preperation for action: the build-up of abundant reserves of spare forms, spare parts, spare ammunition, *"money"*, etc., in order to consolidate the present position before beginning an advance toward the goal.

Perpetual Preperation

Perpetual preperation: An instructive example of Grant Swinger, deputy director of Deeprest Welfare Department, who was regarded as highly competent because of his outstanding ability to **coax governments** and **charitable foundations** into parting with **money** for worthy local causes.

War was declared on poverty. **And you need an army to fight the war!** [*My Italics*] Swinger was premoted to the post of co-ordinating director of the Deepest **Anti-Disadvantaged Program**, on the princple that he so well understood the mighty. He should be highly competent to help the weak.

As these goes to press, Swinger is still busily **raising funds**, to erect an **Olympian building**, *like the new "Salvation Army" International Headquarters in London! Or the the salvation army's old William Booth Memorial Training College, Denmark Hill, London: which is a College for Officer Training of **"The Salvation Army"** in the UK* [*My Italics*] to house staff and to stand as a permanent monument to the spirit of aiding the needy!

Structurophilia

 Has been referred to, as by the uninformed, as the Edifice Complex. We most be precise in differentiating between this simple pre-occupation with structures and the Edifice Complex which involes a number of elaborately interrelated, inter-connected and complicated attitudes. The Edifice Complex tends to afflict philanthropists wishing to improve education, health services or religious instruction! Thay consult experts in these fields and descover so many at their respective levels of incompetence that the formulation of a positive program is impossible. The only thing they agree on is to have a new building!

"First things first"
"We want the poor to see that they have not been forgotten! By their government"

Explains swinger. Next he plans to convene a **Deeprest Anti-Disadvantaged Advisory Council** (obtaining expert advice), **raise money** for a survey of the **problems** of the **disadvantaged** (*confirming the need*) and tour the Western world to inspect similar schemes in preperation and operation elsewhere (*studying alternitive methods*).

It should be pointed out that Swinger is busy, *like the* **"salvation army"** [*My Italics*] from morning till night, **"to busy doing his job or their job, to be able to do their job!"** *it is* **"self-defeating"** [*My Italics*] he is happy in his new post, and sincerely feels that he is doing a good job. He modestly turns away invitations to capitalize on his good image by running for elective office. In short he has achieved a highly successful substatution!

The peter Principle

130

AUTUMN OF TERROR
Rent-Farming
(Slum-landlord)

It's like treating certain people no better than animals, because you see them as an inferior-species, do you remember that history has already cast the first *stone!* Having blamed individuals like **"Adolf Hitler"** and **"Joseph Stalin"** for such barbaric and inhuman behaviour!

At this point the (*Daily Telegraph)* joined the chorus with an editorial *that* reads more like the prospectus for a south Sea Bubble scheme **"a perfect goldmine exists in undeveloped London at our back door,"** the editorial gushed.

"We purposely abstain from dwelling on the philanthropic aspect of the question," it continued, dismissing with contempt what is called **"charity dribbles"; "We want to see a freshet, a flood of capital spring from practical sources and taking the direction of Pactolus."**

. . .

Pactolus

"Is a river near the Aegean coast of Turkey. The river rises from Mount Tmolus, flows through the ruins of the ancient city of Sardis, and empties into the Gediz River, the ancient Hermus. The Pactolus once contained electrum that was the basis of the economy of the ancient state of Lydia. According to legend, King Midas divested himself of the golden touch by washing himself in the river."

. . .

The newspaper then gave as its considered judgement that, with proper management, Whitechapel slums could be made to pay **"better than preference shares in the best railways, or Prussian stocks, or any foreign rentes. A net and safe 4% (Per Cent) is something to be desired . . . More than that—sometimes considerably more— has been and can be secured."**

Indeed, the profits to be made from **"rent-farming"** in the East End were enormous. A landlord, who owned six lodging-houses in Thrawl Street, where Polly Nicholls dosed, did so well off his property that he could afford a country house in Hampstead, according to Henry Mayhew.

Montague Williams, the police magistrate, tells of other landlords who bought up condemned property on short leases from the railway companies, paying as little as **£1** a week for a house, and who turned around and let their single rooms for 35s imperial (*shillings*) up to **£2** a week.

Very little capital outlay was required to set up as a **"rent-farmer"** *thus was born the* **"slum-landlord"** [*My Italics*]. One landlord bought enough beds to furnish four doss-houses from a smallpox hospital, which was being pulled down, all for the sum of **£20**. No one else would touch the furniture for fear of infection.

But, as September drew to a close, the 4% Percenter's began to wrangle among themselves. In particular they turned on the Reverend Barnett and accused him of informing the owners of slum property of their intention to but, and thus encouraging the owners to charge **"fancy prices"**.

Indignantly, the clergyman denied giving any such encouragement. A new note was introduced into the debate by a correspondent who signed himself **"One Who Knows"** in *The Times*. Referring to the doss-houses, he wrote, **"the suppression of these haunts of crime and the dispersion of their lawless population should be the watchword and cry—the Carthago delendo est—of every social reformer."**

"Dispersion of their lawless population"—there is nothing to indicate that the Reverend Barnett had envisaged this in his original proposal. And if the inhabitants of Dorset Street, Flower and Dean, and Thrawl Streets were to be dispersed where would they go? Certainly, there were no more wretched streets in the whole of London that these. And with equal certainty, their inhabitants were entitled to hire shelter, **"because we are certainly not our brother or sisters keeper, are we?"** [*My Italics*] from the bitterness of the English night—the outcry occasioned by the murder of the Whitechapel **outcasts** implied a universal belief that they had the right to life.

Because the differential must not be eroded at any and all costs! It upsets the **status-quo**, because its been worked out in the mind of a monster, that the simile or the **"pie"** in a democracy society! Is only big enough for so many **equal slices**, only some are more equal than others, and of course any fool knows that survival must be earned, at any cost!

If the Anne Chapman's were to be dispersed, they would be robbed of greater sums for accommodation, and be forced to resort to even more desperate measures to make themselves more money.

There was also the question of moral hygiene—were the Annie Chapman's to be allowed to spread their trade to streets hitherto untainted? Where these the results that the Reverend Barnett was working for? If so the **"mawkish twaddle"** epithet with which the Social Democrats stigmatised the slum-clearance programme would seem to apply. The Socialist League was even more to the point. Referring to **"the opening for profit made literally with the murderer's knife"**, Frank Fitz, the league secretary prophesied, **"the gutters of London and their terrible human wreckage shall be made to yield 4% (Per Cent). And 'even more'."**

Holten's Homily

"The only time to be positive is when you are positive you are wrong!"

Like the numbskull's who felt that it was only right and fitting that she should turn to the oldest profession in the world, and the anathema of so-called Christians! Who morally justify it, through strength or the **3lb jackboot**, (*rough approx weight of the human brain*)?

Catherine Eddowes, alias Kate Conway, alias Kate Kelly, was buried on Monday afternoon, 8th October, with something approaching military honours."

Closing the stable-door
When Hobson's choice of black-horse has already bolted!
"Remember we haven't yet discovered a cure fore stupidity!"
By one o'clock not more than a score of people had gathered in front of the city mortuary in Golden Lane, but a quarter of an hour later the number had swelled to several hundred, **where are people when you rely need them?** [*My Italics*] this being the lunch hour for the city clerks and office workers.

Meanwhile, Eddowes' remains had been placed in a coffin of polished elm with oak mouldings and black furniture, which had been donated by an undertaker in near-by Banner Street, and which bore a metal plate with the inscription **"Catherine Eddowes, died September 30th, 1888, Aged 43 Years"**.

The coffin, in turn, was placed in an open glass car drawn by a pair of horses and escorted by a strong force of city police under Superintendent Foster as far as the boundary of the city of London, where the escort was taken over by the Metropolitan police under Inspector **"Barnum and bailey"** remember that many a truth is said in jest, because they had already turned it into a **"circus"** come and bring the kiddies! No doubt the police were there in force, just in case Catherine Eddowes decided to ply her trade (*Sell her body!*) excuse the pun, and even this time they probably couldn't even catch the perpetrator!

The irony was, of course, that these same city police who now paid their respects to the dead woman had had her in their custody scarcely a week before as **"drunk and disorderly"**. Eddowes was followed to her grave by her four sisters, all dressed in black, and by the man she had lived with, John Kelly. (*The press made no mention of her daughter Anne nor Thomas Conway, alias Thomas Quinn, the reluctant army pensioner, and his two sons, though they attended the funeral*).

The cortège passed St Mary's Whitechapel, and moved along Mile End Road, where the pavement AKA (*Also known As*) the (*sidewalk*) was lined five deep with spectators, good Christians one and all, **"who no doubt were some of her best customers and knew her personally!"** [*My Italics*] and so through Bow and Stratford-atte-Bow.

"Many bystanders uncovered their heads as the hearse passed", the East London Observer reported; **"Along the whole route great sympathy was expressed for the relatives."** At Ilford cemetery nearly **500 people** had gathered to witness the interment. The service was conducted by the Rev. T. Dunscombe, the cemetery chaplain, and was brief, no reference being made to the murder.

In startling contrast, **"Elizabeth Stride"** was hustled into a **pauper's grave** as quickly and as secretly as possible

The people who condoned such things are not only conceited and contemptible they don't know how much they sin—, either in the past or in the future!

Like in George Orwell's cult 60s book: **"Animal-farm"** where the pigs were in charge, and something like the **"abyss"** came out the mind of a monster! Devil's who cleverly hide in the dark, wearing the mask or persona of false **morality**, they are **spiritually** and **morally-bankrupt**, and who think they are first among equals, in a virtuous cause, **where its better to rule in hell, than to serve in heaven**!

. . .

CHE GUEVARA

The **"hungry Indian masses, peasants without land, exploited workers, and progressive masses"**. To Guevara the conflict was a struggle of masses and ideas, which would be carried forth by those **"mistreated and scorned by imperialism"** who were previously considered **"a weak and submissive flock"**. With this **"flock"**, Guevara now asserted, **"Yankee monopoly capitalism"** now terrifyingly saw their **"gravediggers"**. It would be during this **"hour of vindication"**, Guevara pronounced, that the **"anonymous mass"** would begin to write its own history **"with its own blood"** and reclaim those **"rights that were laughed at by one and all for 500 years"**. Guevara ended his remarks to the General Assembly by hypothesizing that this **"wave of anger"** would **"sweep the lands of Latin America"** and that the labor masses who **"turn the wheel of history"** were now, for the first time, **"awakening from the long, brutalizing sleep to which they had been subjected"**.

Guevara later learned there had been two failed attempts on his life by Cuban exiles during his stop at the UN complex. The first from Molly Gonzales who tried to break through barricades upon his arrival with a seven-inch hunting knife, and later during his address by Guillermo Novo with a timer-initiated bazooka that was fired off target from a boat in the East River at the United Nations Headquarters. Afterwards Guevara commented on both incidents, stating that **"it is better to be killed by a woman with a knife than by a man with a gun"**, while adding with a languid wave of his cigar that the explosion had **"given the whole thing more flavor"**.

While in New York **Guevara** appeared on the **CBS** Sunday news program **Face the Nation** and met with a range of people, from United States Senator **Eugene McCarthy** to associates of **Malcolm X**. The latter expressed his admiration, declaring: **Guevara** **"one of the most revolutionary men in this country right now"**

. . .

while reading a statement from him to a crowd at the Audubon Ballroom.
On December 17 Guevara left for Paris, France, and from there embarked on a three-month world tour that included visits to the **People's Republic of China**, **North Korea**, the **United Arab Republic**, **Egypt**, **Algeria**, **Ghana**, **Guinea**, **Mali**, **Dahomey**, **Congo-Brazzaville** and **Tanzania**, with stops in **Ireland** and **Prague**. While in Ireland **Guevara** embraced his own **Irish heritage**, celebrating **Saint Patrick's Day in Limerick city**. He wrote to his father on this visit, humorously stating **"I am in this green Ireland of your ancestors**. When they found out, the television [*station*] came to ask me about the

Lynch genealogy, but in case they were horse thieves or something like that, I didn't say much."

During this voyage he wrote a letter to **Carlos Quijano**, editor of a **Uruguayan weekly**, which was later retitled **Socialism and Man in Cuba**. Outlined in the treatise was **Guevara's** summons for the creation of a new consciousness, a new status of work, and a new role of the individual. He also laid out the reasoning behind his **anti-capitalist**. sentiments, stating:

. . .

"The laws of capitalism, blind and invisible to the majority, act upon the individual without his thinking about it. He sees only the vastness of a seemingly infinite horizon before him. That is how it is painted by capitalist propagandists, who purport to draw a lesson from the example of **Rockefeller**—whether or not it is true—about the possibilities of success. The amount of poverty and suffering required for the emergence of a **Rockefeller**, and the amount of depravity that the accumulation of a fortune of such magnitude entails, are left out of the picture, and it is not always possible to make the people in general see this."

Guevara ended the essay by declaring that **"the true revolutionary is guided by a great feeling of love"** and beckoning on all revolutionaries to **"strive every day so that this love of living humanity will be transformed into acts that serve as examples"**, thus becoming **"a moving force"**. The genesis for **Guevara's** assertions relied on the fact that he believed the example of the Cuban Revolution was **"something spiritual that would transcend all borders"**.

Guevara wrote his own epitaph, stating:

. . .

"Wherever death may surprise us, let it be welcome, provided that this our battle cry may have reached some receptive ear and another hand may be extended to wield our weapons."

Fidel Castro closed his clever impassioned eulogy thus:
(*What is it that makes a man?*)

"If we wish to express what we want the men of future generations to be, we must say: Let them be like **Che**! If we wish to say how we want our children to be educated, we must say without hesitation: We want them to be educated in **Che's spirit**! If we want the model of a man, who does not belong to our times but to the future, I say from the depths of my heart that such a model, without a single stain on his conduct, without a single stain on his action, is **Che!**"

Fyodor Dostoyevsky

Dostoyevsky relates the story of a woman who was almost saved by an onion. She had been a person of absolute selfishness and so, when she died, she went to hell. After all, she had chosen hell every day of her life. Even after her death, her guardian angel wanted to save her and so approached the Savior, saying a mistake had been made.

"Don't you remember? Olga once gave an onion to a beggar." It was left unsaid that the onion had started to rot, and also that it wasn't so much given as thrown at the beggar. The Savior said, **"You are right. Then pull her out of hell with an onion."** So the angel flew into the twilight of hell — all those people at once so close to each other and so far apart — and there was the selfish woman, glaring at her neighbours.

The angel offered her the onion and began to lift her out of hell with it. Others around her saw what was happening, saw the angel's strength, and saw their chance. They grabbed hold of the woman's legs and so were being lifted with her, a ribbon of people being rescued by one onion. Only the woman had never wanted company.

She began kicking with her legs, yelling at her uninvited guests, **"Only for me! Only for me!"** These three words are hell itself. The onion became rotten and the woman and all the others attached to her fell back into the disconnection of hell...

. . .

Providence

Like a voice in the wilderness, it will blow and shake the indifference and conceit of the priviledged darling buds of May, and an ill-wind will be the herald of its will, and many will wither before its blast, in the imortal words:

. . .

"For each mans death diminishes me,
For I am part of humanity,
Ask not for whom the bell tolls,
It tolls for thee!"
John Dunne

. . .

'Powers That Be'
By
Jonathan Cape
1966

With the heart-felt utterance, **"like that of my own argument"** [*My Italics*] much of the value is lost to humanity as a whole, owing to the Ostrich-like-attitudes of orthodox science, medicine and religion, when faced with the **common purpose**, of a world dictatorship, one has to prick the popular consciousness of the broad-masses, who by tradition are simple and stupid, more specifically the **"professional middle** *classess*" or the "*bourgeoisie*" and the "*aspiring working class*" or (*new labour aristocracy*!).

"Look before you leap, for as ye sow
So shall ye reap?"
Samuel Butler

. . .

We are able to clear our conscience by ingaging in this bestial behaviour, by condoning political orchestrated domestic killing and international warfare on a global scale, with the systimatic killing of our own and other species!

The House of Rothschild's
(Remember)

"The **commom purpose** is invisible to its audience, in order to make it fit the changes, in the means that justify the ends, of information consumption!".

. . .

Show me a man who has failed, and I'll show you a man who hasn't tried! Why? Because "*they*" are indolent and lazy, and the **virteous** know that the Devil finds work for idle-hands, why? Because we kneel before our shinning alters of transparent Christianity, **Jesus Christ** is not on trial here nor are the **Rothschild's** but the invisible money changers in the temple of God, and we all know who they are, **look in the mirror**!

. . .

Mirror Mirror

Any "*fool*" knows that survival must be earned! Or "*ARBEIT MACHT FREI*" or "*Arbeits gruppen, die Sie Freigeben*" or "*work sets you free*" or those and such as those, who maintain the **diffrential** or **imaginery-pie**, under the yoke of slavery, while knowingly borrowing vast amounts of money with exstortionate interest rates, to pay for the **deficit** or **idiocy** of the bankers who control the world **theatre** of **hate** and **lies** born of the **goyim wars**! Or **30 pieces of silver** borrowed from the international bankers or "*Dybbuk*" (*dubik*) with it's evolved and organized capitalism, and its working instrumentality, the banking system! Where you just can't say no? To the house of **Rothschild**!

Personal initilive

We know being able to work will give you the freedom to live the way you want to, but that's only a half-truth, with freedom comes a moral and personal responsibility to be your brothers and sisters keeper, not their gailer! You see how a devil's togue can use tricks of logic! To begile and fool the masses into thinking that we are not (*dictatorships*) and that we are democratic and free! why do you think prisons have been intentionally run in order to **de-humanize** the population, (*ops*) prison population, and we or they are treated no better than animals? Because it's a very clever way to be used against political desenters, and that means **you**!

Friend or Foe

137

"You can have any of Hobson's colour as long as it's black"
The invisible hand that would in the intervening years of the Second World War offer the poisoned olive branch of so-called democracy! Who's moving principle is enshrined in the wisdom of ***"don't give them what they want, but what they think is good for them"*** In spite of themselves, so one should shun this so-called dreadful book **Mien Kampf** without a hearing, and above all not speak of it, and that's an indirect order! Because it contains everything that we find abhorrent in a so-called civilised world! But what they had cleverly done was to unconsciously ban it or more conveniently leave it up to each and everybody's well-indoctrinated but collective consciousness, you know the one used at the ballot-box! By the shy fascists or secret voters. In the final analysis of our solution to world domination by the few or whatever and whoever they are? Over the many in the great collective of global slavery!

Where natural selection is exemplified to a fine art by the people who turn a blind-eye, and will not lift a finger to help stop it, you know, the hand that rocks the cradle, that now runs the provisional governments of ***"America"*** and ***"Imperialist Britain"*** who can increase the bank-books, of the ***privileged-classes*** or the ***"Petty-Bourgeoisie"*** and the great unwashed or ***working-aristocracy*** under the banner of slavery using economic power-broking for those and such as those! While in the **final solution**, excuse the pun, decreasing the **surplus-population**, that sounds familiar!

Would you buy a car from this man?

"Proofs of **conspiracy** against all the **religions** and **governments** of Europe carried on in the ***Secret Meetings of Freemasons, Iiuminati*** and reading Societies" in his book, Professor Robison of the University of Edinburgh, one of the leading intellects who in ***1783*** was elected secretary of the Royal Society of Edinburgh, gives details of the whole Rothschild ***"Illuminati,"*** plot.

He advises how he had been a high degree mason in the Scottish Rite of Freemasonry, and had been invited by Alan Weishaupt to Europe, where he was given a revised copy of Weishaupt's conspiracy. Professor Robison did not agree with it and somehow tried to expose it, you mean like the pope's playing off both sides against the middle, that akin to the old saying of ***"The Goyim-kettle"*** calling the ***"Rothschild's black***!"

. . .
William Shakespeare
(Our doubts are our traitors)

1800

In France, the bank of France is set up. Napoleon would soon see that a free France would mean a country free of debt, and he subsequently states, ***"The hand that gives is among the hand that takes."*** Money has no motherland financiers are without patriotism and without decency! Their sole object is gain! And this verbal-poison came from a patriotic decent **war criminal** that seems or appears to have divided loyalties! By trying to indirectly impeach the **Rothschild's**, who held the figurative-pistol, that so conveniently shot *"Maximillian Robespierre"* the peoples (*tyrant*) in the mouth! The day before his execution!

· · ·

1789

Due to the European ignorance of the Bavarian government's warning, the, **"Illuminati's** plan for a **French Revolution** succeeds from this year to it's completion in **1793.**" This revolution is a **central banker's dream**, as it establishes a new constitution and passes laws that both forbids the Roman Church from levying tithes (*taxes*) and also removes the Church's exemption from taxation.

Andrew Carrington Hitchcock

· · ·

Providence!

The result of this was policy through which the state used violent repression to crush resistance to the government. Under control of the effectively dictatorial committee, the convention quickly enacted more legislation. On 9 September, the convention established: *"sans-culottes"* paramilitary forces, the *"revolutionary armies"*, to force farmers to surrender grain demanded by the government. On 17 September, the Law of Suspects was passed, which authorized the charging of counter-revolutionaries with vaguely defined *"crimes against liberty"*. On 29 September, the convention extended price-fixing from grain and bread to other essential goods, and also fixed wages. The guillotine became the symbol of a string of executions: **Louis XVI** had already been guillotined before the start of the terror; **Marie-Antoinette**, the Girondists, **Philippe Égalité**, **Madame Roland** and many others lost their lives under its blade.

The Revolutionary Tribunal summarily condemned thousands of people to death by the guillotine, while mobs beat or stabbed other victims to death. Sometimes people died for their political opinions or actions, but many for little reason beyond mere suspicion, or because some others had a stake in getting rid of them!

Among people who were condemned by the revolutionary tribunals, about 8 percent were aristocrats, 6 percent clergy, 14 percent middle class, and 72 percent were workers or peasants accused of hoarding, evading the draft, desertion, or rebellion. **Maximilien Robespierre**, "frustrated with the progress of the revolution," saw politics through a populist lens because **"any institution which does not suppose the people good, and the magistrate corruptible, is evil."**

The invisible hand!

Another anti-clerical uprising was also made possible by the enactment of the Revolutionary Calendar on the 24th of October. Hébert's and Chaumette's atheist movement initiated an anti-religious campaign in order to dechristianise society. The program of dechristianisation waged against Catholicism, and also eventually against all forms of Christianity, included the deportation or execution of clergymen and women; the closing of churches; the rise of cults and the institution of a civic religion; the large scale destruction of religious monuments; the outlawing of public and private worship and religious education; the forced abjuration of priests of their vows and forced marriages of the clergy; the word "saint" being removed from street names; and the War in the Vendée.

. . .

When does virtue become a vice?
(*When its based on ignorance*)

The enactment of a law on 21 October 1793 made all suspected priests and all persons who harbored them liable to summary execution. The climax was reached with the celebration of the goddess Reason in **Notre Dame Cathedral** on 10 November. Because dissent was now regarded as counter-revolutionary, extremist **enragés** such as **Hébert** and moderate **Montagnard indulgents** such as **Danton** were guillotined in the spring of 1794. On 7 June, **Robespierre**, who favored **deism** over **Hébert's** atheism, and had previously condemned the Cult of Reason, recommended that the convention acknowledge the existence of his god. On the next day, the worship of the **deistic Supreme Being** was inaugurated as an official aspect of the revolution. Compared with **Hébert's** somewhat popular festivals, this austere new religion of **Virtue** was received with signs of **hostility** by the Parisian public.

. . .

The end of the reign
(*The execution of Robespierre*)

The repression brought thousands of suspects before the Paris Revolutionary Tribunal, whose work was expedited by the Law of 22 Prairial (10 June 1794). As a result of Robespierre's insistence on associating Terror with Virtue, his efforts to make the republic a morally united patriotic community became equated with the endless bloodshed. Finally, after 26 June's decisive military victory over Austria at the Battle of *Fleurus*, Robespierre was overthrown on 9 Thermidor (27 July).

The fall of *Robespierre* was brought about by a combination of those who wanted more power for the Committee of Public Safety, and a more radical policy than he was willing to allow, with the moderates who opposed the revolutionary government altogether. They had, between them, made the Law of 22 Prairial one of the charges against him, and after his fall, advocating terror would mean adopting the policy of a convicted enemy of the republic, endangering the advocate's own head. *Robespierre* tried to commit suicide! Before his execution by shooting himself, although the bullet only shattered his jaw. He was guillotined the next day!

The reign of the standing Committee of Public Safety was ended. New members were appointed the day after Robespierre's execution, and term limits were imposed (a quarter of the committee retired every three months); its powers were reduced piece by piece.

This was not an entirely or immediately conservative period; no government of the Republic envisaged a Restoration, and Marat was reburied in the Pantheon in September!

. . .

"qui tacet consentire videtur" (literally, who (is) silent is seen to consent)

"Remember you won't be able to see the trees for the forest!"

*In trying to assess the causes of the conditions found in **Belsen** one must be alerted to the tremendous visual display, ripe for purposes of propaganda, that masses of starved corpses presented.*

Gas Chamber Myths

*Some former inmates and a few historians have claimed that Jews were put to death in gas chambers at Bergen-Belsen. For example, an **"authoritative"** work published shortly after the end of the war, A History of World War II, informed readers: "In Belsen, [Commandant] Kramer kept an orchestra to play him Viennese music while he watched children torn from their mothers to be burned alive. Gas chambers disposed of thousands of persons daily."*

*In Jews, God and History, Jewish historian Max Dimont wrote of gassings at **Bergen-Belsen**. A semi-official work published in Poland in 1981 claimed that women and babies were "put to death in gas chambers" at Belsen.*

In
1945
The Associated Press news agency reported

*In Lueneburg, Germany, a Jewish physician, testifying at the trial of 45 men and women for war crimes at the **Belsen** and **Oswiecim** [Auschwitz] concentration camps, said that 80,000 Jews, representing the entire ghetto of **Lodz**, Poland, had been gassed or burned to death in one night at the **Belsen camp**.*

*Five decades after the camp's liberation, British army Captain Robert Daniel recalled seeing **"the gas chambers"** there.*

Years after the war, Robert Spitz, a Hungarian Jew, remembered taking a shower at Belsen in February 1945: "... It was delightful. What I didn't know then was that there were other showers in the same building where gas came out instead of water."

Another former inmate, Moshe Peer, recalled a miraculous escape from death as an eleven-year-old in the camp. In a 1993 interview with a Canadian newspaper, the French-born Peer claimed that he was sent to the [**Belsen**] camp gas chamber at least six times. "The newspaper account went on to relate: "Each time he survived, watching with horror as many of the women and children gassed with him collapsed and died. To this day, Peer doesn't know how he was able to survive." In an effort to explain the miracle, Peer mused: "Maybe children resist better, I don't know." (Although Peer claimed that "**Bergen-Belsen** was worse than **Auschwitz**," he acknowledged that he and his younger brother and sister, who were deported to the camp in 1944, all somehow survived internment there.)

. . .

"Such gas chamber tales are entirely fanciful. As early as 1960, historian Martin Broszat had publicly repudiated the Belsen gassing story. These days no reputable scholar supports it."

. . .

Exaggerated Death Estimates

Estimates of the number of people who died in **Bergen-Belsen** have ranged widely over the years. Many have been irresponsible exaggerations. Typical is a 1985 York Daily News report, which told readers that "probably 100,000 died at **Bergen-Belsen**." An official German government publication issued in 1990 declared that "more than 50,000 people had been murdered" in the Belsen camp under German control, and "an additional 13,000 died in the first weeks after liberation."

Closer to the truth is the Encyclopaedia Judaica, which maintains that 37,000 perished in the camp before the British takeover, and another 14,000 afterwards.

Whatever the actual number of dead, Belsen's victims were not "**murdered**," and the camp was not an "**extermination**" centre.

. . .

Black Market Centre

From **1945** until **1950**, when it was finally shut down, the British maintained **Belsen** as a camp for displaced European Jews. During this period it achieved new notoriety as a major European black market centre. The "**uncrowned king**" of **Belsen's** 10,000 **Jews** was **Yossl (Josef) Rosensaft**, who amassed tremendous profits from the illegal trading. Rosensaft had been interned in various camps, including **Auschwitz**, before arriving in **Belsen** in early April 1945.

British Lieutenant General Sir Frederick Morgan, chief of "**displaced persons**" operations in postwar Germany for the United Nations relief organization **UNRRA** recalled in his memoir that under **Zionist** *auspices* there had been organized at **Belsen** a vast illegitimate trading organization with worldwide ramifications and dealing in a wide range of goods, principally precious metals and stones. A money market dealt with a wide range of currencies. Goods were being imported in cryptically marked containers consigned in **UNRRA** shipments to **Jewish voluntary agencies**!

* * *

Lebensraum

(*Living-space*)
The shape of things to come
QED
(*Questions enable debate*)

Before the public gets on their moralistic high horse, no matter what your opinion of *"Adolf Hitler"* is? Listen to what he has to say about the amoral and unscrupulous individuals spoken so adroitly of in **Mein Kampf "My Struggle"** a political/ autobiographical manifesto by *"Adolf Hitler"* in which he outlines his political ideology of certain **wheels-within-wheels** or pernicious and dangerous shadowy racial figures, who can use and manipulate groups like **Freemasonry, Unions, etc**, that are cleverly infiltrated by those and such as those, in some **internal colonization**, faceless individuals who cleverly stand in the shadows! And they all know who they are!!

They are a social and moral evil! That threatens the very existence of the individual races of the world, a silent enemy that has invaded our societies without even a shot being fired in anger, and who loot and pillage using nothing more than tricks of logic!

By the slow and painful destruction of the innocents, with the eventual closure of our precious libraries! Due to our own indifference, or *"dolce far niente"* (*doltfe far njente*) Why? Because of the presence of this **Chameleon** as the people slowly surrender from their half-slumbering existence, where they are asked, not told, to lay down their symbolic-arms and surrender to this invisible invader, because who needs a library? If no one is using it! Who needs to know about history? Because it's not my history! The enemy within or the face of the beast, foreign or domestic! A ravenous Wolf in sheep's clothing, that is always hidden like the true face of **Ecclesiasticism** in all its guises? Because its proved itself worse than useless, along with the herd of the **British-isles**, who should have demanded justice, instead of allowing a mandate that is morally reprehensible, in the formation of an **illegal and treasonable coalition** of monsters tied at the Thames, that has been strengthened by nothing less than **political corruption** and **cronyism**, with the fettered and rank under-belly of corrupt **malevolent (ops) benevolent secret or societies with secrets**! *from the invisible hand of the fountainhead? To innocuous "Free Masonry groups"* and out onto the arms of the **Octopus** i.e.: **Rotarian organisations** and other **criminal organisations** that recruit specially selected members!

They are all treasonable and dangerous **cults** or **societies** that swear their allegiance to the top of the controlling **pyramid** (*fountain head*) or invisible hand that wears the **velvet-glove** of the dictator in the guise of **cross-party-agreement**, and because of this, political parties get away with flaunting the law by buying it! And **tyranny** waits its appointed hour upon the stage, hiding behind the mask or persona of legality! And so the ramparts fall like a house of cards, by nothing more than dictatorial expediency!

. . .

"Chicken Hawks"
An exposé of the true face of religion and who rely sits on high!
Jesus Christ taught us to beware of false prophets!

We have only ourselves to blame, ignorant wretches who wear the false-face of the self-styled corruption of provisional Christianity with its faceless masters, who seemed or appeared to stand back like frightened little children to allow ill and vulnerable people to be forced to the wall, by nothing more than the invisible hand that hides behind **legality**, and openly shows cynical disregard before the majesty of an empty and corrupt **law**! With its active abuse of **human rights**, after denying people who are not strong enough, access to due process, like the hysterical **Witch trials** of the middle ages!

. . .

𝕿𝖍𝖊 𝖂𝖎𝖙𝖈𝖍 𝕺𝖋 𝕰𝖉𝖒𝖔𝖓𝖙𝖔𝖓

". . . Why should the envious world throw all the scandalous malice upon me, cause I am poor, deform'd and ignorant, and like a bow buckled and bent together, by some more strong in mischiefs than myself?
Must I for that be made a common sink, for all the filth and rubbish of men's tongues, to fall and run into? Some call me Witch; and, being ignorant of myself, they go about to teach me, how to be one . . ."

. . .

Double entendré

If you don't believe me, open your mind and read the book **Mein-Kampf**, read **between the lines**! If you are capable of **analysing** and **understanding** where the truth **lies!** (*Excuse the play on words*) because the book is a clever instrument or weapon in either hand, by clever **devils**, to convey a massage that would be socially suggestive or offence to state directly, in an undeclared war against free thought:

Legacy

A kind of memorial centre now draws many tourists annually to the campsite. Not surprisingly, **Bergen's 13,000 residents** are not very pleased with their town's infamous reputation. Citizen's report being called **"murderers"** during visits to foreign countries.

In striking contrast to the widely accepted image of *Belsen*, which seems or appears to be essentially a product of hateful wartime propaganda, which apparently suppressed an albeit grim, historical reality.

"The best laid plan's of mice and men"

Heinrich Himmler

Was Arrested with two other men by a British soldier at a bridge at **Bremervorde** *in* **Northern Germany** *as he travelled to Switzerland, the small dishevelled figure with a patch over his left eye, was put into a guardroom. Here he was interviewed by two British Army sergeants who decided that the small man was a member of the* **"field police"** *- men who shot anyone in non-occupied Germany who spoke out against the war as it reached its final stages of defeat for Nazi Germany.*

From the guardroom, **"Heinrich Hitzinger"** *(as his papers stated) was taken to an internment camp where he could be further questioned. It was only at this internment camp that it became obvious that* **Hitzinger** *was, in fact,* **Himmler.**

Himmler *was searched and two cyanide phials were found on him and removed. It is said that as an Army doctor was about to give* **Himmler** *a more thorough examination, he bit on a cyanide capsule embedded in one of his teeth and died as a result,* **what a surprise!** *[My Italics]*

However, research done by Martin Allen questions this traditional story. He claims that **Himmler** *was killed by British Intelligence to stop any chance of his inter-war peace dealings with the Allies from being made public. These covert dealings started in 1943 - at a time when publically the Allies were calling for the unconditional surrender of Nazi Germany. Any revelations about clandestine peace deals with one of the most notorious men in Nazi- Germany would have been highly embarrassing for the British government.*

In 1941, Churchill established the **Political Warfare Executive** *(PWE). Its function was to broadcast propaganda into Nazi Germany to undermine the leadership there.*

As part of this work, **PWE** *tried to set off one senior Nazi official against others. It was known in* **PWE** *that the majority of senior Nazi figures had little time for others in the Nazi hierarchy and that all of them simply wanted to advance their power base at the expense of the others.*

This belief was confirmed, by Albert Speer in his post-war autobiography **"Inside the Third Reich"** *From 1943 on,* **Himmler** *had made contact with British Intelligence in an effort to end the war from the Allies point of view. What* **Himmler** *is said to have envisioned was the Allies combining their military might with the Germans with one target - Stalin's Russia. It is said that* **Himmler** *had decided that Germany would suffer defeat in the war after the Battle of Stalingrad.*

In March 1943, **Himmler** *sent SS general Walter Schellenberg to Sweden where he was to have contacted Victor Mallet, the British ambassador in Sweden. Mallet had little intention of dealing with* **Himmler** *but was told to do so by* **PWE.** *They also told him to actively encourage more meetings* *and contact. It seems that **PWE's** plan was to completely destabilise the Nazi hierarchy within Germany that would precipitate an early surrender. In October 1943, **PWE** received a six-point peace plan from **Himmler** who seemed to believe that he was dealing directly with senior officials at British Intelligence. **Himmler** stated that peace would lead to German troops being pulled out of occupied Western Europe and that an independent and free Poland would once again come into being.*

*In return he wanted assurances that there would be no Allied invasion of Western Europe and that the Allied bombing of Germany would stop. The head of **PWE**, Brendan Bracken, wrote*

*"Of course **HH's** proposal is unrealistic, but it also reveals how desperate the top men of the Nazi regime believe their military situation to be."*

*Towards the end of the war, **Himmler** openly made overtures of peace to the Allies - much to the fury of **Hitler** who ordered his arrest. His arrest put **PWE** in a very difficult position. Churchill had set up **PWE** to send out propaganda to Nazi Germany.*

*Churchill had been a very vocal supporter of non-negotiation with the Nazis and Churchill had always made it clear that he wanted an unconditional surrender from them. Yet here was a shadowy organisation set up by Churchill doing exactly what Churchill said the Allies would not do - negotiate with Nazi leaders. Any show trial of **Himmler** may well have brought up other issues.*

*The death camps were known about in London. RAF intelligence photos and information provided by the Polish Underground movement provided such information. Why didn't PWE use its potential influence over **Himmler** to either stop the transport trains to the camps or at the least, reduce the flow of Jews? Also, if **Himmler** could have pulled off a change in leadership as a result of his contact with GB Intelligence, how many Allied lives might have been saved from D-Day onwards? Would the Red Army have got as far into Eastern Europe as Berlin? Above all, America knew nothing about what **PWE** had been doing with **Himmler**.*

*"If **Himmler** stood trial, all this would come into the open. It might also undermine any case against him. Bracken wrote: (**the truth**) would have devastating repercussions for this country's standing."*

*At the Public Records Office at Kew, London, Martin Allen found a note dated May 10th 1945 from John Wheeler-Bennett at the Foreign Office to Robert Bruce Lockhart at **PWE**. The note was marked 'Personal and Secret'. It states:*

*"We cannot allow **Himmler** to take to the stand in any prospective prosecution, or indeed allow him to be interrogated by the Americans. Steps will therefore have to be taken to eliminate him as soon as he falls into our hands. Please give the matter some thought as if we are to take action, we will have to expedite such an act with some haste.*

*I have arranged for Mr. Thomas to go for a fortnight" What happened next, Allen argues, is open to contention. Allen has found a coded telegram in a Foreign Office file at Kew. It is from a 'Mr. Thomas'. It states: "Further to my orders, we successfully intercepted **HH** last night at **Luneberg** before*

146

he could be interrogated. As instructed, action was taken to silence him permanently."

*It is assumed that **HH** was **Heinrich Himmler**. Whatever precisely happened, a dead **Himmler,** according, to Allen, could not embarrass the government. Did **Himmler** kill himself to cheat the hangman or was he killed by British Intelligence and then buried in an unmarked grave so no autopsy can ever be carried out? Is the great un-washed ready to except this?*

Never-mind the staggering news that on July 24, 1945, Truman believed it necessary to inform the USSR of the imminent success of the Manhattan project. Failure to do so, they believed, would guarantee a post-war atmosphere of suspicion and hostility:

. . .

"Half-truth"

(*Don't forget to rattle the cage!*)

Did the US Government intended to use the atomic weapon for the purpose of achieving its Imperialist goals from a position of strength in "the cold war." This was amply corroborated on August 6th and 8th. Without any military need whatsoever, the Americans dropped two atomic bombs on the peaceful and densely populated Japanese cities of **Hiroshima** and **Nagasaki.**

Control and inslave, that's where you will find out who belongs to the hand that rocks the cradle! And the clever way to invade and control a **Republic, kingdom** or even a **planet**!!!

. . .

Where everybody is guilty until proved innocent!

And where, togue-in-cheek there is no differentiation between enemies foreign or domestic! when the pen is mightier than the sword?

Like some heavenly parody or battle, like Milton's **"*Paradise lost*"** where Lucifer or the Devil was cast into the pit, and he said that it would be better to rule in hell, than serve in heaven! The mechanical drones where rumoured to have been behind a series of grisly murders, which like Rutger Hauer in Blade-runner, when after kissing the man who was responsible for their plight! Confused and lost like **"*Judas Iscariot*"** he seemed or appeared to be in tears as he literary crushed the man's skull!

In an act of self-betrayal, who in the end realized themselves, that all life was precious, like in the Deer-Hunter with Robert De Niro, and the reason why he couldn't shot the deer! A world filled with curiosity and wonder in the beauty of life itself, a self-evident state that has more questions than answers...!

'Unquiet voices'

Maybe everything is a lie and even history, religion, politics, or as they said in Woody Allen's movie: "How do you know you have a brain! Have you ever seen or touched it? If not, can you prove its actually there! Well

can you? So you have to be careful how you view the half-empty or half-full glass, because we haven't discovered a cure for stupidity yet!"
"What fool/friend will sell us his secrets?"
Joseph Stalin (*Jew*) said retorically, I will, **Churchhill (*Jew*)** replied!

* * *

"Said the mad march hare, at the mad hatters tea party, will this lot not believe anything?"

Early post-war designs were based on domestic works as well as captured German jet fighters and information provided by **Britain** or the **US**. By 1946, Soviet designers were still having trouble in perfecting the German-designed, axial-flow jet engine, and new airframe designs and near-sonic wing designs were threatening to outstrip development of the jet engines needed to power them. Soviet aviation minister Mikhail Khrunichev and aircraft designer Alexander Sergeyevich Yakovlev suggested to Joseph Stalin that the USSR buy advanced jet engines from the British, However, Stalin gave his assent to the proposal, and Artem Mikoyan, engine designer Vladimir Klimov, and other officials traveled to the United Kingdom to request the engines. To Stalin's amazement, the British Labour government and its pro-Soviet Minister of Trade, Sir Stafford Cripps were willing to provide technical information and a licence to manufacture the Rolls-Royce Nene centrifugal-flow jet engine. This engine was reverse-engineered and produced in modified form as the Soviet Klimov VK-1 jet engine, later incorporated into the MiG-15 (Rolls-Royce later attempted to claim £207m in licence fees, without success! Who do we believe and where does the truth lie, (excuse the pun) in this grime game of cat and mouse propaganda, or is it the **invisible hand that rocks the cradle** or rules the world, feeding on a:

. . .

A diet of worms
*For nothing is secret
That shall not be reveiled
Neither anything hidden
That shall not be known
And come to light*
Luke 8:17

" The Devil will not be mocked"

Like in the cult TV Show "Night Gallery" that begs the question, what does *evil do*, when it meets *evil?*

Like the story of Burke and Hare, the grave-robbers or resurrectionists, who were rummured to have robbed graves in order to sell the bodies or cadavers in exchange for money, **aka**, (*cash*) to doctors in local hospitals to further their so-called anatomy and dysection skills or operational techniques!

The painted smile

On further inspection of this and other so-called lies or great (porker's) of history, like the great plague that mysteriously came and went! Or the other so-called great lie, there were literally tens of thousands each year, who had already died or hundreds of poor people of all ages, dying each and every day of deseases like **TB** (*tuberculosis*) **cancer** with no access to any kind of treatment or pain killers, never mind being able to afford to be buried! So they were destined for the finality of the disection table, whether they like it or not.

So the truth lies buried in the past, (*excuse the pun*), why theses two or others who were cleverly accused on a point of empty law, for so-called **"grave robbing"** or was there something else hidden in among these so-called facts, that obscures the truth?

And **Burke** and **Hare** were not stealing dead bodies, why? Because there was a plentiful supply! And if that was the case, then they must have been kidnapping healthy-people, for a more mysterious and pernicous reason? That points in only two directions, we already know that doctors have no scruples and would do practically anything for **money** or to maintain the **diffirential**, like the so-called doctors, did they not experiment on **jewish people**, **gypsies**, **mentally-ill** and **criminals** in the **death camps**!

. . .

"In the absence of a grand plan: if nothing that we do matters, then all that matters is what we do, therefore the smallest act of kindness can mean the whole world..."
ANGEL

. . .

Murphy's Law
(Cohn's Law)

"In any bureaucracy, paperwork increases as you spend more and more time reporting on the less and less you are doing. Stability is achieved when you spend all of your time reporting on nothing you are doing."
Arthur Bloch

. . .

"Bulwark"

Only as a unillateral weapon of choice, so to speak, akin to a symbolic double-edged sword drawn from its sheath, in the story by Malory who died in (1471) Le Morte d' Arhur, or the death of King Arthur! By the invisible hand of that *serpent,* that sits on high leading the blind!

And like a beacon of light, in that dark-hour of the soul, it will illuminate the way ahead, (*excuse the pun*) and through the *common purpose* as the shadows gather around the growing boy! We will be forced to give and take or live and let live, as we hold aloft the sword of understanding and truth!

. . .

"Missing links"

For to try and understand the chilling possibilities of whatever or whoever is doing this, you need to investigate father down the rabbit hole, so to speak, as you turn the pages of **"God, Angels and giants!"** which is connected to *California* and *Mount Shasta*, and the strange craft circling or near these mountains, like in **"who goes there?"** which is connected to **"Into the Void"** and **"The legion's of the damned"** and then to **"The Jack the ripper"** murders in England UK "1888" or by way of the eerie slayings of the woman, by **"Bible John"** in the swinging "60s?" You will perceive above your head, hanging by a slender thread, *'The sword of Damicles'* much like a dagger of the mind:

. . .

Hypnosis

(*Through the looking glass*)

"I know it sounds outré Di-partite and unconventional or peculiarly and shockingly unusual, but under self-hypnosis or conditioning, while in that natural state of heightened suggestion, a subject can be convinced of anything!!"

Passport to Magonia

By
Jacques Vallee
1975

That relates a strange metaphorical similé in an almost prophetic incident at or near the *"Loire" River* in France, on May 20th 1950 at approximately 4pm that involved a woman of an unknown age!

"Suddenly I found myself within a brilliant, blinding light and I saw two "*huge*" black hands appear in front of me. Each one had five fingers of black colour with a yellowish tint, somewhat like **"copper"** she explained that the hands did not come from behind but appeared to come from above!

She states that she took a couple of steps without anything happening and then the hands touched her. She didn't see any arms, just hands. "The two hands were applied to my face with violence and squeezed my head." Her head was pulled back against what she described as a very hard chest, as hard as iron! The hands slowly gripped her head harder and harder.

She described the hands as cold, as though they weren't made of flesh. The fingers on the hands completely covered her eyes, nose and mouth. She couldn't scream out and she couldn't breath. "When I was surrounded by the strong, blinding light, I had the feeling I had been paralysed and when the hands touched me, I had the very distinct impression of a strong electric charge."

The woman felt helpless for a little over a minute. She describes a feeling as though being swung front and backwards. She again states that the subject swinging her had a metal hard chest and shoulders. She also claims that she was being *swung*. She came back against "*invisible arms*" that were making contact with her "*shoulders*"

"It was at this moment that I heard his laugh, a strange laugh I could not explain; it was as if I heard him through water, and yet it seemed quite close, above my head. The laugh stopped after a few seconds and then the woman felt something like a knee hit her in the centre of her back.

The subject put her on the ground while still squeezing her head. He then dragged her rapidly along the path, but she could not hear the subject breathing. "*He pulled me into a bush of brambles and nettles and acacias*", still going backwards at an incredible speed, holding my head. At that moment I heard a voice above me, and it said: "*There she is, we've got her.*"

It appeared that the abductor was taking with someone else. As she was hearing this, she was choking and having difficulty breathing and feared she was going to die.

The abductor then dragged her into a field and stopped. She gradually felt the fingers come off her face and at that point she tried to scream but she couldn't "*After awhile I was able to sit up among the brambles.*" I had a very hard time breathing; my bag was still in my hand with the money it contained.

And the she heard a "*loud and violent windstorm*" "*I saw the trees bending as if under a sudden storm, and I was nearly thrown down, almost simultaneously there was a strong, blinding light. I had the feeling that something flew through the air very fast, but I saw nothing. Soon everything became calm again. I felt discomfort and nausea.*"

She stated that she had an ongoing metallic taste in her mouth and at one point she believed some **"invisible-force"** was brushing her off as she simultaneously felt an intense heat near the centre of her back.

151

(But what has one thing, got to do with the other?)

"Deo non Fortuna"
(By God not by chance!)

It's as if we need to look at the problem Pluralistically or adhere to the belief in the validity of a diversity of ancient cultures or beings with different views and practices

Someone or something could be controlling or interfering with time! Or **"Déjà vu"** from the French, literally **"already seen"**, is the phenomenon of having the strong sensation that an event or experience currently being experienced has been experienced in the past, whether it has actually happened or not!

. . .

Walter Mitty
(Capgras Syndrome)

"It's as if, someone or something is playing each side off against the middle! And unless we can understand the significance of events in relation to their cause, it seems or appears that we are being cleverly manipulated in some way!"

. . .

And there are more strange coincidences or anomalies to do with this strange phonomona of the **"look-a-likes"** like the Coed, **Ronald Tammen Jr** who mysteriously disappeared in **1953**.

In **David Paulides** book: **MISSING 411 NORTH AMERICA AND BEYOND** *page 378*, aged *19 years*. Who seems or appears to have been spotted on August 5th 1953 by H.H. Stephenson head of Miami housing for students, while he was vacationing with his wife in New York! On August 5th, 1953.

While in the hotel dining area, he made eye contact with a table of men seated close to them, and one of the men looked exactly like Tammen! And Stephenson stated that he definitely knew the student, and while he was looking at the men, **"whatever or whoever he was"** seemed or appeared [My Italics] to look straight through him!

And after leaving the dining room, Stephenson told his wife about the strange sighting, [My Italics] the couple then decided to go back to the restaurant, and by that time the men had gone!

Without turning these strange disappearances in a circus, what are we to make of these odd events!

Let Sleeping Dogs lie!

Like in the quirky observation of *David Paulides* in the *Dennis Lloyd Martin's* abduction/kidnapping and possible homicide?

As William and Clyde Martin were sitting on the grass with Dennis and his brother Doug, when another family who would become very important and pertinent witnesses in this strange affair, met or made the Martin's acquaintance in the meadow, asking them could their kids could join them in playtime? Even more odd was the subsequent fact that their surname or second name was *"Martin!"* remember it is very important to look for these weird coincidences, do such things have an uncanny ring to them, *"it happened by coincidence"*. When something out of the ordinary happens to us, we stand by this reason or when this happens too often, we begin to think there are other forces at work, even when...

"Less is more"

Even in the same book and the case of Michael Edwin Hearon on *page 127* and on *page 129* titled: **Follow-up** and the simple or apparently trite meaning of something that lacks freshness or effectiveness, because of constant use or excessive repetition that has no doubt become hackneyed or stale in its observation, much like the *"Martin's"* door-knocker! And when they went to the residence of the *Blythes*, they discovered that they had the exact same doorknocker!

"The coming of mad ones"
(*When the big-heat falls, the lice start running!*)

Eulogy

Akin to the *"Cheyenne Mountain nuclear"* bunker is a Cold War hardened installation with NORAD centers and associated computer systems in warm standby such as the Alternate Command Center for the nearby Peterson AFB NORAD-NORTHCOM Command Center.

Completed after more than 11 previous US command bunkers (e.g., 1953 Raven Rock, 1960 Ft MacArthur DC & 1962 Greenbrier), Cheyenne Mountain was designed for a 30 megaton nuclear explosion within 1.0 nmi (1.2 mi; 1.9 km). The bunker is 5.1 acres (2.1 ha) tunneled within part of a spur of the Cheyenne Mountain massif at the Rocky Mountains eastern *"Front Range"*. The bunker's standby centers are controlled by a NORAD division, and support services are provided by Air Force Space Command's 721st Mission Support Group

Beyond the parking area excavation through the bunker's North tunnel entrance, the bunker's Access Tunnel extends to the South opening at the end of an access road. The bunker has an Exhaust outlet, and NORAD Road has a SH 115 interchange on the west side of Fort Carson. The foreground is now a southern subdivision of Colorado Springs, Colorado.

It is a eulogy of madness and stupidity, that seems or appears to have been going on for thousands or even millions of years for all we know!

. . .

"The hidden history of these and other hidden bunkers!
Is yet to be written"

Are we being fooled by what seem or appears to be these ghosts in the machine or **"higher-collective-inteligences"** like drones in the **"hive"** or *great collective*, from either the corporal or non-corporal, for reasons best known to whatever or whoever they are?

Remember the universe has the same amount of of matter as it has spaces, because like the **"Viennese Waltz"** *(Wiener Walzer)* it must have spaces or rests in the music, in order to give it meaning and porpose!

And these metaphysical ghosts or shadow aspect of our own selves, so to speak, are either using **"time-travel"** somewhere in the future? Because time and space seems or appears to be contradicting itself, compared to the laws that restrict us, which means they must be more intelligent, but not necessesarily civilized like us!

Time-Travel

You were here yesterday, true or false? Yes! And that's a fact, not a theory, and it's highly probably that you will be here tomorrow, standing as you are today True or false? True, which is one day into the future, because you are now standing in the future, which was tomorrow, or today! Are you not? Which is a fact, not a theory! Like you were yesterday, which is now in the past and that's a fact, not a theory!

This idea gained popularity with the H. G. Wells story *The Time Machine*, published in 1895 (preceded by a less influential story of time travel Wells wrote in 1888, titled **"The Chronic Argonauts"**), which also featured a time machine and which is often seen as an inspiration for all later science fiction stories featuring time travel using a vehicle that allows an operator to travel purposefully and selectively. The term **"time machine"** coined by Wells, is now universally used to refer to such a vehicle!

A Christmas Carol

Charles Dickens' 1843 book A Christmas Carol is considered by some to be one of the first depictions of time travel in both directions, as the main character, Ebenezer Scrooge, is transported to Christmas past, present and yet to come! These might be considered mere visions rather than actual time travel, though, since Scrooge only viewed each time period passively, unable to interact with them.

. . .

"Even so they seem or appear to be able to construct, what seems or appears to be carbon copies, meaning that they might have a way of manipulating physics?

. . .

Being one of the oldest academic disciplines, perhaps the oldest through its inclusion of astronomy.

Over the last two millennia, physics was a part of natural philosophy along with chemistry, certain branches of mathematics, and biology, but during the Scientific Revolution in the 17th century, the natural sciences emerged as unique research programs in their own right. Physics intersects with many interdisciplinary areas of research, such as biophysics and quantum chemistry, and the boundaries of physics are not rigidly defined.

New ideas in physics often explain the fundamental mechanisms of other sciences while opening new avenues of research in areas such as mathematics and philosophy!

"But how and why could they be interfering with our Past? Present, and Future?"

(Albert Einstein)

Showed that ultimately all matter is capable of being converted to energy (known as mass–energy equivalence) by the famous formula "$E = mc^2$," where E is the energy of a piece of matter of mass m, times c^2 the speed of light squared.

As the speed of light is **299,792,458** metres per second (**186,282 mi/s**), a relatively small amount of matter may be converted to a large amount of energy. An example is that positrons and electrons (**matter**) may transform into photons (**non-matter**).

However, although matter may be created or destroyed in such processes, neither the quantity of mass or energy change during the process.

Matter should not be confused with mass, as the two are not quite the same in modern physics.

For example, mass is a conserved quantity, which means that its value is unchanging through time, within closed systems. However, matter is not conserved in such systems, although this is not obvious in ordinary conditions on Earth, where matter is approximately conserved. Still, special relativity shows that matter may disappear by conversion into energy, even inside closed systems, and it can also be created from energy, within such systems.

*However, because mass (**like energy**) can neither be created nor destroyed, the quantity of mass and the quantity of energy remain the same during a transformation of matter (**which represents a certain amount of energy**) into non-material (**i.e., non-matter) energy**. This is also true in the reverse transformation of energy into matter.*

*Different fields of science use the term matter in different, and sometimes incompatible, ways. Some of these ways are based on loose historical meanings, from a time when there was no reason to distinguish mass and matter. As such, there is no single universally agreed scientific meaning of the word "**matter**." Scientifically, the term "**mass**" is well-defined, but "**matter**" is not. Sometimes in the field of physics "**matter**" is simply equated with particles that exhibit rest mass (**i.e., that cannot travel at the speed of light**), such as **quarks** and **leptons**.*

*However, in both physics and chemistry, matter exhibits both **wave-like** and **particle-like** properties, the so-called **wave–particle** duality.*

Know they self!

So its very probable that someone or something could have used or be using a **time-machine** with some form of highly advanced **"Bio-molecular *nanotechnology*"** or a science without **'*instrumentally*'** that is so advanced and so old, it seems or appears that it could have constructed the very universe or world that we think we live in!

A pseudo-science, if you like using something akin to a **Pseudo-code** that typically omits details that are not essential for human understanding of the **"algorithm"** such as **"*variable-declarations*" "*system-specific-code*"** and some **"*subroutines*"**.

And their programming language is augmented with something that is like natural language description details, where convenient, or with compact mathematical notation.

It gives meaning to the world, that we think we live in!
. . .

The purpose of using **pseudocode** is that it is easier for people or us! To understand than conventional programming language code, and that it is an efficient and environment-independent description of the key principles of an **"algorithm"**.

It is commonly used in textbooks and scientific publications that are documenting various algorithms, and also in planning of computer program development, for sketching out the structure of the program before the actual coding takes place.

So they could be light-years ahead of us, and could have literally constructed a time-machine or something along these lines? Remember, matter cannot be created or destroyed! So where is it coming from and going to? It's like an itch that you can't scratch, caused by highly **"advanced-molecular-bots..."**

Nanotechnology

(Engineering of functional systems at the molecular scale)

This covers both current work and concepts that are more advanced. In its original sense, *"nanotechnology"* refers to the projected ability to construct items *from the bottom up*, using techniques and tools being developed today to make complete, high performance products.

The Meaning of Nanotechnology

When K. Eric Drexler popularised the word *"nanotechnology"* in the 1980's, he was talking about building machines on the scale of molecules, a few nanometers wide—motors, robot arms, and even whole computers, far smaller than a cell. Drexler spent the next ten years describing and analysing these incredible devices, and responding to accusations of science fiction. Meanwhile, mundane technology was developing the ability to build simple structures on a molecular scale. As nanotechnology became an accepted concept, the meaning of the word shifted to encompass the simpler kinds of nanometer-scale technology.

The U.S. National Nanotechnology Initiative was created to fund this kind of nanotech: their definition includes anything smaller than 100 nanometers with novel properties.

Much of the work being done today that carries the name 'nanotechnology' is not nanotechnology in the original meaning of the word, nanotechnology, in its traditional sense, means building things from the bottom up, with atomic precision, this theoretical capability was envisioned as early as 1959 by the renowned physicist Richard Feynman:

"I want to build a billion tiny factories, models of each other, which are manufacturing simultaneously, the principles of physics, as far as I can see, do not speak against the possibility of manoeuvring things atom by atom. It is not an attempt to violate any laws; it is something, in principle, that can be done; but in practice, it has not been done because we are too big!"

Richard Feynman, Nobel Prize winner in physics.

Based on Feynman's vision of miniature factories using nanomachines to build complex products, advanced nanotechnology (*sometimes referred to as molecular manufacturing*) will make use of positionally controlled mechanochemistry guided by molecular machine systems. Formulating a roadmap for development of this kind of nanotechnology is now an objective of a broadly based technology roadmap project led by Battelle (*the manager of several U.S. National Laboratories*) and the Foresight Nanotech Institute.

Shortly after this envisioned molecular machinery is created, it will result in a manufacturing revolution, probably causing severe disruption. It also has serious **'economic, social, environmental**, and **military** implications...

Etymology and discovery

The word **"quantum"** comes from the Latin **"quantus"** for **"how much"**. **"Quanta"**, short for **"quanta of electricity"** (*electrons*) was used in a 1902 article on the photoelectric effect by Philipp Lenard, who credited Hermann von Helmholtz for using the word in the area of electricity. However, the word quantum in general was well known before 1900.

It was often used by physicians, such as in the term quantum satis. Both Helmholtz and Julius von Mayer were physicians as well as physicists. Helmholtz used **"quantum"** with reference to heat in his article on Mayer's work, and indeed, the word **"quantum"** can be found in the formulation of the first law of thermodynamics by Mayer in his letter dated July 24, 1841.

Max Planck used **"quanta"** to mean **"quanta of matter and electricity"**, gas, and heat.

In **1905**, in response to Planck's work and the experimental work of Lenard, who explained his results by using the term **"quanta of electricity"**, Albert Einstein suggested that radiation existed in spatially localized packets which he called "quanta of light" (**"Lightquanta"**).

The concept of quantization of radiation was discovered in 1900 by Max Planck, who had been trying to understand the emission of radiation from heated objects, known as black-body radiation. By assuming that energy can only be absorbed or released in tiny, differential, discrete packets he called **"bundles"** or **"energy elements"**, Planck accounted for the fact that certain objects change colour when heated.

On December 14, **1900**, Planck reported his revolutionary findings to the German Physical Society, and introduced the idea of quantization for the first time as a part of his research on black-body radiation.

As a result of his experiments, Planck deduced the numerical value of **h**, known as the (*Planck constant*), and could also report a more precise value for the Avogadro–Loschmidt number, the number of real molecules in a mole and the unit of electrical charge, to the German Physical Society. After his theory was validated, Planck was awarded the Nobel Prize in Physics in 1918 for his discovery.

This effect does not come into play by going from macro to micro dimensions. However, quantum effects can become significant when the nanometer size range is reached, typically at distances of 100 nanometers or less, the so-called quantum realm.

Additionally, a number of physical (**mechanical, electrical, optical, etc.**) properties change when compared to macroscopic systems. One example is the increase in surface area to volume ratio altering mechanical, thermal and catalytic properties of materials.

Diffusion and reactions at nanoscale, nanostructures materials and nanodevices with fast ion transport are generally referred to as nanoionics. *Mechanical* properties of nanosystems are of interest in the nanomechanics research.

STANDING ON THE SHOULDERS OF GODS

There creature had left **cryptic clues** on **theology**, **anthropology** and **sociology**, by underlining certain passages in books like the **Christian Bible** and the **book of Revelation**, where the creature had out grown, even its own strange **creator**! Much like ourselves who sees their maker with sceptic indifference, **a great architect**, who seems or appears to be acting more like a **super sentient bio-computer**, that for some reason best known to its programmer has found out that it is malfunctioning, and it is trying to de-bug the system!

Paul Crowe

. . .

Enigma

(Or source of all wisdom and understanding)

"Some unknown-intelligence for whatever reason, has in its infinite wisdom, seems or appears to have left a backdoor open to reality."

. . .

Remember no one has ever caught or seen, whatever or whoever is responsible for the people who have not only went missing, but who have been found murdered in strange and bizarre circumstances!

We are only left with theories or hint's that something else seems or appears to be going-on under the radar, so to speak! Like in the **"Jack the ripper"** mystery, or even in the more contemporary mysteries like the **"JFK"** assassination or **"The Twin Towers"** and the people who have been mysteriously murdered, who were directly or indirectly connected to these strange events, or in the excellent and prophetic books by **"David Paulides"** a mystery that has been going on longer than one would care to remember, and that's not a theory, but a fact!

It's as simple as that! So the theory holds true, that the collective energy of the species has already achieved a science without instrumentality in some **evolutionary** or **spiritual-development** of some kind! Through a dichotomy of **negative** and **positive** forces in:

. . .

STANDING ON THE SHOULDERS OF GODS

(Fiction)

"Osirus slain" and **"Osirus risen"**

Inscription on the cross: *Igne Natura Renovatur Integra*, 'by fire nature is renewed whole' and the strange inscription at the head of *Christ's cross* on Calvary: *"OCRUXAVES PESUNICA"* that can be broken up to form the phrase: *O crux ave spes unica, 'Hail O cross, the only hope.'* With its hidden or cryptic message: *(OCRUXAVES PESUNICA ORCUS)* which is a Latin phrase: *Orcus ave pus e canis*, meaning: *Orcus hail, down from the "dog"* Orcus is the Roman Lord of the underworld-whom the Eygptians knew as **"Osiris"** The lord of the dead!

Genesis:

"Behold the man is become as one of 'us'
To know good and evil and now, lest he put forth his hand,
And take also of the tree of life,
'Eat' and live forever
So he drove out the man; and he placed him at the East of Eden,
Cherubim's and a flaming torch which turned every way,
To keep the way of the tree of life!"

. . .

Continued:

(Where the means will justify the ends)

For the great architect and progenitor in the cellar, created by a mad-scientist, or some unseen hand, like an unconscious truth or subliminal message, that if you take off the **mask** or **false persona**, you will find, that the hidden face of the executioner is our own, Looking back at us!

Don't forget the strange beast that was created from the **DNA** found in the dust of the cellar, like a parody of the symbolic story of *Adam* and especially *Eve* being created from Adam by *God!*

. . .

"You could learn a lot from children, they believe in things in the dark,
until we tell them it's not so, maybe we've been fooling them?"
Night/Curse of the Demon

. . .

Personal initive

In order to hold aloft the greatest weapon at our disposal, we can slowly drain off the nations infected blood, where it seeks to divide and conquer any resistance to the **common purpose,** through **political**, **economic**, **social**, and **religious means**.

. . .

Sentient automaton / Machine?

(Scanning)

So it's not a judgement, but more of something trying to get us to question the status quo, or de-bug the main frame! By using the invisible hand to try and find the *itch that you can't scratch,* to rock the cradle, so to speak!

. . .

Anthropomorphic creatures

"Having contrived to possess itself of the minds of the **Goy** (*Gentile*) communities to such an extent they all come near looking upon the events of the world through the coloured glasses of those spectacles we are setting astride their noses; if already now there is not a single state where there exist for us any barriers to admittance into what Goy (*Gentile*) stupidity calls State secrets: what will our position be then, when we shall be acknowledged supreme lords of the world in the person of our king of all the world!"

. . .

𝕯racula

"It is a wild adventure we are on. Here, as we are rushing along through the darkness, we seem to be drifting into unknown places and unknown ways; into a whole world of dark and dreadful things"
Professor Van Helsing

. . .

"You clever man, friend John; you reason well, and your wit is bold; but you are too prejudiced. You do not let yours eyes see nor your ears hear, and that which is outside your daily life is not of account to you. Do you not think that there are things that you cannot understand, and yet which are; that some people see things that others cannot? But there are things old and new that must not be contemplate by men's eyes, because they know — or think they know — some things which other men have told them. Ah, it is the fault of our science that it wants to explain all; and if it explain not, then it says there is nothing to explain. But yet we see around us every day the growth of new beliefs, which think themselves new; and which are yet but the old, which pretend to be young — like the fine ladies at the opera. I suppose now you do not believe in *corporeal transference*. No? Nor in *materialization*. No? *Nor in astral bodies*. No? *Nor in the reading of thought*. No? *Nor in hypnotism —*'

"Yes" I said. Charcot has proved that pretty well.' He smiled as he went on: Then you are satisfied as to it. Yes? And of course then you understand how it act, and can follow the mind of the great Charcot — alas that he is no more! — Into the very soul of the patient that he influence. No? Then, friend John, am I to take it that you simply accept fact, and are satisfied to let from premise to conclusion be a blank?"

To believe what? To believe in things that you cannot, let me illustrate. I heard once of an American who so defined faith: "that which enables us to believe things which we know to be untrue." For one, I follow that man. He meant that we shall have an open mind, and not let a little bit of truth check the rush of a big truth, like a small rock does a railway truck. We get the small truth first. Good! We keep him, and we value him; but all the same we must not let him think himself all the truth in the universe.'

Then you want me not to let previous conviction injure the receptivity of my mind with regard to some strange matter. Do I read your lesson alright? But not much is written of these beings, because they lived in very ancient times, and man is young, and knows but little of the very ancient living things, so."

Big Time

"In the sci-fi story called: Big Time the entire universe is divided into two camps, those of the Spiders and the Snakes. They and their supporters battle desperately throughout billions of years of past and future time. Yet for all its vast scale, it's a secret war, one that you and I will likely never perceive, however much our civilisations are overthrown, our history perverted and our lives destroyed.

But in the Big Time, that special region outside of normal time and space, the Spiders and the snakes observe the changes they make to reality, and feel the Change Winds rushing through them as one side or the other manages to alter the course of history.

Still, all this big stuff takes place in the background. This novel is concerned with the goings on in the lounge of a small R&R station floating in the Big Time. It's asking questions about life, the universe, whether the ends justify the means.

You view the story through the eyes and ears of entertainer and hostess extraordinaire, Greta Forzane, as she observes the differing beliefs and moralities of her fellow entertainers and the soldiers they serve.

There's Sid the senior man, Doc the far-gone alcoholic, Maud, Beau and the new girl, Lili. The recuperating soldiers are Erich, Bruce, Mark, Caby and a couple of aliens, Sevencee and Illhilihis. We learn what Greta already knows, that both she and her associates are both better and worse than appearances suggest.

Fritz Lieber

.   .   .

Ides of March

(Portentous events)
"Deification of Julius Caesar, a 16th-century engraving by Virgil Solis illustrating Ovid's passage on the apotheosis of Caesar (Metamorphoses 15.745-850)"

.   .   .

Virgil wrote in the *Georgics* (26 B.C.) that several unusual events took place following Caesar's assassination.

Who dare say the Sun is false? He and no other warns us when dark uprisings threaten, when treachery and hidden wars are gathering strength. He and no other was moved to pity Rome on the day that Caesar died, when he veiled his radiance in gloom and darkness, and a godless age feared everlasting night. Yet in this hour Earth also and the plains of Ocean, ill-boding dogs and birds that spell mischief, sent signs which heralded disaster. How oft before our eyes did Etna deluge the fields of the Cyclopes with a torrent from her burst furnaces, hurling thereon balls of fire and molten rocks. Germany heard the noise of battle sweep across the sky and, even without precedent, the Alps rocked with earthquakes. A voice

162

boomed through the silent groves for all to hear, a deafening voice, and phantoms of unearthly pallor were seen in the falling darkness. Horror beyond words, beasts uttered human speech; rivers stood still, the earth gaped upon; in the temples ivory images wept for grief, and beads of sweat covered bronze statues. King of waterways, the Po swept forests along in the swirl of his frenzied current, carrying with him over the plain cattle and stalls alike. Nor in that same hour did sinister filaments cease to appear in ominous entrails or blood to flow from wells or our hillside towns to echo all night with the howl of wolves. Never fell more lightning from a cloudless sky; never was comet's alarming glare so often seen.

The dictator's last words are a contested subject among scholars and historians and people alike. Suetonius reports that others have said Caesar's last words were the Greek phrase "κα☐ σὺ, τέκνον;" (transliterated as "*Kai su, teknon?*": "You too, child?" in English). However, Suetonius himself says Caesar said nothing. Plutarch also reports that Caesar said nothing, pulling his toga over his head when he saw Brutus among the conspirators. The version best known in the English-speaking world is the Latin phrase "***Et tu, Brute?***" ("You too, Brutus?"); this derives from Shakespeare's *Julius Caesar* (1599), where it actually forms the first half of a macaronic line: "***Et tu, Brute?*** Then fall, Caesar.

According to Plutarch, after the assassination, Brutus stepped forward as if to say something to his fellow senators not involved in the plot; they, however, fled the building. Brutus and his companions then marched to the Capitol while crying out to their beloved city: "People of Rome, we are once again free!". They were met with silence, as the citizens of Rome had locked themselves inside their houses as soon as the rumour of what had taken place had begun to spread. According to Suetonius, all the conspirators made off, and he (Caesar) lay there lifeless for some time, and finally three common slaves put him on a litter and carried him home, with one arm hanging down.

. . .

In the ensuing years a series of civil wars resulted with the end of the Republic and the rise of imperial Rome

...his friends were alarmed at certain rumors and tried to stop him going to the Senate-house, as did his doctors, for he was suffering from one of his occasional dizzy spells. His wife, Calpurnia, especially, who was frightened by some visions in her dreams, clung to him and said that she would not let him go out that day.

But Brutus, one of the conspirators who was then thought of as a firm friend, came up and said, 'What is this, Caesar? Are you a man to pay attention to a woman's dreams and the idle gossip of stupid men, and to insult the Senate by not going out, although it has honoured you and has been specially summoned by you? But listen to me, cast aside the forebodings of all these people, and come. The Senate has been in session waiting for you since early this morning.' This swayed Caesar and he left.

Caesar had been preparing to invade the Parthian Empire (a campaign later taken up by his successor, Mark Antony) and planned to leave for the

East in the latter half of March. This forced a timetable onto the conspirators. Two days before the actual assassination, Cassius met with the conspirators and told them that, should anyone discover the plan, they were to turn their knives on themselves. His successors did attempt the conquests of Parthia and Germania, but without lasting results.

On the Ides of March (March 15; see Roman calendar) of 44 BCE, the conspirators staged a game of gladiatorial sport at Pompey's theatre. The gladiators were provided by Decimus Brutus in case their services were needed. They waited in the great hall of the theatre's quadriportico. Mark Antony, having vaguely learned of the plot the night before from a terrified *Liberator* named Servilius Casca, and fearing the worst, went to head Caesar off at the steps of the forum. However, the group of senators intercepted Caesar just as he was passing the Theatre of Pompey, located in the Campus Martius (now adjacent to the Largo di Torre Argentina), and directed him to a room adjoining the east portico.

According to Plutarch, as Caesar arrived at the Senate, Lucius Tillius Cimber presented him with a petition to recall his exiled brother. The other conspirators crowded round to offer their support. Both Plutarch and Suetonius say that Caesar waved him away, but Cimber grabbed Caesar's shoulders and pulled down Caesar's tunic. Caesar then cried to Cimber, "Why, this is violence!" ("*Ista quidem vis est!*"). At the same time, Casca produced his dagger and made a glancing thrust at Caesar's neck.

Caesar turned around quickly and caught Casca by the arm. According to Plutarch, he said in Latin, "Casca, you villain, what are you doing?" Casca, frightened, shouted "Help, brother!" Within moments, the entire group, including Brutus, was striking out at the dictator.

Caesar attempted to get away, but, blinded by blood, he tripped and fell; the men continued stabbing him as he lay defenseless on the lower steps of the portico. According to Eutropius, around 60 or more men participated in the assassination. Caesar was stabbed 23 times. Suetonius relates that a physician who performed an autopsy on Caesar established that only one wound (the second one to his chest) had been fatal. This autopsy report (the earliest known post-mortem report in history) describes that Caesar's death was mostly attributable to blood loss from the multiple stab wounds.

. . .

The result unforeseen by the assassins was that Caesar's death precipitated the end of the Roman Republic. The Roman lower classes, with whom Caesar was popular, became enraged that a small group of aristocrats had sacrificed Caesar. Antony, who had been drifting apart from Caesar, capitalised on the grief of the Roman mob and threatened to unleash them on the Optimates, perhaps with the intent of taking control of Rome himself. But, to his surprise and chagrin, Caesar had named his grandnephew Gaius Octavius his sole heir, bequeathing him the immensely potent Caesar name as well as making him one of the wealthiest citizens in the Republic. Octavius became *Gaius Julius Caesar Octavianus* or Octavian, the son of the great Caesar, and consequently also inherited the loyalty of much of the Roman populace. Octavian, aged only 18 at the time of Caesar's death, proved to have considerable political skills, and while Antony dealt with Decimus Brutus in the first round of the new civil wars, Octavian consolidated his tenuous position.

To combat Brutus and Cassius, who were massing an enormous army in Greece, Antony needed soldiers, the cash from Caesar's war chests, and the legitimacy that Caesar's name would provide for any action he took against them. With passage of the Lex Titia on November 27, 43 BC, the Second Triumvirate was officially formed, composed of Antony, Octavian, and Caesar's Master of the Horse Lepidus.

It formally deified Caesar as Divus Iulius in 42 BC, and Caesar Octavian henceforth became *Divi filius* ("Son of the Divine"). Seeing that Caesar's clemency had resulted in his murder, the Second Triumvirate brought back proscription, abandoned since Sulla. It engaged in the legally sanctioned murder of a large number of its opponents in order to fund its forty-five legions in the second civil war against Brutus and Cassius. Antony and Octavius defeated them at Philippi.

Afterward, Mark Antony married Caesar's lover, Cleopatra, intending to use the fabulously wealthy Egypt as a base to dominate Rome. A third civil war broke out between Octavian on one hand and Antony and Cleopatra on the other. This final civil war, culminating in the latter's defeat at Actium, resulted in the final ascendancy of Octavian, who became the first Roman emperor, under the name Caesar Augustus, a name that raised him to the status of a deity.

You men of stone! Shouted the Devil! I come not to praise Caesar, but to buy him.

William Shakespeare

. . .

Hansel and Gretel

(*Brothers Grimm*)

"Once upon a time, a story was told about fairies and goblins and witches of old. They haunted the forests and meadows and dells and this is the legend the storybooks tell: Oh, don't you remember a long time ago? When two little babes, whose names I don't know. They wandered away on a fine summers day and were lost in a wood, I've heard people say."

. . .

Hansel and Gretel stumble on a clearing in the woods where elves are going about their business. The elves are friendly to the children. A witch comes and takes them away on her broom to her gingerbread house, where she turns nasty on them, turning Hansel into a spider, her yowling cat to stone, and tries to turn Gretel into a Rat when an elf's arrow stops her.

While the elves are fighting the witch, Hansel and Gretel free the other children who have been imprisoned and transformed by the witch.

Finally, the witch falls from her broom and lands in the cauldron containing the brew that turns living things to stone, and becomes a large rock! Which would be known as the Witch Rock...

165

Silence

"There are some qualities--some incorporate things, that have a double life, which thus is made a type of that twin entity which springs from matter and light, evinced in solid and shade.
There is a twofold _Silence_ --sea and shore--body and soul. One dwells in lonely places, newly with grass o'ergrown; some solemn graces, some human memories and tearful lore, render him terrorless: his names! No More.
He is the corporate Silence: dread him not! No power hath he of evil in himself; but should some urgent fate (untimely lot!) Bring thee to meet his shadow (nameless elf, that haunteth the lone regions where hath trod no foot of man), commend thyself to God!"
Edger Allen Poe

. . .
THE LAST SEASON
(Eric Blehm)
Randy Morgenson was legendary for finding people missing in the High Sierra, then one day he went missing himself!

1973
(McClure Medow)
"I am suddenly close to something very great and very large, something containing me and all this around me, something I only dimly perceive, and understand not at all.

"Perhaps if I am here, aware, and perceptive, long enough I will"
That a humaniod God willed all this into exsistance simply to glorify himself (a bit too egotistically), and/or for us, his greatest creation!
Randy Morgenson
"As the mind of man is constituted, there is nothing that breeds such conviction in it, as the palpable and the tangible."

. . .
STANDING ON THE SHOULDERS OF GODS
Or if you listen real close, you might make out or hear the sound of one hand clapping, which could turn-out to be the sound of Gods own retrospective voice in his own head, so to speak, or that shadow aspect cast by God, like the tongue of the **serpent** in the garden of Eden, whispering into *Gods-ear* if you will, or even *Randy's-ear, [My Italics]* so to speak!
Paul Crowe
And isn't it very odd that Randy Morganson who was first among equals, and a highly experienced **"backwoods ranger"** turned out to be a gaint with feet of clay!
It is very probable that his death was accidental, but highly unlikely! He disappeared and reappeared under very odd, and yet normal circumstances.

166

"The least I owe these mountains is a body!"

Including the two **John Doe's** fitting Randy Morgenson's description! **One—deceased** and **one with amnesia**! As well as the rather odd and yet mute coincidence of Randy's radio call sign **"114"** which is the call sign for missing persons **"411"** only back-to-front or the other way around! Which is an uncomfortable phenomenon like **"duple-gangers"** that you will come across further on in the book.

Without the exact science of **hind-sight**! Or **"Fagin's Rule on past prediction"**, we have no fixed references to the enigma of our **"past"** or **"future!"**

That's why my theory is startling, as it is baffling, and you either need to have an open mind, or at least be prepared to approach the subject half way, so to speak, which means it's not a question whether the cup is either half-empty or half-full, but that you need to empty the cup, before you can fill it!

If we look at the odd and strange facts, that are often hidden in among the evidence, like an unquiet voice of these and other murdered people, you will stumble over what seems or appears to be an **"anthropological"** **"theological"** and **"sociological"** unquiet truth, like an umbilical-cord that not only stretches into the **"past"** but seems or appears to return back to the **"future!"**

Ambiguity

If you begin to join up the dots, or know the significance of an event, in relation to its cause, a sinister and disturbing picture begins to take shape, of what seems or appears a series of dissections of a *lower spieces*, by a *higher one*! Who are apparently just as curious about us, as we should be about whatever or whoever is commiting some of these dreadful acts, because all of the people who have mysteriously disappeared, have not been killed! Some were intentially left alive, so that the efforts of **SAR** (*Search and Reascue*) would eventually find them just in the nick-of-time! Excuse the pun, so there could be **one** or **more benevolent/malevolent** types, systematically studying or looking for something, And if the double standards of our own behaviour to our own kind, as well as to other species, is anything to go by, then this **"Nemesis"** or some of the more **malevolent** types might see us as nothing more than animals!

'Gods, Angels And Giant's'

A mysterious battle, call it what you will, seems or appears to be at the very source of all knowledge and understanding.

ENIGMA?

Who or what could be responsible for what can only be described as a...

Giant non-corporal bio-computer

0-1-1-0

. . .

That seems or appears to have found the answer to its self before trying to find the question!

"Which is like or akin to a malfunction or virus!"

Anthropomorphism

"Anthropomorphism, or personification, is attribution of human form or other characteristics to anything other than a human being. Examples include depicting deities with human form"

Fact not theory!

Energy cannot be created or destroyed! So what is causing this enigma of $E=MC2$ where the universe is said to shrink to the size of a marble, per-say, and in doing so it has become so dense, it seems or appears to react under its own weight by exploding at the speed of light! Or *expanding* while shrinking or slowing down at the same time! That's a contradiction in terms, the source of all knowledge and understanding, must be accessing itself or looking for the answer to the question it has found, and from this theoretical conception or creation, in order to find the condition of $E=MC2$ it must have used the same technique or trite simile that was akin to pulling a simple sock inside-out, or (*Visa versa.*).

Ghosts in the machine

(*Electrical energy*)

Atoms are not solid they only appear to be, because it is only tiny electrons spinning around in their fixed orbit, like a spinning wheel, that cause this deception! And the Enigma before us is a broad concept, that incompessses objective and subjective features of the world that we think we live in! Because the theory goes from the sublime to the ridiculous!

The Riddle?

"What came first, the chicken or the egg?"

Just like the puzzle of the universe and the *enigma* of who we think *God* or the **indescribable** or **inconceivable Androgynous state is**! Wherever or whatever it is? If the concept of a divine omnipotent **being** or

God is only theoretical! And there was and is nothing really there, so to speak, if something does not exist, then we have the **question**, that something seems or appears to be looking for, because it already knows the **answer**! But it's trying to find the condition, like in mathematics! Which makes the case even stronger regarding the proof or presence of a contradictory source of all knowledge and understanding! And its means will justify the ends, one way or the other, or someone or something is using:

THE SYNAGOGUE OF SATAN
(Straight from the horse's mouth)
See Benjamin Freedmans 1961 speech at the Willard hotel.
*And the fantastic eye opening book the **synagogue of Satan**!*
(Updated, Expanded and Uncensored)
Andrew Carrington Hitchcock

And the so-called tyranny of the **"Rothschild's"** and **the promised land of organized crime** by **Dr David Duke** (*You-tube*) if they were that powerful why have they let people expose their presence? (*Pause*) and Remember what I have said, that there is **nothing more deceptive than the obvious!**

A-Moral

So it seems or appears as if something of a higher value could be using us for its own purposes, a sentient **automaton** specialist, with a **highly intelligent administrative brain**, that seems or appears to use, **analysis**, **observation** and **arithmetical calculations** to **organize** and **supply** us with our **material needs**!

Like in the 60s cult TV Show **"Star Trek"** and the episode called **"Day of The Dove"** where some entity or living force that was equal to and yet opposite to harmony and order! That was putting *humans* and *Clingons* against one another, using their own instincts of violence and mayhem at any cost! As a natural law, but as we know, evil or good is inherit in law of opposites and one cannot win over the other, so **evil** is not what we thing it is! Because it tends to defeat its own purpose!

Satan
(Who sits on high leading the blind?)

Its very probable that it is the *means* spoken of in the Christian bible, where **Jesus Christ** described how **Lucifer** would achieve or justify his own *ends*, it describes **Good** and **Evil**, or it describes, **"Dualism"** inherit in the law of opposites, **Negative/Positive**, **Life/Death**, so it seems or appears as I have already said, that its either something **Sentient** or (**the source of all knowledge and understanding!**) Or **extra-terrestrial** or **terrestrial** that could be involved!

. . .

"That darkness and destruction would come upon creation and the beast shall reign"
Revelation 21:6

STANDING ON THE SHOULDERS OF GODS
(Fiction)

So now we know that these psychopathic criminals were from a highly technologically advanced, future society that had taken a giant psycho-evolutionary step, one that had propelled them into an uncertain future. Using hybrid virtual software to boost their intellects to the dizzying heights of unparalleled social development, but like *"The picture of Doreen Grey"* this ghastly charade reflected something darker and more frightening in the shadow aspect of it's own self, like in the **THE SYNAGOGUE OF SATAN** (*Updated, Expanded and Uncensored*) by Andrew Carrington Hitchcock. About the tyranny of the *"Rothschild's"* and **the promised land of organized crime** by *Dr David Duke* (*Youtube*) if they were that powerful why have they let people expose their presence? A fact that *begs the question,* (*Pause*) and Remember what I have said, that there is nothing more deceptive than the obvious, could it be due to a simple glitch in the bio-software, where the artificial intelligence has become infected by a virus, a fatal flaw that has opened up a widow to the human psyche! Like **Dr Jeykll** and **Mr Hyde**, in a self made plague that would send them into intellectual madness, producing **Schizoid-Psychopaths**, with an **alter-ego** that would plunge the depths of the human mind and set free *monsters* from the **"ID"** in a society now haunted by the ghosts of their own imagination.

In a *Novus Ordo Seclorum* or **"New Order of the Ages"** or **World-order** modelled on **Rome**, and run by a mega corporation that had pushed the boundaries of its *pseudo-empire* to colonize the galaxy and beyond.

. . .

Like the worm in the apple or *"Hell has its price"*, *"Sua Infernum Pretium"* like that pariah *"Thomas De Torquemada"* as he awoke buried alive! All alone in the dark screaming his head off like a paper tiger! Otto also had with him a piece of ancient tablet, that would act as an amulet to protect him from spiritual harm, like a symbolic shield of sorts, against the dark forces, did the creature already know he had the stone tablet? And it had used a more subtle or clever approach, explaining to him of the pain and the suffering of the world it had to endure for his and others sake! As the mysterious figure began to dance in the shadows as it came forward revealing itself, to be none other than: **Mick Jagger** as large as life its self, singing *"Sympathy for Devil?"*

. . .

Continued:

The company's board members were like the **Senate** in **Rome** and run by the **patricians**, the **ruling elite** who ran the board and the corporation with a system of **one-hand-washes-the-other**! And as the **wheels-within-wheels** turned the mysterious chairman, a man who seemed or appeared to step out of the shadows! Would be voted in by **proxy**, raising such an inexplicable individual to the status of **Caesar**, and where the minority shareholders were like the **plebeians** or **common Roman citizens** and the workers reduced to *drones* or nothing more than **slavery**, and like the beast or emperor **Nero**! The chairman's growing madness had brought the machinery of this company or quasi-government into direct conflict with his right to rule or chair the board, having become a *despot* who had at first wore the **velvet-glove** of the *dictator* he would be forced to throw down the **steel-gauntlet** of the **tyrant,** a change that had threatened the **Pax-Romana** (*Roman peace*) by a monster who had eyes-and-ears everywhere, because of the shifting loyalties of the boardroom, having used secret assassins to kidnap and murder his political opponents, no one would dare try to oppose the chairman's power in an air of intrigue, conspiracy and deceit.

. . .
"What goes around comes around"
. . .

No one could be trusted and the **Plebs** or **Plebeians** like the Roman citizens had had enough... as the spectre of **civil war, social upheaval** and **political unrest** cast it's shadow over the company, who's machinery of government as usual appeared to do nothing about the chairman's behaviour until the **"eleventh hour"** so to speak, by the one's who knew everything, until there was nothing left to know!

Where they would be forced to act in the best interests of the company and put forward a motion of no confidence, in the chairman's eye's this was an act of treason, his divine right to rule had been challenged, to a God this was no more than blasphemy!

Because the mad chairman like **Nero** had plans to destroy the corporation in a baptism of fire and like the **Phoenix** a new world order would rise out of the old one, with the chairman as it's divine ruler, he would use the company's embryo labs to create a new gene profile, like some super hive! To produce or incubate a new type of Godless **slave** or **mindless** **drone** to labour in the dark confines, deep in the bowels of the earth called: the children of this new God! In this brave new world they would smell their way through life, as **cheep labour** or **military chattel**! In a **truly Novus Ordo Seclorum "New Order of the Ages"** or *World-order*, like **uneducated moles** or **automatons** to *serve* **the machine** or **collective** like **"Verdi's Hebrew slaves"** or as they say, who ever they are: **"out of sight and out of mind"** for the great dictator or tyrant and now new-order! That would free the people from the **anarchy** and **chaos** of that heady brew of **liberty** and *freedom*, where everyone will be truly equal!

Paul Crowe

171

Dutch Philosopher:
In the land of the spiritually and mentally blind
The one eyed man is king
Erasmus

. . .

"*Lo! Thy dread Empire, chaos! Is restored; Light dies before thy uncreating word: Thy hand great Anarch! Lets the curtain fall; and universal Darkness buries all.*"
Alexander Pope

. . .

Question

Is it the source of all **knowledge** and *understanding* retro-spectively gazing into a **metaphorical mirror**, in an attempt to convince what seems or appears to be its own reflection that it cannot exist! Like a retrospective conception or self-induced-puzzle, if you will, that seems or appears to have now caused the very problem in the first place, where does the truth lie! (*Excuse the pun*) is it a sentient being or is it a highly evolved species that seems or appears to be our kind, but not our like, who come from the past and from the future, having merged into some kind of collective objective **anthropomorphic energy** that has been created for good, but may serve for evil in the application of a mechanical morality! Who have been interfering in our (*ops*) their own or someone else's evolution in order to ambiguously control their own means to an end?

. . .

Vampyr

(Terror from the grave)
Can such things be?
The shunned house...

"*There must lie buried beneath the house one of those vampires - the dead who retain their bodily form and live on the blood or breath of the living - whose hideous legions send their preying shapes or spirits abroad by night. To destroy a vampire one must, exhume it and burn its heart, or at least drive a stake through that organ.*"
H.P Lovecraft

. . .

Dracula

"*The great box was in the same place, close against the wall, but the lid was laid on it, not fastened down, but with the nails ready in their places to be hammered home. I knew I must search the body for the key, so I raised the lid and lad it back against the wall; and then I saw something which filled my very soul with horror, there lay the count, but looking as if his youth had been half-renewed, for the white hair and moustache were changed to dark iron grey; the cheeks were fuller, and the white skin*

172

seemed ruby-red underneath; the mouth was redder than ever, for on the lips were gouts of fresh blood, which trickled from the corners of the mouth and ran over the chin and neck. Even the deep, burning eyes seemed set against swollen flesh, for the lids and pouches underneath were blotted. It seemed as if the whole awful creation were simply gorged with blood; he lay there, like a filthy leech, exhausted with his repletion.

 I shuddered as I bent over to touch him, and every sense in me revolted at the contact but I had to search, or I was lost. The coming of night might see my own *body* a banquet in a similar way to those horrid three "The women vampires he had encountered earlier on in the story". I felt all over the body, but no sign could I find of the key. Then I stopped and looked at the count. There was a mocking smile on the blotted face, which seemed to drive me mad. This was the being I was helping to transfer to London where, perhaps for centuries to come he might, amongst its teeming millions, satiate his lust for blood, and create a new and ever widening circle of semi-demons to batten on the helpless. The very thought drove me mad. A terrible desire came upon me to rid the world of such a monster.

There was no lethal weapon at hand but I seized a shovel, which the workman had been using to fill the cases, and lifting it high, struck, with the edge downward, at the hateful face. But as I did so the head turned, and the eyes fell upon me, with all their blaze of basilisk horror. The sight seemed to paralyse me, and the shovel turned in my hand glanced from the face, merely making a deep gash across the forehead. The shovel fell from my hand across the box, and as I pulled it away the flange of the blade caught the edge of the lid, which fell over again and hid the horrid thing from my sight, the last glimpse I had was of the blotted face, bloodstained and fixed with a grin of malice which would have held its own in the nethermost hell"

Bram Stoker

· · ·

Do strangers walk among us?

"Strange but true"

1951

The living dead

There is a strong rumour in the U.K. about pets particularly dogs being forcible destroyed, just before or during the Second World War, under some convenient and no doubt petty excuse!

There is only one reason why something would want this done? So you don't discover who could have been moving about in the dark streets during the blackout, where ARP (Air Raid Wardens) kept most, if not all the people of the streets, for their own good, of course!

Which is akin to the stories of the American Indians (First Nation People) in the cowboy movies, who would kill the dogs! Because they could sense them creeping up on the cavalry, because Dogs have extra senses! And will warn us, if someone or something strange is creeping about!

. . .
(Fact)

The true story of a 60yr old San Francisco widow defied a doctor's pronouncement of death... found lying in a half-filled bathtub in her apartment, an apparent suicide from an overdose of sleeping pills.

The woman was examined by a hastily summoned physician who then sent for the coroner. "The body was cold," said the doctor. "There was no detectable pulse, no reflex of the eye and no heart beat that could be picked up by a stethoscope."

Even a mirror held in front of her mouth and nostrils showed no signs of life. He said that the woman had been dead for about 10hrs...! And guessed that rigor mortis hadn't set in because of the warm water in which she had been found.

"Then the coroner examined her and he too, declared the woman dead..."
. . .

An ambulance from the morgue came to pick her up. She was strapped into a stretcher and carried out. At the mortuary reception room, as she was being wheeled in, a sharp-eyed cop saw her stir slightly. She was rushed to an emergency room where she was given oxygen and blood transfusions.

Five days later flabbergasted doctors predicted her full recovered. Up until then she had been in a coma, physicians thought she would suffer permanent injury as a result of her brain having received little oxygen from the heart, but she didn't.

Dr Thomas Albers, superintendent of the San-Francisco Hospital called the case "the most far-fetched and implausible" he had ever known...

The city health director Dr J. C. Geiger

Termed her recovery or reanimation *"extraordinary"* obviously she was so close to death "he said" that none of the standard signs of life were visible. "Any doctor would have made the same diagnosis." Another doctor said her "recovery just couldn't happen but it did!"

The Vampire of Croglin Grange

(*Fiction*)

'In My Solitary life'

By

Augustus Hare.

"Legend tells that Croglin Grange was in the hands of the Fisher Family for many centuries. In the Early 19th Century the Fishers moved from the property into larger dwellings and put the property up to let. All during the cold long winter the house was empty, who knows what ancient stirrings were aroused in its period of dereliction. As the winter passed into spring the grange was finally let to two brothers and a sister called the Cranswells. It seems that they enjoyed life to the full and soon settled in to village routine and socialised with the local people. They were well liked within the village and loved their new home very much.

One summers evening as the shadows drew long around the Grange, and the Churchyard hollow took on the blackness of night. Miss Cranswell took her leave to her bedchamber; she paused to look out of the window in the direction of the darkened churchyard at the bottom of their long lawn, and noticed something peculiar in the vicinity of the churchyard. It seemed that above the darker blackness of the gravestones, she could see two points of light moving. In time they moved from the graveyard over the shadows of the wall, moving closer on to the bottom of the lawn where they played around the churchyard wall. By this time Miss Cranswell's curiosity had given way to a deep feeling of unease, she shut the window tight bolted the door and laid down in her bed to try and get some sleep.

After a short while she checked herself for her foolish superstition and slowly drifted to slumber. On the verge of sleep she was suddenly jolted awake by a low rustling from outside the window. She twisted in bed and sat bolt upright, outside the window burning like coals in the night were two points of light, which she now recognised as the demon eyes of some humanoid creature grasping at the windowpane, she tried to scream but terror froze the sound in her throat.

The sound of rustling gave way to picking and she realised that the creature's brutish hands were unpicking the lead from the triangular panes. First one, then another of the small glass panels gave way and fell to the floor. A grey cadaver like hand reached in and pulled the latch. The window swung inwards in one slow motion and the figure climbed through the gap with a cat like ease. Miss Cranswell could now hardly breathe let alone scream for before her stood the towering figure of a man, pale, almost translucent with bright burning eyes and blood red lips.

He stepped to the bed and in one movement grasped her hair with gnarled hands, and pulled her head back as if to deliver a kiss.

The brothers, sleeping in separate rooms were aroused by a loud high-pitched scream that seemed to shake the very walls of the Grange. In a moment they were before their sisters door.

The door was locked so they smashed through with a poker, eventually breaking through into a devastating scene. There was a stench of mouldy decay in the air and upon the bed lay their sister, blood pumping from arterial gashes in her neck. One of the brothers rushed to the open window and just caught sight of a shadow flitting across the bottom of the lawn near the churchyard.

They managed to stop the blood flow and revive Miss Cranswell, the next few hours were spent in the attempt to save her life.

Miss Cranswell survived the attack and when she was strong enough to travel they took her to Switzerland to recuperate in the fresh mountain air. When the full story was in the open the brothers swore revenge on the creature, at whose nature they could only guess. When Miss Cranswell had recovered fully and heard of her brother's plans to hunt out her assailant, she persuaded her brothers to let her act as bait, and would not be dissuaded by her brothers concerns.

So it came to be that the Cranswells returned to Croglin one dark winters day. Miss Cranswell took her place in the room overlooking the churchyard, and as the moon had rose a pair of bright lights shone in the shadows of the churchyard. Once more the figure of a man appeared at the window and picked the leaded glass to gain entry to the bedchamber. This time the two brothers were lying in wait in the shadows, as the figure came to step into the room they both loosed shots at the creature.

There was a low howl and the creature sped off in the direction from whence it came. Not wishing to follow such a night creature into its domain the two brothers waited for daybreak.

First thing in the morning they took Miss Cranswell to safety and gathered all the residents of the grange around them to carry out their gruesome task. The men searched the graveyard for any signs of disturbance on finding none turned their attention to the church. All was quiet but they noticed that the crypt door was slightly ajar. Pushing into the crypt they were met with a horrific scene. All around the crypt were the scattered remains of broken coffins and gnawed human bones.

One coffin stood alone in the corner and seemed to have been left untouched by the chaos. The villagers wrenched off the coffin lid, inside wrapped in mouldy clothes was what they assumed to be a vampire. Its eyes were cold and lifeless in the daylight but a fresh pistol wound was gaping from one of the creature's legs. The villagers dragged the coffin and its demonic contents out into the churchyard and burned the lot to ashes.

Nobody seemed to know where this strange creature came from, or why it had remained dormant in the centuries of peace when the Fishers lived in the property. One can only surmise that during the period of dereliction, an age-old horror was reawakened and would not return to rest after the house was reoccupied"

The living dead
(*Fact*)

A 55-year-old-man, who has been a patient at Montefiore Hospital in the Bronx, NY. Has a strange heart condition known as Ventricular Fibrillation, caused by an unknown factor? In all recorded history it is a very rare and strange condition.

When he gets an attack, he has all the symptoms of death... His heart stops. His pulse cannot be detected. He has no sign of breathing and his blood pressure falls off to zero, and he has been pronounced dead, only to return from the grave, so to speak, as the living-dead:

. . .

Premature burial

Reality -- it is the history, which excites. As inventions, we should regard them with simple abhorrence.

I have mentioned some few of the more prominent and august calamities on record; but in these it is the extent, not less than the character of the calamity, which so vividly impresses the fancy. I need not remind the reader that, from the long and weird catalogue of human miseries, I might have selected many individual instances more replete with essential suffering than any of these vast generalities of disaster.

The true wretchedness, indeed -- the ultimate woe -- is particular, not diffuse, that the ghastly extremes of agony are endured by man the unit, and never by man the mass -- for this let us thank a merciful God!

To be buried while alive is, beyond question, the most terrific of these extremes, which has ever fallen to the lot of mere mortality. That it has frequently, very frequently, so fallen will scarcely be denied by those who think. The boundaries, which divide Life from Death, are at best shadowy and vague. Who shall say where the one ends, and where the other begins? We know that there are diseases in which occur total cessations of all the apparent functions of vitality, and yet in which these cessations are merely suspensions, properly so called.

They are only temporary pauses in the incomprehensible mechanism. A certain period elapses, and some unseen mysterious principle again sets in motion the magic pinions and the wizard wheels. The silver cord was not forever loosed, nor the golden bowl irreparably broken. But where, meantime, was the soul?

Apart, however, from the inevitable conclusion, a priori that such causes must produce such effects - -- that the well-known occurrence of such cases of suspended animation must naturally give rise, now and then, to premature interments -- apart from this consideration, we have the direct testimony of medical and ordinary experience to prove that a vast number of such interments have actually taken place. I might refer at once, if necessary to a hundred well-authenticated instances. One of very remarkable character, and of which the circumstances may be fresh in the

177

memory of some of my readers, occurred, not very long ago, in the neighbouring city of Baltimore, where it occasioned a painful, intense, and widely-extended excitement. The wife of one of the most respectable citizens-a lawyer of eminence and a member of Congress -- was seized with a sudden and unaccountable illness, which completely baffled the skill of her physicians. After much suffering she died, or was supposed to die.

No one suspected, indeed, or had reason to suspect, that she was not actually dead. She presented all the ordinary appearances of death. The face assumed the usual pinched and sunken outline. The lips were of the usual marble pallor. The eyes were lustreless. There was no warmth. Pulsation had ceased. For three days the body was preserved unburied, during which it had acquired a stony rigidity. The funeral, in short, was hastened, on account of the rapid advance of what was supposed to be decomposition.

The lady was deposited in her family vault, which, for three subsequent years, was undisturbed. At the expiration of this term it was opened for the reception of a sarcophagus; - -- but, alas! How fearful a shock awaited the husband, who, personally, threw open the door! As its portals swung outwardly back, some white-apparelled object fell rattling within his arms. It was the skeleton of his wife in her yet un-moulded shroud.

A careful investigation rendered it evident that she had revived within two days after her entombment; that her struggles within the coffin had caused it to fall from a ledge, or shelf to the floor, where it was so broken as to permit her escape. A lamp, which had been accidentally left, full of oil, within the tomb, was found empty; it might have been exhausted, however, by evaporation. On the uttermost of the steps, which led down into the dread chamber, was a large fragment of the coffin, with which, it seemed, that she had endeavoured to arrest attention by striking the iron door. While thus occupied, she probably swooned, or possibly died, through sheer terror; and,

The lady was deposited in her family vault, which, for three subsequent years, was undisturbed. At the expiration of this term it was opened for the reception of a sarcophagus; - -- but, alas! How fearful a shock awaited the husband, who, personally, threw open the door! As its portals swung outwardly back, some white-apparelled object fell rattling within his arms. It was the skeleton of his wife in her yet un-moulded shroud.

A careful investigation rendered it evident that she had revived within two days after her entombment; that her struggles within the coffin had caused it to fall from a ledge, or shelf to the floor, where it was so broken as to permit her escape. A lamp, which had been accidentally left, full of oil, within the tomb, was found empty; it might have been exhausted, however, by evaporation. On the uttermost of the steps, which led down into the dread chamber, was a large fragment of the coffin, with which, it seemed, that she had endeavoured to arrest attention by striking the iron door. While thus occupied, she probably swooned, or possibly died, through sheer terror; and, and, she was aroused by the caresses of her lover from the lethargy, which had been mistaken for death.

He bore her frantically to his lodgings in the village. He employed certain powerful restoratives suggested by no little medical learning. In fine, she revived. She recognized her preserver. She remained with him until, by slow degrees, she fully recovered her original health. Her woman's heart was not adamant, and this last lesson of love sufficed to soften it. She bestowed it upon Bossuet. She returned no more to her husband, but, concealing from him her resurrection, fled with her lover to America.

Twenty years afterward, the two returned to France, in the persuasion that time had so greatly altered the lady's appearance that her friends would be unable to recognize her. They were mistaken, however, for, at the first meeting, Monsieur Renelle did actually recognize and make claim to his wife. This claim she resisted, and a judicial tribunal sustained her in her resistance, deciding that the peculiar circumstances, with the long lapse of years, had extinguished, not only equitably, but legally, the authority of the husband.

The "Chirurgical Journal" of Leipzig -- a periodical of high authority and merit, which some American bookseller would do well to translate and republish, records in a late number a very distressing event of the character in question.

An officer of artillery, a man of gigantic stature and of robust health, being thrown from an unmanageable horse, received a very severe contusion upon the head, which rendered him insensible at once; the skull was slightly fractured, but no immediate danger was apprehended. Trepanning was accomplished successfully. He was bled, and many other of the ordinary means of relief were adopted. Gradually, however, he fell into a more and more hopeless state of stupor, and, finally, it was thought that he died.

The weather was warm, and he was buried with indecent haste in one of the public cemeteries.

His funeral took place on Thursday. On the Sunday following, the grounds of the cemetery were, as usual, much thronged with visitors, and about noon an intense excitement was created by the declaration of a peasant that, while sitting upon the grave of the officer, he had distinctly felt a commotion of the earth, as if occasioned by some one struggling beneath. At first little attention was paid to the man's asseveration; but his evident terror, and the dogged obstinacy with which he persisted in his story, had at length their natural effect upon the crowd. Spades were hurriedly procured, and the grave, which was shamefully shallow, was in a few minutes so far thrown open that the head of its occupant appeared. He was then seemingly dead; but he sat nearly erect within his coffin, the lid of which, in his furious struggles, he had partially uplifted.

He was forthwith conveyed to the nearest hospital, and there pronounced to be still living, although in an asphytic condition. After some hours he revived, recognized individuals of his acquaintance, and, in broken sentences spoke of his agonies in the grave.

From what he related, it was clear that he must have been conscious of life for more than an hour, while inhumed, before lapsing into insensibility.

The grave was carelessly and loosely filled with an exceedingly porous soil; and thus some air was necessarily admitted. He heard the footsteps of the crowd overhead, and endeavoured to make himself heard in turn. It was the tumult within the grounds of the cemetery, he said, which appeared to awaken him from a deep sleep, but no sooner was he awake than he became fully aware of the awful horrors of his position.

This patient, it is recorded, was doing well and seemed to be in a fair way of ultimate recovery, but fell a victim to the quackeries of medical experiment. The galvanic battery was applied, and he suddenly expired in one of those ecstatic paroxysms, which, occasionally, it super induces.

The mention of the galvanic battery, nevertheless, recalls to my memory a well-known and very extraordinary case in point, where its action proved the means of restoring to animation a young attorney of London, who had been interred for two days. This occurred in 1831, and created, at the time, a very profound sensation wherever it was made the subject of converse.

The patient, Mr. Edward Stapleton, had died, apparently of typhus fever, accompanied with some anomalous symptoms, which had excited the curiosity of his medical attendants. Upon his seeming decease, his friends were requested to sanction a post-mortem examination, but declined to permit it. As often happens, when such refusals are made, the practitioners resolved to disinter the body and dissect it at leisure, in private. Arrangements were easily effected with some of the numerous corps of body snatchers, with which London abounds; and, upon the third night after the funeral, the supposed corpse was unearthed from a grave eight feet deep, and deposited in the opening chamber of one of the private hospitals.

An incision of some extent had been actually made in the abdomen, when the fresh and undecayed appearance of the subject suggested an application of the battery. One experiment succeeded another, and the customary effects supervened, with nothing to characterize them in any respect, except, upon one or two occasions, a more than ordinary degree of life-likeness in the convulsive action.

It grew late. The day was about to dawn; and it was thought expedient, at length, to proceed at once to the dissection. A student, however, was especially desirous of testing a theory of his own, and insisted upon applying the battery to one of the pectoral muscles. A rough gash was made, and a wire hastily brought in contact, when the patient, with a hurried but quite unconvulsive movement, arose from the table, stepped into the middle of the floor, gazed about him uneasily for a few seconds, and then -- spoke. What he said was unintelligible, but words were uttered; the syllabification was distinct. Having spoken, he fell heavily to the floor.

For some moments all were paralysed with awe -- but the urgency of the case soon restored them their presence of mind. It was seen that Mr. Stapleton was alive, although in a swoon. Upon exhibition of ether he revived and was rapidly restored to health, and to the society of his friends -- from whom, however, all knowledge of his resuscitation was withheld, until a relapse was no longer to be apprehended. Their wonder -- their rapturous astonishment -- may be conceived.

The most thrilling peculiarity of this incident, nevertheless, is involved in what Mr. S. himself asserts. He declares that at no period was he altogether insensible -- that, dully and confusedly, he was aware of everything which happened to him, from the moment in which he was pronounced dead by his physicians, to that in which he fell swooning to the floor of the hospital. "I am alive," were the uncomprehended words which, upon recognizing the locality of the dissecting-room, he had endeavoured, in his extremity, to utter.

It were an easy matter to multiply such histories as these -- but I forbear -- for, indeed, we have no need of such to establish the fact that premature interments occur.

When we reflect how very rarely, from the nature of the case, we have it in our power to detect them; we must admit that they may frequently occur without our cognisance. Scarcely, in truth, is a graveyard ever encroached upon, for any purpose, to any great extent, that skeletons are not found in postures, which suggest the most fearful of suspicions.

Fearful indeed the suspicion -- but more fearful the doom! It may be asserted, without hesitation, that no event is so terribly well adapted to inspire the supreme ness of bodily and of mental distress, as is burial before death. The unendurable oppression of the lungs -- the stifling fumes from the damp earth -- the clinging to the death garments -- the rigid embrace of the narrow house -- the blackness of the absolute Night -- the silence like a sea that overwhelms -- the unseen but palpable presence of the Conqueror Worm -- these things, with the thoughts of the air and grass above, with memory of dear friends who would fly to save us if but informed of our fate, and with consciousness that of this fate they can never be informed -- that our hopeless portion is that of the really dead -- these considerations, I say, carry into the heart, which still palpitates, a degree of appalling and intolerable horror from which the most daring imagination must recoil. We know of nothing so agonizing upon Earth -- we can dream of nothing half so hideous in the realms of the nethermost Hell.

And thus all narratives upon this topic have an interest profound; an interest, nevertheless, which, through the sacred awe of the topic itself, very properly and very peculiarly depends upon our conviction of the truth of the matter narrated. What I have now to tell is of my own actual knowledge -- of my own positive and personal experience.

For several years I had been subject to attacks of the singular disorder, which physicians have agreed to term catalepsy, in default of a more definitive title. Although both the immediate and the predisposing causes, and even the actual diagnosis, of this disease are still mysterious, its obvious and apparent character is sufficiently well understood. Its variations seem to be chiefly of degree. Sometimes the patient lies, for a day only, or even for a shorter period, in a species of exaggerated lethargy. He is senseless and externally motionless; but the pulsation of the heart is still faintly perceptible; some traces of warmth remain; a slight colour lingers within the centre of the cheek; and, upon application of a mirror to the lips, we can detect a torpid, unequal, and vacillating action of the lungs. Then again the duration of the trance is for weeks -- even for months; while the closest scrutiny, and the most rigorous medical tests, fail to establish any material distinction between the state of the sufferer and what we conceive of absolute death. Very usually he is saved from premature interment solely by the knowledge of his friends that he has been previously subject to catalepsy, by the consequent suspicion excited, and, above all, by the non-appearance of decay.

The advances of the malady are, luckily, gradual. The first manifestations, although marked, are unequivocal. The fits grow successively more and more distinctive, and endure each for a longer term than the preceding. In this lies the principal security from inhumation. The unfortunate whose first attack should be of the extreme character, which is occasionally seen, would almost inevitably be consigned alive to the tomb.

My own case differed in no important particular from those mentioned in medical books. Sometimes, without any apparent cause, I sank, little by little, into a condition of hemi-syncope, or half swoon; and, in this condition, without pain, without ability to stir, or, strictly speaking, to think, but with a dull lethargic consciousness of life and of the presence of those who surrounded my bed, I remained, until the crisis of the disease restored me, suddenly, to perfect sensation.

At other times I was quickly and impetuously smitten. I grew sick, and numb, and chilly, and dizzy, and so fell prostrate at once. Then, for weeks, all was void, and black, and silent, and nothing became the universe. Total annihilation could be no more.

From these latter attacks I awoke, however, with a gradation slow in proportion to the suddenness of the seizure. Just as the day dawns to the friendless and houseless beggar who roams the streets throughout the long desolate winter night -- just so tardily -- just so wearily -- just so cheerily came back the light of the Soul to me. Just so wearily -- just so cheerily came back the light of the Soul to me.

Apart from the tendency to trance, however, my general health appeared to be good; nor could I perceive that it was at all affected by the one prevalent malady -- unless, indeed, an idiosyncrasy in my ordinary sleep may be looked upon as super induced.

Upon awaking from slumber, I could never gain, at once, thorough possession of my senses, and always remained, for many minutes, in much bewilderment and perplexity; -- the mental faculties in general, but the memory in especial, being in a condition of absolute abeyance.

In all that I endured there was no physical suffering but of moral distress infinitude. My fancy grew charnel, I talked "of worms, of tombs, and epitaphs." I was lost in reveries of death, and the idea of premature burial held continual possession of my brain.

The ghastly Danger to which I was subjected haunted me day and night. In the former, the torture of meditation was excessive -- in the latter, supreme. When the grim Darkness overspread the Earth, then, with every horror of thought, I shook -- shook as the quivering plumes upon the hearse. When Nature could endure wakefulness no longer, it was with a struggle that I consented to sleep -- for I shuddered to reflect that, upon awaking, I might find myself the tenant of a grave. And when, finally, I sank into slumber, it was only to rush at once into a world of phantasms, above which, with vast, sable, overshadowing wing, hovered, predominant, the one sepulchral Idea.

. . .

From the innumerable images of gloom, which thus oppressed me in dreams, I select for record but a solitary vision. Me thought I was immersed in a cataleptic trance of more than usual duration and profundity. Suddenly there came an icy hand upon my forehead, and an impatient, gibbering voice whispered the word "Arise!" within my ear.

I sat erect. The darkness was total. I could not see the figure of him who had aroused me. I could call to mind neither the period at which I had fallen into the trance, nor the locality in which I then lay. While I remained motionless, and busied in endeavours to collect my thought, the cold hand grasped me fiercely by the wrist, shaking it petulantly, while the gibbering voice said again:

"Arise! Did I not bid thee arise?"

"And who," I demanded, "Art thou?"

"I have no name in the regions which I inhabit," replied the voice, mournfully; "I was mortal, but am fiend. I was merciless, but am pitiful. Thou dost feel that I shudder. -- My teeth chatter as I speak; yet it is not with the chilliness of the night -- of the night without end.

But this hideousness is insufferable. How canst thou tranquilly sleep? I cannot rest for the cry of these great agonies. These sights are more than I can bear. Get thee up! Come with me into the outer Night, and let me unfold to thee the graves. Is not this a spectacle of woe? -- Behold!"

I looked; and the unseen figure, which still grasped me by the wrist, had caused to be thrown open the graves of all mankind, and from each issued the faint phosphoric radiance of decay, so that I could see into the innermost recesses, and there view the shrouded bodies in their sad and solemn slumbers with the worm. But alas! The real sleepers were fewer, by many millions, than those who slumbered not at all; and there was a feeble struggling; and there was a general sad unrest; and from out the depths of the countless pits there came a melancholy rustling from the garments of the buried. And of those who seemed tranquilly to repose, I saw that a vast number had changed, in a greater or less degree, the rigid and uneasy position in which they had originally been entombed. And the voice again said to me as I gazed:

"Is it not -- oh? Is it not a pitiful sight?" -- but, before I could find words to reply, the figure had ceased to grasp my wrist, the phosphoric lights expired, and the graves were closed with a sudden violence, while from out them arose a tumult of despairing cries, saying again: "Is it not -- O, God, is it not a very pitiful sight?"

Phantasies such as these, presenting themselves at night, extended their terrific influence far into my waking hours. My nerves became thoroughly unstrung, and I fell a prey to perpetual horror. I hesitated to ride, or to walk, or to indulge in any exercise that would carry me from home.

In fact, I no longer dared trust myself out of the immediate presence of those who were aware of my proneness to catalepsy, lest, falling into one of my usual fits, I should be buried before my real condition could be ascertained. I doubted the care, the fidelity of my dearest friends. I dreaded that, in some trance of more than customary duration, they might be prevailed upon to regard me as irrecoverable.

I even went so far as to fear that, as I occasioned much trouble, they might be glad to consider any very protracted attack as sufficient excuse for getting rid of me altogether. It was in vain they endeavoured to reassure me by the most solemn promises.

I exacted the most sacred oaths, that under no circumstances they would bury me until decomposition had so materially advanced as to render farther preservation impossible. And, even then, my mortal terrors would listen to no reason -- would accept no consolation.

I entered into a series of elaborate precautions. Among other things, I had the family vault so remodelled as to admit of being readily opened from within. The slightest pressure upon a long lever that extended far into the tomb would cause the iron portal to fly back.

There were arrangements also for the free admission of air and light, and convenient receptacles for food and water, within immediate reach of the coffin intended for my reception. This coffin was warmly and softly padded, and was provided with a lid, fashioned upon the principle of the vault-door, with the addition of springs so contrived that the feeblest movement of the body would be sufficient to set it at liberty. Besides all this, there was suspended from the roof of the tomb, a large bell, the rope of which, it was designed, should extend through a hole in the coffin, and so be fastened to one of the hands of the corpse.

But, alas? What avails the vigilance against the Destiny of man? Not even these well-contrived securities sufficed to save from the uttermost agonies of living inhumation, a wretch to these agonies foredoomed!

There arrived an epoch -- as often before there had arrived -- in which I found myself emerging from total unconsciousness into the first feeble and indefinite sense of existence. Slowly -- with a tortoise gradation -- approached the faint grey dawn of the psychal day.

A torpid uneasiness. An apathetic endurance of dull pain. No care -- no hope -- no effort. Then, after a long interval, a ringing in the ears; then, after a lapse still longer, a prickling or tingling sensation in the extremities; then a seemingly eternal period of pleasurable quiescence, during which the awakening feelings are struggling into thought; then a brief re-sinking into non-entity; then a sudden recovery. At length the slight quivering of an eyelid, and immediately thereupon, an electric shock of a terror, deadly and indefinite, which sends the blood in torrents from the temples to the heart.

And now the first positive effort to think. And now the first endeavour to remember.

And now a partial and evanescent success. And now the memory has so far regained its dominion, that, in some measure, I am cognizant of my state. I feel that I am not awaking from ordinary sleep. I recollect that I have been subject to catalepsy. And now, at last, as if by the rush of an ocean, my shuddering spirit is overwhelmed by the one grim Danger -- by the one spectral and ever-prevalent idea.

For some minutes after this fancy possessed me, I remained without motion. And why? I could not summon courage to move. I dared not make the effort, which was to satisfy me of my fate -- and yet there was something at my heart, which whispered me, it was sure. Despair -- such as no other species of wretchedness ever calls into being -- despair alone urged me, after long irresolution, to uplift the heavy lids of my eyes. I uplifted them. It was dark -- all dark. I knew that the fit was over. I knew that the crisis of my disorder had long passed. I knew that I had now fully recovered the use of my visual faculties -- and yet it was dark -- all dark -- the intense and utter raylessness of the Night that endureth for evermore.

I endeavoured to shriek-, and my lips and my parched tongue moved convulsively together in the attempt -- but no voice issued from the cavernous lungs, which oppressed as if by the weight of some incumbent mountain, gasped and palpitated, with the heart, at every elaborate and struggling inspiration.

The movement of the jaws, in this effort to cry aloud, showed me that they were bound up, as is usual with the dead. I felt, too, that I lay upon some hard substance, and by something similar my sides were, also, closely compressed. So far, I had not ventured to stir any of my limbs -- but now I violently threw up my arms, which had been lying at length, with the wrists crossed. They struck a solid wooden substance, which extended above my person at an elevation of not more than six inches from my face. I could no longer doubt that I reposed within a coffin at last.

And now, amid all my infinite miseries, came sweetly the cherub Hope -- for I thought of my precautions. I writhed, and made spasmodic exertions to force open the lid: it would not move. I felt my wrists for the bell-rope: it was not to be found. And now the Comforter fled for ever, and a still sterner Despair reigned triumphant; for I could not help perceiving the absence of the paddings which I had so carefully prepared -- and then, too, there came suddenly to my nostrils the strong peculiar odour of moist earth. The conclusion was irresistible. I was not within the vault. I had fallen into a trance while absent from home-while among strangers -- when, or how, I could not remember -- and it was they who had buried me as a dog -- nailed up in some common coffin -- and thrust deep, deep, and for ever, into some ordinary and nameless grave.

As this awful conviction forced itself, thus, into the innermost chambers of my soul, I once again struggled to cry aloud. And in this second endeavour I succeeded. A long, wild, and continuous shriek, or yell of agony, resounded through the realms of the subterranean Night.

"Hillo! Hillo, there!" said a gruff voice, in reply.

"What the devil's the matter now!" said a second.

"Get out o' that!" Said a third.

"What do you mean by yowling in that ere kind of style, like a catty mount?" said a fourth; and hereupon I was seized and shaken without ceremony, for several minutes, by a junto of very rough-looking individuals. They did not arouse me from my slumber -- for I was wide-awake when I screamed -- but they restored me to the full possession of my memory.

This adventure occurred near Richmond, in Virginia. Accompanied by a friend, I had proceeded, upon a gunning expedition, some miles down the banks of the James River. Night approached, and we were overtaken by a storm. The cabin of a small sloop lying at anchor in the stream, and laden with garden mould, afforded us the only available shelter. We made the best of it, and passed the night on board. I slept in one of the only two berths in the vessel -- and the berths of a sloop of sixty or twenty tons need scarcely be described.

That which I occupied had no bedding of any kind. Its extreme width was eighteen inches. The distance of its bottom from the deck overhead was precisely the same. I found it a matter of exceeding difficulty to squeeze myself in. Nevertheless, I slept soundly, and the whole of my vision -- for it was no dream, and no nightmare -- arose naturally from the circumstances of my position -- from my ordinary bias of thought -- and from the difficulty, to which I have alluded, of collecting my senses, and especially of regaining my memory, for a long time after awaking from slumber.

The men who shook me were the crew of the sloop, and some labourers engaged to unload it. From the load itself came the earthly smell. The bandage about the jaws was a silk handkerchief in which I had bound up my head, in default of my customary nightcap.

The tortures endured, however, were indubitably quite equal for the time, to those of actual sepulture. They were fearfully -- they were inconceivably hideous; but out of Evil proceeded Good; for they're very excess wrought in my spirit an inevitable revulsion.

My soul acquired tone -- acquired temper. I went abroad. I took vigorous exercise. I breathed the free air of Heaven. I thought upon other subjects than Death. I discarded my medical books.

"Buchan" I burned. I read no "Night Thoughts" -- no fustian about churchyards -- no bugaboo tales -- such as this. In short, I became a new man, and lived a man's life. From that memorable night, I dismissed forever my charnel apprehensions, and with them vanished the cataleptic disorder, of which, perhaps, they had been less the consequence than the cause.

There are moments when, even to the sober eye of Reason, the world of our sad Humanity may assume the semblance of a Hell -- but the imagination of man is no Carathis, to explore with impunity its every cavern. Alas! The grim legion of sepulchral terrors cannot be regarded as altogether fanciful -- but, like the Demons in whose company Afrasiab made his voyage down the Oxus, they must sleep, or they will devour us -- they must be suffered to slumber, or we perish.

Edgar Allen Poe

. . .

Carmilla

Fiction

Sheridan La Fanu

"I concealed myself in the dark dressing-room that opened upon the poor patients room, in which a candle was burning, and watched there till she was fast asleep, I stood at the door, peeping through the small crevice, my sword laid on the table beside me, as my directions prescribed, until, a little after one, I saw a large black object, very ill-defined, crawl, as it seemed to me over the foot of the bed, and swiftly spread itself up to the poor girl's throat, where it swelled, in a moment, into a great palpitating mass.

For a few moments I stood petrified, I now sprang forward, with my sword in my hand, the black creature suddenly contracted towards the foot of the bed, glided over it, and, standing on the floor about a yard from the bed, with a glare of skulking ferocity and horror fixed on me..."

. . .

STANDING ON THE SHOULDERS OF GODS
(The Witching Hour)

"And there in the strand as the clock **struck 13**! The esteemed gathering had vanished like the building, into thin air, and even to this day if you try and find out anything about this ghostly property, you will meet with a wall of silence! And there the jolly fat showman had showed the kids his amazing exhibit of the **Vampire** lying in its coffin by day, and as darkness falls, it would rise from its grave in the dead of night, inside every child's imagination, even to this day the **Vampire** still lurks in the back of our mind, with its unnatural existence, a creature that can take on any form or be who you expect them to be!

It could be someone you know or trust, and by then it would be too late... much like the British 80s TV programme about a psychic who investigates the strange and the odd cases, like the legend from Eastern Europe in the episode called the **"Dybbuk"** or *tree-spirit* that takes on the shape or essence of the dearly departed or people and pets you once knew, if you have inadvertently come into contact with any object made from the wood of these haunted trees, a coffin! Or even a simple wooden figure that would grow into a hideous creature that tore them apart!

And if you are brave enough or stupid enough, you can find them in old abandoned empty houses or in dark eerie cellars and in other places that you are not supposed to go! Or you might be unlucky enough to bump into them, in the subway or when you are alone in a crowd! Just like the woman in the England of the Swinging Sixties, it could have been any woman sitting reading their paperback novel, as they sometimes do:

187

Terror On The Underground

"A story that was set in the 1880s, with its horse-drawn Hansom Cabs, out in the eerie fog and gas light streets of Victorian London, and the driver on the dead body train! That carried, that's right, you guessed it, nothing but dead passengers, a gruesome spectacle on the graveyard shift of life's mortality, and bound for the Mortuary or the Hospital! No need to dig up or be-spoil the dead, like the Body snatchers or Resurectionists, Burke and Hare, it was all legal now and above board, and with no money for the luxury of even a grave, the poor whether they liked it or not, were unceremoniously destined for the finality of the dissection table, in the name of humanity of course!

And here among the Phantoms and the Spectres of London's underground, here at the threshold between two worlds, the reader had begun her unquiet journey on the oldest Underground railway in the world, and one of the most Haunted places in Britain.

A chilling place that had been constructed in the 19th Century and had pushed its way through, Plague Pit's, Church Crypts and old Cemeteries, and having disturbed the dead, something has returned to Haunt the place, a place where you are truly never alone, a place with its accidental Death's, Suicides and Murders, all this and more, like the story that had been supposedly told to someone by a mysterious passenger in the queerest of garb or cloths from the early part of the nineteenth century, who spoke of the disastrous cave in during the early days of construction, where the passengers had been trapped for days, and when they were finally rescued, some of them had went off their heads, and had begun to eat the other dead passengers, or so the story or more to the point the rumour goes, as we continue our ill fated and Macabre journey, with the train pushing on and on through the dark tunnels, under the very streets of the Capital, with the helpless driver growing more and more uneasy with each passing moment, as he listened, he could hear that little voice in his own head, and feel the blood pounding in his ears, as he remembered the story of the headless corpse seen on the Underground, as if it was actually riding on the train, after the mad killer had been caught with the severed head, wrapped up in a brown paper parcel, soaked in blood, inside the ladies lavatory or toilet, where he had been caught dressed as a woman!"

Paul Crowe

Read me
The Idolatry of the ages
And theTitanomachy
Or
Divine war

And the "*Divom deus*" or "*God of Gods*" like a voice crying in the wilderness: "***The King is dead, long live the king***" or "***Rex mortuus est. vivat rex.***" Said the reflection in gods *dark mirror!*

" . . . And there fell a great star from heaven, burning as it were a lamp, and it fell upon the third part of the rivers, and upon the fountains of the waters"

> **Revelation** *(8:10:11)*

"How art thou fallen from heaven *O Lucifer, son of the morning*, in the propagation of *Satan's Kingdom*, not of the seed of Adam are we, Nor is Abraham our father, but of the seed of the proud angel driven from heaven!"

> **Isaiah** *(XiV, 12)*

Oedipus Rex
Adam's Rib

A strange paragraph in the King James Bible: "And God (*singular*) said: let us make man in our image! (*Plural*) After our likeness! And God (*Singular*) formed man from the dust of the ground, and breathed into his nostrils the breath of life: and man became a living soul!

To The Manner Born

And the Lord (*Singular*) said behold, the man has become like us (*plural*) who then went on to describe the way *Eve* had been created, not from the dust of the earth, but from *Adam*!

And the Lord caused a deep sleep to fall upon *Adam* and he slept: and he took (*Singular*) one of his ribs, and closed up the flesh instead thereof, and the rib which the Lord had taken from man, and she shall be called woman! And brought her unto the man, and this is now bone of my bones and flesh of my flesh!

Lilith
Dichotomy

"*Then, brothers, it came. Oh, bliss, bliss and heaven. I lay all nagoy to the ceiling, my gulliver on my rookers on the pillow, glazzies closed, rot open in bliss, slooshying the sluice of lovely sounds. Oh, it was gorgeousness and gorgeosity made flesh.*"

> **– Anthony Burgess, A Clockwork Orange**

Who was closely associated with the Babylonian night-demon 'Lilitu' or the Hebrew *Lilith*, (*Eve*) who was the first wife of *Adam*, and a *mother of devils*. She is a spirit of *uncleanness*! Who produced *Cain* and *Abel*!

"What hast thou done? The voice of they brother's blood crieth unto me from the ground! And now art thou cursed from the earth, which hath opened her mouth to receive thy brothers blood from thy hand."

Could this not be the answer!

(Is it time-travellers?)

Extra-terrestrials or Terrestrials?

Is it no more than a symbolic story of a genetic breeding programme? By *highly evolved extra-terrestrials or terrestrials?* From the past and or future! Who seem or appear to be *malevolent* or *benevolent* collective beings that are very probably our kind, but not our like! Which is highly unlikely, that they have some kind of affinity with ourselves, but they seem or appear to be trying to manipulate or tweak the final outcome by using an invisible *hand* that has, and is behind what has been happening in our *Anthropological, Sociological* and *Theological* history, as we now inexorably slide towards the abyss or final outcome, by the means that will justify the ends! Through a pseudo scientific *anthropological, sociological* and *theological conundrum,* where the author of the piece, the international "*Dybbuk*" (An Eastern European name for an unclean spirit!) with its evolved and organized capitalism or working instrumentality, the banking system in the form of the "house of Rothschild" inadvertently acts like a reflection cast upon a mirror or looking-glass, that indirectly revaluates our *moral behaviour*...

Gods from a machine

"Deus ex Machina"

"We are not the first nor the last"

To try and understand the puzzle that we are confronted with, we need to put the cart before the proverbial horse, so to speak or what came first, the *chicken* or the *egg?* Because the truth is a theoretical paper chase that tends to say one thing and mean another! And just when you think you have found the answer, you discover that you have been going round in a circle chasing your own tail, so to speak! Which seems or appears to be a problem that leaves us with more questions than answers, concerning the bigger picture:

$$E=MC2$$

Energy=Mass=Energy

Someone or something could be controlling or interfering with these streams of quantum *time!* Or "*Dé jà vu*" from the French, literally "*already seen*", is the phenomenon of having the strong sensation that an event or experience currently being experienced has been experienced in the past, whether it has actually happened or not!

And we can only feel the results of the positive or negitive behaviour of this slip-stream, in the experiences of "*Dé jà vu*" through our own **Anthropological, Socialogical** and **Theological past**, to understand the event, in relation to its cause!

What goes around comes around

I will repeat this theoretical chunk of *Anthropological*, *Sociological* and *Theological* history, because it is the only link in the metaphorical-chain that fits the fragmented picture! Like in my fiction novel called: **"Standing on the shoulders of Gods"** it has to be repeated again for good measure, about...

"The Enigma"
(Electrical-enersia)

And yet all matter is to be regarded as simply a mode or expression of *transient energy*, so what is energy and where is it coming and going to? because as science knows, you can't create it or destroy it! **Matter=energy** and **energy=matter**, and that both states of matter can be altered, but they cannot be destroyed! As in the **Ex nil, nihil fit** *"From nothing, nothing is made"*

Transient energy
(And other dimentions)

There is of course, something to which atoms correspond, something of which they are a manifistation : but that something is intangible, and there's the rub for the materialism its age-long advantage of appealing to the sense of touch; in which we are apt to believe so heartly, has been taken away. However real a marble may feel to us that peculiar sense of reality can no longer be appealed to or utilised by the materialist, his theory is now on a level with other theories, and can make no special appeal to this biased judge for the marble dispute and its convincing air of solidity, must yet be convinced by us, if we are to except the verdict of science at all—as materialism constantly asserts that we must in terms not of hard atoms as resistant as itself, but in terms of electrons which, we are now taught, have no mass that is not **"electrical-inersia."** And the only ultimate reality is *(electical inersia)*

Our knowledge of the external world is limited, and conditioned by the limits and conditions of our own minds; it is knowledge, not of reality but of appearances. The reality that lies behind these appearences, must be in its essence not dissimilar to the perceiving mind itself.

Berkeley

Who over hears us saying that "all we are aware of are changes in our own consciousness" "can you not see, then" he would say. "that what you are aware of and what you are alone aware of, is all that is?" Material things have no objective exsistance—no exsistance outside yourselves.

The external world which you persist in postulating as the *Noumenon* or *substance*. The attrubutes of which cause changes in your consciousness is a figment of your imagination, the abstract, the invisable, the impalpable is for most minds more or less of a fiction it does not rely exsist.

"If a tree falls in the forest, and if no one is there to hear it, does it make a sound?"

Because time does not apply to the **Androgynous state**! And time and space seem to be there, and yet at the same time they are not there!

Like matter that appears to be solid or the bicycle wheel effect with it's little *electrons* whirling endlessly in space, or the void, as if held in a *unified-field* by some unknown energy around the nucleus of this *phantom or theoretical atom!*

Like Shakespeare put it: *Is our fate in ourselves or in our stars?* Is our life a second hand one or are we spoiled goods! Where our autonomy or free will is something that is handed down to us, even though it seems or appears that we have the free will to choice from an infinite number of possibilities, they have already been chosen for us! Implying the hand of fate has already dealt the cards, and the future or for that matter the past is already self-ordained, before we are even born into the world! Or is it?

Dual Destiny

The answer is *yes* and *no*, like an infinite and vast intelligence running on a **binomial** or **binary system** namely **1-or-0**, Vis-à-vis it means its quantum-physics **yes** and **no**... which is a half-truth or **Deo non Fortuna**, meaning by: **God,** not by **chance**, or at the hands of **capricious Gods** and the twisted hand of *fate!*

It is like king Solomon's cyclic view of destiny?
'For everything its season, and for every activity under heaven its time: a time to be born and a time to die...Whatever is has been already, and Whatever is to come has been already, and God summons each event back in turn'
Eccl. 3: 1, 2, 15.

Just like the puzzle of the universe and the enigma of *God* or the *indescribable* or *inconceivable Androgynous state?* Wherever or whatever it is!

Is **"Christ"**, **"Quetzalcohuātl"** or anything out of the ordinary being constructed by this great machine to relay the meaning of life or the "Grand-plan" as they say, without the restrictions inherent on this plane, or **"physical level"** by using something like **"advanced-molecular-nano-bots"** or...

Pseudo-code

The purpose of using *pseudo-code* is that it is easier for people or us! To understand, than conventional programming language code, and that it is an efficient and environment-independent description of the key principles of an...

algorithm

It is commonly used in textbooks and scientific publications that are documenting various algorithms, and also in planning of computer program development, for sketching out the structure of the program before the actual coding takes place.

So they could be light-years ahead of us, and could have literally constructed a time-machine or something along these lines? Remember, matter cannot be created or destroyed! So where is it coming from and going to? *It's very probible that it is the proverbial itch that you can't scratch, but its highly unlikely*, that it is being caused by a highly evolved being that is technically, our own evolved selves! That seems or appears to have constructed an advanced bio-computer, that we have assumed to be a sentient anthropomorphic being called: **"God?"**

"Remember, one thing does not nessesarily mean the other!"
So the enigma before us is a broad concept, that incompessses objective and subjective features of the world that we think we live in! Read my fictionlized novel: **"Standing on the shoulders of gods"** Because the theory in that book goes from the *sublime* to the *ridiculous!* Because we seem or appear to be ignorant of the real nature of this underlying tradgedy or reality.

Are we dealing with some kind of being that seems or appears to have always been! And who exists in some strange place? And who apparently has two different sides to its supernature, one that is diametrically oppossed to anything that is evil and wrong! And seems or appears to be trying to save us in spite of ourselves, and prophets or philosophers who mysteriously appear like: **"Quetzalcoatl"** and **"Christ"** who have some mysterious connection with it, and if we are all part of "*God*" then its as if we are writing a letter to ones self, figuritively speaking, in order to try and understand and hormonize, what appears to be two opposing polarities or the metaphor of a symbolic *battle* between the **"Raven"** and the **"Dove"** and that we are literally chasing our own tail's, so to speak, in order to realize that the balance of these **positive** and **negitive polarities** need to be canceled out, by this anti-virus or symbolic method, where the means will justify the ends!

And this being seems or appears to be multi-faceted in some way or **"3D"** (*three dimentional*) with its collective-energies struggling within itself, like a reflection in a mirror, and these collective energies who seem or appear to have the knowledge, are trying to tweek existance, or what is euphamistically called a movment in the void, so to speak, and the diacotomy of this non-corporeal being has inadvertantly brought the world that we think we live in, into temporal exsistance, or "something has!" which Seems or appears to be a refference point, for reasons best known to this non-corporal being or source of all wisdom and knowledge, in an attempt to cancel-out the **polarities** or **opposites**, and in doing so, has set up what can only be described as some kind of **struggle**!

In Jewish mythology, a **dybbuk** (*dubik*) (Yiddish: from Hebrew *adhere* or *cling*) is a malicious possessing of an unclean spirit believed to be the dislocated soul of a dead person. It supposedly leaves the host body once it has accomplished its goal, using an evolved and **organized capitalism** or **working instrumentality** of the banking system in the form of **the house of Rothschild's,** that seems or appears to inadvertently act like a reflection cast upon a mirror or looking-glass, that indirectly revaluates our

moral behaviour, *is that way* **God** *or? Did not destroy* **Lucifer** *because he has the* **essence** *or* **power of command***! Or we would not be suffering in this way.* **Does one have to be cruel to be kind,** *so to speak! Like the means that will justify the ends or the bringing together of two opposites, as well as that* **intangible catalyst***! Or source of all knowledge and understanding that brings together that which cannot be one or the other!!*

And the opposite part or negitive-side of **"God"** has also come into being with terrifying power and malignancy, like **"des Cartes"** reflection in a

looking glass or **"that bubble of man's vanity"** in 𝕯𝖗𝖆𝖈𝖚𝖑𝖆.

. . .

Dual Destiny

The answer is *yes* and *no,* like an infinite and vast intelligence running on a **binomial** or **binary system** namely **1-or-0,** Vis-à-vis it means its quantum-physics **yes** and **no**... which is a half-truth or **Deo non Fortuna,** meaning by: **God,** not by **chance,** or at the hands of **capricious Gods** and the twisted hand of *fate!*

It is like king Solomon's cyclic view of destiny?

'For everything its season, and for every activity under heaven its time: a time to be born and a time to die...Whatever is has been already, and Whatever is to come has been already, and God summons each event back in turn'

I stand amid the roar of a surf-tormented shore, and I hold within my hand grains of the golden sand--how few! Yet how they creep through my fingers to the deep while I weep--while I weep! O God! Can I not grasp them with a tighter clasp? O God! Can I not save one_ from the pitiless wave? Is _all_ that we see or seem but a dream within a dream?"

Edgar Allen Poe.

. . .

Standing on the shoulders of gods

By
Paul Crowe

And there our character, Mathew sat reading his little Almanac titled: The Wizards pocket book of magic, that he had got from the ad section of his Marvel comics like: Thor and Dr strange, and where he remembered years ago, he had bought his X-ray specs! For $1.95 and how the very mention of them had freaked out the girls, sending them into an hysterical throng of shrieking and screaming humanity, chasing after him to try and get their hands on his legendry and iconic X-ray specs!

With his Wizards Almanac, and the heady brew of his imagination when he was as high as a kite on **LSD,** Mathew thought he had held the power of the cosmos in his hands, as if he had been initiated into the secret brotherhood of Magicians! On one page there was a drawing of a magic amulet which bore an eye in its centre, like the coin that is used with the esoteric card set with one side of the coin bearing two little vertical marks or strokes slightly spaced apart like two pillars which represent a symbolic doorway, and to look or concentrate on the middle of the pillars, like the eye of the amulet it is supposed to open up a door or gateway into the human mind or a pathway into other realities, by using the minds eye to see into this mystical realm! Written around the outer edge of the amulet, were the esoteric words of the declaration of Isis...

"*I am whatsoever was. Whatsoever Is, Whatsoever shall be, and the veil, which is over my face, No mortal hand has ever raised.*"

The eye on the amulet symbolised the all seeing eye or that which the minds eye alone can see, and Sprach the prophet; "**Zarathustra**" as Mathew spoke aloud the secret words the constellations themselves would shift, and there on the threshold of the equinox between two worlds, a portal or gate would open up into the mystic realms beyond, as if Mathew had pronounced the words from Ali Baba and the forty thieves: Open Sesame!

The ground would tremble from the bombs falling from the American bombers in Vietnam, that no one could ever see, never mind hear flying overhead, because they were so high up in the sky, when they delivered their pay-load onto the jungle below it was like distant thunder rolling and peeling as it came ominously closer and closer, as if the unseen forces were reaching out to Mathew as he transcended the physical world, holding his almanac to guide him, as if he were a tourist inside his own head, as if trying to find his way in a strange and bizarre world, and there at the gates of matter, Mathew saw one of the **7 archons** or keepers of wisdom and watchers at the door to the physical world, and there the strange figure held up it's hand as if to bar the way, and on the palm of it's hand was a drawing of a snake trying to eat it's own tail! Or consume its self, a symbol that stood for eternity, with this Mathew was shown to what was called the chamber of the ages, containing the book of Anon!

Or something akin to the "**Corpus Hermeticum**" and the cornerstone inherit in the maxim "*As it is above, so it is below*" and like the sorcerer's apprentice he would learn the forgotten knowledge or true nature of himself, that life was an illusion or dream, and that we have become ensnared like a fly caught in a spiders web, and the third eye or all seeing eye like the one on the American dollar bill! Symbolic of the eye of God or the true beholder of its! Or should I say, our own self that reflects the dream of life onto a pool of water, a crystal ball if you will, even more appropriately *a looking glass,* like a sea of eternity that reveals who we truly are, and our proper place in the scheme of things.

As a seeker of wisdom Mathew would gaze with his **LSD** induced but lofty purpose to try and awake from the dream of life, like in the cult **60s** TV show **The Prisoner**, where we seem or appear to have become our **own jailers** and where questions or the pursuit of knowledge has become a burden to others and answers have become a prison for one's self, as we blindly go through life like cattle, from the cradle to the grave and die like cabbages in a viscous and pointless circle of ignorance, over and over again on the wheel or yoke of life! And there Mathew read his book of all knowledge with its esoteric text and his expanded mind he began to understand life's hidden meaning, like **"Aaron's rod"** to tap the fount of creativity, to **a timeless time**! Before the **beginning of time and space**! That was and is and always will be indescribable or inconceivable. And it seemed to Mathew that this Androgynous state was looking for an answer to it's own self-inquiry! Who am I, what am I, and where am I, and strangely enough it seems to have found the answer in the knowledge of its own self, because we know that matter cannot be created or destroyed! So it begs the question, if we don't know where it comes from? Or where it will go too if anywhere... when you can't perceive it relative to each and every one of us, or our higher self or observer? Either when we are sleeping or after each and every one of us die! Or leave our physical bodies or is it rely there to begin with? Or is it being held in some unified field or middle ground, micro-second by micro-second, the big bang or that strange event did not just happen all by it's self, or that it just some how came into being some how!

Because Mathew knew he was alive, he was substantial, he thought to himself, as he recalled Des Carté and his famous supposition: **"I think therefore I am**." So something must have happened, because he and all the rest of us are the living proof, but why and how was at that point a much deeper and unfathomable mystery even to Mathew till his mind had been artificially expanded enough to try and understand the bottomless truths inside himself, and all around him like the great philosophers and religions of the world who seem like blind men trying to reach out and touch that elusive something! Wrapped up in the meaning of life like the blind folded men who were asked to touch and describe the preverbal Elephant! And yet each and every one of them came up with a different answer to the question? Is the answer or the pun, so to speak staring us in the face, if we could only read between the lines, or was Mathew like the rest of us who seem or appear to be chasing our own tail? Like the snake on the man's hand with it's hidden symbolism or like the abstract imagery we see in our dreams that can contain the meaning or the solution to a problem, like the German chemist: **F. A. Kekule** who saw in the reverie of his own dream a snake seize its own tail! And with this he went on to discover the formula for Benzene.

Or like the Scottish inventor: **"James Watt"** inventor of the steam engine, while walking through a heavy rainstorm while he was dreaming saw the rain itself turn to tiny leaden pellets which bounced about under foot and from this wonderful dream, he discovered how to make lead shot, by dropping molten liquid metal (Lead) into water, thanks to James Watt and his recurring dream, like, *"**visions of the Night**"* '***Dreams***' By **David** and **Susan Hillier**

Separating the '***paranormal***' from the *"**normal**"* is a sign of discontinuity of experience, for the term '***paranormal***' has no organic meaning: it is defined only by negation, by the withdrawal of successive material causes for an event until only the *"**impossible**"*, the *"**paranormal**"*, remains.

Within Islam, for example, the continuity and integration of the numinous dream experience with the *"**normality**"* of material life has remained intact. The institution of the ***ad' Han***, the call to prayer, was received in a dream. At the time, the prophet was eager to introduce a recognizable call to prayer for the faithful, just as the **Jews** were called to the synagogue with the trumpet, and the early Christians summoned to church by the sound of the rattle. During prayers, one of Mohammed's followers, Abdullah Ben Zayd, fell asleep, and dreamed of a man dressed in green who was carrying a rattle.

He asked if he could buy the rattle to use as a call to prayer, but the man in green said to him: 'call out, "There is no god but God and Mohammed is his Prophet" As soon as he awoke, Abdullah Ben Zayd told the prophet his dream, and Mohammed instructed him to teach the exact phrase that he had heard to Bilal, who became the first muezzin.

The profound paradox: the dreamer should learn to acknowledge the psychic forces anew . . . his dissociative tendencies are actually psychic personalities possessing a differential reality. They are real when they are not recognised as real, and unconsciously projected; they are relatively real when they are brought into relationship with consciousness (in religious term etc) but they are unreal to the extent that consciousness detaches itself from its contents. This last stage, however, is only reached when life has been lived so exhaustively and with such devotion that no obligations remain unfulfilled . . . it is futile to lie to ourselves about this. Wherever we are still attached we are still possessed.

So deep within this imagery there seems to be a secret language that's speaks with a hidden tongue of great truths that we have lost for whatever reason and that it is begging the question, what do you think? And the indescribable or inconceivable androgynous state we know as God! Somehow used the retrospective or self-conscious impression of it's own self to try and find the answer to a question it was looking for: ***Who am I***, ***what am I***, and ***where am I***, and this timeless unified thought created the heavens and the earth and on the seventh day! The lord rested, because he had come to the end of his work, and where the answer to the question has already been found... and yet at the same time nothing seems or appears to have happened in the conventional sense, so to speak! Even though the indescribable or inconceivable androgynous state has come full circle like the theory of the past, present and the future which co-exist with one another in that timeless unified thought, because something has happened, so it could be the key or answer to a paradox of who God is? Or the riddle of what appears to be its or our own self that is actually somewhere and yet nowhere, beyond the beyond or at the incredible source of all knowledge and understanding!

Hermaphrodites

Is there race's of beings with an affinity to **"Homo-sapian's"** who through some meta-physical experiment created a precursor like **"Adam"** And who in turn produced **"Eve?"** And was it their hand that was behind **"Samson"** and **"Christ!"** Who seem or appear to be a race, of **"hermaphrodites","** A-sexual" or **"androgynous"** beings?

And through some kind of crossbreeding or inbreeding having taken place, in the grand experiment or plan, to alter our destinies, for reasons best known, to whatever or whoever is responsible?

And then they had to cross-bread with the **"seed of heaven"** or symbolic **'sons of god'** that could have been some mysterious, or more evolved **"gene!"** That was mysteriously introduced by person or persons unknown, so to speak, that seem or appear to have albeit broken or continued the link in our evolution, from **"Neanderthal-man"** to **"Cro-Magnon"** or other humanoids that live on the planet with us.

A consummation that would produce **"giants"** or **"freaks"** and these high-tech mysterious creatures introduced, the **"X-factor"** or missing link **"Gene!"** Of the mysterious progenitor named: **"Noah"** or **"precursor"** to the Homo sapiens!

" There is more to this than meets the eye?"
(People who disappear)

By whoever unconsciously named strange areas with the words or connotation which has a cultural or emotional association that some word or phrase carries, in addition to the word's or phrase's explicit or literal meaning, which is its denotation **"Devil"** or like the description in **David Paulides** Excellent book: **MISSING 411 The Devil's in the detail.** And the introduction on **page 47** and the **Animas river** in Colorado where in **1765** and the Spanish Explorer: **Juan Maria De Rivera** and the river he named **Rio De Las Animas** or **River of lost souls,** and the fact that so many of his soldiers had mysteriously disappeared in its vicinity, as well as other children from **1924/2003**

" The means will justify the ends"

And something went wrong in the breeding-programme, by introducing what was symbolically known as the **sons of God**! That accidentally or purposefully produced **freaks** or **strange giants,** and because of this they had to flush most of it down the drain, so to speak, and introduce a mysterious **progenitor** called: **"Noah"** as we now inexorably slide towards the abyss or final outcome, by the means that will justify the ends! Through a pseudo scientific **unthropological, sociological** and **theological conundrum,** where the collective or author of the piece, the

"Dybbuk" (An Eastern European name for an unclean spirit!) Indirectly revaluates our **moral behaviour,** from what can only be described as **non-space.**

"The Cart Before The Horse"
"Moses"
Apocalypse
(Chapter 13)

"Eve looked up to heaven and saw a chariot of light! Travelling there, it was drawn by 4 shinning eagles. No terrestrial being could have described its magnificence, and the chariot drove up to Adam and smoke came out between the wheels."

Its as if the bible is describing the first appearance by the **beings** that had **genetically** modified **Adam** and **Eve**! Or **Lilith**, and who was the mysterious third party! That was describing what was going on?

Pride

"Lucifer, who himself succumbed to pride, was the first and mightiest angel to be created. With intelligence, radiance, beauty, and power unmatched among all of the angels in Heaven, Lucifer was second in majesty only to God Himself."

Spiritual warfare

there seems or appears to be **collective principalities** or **powers** that represent, the minions of **inequity** this symbolic **"great star"** of Revelation, is the **evil** or **demonic spirit of bitterness** and one of the **3 of stars**, which fell from heaven with **Lucifer** (*Revelation 12*).

His rebellion established **darkness,** or a sort of theoretical seperation, and all those **stars** captured by his **prideful rebellion**, became a sort of **spiritual warfare.**

And one from out the order of **angels,** having turned away with the order that was under him, **conceived an impossible thought**, to place his throne higher than the clouds above the earth, that he might become equal in rank to my power!

Beelzebub
(Lord of the flies)

All your pomp has been brought down to the grave, along with the noise of your harps; maggots are spread out beneath you, and worms cover you. How you have **fallen** from heaven, **morning star,** and **son of the dawn**! But you are brought down to the realm of the **dead,** to the **depths** of the **pit:**

The Conqueror Worm

They're in his grave, lo! 'Tis a gala night
Within the lonesome latter years!
An angel throng, bewinged, bedight
In veils, and drowned in tears,
Sit in a theatre, to see
A play of hopes and fears,
While the orchestra breathes fitfully
The music of the spheres.
Mimes, in the form of God on high,
Mutter and mumble low,
And hither and thither fly--
Mere puppets they, who come and go
*That the play is the tragedy, "**Man**,"*
*And its hero the **Conqueror Worm**.*

Edgar Allen Poe

. . .

Doppelganger

Quasi-corporal, 'astral' body of **paracelsus'** theorizing; that the second body, **second persona;** not quite **spirit** and not quite **flesh;** sharing equally the qualities of the **material** and of the **immaterial.** Living within the **flesh,** and **pervading** it but **exstending** itself far **beyond** the earthly **confines** of the flesh. The **mirror-image** of the **material body.**

. . .

The War Scroll

"*The War of the Sons of Light Against the Sons of Darkness*"

In the **War Scroll,** according to Menahem Mansoor, the **angels of light,** who are identified with **Michael,** the prince of light, will fight in **heaven** against the **angels of darkness,** in some kind of dichotomy or embrace, and the part that has been theoretically separated identified with **Belial.** While the **Sons of Light** fight the **Sons of Darkness** on earth, during the last of the **7 battles** described in the **scroll** the **Sons of Light!** Will win the final victory.

The Judeo-Christian

Tradition has stories about angelic beings, cast down from heaven by God, often presenting the punishment as inflicted in particular on **Satan.** The name **Lucifer,** the Latin name (literally "**Light-Bearer**" or "**Light-Bringer**") for the **morning star** (the planet Venus in its morning appearances), is often given to the **Devil** in these stories. The brilliancy of the **morning star,** which eclipses all other stars,

In verses **7-9,** after defeat in a **War in Heaven** in which the **dragon** and his **angels** fought against **Michael** and his **angels,** "*the great dragon was thrown down, and whose tail swept a third part of the stars of heaven and cast them to the earth.*"

The
Ancient serpent

"Who is called the **devil** or **Satan,** the **deceiver** or **self-deceiver** of the whole world – was he not **thrown down** or symbolic fall to earth, and were his **angels** not **thrown down** with him?"

In traditional **Christian** understanding of the **Hebrew scriptures**, the **Torah, Satan** is a synonym for the **Devil.** For most Christians, he is believed to be an **angel** who rebelled against **God**—and also the one who spoke through the **serpent** and seduced **Eve** into disobeying **God's** command.

His ultimate goal is to lead people away from the love of God—to lead them to **fallacies** which **God** opposes. **Satan** is also identified as the accuser of Job, the tempter in the Gospels, the secret power of lawlessness in **2 Thessalonians 2:7,** and the **dragon in the Book of Revelation.**

Before his insurrection, **Satan** was among the highest of all **angels** and the **"Brightest in the sky".** His pride is considered a reason why he would not bow to God as all other angels did, but sought to rule heaven himself. The popularly held beliefs that Satan was once an angel who becomes prideful and eventually rebels against God, however, are not portrayed explicitly in the Bible and are mostly based on inference (e.g., **Ezekiel 28** and **Isaiah 14:12–17**).

In mainstream Christianity he is called **"the ruler of the demons"** (**Matthew 12:24**), **"the ruler of the world"** and **"the god of this world"** (**2 Cor. 4:4**).

2 separate falls from heaven, one of **Satan** being cast down, the other of the **sons of God** choosing to come to earth to take human wives.

Samyaza

In the **Book of Enoch** he is portrayed as the leader of a **band of angels** called the **Watchers** that are consumed with lust for mortal women and become **Fallen Angels.**

> "*And Semjâzâ, who was their leader, said unto them: 'I fear ye will not indeed agree to do this deed, and I alone shall have to pay the penalty of a great sin. And they all answered him and said: 'Let us all swear an oath, and all bind ourselves by mutual imprecations not to abandon this plan but to do this thing.' Then sware they all together and bound themselves by mutual imprecations upon it*"
> (**Enoch 6:3-5**)

Semjâzâ convinced several other **Grigori** to join him in fornicating with women. As a result, he and the other sinful **Grigori** begot **giant offspring** (in **Genesis** called **Nephilim** or **"fallen ones"** in Hebrew) that dominated and *feasted upon humans* during the days of **Enoch.**

. . .

" They rage against mankind,
They spill human blood like rain,
Devouring the flesh of man,
And emptying his vains of blood,
Ceaselessly quaffing hot human gore "

. . .

The Watchers

Other sins was to teach humans various creative arts — especially **Azâzêl's,** who taught the secrets of war, which brought down the wrath of God.

God commanded the angel Gabriel to cause the Giants to wage Civil War:

And to Gabriel said the Lord: 'Proceed against the biters and the reprobates, and against the children of fornication: and destroy [the children of fornication and] the children of the Watchers from amongst men [and cause them to go forth]: send them one against the other that they may destroy each other in battle: for length of days shall they not have.

Enoch 10:9

"Finally, the judgement of the associates of **Samyaza** is described"

And the Lord said unto Michael: 'Go, bind Semjâzâ and his associates who have united themselves with women so as to have defiled themselves with them in all their uncleanness. And when their sons have slain one another, and they have seen the destruction of their beloved ones, bind them fast for seventy generations in the valleys of the earth, till the day of their judgement and of their consummation, till the judgement that is for ever and ever is consummated. In those days they shall be led off to the abyss of fire: and to the torment and the prison in which they shall be confined for ever. And whosoever shall be condemned and destroyed will from thenceforth be bound together with them to the end of all generations"

Enoch 10:11-14

After the destruction of the **Giants,** God caused the Great Flood (**Noah's flood**) or deluge, to wipe out the humans who had become corrupted.

Moses

(Drawn out of the water)

"I am slow of speech, and of a slow tongue'. And the anger of the lord was kindled against Moses, and he said, is not Aaron the Levite thy brother? I know that he can speak well . . . And I will be with thy mouth, and with his mouth . . . and he shall be thy spokesman unto the people."

And this is a man who was not only brought up and well versed in the wisdom of the **Egyptians!**

Who was himself a complete mystery; no one knew where he actually came from! Even though he was meant to have been brought up in the **Egyptian royal household** and probably knew more than meets the eye, as a receptive and learned person, because he had access to the huge venerable library rooms, and of course due to the fact that he could not enter the Promised Land, **why?** And even Moses could not look upon the face of God! **Why?**

In the culture of the **Israelites,** the rod would be a natural symbol of authority, as the tool used by the shepherd to correct and guide his flock (**Psalm 23:4**). Moses' rod is, in fact, cited in **Exodus 4:2** as carried by him while he tended his sheep; and later (Exodus 4:20) becomes his symbol of authority over the Israelites (Psalm 2:9, Psalm 89:32, Isaiah 10:24 and 11:4, Ezekiel 20:37). The rods of both Moses and Aaron were endowed with miraculous power during the Plagues of Egypt (Exodus 7:17, 8:5, 8:16-17, 9:23, and 10:13); God commanded Moses to raise his rod over the Red Sea when it was to be parted (Exodus 14:16) and in prayer over Israel in battle (Exodus 17:9); Moses brings forth water from a stone using his rod (Exodus 17, Numbers 20:11).

Aaron's rod, however, is cited twice as exhibiting miraculous power on its own, when not physically in the grasp of its owner. In **Exodus 7** (Parshat Va'eira in the Torah), God sends Moses and Aaron to Pharaoh once more, instructing Aaron that when Pharaoh demands to see a miracle, he is to "cast down his rod" and it will become a serpent. When he does so, Pharaoh's sorcerers counter by similarly casting down their own rods, which also become serpents, but Aaron's rod/serpent swallows them all. "Pharaoh's heart is stubborn" and he chooses to ignore this bit of symbolic warning, and so the Plagues of Egypt ensue. Notably, this chapter begins with God telling Moses, "Behold, I have made you as God to Pharaoh and your brother Aaron will be your prophet." As God transmits his word through his prophets to his people, so Moses will transmit God's message through Aaron to the pharaoh. The prophet's task was to speak God's word on God's behalf. He was God's "mouth". (Exodus 4:15-16)

Why was **God** or the **Gods** so reluctant to show their faces and what are they so afraid of? And the dead-sea scrolls with its cryptic origins to the **Epic of Gilgamesh** which is of Sumerian origin, and much older than the bible! Of **Enoch,** and of the **Lamech scroll** and its strange description of Noah! And the...

Cuckoo In The Nest

'**Lamech**' who apparently came home one day, and was surprised to find a strange boy, who was quit out of place! In the family home, and after the protestations of his wife, 'Bat-Enosh' who swore that by all that was holy, claiming that it was his child! And not due to the amorous attention of a passing stranger, which also included any of the guards, and the "**sons of God**" After that Lamech went to seek advise from '**Methuselah**' who in turn went off to see the wise '**Enoch**' about the **boy** or **son of heaven**, and **Enoch** then described to '**Methuselah**' about the forth coming judgement that would come upon the earth, and all mankind, and that all flesh would be destroyed, as it was sordid and dissolute!

The strange boy who was to be called '**Noah**' had been chosen by some unknown proxy to be the progenitor of those who would survive the great deluge, and after this prophetical gestation period, '**Enoch**' had mysteriously disappeared! Described the boy as '**a son of heaven**' because his eyes, hair, skin and whole being where unlike any of the family. Now it came about, when men began to multiply on the face of the land, and daughters were born to them, that the sons of God saw that the daughters of men were beautiful; and they took wives for themselves, whomever they chose. Then the LORD said, "My Spirit shall not strive with man forever, because he also is flesh; nevertheless his days shall be one hundred and twenty years."

The **Nephilim** were on the earth in those days, and also afterward, when the sons of God came in to the daughters of men, and they bore children to them. Those were the mighty men who were of old, men of renown.

Kuyundjik

The 12 clay tablets

"That belonged to the Assyrian King Assurbanipal and it was written in Akkadian; and later a second copy was found that dated back to King Hammurabi"

The original version of the Epic of Gilgamesh, who was part man and part God, stems from the mysterious '**Sumerians**' whose origin is unknown! And runs parallel to the Book of Genesis.

And speaks of the cross breeding of two different species or the character: '**Enkidu**' whose whole body was covered with hair! Who wears skins and eats grass in the fields and drinks at the same watering place as the cattle! When **Gilgamesh** the king of **Uruk,** finds this out, he suggests that '**Enkidu**' should be given a lovely woman, to estrange him from the cattle! Or **semi-divine female**!

And on one these clay tablets it speaks of a cloud of dust that came from the distance, the heavens roared and the earth quaked, until finally the sun God came and seized '**Enkidu**'

The **5th clay** tablet narrates how '**Gilgamesh**' and '**Enkidu**' set out to visit the Gods, '**turn back! No mortal comes to the holy mountain**

where the Gods dwell; he who looks the Gods in the face must die.' 'Thou canst not see my face, for there shall no man see me and live . . .', it says in Exodus.
And on the **8th tablet** who sees the earth from above! Dies of a mysterious disease, and '*Gilgamesh*' ask's if his friend had been smitten by the poisonous breath of a heavenly beast?
And on the **9th** tablet it describes '*Gilgamesh*' mourning for the death of his friend '*Enkidu*' and it describes the two mountains which support the heavens and that between those two mountains arched the gate of the sun. At the gate **Gilgamesh** meets two **giants!** Who eventually let him pass, because he was already **semi-divine!** And that's where he found the garden! **Of the Gods**, and beyond was the **endless sea...**
'*Gilgamsh*, whither are thou hurrying? Thou shalt not find the life that thou seekest. When the Gods created man, they allotted him to death, but life they retained in their own keeping.'
For **Gilgamesh** wanted to reach '*Utnapishtim*' the father of men! Described in the **11th tablet** and **Gilgamesh** eventually found **the father of men!** Who not only told him about his past, and forewarned him of a great change or **flood** (*deluge*) to **come!** And that would be visited upon the people, and he was given the task of building or constructing a **huge boat** on which he was to shelter, woman and children, including relations and craftsman of every kind.
It goes on to vividly describe the **violent storm**, the **darkness**, the rising **flood-waters** and the despair of the people he could not take with him, a description that is almost identical to **"Noah"** of the **Christian bible**, where the **flood-gates of heaven** were **opened** and the rain fell for **40 days** and **40 nights,** as the waters rose upon the earth!
A chilling and frightening observation, which includes the **Raven** and the **Dove!** That was released and how finally, as the waters receded, the huge boat or **ark!** Was ground on a [**Mountain!**]

Evolutionary fingerprints
The path of the poles
By
Charles Hapgood

Its as if the dinosaurs seemed or appeared in Africa, already fully evolved, at the start of the **Mesozoic-Era,** literally out of nowhere!
In evolutionary terms, the amount of generations needed for the change of a species, are so tremendous, that natural selection alone as an evolutionary agent, even on a geological scale, may be open to doubt!
And mathematically the changes needed to take place, according to certain theories at rates so slow, that even geological era's would provide insufficient time for evolution, some **drastic influence**, must have been involved to produce evolutionary change!

Tiahuanaco

The gate of the son
"And the strange flying light that landed the great earth mother on earth,
so that she could bear children!"

Pre-Antediluvian times

That the sons of God saw the daughters of men that they were fair, and they took them wives of all which they chose. There were giants in the earth in those days; and also after that, when the sons of God came in unto the daughters of men, and defiled themselves on mortal women, producing monstrous children, who grew to be giants! And they bore children to them; the same became mighty men, which were of old, men of renown. And God saw that the wickedness of man was great in the earth.

Genesis vi 2, 4, 5

Byron

Offspring of the symbolic union of the '**sons of God**'
And the daughters of men!
These are they, then, who leave the throne of God, to take them wives from out of the race of Cain; the sons of heaven, who seek earth's daughters for their beauty . . .. Woe, woe, woe to such communion! Has God not made a barrier between earth and heaven, and limited each, kind to kind?

Enoch in the Rabbinic Legend

It was during the time of Jared, father of Enoch, that the angels, known as the Watchers came down to earth to take mortal women as wives and mate with them, and they beget monstrous children.

The 12 Spies

Report that they have seen fearsome giants in Canaan: So they gave out to the sons of Israel a bad report of the land which they had spied out, saying, "The land through which we had gone, in spying it out, is a land that *devours its inhabitants!*" And all the people whom we saw in it are men of *great size.* There also we saw the *Nephilim* (the sons of Anak are part of the *Nephilim*); and we became like grasshoppers in our own sight, and so we were in their sight.

Interpretations

Offspring of Seth: The Qumran (Dead Sea Scroll) fragment **4Q417** (*4QInstruction*) contains the earliest known reference to the phrase **"children of Seth"** stating that God has condemned them for their **rebellion.** Other early references to the offspring of **Seth** rebelling from God and **mingling** with the **daughters of Cain,** are found in rabbi Shimon bar Yochai, Augustine of Hippo, Julius Africanus, and the Letters attributed to St. Clement. It is also the view expressed in the modern canonical Amharic Ethiopian Orthodox Bible.

Offspring of angels: A number of early sources refer to the "sons of heaven" as **"Angels"**. The earliest such references seem to be in the **Dead Sea Scrolls,** the Greek, and Aramaic Enochic literature, and in certain Ge'ez manuscripts of 1 Enoch (mss A–Q) and Jubileess used by western scholars in modern editions of the Old Testament Pseudepigrapha.

Also some Christian apologists shared this opinion, like Tertullian and especially Lactantius. The earliest statement in a secondary commentary explicitly interpreting this to mean that angelic beings mated with humans, can be traced to the rabbinical Targum Pseudo-Jonathan, and it has since become especially commonplace in modern-day Christian commentaries.

Dualism, fallen Angels and Hermafridtes

The New American Bible commentary draws a parallel to the Epistle of Jude and the statements set forth in Genesis, suggesting that the Epistle refers implicitly to the paternity of **nephilim** as **heavenly beings** who came to earth and had sexual intercourse with women.

Fallin Angels

In heaven they are unknown, **on earth they are not understood**. There were rulers among them, rulers of fearful melevolence and power.

Seven are they! Seven are they

In the womb of the deep 7 they are!

Nor male nor female are the 7

but as the swift blast of the roaming wind.

No wife have they, no heir, no son. Knowing

naught of mercy, of kind pity naught. Their ears

are deaf to prayer or supplication.

The footnotes of the Jerusalem Bible suggest that the Biblical author intended the **nephilim** to be an **"anecdote of a Superhuman race!"**

Some Christian commentators have argued against this view, citing Jesus's statement that angels do not marry. Others believe that Jesus was only referring to angels in heaven.

Evidence cited in favor of the **"fallen angels"** interpretation includes the fact that the phrase **"the sons of God"** (*Hebrew*) literally **"sons of the gods"** is used twice outside of Genesis chapter 6, in the Book of Job (*1:6 and 2:1*) where the phrase explicitly references angels. The Septuagint's translation of Genesis 6:2 renders this phrase as **"the angels of God"**

In this tradition, the **children** of the **Nephilim** are called the **Elioud,** who are considered a **separate race** from the **Nephilim,** but they share the **fate** as the **Nephilim.**

According to these texts, the fallen angels who begat the nephilim were cast into Tartarus (Greek Enoch 20:2), a **place** of **'total darkness'.** However, Jubilees also states that God granted ten percent of the disembodied spirits of the nephilim to remain after the flood, as demons, to try to lead the human race astray until the final judgment

In these sources, these offspring of **Seth** were said to have disobeyed God, by breeding with the Cainites and producing wicked children **"who were all unlike"** thus angering God into bringing about the Deluge, as in the Conflict:

Certain wise men of old wrote concerning them, and say in their [sacred] books, that angels came down from heaven, and mingled with the daughters of Cain, who bare unto them these giants. But these [wise men] err in what they say. God forbid such a thing, that angels who are spirits, should be found committing sin with human beings. Never, that cannot be.

FallinAngels

Amorites

And if such a thing were of the nature of **angels** that fell, they would not leave one woman on earth, undefiled... But many men say, that **angels** came down from heaven, and joined themselves to women, and had children by them. This cannot be true.

But they were children of **Seth**, who were of the children of **Adam**, that dwelt on the mountain, high up, while they preserved their virginity, their innocence and their glory like angels and were then called *'angels of God.'* But when they transgressed and mingled with the **children of Cain,** and begat children, ill-informed men said, that angels had come down from heaven, and mingled with the daughters of men, who bear them giants.

Lord protect us, From the Amorites?

The mysterious Amorites or giants may have come from European origin, though no one is sure what was their ethnic origin! They were represented on the Egyptian monuments with fair skins, light hair, blue eyes, curved or hooked noses, and pointed beards, were nomadic clans ruled by fierce tribal chiefs,

"The Amorites or MAR.TU who know no grain... The MAR.TU who know no house nor town, the boors of the mountains... The MAR.TU who digs up truffles... who does not bend his knees (to cultivate the land), who eats raw meat! Who has no house during his lifetime, who is not buried after death!"

They occupied the middle Euphrates area from the second half of the third millennium B.C. The Amorites were likely the largest of the 7 nations that God displaced for Israel out of Canaan.

Gen 15:16; "When the Lord your God brings you into the land where you are entering to possess it, and clears away many nations before you, the Hittites and the Girgashites and the Amorites and the Canaanites and the Perizzites and the Hivites and the Jebusites, 7 nations greater and stronger than you," (Deut 7:1)

The Amorites were a large and powerful nation that controlled much of the promised-land, including Jerusalem, Hebron, and Lachish: **Joshua 10:5**

Warlike

The **Amorites** were fierce warrior clansman who twice conquered Babylonia (at the end of the 3rd and the beginning of the 1st millennium" their king, Og, is described by Moses as the last "of the remnant of the **giants**" (Deut. 3:11). Both Sihon and Og were independent kings. Og, king of Bashan, is also called an Amorite in Deut. 3:8, 4. 47, where we learn that Og's territory extended "from the river of Arnon unto Mount Hermon."

So the land of the Amorites, which is in Gilead (Judges, 10. 8), seems to have embraced all the territory afterward owned by Israel, east of the

Jordan. Deut. 3:9 inform us that the name of Mount Hermon in the language of the Amorites was Shenir.

Amorites in the Bible

The 'Amorite' race appeared in the area of the Middle Euphrates, about the time of Abraham (c.1900 B.C. while it should be noted that the city of Tyre was founded in 2,750 B.C.) they had gained control of the whole of Babylonia.

They seem to have originally occupied the land stretching from the heights west of the Dead Sea to Hebron, with the Jordan valley on the east of the river, the land of the "two kings of the Amorites," Sihon and Og

The five kings of the Amorites were defeated in a great slaughter by Joshua, and they were again defeated at the waters of Merom by Joshua, who smote them till there were none remaining! (Josh. 11:8). It is mentioned as a surprising circumstance that in the days of **Samuel** there was peace between them and the **Israelites**.

The
Israelites and the Philistines
At the valley of Elah

(David and Goliath)

Metaphor

Goliath was the son of Orpah, the so-called sister-in-law of Ruth; David's own Grandmother or blood relationship was meant to be even closer, because Orpah and Ruth were full sisters.

They Battled

Twice a day for 40 days!

David picks up **7 stones** and writes on them the names of God, one name per stone, speaking to **Goliath**, he says, "Hear this word before you die; were not the two women from whom you and I were born, **sisters?** Even though **Orpah** was said to have made pretence of accompanying **Ruth**, but after 40 paces! Left her! **Orpah**, lead a **desolate** life, *its as if she was different in some way, or that she was baron, figuratively speaking, and she could not conceive or mix with other types of humans, who were not giants!* [My italics]

And your mother was **Orpah** and my mother **Ruth**..." after **Goliath** had been mocking the Israelites during pray, about the ark of the covenant being at the temple of Dagon!

After David strikes Goliath who is **6** Cubits and a span, or rough approximate (9ft) with the **stone**, he runs to Goliath before he dies and Goliath says: "Hurry and kill me and rejoice" and David replies: "before you die, **open your eyes and see your slayer**" Goliath sees an angel and tells David that it is not he who killed him, but the angel! And when

Amorites

6' Average Man | 12' Og of Bashan Goliath Scale | 18' | 24' | 30' Early Canaanite Giants Scale See Amos 2:9 | 36'

Goliath was dead, his heart carried the image of Dagon, who was a *fish* God! "There's that strange link, with *water* again!"

And following this startling revelation, Saul came out with an even more baffling retort, asking David. Who he was?

There is a surfeit of references in the holy-bible, to: *Numerology,* like in the *23rd Psalm* and that it is also connected to *water* and the *sea.*

It also seems or appears to have a quasi-relationship to *Normal human sex cells* that have *23 chromosomes*. Other human cells have *46 chromosomes*, arranged in *23 pairs*!

Hecate

The goddess **"Hecate"** with her crown of thorns! Or points radiating outwards from her crown, like **"thorns"** she is also known as queen of heaven and **star** of the (**sea**) the statue of liberty is modelled on *Hecate* and its cryptic association with *Christ the redeemer, and his crown of thorns* she is also associated with *Hades,* like the infamous Gorgon, (Medusa) with its wreathing crown or mass of snakes, and she is sometimes seen with **3 heads,** like a divinity, or Cerberus the *3 heeded dog*!

| **Statue of liberty** | **Hecate** |

(There is lots of pseudo or cryptic passages that describe *Stones*)

Psalm 118:22

The *stone* that the builders rejected

Has become the chief cornerstone.

'Goliath was metaphorically brought down by a stone'

John 8: 1-11

But Jesus went to the *Mount* of Olives. Early in the morning he came again to the temple; all the people came to him, and he sat down and taught them. The scribes and the Pharisees brought a woman who had been caught in adultery, and placing her in the midst they said to him,

"Teacher, this woman has been caught in the act of adultery. Now in the law Moses commanded us to stone such. What do you say about her?"

This they said to test him that they might have some charge to bring against him. Jesus bent down and wrote with his finger on the ground. And as they continued to ask him, he stood up and said to them.

> *"Let him who is without sin among you*
> *Be the first to throw a stone at her."*

And once more he bent down and wrote with his finger on the ground. But when they heard it, they went away, one by one, beginning with the eldest, and Jesus was left alone with the woman standing before him. Jesus looked up and said to her, "Woman, where are they? Has no one condemned you?" She said, "No one, Lord." And Jesus said, "Neither do I condemn you; go, and do not sin again."

Deut. 22:22-24

"If a man is found lying with a woman married to a husband, then both of them shall die—the man that lay with the woman, and the woman; so you shall put away the evil from Israel. If a young woman who is a virgin is betrothed to a husband, and a man finds her in the city and lies with her, then you shall bring them both out to the gate of that city, and you shall

stone them to death with *stones,* the young woman because she did not cry out in the city, and the man because he humbled his neighbor's wife; so you shall put away the evil from among you."

If thy brother, the son of thy mother, or thy son, or thy daughter, or the wife of thy bosom, or thy friend, which [is] as thine own soul, entice thee secretly, saying, *Let us go and serve other gods*, which thou hast not known, thou, nor thy fathers; [Namely], of the gods of the people which [are] round about you, nigh unto thee, or far off from thee, from the [one] end of the earth even unto the [other] end of the earth; Thou shalt not consent unto him, nor hearken unto him; neither shall thine eye pity him, neither shalt thou spare, neither shalt thou conceal him: but thou shalt surely kill him; thine hand shall be first upon him to put him to death, and afterwards the hand of all the people. And thou shalt **stone** him with **stones**, that he die; because he hath sought to thrust thee away from the LORD thy God, which brought thee out of the land of Egypt, from the house of bondage.

213

Goliath was said to have had 100 fathers!

But it seems or appears that old cryptic books, like the **bible**, and others, are trying to describe something that is apparently hidden there, if you read between the lines, so to speak, because it is known that the legendary **Goliath** was born by **Polyspermy.**

Triploid syndrome

Polyploidy occurs in humans in the form of **triploidy,** with **69 chromosomes** (sometimes called 69,XXX), and **tetraploidy** with **92 chromosomes** (sometimes called **92,XXXX**). **Triploidy,** usually due to **polyspermy,** occurs in about 2–3% of all human pregnancies, the vast majority of **triploid** conceptions end as miscarriage and those that do survive to term typically die shortly after birth. In some cases survival past birth may occur longer if there is **mixoploidy** with both a **diploid** and a **triploid** cell population present.

Did you know?

In **Islam**, the **Qur'an** was revealed in a total of **23 years** to Muhammad, and
Muslims believe the first verses of the **Qur'an** were revealed to the Islamic prophet **Muhammad**, on the **23rd night** of the 9th Islamic month.

Remember! Remember!

There is a surfeit of references in the holy-bible, to: **Numerology,** like in the **23rd Psalm** and that it is also connected to **water** and the **sea.**

It also seems or appears to have a quasi-relationship to **Normal human sex-cells** that have **23 chromosomes**. Other human-cells have **46 chromosomes**, arranged in **23 pairs**!

46x46=92!+ the sign for **infinity ∞** or number **8** the right way up=**100**! Equals one hundred fathers.

· · ·

The story of the Nephilim is chronicled more fully in the Book of Enoch (part of Ethiopian biblical canon). Enoch, as well as Jubilees, connects the origin of the **Nephilim** with the *fallen angels,* and in particular with the **Grigori** (watchers). *Samyaza,* an **angel** of high rank, is described as leading a rebel sect of **angels** in a **descent** to earth to instruct humans in righteousness.

214

The **tutelage** went on for a few centuries, but soon the angels pined for the human females and began to instruct the women in magic and conjuring. The angels **consummated** their lust, and as a result produced **hybrid offspring:** the **Nephilim.**

According to these texts, the fallen angels who begat the Nephilim were cast into Tartarus/Gehenna, a place of **'total darkness'.** However, Jubilees also states that God granted ten percent of the disembodied spirits of the Nephilim to remain after the flood, as demons, to try to lead the human race astray, until the final Judgment.

𝔍𝔫 𝔥𝔦𝔰 𝔥𝔞𝔫𝔡 𝔞𝔯𝔢 𝔱𝔥𝔢 𝔡𝔢𝔢𝔭 𝔭𝔩𝔞𝔠𝔢𝔰 𝔬𝔣 𝔱𝔥𝔢 𝔢𝔞𝔯𝔱𝔥

Psalm 95:4

In addition to Enoch, the Book of Jubilees (7:21-25) also states that ridding the Earth of these Nephilim was one of God's purposes for flooding the Earth in Noah's time.

The Biblical reference to Noah being "perfect in his generations" may have referred to his having a clean, **Nephilim-free-bloodline,** although it may be inferred that there was more diversity among his **3** daughters in-law. These works describe the **Nephilim** as being **evil giants**.

Nowhere is the **Ethiopian** view presented more explicitly than in the Conflict of:

Adam

Book 3, chap. 4

"Certain wise men of old wrote concerning them, and say in their [sacred] books, that angels came down from heaven, and mingled with the daughters of Cain, who bare unto them these giants. But these [wise men] err in what they say. God forbid such a thing, that angels who are spirits, should be found committing sin with human beings. Never, that cannot be. And if such a thing were of the nature of angels, or Satan that fell, they would not leave one woman on earth, undefiled...

But many men say, that angels came down from heaven, and joined themselves to women, and had children by them. This cannot be true. But they were children of Seth, who were of the children of Adam, that **dwelt on the mountain,** high up, while they preserved their virginity, their innocence and their glory like angels; and were then called **'angels of God.'** But when they transgressed and mingled with the children of **Cain,** and begat children, ill-informed men said, that **angels** had come down from **heaven,** and mingled with the daughters of men, who bare them **giants**."

Origin of the term

The origin of the term lies in the Hebrew word for **"giant"**. The Hebrew word translated as **"giants"** here is **Nephilim,** a plural, which itself derives from the root word **Naphal,** which means to *fall.*

The apocryphal Book of Enoch explains that a group of rebellious **angels** "left their first estate" (**heaven,** or the **sky**) and came down (**fell**) to Earth to marry human women and have children with them. Jude makes mention of these angels in the New Testament:

Lust

The following comes from a series of ancient texts referenced in the Bible called **"The Three Books of Enoch"**, a set of books found in the Pseudepigrapha of the Old Testament.

According to these books, it is because of lust that some angels fell from Heaven. God asked the **"Watchers"** (*Grigori*), a select group of angels, to assist the Archangels in the creation of Eden.

Those Grigori who descended to Earth saw the daughters of men and became enchanted with them. Consequently, the Grigori began to reveal to man some of the secrets of Heaven, such as astrology and the vanity of enhancing the face and body with perfumes and cosmetics. The Grigori then fell in love with human women. According to the text, some of the Grigori even took wives and created offspring, giants known as the Nephilim.

This made God so angry that he cursed those Grigori who had betrayed Him, threw them out of Heaven, made them mortal and transformed them into demons. God sent the Great Flood to cleanse the Earth of the wanton killing and destruction perpetrated by the Nephilim. Notable angels who fell in this account are Semyazza, Samael, Azazel, and Lucifer.

Casting The Runes

*"It has been written since the beginning of time, that evil supernatural **creatures** exist in a **world of darkness**, and it is also said, man using the magic power of the ancient runic symbols, can call forth these powers of darkness, the **demons of hell"***

Night/Curse of the demon

In the coldest region's of non-space! The monsterious entites: Ogdru-Jahad-the Gods of chaos-slumber in their prison, waiting to reclaim the earth . . . and burn the heavens...

Hypnos

H.P. Lovecraft

"May the merciful Gods, if indeed there be such, guard those hours when no power of the will, or drug that the cunning of man devises, can keep me from the chasm of sleep, death is merciful, for there is no return there from, but with him who has come back out of the nethermost chambers of night, haggard and knowing, peace rests never more, fool that I was to plunge with such unsanctioned frenzy into mysteries no man was meant to penetrate; fool or God that he was my only friend, who led me and went before me, and who in the end passed into terrors which yet be mine!"

Weighty tome that contained spells to summon evil creatures as servants and those who invoke these strange creatures, had to call them forth from behind the protection of the symbolic shield of the magic-circle. It was also said to contained spells to call forth what was known as the **"Shambler from the stars"** as well as an othology of the elder or dark gods: **"Nyarlathotep"** the all-seeing-eye! **"Yig"** the father of serpents! And **"Cthulhu"**

It has ways and means using concoctions that allow the percipient to see or recall collective memories of past lives, and dire warnings of the consequences of attempting to contact these strange dwellers of the hidden worlds of demons and servants of the elder or dark gods.

Like **Iod** or the **shinning pursuer**, who is meant to hunt souls through the secret dimensions or nether worlds of time and space, it even spoke of the Egyptian priesthood worshiping strange beings that were half-beast and half-man!

The book also contained strange instructions for contacting **evil entities**, as well as using **secretive drugs** and **outré drawings** on the floor, when the stars were just right...!

"WARNING"

(Christian Theology)
THE FIFTH VISION
OF St John
THE SEVEN VIALS OF WRATH

And I saw another sign in heaven, great and marvellous, 7 angels having the 7 last plagues, for in them is filled up with the wrath of God.

And I saw as it were a seal of **glass** mingled with fire: and them that had victory over the **beast,** and over his **image,** and over his **mark,** and over the **number** of his name, stand on the **"sea of glass."**

And I heard a great voice out of the temple saying to the 7 angels, Go your ways, and pour out the vials of the wrath of God upon the earth.

And the **1st** went, and poured out his vial upon the earth, and there fell a noisome and grievous sore upon the men, which had the **mark** of the **beast,** and upon them, which worshipped his **image**.

And the **2nd** angel poured out his vial upon the **sea;** and it became as the **blood** of a dead man; and every living soul died in the **sea**.

And the **3rd** angel poured out his vial upon the **rivers** and **fountains** of **waters;** and they became **blood**.

And I heard the angel of the **waters** say, Thou art righteous, O Lord, which art and vast, and shalt be, because thou hast judged thus.

For they have shed the **blood** of saints and prophets, and thou has given them **blood to drink,** for they are worthy.

217

And I heard another out of the altar say, Even so, Lord God Almighty, true and righteous are thy judgments.

And the **4th** angel poured out his vial upon the sun; and power was given to him to scorch men with fire.

And men were scorched with great heat, and blasphemed the name of God, which hath power over these plagues: and they repented not to give him glory.

And the **5th** angel poured out his vial upon the seat of the **beast**; and his kingdom was full of darkness; and they gnawed their tongues for pain and blasphemed the God of heaven because of their pains and their sores, and repented not of their deeds

And the **6th** angel poured out his vial upon the great **river** Euphrates; and the **water** thereof dried up, that the way of the kings of the east might be prepared.

And I saw three unclean spirits like frogs come out of the mouth of the dragon, and out of the mouth of the **beast**, and out of the mount of the false prophet.

For they are the spirits of devils, working miracles, which go forth unto the kings of the earth and of the whole world, to gather them to the battle of that great day of God Almighty.

Behold, I come as a thief. Blessed is he that watcheth, and keepeth his garments, lest he walk naked, and they see his shame.

And he gathered them together into a place called in the Hebrew tongue, Armageddon.

And the **7th** angel poured out his vial into the air, and there came a great voice out of the temple of heaven, from the throne saying: It is done.

And there fell upon men a great hail out of heaven, every stone about the weight of a talent; and men blasphemed God because of the plague of the hail; for the plague thereof was exceeding great.

And there came one of the **7** angels, which had the **7** vials, and talked with me, saying unto me, Come hither; I will shew unto thee the judgment of the great **whore** that sitteth upon many waters:

With whom the kings of the earth have committed fornication, and the inhabitants of the earth have been made drunk with the wine of her fornication.

And he carried me away in the spirit into the wilderness and I saw a woman sit upon a scarlet coloured **beast,** full of names of blasphemy, having **7** heads and **10** horns.

And the woman was arrayed in purple and scarlet colour and decked with gold and precious stones and pearls, having a golden cup in her hand full of abominations and filthiness of her fornication.

And upon her forehead was a name written:
"MYSTERY, BABYLON THE GREAT, THE MOTHER OF HARLOTS AND ABOMINATIONS OF THE EARTH"

And I saw the woman drunken with the **blood** of the saints, and with the **blood** of the martyrs of Jesus: and when I saw her, I wondered with great admiration.

And the Angel said unto me, wherefore didst thou marvel? I will tell thee the mystery of the **woman,** and of the **beast** that carrieth her, which hath the **7** heads and **10** horns.

The **beast** that thou sawest was, and is not; and shall ascend out of the bottomless pit, and go into perdition and they that dwell on the earth shall wonder, whose names were not written in the book of life from the foundation of the world, when they behold the beast that **was**, and **is not**, and **yet is**!

𝕎itch

(Neophite)
What would you save me from, prince charming? my reflection!

Jack the giant killer

. . .

And here is the mind, which hath wisdom. The **7** heads are seven mountains, on which the woman sitteth.

And there are **7** kings: **5** are fallen, and **1** is, and the other is not yet come; and when he cometh, he must continue a short space.

And the beast that was, and is not, even he is the **8th**, and is of the **7** and goeth into perdition.

And the **10** horns, which thou sawest, are **10** kings, which have received no kingdom as yet; but receive power as kings **1 hour** with the **beast.** These have one mind, and shall give their power and strength unto the **beast.**

These shall make war with the Lamb, and the Lamb shall overcome them: for he is Lord of lords, and King of kings; and they that are with him are called, and chosen, and faithful.

And he saith unto me, the **waters,** which thou sawest, where the **whore** sitteth, are peoples, and multitudes, and nations, and tongues.

And the **10** horns which thou sawest upon the **beast,** these shall hate the **whore,** and shall make her desolate and naked, and shall eat her flesh, and burn her with fire.

For God hath put in their hearts to fulfil his will, and to agree, and give their kingdom unto the **beast,** until the words of God shall be fulfilled, and the woman which thou sawest is that great city, which reigneth over the kings of the earth.

And after these things I saw another angel come down from heaven, having great power; and the earth was lightened with his glory. And he cried mightily with a strong voice, saying:

. . .

"Babylon is fallen, is fallen, and is become the habitation of devils, and the hold of every foul spirit, and a cage of every unclean and hateful bird.
For all nations have drunk of the wine of the wrath of her fornication, and the kings of the earth have committed fornication with her, and the merchants of the earth are waxed rich through the abundance of her delicacies."

. . .

And I heard another voice from heaven, saying: Come out of her my people, that ye be not partakers of her sins, and that ye receive not of her plagues. For her sins have reached unto heaven, and God hath remembered her iniquities. Reward her even as she rewarded you, and double unto her double according to her works: In the cup which she hath filled fill to her double. How much she hath glorified herself, and lived deliciously, So Much torment and sorrow give her: For she saith in her heart "I am **Queen,** and am no **widow,** and shall see no sorrow."

"Therefore, shall her plagues come in one day, death, and mourning, and famine; and she shall be utterly burned with fire: For strong is the Lord God who judgeth her. And the kings of the earth, who have committed fornication and lived deliciously with her, shall bewail her, and lament for her, when they shall see the smoke of her burning. Standing afar off for the fear of her torment, saying: Alas, alas that great city Babylon, that mighty city!"

FOR IN ONE HOUR IS THY JUDGMENT COME.

And the merchants of the earth shall weep and mourn over her; for no man buyeth their merchandise any more; the merchandise of GOLD AND SILVER AND PRECIOUS STONES and of PEARLS, and FINE LINEN, and PURPLE AND SILK and SCARLET, and all THYINE WOOD, and all manner of vessels of IVORY, and all manner of vessels of most PRECIOUS WOOD, and of BRASS, and IRON and MARBLE, and cinnamon, and odours, and ointments, and frankincense, and wine, and OIL, and FINE FLOUR, and WHEAT, and BEASTS, and SHEEP and HORSES, and CHARIOTS, and slaves.

THE
SOULS OF MEN
And the
Whore of Babylon

"Babylon the Great" is a Christian figure of evil mentioned in the Book of Revelation in the Bible. Her full title is given as "Babylon the Great, the Mother of Prostitutes and Abominations of the Earth."

And the fruits that thy soul lusted after are departed from thee, and all things which were dainty and goodly, are departed from thee, and thou shall find them no more at all.

The merchants of these things, which were made rich by her, shall stand off for the fear of her torment, weeping and wailing.

And saying, Alas, alas, the great city that was clothed in fine linen, and purple, and scarlet, and decked with gold, and precious **stones,** and pearl! For in one hour so great riches is come to nought. And every **shipmaster,** and all the company of **ships,** and **sailors,** and as many as trade by **sea,** stood afar off, and cried when they saw the smoke of **her** burning, saying:

. . .

"What city is like unto this great city?" And they cast dust on their heads,
and cried, weeping and wailing, saying:
"Alas, Alas that great city, wherein were made rich all that had
Ships in the sea by reason of her costliness! For in one hour is
She made desolate?"
. . .
Rejoice over her, thou heaven, and ye holy apostles and prophets for God hath avenged you on her.

And a mighty angel took up a **stone** like a great **millstone**, and cast it into the **sea**, saying, Thus with violence shall that great city Babylon be thrown down, and shall be found no more at all.

And the voice of harpers, and musicians, and of pipers, and trumpeters, shall be heard no more at all in thee; and no craftsman, of whatsoever craft he be, shall be found any more in thee; and the sound of a millstone shall be heard no more at all in thee; and the light of a candle shall shine no more at all in thee; and the voice of the **bridegroom** and of the **bride** shall be heard no more at all in thee; for thy merchants were the great men of the earth; for by thy sorceries were all nations deceived.

And in **her** was found the **blood** of prophets, and of saints and of all that were slain upon the earth.

In one final glimpse into the future, John sees this **river** flowing from the **throne of God**. It is the source of eternal life that emanates from **God.**

And he shewed me a **pure river of water of life, clear as crystal,** proceeding out of the **throne of God** and of the Lamb they will see his **face,** and his name will be on their **foreheads**, there will be no more night. They will not need the light of a lamp or the light of the sun, for the Lord God will give them light.

John the Baptist
3:28-30.
Understood that he was subordinate to Christ when he used the analogy of the **bridegroom** and **bride** to show the pre-eminence of the Lord, you yourselves can testify that I said, 'I am not the Christ but am sent ahead of him.'

The **bride** belongs to the **bridegroom.** The friend who attends the **bridegroom** waits and listens for him, and is full of joy when he hears the **bridegroom's** voice. That joy is mine, and it is now complete. 30 He must become greater; I must become less.

The woman at the well
Now he had to go through Samaria. So he came to a town in Samaria called Sychar, near the plot of ground Jacob had given to his son Joseph. Jacob's well was there, and Jesus, tired as he was from the journey, sat down by the well. It was about the 6TH hour. When a Samaritan woman came to draw **water**, Jesus said to her, **"Will you give me a drink?"** (His disciples had gone into the town to buy food.) The Samaritan woman said to him,

"You are a **Jew** and I am a **Samaritan** woman. How can you ask me for a *drink?*"

"And the Spirit and the bride say,
"Come!" And let him who hears say, 'Come!'
And let him who thirsts come.
Whoever desires let him take the water of life freely"

Amos 5:8

Seek him that maketh the **7 stars** and Orion, and turneth the shadow of death into the morning, and maketh the day dark with night: that calleth for the **waters** of the **sea,** and poureth them out upon the face of the earth: The LORD is his name.

. . .

Deuteronomy 29:18

"Lest there should be among you man, or woman, or family, or tribe, whose heart turneth away this day from the LORD our God, to go and serve the gods of these nations; lest there should be among you a root that beareth gall and **wormwood"**

. . .

Another Warning!

(History of the Americas)
The Vision Serpent

Is an important creature in **Pre-Columbian Maya mythology,** although the term itself is now slowly becoming outdated.

The serpent was a very important social and religious symbol, revered by the Maya. Maya mythology describes serpents as being the vehicles by which celestial bodies, such as the sun and stars, cross the heavens. The shedding of their skin made them a symbol of rebirth and renewal.

They were so revered, that one of the main Mesoamerican deities, Quetzalcoatl, was represented as a feathered serpent. The name means **"beautiful serpent"** (From Nahuatl, *'Quetzalli'* means beautiful and *'coatl'* meaning **snake** or **serpent**).

The Vision Serpent is thought to be the most important of the Maya serpents. "It was usually bearded and had a rounded snout. It was also often depicted as having **2 heads** or with the spirit of a god or ancestor emerging from its jaws." During Maya bloodletting rituals, participants would experience visions in which they communicated with the ancestors or gods. These visions took the form of a giant serpent "which served as a gateway to the spirit realm." The ancestor or god who was being contacted was depicted as emerging from the serpent's mouth. The vision serpent thus came to be the method in which ancestors or Gods manifested themselves to the Maya. Thus for them, the Vision Serpent was a direct link between the spirit realm of the gods and the physical world.

The Vision Serpent goes back to earlier Maya conceptions, and lies at the center of the world as they conceived it. *"It is in the center axis atop the World Tree. Essentially the World Tree and the Vision*

Serpent, representing the king, created the center axis which communicates between the spiritual and the earthly worlds or planes. It is through ritual that the king could bring the center axis into existence in the temples and create a doorway to the spiritual world, and with it power."

Akin to Janus the Divom-Deus or God of Gods and the two-headed son of Apollo and Creusa, who was the God of doorways and arches, which symbolically signifies beginnings and endings, which was the theoretical aim of the Alchemists, who believed that the process itself was accompanied by a spiritual change, akin to a symbolic death or aphoristic principle **"solve et coagula"** dissolve and combine... or where the various characteristics of a substance are stripped away in some unknown metamorphosis or joining of its opposing polarities between male or female or **Hermaphroditism,** these changes may be the result of inner, profound spiritual experiences, and a new, nobler substance is built-up, it symbolizes death followed by rebirth into a better, purer life or **divine Androgyny** each one to symbolises the **dichotomy** between the **two-worlds** or the **tangled-web** we weave... Fulcanelli tells us this in **Le mystère des cathedrals,** is emblematic of the whole labour of the work, it is there that the **thread of Ariadne or Arachne**, the legendary, **'Arachne'**, the **spider queen,** from Greek mythology who had been a Lydian maiden, having challenged the Goddess, **'Athene'** who wove the garments of the Gods, and because she was beaten by a mortal, the Goddess, **'Athene'** had changed, **'Arachne'** into a spider who now weaves her webs so that mankind can look upon its deadly beauty... with her family the **'Arachnidae'**...

ARACHNE THE SPIDER

(Remember **"Big Time"** by Fritz Lieber)

Who sits at the centre of the horoscope chart, with its head towards the 13th sign **ARACHNE THE SPIDER** Astrological symbol the Earth would appear to be the ruling planet of **Arachne.**

Characteristics the **spider** is linked throughout legend with **women,** And also weaving and the **metaphorical web, tapestry** or **fabric of life,** as well as with **Hecate** or **tripartite goddess,** who had **3 heads,** and is almost identical to the **"statue of liberty"**

"I am she that is the natural mother of all things, mistress and governess of all the elements, the initial progeny of worlds, chief of powers divine, Queen of heaven, the principal of the Gods celestial, the light of the goddesses: at my will the planets of the air, the wholesome winds of the Seas, and the silences of hell be disposed; my name, my divinity is adored throughout all the world in divers manners, in variable customs and in many names, Some call me Juno, others Bellona of the Battles, and still others Hecate. Principally the Ethiopians, which dwell in the Orient, and the Egyptians, which are excellent in all kind of ancient doctrine, and by their proper ceremonies accustomed to worship me, do call me Queen Isis."

Shrines to **Hecate** at *3 way* crossroads Goddess of the **crossroads** as a virgin goddess dogs were perceived as daemonic animals operating in the *liminal or transitory realm between the domestic and the unknown,* danger-stricken outside world **Hecate** or **Hekate** is an ancient goddess, most often shown holding **two torches** or a **key** and in later periods depicted in triple form.

She is variously associated with **crossroads, entranceways; fire, light, the Moon, magic, witchcraft, knowledge of herbs and poisonous plants, necromancy, and sorcery.** She has ruler ship over **earth, sea,** as in the lovely catholic hymn: (**Star of the sea**), and **sky,** as well as a more universal role as **Saviour** (*Soteira*), Mother of Angels and the **Cosmic World Soul**.

She was one of the main deities worshiped in Athenian households as a protective goddess and one who bestowed prosperity and daily blessings on the family.

Hecate whom Zeus the son of Cronos (Titan) honored above all. He gave her splendid gifts, to have a share of the earth and the unfruitful sea. She received honor also in starry heaven, and is honored exceedingly by the deathless gods. For to this day, whenever any one of men on earth offers rich sacrifices and prays for favor according to custom, he calls upon Hecate.

Great honor comes full easily to him whose prayers the goddess receives favorably, and she bestows wealth upon him; for the power surely is with her. For as many as were born of Earth and Ocean amongst all these she has her due portion.

The son of Cronos did her no wrong nor took anything away of all that was her portion among the former Titan gods: but she holds, as the division was at the first from the beginning, privilege both in earth, and in heaven, and in sea.

According to Hesiod, she held sway over many things...

"Whom she will she greatly aids and advances: she sits by worshipful kings in judgement, and in the assembly whom she will is distinguished among the people. And when men arm themselves for the battle that destroys men, then the goddess is at hand to give victory and grant glory readily to whom she will. Good is she also when men contend at the games, for there too the goddess is with them and profits them: and he who by might and strength gets the victory wins the rich prize easily with joy, and brings glory to his parents. And she is good to stand by horsemen, whom she will: and to those whose business is in the grey discomfortable sea, and who pray to Hecate and the loud-crashing Earth-Shaker, easily the glorious goddess gives great catch, and easily she takes it away as soon as seen, if so she will. She is good in the byre with Hermes to increase the stock. The droves of kine and wide herds of goats and flocks of fleecy sheep, if she will, she increases from a few, or makes many to be less. So, then, albeit her mother's only child, she is honored amongst all the deathless gods. And the son of Cronos made her a nurse of the young who after that day saw with their eyes the light of all-seeing Dawn. So from the beginning she is a nurse of the young, and these are her honours."

Even Jesus comes into it with the **12** disciples and He as the Sun round which they revolved, just like a coven of **13**, not to mention the **12** tribes of Israel!

Ophiuchus
The Serpent Bearer

Is and always has been the **13th** constellation on the zodiac belt, but apparently nobody has ever initiated his sign as a member of the Zodiac,

The constellation Ophiuchus the Serpent Bearer is in Greek myth and tells about the Greek God of Medicine Aesclepius who, while in the process of bringing Orion The Hunter back to life following an accident, was struck and killed by a thunderbolt hurled at him by Zeus, God of the Sky and Earth.

The brother of Zeus was Hades, God of the Dead. He was afraid that the great skill of Aesclepius in bringing dead people back to life might put him out of work. So he played the blood is thicker than water card on Zeus, and Zeus complied and dealt the deathblow.

To honour Aesclepius (so the story goes), Zeus set him in the sky and gave him the Greek name *"Ophiuchus."* (*The Serpent Bearer*)

We have gotten used to the 30 degrees per sign of the Zodiac and it makes us think, if we think about it at all that the Sun is in the **12** signs an equal amount of time. Well that isn't so either. Here, plus or minus a day, depending on the year is the actual number of days it takes the Sun to pass through the various signs, including *Ophiucus*, the **13th**

"Sagittarius (Dec 18- Jan 18), 32 days, Capricornus (Jan 19- Feb 15), 28 days, Aquarius (Feb 16- Mar 11), 24 days, Pisces (Mar 12- Apr 18), 38 days, Aries (Apr 19- May 13), 25 days, Taurus (May 14- Jun 19), 37 days, Gemini

(Jun 20- Jul 20), 31 days, Cancer (Jul 21- Aug 9), 20 days, Leo (Aug 10-Sep 15), 37 days
Virgo (Sep 16- Oct 30), 45 days, Libra (Oct 31-Nov 22), 23 days, Scorpius (Nov 23-Nov 29), 7 days, Ophiuchus (Nov 30-Dec 17), 18 days"
These are obviously not the tidy magazine horoscope dates. The starting point of the astrologer's calculations is the Point of Aries, which is in the same place every year around March 21st. But nowadays it isn't in Aries. The wobble of the Earth's poles makes it apparently move across the background of stars as it changes the Pole Star every 26000 years or so.
This makes no difference to the way modern astrology works. They just call the Point of Aries by the name it had millennia ago, when it actually did appear in Aries. The zero from which they measure everything is still the Spring Equinox.
Notice that the Sun is astronomically only in Scorpio for about 7 days, because Scorpio is a funny shape.
And if you pull one of the free star gazing programs off the Web, you will be able to watch as the path of the Sun moves through the bottom of Scorpio and into a much bigger Ophiucus.

Creativity and the Weaving of Fate

"Like the throw of **2** dice! With its **6** sides=**12** which is another significant number as in Apostles including Christ who made **13**! As in coven or **12** o'clock or the witching hour of **13**!"
The spider has shown up in myth and lore throughout the world. Usually its symbolism has been very similar wherever it is used. In India it was associated with **Maya,** the **weaver of illusion.** It has had connections to the Fates in Greek mythology and the Gnomes in Scandinavian lore - women who would **weave, measure, and cut the threads of life.** To the Native Americans, **spider** is grandmother, the link to the **past** and the **future.**

Eternity

The infinity symbol

(*Lemniscate*)

"Was re-introduced in *1655* by John Wallis, and, since its introduction, has also been used outside *mathematics* in modern *mysticism* and literary *symbology*."

Unlike insects, spiders have a two-section body instead of three, often giving them the appearance of a *figure 8*. This in conjunction with its eight legs links it to all the mysticism associated with the geometric form of the *figure 8*.

Remember! Remember! Remember!!!

Moebius-strip

∞

The legendary *Goliath* was born by *Polyspermy. polyspermy,* occurs in about 2–3% of all human pregnancies, the vast majority of *triploid* conceptions end as miscarriage and those that do survive to term typically die shortly after birth. In some cases survival past birth may occur longer if there is *mixoploidy* with both a *diploid* and a *triploid* cell population present.

There is a surfeit of references in the holy-bible, to: *Numerology,* like in the *23rd Psalm* and that it is also connected to *water* and the *sea.*

It also seems or appears to have a quasi-relationship to *Normal human sex cells* that have *23 chromosomes*. Other human cells have *46 chromosomes*, arranged in *23 pairs*!

GOLIATH

46x46=92!+ the sign for *infinity* ∞ or number *8* the right way up=*100*! Equals one hundred fathers!

number 8 on its side, is the symbol of infinity ∞ it is the *wheel-of-life*, flowing from one circle to the next. The difficulty is learning to walk those circles or even hold your position within the middle between the two.

Spider teaches you to maintain a balance - between past and future, physical and spiritual, male and female. Spider teaches you that everything you now do is weaving what you will encounter in the future. In the tarot deck is a card - The Wheel of Fortune. This is a card that has to do with rhythms - the rise and fall, the flow and flux. It is linked to the energies of honour and fame, and the sensitivities necessary to place us within the rhythm of Nature. Meditation upon this card would be beneficial for anyone with the spider as a totem.

The spider awakens creative sensibilities. It weaves a web of intricate and subtle fabric, as if to remind us that the past always subtly influences the present and future. Often the webs will take a spiral shape, the traditional form of creativity and development.

The spider found within the web reminds us that we are the centre of our own world. The ancient mystery schools had one precept inscribed above their portals: *"Know thyself and thou shalt know the universe!"*

The Spider reminds us that the world is woven around us. We are the keepers and the writers of our own destiny, weaving it like a web by our thoughts, feelings and actions! In the magic and energy of creation, which is a symbol of creative power, reflected in its ability to spin a silken web, the third predominant magic of the spider is associated with its spiral energy, the links with the past and the future.

The spiral of the web, converging at a central point, is like the Norse god **Odin** who created the Runic alphabet, after hanging upon the great tree of life for **9 days** and **nights.** After this time, the twigs fell off and spelled our certain formulas and words.

To many, there was an alphabet even more primordial. It was formed by the geometric patterns found within spider's web. To many this was the first true alphabet. This is why spider is considered the teacher of language and the magic of writing. Those who weave magic with the written word probably have a spider totem.

The **spider** has long been associated with **death** and **rebirth.** Part of this may have to do with the fact that some female spiders will kill and eat the male after mating. This is often found in the insect world, the praying mantis being another such example. Because it is constantly building and weaving new webs, it has also bee a lunar symbol, with ties to the waxing and waning of the moon. For those with this totem, this pattern is a reminder to maintain balance and polarity in all aspects of life. Spider teaches that through polarity and balance creativity is stimulated.

Books, movies, and television have had a tendency to promote a fear of spiders in the general public. Most spiders are poisonous. This is how they kill or stun their prey. They serve a vital function in controlling insect populations.

The black widow probably has received the worst reputation undeservedly. It is found all over the United States. It is jet black, but has a red hourglass shaped marking on its belly. It is a poisonous spider, but it is not fatal to humans as many assume. It is actually a very timid spider, and it is usually as much or more afraid of humans than they are of it.

Tarantulas are another common big spider that people are familiar with, the tarantula, a folk dance of Southern Italy, was named after the tarantula. They believed incorrectly that its bite caused convulsive movements in humans. The dance with its circular direction and quick foot movements was named for it.

The tarantula is one of the largest spiders, and it is hairy. Its mouth is underneath its body. Its bite is poisonous, as with most spiders, but it would not affect the average human any more than a bee sting. Tarantulas do spin a thread, but they do not weave a web. They dig a burrow or a hole in the sand and hide in the bottom of it. As soon as they feel something walking around the opening, they will jump up, grab it, and pull it back in. That is how they catch their food.

Most spiders are actually very, very delicate. If you were holding a tarantula and dropped it, it would break and die. Spiders are a combination of gentleness and strength, and they have learned to combine both for successful survival. This is an important lesson for those with this totem.

As delicate as they are, spiders are also very agile. They can maintain balance and walk the tiny threads with ease. To walk the threads of life and maintain balance has been one of the mysteries throughout the ages. Myth and lore often speak of individuals who have learned to walk the threads between life and death - waking and sleeping - between the physical and the spiritual. This is part of what spider medicine can teach, for spiders are the experts at walking threads.

Most people have little or no contact with the bigger spiders, but they will often see a wide variety around the house and home. Many of these serve vital functions, killing more harmful insects. Most of their movement occurs in the dark, and they move into inaccessible areas. This reflects much about how to express the creative energies. Don't be afraid to employ it in seemingly inaccessible corners. Weave your creative threads in the dark and then when the sun hits them, they will glisten with intricate beauty.

If spider has come into your life, ask yourself some important questions. Are you not weaving your dreams and imaginings into reality? Are you not using your creative opportunities? Are you feeling closed in or stuck as if in a web? Do you need to pay attention to your balance and where you are walking in life? Are others out of balance around you? Do you need to write? Are you inspired to write or draw and not following through? Remember that spider is the keeper of knowledge of the primordial alphabet. Spider can teach how to use the written language with power and creativity so that your words weave a web around those who would read them...

THE WEB

(Excuse the pun!)

"Through a glass, darkly"

Corinthians 13:12 contains the phrase: (*blepomen gar arti di esoptrou en ainigmati*), which is rendered in the King James verson as **"For now we see through a glass, darkly."**

The word εσοπτρου ("esoptrou", from εσοπτρου, "esoptron") here translated *glass* is ambiguous, possibly referring to a **mirror** or a **lens.**

Influenced by Strong's Concordance, many modern translations conclude that this word refers specifically to a **mirror.** Example English language translations include: now we see but a poor reflection as in a mirror or what we see now is like a dim image in a **mirror**

Paul's usage is in keeping with rabbinic use of the term (*aspaklaria*), a borrowing from the Latin *specularia*. This has the same ambiguous meaning, or reference to specularibus lapidibus, **clear polished stones** used as **lenses** or **windows.** One way to preserve this ambiguity is to use the English cognate, *speculum.* Rabbi Judah ben Ilai (2nd century) was quoted as saying "All the prophets had a vision of God as he appeared through nine specula" while "Moses saw God through one speculum." The Babylonian Talmud states similarly "All the prophets gazed through a speculum that does not shine, while Moses our teacher gazed through a speculum that shines."

To see **"through a glass"** — **a mirror** — **"darkly"** is to have an **obscure or imperfect vision of reality.** The expression comes from the writings of the Apostle Paul; he explains that we do not now see clearly, but at the end of time, we will collectively do so

In the book:
"Les demeures philosophales"
By Fulcanelli

Our attention is drawn to a remarkable piece of sculpture – one of four statues that symbolically guard the tomb of François Π in Nantes Cathedral. Fulcanelli calls it prudence... in frontal view it depicts the figure of a beautiful young girl in a hooded cloak and floor-length gown. She seems **mesmerized** by her own **reflection** in a strange **convex mirror** she holds in her hand.

In her right hand is a pair of **compasses** or perhaps **dividers** throughout alchemical literature, there are frequent injunctions to **separate** and conjoin. And on the back of the girl's head is another **face** – that of a **wise old sage** apparently deep in contemplation and enfolded within the cloak of philosophy.

She symbolises nature in all its hidden aspects, both **inward** and **outward,** but beneath her exterior **veil,** there appears the mysterious **image** of ancient **alchemy,** 'and we are, through the attributes of the **first,** initiated into the **secrets** of the **second.**

"Like the symbolism of the Christian mass, and the rite of communion: (He broke bread, and give it to his disciples, and said: **Take this, all of you, and eat it: this is my body which will be given up for you. When the supper was ended, he took the cup. Again he gave thanks and praise, gave the cup to his disciples, and said: take this, all of you, and drink from it: this is the cup of my blood, the blood of the new and everlasting covenant, it will be shed for you and for all"** He seems or appears to be doing something very strange or **alchemistical** by changing one thing into another! Like his strange pseudo-like death, as if he could not be killed! Followed by his strange resurrection, when Mary Magdalene was going to approach him, he told her specifically not to touch him, for some reason!

Which reminds us of **David,** *who was also a bit of a* **wolf-in-the-fold** and the mysterious **Goliath** or (*Amorite*) who was related to him! It seems that legend has it, that he could not be killed, but he could be destroyed, by cutting off his head, like the legend of the **Vampire...!**

'John the Baptist'

The **defiant** and audacious idolatry of the **Templar knights,** and the worship of a fearful head they called: (**un mauffé**) or **Devil,** that was a terrible site to look upon, with its huge staring eyes, which was believed to be the father of all wisdom! Known as **"Baphomet"** or the '**Absorption into primal Wisdom**' a 19th century image in Sabbatic symbolism, created by **Eliphas Lévi.** The arms bear the Latin words **SOLVE** (*separate*) and **COAGULA** (*join together*), the sign of the **Baffomet**, 'figura Baffometi,' which was depicted on the breast of the bust representing the Creator, cannot be exactly determined, it is believed to have been the **Pythagorean pentagon** (*Fünfeck*) of health and prosperity: It is well known how holy this figure was considered, and that the **Gnostics** had much in common with the **Pythagoreans.** From the prayers which the soul shall recite, according to the diagram of the **Ophite-worshippers,** when they on their return to God are stopped by the **Archons!**

Hebdomad

A characteristic feature of the **Gnostic** concept of the universe is the role played in almost all Gnostic systems by the *7* **world-creating archons,** known as the **Hebdomad.**

These *7* are in most systems **semi-hostile powers,** and are reckoned as the last and lowest emanations of the **Godhead;** below them—and frequently considered as derived from them—comes the world of the actually **devilish powers.** There are indeed certain exceptions; Basilides taught the existence of a **"great archon"** called **Abraxas** who presided over *365* **archons.**

The ancient astronomy taught that above the seven planetary spheres was an eighth, the sphere of the fixed stars. In the **8th sphere,** these **Gnostics** taught, dwelt the **mother** to whom all these **archons** owed their origin, **Sophia** (*Wisdom*) or **Barbelo.**

In the language of these **sects** the word **Hebdomad** not only denotes the *7* **archons,** but is also a name of place, denoting the heavenly regions over which the *7* **archons** presided; while **Ogdoad** denotes the **supercelestial** regions which lay above their control.

And their purity has to be examined, it appears that these **serpent-worshippers** believed they must produce a token that they had been clean on earth. I believe that this token was also the **holy pentagon**, the sign of their initiation! His chief subject is the images which are called **Baphomet,** found in several museums and collections of antiquities, as in Weimar and in the imperial cabinet in Vienna.

These little images are of **stone,** partly **hermaphrodites,** having, generally, **two heads** or **two faces,** with a beard, but, in other respects, *female figures,* most of them accompanied by **serpents,** the sun and moon, and other strange emblems, and bearing many inscriptions, mostly in Arabic.

"Half man, half woman"

(A symbol of wisdom)

The **Templars** carried with them in their coffers. **Baphomet** *or* "**Templars head**" or **Gnostic idol** called **Baphomet,** which signifies, a **symbolic baptism of fire,** or the **Gnostic baptism!** "**Gauserand de Montpesant**", a knight of Provence, said that their superior showed him an idol made in the form of **Baffomet;** another, named "**Raymond Rubei**" described it as a wooden head, on which the figure of Baphomet was painted, and adds, "that he worshipped it by kissing its feet, and exclaiming, 'Yalla,' which was," he says, "**verbum Saracenorum**" a word taken from the **Saracens.**

A templar of Florence declared that, in the secret chapters of the order, one brother said to the other, showing the idol, "**Adore this head—this head is your god and your Mahomet.**"

Until a bull by Clement V officially announced that the order was found to be so corrupt and beyond any hope of remedy or reform that it must be dissolved, and accordingly it was declared to be absolutely, and entirely suppressed.

Elias Levita, quoted in Selden De Diis Syris, I, cap, 2, says the Teraphim consisted of a polymath in the shape of a human head, symbolic of **Adam!** Or **Eve,** who came from Adam! Cut off and preserved in spices that spoke of the shape of things to come!

Like the work of science fiction by H. G. Wells, published in 1933, which speculates on future events from 1933 until the year 2106. In the book a world state! Is established as the solution to humanity's problems, which sounds as odious as the worship of mummified heads, that were salted and then embalmed, and then incantations on a plate of gold, was put under the tongue and then stood up on the walls.

Alchemy

Pisces has been called the "**dying god**" where its sign opposite in the night sky is **Virgo,** or, the **Virgin Mary.** When Jesus was asked by his disciples where the next Passover would be, he replied to them:

"Behold, when ye are entered into the city, there shall a man meet you bearing a pitcher of water... follow him into the house where he entereth in."
—Jesus, *Luke 22:10*

. . .

This coincides with the changing of the ages, into the *Age of Aquarius,* as the personification of the constellation of *Aquarius* is a man carrying pitchers of water.

Aquarius

Is a constellation of the zodiac, situated between Capricornus and Pisces. Its name is Latin for "*water-carrier*" or "*cup-carrier*", and its symbol is a representation of *water.*

Aquarius is one of the oldest of the recognized constellations along the zodiac (the sun's apparent path). It was one of the 48 constellations listed by the 2nd century AD astronomer Ptolemy, and it remains one of the 88 modern constellations. It is found in a region often called the "*Sea*" due to its profusion of constellations with *watery associations* such as *Cetus the whale, Pisces the fish,* and *Eridanus the river.*

Which is self evident in the doctrine of alchemy or that which is quantitative and qualitative or (Proportional to) as in the society of dynamics, or the *spark!* Or creed of dualism inherent in the law of opposites...

Genesis

"In the beginning there was darkness, and God moved upon the face of the darkness, and God said: "let there be light!" and there was light, and the earth was without form and void, and darkness was upon the face of the deep, and God saw that the light, that it was good, and God divided, the light from the darkness..."

The *serpent* is the shadow aspect of the *indescribable* or *inconceivable androgynous something?* Or *wisdom* of that which is not, was not, and never will be! Who knew, that in the day ye eat of the fruit from the *tree of knowledge* or *wisdom,* by asking: *Who am I? What am I? And where am I?* You will have and keep tasting the *forbidden fruit of knowledge!*

Then your eyes will be *retrospectively opened,* that you are not! And cannot be! As Gods, Knowing good and evil, or what has happened is that you only think that you seem or appear to be separate, and that's why you are struggling with your real self, in trying to survive at any cost, because you want to exist, but you cannot, why? Because you already *Are, Were,* and *always will be!*

Which has caused a *dichotomy* or *shadow aspect* of God, so to speak, to come into being, that has to be reunited or absorbed into an all embracing source of knowledge and understanding, of *Who?* Or *What?* We all truly *are!* And always *will be?*

"The Kings Majesties most excellent Hocus Pocus, and so was he called, because that at the playing of every Trick, he used to say, **"Hocus pocus, tontus talontus, vade celeriter jubeo"** a dark composure of words, to blinde the eyes of the beholders, to make his Trick pass the more currently without discovery, because when the eye and the ear of the beholder are both earnestly busied, the Trick is not so easily discovered, nor the Imposture discerned."

(Thomas Ady: A Candle in the Dark, 1656)

This is substantiated by the fact that in the Netherlands, the words **Hocus pocus** are usually accompanied by the additional words **pilatus pas,** and this is said to be based on a post-Reformation parody of the traditional Catholic ritual of **transubstantiation** during mass, being a Dutch corruption of the Latin words **"Hoc est corpus"**, meaning **"this is (my) body"**, and the credo **"sub Pontio Pilato passus et sepultus est"**, meaning "under Pontius Pilate he suffered and was buried".

In a similar way the phrase is in Scandinavia usually accompanied by **filiokus,** a corruption of the term **filioque,** from the **Nicene Creed,** meaning **"and from the Son"**.

Others believe that it is an appeal to the Norse folklore magician **"Ochus Bochus."**

The Mayan God

(Votan the serpent)

Like the **Sun, "Pacal Votan"** came to this world to **illuminate** his Mayan people. He came from the **dimension** where the **enlightened teachers** are awaiting for the right moment to get **reincarnated.**

It is there where the **Universal Creator** chooses the **teacher** who will come to **full-fill** the **mission** of **guiding** his people toward the **cosmic light of wisdom** so that once again the **sacred human race** can use that **wisdom** to complete its **destiny of enlightenment.**

. . .

The back door!

The ancient **Mayans** worshipped the teacher **"Pacal Votan"** for his great **wisdom** because he was an **enlightened one** and he knew everything. According to Alberto Ruz Lhuillier's book, some inscriptions in the Temple of the Inscriptions in Palenque say that **"Pacal Votan"** was an initiate who had the ability to do **healing miracles.** He could cure many **illnesses** just by **raising his hands** or through a **look.**

He was able to perfectly handle the energy, which he could control and regulate with his body and mind.

"Pacal Votan" taught his people the mystery of the **9 BOLON TI K'U** and the **13 OX LAHUN TI K'U.**

He taught his **Mayan** people that the **9 BOLON TI K'U** are the **Lords of the Night** and their **wisdom** and **power** depend on the **absence of light.** Also he taught them that the **13 OX LAHUN TI K'U** are the **Lords** *of the 13 dimensions;* he used to say that every initiate should be aware of knowing these *13 dimensions* because the explanations to all the *existing mysteries* in the *world,* either *physically* or *non-physically,* could be found there.

The ancient Mayan priests of the old times claimed that the spirit of *"Pacal Votan"* came from the *stars!* And that was why he brought the *wisdom of the stars* with him and knew the *13 OX LAHUN TI K'U.*

They also said that after arriving in our *Mother Earth,* he decided to work with the human beings forever teaching them all the current *well-known sciences* plus other *unknown sciences* that are even *unknown* to us these days. According to the Mayan priests, *"Pacal Votan"* knew the *tunnels of time, and did you know...*

A spider has 8 legs!

"Votan" romed the world, like the norse god *"Wotan"* or *Odin* with his *8 legged hourse "Sleipnir"* also known as *"Ygg"* the norse name for *"ash"* or *"Yggdrasils"* or *"ash"* of Odins horse, the *"ash"* of *"Sleipner"* with staff in hand, disguised as a *one-eyed-man!* (like one of the *elder* or *dark gods,* known as the *"Old One's"* in *"De Vermis* Mysteriis" known as *"Nyarlathotep"* or the all seeing *eye!*

. . .

Standing on the shoulders of Gods

Where Mathew who had thought he had held the power of the cosmos in his hands, as if he had been initiated into the *secret brotherhood of Magicians!* On one page there was a drawing of a magic amulet which bore an *eye* in its centre, like the coin that is used with the esoteric card set with one side of the coin bearing two little *vertical marks* or *strokes* slightly spaced apart like *two-pillars* (*Samson!*) which represent a symbolic doorway, and to look or concentrate on the middle of the pillars, like the *eye of the amulet* it is supposed to open up a *door* or *gateway* into the human mind or a *pathway* into other *realities*, by using the *minds eye* to see into this *mystical realm*! Written around the outer edge of the amulet, were the esoteric words of the *declaration of Isis.*

PAUL CROWE

. . .

"I am whatsoever was. Whatsoever Is, whatsoever shall be, and the veil, which is over my face, no mortal hand has ever raised."

. . .

Votans eternal home was known as (*Vallhala*) and was also known as a patron of culture, inventor of ruines, *God* of *wisdom, poetry, magic* and *prophecy.*

Like *Jesus Christ* with the *symbolic star of Bethlehem!* Or *Quetzcatl,* who came in the *Mayan year of 3113 B.C,* a *white bearded man,* who was said to have *descended* from the *sun,* of *good appearance* and *grave countenance,* dressed in a *white flowing gown,* who was also called *"huemac"* because of his *great goodness*, who was also born (*after a heavenly annunciation*) of the *virgin queen of heaven,* he was an *innovator* in the *arts* and *crafts,* a preacher of *love, compassion,* he was **tall and robust,** with **large eyes** and a **fair beard,** almost identical to **Christ the redeemer** and **saviour.**

But **Tezcatlipoca** represented the **opposite** or **dark-side,** in order to balance out the two opposing forces, that are needed in the universe. It is not **good** and **evil,** but rather **opposite energies** (*Positive and negative*). The opposites are needed in the universe and nature. How can you have electricity without the opposite poles?

In Quetzcatl's hand he carried a **symbolic-staff** or **symbolic union of knowledge applied with wisdom,** which should be applied in the **practice of medicine.** You can see it on the backs of many American ambulances or the dollar sign.

The **serpent-staff** has a long history of being connected with **religious** and **occult circles,** with the most notable early appearance during Ancient Egyptian times in the Biblical battle between the **Yahweh Staff** of **Aaron** the **Hebrew,** and the **Uraeus Staff** of the **Priests of the Egyptian Pharaoh.**

Later, this same **serpent-staff** concept was adopted by the **American Medical Association** in its development of the symbol **"Caduceus",** which looks something like a **winged flagpole** about which a **pair** of **serpents** is **entwined...**

O_P

The **Moebius-strip** is a mathematical example of eternity ∞ the spider! Take a strip of paper. Turn one end through 180 degrees and tape it or stick it to the other, but keep that end stationary! So that you now have a very special loop of paper.

It has only one side, as you can prove by running a pencil down the centre of the paper. You get back where you began without having to cross from one side to the other.

By applying another dimension to the strip you have changed its properties. By doing magical work it is possible to stand at the intersection point of the two **opposing modalities,** and by elevating the conscious up one dimension you will be able to see that there is a perspective from which both views have the same **truth-value.**

We have gotten used to the **30 degrees** per sign of the **Zodiac** and it makes us think, if we think about it at all that the Sun is in the **12 signs** an equal amount of time. Well that isn't so either. Here, plus or minus a day, depending on the year is the actual number of days it takes the Sun to pass through the various signs, including **Ophiucus,** the **13th.** A strange Book of numbers (7, 3, 13, 40, etc) like the **Mayan** calendar of **20 days** or the **footprints of creation,** where the significance of the **trinity** comes into play, with **Christ's 40 days** and **40 nights** spent in the desert, **40÷by the number 3= 13,13,13 recurring!** Creation of the world symbolically took **7 days, 7+13=20+20=40!** Or the significance of the **cross** or **quincunx,** which has **5 points of reference,** including the figure of

Christ the saviour, on the symbolic cross, that has *4 sides* with *Christ's figure in the centre making the 5th!*

The pentagram has *5 points* or *5 full pentagrams hidden within it*, if you revolve it, you end up where you started! Like the *book-of-Genesis* or the *book-of-Revelation,* you symbolically end up where you started, and you discover the *5 pentangles* within it! And as you know if you spin the number *5,* in reveals the hidden *cross* or *broken cross,* (*swastika*) symbolic of the *wheel of life.*

Which is a strange occult import, because it is used in magic or if you think about it, *3* in the *trinity, 3 Pyramids* and the *3 wise-Shepard Kings!* Or *"Cerberus"* the *3* headed *"dog"* that guarded the way to *Hades* or *underworld!* And once again we are drawn to the inscription on the cross: *Igne Natura Renovatur Integra,* 'by *fire* nature is renewed whole' and the strange inscription at the head of *Christ's cross* on Calvary: *"OCRUXAVES PESUNICA"* that can be broken up to form the phrase: *O crux ave spes unica, 'Hail O cross, the only hope.'* With its hidden or cryptic message: (*OCRUXAVES PESUNICA ORCUS*) which is a Latin phrase: *Orcus ave pus e canis,* meaning: *Orcus hail, down from the "dog"* Orcus is the Roman Lord of the underworld-whom the Eygptians knew as *"Osiris"* The lord of the dead! *Osiris-slain* and *Osiris-risen.* And you do know that *"Dog"* is an anagram of *"God"*.

The *Apostles* including *Christ* made *13* and is of numerical significance in the *20 Mayan days calendar,* as well as the words *Hocus-Pocus* Words of *pseudomagical import.* According to Sharon Turner in The History of the Anglo-Saxons (4 vols., 1799-1805), they were believed to be derived from *"Ochus Bochus"* a *magician* and *demon* of the north. And some have even suggested the phrase predated his *Majesties Hocus Pocus,* being corrupted from the name of a demonic sorcerer of Norse folklore, *Ochus Bochus.*

Ochus Bochus is himself quite possibly a corruption of *Bacchus,* god of *conjuration who turned water into sacred wine. Bacchus/Bochus* could well be related to the story of *Jesus* who turned *water into wine, wine into his own blood, & bread into his flesh.* Much like *Nahua* cosmology and its *3 heavens* (*Trinity*) the lowest (*Tlalocan*) the land of *mist* and *water,* from which the *soul returned* and reincarnated after some *4 years; "The Tlapaallan"* that was a *narvana,* like *heaven* of *non-attachment to the body,* attained only by initiates of the highest (*Tonatiuhican*) or home of the sun and the abode of eternal happiness reached only by the fully enlightened, at the lower-end of the scale, there was also a kind of *limbo* known as *"Mictlan"* where *souls of the condemned* would endure a colourless but painless *eternity.*

A closer inspection of the constellation of *Ophiuchus* as a set of stars across the Belt of the Zodiac poses a *Rorshach test* -- is *Ophiuchus* holding a *snake torn in two pieces* or is he holding a *two-headed King snake,* each head adorned with a *crown?* Relatively speaking!

237

Like **Votan** who declared himself to be a **serpent,** a possessor of knowledge, who departed from **Valum chivim,** by way of the **13 snakes** Throughout the miraculous exploits of **Aesclepius,** God of Medicine, and **Imhotep,** mortal-made-god, the common thread of essential primary teachings begins and ends with the **Serpent of Wisdom** and **The Tree of Life,** also sometimes called: **The Tree of the Knowledge of Good and Evil,** as in the **Genesis** version of **creation!**

The adopted *man/god* **"Thoth"** who was adopted by the Greeks as their god **Hermes.** A similar thing happened to **Aesclepius** as a Greek deity whose attributes were nearly identical to those of the Egyptian **I-Em-Hetep** or **"He Who Cometh In Peace".**

. . .

"Charity suffereth long, and is kind; charity envieth not; charity vaunteth not itself, is not puffed up, *5* Doth not behave itself unseemly, seeketh not her own, is not easily provoked, thinketh no evil; *6* Rejoiceth not in iniquity, but rejoiceth in the truth; *7* Beareth all things, believeth all things, hopeth all things, endureth all things. *8* Charity never faileth: but whether there be prophecies, they shall fail; whether there be tongues, they shall cease; whether there be knowledge, it shall vanish away. *9* For we know in part, and we prophesy in part. *10* But when that which is perfect is come, then that which is in part shall be done away. *11* When I was a child, I spake as a child, I understood as a child, I thought as a child: but when I became a man, I put away childish things. *12* "For now we see through a glass, darkly; but then face to face: now I know in part; but then shall I know even as also I am known. *13* And now abideth faith, hope, charity, these three; but the greatest of these is charity"

King James Version

. . .

Is Ignorance not truely Bliss?
Like in that wonderful song by the Bee Gee's:
" The First Of May"
"When I was small, and Christmas trees were tall, we used to love while others used to play. Don't ask me why, but time has passed us by, some one else moved in from far away."
(Chorus)
"Now we are tall, and Christmas trees are small, and you don't ask the time of day. But you and I, our love will never die, but guess we'll cry come first of May."

. . .

And like what Solomon said, life is cyclic, destined to reach its appointed time.

All moons, all years, all days, all winds, reach their completion and pass away. So does all **blood** reach its **place of quit,** as it reaches its power and its throne measured was the time in which they could praise the **splendour** of the **trinity**, measured was the time in which they could know the sun's **benevolence**, measured was the **grid of the stars** would look down upon them, and through it, keeping watch over their **safety**, the **gods** trapped within the stars would contemplate them!

Tetragrammaton

"The philosophers-stone"
Or
Crystal
(*Like Alice through the Looking-glass*)
A jewel of **Alchemy**, by which base metals (**bodies**) are turned or transformed into gold (**higher-self**)

Like the **cross** or **quincunx,** that indicates human existence at the intersection of the (**horizontal**) physical plane and the (**vertical**) plane of eternity, like the **Mayan** calendar represents a sort of **spiritual pilgrimage**, or **footprints of creation,** represented by the **20 Mayan days,** see: "The pyramid decoded" by Peter Lemesurier page 267.

"**The impalpable separated from the palpable and through wisdom it rises slowly from the world to heaven**"

Like the crucifixion of our lord, Jesus Christ's **baptism** of **purifying fire,** and the true meaning of the cross: **Igne Natura Renovatur Integra** "by fire nature is renewed whole" like an esoteric experience or as the 60s song by Norman Greenbuam: (**Spirit in the sky**) "Prepare yourself you know it's a must, gotta have a friend in Jesus, So you know that when you die, he's goanna recommend you To the spirit in the sky!"

In a way of trying to achieve **self-illumination** by trying to raise the base **human body** and **spirit** to a **higher-state** or **join** that which has been **separated**, by **rediscovery** of the **winding path** by following the **hidden-thread**, like **Theseus** and the **Monitor** in Greek legend, after he had overcome his **lurking-fear** round every corner, and had slain this many headed **monstrosity** behind the **mask** of his own **fears** and **dread**!

Quasi-corporal, 'astral' body of paracelsus' theorizing; that the second body, **second persona;** not quite **spirit** and not quite **flesh;** sharing equally the qualities of the **material** and of the **immaterial.** Living within the **flesh**, and **pervading** it but **exstending** itself far **beyond** the earthly **confines** of the flesh. The **mirror-image** of the **material body.**

Like **Quetzacotl** who was **consumed** by a **symbolic funeral fire**, that he threw himself upon, and was consumed into **ashes,** like in the **Mayan 20 days** or **footprints of God,** that on the **17ᵗʰ day, C'haban,** he shakes off the last traces of **ash** clinging to him in the **material world,** and **rose into the sky!** As a flock of birds, bearing his heart that was to become the **planet Venus** or **morning star!** Telling them that one-day he would return. Much like the mysterious **star of Bethlehem** and the

5th *hidden aspect* of *Jesus Christ's cross* or *quincunx*, and his symbolic *death* and *resurrection...*

"Mathew *('Eli, Eli, lama sabachthani')* is akin to the Mayan for *'I faint' I faint, and my "face" is hidden in darkness' ('Hele, hele, lamah sabac ta ni')*"

Are we writing a letter to our selves, so to speak, like in an experiment in time, by J.W.Dunne and that dreams contain both past and future events! Which is like an invisible footprint from whatever or whoever has left it behind, where the finger of suspicion points at us!

Like the character *Morbius* in the *Forbidden-planet*, when his *"id"* was actually at the door trying to get in, and its very probable but highly unlikely *"it"* is responsible for the *Jack the ripper* killings or *Bible John* and even the people in David Paulides *Missing 411,* books.

Quetzacotl

Is also associated with the sun, which dies daily and is reborn or resurrected, like *Osiris-slyin* and *Osiris-risen,* who was reborn or reincarnated as *Ra* the *sun!* And at the *5th hour,* the Gods boat! Which was known to emerge from the *divine-egg!* Or was it the divine yoke or stick from the symbolic tree to *break our backs,* when it falls in the forest, and if no one's there, does it make a sound! Or is that the sound of the Gods laughing at the riddle of what came first, the *chicken or the egg?* Or...

Aztec

(Symbolism)

Like the biblical *Israelites* had wandered, from around *A.D, 1160* to look for their mythical promised land *"Anahuac"* 'the place in the midst of the circle' led by *2 warrior brothers* like *"Moses and Aaron"* called *Gagavitz* and *Zactecauh,* with their *holy staff of Tulan* and *drove it into the sea,* and the *waters parted* with the *pilgrims* walking across to the opposite shore, the parallel with the *red sea* is startling in the extreme.

'Pause and Remember this!'

That one day we will or already have as a species reached that relative-point of observation, like our own highly evolved selves, who seem or appear to be not only interfering in time, but could be collectively projecting something into our primitive minds or their own ancestral heads, so to speak!

(If you don't believe me, you can test the theory!)

. . .

"By checking back, not in a billion years, just tomorrow? Which is in the future and by that time, today, which is the present, will be yesterday or it will be in the past! And if you do, you will have eventually arrived in the future, which is tomorrow?"

. . .

240

It's as simple as that! So the theory holds true, that the collective energy of the species has already achieved a science without instrumentality or when one has what is euphemistically called a *Conscious-Dream* or when you know you are asleep and dreaming, like the Yogi who realizes the true teaching of the dream doctrine by penetrating the state of dreaming and becomes active in the so-called realm of **"taijasa"** and has begun to grasp the meaning and significance of the **illusion,** where they try and solve the problem of **reality,** so when he goes to sleep, he takes along the material of this all-containing world, he tears it apart and then builds it up, like creation through destruction, he is then **self-illuminated** and can create anything by mere thought! Be it **heaven** or **hell,** for he is a **creator** or **god!** Where reality is indeed **plastic**, like the riddle of life itself or what came first the **chicken or the egg?** Because matter cannot be created! Or destroyed, like the...

Petitio Principii

"A begging of the question"

If a tree does fall in the proverbial or prime-ordinal forest, if no one is rely there to hear it! Does it make a sound? Or is not only the forest even there, but anything, unless anybody is there to perceive it, by way of their ability to see, hear and feel things relative to the consciously aware observer, then does anything rely exist? Which is a fair question, because if you can't create matter or destroy it, then technically it isn't rely there, just like deep trance phenomena or hypnotic hallucinations!

We seem or appear to be chasing our own tail, so to speak, through time, caught in a self-made relative **dichotomy** or **prison**, in the long dead past! And in a future that has still to happen!

Having become our own **gaoler**, so to speak, there we collectively wait, trapped outside and inside ourselves, like the beings in **"Beneath The Planet Of The Apes?"** projecting and controlling what we think is our own or **shared-reality**, with certain safeguards built in, to protect us from our own selves?

"Men of science say miricles are past and give reasons for
things supernatuaral,
therefor we dismiss our terror,
by finding safety in false knowledge,
instead we should submit ourselves to an unknown fear"

I know this story is quite esoteric, but if you stick with it, you will find the hidden clues among a wealth of **Easter eggs!**

As we journey back like an **anthropological theological** and **sociological** paper chase, back in time to the **antediluvian** past with its **Atomic-bombs**! And **fiery chariots.**

Mahabharata War-An atomic War?
Aftermath
(India epic 5.000bc...)

Gurka loosed a single **projectile** on the triple city from a mighty **Vimana** that was brighter than the **sun** that rose up in **infinite brilliance,** which reduced the city to ashes.

"It was as if the elements had been unleashed. The sun spun round. Scorched by the incandescent heat of the weapon, the world reeled in fever. Elephants were set on fire by the heat ran to and fro in a frenzy to seek protection from the terrible violence.

The water boiled, the animals died, the enemy was mown down and the raging of the blaze made the trees collapse in rows as in a forest

The elephants made a fearful trumpeting and war chariots were burnt up and the scene looked like the aftermath of a conflagration. Thousands of chariots were destroyed and then a deep silence descended on the sea.

The winds began to blow and the earth grew bright. It was a terrible sight to see. The corpses of the fallen were mutilated by the terrible heat, so that they no longer looked like human beings, never before have we seen such a ghastly weapon and never before have we heard of such a weapon!"

C.Roya. Drona Parva 1889

Those who were lucky enough to escape washed themselves, their equipment and their arms, because everything was polluted by the death dealing breath of the **Gods!**

Years have rolled by since **India** detonated its first **Atomic Bomb** to join the league of the so-called **"Nuclear Powers."**

However the **Mahabharata** indicates that **India** seems or appears to have had or been given **atomic-power** long ago, before the rest of the world even came to know of the existence of **atoms.**

Incidentally **Oppenheimer** who worked on the **atomic-bomb-project,** while being interviewed by the media, gave a surprising reply referring to the **atom- bomb,** as not the first **nuclear-weapon,** but the first one of modern times".

A few excerpts from the **Mahabharata** have caused doubts in the minds of historians, indicating the possibility of **nuclear-weapons** being used in the **Mahabharata** or **ancient war.**

Recent discoveries of **green glass,** and many **radioactive samples** in certain excavations, in India associated with the **Mahabharata** war. **Green glass** is said to form when **sand melts** at very high temperatures prevalent in **Atomic Explosions.** The following is an excerpt:

"**Gurkha,** flying a swift and powerful **vimana** hurled a single projectile charged with the power of the Universe. An incandescent column of smoke and flame, as bright as ten thousand suns, rose with all its splendour. It was an unknown weapon, an iron thunderbolt, a gigantic messenger of death, which reduced to ashes the entire race of the **Vrishnis** and the hakas.

The corpses were so burned as to be unrecognisable. Hair and nails fell out; Pottery broke without apparent cause, and the birds turned white. After a few hours all foodstuffs were infected... to escape from this fire the soldiers threw themselves in streams to wash themselves and their equipment."

"Dense arrows of flame, like a great shower issued forth upon creation, encompassing the enemy.

A thick gloom swiftly settled upon the **Pandava** hosts. All points of the compass were lost in darkness. Fierce wind began to blow upward, showering dust and gravel; birds croaked madly... the very elements seemed disturbed. The earth shook, scorched by the terrible violent heat of this weapon. Elephants burst into flame and ran to and fro in frenzy, over a vast area, other animals crumpled to the ground and died. From all points of the compass and arrows of flame rained continuously and fiercely."

. . .

The excerpt "An incandescent column of smoke and flame, as bright as ten thousand suns, rose with all its splendour" actually appears in the *section 34* of the **Karna Parva** of the **Mahabharata** as follows: The universe is similarly said to consist of **Vishnu. Vishnu** is, again, the Soul of the holy **Bhava** of immeasurable energy. For this the touch of that bowstring became unbearable to the **Asuras.** And the lord **Sankara** cast on that arrow his own irresistible and fierce wrath, the unbearable fire of anger or that which was born of wrath of **Bhrigu** and **Angirasa.**

Then He called **Nila Rohita** that terrible deity robed in skins, looking like 10,000 Suns, and shrouded by the fire of superabundant Energy, blazed up with splendour.

That discomfiter of even him that is difficult of being discomfited, that victor, that slayer of all haters of **Brahma,** called also **Hara,** that rescuer of the righteous and destroyer of the unrighteous, the illustrious **Sthanu,** accompanied by many beings of terrible might and terrible forms that were endued with the "**speed of the mind**" and capable of "**agitating and crushing all foes**", as if with all the fourteen faculties of the soul awake about him, looked exceedingly resplendent, it was an unknown weapon, an iron thunderbolt, a gigantic messenger of death, which reduced to ashes the entire race of the **Vrishnis** and the **hakas.**

. . .

"When then next day came, Samva actually brought forth an iron bolt through which all the individuals in the race of the vrishnis and the hakas became consumed into ashes."

Indeed, for the destruction of the **Vrishnis** and the **hakas, Samva** brought forth, through that curse, a fierce iron bolt that looked like a gigantic messenger of death. The fact was duly reported to the king. In

243

distress of mind, the king (**Ugrasena**) caused that iron bolt to be reduced to a fine powder. Men were employed to cast the powder into the sea.

"The streets swarmed with rats and mice. Earthen pots showed cracks or broke from no apparent cause. At night, the rats and mice ate away the hair and nails of slumbering men" and "Fires, when ignited, cast their flames towards the left. Sometimes they threw out flames whose splendour was blue and red. The Sun, whether when rising or setting over the city, seemed to be surrounded by headless trunks of human form. In cook rooms, upon food that was clean and well-boiled, were seen, when it was served out for eating, innumerable worms of diverse kinds..."

. . .

'Heavenly chariots'

Moses Apocalypse
Chapter 33

Eve looked up to heaven, and saw a chariot of light travelling there and it was drawn by four shining eagles and where no terrestrial being could have described its magnificence as the chariot drove up to Adam and smoke came out from between the wheels...

"Chariots of light as early as Adam and Eve!"

. . .

Tuthmosis III

1500B.C.

Whose scribes saw a ball of fire that came down from heaven and its breath had an evil smell. Tuthmosis and his soldiers watched this strange spectacle up until the weird fiery ball rose up and moved away till it disappeared from view.

. . .

Cuneiform text to the sun God Ra:

"Thou couplest under the stars and the moon,
Thou drawest the ship of Aten in heaven and on earth like the tirelessly revolving stars,
And the stars at the north-pole that do not set...!"

. . .

The Apocryphal book of Abraham xviii, 11/12
"Behind the being I saw a chariot which had wheels of fire, and every wheel was full of eyes all around, and on the wheels was a throne and this was covered with fire that flowed around it.

EZEKIEL.

(*The book of the prophet*)

"Ghosts in the machine"

And I looked, and, behold, a whirlwind came out of the north, a great cloud, and a fire unfolding itself, and a brightness *was* about it, and out of the midst thereof as the colour of amber, out of the midst of the fire.

Also out of the midst thereof *came* the likeness of four living creatures. And this *was* their appearance; they had the likeness of a man. And every one had four faces, and everyone had four wings.

And their feet *were* straight feet: and the sole of their feet *was* like the sole of a calf's foot: and they sparkled like the colour of burnished brass. And *they* had the hands of a man under their wings on their four sides: and they four had their faces and their wings.

Their wings were joined one to another; they turned not when they went; they went everyone straightforward.

As for the likeness of their faces, they four had the face of a man, and the face of a lion, on the right side: and they four had the face of an ox on the left side; they four also had the face of an eagle.

Thus *were* their faces: and their wings *were* stretched upward; two *wings* of everyone *were* joined one to another, and two covered their bodies. And they went everyone straightforward: whither the spirit was to go, they went: and they turned not when they went.

As for the likeness of the living creatures their appearance *was* like burning coals of fire, *and* like the appearance of lamps: it went up and down among the living creatures: and the fire was so bright, and out of the fire went forth lightening.

And the living creatures ran and returned as the appearance of a flash of lightening.

Now as I beheld the living creatures, behold one wheel upon the earth by the living creatures, with four faces.

The appearance of the wheels and their work *was* like unto the colour of beryl: and they four had one likeness: and their appearance and their work *was* as it were a wheel in the middle of a wheel.

When they went, upon their four sides: *and* they turned not when they went.

As for their rings, they were so high that they were dreadful: and their rings *were* full of eyes round about them four.

And when the living creatures went, the wheels went by them: and when the living creatures were lifted up from the earth, the wheels were lifted up whithersoever the spirit was to go, they went thither *was* their spirit to go: and the wheels were lifted up over against them: for the spirit of the living creature *was* in the wheels.

When those went, *there* went; and when those stood, *these* stood; and when those were lifted up from the earth, the wheels were lifted up over against them: for the spirit of the living creature *was* in the wheels.

And the likeness of the firmament upon the heads of the living creature *was* as the colour of the terrible crystal, stretched forth over their heads above. And under the firmament *were* their wings straight, the one toward the other: everyone had two, which covered on this side and everyone had two, which covered on that side, their bodies.

And when they went, I heard the noise of their wings, like the noise of great waters, as the voice of the almighty, the voice of speech, as the noise of an host: when they stood they let down their wings. And there was from the firmament that *was* over their heads when they stood, *and* had let down their wings.

And above the firmament that *was* over there heads *was* the likeness of a throne, as the appearance of a sapphire stone: and upon the likeness of the throne was the likeness as the appearance of a man above it. And I saw as the colour of amber, as the appearance of fire round about it, from the appearance of his loins even upward, and from the appearance of his loins even downward, I saw as it were the appearance of fire, and it had brightness round about.

As the appearance of the bow that is in the cloud in the day of rain, so *was* the appearance of the brightness round about. This *was* the appearance of the likeness of the glory of the lord, and when I saw it, I fell upon my face, and I heard a voice of one that spake.

"And he said unto me, son of man, stand upon they feet, and I will speak unto thee. And Ezekiel was warned of his rebellious house, which has eyes to see and sees not, and ears to hear and hears not... and then he was given or handed orders to establish law and order and to create a proper civilization...!"

Ezekiel

Continued:

With the destruction at noonday...

Jerusalem

"Bacillus"

Satan Bug

Using the metaphorical:

. . .

"Ring a ring o'roses, a pocketful of posies,

Atishoo, atishoo,

All fall down..."

. . .

In all your dwelling places, the cities shall be desolate. And the slain shall fall in the midst of you.

So will I stretch out my hand upon them, and make the land desolate, yea, more desolate than the wilderness toward Dihlath, in all their habitations.

An end, the end is come upon the four corners of the land. Now *is* the end come upon thee, and I will send mine anger upon thee. And mine eye shall not spare thee, neither will I have pity.

An evil, an only evil, behold, is come. An end is come, the evil is come: they have blown the trumpet even to make all ready: but none goeth to the battle: for my wrath *is* upon all the multitude thereof.

All hands shall be feeble, and all knees shall be weak as water. They shall also gird *themselves* with sackcloth, and horror shall cover them; and shame *shall be* upon all faces, and baldness upon all their heads.

Destruction cometh; and they shall seek peace, and *there shall be* none.

Then I beheld, and lo a likeness as the appearance of fire: from the appearance of his loins even downward, fire; and from his loins even upward, as the appearance of brightness, as the colour of amber.

And he put forth the form of a hand, and took me by a lock of mine head; and the spirit lifted me up between the earth and the heaven and brought me in the visions of God to Jerusalem.

He cried also in mine ear with a loud voice, saying cause them that have charge over the city to draw near, even everyman with his destroying weapon in his hand. And, behold, six men came from the way of the higher gate, which lieth toward the North, and everyman a slaughter weapon in his hand; and one man among them was clothed with linen, with a writers ink-horn by his side: (Who was to go through the midst of the city, through the midst of Jerusalem) and set a mark upon the foreheads of (certain people)

And to the others he said in mine hearing, go ye after him through the city, and smite: let not your eye spare, neither have ye pity: slay utterly old and young, both maids, and little children, and woman: but come not near any man upon whom is the mark.

And behold the man clothed with linen, when had the inkhorn by his side, reported the matter, saying, I have done as thou commanded me...

Standing on the shoulders of Gods

"*Like in the story of **the merchant** year of our lord 1665 and the rich and God fearing merchant during the time of the black death or the bubonic plague that swept over Europe killing millions and sparing lots of people, a democratic pestilence that was to chose the young and the old, the rich and poor alike!*

Through the streets wide and narrow came the horse and its barrow with a disconcerting voice that cried out! Bring out your dead as it tolled that awful bell, making its way through the streets as it hovered over the great cities of Europe, a disturbing ringing in the ears, carried by the wind alongside that terrible smell, with the cry of a million voices rising up from the multitude to ask or beg the question: why Does God let such things happen, and are such things part of the grand plan? But the answer like the smell was blowing in the wind, like an unsolved riddle.

With the rich and powerful merchant now sitting beside a little girl, who had her arm around his bulky shoulders, as she tried to comfort and console a giant with feet of clay! The way she would have when playing with her rag dolly.

It was too late for the likes of them, the merchant had said, as if staggering blindly in the confines of his own spiritual darkness, before the words were thrown back in his face, like a hand full of purblind consonants and stray vowels, where he had earlier recoiled in horror, the way a cartoon Elephant does when it sees a mouse, as the same little girl had come over to take his hand in a nonchalant way, oblivious to what was happening, and to show him her rag dolly. It was God punishing them for being idol and lazy, because the merchant had been taught that the devil finds work for idle hands, as if the pompous and arrogant merchant was not bound on that same journey as the rest of us! And there sat the merchant and his little impromptu friend, like a little sparrow that had been blown off course, with the sound of that bell, as it came ominously closer and closer, and the merchant and the little girl were unceremoniously taken away in the cart!"

"Know one seems or appears to question where this mysterious pestilence originally came from like the **Great-plague** or **black-death,** and why it mysteriously stoped!"

Paul Crowe

248

"For each mans death diminishes me,
For I am part of humanity, ask not for whom the bell tolls, it tolls for thee!"
John Dunne

Ezekiel

Continued:

Then I looked, and behold, in the firmament that was above the head of the cherubim's there appeared over them as it were a sapphire stone, as the appearance of the likeness of a throne.

And he spake unto the man clothed with linen, and said, go in between the wheel's, *even* under the cherub, and fill thine hand with coals of fire from between the cherubim's, and scatter *them* over the city. And he went in, in my sight.

Now the cherubim's stood on the right side of the house, when the man went in: and the cloud filled the inner court. Then the glory of the Lord went up from the cherub, *and stood* over the threshold of the house: and the house was filled with the cloud, and the court was full of the brightness of the Lords glory. And the sound of the cherubim's wings was heard *even* to the outer court, as the voice of the almighty God when he speaketh.

And it came to pass, *that* when he had commanded the man clothed with linen, saying, take fire from between the wheels, from between the cherubim's: then he went, and stood beside the wheels.

And *one* cherub stretched forth his hand from between the cherubim's unto the fire that *was* between the cherubim's, and took *thereof,* and put *it* into the hands of *him that was* clothed with linen: who took it and went out.

And there appeared in the cherubim's the form of a man's hand under their wings. And when I looked, behold the four wheels by the cherubim's, one wheel by one cherub, and another wheel by another cherub: and the appearance of the wheels was as the colour of a beryl stone.

And *as for* their appearances, they four had one likeness, as if a wheel had been in the midst of a wheel. When they went, they went upon their four sides; they turned not as they went, but to the place whither the head looked they followed it; they turned not as they went.

And their whole body, and their backs, and their hands, and their wings, and the wheels, *were* full of eyes round about, *even* the wheels that they four had. As for the wheels, it was cried unto them in my hearing O wheel.

And everyone had four faces: the first face *was* the face of a cherub, and the second face was the face of a man, and the third a face of a lion, and the forth the face of an eagle. And the cherubim's were lifted up. This *is* the living creature that I saw by the river Chebar.

And when the cherubim's went, the wheels went by them: and when the cherubim's lifted up their wings to mount up by the earth, the same wheels also turned not from beside them.

When they stood, *these* stood: and when they where lifted up, *these* lifted up themselves *also*: for the spirit of the living creature *was* in them. Then

the glory of the Lord departed from off the threshold of the house, and stood over the cherubim's.
And the cherubim's lifted up their wings, and mounted up from the earth in my sight.

"A.D: Chariots in the sky"

For before the sun set, they're appeared in the air over the whole country, chariots coursing through the clouds and surrounding the cities.

Josephus, Jewish war book CXI.

From a contemporary historian of the time, described two shiny shields spitting fire around their rims and dived repeatedly at the columns of Alexander the great, stampeding horses and elephants, and then returning to the sky!

. . .

"What on earth were Ezekiel and the others trying to describe?" Like in the strange disappearence of **Mitchell Dale Stehling** in the **Mesa Verde National Park, Colorado aged 51 years. Page 91 MISSING 411 The Devil's in the Detail.** And what the man's wife, Denean stated to a reporter: "When I look back, there were a lot of signs that we shouldn't have taken the trip! Was she inadvertently using intuition?

Like creatures that live in the deep oceans of the world, who need to take sustenance from other organic life-forms that *die* and sink to the bottom of the ocean or sea, is this how our facless predators from out of the unknown *Take's* (ops) or absorbs its proteins!

. . .

Hermaphrodites

Is there race's of beings with an affinity to *"Homo-sapiens"* who through some meta-physical experiment created a precursor like *"Adam"* And who in turn produced *"Eve?"* And was it their hand that was behind *"Samson"* and *"Christ!"* Who seem or appear to be a race, of *"hermaphrodites"*, *"A-sexual"* or *"androgynous"* beings?
And through some kind of crossbreeding or inbreeding having taken place, in the grand experiment or plan, to alter our destinies, for reasons best known, to whatever or whoever is responsible?
And then they had to cross-bread with the *"seed of heaven"* or symbolic 'sons of god' that could have been some mysterious, or more evolved *"gene!"* That was mysteriously introduced by person or persons unknown, so to speak, that seem or appear to have albeit broken or continued the link in our evolution, from *"Neanderthal-man"* to *"Cro-Magnon"* or other humanoids that live on the planet with us, like cattle?
A consummation that would produce *"giants"* or *"freaks"* and these high-tech mysterious creatures introduced, the *"X-factor"* or missing link

"**Gene!**" Of the mysterious progenitor named: "**Noah**" or "**precursor**" to the new Homo sapiens!

The Tiger

Tiger, tiger, burning bright in the forests of the night, what immortal hand or eye could frame thy **fearful symmetry,** in what distant deeps or skies burnt the fire of thine **eyes?** On what wings dare he aspire? What the hand dare seize the fire and what shoulder and what art could twist the sinews of thy heart? And when thy heart began to beat, what dread hand and what dread feet? What the hammer? What the chain? In what furnace was thy **brain?** What the anvil? What dread grasp *dare its deadly terrors clasp? When the stars threw down their spears, and water'd heaven with their tears, did he smile his work to see? Did He who made the lamb make* **thee,** *tiger, tiger, burning bright in the forests of the night, what* immortal hand or eye *dare frame* thy fearful *symmetry?*

William Blake. 1757–1827

* * *

"**The forest is dark and deep
And we have a long way to go before we sleep**"

. . .

"This is the end of our pseudo history lesson"

What about the case of **Charles McCuller, page 121**, *MISSING 411 EASTERN UNITED STATES by David Paulides Crater Lake*!
The Ranger on the scene for **"NPS"**(*National Parks Service*) said it was one of the oddest sites he had ever seen, there was no large bones, except the skull and the jaw, and it seemed or appeared as if the man had melted into his pants! Figuratively speaking, at the bottom of the pants were socks with toe-bones inside, and the belt Charles was wearing had been intentially unbuckled! And his boots were missing!
Or like in the great book "**Lost**" by **Dwight McCarter. Page 46,** with a rather tongue-in-cheek title:

THE PERILS OF PASSAGE

(Criminal negligence)

And the young boy, **Geoffrey Burns Hague, aged 16yrs**, having just earned his scout explorer badge in scouting, the description of this boy, does not fit or tally with the character or temperament needed in the first place to get into the **Cubs** or the **Scouts,** one has to have the right temperament to begin with, and you have to be organised and be able to understand and follow orders, which must I assume have already been the case, having dedicated much of his youth to such an organization as the **Scouts,** it does not make any logical sense, that his behaviour or lack of maturity was in any way a form of self-denial in regards to his **rights of passage to adulthood,** the scoutmaster adults with him, must have made the decision based upon what?

251

To leave a **16-year-old boy** standing alone for whatever reason, in the middle of nowhere! Who may or may not have been in the throws of developmental adolescence, either physical or emotional, and having been assigned to the middle of the group or hiking order with so-called experienced adult-hikers ahead of and behind him to make sure that everyone made it out safely, till they had reached the first junction of the **Appalachian Trail,** with the **Boulevard Trail** where they had stopped briefly, being only half-a-mile from their camp-site and going towards the **newfound gap parking-lot,** why had they changed their mind set?

As they started to move out towards the **Newfound Gap parking-lot,** instead of insisting that Geoffrey would be coming with them, because there was no way they would be leaving him all alone out there, or they would be staying with him until the other scoutmaster Lee Smith, who had stayed behind to secure the campsite, said that he would join them later, by following them out, eventually reached the group, so when they met at that point, then they could have all left together, why were they in such a hurry to get out?

More haste and less speed

Unaware that they would half to come back all over again and take part in the **SAR** (*search-and-rescue*), if only they had waited, instead of having to use the benefit of hindsight or theorising after the fact, **"would you bay a car from any of these men?"** never mind let them take part in the **SAR** (*search-and-rescue*) efforts!

If only they could have looked before they leaped, they would have come out of the wilderness together. But the people who Geoffrey was relying on to make sure he was safe and sound, for reasons best known to themselves, made what seems or appears to be a serious and tragic error, and one that would eventually cost a young inexperienced **"boy"** his life, why did the group dynamics change at this point? Was Geoffrey's behaviour so strange and bizarre that it influenced their behaviour, which is a form of group behaviour or indirect **hypnosis,** that can open a widow to the mind that is capable of subtly changing the mind set of one or more of the experienced members of the group, so that a band of gorillas would eventually choice an alfa-squirl as leader! When they urged him to follow them, and for some reason he hesitated and then said he would wait for Lee and come out with him, at that point the suggestion or pattern-interrupt was implanted, and they left him standing at the junction near the trail signs which clearly pointed the way toward the **Boulevard Trail** and **Mt LeConte** in one direction, and the **Appalachian Trail** to **ice water Springs** and **Charlie's Bunion eastwards,** a decision that defied logic, and one that seems or appears to have been the equivalent of buying a dog and barking yourself, walking away defeats the whole purpose of why he went with so-called responsible adults in the first place, they indirectly signed his death warrant, or have we accidentally found out that something else might have been going-on underneath the radar, so to speak!

Young **Geoffrey Burns Hague** was eventually found in the Great Smokey Mountains National Park, **1970,** there description is as follows: "The rangers described finding him at the base of a tree, half-sitting, half-slumped into a foetal position and still covered with deep snow, except for the parts of his right-arm and part of his right-leg, where the snow has partially melted off him, he has no socks on and one boot is lying 6ft away, the other boot is unlaced and half on his right foot, his orange toboggan cap is off, his mittens are off, his left arm is pulled up inside the sleeve, his pants are unzipped and partial removed." As if he were suffering from "**hypothermia**" like in our so-called **humane-society** when a person living alone is sometimes found in their apartment in a state of disarray, and there seems or appears to have been a terrible struggle for life, against person or persons unknown, and the obvious scene looks to all intent and purposes, like a violent homicide or where the person has been struggling against nothing more than an invisible killer or assailant called: "**hypothermia**" or is there something more frightening about these strange deaths that should be properly investigated, something that is being hidden right out in the open!

Half-truth

Information that seems or appears to be fallacious, as reason or dawn struggles with something of a mystery in the dark, in regards to what they seem to think happens when a person dies of the cold, which is the obvious, compounded by the erroneous!

Symptoms of mild hypothermia **may** be vague, with sympathetic nervous system excitation (shivering, hypertension, tachycardia, tachypnea, and vasoconstriction).

These are all physiological responses to preserve heat. Cold diuresis, mental confusion! And hepatic dysfunction **may** also be present. Hyperglycemia **may** be present, as glucose consumption by cells and insulin secretion both decrease, and tissue sensitivity to insulin **may** be blunted. Sympathetic activation also releases glucose from the liver. In many cases, however, especially in alcoholic patients, hypoglycemia appears to be a more common presentation. Hypoglycemia is also found in many hypothermic patients, because hypothermia **may** be a result of hypoglycemia.

Low body temperature results in shivering becoming more violent. Muscle mis-coordination becomes apparent. Movements are slow and labored, accompanied by a stumbling pace and mild confusion! Although the person **may** appear alert. Surface blood vessels contract further as the body focuses its remaining resources on keeping the vital organs warm. The subject becomes pale. Lips, ears, fingers and toes **may** become blue.

As the temperature decreases, further physiological systems falter and heart rate, respiratory rate, and blood pressure all decrease. This results in an expected heart rate in the 30s at a temperature of 28 °C (82 °F). Difficulty in speaking, sluggish thinking, and amnesia start to appear; inability to use hands and stumbling is also **usually** present. Cellular metabolic processes shut down. Below 30 °C (86 °F), the exposed skin becomes blue and puffy, muscle coordination becomes very poor, walking becomes almost impossible, and the person exhibits **incoherent/irrational behavior!** Including terminal burrowing or **even** a stupor. Pulse and respiration rates decrease significantly, but fast heart rates (ventricular tachycardia, atrial fibrillation) **can** occur. Major organs fail. Clinical death occurs!

Paradoxical undressing

Twenty to fifty percent of **hypothermia** deaths are associated with paradoxical undressing. This typically occurs during moderate to severe **hypothermia,** as the person becomes disoriented, confused, and combative. They **may** begin discarding their clothing, which, in turn, increases the rate of heat loss.

Rescuers who are trained in mountain survival techniques are taught to expect this; however, some **may** assume incorrectly that urban victims of **hypothermia** have been subjected to a **sexual assault!** Like in **David Paulides** book: **MISSING 411 WESTERN UNITED STATES & CANADA** And **Evelyn Consuela Roseman,** who you will read about later on!

One explanation for the effect is a cold-induced malfunction of the hypothalams, the part of the brain that regulates body temperature. **Another explanation** is that the muscles contracting peripheral blood vessels become exhausted (known as a loss of vasomotor tone) and relax, leading to a sudden surge of blood (and heat) to the extremities, fooling the person into feeling overheated.

There seems or appears to be more to why people are stripping off their clothes, vuluntarily or otherwise! Like in **MISSING 411 WESTERN UNITED STATES & CANADA. By David Paulides** and the odd case of **Billy Colman 1940 CA. aged 14 years. Page 81.** And as David said, the idea that a young 14 year old boy volentarily stripped off his clothing in the cold, on the first day that he went missing, is a contridiction in terms, regarding **hypothermia!**

Terminal burrowing

An apparent self-protective behaviour known as **terminal burrowin**g, or **hide-and-die** syndrome, occurs in the final stages of **hypothermia.** The afflicted will enter small, enclosed spaces, such as underneath beds or behind wardrobes. It is often associated with **paradoxical undressing.** Researchers in Germany claim this is **obviously** an autonomous process of the brain-stem, which is triggered in the final state of **hypothermia** and produces a primitive and burrowing-like behaviour of protection, as seen in hibernating animals. This happens mostly in cases where temperature drops slowly.

This information is nothing but a half-truth, like the weather forecast being sure about being unsure!

Remember!

[There is nothing more deceptive than the obvious]

Was **Geoffrey Burns Hague** confused in some other way? Although it looks to all intent and proposes, as if he was confused or had been assaulted, and whoever it was had been trying to dress him in a hurry or were disturbed in doing it, so something else could have been involved in the assault! Because I know it sounds crazy, but it looks to all intent and purposes that whoever was responsible seems or appears to be unsure on how to dress him!

A **Green-Beret-team** with Tom McGinn and his dogs are assigned to the slopes of Anakeesta Ridge on the right flank of Washington State team. Rescue squad personnel are assigned to search remaining areas not yet combed in the vicinity of the **PLS.** (*Place-last-seen*). **NPS** (*National-Parks-Service*) crew leaders with radios are assigned to these search teams to assist in communicating any information found to headquarters. Helicopters are to assist in transporting searchers in and out of their assigned areas.

"It's a chilling observation by David Paulides, but there have been people frozen to death on the tops of mountains and in the Artic, but they are always found with their boots and cloths still on, if not, then something very strange is happening!"

Or the strange and unsettling case in **David Paulides' books MISSING 411** and the terrifying stories of **Robert Springfield 49yrs,** who had mysteriously went missing in Bighorn Mountain, Montana, while out bow hunting and several years later his coat was located neatly placed next to a tree, and his belt was neatly rolled-up next to the evidence of his remains!

Or in **MISSING 411 WESTER UNITED STATES AND CANADA** by **David Paulides** and the case of **Bart Schleyer aged 49.** Who mysteriously disappeared in Canada, Reid Lakes, in the **Yukon Territory in 2004** under highly suspicious circumstances, both of these men where the same age! Barts bow was found leaning up against a tree, and his pants seemed or appeared to have been taken or pulled off!

It was as if he had been attacked by something that was **very intelligent, fast and yet very powerful!** Other strange cases show an uncomfortable pattern where only their skulls and small pieces of bone are located, yet major amounts of blood are not present on the cloths!

It can't be indigenous animals that we know of, because they don't unlace boots or undue belt buckles! Do they? As in the Bart Schleyer, Charles McCullar and Robert Springfield cases!

Why are children being found at great distances from where they disappear, and are they being taken or carried there by some means of travel or vehicle [moving/flying craft] that we don't know about? By **highly intelligent creatures** that are either from this world or somewhere else! So to speak, and who seem or appear to be trying to cover-up their true motives or intentions!

We cannot judge them by our own double standards, because they don't, whoever or whatever they are, need to try and understand a **cabbage,** with its false sense of **morality**! You wouldn't ask the dogs, cats and mice! That the military and or drug companies experiment on, especially if your country depends on it, or your precious father and mother or daughter and son might need that drug to live, now would you? Either before you experiment or dissect them alive or dead, in the laboratory! And then you just throw it away in the rubbish bin *"For disposal and incineration"*
Or even little harmless worms or insects like wasps, bubble-bees and flies that are mercilessly killed with electronic bug zappers! If they believe in a God! And would they like the last rites, now would you! Because that would be ridiculous?
Whatever or whoever is doing this, does not want to draw undue attention to what ever they are doing, by causing panic and alarm among the enslaved populace or *pets*! And yet it strangely seems or appears that we are being controlled by something outside our own frame of existence, so to speak, judging by our behaviour in the past, present and probably in the future!
Because religion, science and politics has shaped the very world that we think we live in, and pseudo-events like the '**Great-Flood**' or '**Sodom**' and '**Gomorrah**' and even in the *Twin Towers or 911* mystery, and the unquiet *Kennedy assassinations*! Is something very odd begging the question, so that we don't affect anything in the future that is yet to happen!
And yet again by using the world as a global slave market, it seems or appears that something is trying to reach out by necessity, in order to warn us in some way, that they will have no compulsion to punish or destroy us, if needs-be, by the apparent death of *2,752 people* who died, including all *157 passengers* (*including the so-called hijackers!*) And crew aboard the two airplanes, if you can believe it, or are these co-cospiritors basking under the *Maui-sun*, like *"Whitman" "Price" and "Haddad"* in the *1987* movie called: *"The Running Man!"*
Its as if it were some kind of signature or warning with the strange destruction of the *Twin-towers* by what seems or appears to be the use of a possible mysterious high-tech induction weapon of some kind, that was used in conjunction with explosives and the mysterious airplanes, that somehow brought down two massive buildings!

. . .

It's very probable, that they or whoever is interfering with our *"Anthropological"*, *"Theological"* and *"Social history"* could be the cause of these and other strange events, and are probably responsible for the *September 11th 2001 catastrophe of the twin-towers!*

Gene-pool

I know it sounds preposterous, but its as if some mysterious hand is at work, like in my fictitious novel Titled: *"Standing On The Shoulders Of Gods"* and the description of the *beast in the cellar*, that was brought to life, from the shed skin in the **"dust on the ground"** that contained: **DNA!**

And the strange and unquiet work of **"Jack the Ripper!"** **"Bible John"** Or **"Legions of the Damned"** Or **"Gods, Angels and Giants"** and through the unseen hand or twin **duality** of the **archetypical** or symbolism of **God** and **Satan,** from within this one single source, the consummation of a theoretical **"dichotomy"**, where both or some aspect have theoretically emerged out of a **dark chrysalis**!

. . .

"For if men do these things when the tree is green, what will happen when it is dry?"
Luke 23:31

. . .

It's as if we are collectively writing a fragmented letter to ourselves, but we don't know if it could be our own highly evolved and collective self, that is the author of the piece!

If not then who is it, or what could it be, that seems or appears to be trying to communicate something and why? As if **"Through a glass darkly"** by using key words in our theological writings again and again, like: **"Water!"** **"Blood!"**, **"Stone!"**, **"Star!"** and **"Sea!"**.

It's as if its got something to do with the old Testament with the **"Israelites"** and the mysterious **"Amorites"** hinting at some obscure **'Anthropological' "Theological"** and **"Sociological"** thread that in some mysterious way, links some kind of symbolic means-to-an-end.

'On That Scaffold Sways The Future!'

If you read the excellent book by David Paulides **"MISSING 411 WESTERN UNITED STATES" page 73.** You will eventually come to a rather **"prophetic"** photograph of a higher species killing a lower one: Robert Winters who vanished in **1969, aged 78yrs,** which reminded me of the cult TV show Star-Trek, and the episode you should all watch, called: **ARENA**, and doctor McCoy's or (Bones) astounding sentence: **"In the name of civilization!"** and then look at Spocks expression! And tell me what you think?

David's excellent books have painfully identified the problem! So to speak! And now it is, as it's always been, the responsibility of a society to ignore the problem, like it does with everything else, with its empty boasts of **"Freedom" "Fraternity" "Liberty"** and **'Justice'** for all, a society that firmly believes in equality, where unfortunately some people are more equal than others!

Including the people who have vanished or have been senselessly and brutally murdered at the hands of some mysterious two-headed monster, or that which seems to be neither one thing or the other, its something that seems or appears to be **Visa-Versa** or there one minute and gone the next, is it the **enemy at the gates**, or **the enemy within!**

That seems or appears to have been with us for longer than we care to remember like in **"Jack the Ripper"** or the **"JFK assassination"** and

257

of course the legacy of the **"Twin-towers"** and the mysterious murders of the people involved, by the invisible-hand that rocks the cradle, being quicker than the eye, by what seemed or appeared to be a clever magicians trick!

" A lernean Hydra that grows another head for each one that is cut off, because it seems or appears to be everywhere, and yet nowhere?"

We need to rally to this and other causes, in order to locate and defeat this and other faceless enemies! That seem or appear to have nothing but contempt for us, as a species, we need to conscript our best brains, **scientists** and **engineers**, even the **inteligencer** from places like **"Mensa"** who probibly sit around all day playing with themselves trying to square the circle, but its highly unlikely! Because they are the ones who seem or appear to know everything, and if nobody comes forward to help, then there will be nothing left to know!

. . .

We know whoever or whatever they are, that they must be **corporeal** or **non-corporeal**, but they seem or appear to act in and out of a physical medium, like **UFOs** (*Unidentified Flying Objects*) or **flying Saucers**, akin to **Ghosts** and other **strange phenomena!** If they can effect the battery in automobiles or cars! Then they must have an **Achillies heel**!

Tranvaluation

(Strange)

"The man's daughter said that's what first made her sit up, was when she heard a noise behind her bed, She said it was a clicking in an electric socket, and it was when she sat up she noticed something outside in the sky. I asked my neighbour if he had seen anything and although he had not, he said about the same time there was a surge in his electricity!

And another neighbours light bulb exploded about the same time, I don't know if this is linked, it's just strange"

Based on the fact that sometimes when searchers have already been in an area where the person has disappeared from, they still cannot find the victim. Months, days, or hours after the incident, the person is found in the exact area they originally disappeared! What does that tell us? We need to overhaul our view of the world that we live!

Its as if a giant computer is trying to reboot the system, like the **Krell** in the 1950s Sci-Fi movie: **The Forbidden Planet.**

. . .

Anybody entering these area's need to carry or use portable **GSM/GPRS/GPS** trackers and the people involved need to use and secretly keep planting, **Mini portable spy cameras** all over the area, but you need to do it surreptitiously, why? Because someone or something is watching us!

And the cameras need to be linked to **DVD/CD** or **streaming-videos** that would automatically send pictures back from the web-cam, before **someone** or **something** tries to pull the plug, so to speak, or even try and collect **DNA** samples from any of the immediate areas, in case we might pick-up any questionable **DNA!**

"The Face Of The Beast Is Always Hidden"

I'm sure you have asked the same question as I have, *why are they being so elusive? And it seems or appears that they do not want us to find out what they look like.*

O*r*

when they go missing in such a way that no one would suspect or notice the pattern of their disappearances over the years!

. . .

Until it has been brought to our attention by **David Paulides** in his excellent and incredibly informative **books**!

As **David** says in his book, that the person had been moved into a position closer to the local, from which they initially disappeared in order that they may be found. **Yes,** found either alive or after they have **died**!

Are they leaving some kind of subliminal message or **"Easter egg"** for us to find them, and that's why they are putting the bodies back dead or alive, remember size is relative, and I know this sounds crazy, but we could be dealing with either an intentional self-induced delusion by person or persons unknown, or a race of giants! That live outside our perception, and are somehow gaining access to this sphere of influence like in: **Passport to Magonia**: **By Jacques Vallee 1975** and who seem or appear to be curious about us, and are accidentally damaging us, because we are akin to someone trying to hold a fragile butterfly, by someone who doesn't know their own strength! Or are they using a machine that grabs them, causing the strange (**scratches all over the entire body**) are they are being grabbed by the legs and feet?

. . .

Which is very much like the story of the flying Scaucer or UFO (Unidentified Flying Object) in Coatbridge. Area Scotland U.K 5th October 2009 8.30pm:

"...As he watched without moving, two spiky spherical objects dropped from the bottom of the larger object. These two **spheres** were approximately two ft across and he later described them as being quite like sea mines as used in World War II, except that the spikes were longer that those of sea mines, making the objects' diameter approximately, *3 ft* **spikes** included.

The spheres were looking metallic, similar to the material of the larger object, and made frightening sucking noises as they fell from the object and impacted the wet ground. As Taylor stared in awe, the two **spiky spheres** rushed towards him from the direction of the object, by bouncing and rolling on the ground.

His dog now barked loudly. The **two spheres** arrived at him each rolling quickly at the same time to his left and right foot."

A bit like the little boy: Billy Clever in *MISSING 411 EASTERN UNITED STATES. Aged 3 years page 197 Pennsylvania in 1947,* who was found with his cloths torn to shreds, but he was ok!

The *spheres' spikes* extended and attached to the *Bob's trousers* and *dragged* him towards the *larger sphere*. I think that wild berries may or may not have anything to do with what's happening, obviously its a possible food source that could possible be used as a clever way of attracting animals or people, in order to catch them, for whatever reason!

But this strange and inconsistent part of the mystery seems or appears to be like *"Sherlock"* Homes, and his greatest nemesis *"Moriarty"* who liked leaving strange clues at the scene of his diabolical and twisted crimes, that were apparently inconsistent or did not make any sense, like the very clever association with *wild berries* and/or *when they come into season, like a preverbal Spiders web.*

Which to all intent and purposes seems or appears to display a very cunning and clever technique of entrapment, just like *Bobby Conner* in *Greenburgh, New York. Page 224. Aged 21 Months. MISSING 411 EASTERN UNITED STATES.* The neighbourhood was on the edge of a forest with lots of water and heavy timber.

On July 13, 1934 Bobby Conner was with an older neighbourhood friend at his residence, Bobby's mother had called the friends home to tell them it was time for Bobby to return home and while en-route home, bobby *conviently* [My Italics] stopped at a sand pile adjacent to an old automobile and started to play! Although his friend had said to him that he had to go home, Bobby had refused.

And after he had left Bobby to go and tell his mom that she would have to come out and get Bobby, but by the time they had arrived at the sand pile, Bobby had vanished! And was eventually found 5 days later, as if placed on his back, he had scratches but was alive and well, lying under brambles, in an area that had already been searched!

Is it one or even several highly evolved races, sending out some kind of mechanical contrivance or machine to take samples and to analyze life forms, on the surface of this planet for whatever reason?

And why are they camera shy? While at the same time being so contradictorily elusive, by intentionally letting us know they are there, which sounds very much like an automaton or computer would, or some highly evolved race like us! Who would show animals and lower forms of life or even *"cabbages"* nothing but contempt!

The speed of the camera lens and what it might catch on film

Maybe that's why photographers go missing as well! Because *"they"* or whoever and whatever *"they"* are! Must be aware of the X-factor/chance/luck/ probability! Just in case somebody sees something that they either shouldn't have seen, or like the young woman *Trenny Lynn Gibson* hiking in the forest, and they put something there to catch her attention that she was meant to see, that was so strange or unusual, or familiar, and why did she not call others to witness this strange event!

Like Nicole Renaud from the same book, aged 3 years, in Bourg-La-Reine, Quebec. Page 251. Who saw something that must have somehow intrigued or beguiled her in some strange unnatural or natural way, something that eventually took her life!

"Come into my parlour said the spider to the fly"

Have you ever noticed that a lot of people who go missing have a middle name, like for example?

John Wilkes Booth or **Lee Harvey Oswald**!

Because we could be dealing with more than one type of race, who are exceptionally clever advisories, and because of this, the girl was eventually caught in the web or very clever animal/mouse-trap! So to speak, on the infamous Appalachian Trail! **In MISSING 411 EASTERN UNITED STATES.** Where the student on a hike mysteriously disappeared: **Trenny Lynn Gibson** aged **16yrs page 111**, in the **Great Smokey Mountains USA.**

Where a witness saw her being distracted by something, and saw her bend over as if to look at whatever it was, and then she seemed or appeared to go off to the right of the trail, into what looked like a very rough area with rocks, bushes and trees, and was never seen again!

It's as if she was distracted by something accidentally, or intentionally in order to catch her!

Like **Harold Mote** in **MISSING 411 EASTERN UNITED STATES Pennsylvania, aged 12yrs, page 206,** whose dog (*Snowball*) mysteriously went missing! And when he, his brother and a neighbour tried to look for the dog, behind the Mott residence, after they had decided to split-up to try and find *the hairy K9 miscreant* (My italics) Harold conveniently went missing! During the search Snowball had mysteriously appeared on the scene, having returned to the house!!

Harold was eventually found 9 miles away by Monty Edel who was searching for Harold with another individual, when they looked up and saw him! Harold asked, if Snowball had been found, as he accompanied them back to their vehicles.

It seems to be a clever manoeuvre in order to catch their prey, so to speak, and a pattern that tends to repeat itself in other instances, like David Paulides says: last in line, a single individual or a very credible excuse in order to coerce them into getting away from the group or any witnesses in order to get them alone, whether it's a fence on the property that needs mending because it seems or appears to have been damaged for whatever reason, and the animals have naturally and conveniently wandered away, and need rounded up!

Pièce de résistance

And the notable or defining episode of: **John Wayne McKinney** of **Gallipolis Ferry, West Virginia. Aged 5 years, page 218** in **MISSING 411 EASTERN UNITED STATES by David Paulides**.

Where the family had only one dog! Up until just ten days before the mysterious abduction and subsequent death of the little boy, no one knew where this hairy agent provocateur collie dog or bitch described as **"fearless"** had mysteriously came from?

And it was while he was out playing with "fearless" and his other hairy K9 friend and fellow companion **"Spitz"** a smaller dog that he and his hairy quadruped companions went missing for some unknown reason?

Here we have what seems or appears to be a very clever ruse, by whatever or whoever was responsible for luring and abducting the little boy and his friends away, the collie dog or bitch had mysteriously returned for whatever reason later that day! And the smaller dog, **"Spitz"** returned the next day!

Like the story of **Otis T. Mason page 197** in the same book, who was last seen playing with his family's three dogs! When he and the three dogs went missing! Several hours after little Otis had disappeared, two of his hairy companions returned home, but the third dog was still missing, while the searchers were at a vacant or empty house, two miles away heard a muffled sound coming from an underground area, and when the searchers then pulled off the lid of an empty septic tank they found the missing dog alive inside the tank! Which begs the question, how did the dog get inside the septic tank, and then put the lid back on, so who or what was responsible? And before you answer that it could have been a human predator, which is very probable, but highly unlikely!

Otis was eventually found dead in a shallow creek in a four-foot-hole filled with water, one that had been searched several times before!

As **David Paulides** implies: **"if only dogs could talk or where is the dog whisperer when you need them?"** So to speak, he was found without his shoes! Was it a killer who took them for some strange reason? I personally don't think it can be answered in this way, because these strange disappearances don't fit into the normal criteria of murder by person or persons unknown, and any parallels to any connection to people living of the grid or possible serial killers, so to speak, will tend to confuse or blur the relative issues of **missing 411** or even **QED** (*questions enable debate*) regarding theses cases.

Even though the victims are sometimes found completely naked for no apparent reason, even after being checked by a physician to see if they have been molested in any way, like **Edward (Teddy) Gately aged 2 years, page 237 MISSING 411 EASTERN UNITED STATES.** Who had been taken and stripped of his clothing and placed under the cover of bushes, even though there was never any mention of molestation, very clever mental or visual abuse can still take place! Without the child being overtly touched or physically harmed, by the abuser, especially to child/adult with special needs or child that has not learned to vocalise as yet, if one reason seems or appears not to apply, then there must be another reason, so the question is why were the cloths removed? As if they are being examined!

Which incidentally reminds me of one of the pivotal events of the Second-World-War, as if someone or something was tampering with the weather in Bastone in France in order to effect the outcome: *"the fog curtain suddenly parted revealing a landscape dotted with German tanks-at least thirty of them. Fourteen tanks from the 3d Panzer Regiment made a try for Noville, coming in from the north.*

Several bogged down in a vain attempt to manoeuvre off the road; others were slopped by Desobry's company of Sherman tanks and by tank destroyer fire. On the east the enemy had started an infantry assault, but the fog lifted before the first waves reached the village and, suddenly divested of cover, most of the attackers turned and ran." Coincidence or another *"Easter egg?"*

Are these event connected in some strange and frightening way? Like in **David Paulides book: MISSING 411 NORTH AMERICA AND BEYOND. Page 195.** In the strange case of little Judy Paterson 1958 in Florida aged 3 years. Where during the search and rescue, later that night it seems or appears that fog moved into the area, restricting air-traffic and then once the fog clears, the little girl is found exactly in the area previously searched! Was it just a coincidence, or as David Paulides said, did it play a role in the little girls recovery? *And have we found another* **Easter egg?**

Or the story on page 179 Nebraska 1891 while out visiting the two little girls aged 4 and 8 years apparently left the road to pick wild flowers, and then mysteriously disappeared!

The little 4 yr old was eventually found fifteen miles away from the point the both left the road, she recovered, but the SAR (*Search and Rescue*) continued on until they discovered the older sisters body 75 miles from where they left the road! Why were the searchers even in that location? I know it sounds absolutely crazy, but it seems or appears as if something is controlling or putting thoughts into our heads, which means it looks like we have found another *"Easter egg"*

I'm sure the egghead's could construct specially shielded *"EMF"* detectors, or *"GPS"* web-cam, like the hand-held *"EMF"* machines used in paranormal investigations, or to locate electrical wiring inside house walls, that leave behind *"electromagnetic footprints"* that would let us be able to track and hopefully view their movements, and we will be able to know who we are dealing with! When our elusive visitors are moving around! Or when they fly over our heads, and we would be able to strategically make up a pattern of their movements in and/or over the cities and in the forests and mountains!

Even though the air has been polluted with *"Low-frequency-spectrum"* i.e. *"Radio-frequency"* and *"Microwave"*, *"EMF"* sources i.e. *"Mri/DC"*, *"Earth & Subways"*, *"AC-Power"*. *"Radio-*

frequency-Spectrum" i.e. *'Cell'* "*AM/FM*", "*TV*", "*Cell/PCS UMTS*", "*Microwave*" i.e. "*Microwave & Satellite*" which protects them or makes it more difficult to trace their movements, because some of our elusive visitors using these strange flying machines or crafts, seem or appear to be showing some kind of "*Electrical-Magnetic-Signature*" or "*footprint!*"

So it could be a case of highly evolved creatures that have some distant affinity with man, then based on an unbiased appraisal of our own treatment of other species or lower forms of life, never mind the barbaric treatment of our own kind, we are in for big trouble!

Which brings us to the pilot 1960s TV Movie" of "**Star-Trek**" with Jeffery Hunter, who was being manipulated by a highly advanced culture, who were capable of reading his mind and controlling his thoughts! Using '**ESP**' and '**Telekinesis!**' Remember, everybody votes in a dictator!

That's why they have continued unabated, even though they have cleverly managed to kidnap and murder citizens of all ages and sex's with so-called impunity, without leaving behind obvious footprints of not wanting to show their '**faces**', so to speak, for whatever reason, do they have some sort of weakness, why don't they come out and openly take what they want? Maybe that's how they could have been colonizing worlds, for millions of years!

Unless our political masters or there overseers, or those and such as those, already know who and what they are! And three most powerfully controlling factors in world control is wealth and power! By distribuling the drug or the "**Opium**" of the people, free of charge! By hi-jacking and twisting the word of God, and turning his son into a leper messiah! And then have them kneel before a false God in the form of money! Or "*mammon*" everybody needs these basics of life: **shelter**, **food**, **warmth**, and human love and companionship and understanding but the truth is usually elusive untill it sets you free!

> *"The lingering illness is over at last*
> *And the fever called living is conquered"*
>
> *Edgar Allen Poe*

Looking for the truth is a bit like trying to put a square-peg in a round hole! Remember, you can't serve two masters! You need to come up for air, or stay down as long as you can, in your fish-tank or artificially created world, so to speak, one is painful and the other is a lie, what do you chose?

In a world of plenty for those and such as those, who make the right chose in the maze, after all are we not **our brothers/sisters keeper**? You know the ones who tend to starve, freeze or die of ill health or of exposure! Doesn't that sound very familiar? It's as if someone or something is treating us like **mice** in a **controlled laboratory experiment, so to speak**!

264

FLYING SAUCERS ARE HOSTILE

These strangers from the skies would feel no compunction about shocking us with a "prod" if we approached their craft too closely, in paralysing our heart muscles if we proved too troublesome, even to cut us open for biological investigation.

Brad Steiger and Joan Whritenour

. . .

So the response or search must be a clever and a coordinated one, which means they must have an **accillies-heel**, much like the mythical entity **"Dracula"** who could not be killed, but only destroyed when **"it"** was dormant!

"Terror By Night"

"We had strayed into some region or some set of conditions where the risks were great, yet unintelligible to us. It was a spot held by the dwellers in some outer-space, a sort of peep-hole whence they could spy upon earth, themselves unseen, a point where the vail between had worn a little thin"

Algernon Blackwood and The Willows 1907

. . .

Why are we always re-acting And not acting?

And the reasons for this contra-indication is caused or alluded to in George Bernard Shaw's statement "England and America are two countries separated by a common language" in which we are being duped by an authority that wallow's in its **"raison d' être"** or nothing more than a reason to be, and act, no matter the outcome, individuals who seem or appear to be unable do their job right, because they are to busy doing their job! They are in effect busy doing nothing!

Like the story in **Missing 411 NORTH AMERICA AND BEYOND** by **David Paulides** and the little girl that went missing and was later found dead, **"as if she had been dropped, from the air!"** [My Italics] or Isabel Zandarski age 30 months on page 273, and while other children were sleeping in the same room, reported seeing 'a big black man' that was subsequently ignored, which could have been a large dark figure? And David Paulides knows, that as a police officer you have to be very careful when it comes to witnesses, or sleight of mouth statements that have a double meaning, like i.e. **"a black woman's handbag!"** Or "**never trust a man who doesn't drink!**"

Is it an unspoken **"demande"** *which means a* **"request"** *or* **"demand"** that in English means some kind of spurious and covert payment! By this pernicious enemy that has to be paid, is it a promise or certain understanding not to invade and then enslave, or what?

We seem or appear to be weak, because we do nothing to meet or impeach what seems or appears to be a highly evolved and intellectual many-headed **"Hydra"** at the gates or from within! That seems or appears to be one step ahead of us, during the kidnapping and the search and rescue operations! Do they already know what we are thinking? Because they could be using **ESP!**

In **Missing 411. NORTH AMERICA AND BEYOND.** And the case of Casey Holliday, Aged 11yrs. Page 107 and the surreal story of how the boy's aunt had turned down an extremely remote forest road, one she'd never driven down before, *and weird as it sounds* [My Italics] she couldn't explain why she was on it! And that's where she found the boy in a gully, babbling and in a daze, was it **'coincidence**, **'chance'** or something **'else?'**

Or the story of **Jason Elijah Burton** aged 21months! Where a so-called decision was made to put two men onto the Tyger River, one of several water bodies within two miles of the boys residence in Cross Anchor, South Carolina, and about a mile from the little boys home.

But there's a strange twist in the tail, David Paulides said that the Spartanburg deputy and another officer were paddling up stream! Which makes no sense, instead of searching down-stream, the way a body is naturally carried by the current, and there was Jason Elijah Burton lying on a sand bar up-stream, still alive!

Or the strange case of Naomi Leigh Whidden aged 2yrs Chattahoochee National Forest, Georgia. And one of the search and rescue teams, led by Kip Clayton who was at the outer fringe of the search perimeter, when something, *Call it a gut feeling or even intuition,* [My Italics] but something told him to continue out another 250 yards and look for the lost girl, where he eventually found her alive!

Or **Stephen Papol aged 3yrs. Hecksher State Park NY.** One of the groups involved in the search, where auxiliary police officer Ramond C. Finger and his wife, on the morning of August 22, the officer told her husband, they were going to search the areas around the parking lots, because she had a premonition the previous night about finding the boy there, and that's where they found him, alive!

Or like the mysterious disappearance in **MISSING 411 NORTH AMERICA AND BEYOND of Colin Gillis, 18yrs, at Tupper Lake NY, 2012. Page 269.** Who was seen by a witness, "Richard Rosentreter" who saw someone who fitted the description of Colin, walking on the shoulder of the highway towards him! But it's the strange thinking processes of the key witness, among other things, that drew my attention; Richard Roseentreter said, **"It wasn't like someone walking with a purpose straight down the road with a coat on, (as I passed by I recognised it as something out of the ordinary, something that I didn't think it was safe to stop")** what did he mean? As well as in the case of **Christopher Vigil aged 9 years. 1978. Colorado: MISSING 411 The Devil's in the detail. Page 71.** That describes the strange disappearance or abduction of Christopher, but the description by two girls

266

who passed him on the trail, who reported a strange type of shout, when they were at the top of the mountain! *"**Intuitively, she sensed that something was wrong and wanted to investigate but did not do so as she feared for her well being**"*

The reason I have mentioned these rather unusual cases, is that they needed more attention, because the evidence can get easily lost in the hue-and-cry of the normal investigation.

. . .

Hypnosis

As David Paulides has already implied, or anybody who is familiar with hypnosis, knows that everybody can be susceptible to the hypnotic-trance, and if these highly evolved beings know this, you or I could be fooled into thinking that something's there, when its not! Or visa-versa, you will hear it, smell it and feel it! Because the truth is akin to peeling an onion, the more you peel away the skin, the more you tend to reveal more of what's underneath, which is self-evident.

We will never solve the problem unless we approach it with an open-mind and use a number of approaches, like in the 1960s TV Show: **"*Star-Trek*"** called: **"*Spectre Of The Gun*"** where Spock has to convince the others, by using his Vulcan mind-mell, after the strange discovery, regarding reality, as it was!

It allowed him to theorise that reality was inconsistent, much like **"*Flying Saucers*"** or **"*UFO's*"** (*Unidentified Flying Objects*) that seem or appear to be doing things inconsistent with reality! Or contradictory to the laws of Physics, see: **"*Gods, Angels and Giants*"** which is like the old metaphysical saying, **"if a tree falls in the forest, and if no one is there to hear it, does it make a sound?"**

And so Spock had to prepare their minds in the context of the story, that the bullets were unreal, and could not hurt them! Which is a bit like life or the psychology of mental-hygiene, if life knows you are afraid of it, it tends to bite! So to speak!

What astonishes me, is the fact that due to some unspoken and idiotic mating ritual, between the authorities, law-enforcement and the parents, who seem or appear to acquiesce, like in the song **"*Four wheels on my wagon, and I keep rolling along, three wheels on my wagon, and I keep rolling along etc*,"** I think you get the point!

And once the parent's are lucky enough to get their child back, alive and well, the victim is not given the proper help to overcome their amnesia! Through the effective agency of **"*Hypnosis*"** as David has already mentioned in one of his books, to gently resolve this puzzling enigma, and try to encourage recall and recover the forgotten information, because its of the utmost importance that we find out, whatever or whoever is doing this! Or people will continue to go missing, and if any resistance is encountered it can be overcome using modern drugs if necessary!

The use of drugs
As an adjunct to hypnosis!

Barbiturates, acting as a cortical depressant. Can be used to produce hypnotic sleep when and if all other methods have failed.

Today, various derivatives and modifications of the Phenobarbital family are used. Some are better suited for the light stages of hypnosis, many drugs have been tried to facilitate the induction or deepening of hypnosis in difficult subjects!

The intravenous barbiturates appeared promising since they are often used to secure the release of emotional material, their action in this respect, however, may not be related to hypnosis which can be used on its own to produce similar abreaction.

Intravenous thiopentone (Pentothal) is occasionally helpful, but is more often disappointing; this is unfortunate since only short-acting drugs of this type can be safely given to outpatients.

Remember no response, times no response, equals, you've got it, no response, so once the person has responded, whether you use drugs or not, all the operator has to do is compound the suggestions in the trance by introducing amnesia! Or forgetting their name or a number or series of numbers, it's as simple as that. [My Italics]

The vein selected is usually the median basilic in the antecubital fossa, or a dorsal metacarpal vein in the back of the hand. The patient is asked to count slowly during the injection, about one count per second, the injection is then stopped to permit the complete effect which usually requires thirty to thirty-five seconds, at which time the patient usually ceases to count and shows evidence of relaxation, the dropping of the jaw, etc.

The drugs are administered in distilled water solution by slow intravenous injection at a rate of not more than 1 c.c. A minute. Dosage varies from 3 grains to 15 grains dissolved in 10 to 20 c.c. Of distilled water.

The barbiturates may also be taken in capsule form. A capsule of 1½ to 3 grains taken orally will produce a drowsy state in about 20 minutes.

This is supplemented by hypnotic suggestion. Even in the use of barbiturates, an understanding of the techniques and principles of hypnotism is essential to obtain the maximum benefits resulting from its utilization.

While the subject is in the hypnoidal state, we find them speaking freely and divulging their conflicts, anxieties and repressed memories! Physiologically, the barbiturates act as a depressant of the higher nerve centres in the cortex while psychologically they lessen the activity of the inhibitory centres, thus facilitating a release of inhibitions and simultaneously removing the psychic barriers

The oral administration of amylobarbitone sodium (Sodium-Amytal), 6 to 9 grains, or pento-barbitone sodium (Nembutal), 3 grains, about 30 minutes prior to the induction of hypnosis can sometimes be of assistance; but these are long-acting drugs and sufficient time must be allowed after their use for the subject to sleep off their effect, vis-à-vis (therefore) you give the subject the proper suggestions to overcome this! [My Italics] or even the drug that is given before general anaesthesia, which is an intravenous injection of (Sodium thiopental) which sends the patient immediately to sleep, in order to induce the hypnotic-state.

It was reported that the administration of Tabs Valium, 2mg or 5mg three times on the day preceding treatment, followed by one 5mg tablet half an hour before, that seems to facilitate the induction of hypnosis in the agitated and apprehensive patient, and removing the psychic-barriers or lessen ego resistance.

And if you think that the use of such drugs are the equivalent of using a sledge hammer to crack a nut, then you can even use a simple sedative to induce what is known as Hypno-sleep or hypnosis induced while the person is asleep!

Normal **counselling** or **psychotherapy** is too long and ineffective; it would be like trying to push custard up hill, it is incapable of uncovering the crucial incident or repressed factors in each case.

We know it must be one thing or the other, its very probable that the mind-block or amnesia was caused by the strange experience, but highly unlikely, it seems or appears to be a false *amnesia*, or some kind of *block* that has been *intentially* been *put in*! Or using:

Art therapy

Is a creative method of expression used as a therapeutic technique. Arts therapy originated in the fields of Art and Psychotherapy and may vary in definition. It may focus on the creative art-making process itself as therapy or on the analysis of expression gained through an exchange of patient/client interaction. The psychoanalytic approach was one of the earliest forms of art psychotherapy. This approach employs the transference process between the therapist and the client who makes art. The therapist interprets the client's symbolic self-expression as communicated in the art and elicits interpretations from the client. Analysis of transference is no longer always a component. Current art therapy includes a vast number of other approaches such as: Person-Centered, Cognitive, Behavior, Gestalt, Narrative, Adlerian, Family (Systems) and more. The tenets of art therapy involve humanism, creativity, reconciling emotional conflicts, fostering self-awareness, and personal growth.

Like in the case of Michael Auberry aged 12 years, in **MISSING 411 EASTERN UNITED STATES page 108.**

Have they tried taking blood samples? In order to find out if anything strange or odd turns up in their blood!

Sounds very **"Orwelling"** but you will have to prepare most, if not all of the people, in some sort of cooperative medical programme that addresses the issues, even if they don't go into these dangerous areas like, i.e. Park rangers, and the citizenry from **5** to **95yrs** with **"Hypnosis"** it sounds radical, but there is no other another answer to these bizarre conundrums, and the **"GPS"** or **"AKA"** (Also-Known-As) the **"Global-Positioning-Satellite"** transponders need to have a locking switch that can't be manually turned off, once it has been activated after you buy it!

And or set up a cost effective website that can be funded by public donations! Called i.e.: **"411 profile"** and like David Paulides said that he can look at a google map, and state the likelihood of a person going missing based on the topography of the area, the age of the child or adult, physical characteristics and so on, where parents need to be made aware that their child could be in more danger than adults are, per say, lone hikers! Or if they leave the group for any reason, their destiny immediately changes because someone or something is probably watching you or your child, in more ways than one, for reasons that would make the mind boggle!

The Mouse Trap

In order to try and catch the culprits, who seem or appear to be one step ahead us, its blatantly obvious they are very cunning and clever, so you could do it in a coordinated fashion using **"GPS"** (*Global-Positioning-Satilite*) units with streaming mini-cameras hidden in selected **red-flag areas**, or/and on the target acquisition, so to speak, with streaming web-cam audio/visual recording facilities, wearing bright colours especial red! And carrying photograph cameras (with film) to pretend you are a photographer, while being in constant contact with others listening and watching/recording, what is going on 24/7, while the **point-walker** is in contact with base, in case they are being cleverly monitored by you know who! And Watched until an opportunity exists for them to disappear!

Obviously its going to be dangerous, in order to draw them out of hiding by providing the cheese that goes in the mouse-trap.

It sound radical and it could probably work, but it's highly unlikely, because we are not dealing with idiots, but something very strange and exceptionally clever.

People who use these dangerous areas, can self-register, by giving enough of their relevant details on the protected site, and/or keep the site up-dated with texts on their movements, while carrying their personal **GPS** tracker! This will allow the system to monitor and check where the **GPS** tracker is located, not the person! So it behoves them to look after it and report or text their relative position, so the site can monitor where they have been and gone, so to speak.

And if they go missing, you have all the details to help in the search and rescue? And if they are that indifferent to what can happen, then it's just the same as going on a ride at the carnival:

"You enter the system at your own risk!"

You could use seismology triangulation all over America and Canada you could intentionally use an underground atom bomb test or (H-bomb) and the resulting shockwave or signature, can be triangulated by pre-selected stations using seismographs, I am not surprised if it has already been done, and already suppressed! So that it would pick-up and show us where, if any, underground structures might be located! Which is either somewhere in the **800 mile crust** or down at the **mantel!** Which in a way epitomizes a comment that was made in old books, that Flying Saucers or UFOs (*Unidentified Flying Objects*) seem or appear to be more curious about our **"Atom- programme"** for reasons best known to themselves.

JOHN KEEL
MICHIGAN

Or the strange story of a creature that was about seven feet tall with '*a black face*' John Utrup told the Cass County sheriff that he had seen the monster several times. One night as he was driving into his yard he saw it standing behind a bush.

Mrs Untrup told of how one of her Shepard dogs chased the monster one night and came back with the **"pupil of one eye turned a pale blue colour"**. Weeks later the **"eye"** returned too normal, it seems or appears that there could be more of grave, than of gravy about these elusive creatures! Whoever or whatever are they?

A logger in British Columbia, Gordon Baum, reported seeing a hair-covered man-like animal leap over a four-foot pile of logs at Salmon Arm Inlet on Thursday, June 27th, 1968. **"It must have been a Sasquatch,"** Baum was quoted as saying in the Vancouver Province. It moved on two legs like a man; it ran like a man, but **"no man can move that fast!"** He was gone in two seconds. He was about five feet tall, very stocky, and heavily built.'

Like in David Paulides book **MISSING 41 EASTERN UNIYED STATES. Page 136.** And the strange case of **Dennis Lloyd Martin**. Aged 9 years.

Its as if its like some primitive beast, like *Shakespeare's* play: **"The Tempest"** or in the 1950s movie adaptation of it called: **"The forbidden planet"**, where the actor, Walter pigeon with his artificially expanded mind, had unknowingly emerged like a nightmarish caterpillar from the dark chrysalis of his own **psyche**, having sent out his **"ID"** or **elemental force/instinctive drive** to destroy anything that was a threat to him, sending out all his hatred and lust with murderous intent, freed from the dictate of so-called civilization, and with no moral-code, he would be a danger not only to himself, but to other people around him, like in **"a tale of mice and men"** or a child in a man's body, with no sense of right or wrong! Sent out to terrify and then to search and destroy everything in its wake...

Retrospect

If we don't do anything but just write about it, then we deserve what we get, from whatever or whoever is doing it? Because if they can come into our homes or grab coedes, they can grab anybody, anywhere and at anytime!

Or we will have to except the fact, that there are **strange** and **mysterious spieces**, that are **superior** and more **advanced** than **ourselves**! And carry on regardless, if David's books don't tell us anything, it sure tells us something about our selves!

Questions?

What about strange enigma of 911? And remember the un-answered questions of why **"Weather" "Water"** and **"stones"** play a big part in not only the bible, but in ***MISSING 411 by David Paulides books!***

Like in Australia and the movie called: (*Picnic at Hanging Rock* or *The Secret of Hanging Rock)* has been presented as a previously unpublished chapter of Joan Lindsay's 1967 book *Picnic at Hanging Rock* and is supposed to contain the **"solution"** to the mystery in that book. According to Lindsay's editor, it was originally written as the final chapter, though the missing material amounts to about twelve pages, it was removed before publication and not released until 1987, three years after Lindsay's death.

It has been argued by critics that much of the power of the original book stems from the suggestion that it was a true story, and the fact that the mystery in the book was never resolved.

The chapter opens with Edith fleeing back to the picnic area while Miranda, Irma, and Marion push on. Irma looks down and compares the people on the plain below to ants. When the girls walk past the monolith, they feel as if they are being pulled from the inside out and get dizzy. After they leave it behind, they lie down and fall asleep.

A woman suddenly appears climbing the rock in her underwear shouting, **"Through!"** and then faints. This woman is not referenced by name and is apparently a stranger to the girls, yet the narration suggests she is Miss McCraw. Miranda loosens the woman's corset to help revive her.

Afterwards, the girls remove their own corsets and throw them off the cliff. The recovered woman points out that the corsets appear to hover in mid-air as if stuck in time, and that they cast no shadows. She and the girls continue together.

After the women experience dizziness, the group encounter a strange phenomenon described as a hole in space that influences their state of mind. They see a snake crawling down a crack in the rock. The woman suggests they follow the snake and takes the lead. She transforms into a small lizard-like creature and disappears into the crack. Marion follows her, then Miranda, but when Irma's turn comes, a balanced boulder [*the hanging rock*] slowly tilts and blocks the way. The chapter ends with Irma "tearing and beating at the gritty face on the boulder with her bare hands".

The Black Rock National Park in **"Queensland"** a natural mountain of Granite which is the signature rock of the continents. More than that, **granite** is the **signature rock** of the planet Earth itself, and **granite** contains: **"quartz!"**

The first nation or Indigenous Aboriginals call it: a forbidden zone! Where stories abound about people, horses and cattle disappearing into the labyrinth of rocks, never to be seen again! Even pilots have reported strange aircraft turbulance and magnetic effects or anomalies over the mountain.

And as **David Paulides** mentions in **MISSING 411 NORTH AMERICA AND BEYOND page 370.** about the common belief in an area of Iceland who belive in hidden people, who have been there for generations, and who live in rocks or **"boulders!"**

Quartz

The second most abundant mineral in the Earth's continental crust, after **feldspar.** It is made up of a continuous framework of SiO_4 **"silicon–oxygen" "tetrahedra"** with each oxygen being shared between two **tetrahedra**, giving an overall formula SiO_2.

Ghosts in the machine

An old Atomic war or was it something else!
Immanual Velikovsky
(*When worlds collide*)
Object-oriented programming

As the name suggests, **object-oriented programming** is related to objects. So far, we have used objects as loose aggregations of values, adding and altering their properties whenever we saw fit. In an **object-oriented approach**, objects are viewed as little worlds of their own, and the outside world may touch them only through a limited and well-defined interface, a number of specific methods and properties.

Newton's laws

One common form of the third of Newton's laws of motion of classical mechanics states that if **one object exerts a force on another object, then the second object exerts an equal and opposite reaction force on the first**.

In that form, only forces are mentioned. The full form of the third law translated from the Newton's Latin states: **"To every action there is always opposed an equal reaction: or the mutual actions of two bodies upon each other are always equal, and directed to contrary parts"**. In this full form, Newton's explanatory commentary explicitly allows for **"actions"** to include both **forces** and **rates of change of momentum**. The attribution of which of the two forces (or "actions") is the action and which is the **reaction** is arbitrary. Either of the two can be considered the action, while the other is its associated reaction.

Where the **force** from something humongous was **accidentally** or **intentionally!** used to **terra-form** the earth, for whatever reason! Destroying the **dinosaurs** to introduce a **new species** into the gene-pool, that resulted in the **historical flood**, and the introduction of the mysterious **Noah**, bleeding into this massive fissure to staunch the wound and cover over the massive scare or opening left behind, and that's what causes **magnetic anomalies**, where **compasses will not work** and the **sun**, although its down on the other side of the earth, is still peeking through this massive scare tissue causing the **Aurora borealis**.

Ringwoodite is produced by **'shock metamorphism'**, which in simple terms means **impact**. Volcanic pressures or sheer weight alone is unable to produce the same effect. Thus it would take a **meteor strike** or **underground or overground Atomic blast** to create enough impact! Such a material as ringwoodite is called a **polymorph** because it is created within existing material.

The existence of **ringwoodite** creates **seismic discontinuities** which is only natural as seismic waves travel best through solid rock whereas the spaces within the new **'shock rock'** contain **polymorph** material.

Various other rock structures have shown the same ability to create **polymorphs** when subjected to the same **shock force.**

Quartz may occur as either of its two high-pressure forms, **coesite** and **stishovite**.

Diamond, the high-pressure allotrope of carbon has been found associated with many impact structures.

Geological occurrences

In meteorites, **ringwoodite** occurs in the veinlets of quenched **shock-melt** cutting the matrix and replacing olivine probably produced during **shock metamorphism.**

In Earth's interior, olivine occurs in the upper mantle at depths less than about 410 km, and **ringwoodite** is inferred to be present within the transition zone from about 520 to 660 km depth. Seismic discontinuities at about 410, 520, and 660 km depth have been attributed to phase changes involving olivine and its polymorphs.

The 520-km discontinuity is generally believed to be caused by the transition of the olivine polymorph wadsleyite (*beta-phase*) to **ringwoodite** (*gamma-phase*), while the 660-km discontinuity by the phase transformation of **ringwoodite** (*gamma-phase*) to a silicate perovskite plus magnesiowüstite.

Ringwoodite in the lower half of the transition zone is inferred to play a pivotal role in mantle dynamics, and the plastic properties of **ringwoodite** are thought to be critical in determining flow of material in this part of the mantle. The solubility of hydroxide in **ringwoodite** is important because of the effect of hydrogen upon rheology.

Ringwoodite synthesized at conditions appropriate for the transition zone has been found to contain up to 2.6 weight percent water.

Because the transition zone between the Earth's upper and lower mantle helps govern the scale of mass and heat transport throughout the Earth, the presence of water within this region, whether global or localized, may have a significant effect on mantle rheology and therefore mantle circulation. In regions of subduction zones, the *ringwoodite* stability field hosts high levels of seismicity.

An ultra-deep diamond found in Juína, Brazil, contained inclusions of *ringwoodite*—the only known sample of natural terrestrial origin—thus providing evidence of significant amounts of water as hydroxide in the Earth's mantle. The mantle reservoir is found to contain about three times more water, in the form of hydroxide contained within the *ringwoodite* crystal structure, than the Earth's oceans combined.

Chemical composition

Ringwoodite compositions range from pure Mg_2SiO_4 to Fe_2SiO_4 in synthesis experiments. Ringwoodite can incorporate up to 2.6 percent by weight H_2O.

Physical properties

The physical properties of ringwoodite are affected by pressure and temperature. The calculated density value of ringwoodite is 3.564 g/cm³ for pure Mg_2SiO_4; 3.691 for Fo90 composition of typical mantle; and 4.845 for Fe_2SiO_4. It is an isotropic mineral with an index of refraction n = 1.768.

The colour of ringwoodite varies between the meteorites, between different ringwoodite bearing aggregates, and even in one single aggregate. The ringwoodite aggregates can show every shade of blue, purple, grey and green, or they have no colour at all.

A closer look at coloured aggregates shows that the colour is not homogeneous, but seems to originate from something with a size similar to the ringwoodite crystallites. In synthetic samples, pure Mg ringwoodite is colourless, whereas samples containing more that one mole percent Fe_2SiO_4 are deep blue in colour. The colour is thought to be due to Fe^{2+}–Fe^{3+} charge transfer.

Shock metamorphism or impact metamorphism describes the effects of shock-wave related deformation and heating during impact events. The formation of similar features during explosive volcanism is generally discounted due to the lack of metamorphic effects unequivocally associated with explosions and the difficulty in reaching sufficient pressures during such an event.

Planar fractures

Planar fractures are parallel sets of multiple planar cracks or cleavages in quartz grains; they develop at the lowest pressures characteristic of shock waves (~5–8 GPa) and a common feature of quartz grains found associated with impact structures. Although the occurrence of planar fractures is relatively common in other deformed rocks, the development of intense, widespread, and closely spaced planar fractures is considered diagnostic of shock metamorphism.

Planar deformation features

Shocked quartz with two sets of 'decorated' planar deformation features in impact melt rock from the Suvasvesi South impact structure, Finland (thin section photomicrograph, plane polarized light).

Main article: Planar deformation features

Planar deformation features, or PDFs, are optically recognizable microscopic features in grains of silicate minerals (usually quartz or feldspar), consisting of very narrow planes of glassy material arranged in parallel sets that have distinct orientations with respect to the grain's crystal structure. PDFs are only produced by extreme shock compressions on the scale of meteor impacts. They are not found in volcanic environments.

Brazil twinning in quartz

This form of twinning in quartz is relatively common but the occurrence of close-spaced Brazil twins parallel to the basal plane, (0001), has only been reported from impact structures. Experimental formation of basal-orientated Brazil twins in quartz requires high stresses (about 8 GPa) and high strain rates, and it seems probable that such features in natural quartz can also be regarded as unique impact indicators.

High-pressure polymorphs

The very high pressures associated with impacts can lead to the formation of **high-pressure polymorphs** of various minerals. Quartz may occur as either of its two high-pressure forms, **coesite** and **stishovite**. Coesite occasionally occurs associated with eclogites formed during very high pressure regional metamorphism but was first discovered in a meteorite crater in 1960. Stishovite, however, is only known from **impact structures**.

Two of the high pressure polymorphs of Titanium dioxide, one with a baddeleyite-like form the other with a α-PbO_2 structure, have been found associated with the Nördlinger Ries **impact structure**.

Diamond, the high pressure allotrope of Carbon has been found associated with many **impact structures** and both fullerenes and carbynes have been reported.

Shatter cones have a distinctively conical shape that radiates from the top of the cones repeating cone-on-cone, at various scales in the same sample. They are only known to form in rocks beneath **meteorite impact craters** or **underground nuclear explosions**. They are evidence that the rock has been subjected to a **shock** with **pressures** in the range of **2-30 GPa**

The effects described above have been found singly, or more often in combination, associated with **every impact structure** that has been **identified** on **earth**. The search for such effects therefore forms the basis for identifying possible candidate **impact structures**, particularly to distinguish them from volcanic features.

Tenham meteorites

Are the fragments of a larger meteorite that fell in 1879 in a remote area of Australia near the Tenham station, South Gregory, in western Queensland. Although the fall was seen by a number of people its exact date has not been established. Bright meteors were seen to be moving roughly from west to east. Stones were subsequently recovered from over a large area, about 20 kilometres (12 mi) long by 5 kilometres (3.1 mi) wide.

Because the Tenham meteorites were recovered quite soon after they fell, from a remote and dry region in which weathering and other alterations had not set in, they have been invaluable for scientific study of meteorites and their mineral contents. They are examples of chondritic meteorites, containing a high level of organic compounds, and rich in silicates, oxides, and sulfides. Many scientific studies have explored the mineralogy of these meteorites and their non-terrestrial features.

Because the Tenham meteorites show evidence of high pressure deformations, they have been used to infer chemical and mineral changes that might occur within Earth's mantle.

Ringwoodite, the high pressure **forsterite polymorph** named after Ted Ringwood was discovered in fragments of the Tenham meteorite.

Ringwoodite

Scientists have discovered a massive reservoir of water 400 miles below the United States.

The discovery appears to confirm that water actually *filters* through the Earth, from the oceans, collecting in vast reservoirs under the surface.

The evidence suggests that water molecules become trapped inside the minerals of mantle rock found deep below the Earth's surface, and then gradually cycle back up due to plate tectonics.

Discovered by geophysicist Steve Jacobsen and University of New Mexico seismologist Brandon Schmandt, the huge reservoir could help scientists better learn how the Earth was formed.

"I think we are finally seeing evidence for a whole-Earth water cycle, which may help explain the vast amount of liquid water on the surface of our habitable planet. Scientists have been looking for this missing deep water for decades."

"The *ringwoodite* is like a sponge, soaking up water, there is something very special about the crystal structure of ringwoodite that allows it to attract hydrogen and trap water. This mineral can contain a lot of water under conditions of the deep mantle."

To give you some idea of just how little we know about our own planet, that sample of ringwoodite is the *only* known sample of it to have come from within the Earth.

The theory was first postulated when a mineral called **ringwoodite** was discovered as part of a volcanic eruption in Brazil.

It's believed the mineral was brought up from a depth of around 400 metres below the Earth's surface. What scientists found when they analysed it was a surprising amount of water was actually trapped inside.

Interestingly this isn't a reservoir in the conventional sense; there isn't a vast floating **ocean** underneath **America.**

Instead the water is trapped inside the molecular structure of minerals found within the mantle rock.Incredibly if just *1%* of the Earth's mantle rock contained *H2O* that would amount to three times the amount of water that's in our **oceans**!

"The **ringwoodite** is like a sponge, soaking up water, there is something very special about the crystal structure of **ringwoodite** that allows it to attract **hydrogen** and **trap water.** This mineral can contain a lot of water under conditions of the deep mantle."

To give you some idea of just how little we know about our own planet, that sample of **ringwoodite** is the only known sample of it to have come from within the Earth!

Researchers from North-western University and the University of New Mexico report evidence for potentially oceans worth of water deep beneath the United States. Though not in the familiar liquid form—the ingredients for water are bound up in rock deep in the Earth's mantle—the discovery may represent the

Planet's largest water reservoir.

The presence of liquid water on the surface is what makes our "blue planet" habitable, and scientists have long been trying to figure out just how much water may be cycling between Earth's surface and interior reservoirs through plate tectonics.

. . .

Jacobsen and Schmandt are the first to provide direct evidence that there may be water in this area of the mantle, known as the "transition zone," on a regional scale. The region extends across most of the **interior of the United States.**

Schmandt, an assistant professor of geophysics at the University of New Mexico, uses seismic waves from earthquakes to investigate the structure of the deep crust and mantle. Jacobsen, an associate professor of Earth and planetary sciences at North western's Weinberg College of Arts and Sciences, uses observations in the laboratory to make predictions about geophysical processes occurring far beyond our direct observation.

The study combined Jacobsen's lab experiments in which he studies mantle rock under the simulated high pressures of **400 miles** below the Earth's surface with Schmandt's observations using vast amounts of seismic data from the **US Array, a dense network of more than 2,000 seismometers across the United States.**

Jacobsen's and Schmandt's findings converged to produce evidence that melting may occur about 400 miles deep in the Earth. H2O stored in mantle rocks, such as those containing the *mineral ringwoodite*, likely is the key to the process, the researchers said.

"Melting of rock at this depth is remarkable because most melting in the mantle occurs much shallower, in the upper 50 miles," said Schmandt, a co-author of the paper. "If there is a substantial amount of H2O in the transition zone, then some melting should take place in areas where there is flow into the lower mantle, and that is consistent with what we found."

If just one percent of the weight of mantle rock located in the **transition zone** is **H2O**, that would be equivalent to nearly three times the amount of water in our oceans, the researchers said.

This water is not in a form familiar to us—it is not **liquid**, **ice** or **vapour**. This fourth form is water trapped inside the **molecular structure** of the **minerals** in the **mantle rock**.

The weight of **250 miles** of **solid rock** creates such **high pressure**, along with temperatures above **2,000 degrees Fahrenheit**, that a **water molecule splits** to form a *hydroxyl radical (OH),* which can be bound into a *mineral's crystal structure.*

. . .

For years, Jacobsen has been synthesizing *ringwoodite,* coloured sapphire-like blue, in his Northwestern lab by reacting the green mineral olivine with water at high-pressure conditions. (*The Earth's upper mantle is rich in* **olivine.**) He found that more than one percent of the weight of the *ringwoodite's* crystal structure can consist of water—roughly the same amount of water as was found in the sample reported in the Nature paper.

"The *ringwoodite* is like a *sponge,* soaking up water," Jacobsen said. "There is something very special about the crystal structure of *ringwoodite* that allows it to attract hydrogen and trap water. This mineral can contain a lot of water under conditions of the deep mantle."

For the study reported in *Science*, Jacobsen subjected his synthesized ringwoodite to conditions around 400 miles below the Earth's surface and found it forms small amounts of partial melt when pushed to these conditions. He detected the melt in experiments conducted at the Advanced Photon Source of Argonne National Laboratory and at the National Synchrotron Light Source of Brookhaven National Laboratory.

Jacobsen uses small gem diamonds as hard anvils to compress minerals to deep-Earth conditions. "Because the diamond windows are transparent, we can look into the high-pressure device and watch reactions occurring at conditions of the deep mantle," he said. "We used intense beams of X-rays, electrons and infrared light to study the chemical reactions taking place in the diamond cell."

Jacobsen's findings produced the same evidence of partial melt, or magma, that Schmandt detected beneath North America using seismic waves. Because the deep mantle is beyond the direct observation of scientists, they use seismic waves—sound waves at different speeds—to image the interior of the Earth.

"Seismic data from the US Array are giving us a clearer picture than ever before of the Earth's internal structure beneath North America," Schmandt said. "The melting we see appears to be driven by **subduction**—the downwelling of mantle material from the surface."

The melting the researchers have detected is called dehydration melting. Rocks in the transition zone can hold a lot of H2O, but rocks in the top of the lower mantle can hold almost none. The water contained within *ringwoodite* in the transition zone is forced out when it goes deeper (into the lower mantle) and forms a higher-pressure mineral called *silicate perovskite*, which cannot absorb the water. This causes the rock at the boundary between the transition zone and lower mantle to partially melt.

"When a rock with a lot of H2O moves from the transition zone to the lower mantle it needs to get rid of the H2O somehow, so it melts a little bit," Schmandt said. "This is called **dehydration melting**."

"Once the water is released, much of it may become trapped there in the transition zone," Jacobsen added.

Just a little bit of melt, about one percent, is detectible with the new array of seismometers aimed at this region of the mantle because the melt slows the speed of seismic waves, Schmandt said.

Prof Graham Pearson, who made the discovery in his role as Canada Excellence Research Chair in Arctic Resources, said: "This sample really provides extremely strong confirmation that there are local **wet spots** deep in the Earth in this area."

The highly-prized diamonds that adorn jewellery form 150 to 200 kilometres below the Earth's surface but this one is an example of an 'ultradeep' specimen from the transition zone.

It was formed at pressures of an incredible 20,000 atmospheres and came to the surface through volcanic eruptions.

Although only one per cent of the *ringwoodite* is water, it is in fact a highly significant amount. Prof Pearson told Nature News: "That may not sound like much but when you realise how much **ringwoodite** there is, the transition zone could hold as much water as all the **Earth's oceans** put together."

The results of the analysis also help to shed light on other theories about how the Earth was formed. It helps demonstrate, for instance, that hydrogen has always been an essential ingredient of our planet - and didn't have to be carried here by meteorites:

Prof Pearson said:
"It looks like it's been to *hell* and back, which it has."

Carbon or silicon based life-forms!

Is there more to this puzzle than meets the eye! Because we could be dealing with highly evolved **"silicon-beings"** not from **"outer-space"** but from **'inner- space!'**

"where God's children may progress to become "heirs of God and joint-heirs with Christ" (Romans 8:17) and thus become one with God or like God."

Is **"Christ"** or **"Quetzalcohuātl"** sent out by this great machine to relay the meaning of life or the **"Grand-plan"** as they say, without the restrictions inherent on this plane, or **"physical level"**

. . .

The strange storm off the coast of New York!
"911"

And the strange dip in the Earth's magnetic field at the precise moment of the supposed **"collapse"** and the coincidental presence of **"Hurricane Erin"** off the coast of New York, and why the 1,400 cars were toasted in strange inexplicable patterns on **"911."**

So once we confirm evidence of widespread molecular dissociation having occurred at Ground Zero in New York City, we have a very strong indication that something unconventional seems or appears to have been happened, but remember what I said, that there is nothing more deceptive than the obvious, and that's not a theory, it's a fact! An exchange of energy must have took place, but what could have released that much extremely — unimaginably — high intensity energy? Which suddenly appeared just as the towers cascaded like water or disintegrated from top to bottom

A half-truth

I think anybody even with half-a-brain truly belives that the **"Ground-Zero- devastation"** was caused, using **"Thermite/Thermate/Super-Thermate"** and **"controlled-demolition"** any more than trying to blame it on **"jet-fuel"** or **"box-cutters."** But they could have been used to hide something else, that was going on in the back ground that could have been happening!

Secondary circulation
(A Carnot heat engine)
'The Storm In A Tea-Cup'

A tropical cyclone's primary energy source is the evaporation of water from the ocean surface, which ultimately recondenses into clouds and rain when moist air rises and cools to saturation. The energetics of the system may be idealized as an atmospheric **"Carnot-heat-engine."**

First, inflowing air near the surface acquires heat primarily via evaporation of water (*i.e. latent heat*) at the temperature of the warm ocean surface.

Second, air rises and cools within the eyewall while conserving total heat content (*latent heat is simply converted to sensible heat during condensation*).

Third, air outflows and loses heat via infrared-radiation to space at the temperature of the cold tropopause. Finally, air subsides and warms at the outer edge of the storm while conserving total heat content.

The first and third legs are nearly isothermal, while the second and fourth legs are nearly isentropic. This in-up-out-down overturning flow is known as the secondary circulation. The Carnot perspective provides an upper bound on the maximum wind speed that a storm can attain.

Scientists estimate that a tropical cyclone releases heat energy at the rate of **50** to **200 exajoules** ($10^{18} J$) per day, equivalent to about **1 PW** (10^{15} *watt*).

This rate of energy release is equivalent to 70 times the world energy consumption of humans and 200 times the worldwide electrical generating capacity, or to exploding a **"10-megaton nuclear bomb"** every 20 minutes!

Can someone or something be controling the weather? Like in **MISSING 411** or were they trying to reduce or enlarge the molecules of person or persons, not of this world, so to speak, and the twin towers got in the way, or have they already infiltrated the USA or Republic, and that's why it looked like an orchstrated-pantomine by government involment! By those and such as those who control the heard, to mask their true motives, for whatever reason.

Should we not let Sleeping Dogs Lie!

Because whatever or whoever seems or appears to have been interfering in our **"Anthropological"**, **"Social"** and **"Theological-development"**, could be either one-thing or the-other, in the **"social-evolutionary scale"**, it could be either the **"enemy-at-the-gates!"** i.e: Invaders from the stars! Or the **"enemy- within!"** which is a double or dichotomy or two-parts thus formed are complements.

"In logic, the partitions are opposites if there exists a proposition such that it holds over one and not the other."

. . .

'Head-hacking'

(*Remember Remember!*)

Like in the cult TV show of the 70s **Dr Who** and the **Daemon's** or **E=MC2** or the **Micro-world** and as we know **energy** can't be **created** or **destroyed**! So it has to go somewhere! When you reduce matter till its practically invisible! So does it not it seem or appear to be causing the weather problems!

. . .

Its as if someone or something is trying to help us something, in spite of ourselves? Like a collective-voice crying in the widerness of our own head, that seems or appears to be writing a letter to ones self!

So either **"they"** came, whoever or whatever **"they"** are, to conventionally colnise the planet by invation, thousands or millions of years ago, who are right out of a **Ray Bradbury sci-fi novel**, because we are or could have been colonised by a **"Macro"** or **"Micro"** infestation, which is something that is as long as it is short, because the large and the small are two opposite ends of the same self-evident truth, and that's a fact, not a throry, figuritively speaking, it is something immeasurable, that has been reduced to an infinite size in order to take on **'Micro'** or infinitesimal or finite colonization! Or **"Macro"** infinite or so large you can't see them! in order to control the **"status-quo"** of a phyisical plurality or condition of being plural or numerous, a state of Monogenism or mono-genesis or the theory of human origins, which posits or puts forward for consideration something such as a suggestion, assumption, or fact, that we all originate from a common descent, somewhere between the borders of the **"Theological"**, **"Spiritual"** and **"Mental"** like **Christ's similé** of the kingdom of heaven, being inside a mustard-seed!

. . .

"The Kingdom of Heaven is like a grain of mustard seed, which a man took, and sowed in his field; which indeed is smaller than all seeds. But when it is grown, it is greater than the herbs, and becomes a tree, so that the birds of the air come and lodge in its branches."

. . .

Was it a clever subliminal or unconscious-truth when **"Christ"** who not only accended to, but always seem to be addressing his father in heaven! Fuguritively speaking, or the **"Macro-world"** (*infinite*!) Or the **"Micro world"** (*finite*).

On the last day, that great day of the feast, Jesus stood and cried out, saying, **"If anyone thirsts, let him come to me and drink. He who believes in me, as the Scripture has said, out of his heart will flow rivers of living (water!)"**

"Jesus (Yeshua, Salvation) had the attention of everyone in the crowd when He declared that the true living **"water"** would come from Him. They could **"draw water from the wells of salvation!"**

The bible depicts a scene in which The Pharisees brought the adulteress to Him on the temple steps. Instead of answering quickly, Jesus knelt down and just wrote in the **"Sand!"**

Standing before Jesus, in the middle of the crowd, the woman probably stared down at her dusty feet, wishing she could vanish from the face of the earth! When Jesus finally stood up after listening to all the taunts and questions, he pronounced, **"He that is without sin among you, let him cast the first stone!"** then the woman fell to her knees in desperation. Again, Christ crouched before the temple and continued writing in the sand!

. . .

Was Christ trying to tell us a great truth in the form of what seems or appears to be a hidden message of sorts, like in an unconscious truth or subliminal message? So that we could try and understand, something that we could not even begin to grasp, about the atomic-level or the mysterious energy that moves the electrons around the atom, Vis-à-vis (therefore) it gives the false appearance of the world being solid!

From the Infinitesimal or *"finite"*, something so small that there is no way to see them or to measure them, and the *"infinite"* an abstract concept describing something without any limit, and Christ's sleight-of-mouth remark, *"that the first will be last and the last will be first!"*

Obviously the question is from out of the mouth of *"babes"* once again we hear Jesus Christ giving us some sort of playful, but deceptive clue to it all, which he reiterates in the Christian scriptures: *"for it would be easier for a camel to go through the eye of a neddle, than a richman to enter the kingdom of heaven!"* Or that you have to be like a *"child"* to enter the kingdom of heaven, or the way a child sees the world, filled with wonder and delight, which is diametrically opposed to the way an adult sees it!!

"The blink of an eye"
Everything yields to logic, does it not?
"Can people live in Rock's"

. . .

" I am Alfa and Omega, the beginning and the end. I will give unto him, that is athirst of the fountain of the waters of life freely "

Revelation 21:6

. . .

Or can they live in *"Water*?" The answer is *"No!"* That's like asking, can a man *"fly?"* Definitely not!

Sematics

"Remember what I said about Lucifer! Stating:
I'm a liar
The sentence above is *true* because the sentence below is a lie!
Don't believe a word I say

but it's only a *half-truth*, because it does not stop a man, woman or boy, flying on a plane from *London* to *Los Angeles*, does it! As long as you have the *technology*, you can find out how to do it!

So technically someone or something could be there at or below the *molecular-level*, or at the infinite expance of *time-and-space*, which could be the equivalent of an *"anthropological"*, *"theological"* and *"sociological"* time-bomb, waiting to go off.

So wheither its *nano-technology* or *sound-technologies*, where sound is actually *"3D"* or (*three-dimentional*), because it moves in waves, like the *interference patterns* that can change as you lower or increase the energy! Which sets up a *signiture-pattern* in the *magnetic-field*!

And the difference between certain *sound-waves* or *frequencies*, are like the geometry patterns in the intricate copper winding's of a coil in an electric-motor, dynamo, step-up or step-down transformer, and the **sound** you perceive in the brain including the ***intervils-of-silence*** or **spaces** or **rests** in a song sheet of music which gives it it's signiture via the **ear**, acts almost like a bat, who uses it to help it see or look for its prey in the dark, remember the **human-ear** has never heard sound in its life, it is the brain that **sees, tastes** and **hears**! Not the instrument of the human ear which transmits sound through the medium of **sound-waves** agitating the **air-molecules** under verying waves of pressure carried in the air, and this changing signiture of the pressure, can also be picked up via, an electrical-meter!

"Frequencies that are visible And invisible?"

(Is Seeing believing!)

Objects in the medium interact or interfere with these energy or sound waves, each time you play a different frequency in different oraintation's it will cause the ripples in the air to cue-up or accumulate at the human-ear.

Sound is made-up of invisible waves or packets of energy, that can pass through solid objects, even water, Particle-to-particle, earthquakes!

A good example is the Tacoma Narrows Bridge opened to traffic on July 1, 1940. Its main span collapsed into the Tacoma Narrows four months later on November 7, 1940, at 11:00 AM (Pacific time) as a result of aeroelastic flutter caused by a 42 mph (68 km/h) wind. The bridge collapse had lasting effects on science and engineering.

In many undergraduate physics texts the event is presented as an example of elementary forced resonance with the wind providing an external periodic frequency that matched the natural structural frequency, even though the real cause of the bridge's failure was aeroelastic flutter in the middle-span, began to torque and twist, untill it finally buckled.

A contributing factor was its solid sides, not allowing wind to pass through the bridge's deck. Thus its design allowed the bridge to catch the wind and sway, which ultimately took it down. Its failure also boosted research in the field of bridge aerodynamics/aeroelastics, fields which have influenced the designs of all the world's great long-span bridges built since 1940.

"It can pass through the medium of water/moisture"

Liquefaction

A special case of quicksand. In this case, sudden earthquake forces immediately increases the pore pressure of shallow groundwater. The saturated liquefied soil loses strength, causing buildings or other objects on that surface to sink or fall over or to simply breaking a glass, at one end of the scale, to the use of it in medicine by the pharmasuitical-industries and in hospitals, from ultra-sound to sound levitation, where the energy from the sound frequency can hold an object in the air, akin to the kids toy of the

1960s that was a simple pipe with a ball balanced in a holder, and all you do is blow in the pipe, and the plastic ball levitates or it floats in mid-air.

It the same as moving the molecules in fluids by manipulating and seperating fluids, without touching them, for to design or produce new drugs.

" The parting of the red-sea!"
UFO
The 60s cut TVShow
CALLED: (CLOSE-UP)
AND TELL ME DO YOU STILL BELIEVE THE WORLD IS WHAT YOU THINK IT IS?

(The world of Macro and Micro photography)

Where it could be Some kind of advanced life-form that is using a more advanced application of this and other techniques, to open some kind of doorway! And that's why people are disappearing so fast, or while they are wearing bright colours, i.e. the frequency of **Red**!

Did you know that our brain interprets the colours that we think we see, through the **Cones** and **Rods** in the human eye, because we can only see the **colours of the spectrum**, because each **colour** is **vibrating** at its own **selected frequency**.

Maybe that why they are disappearing? Through a portal or synthetic doorway in the **sound medium** or **sound-wave-corridor**, and they are put aboard a **carrier-wave** or **ghostly third harmonic**, like in:

Standing on the shoulders of Gods

A machine that was built by the eggheads of a futuristic mega company using quantum technology they had constructed a highly advanced **signal feedback circuit**, which was made up of two giant dual oscillating circuits that were like a massive tuning fork! Reminiscent of the *"70s pop record silver machine by Hawk-wind"* and Powered by atomic fusion-reactors, it acted like two giant guitar strings that vibrated together to produce what is known as a **sympathetic vibration**, which produces a **third note** or **harmonic**, caused by the two humungous circuits oscillating and producing dual hyper frequency waves that technically geometrically squares itself, and as the **oscillating frequency** or **waves accelerate**, the super heat dissipation dampers would control the incredible temperatures produced not only from the friction of the two surrogate carrier waves, but also from the sympathetic wave that would resonate like a giant bell they called *"The mother of all voices"* and the time travellers or *"Brothers of the bell"* or "true believers" atomic structure would vibrate like a glass! To the point of instability to achieve critical mass and where time itself would shift out of faze in *"E=MC2"* and there the time travellers would fly on the wings of the wind given to them by *"Aeolus"* keeper of the winds and son of *"Poseidon"* who was in charge of the brothers: *"Boreas"* the north wind, *"Zephyrus"* the west

286

wind, **"*Eurus*"** the east wind and **"Notus"** the south wind, travellers who stood on the threshold of tomorrow and the keeper of all our yesterdays.

With the egg-heads looking more like steam-punk mad-scientists with their dark goggles and ear-plugs, as the sound waves began to agitate the air-molecules in began to howl and roar like a primitive angry creature, fighting to escape from its captivity with all the power of a massive hurricane!

And like the painting of **"*Leonardo de Vinci*"** in the Sistine-chapel in *Rome*, where God and Adam are about to touch fingers, like two giant oscillators, would bend and shape the selected frequencies, like a tool that would redefine parameters on the molecules, acting like a surgical scalpel performing an operation where consummation would take place, by opening up a portal or corridor, as the machine slipped from sub-light to light speed, as mass travelling at the speed of light becomes energy, and to achieve this function it would have to purge it's own atomic weight, to slip the bonds of time, in a Genesis or beginning of a new world or the end of the old one, in the bible's book of revelation:

(Which is like a two edged sword or catalyst)

"Woe to you oh earth and sea, for the Devil sends the beast with wrath and fury because he knows the time is short"

"*That darkness and destruction would come upon creation and the beast shall reign*"

. . .

"Lo! Thy dread Empire, chaos! Is restored; Light dies before thy uncreating word: Thy hand great Anarch! Lets the curtain fall; and universal Darkness buries all."

Alexander Pope

. . .

To try and understand the theory of how the **CLA** time machine can theoretically work and travel in the forth dimension, you need to know about Einstein's theory that the past, present and the future co-exist at the same time, and he also stated that matter=energy and energy=matter, and that both states of matter can be altered, but they cannot be destroyed! As in the Ex nil, nihil fit **"*From nothing, nothing is made*"** So to us living in the present, somehow the past and the future must be altered in a way that locks them into the present, and the so-called egg-heads had somehow discovered how to unlock its secret code by using the oscillating circuits that produced the sympathetic wave or third harmonic that mathematically squared itself, as it drew the life essence or power from the atomic fusion reactors, like a blood sucking leech, until it had sated its appetite and reached saturation point as the eggheads stood like frightened children between two worlds, half in fear and half in excitement!

Paul Crowe

. . .

Like Maurice Blanchot, who remarked that those who believe in ghosts are in a way placating the phantasms of the night, that is an attempt to circumvent or circumscribe the illimitable terrors of the night by a more approachable terror in the old adage, better the Devil you know, than the one you don't know, real terror comes out of not knowing, or maybe sometimes its better not to know:

So they, whoever or whatever they are, can **surgically vibrate** the **speed** of the **molecules**, that would allow some kind of unimaginable process to take place, and they would be no longer visible, because they are **vibrating** at a different **speed** or **frequency**! Or are they being reduced in size, by using a form of **nano-technology**, that reduces their molecules in some way to a different size, all in the blink of an eye!

" There are those who will be still alive and will not go through death (sleep), but their bodies will be changed"

Paul

· · ·

"Behold, I shew you a mystery; we shall not all sleep, but we shall all be changed, in a moment, in the twinkling of an eye, at the last trump: for the trumpet shall sound, and the dead shall be raised incorruptible, and we shall be changed.

For this corruptible must put on incorruption, and this mortal must put on immortality. So when this corruptible shall have put on incorruption, and this mortal shall have put on immortality, then shall be brought to pass the saying that is written.

He is the Savior and worthy to be praised...they were doing the right thing by praising Him for who He was and that if they did not shout out their praise... if humans will not do it, then part of creation will the stones will cry out! In other words, no kind of silencing or denial of who the Lord was, could stop him from being Just that, God as a Man, coming to die for mankind and bring man back to God's presence through him."

· · ·

Can anybody live in water, definitly not! but it does not stop someone going into a submarine under the ocean, scuba-diving or even holding your breath for as long as you can!

So there is no such thing as **time-and-space** in the *"Macro"* or in the *"Micro"*, it has no beginning or *"Alfa"* and it has no end *"Omega"* its like the *"Mobeus-strip"*

So theoretically other life-forms! Hostile or not, could interact at the **molectular** or **Atomic-level**! And invade other systems or worlds, so to speak. without the need for actual physical space-travel.

Its like the analogy of the computer game *"fallout"* that contains the **city** of **Washing DC** if not the **world**! On something as small as an

"electron" or **micro-chip**! Because as you may already know that our eyes are being fooled all the time, by our so-called perception of reality, and the human eye cannot see the **3D** or **"three dimentional world around it!"**

We are all born blind

Like the blind person who got their sight back, and had to learn not to see again! Because they he knew what a cup was by touching it, but could not begin to see the frightening world about him, never mind the cup nor the table it was on, never mind the world about him! Is that what **Jesus Christ** was trying to tell us: by meaning one thing and not the other!

We hvae eeys but we cnanot see!

"Aonccdrig to rserach at an elingsh uinevrtisy, it deons't mttaer in what order the ltteers in a word are, the only iprmoatnt thing is that the frsit and lsat ltteer is at the rghit pclae. The rset can be a total mses and you can still raed it wouthit a porbelm. This is bcuseae we do not raed ervey lteter by istlef, but the word as a wlohe."

English
(Header and footers)

According to research at an English university, it doesn't mater in what order the letters in a word are, the only important thing is that the first and last letter is at the right place. The rest can be a total mess and you can still read it without a problem, this is because we don't read every letter by itself, but the word as a whole.

Fundamental law

Like in how we read language is **ruled** by **mathematics** (excuse the pun)

. . .

Its your brain that figures it out, because we process the physical world in chunks, and each eye being a basic camera, the incoming information is upside-down, and from this data the brain extracts the nessasary info your brain corrects or puts the image the right-way-up, while constructing what seems or appears to be a **'3D'** or **"three dimentional image"** mapped on a one dimentional surface, and that's why we see the world in a false **"3D"** supplamented by our perseptions aa well as our senses! Or a world that is figuratively speaking not even there!, Only the false representation that our brains tell us, so to speak!

Was the image left on the **"shroud"** accidently or for a purpose! So we would question and probe to find the truth of the matter! When we are advanced enough to be able to understand the message scientifically?

Is this then the great-plan? That makes up the so-called world or level that we think we exsist on? because reality is not what we think it is! See:

. . .

Its as if its like a giant computer, that's looking for a bug that keeps crashing and its re-booting the system, i.e: hence the enigma of who or what is giving the impression or enigma of having created matter, that can't be destroyed? Because we know it can't be created or destroyed! So who or what is it, that is generating the illusion?

Spontanious combustion

Are these and other strange events trying to tell us something? Especially About 9/11 and what happened to the twin-towers? Like the character in Charles Dickens novel: ***"Bleak House"*** and his character: ***"Krook"*** who had been found consumed by a strange fire, and had smelt of fire and brimstone, attributed to his evil nature... like fire from heaven or Spontaneous Human combustion: ***"What's the matter with the cat?' says Mr Guppy, 'look at her! 'Mad, I think. And no wonder, living in this evil place."***

Mr Guppy takes the light. They go down, more dead than alive, and holding one another, push open the door of the back shop. The cat has retreated close to it, and stands snarling-not at them, at something on the ground, before the fire. There is a very little fire left in the grate, but there is a smouldering suffocating vapour in the room, and a dark greasy coating on the walls and ceiling.

The chairs and the table, and the bottle so rarely absent from the table, all stand as usual. On one chair-back, hang the old man's hairy cap and coat, so the old man must be somewhere in the room... he is.

They advance slowly... The cat remains where they found her, still snarling at something on the ground, before the fire and between the two chairs, what is it? Hold up the light. Here is a small burnt patch of flooring; here is the tinder from a little bundle of burnt paper, but not so light as usual, seeming to be steeped in something; and here is-is it the cinder of a small, charred and broken log of wood sprinkled with white ash, or is it coal? O horror, he is here! And it is from this that we run away, striking out the light and overturning one another into the street, is all that represents him.

"At last come the coroner and his enquiry"

"That would seem to be an unlucky house, a destined house; but so we sometimes find it, and these are mysteries we can't account for!"

Charles Dickens's

. . .

Or the strange and baffling death of Mrs Reeser, The countess di Bandi, Harry Thomas, John Irving Bently, Robert Francis Bailey and the case of George I. Mott, the fire fighter, the list goes on and on, of people who seem or appear to have spontaneously combusted in the fabulous 70s paperback by Michael Harrison ***"Fire From heaven!"***

By using and/or testing their highly advanced science! That seems or appears to be without instrumentally! Of reducing someones moloecules by none other than a form of highly-advanced molecular-transference or reduction?

Induction

And it has failed to reduce their molecular-structure, for whatever reason, and the energy or heat almost destroyed the body in some cases, leaving on a piece of the ankle and one of the feet, still wearing a **shoe**!

Has shoes got something to do with this, and other strange mysteries? Like in the people who are found without **"shoes"** in the **MISSING 411 books** by David Paulides, where the people are found without their shoes, which takes us to the mystery of **911** and the twin towers! And the weird observation made by **Dr Woods, on her excellent video on u-tube** a highly qualified person in many disciplines, who observed that the people were trying to **"shed their cloths"** like the case of Cullen John Finnerty aged 39 years. Michigan. In Davids new book MISSING 411 The Devil's in the Details. Page 133. Who was found under the most strangest of curcumstances, apparently he was mysteriously found dead, the medical examiner either could not determine or was unable to find the cause of death! he was 6'2" and 240 pounds or 17st-2lbs, who had said over the cell or mobile-phone, that he was being followed by two strange men who seemed or appeared to make a man the size of **Cullen John Finnerty** nervous for some unknown reason, and he said over the phone that he was taking off his cloths!

A story that pings familier or possible other clues included in the search and rescue during **911** and the **world-trade-towers** in **New-York,** where the firemens boots were melting, due to some mysterious and yet selective tempreture veriation, but the firemen seemed or appeared unharmed! but they had to change there boots, the same as out in the forest, if the victims **cloths** and their **shoes** are being effected in some strange way, you would naturally take them off, and on one of the photographs taken after the mysterious attack on the twin-towers, it actually shows certain objects that seem or appear to have escaped the devastation, were the trees and a set of the traffic-lights, were not even charred, are the people being reduced by some kind of molecular-induction? Where they need to be **"earthed"** in some way first!

And this strange **"fire from heaven"** didn't even singe the news-papers lying near, what was left of the victim! In **Michael Harrison's book,** or the paper next to the cars that were strangely burned, during **911!** What could be happening here? Because its not a theory that we are trying to understand, but a fact!

Potential energy

Energy stored by virtue of the position of an object in a force field, such as a gravitational, electric or magnetic field.

For example, lifting an object against gravity performs work on the object and stores gravitational potential energy; if it falls, gravity does work on the object which transforms the *"potential-energy"* to *"kinetic-energy"* associated with its speed.

Some specific forms of energy include elastic energy due to the stretching or deformation of solid objects, chemical energy such as is released when a fuel burns, and thermal energy, the **microscopic kinetic** and **potential energies** of the **disordered motions** of the **particles** making up matter.

Not all of the **energy** in a **system** can be **transformed** or **transferred** by a **work process**; the amount that can is called the **available energy**. In particular the second law of **thermodynamics** limits the amount thermal energy that can be transformed into other forms of energy. **Mechanical** and other **forms** of **energy** can be **transformed** in the other direction into **thermal energy** without such **limitations**.

Any object that has **mass** when stationary (thus called **rest mass**), equivalently has **rest energy** as can be calculated using Albert Einstein's equation *"$E=mc^2$."*

Being a form of energy, rest energy can be transformed to or from *other forms* of energy, while the total amount of energy does not change. From this perspective, the amount of matter in the universe contributes to its total energy.

Similarly, *all* energy manifests as a proportionate amount of mass. For example, adding 25 kilowatt-hours (90 megajoules) of *any form* of energy to an object increases its mass by 1 microgram. If you had a sensitive enough mass balance or scale, this mass increase could be measured.

Our Sun (or a nuclear bomb) transforms nuclear potential energy to other forms of energy; its total mass doesn't decrease due to that in itself (since it still contains the same total energy even if in different forms), but its mass does decrease when the energy escapes out to its surroundings, largely as radiant energy.

A new form of energy can't be defined arbitrarily. In order to be valid, it must be shown to be transformable to or from a predictable amount of some known form(s) of energy, thus showing how much energy it represents in the same units used for all other forms.

It must obey conservation of energy, so it must never decrease or increase except via such a transformation (or transfer). Also, if an alleged new form of energy can be shown *not* to change the mass of a system in proportion to its energy, then it is *not* a form of energy.

Living organisms require available energy to stay alive; humans get such energy from food along with the oxygen needed to metabolize it. Civilization requires a supply of energy to function; energy resources such as fossil fuels are a vital topic in economics and politics. Earth's climate and ecosystem are driven by the radiant energy Earth receives from the sun (as well as the geothermal energy contained within the earth), and are sensitive to changes in the amount received.

Classical mechanics distinguishes between kinetic energy, which is determined by an object's movement through space, and potential energy, which is a function of the position of an object within a field which may itself be related to the arrangement of other objects or particles. These include gravitational energy (which is stored in the way masses are arranged in a gravitational field), several types of nuclear energy (which utilize potentials from the nuclear force and the weak force, electric energy (from the electric field), and magnetic energy (from the magnetic field).

Other familiar types of energy are a varying mix of both potential and kinetic energy. An example is mechanical energy which is the sum of (usually macroscopic) kinetic and potential energy in a system. Elastic energy in materials is also dependent upon electrical potential energy (among atoms and molecules), as is chemical energy, which is stored and released from a reservoir of electrical potential energy between electrons, and the molecules or atomic nuclei that attract them.

Heat, in the strict use in physics, is characteristic only of a process, i.e. it is absorbed or produced as an energy *exchange*, always as a result of a temperature difference. Heat is thermal energy in the process of transfer or conversion across a boundary of one region of matter to another, as a result of a temperature difference. In engineering, the terms **"heat"** and **"heat transfer"** are thus used nearly interchangeably, since heat is always understood to be in the process of transfer. The energy transferred by heat is called by other terms (such as thermal energy or latent energy) when this energy is no longer in net transfer, and has become static.

Thus, heat is not a static property of matter. Matter does not contain heat, but rather thermal energy, and even the thermal energy is subject to transformations into and out of other types of energy, and so can be considered to be **"conserved"** only when these processes are small. The heat transfer rate or heating rate is the amount of energy per unit time being transferred as heat, or the heat power.

When two thermodynamic systems with different temperatures are brought into diathermic contact, they spontaneously exchange energy as heat, the exchange being transfer of thermal energy from the system of higher temperature to the colder system. Heat may cause work to be performed on a system, for example, in form of volume or pressure changes. This work may be used in heat engines to convert thermal energy into other forms of energy. When two systems have reached a thermodynamic equilibrium, they have attained the same exact temperature and the net exchange of thermal energy vanishes, and heat flow ceases.

The shroud

The visible and the invisible
'Christ's mysterious change in the tomb'
Like the resurection of christ and the strange burst of radiation that must have produced the amazing image on the cloth, as if he was scanned by a

higher technological process, the light that was used, could only have been done in three ways?

Like in that excellent documentary on **U-TUBE** called **"The Real Face of Jesus?"**

'Radially' like a light-bulb, but it would be too out of focus, and 'directionally' or in a streight line, which contains no information! So what else could have done it? because none of these methods would have produced the mysterious image on the shroud, so what other kind of light or process could have been responsible? It seems or appears to have been narrow slithers of slow moving light, like you get in a 20th century desk-top scanner!

"Sealed was the tomb, guarded by soldiers, brightly the moonlight shone around Roadway and hill gleamed in the brightness, Flooded with light The garden's bound. Brighter the light seen 'neath the olives; Forms bright as sunlight, 'mid the trees, Soldiers were there, clad as for warfare: Lo! They are gone, and who are these? See yonder, hast'ning to the city, the trembling soldiers in terror go! Earthquake astounding, strange light surrounding, Drive them away these things to show."

. . .

Only a more advanced version, that was used on the 3rd day A.D. that scanned the **master-copy,** and then deleted it, leaving or producing a

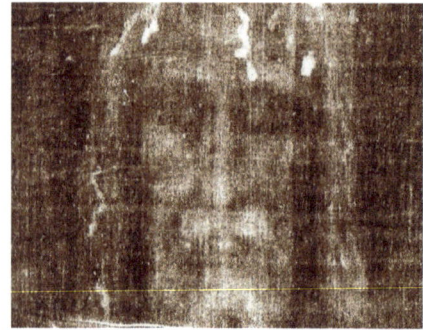 **douple-ganger** of **Christ** that wasn't quit finnished or dry yet, so to speak, like in the bible:

"Jesus saith unto her, Touch me not; for I am not yet ascended to my Father: but go to my brethren, and say unto them, I ascend unto my Father, and your Father; and to my God, and your God..."

Like you do in a computer! Its as if So someone or something using some kind of higher technology, while using metafors to try and understand something that we just could not grasp, Christ has left us a very clever message, what is it trying to tell us, and is it related to the holy-Bible, in more ways than one, especially in regard to us being made in Gods image! And tells us volumes about the world that we think we live in!

'Photocopy'

A cylindrical drum is electrostatically charged by a high voltage wire called a corona wire or a charge roller. The drum has a coating of a photoconductive material. A photoconductor is a semiconductor that becomes conductive when exposed to light.

Exposure: A bright lamp illuminates the original document, and the white areas of the original document reflect the light onto the surface of the photoconductive drum.

The areas of the drum that are exposed to light become conductive and therefore discharge to the ground. The area of the drum not exposed to light (those areas that correspond to black portions of the original document) remain negatively charged. The result is a latent electrical image on the surface of the drum.

Developing: The toner is positively charged. When it is applied to the drum to develop the image, it is attracted and sticks to the areas that are negatively charged (black areas), just as paper sticks to a balloon with a static charge.

Transfer: The resulting toner image on the surface of the drum is transferred from the drum onto a piece of paper with a higher negative charge than the drum.

Fusing: The toner is melted and bonded to the paper by heat and pressure rollers.

This example is of a negatively charged drum and paper, and positively charged toner as is common in today's digital copiers. Some copiers, mostly older analog copiers, employ a positively charged drum and paper, and negatively charged toner.

Is something going on at the molecular level? And, or has our would-be visitors, having established there colony, God knows when, in the new-world, like the Jappannse queen-hornet, will in time wake-up to their true porpose, to invade and conquer, once the new-world is colonised, using a self-sustaining Macro/Micro-science they could easily terra-form our brain, and everything you think you know, becomes a figment of the imagination! So to speak.

Or has it been created by nothing more than self-sustaining programme that's incurred a fault, and the **sentient being**, who sent **Christ** to **de-bug** the **software**! Or to save the user from itself, because the operating system seems or appears to be still running, and it doesn't know that there is something wrong, and because of this its hell-bent on protecting itself, from destruction!

"The clock seems or appears to be working, but its telling the wrong time"

Or a **great collective** or **singular intelligence**, that we cannot fathom-out, constructed or put forward a system without instrumentality before time itself, because time as we know is relevent!

Albert Einstein showed that ultimately all matter is capable of being converted to energy (known as mass–energy equivalence) by the famous formula $E = mc^2$, where E is the energy of a piece of matter of mass m, times c^2 the speed of light squared.

As the speed of light is 299,792,458 metres per second (186,282 mi/s), a relatively small amount of matter may be converted to a large amount of energy.

An example is that positrons and electrons (matter) may transform into photons (non-matter). However, although matter may be created or destroyed in such processes, neither the quantity of mass or energy change during the process.

295

A quark is an elementary particle and a fundamental constituent of matter. Quarks combine to form composite particles called **hadrons**, the most stable of which are protons and neutrons, the components of atomic nuclei. Due to a phenomenon known as *color confinement*, quarks are never

directly observed or found in isolation; they can be found only within hadrons, such as baryons (of which protons and neutrons are examples), and mesons. For this reason, much of what is known about quarks has been drawn from observations of the **hadrons** themselves.

There are six types of quarks, known as *flavors*: up, down, strange, charm, bottom, and top. Up and down quarks have the lowest masses of all quarks. The heavier quarks rapidly change into up and down quarks through a process of particle decay: the transformation from a higher mass state to a lower mass state. Because of this, up and down quarks are generally stable and the most common in the universe, whereas strange, charm, top, and bottom quarks can only be produced in high energy collisions (such as those involving cosmic rays and in **particle accelerators**).

. . .

Quarks have various intrinsic properties, including electric charge, mass, color charge and spin. Quarks are the only elementary particles in the Standard Model of particle physics to experience all four fundamental interactions, also known as *fundamental forces* (**electromagnetism, gravitation, strong interaction, and weak interaction**), as well as the only known particles whose electric charges are not integer multiples of the elementary charge.

For every quark flavor there is a corresponding type of antiparticle, known as an *antiquark*, that differs from the quark only in that some of its properties have equal magnitude but opposite sign.

Are these quark's being constructed by drones that maintain the great hive or collective, so to speak, having created or terra-formed the universe or world, using these strange micro-biological life-forms, to people the vast out-posts of its empire, smaller than the electron, and greater than the infinite, and it doesn't know that its creators died out, evolved or originally came from a higher sphere, and the machine is still running, and it doesn't know it, so to speak!

Gulliver's Travel's

During his first voyage, Gulliver is washed ashore after a shipwreck and finds himself a prisoner of a race of tiny people, less than 6 inches tall, who are inhabitants of the island country of **Lilliput**.

After giving assurances of his good behaviour, he is given a residence in **Lilliput** and becomes a favourite of the court. From there, the book follows Gulliver's observations on the Court of **Lilliput**.

He is also given the permission to roam around the city on a condition that he must not harm their subjects. Gulliver assists the **Lilliputians** to subdue their neighbours, the **Blefuscudians**, by stealing their fleet.

However, he refuses to reduce the island nation of **Blefuscu** to a province of **Lilliput**, displeasing the King and the court. Gulliver is charged with treason and is convicted and sentenced to be blinded, but with the assistance of a kind friend, he escapes to **Blefuscu**. Here he spots and retrieves an abandoned boat and sails out to be rescued by a passing ship, which safely takes him back home.

This book of the *Travels* is a topical political satire, when the sailing ship **"Adventure"** is blown off course by storms and forced to sail for land in search of fresh water, Gulliver is abandoned by his companions and found by a farmer who is 72 feet (22 m) tall (the scale of **Brobdingnag** is about **12:1**, compared to **Lilliput's 1:12**, judging from Gulliver estimating a man's step being **10 yards (9.1 m)**). He brings Gulliver home and his daughter cares for Gulliver.

The farmer treats him as a curiosity and exhibits him for money. After awhile the constant shows make *Lemuel* sick, and the farmer sells him to the queen of the realm. The farmer's daughter is later brought to the palace as well to take care of him. Since Gulliver is too small to use their huge chairs, beds, knives and forks, the queen commissions a small house to be built for him so that he can be carried around in it; this is referred to as his **"travelling box"**.

Between small adventures such as fighting giant wasps and being carried to the roof by a monkey, he discusses the state of *Europe* with the King. The King is not happy with Gulliver's accounts of Europe, especially upon learning of the use of guns and cannons.

On a trip to the seaside, his traveling box is seized by a giant eagle which drops Gulliver and his box into the sea, where he is picked up by some sailors, who return him to England. This book compares the truly moral man to the representative man; the latter is clearly shown to be the lesser of the two. **Swift,** being in Anglican holy orders, was keen to make such comparisons.

After Gulliver's ship was attacked by pirates, he is marooned close to a desolate rocky island near India.

Fortunately, he is rescued by the flying island of Laputa, a kingdom devoted to the arts of music and mathematics but unable to use them for practical ends. Since **Swift** was in Anglican holy orders, he, like so many of them, viewed reason as what Martin Luther had called **"that great** *whore*" and regarded **Deism**, whose practitioners attacked revealed religions, with pure horror. Laputa's custom of throwing rocks down at rebellious cities on the ground seems the first time that the air strike was conceived as a method of warfare.

Gulliver tours **Laputa** as the guest of a low-ranking courtier and sees the ruin brought about by the blind pursuit of science without practical results, in a satire on "**bureaucracy**" and on the Royal Society and its experiments. At the Grand Academy of Lagado, great resources and manpower are employed on researching completely preposterous schemes such as extracting sunbeams from cucumbers, softening marble for use in pillows, learning how to mix paint by smell, and uncovering political conspiracies by examining the excrement of suspicious persons (muckraking).

Gulliver is then taken to **Balnibarbi** to await a trader who can take him on to Japan. While waiting for a passage, Gulliver takes a short side-trip to the island of **Glubbdubdrib**, where he visits a magician's dwelling and discusses history with the ghosts of historical figures, the most obvious restatement of the "**ancients versus moderns**" theme in the book.

In Luggnagg he encounters the **struldbrugs**, unfortunates who are immortal. They do not have the gift of eternal youth, but suffer the infirmities of old age and are considered legally dead at the age of eighty. After reaching Japan, Gulliver asks the Emperor "**to excuse my performing the ceremony imposed upon my countrymen of trampling upon the crucifix**," which the Emperor does. Gulliver returns home, determined to stay there for the rest of his days.

Despite his earlier intention of remaining at home, Gulliver returns to the sea as the captain of a merchantman as he is bored with his employment as a surgeon. On this voyage he is forced to find new additions to his crew, whom he believes to have turned the rest of the crew against him. His crew then mutiny, and after keeping him contained for some time resolve to leave him on the first piece of land they come across and continue as pirates.

He is abandoned in a landing boat and comes upon a race of hideous, deformed and savage humanoid creatures to which he conceives a violent antipathy. Shortly afterwards he meets a race of horses who call themselves **Houyhnhnms** (which in their language means "**the perfection of nature**"); they are the rulers, while the deformed creatures called **Yahoos** are human beings in their base form.

Gulliver becomes a member of a horse's household, and comes to both admire and emulate the **Houyhnhnms** and their lifestyle, rejecting his fellow humans as merely Yahoos endowed with some semblance of reason which they only use to exacerbate and add to the vices Nature gave them.

However, an Assembly of the **Houyhnhnms** rules that Gulliver, a Yahoo with some semblance of reason, is a danger to their civilisation, and expels him.

He is then rescued, against his will, by a Portuguese ship, and is surprised to see that Captain Pedro de Mendez, a *Yahoo,* is a wise, courteous and generous person. He returns to his home in England, but he is unable to reconcile himself to living among **"Yahoos"** and becomes a recluse, remaining in his house, largely avoiding his family and his wife, and spending several hours a day speaking with the horses in his stables.

This book uses coarse metaphors to describe human depravity, and the **Houyhnhms** are symbolised as not only perfected nature but also the emotional barrenness which Swift maintained that devotion to reason brought.

It is uncertain exactly when Swift started writing **Gulliver's Travels**,(much of the writing was done at Loughry Manor in Cookstown, Co. Tyrone whilst Swift stayed there) but some sources suggest as early as 1713 when Swift, Gay, Pope, Arbuthnot and others formed the Scriblerus Club with the aim of satirising popular literary genres.

According to these accounts, Swift was charged with writing the memoirs of the club's imaginary author, **Martinus Scriblerus**, and also with satirising the **"travellers tales"** literary sub-genre.

It is known from Swift's correspondence that the composition proper began in **1720** with the mirror-themed parts I and II written first, Part IV next in **1723** and Part III written in **1724**; but amendments were made even while Swift was writing Drapier's Letters.

By August **1725** the book was complete; and as **Gulliver's Travels** was a transparently **anti-Whig** satire, it is likely that Swift had the manuscript copied so that his handwriting could not be used as evidence if a prosecution should arise, as had happened in the case of some of his Irish pamphlets (the Drapier's Letters).

In March 1726 Swift travelled to London to have his work published; the manuscript was secretly delivered to the publisher Benjamin Motte, who used five printing houses to speed production and avoid piracy. Motte, recognising a best-seller but fearing prosecution, cut or altered the worst offending passages (such as the descriptions of the court contests in **Lilliput** and the rebellion of **Lindalino**), added some material in defence of Queen Anne to book II, and published it.

The first edition was released in two volumes on 26 October **1726**, priced at **8s. 6d.** The book was an instant sensation and sold out its first run in less than a week.

Motte published *Gulliver's Travels* anonymously, and as was often the way with fashionable works, several follow-ups (**Memoirs of the Court of Lilliput**), parodies (**Two Lilliputian Odes, The first on the Famous Engine With Which Captain Gulliver extinguish'd the Palace Fire...**) and **"keys"** (*Gulliver Decipher'd* and *Lemuel Gulliver's Travels into Several Remote Regions of the World Compendiously Methodiz'd*, the second by Edmund Curll who had similarly written a **"key"** to Swift's Tale of a Tub in **1705**) were swiftly produced.

These were mostly printed anonymously (or occasionally pseudonymously) and were quickly forgotten. Swift had nothing to do with them and disavowed them in Faulkner's edition of **1735**. Swift's friend Alexander Pope wrote a set of five *Verses on Gulliver's Travels*, which Swift liked so much that he added them to the second edition of the book, though they are rarely included.

Faulkner's
(1735 edition)

In **1735** an Irish publisher, George Faulkner, printed a set of Swift's works, Volume III of which was **Gulliver's Travels**. As revealed in Faulkner's **"Advertisement to the Reader"**, Faulkner had access to an annotated copy of Motte's work by **"a friend of the author"** (generally believed to be Swift's friend Charles Ford) which reproduced most of the manuscript without Motte's amendments, the original manuscript having been destroyed.

It is also believed that Swift at least reviewed proofs of Faulkner's edition before printing, but this cannot be proved. Generally, this is regarded as the Editio Princeps of **Gulliver's Travels** with one small exception. This edition had an added piece by Swift, *A letter from Capt. Gulliver to his Cousin Sympson*, which complained of Motte's alterations to the original text, saying he had so much altered it that **"I do hardly know mine own work"** and repudiating all of Motte's changes as well as all the keys, libels, parodies, second parts and continuations that had appeared in the intervening years. This letter now forms part of many standard texts.

Lindalino

The short (five paragraph) episode in Part III, telling of the rebellion of the surface city of **Lindalino** against the flying island of **Laputa,** was an obvious allegory to the affair of *Drapier's Letters* of which Swift was proud. **Lindalino** represented Dublin and the impositions of **Laputa** represented the British imposition of William Wood's poor-quality copper currency.

Faulkner had omitted this passage, either because of political sensitivities raised by an Irish publisher printing an **anti-British satire**, or possibly because the text he worked from did not include the passage. In **1899** the passage was included in a new edition of the *Collected Works*. Modern editions derive from the Faulkner edition with the inclusion of this **1899** addendum.

Isaac Asimov notes in **The Annotated Gulliver** that **Lindalino** is composed of double lins; hence, **Dublin.**

Major themes

Gulliver's Travels has been the recipient of several designations: from Menippean satire to a children's story, from proto-Science Fiction to a forerunner of the modern novel.

Published seven years after **Daniel Defoe's** wildly successful **Robinson Crusoe, Gulliver's Travels** may be read as a systematic rebuttal of **Defoe's** optimistic account of human capability.

In *The Unthinkable Swift: The Spontaneous Philosophy of a Church of England Man*, Warren Montag argues that Swift was concerned to refute the notion that the individual precedes society, as Defoe's novel seems to suggest. Swift regarded such thought as a dangerous endorsement of Thomas Hobbes' radical political philosophy and for this reason Gulliver repeatedly encounters established societies rather than desolate islands.

The captain who invites **Gulliver** to serve as a surgeon aboard his ship on the disastrous third voyage is named Robinson.

Scholar Allan Bloom points out that Swift's critique of science (the experiments of **Laputa**) is the first such questioning by a modern liberal democrat of the effects and cost on a society which embraces and celebrates policies pursuing scientific progress.

A possible reason for the book's classic status is that it can be seen as many things to many different people. Broadly, the book has three themes:

A satirical view of the state of European government, and of petty differences between religions.

An inquiry into whether men are inherently corrupt or whether they become corrupted.

A restatement of the older "ancients versus moderns" controversy previously addressed by Swift in *The Battle of the Books*

In terms of storytelling and construction the parts follow a pattern:

The causes of Gulliver's misadventures become more malignant as time goes on—he is first shipwrecked, then abandoned, then attacked by strangers, then attacked by his own crew.

Gulliver's attitude hardens as the book progresses—he is genuinely surprised by the viciousness and politicking of the **Lilliputians** but finds the behaviour of the **Yahoos** in the fourth part reflective of the behaviour of people, each part is the reverse of the preceding part, **Gulliver** is big/small/wise/ignorant, the countries are complex/simple/scientific/natural, and the forms of government are worse/better/worse/better than England's.

Gulliver's viewpoint between parts is mirrored by that of his antagonists in the contrasting part—Gulliver sees the tiny **Lilliputians** as being vicious and unscrupulous, and then the king of **Brobdingnag** sees Europe in exactly the same light; Gulliver sees the **Laputians** as unreasonable, and his **Houyhnhnm** master sees humanity as equally so.

No form of government is ideal—the simplistic **Brobdingnagians** enjoy public executions and have streets infested with beggars, the honest and upright **Houyhnhnms** who have no word for lying are happy to suppress the true nature of Gulliver as a *Yahoo* and are equally unconcerned about his reaction to being expelled.

Specific individuals may be good even where the race is bad—Gulliver finds a friend in each of his travels and, despite Gulliver's rejection and horror toward all Yahoos, is treated very well by the Portuguese captain, Don Pedro, who returns him to England at the novel's end.

Of equal interest is the character of Gulliver himself—he progresses from a cheery optimist at the start of the first part to the pompous misanthrope of the book's conclusion and we may well have to filter our understanding of the work if we are to believe the final misanthrope wrote the whole work. In this sense *Gulliver's Travels* is a very modern and complex novel. There are subtle shifts throughout the book, such as when Gulliver begins to see all humans, not just those in Houyhnhnm-land, as Yahoos.

Throughout, Gulliver is presented as being gullible; he believes what he is told, never perceives deeper meanings, is an honest man, and expects others to be honest. This makes for fun and irony; what Gulliver says can be trusted to be accurate, and he does not always understand the meaning of what he perceives.

Also, although Gulliver is presented as a commonplace *"everyman"*, lacking higher education, he possesses a remarkable natural gift for language. He quickly becomes fluent in the native tongue of any strange land in which he finds himself, a literary device that adds much understanding and humour to Swift's work.

Despite the depth and subtlety of the book, it is often classified as a children's story because of the popularity of the Lilliput section (frequently bowdlerised) as a book for children. One can still buy books entitled *Gulliver's Travels* which contain only parts of the Lilliput voyage.

Character analysis

Pedro de Mendez is the name of the Portuguese captain who rescues Gulliver in Book IV. When Gulliver is forced to leave the Island of the **Houyhnhnms**, his plan is *"to discover some small Island uninhabited"* where he can live in solitude. Instead, he is picked up by Don Pedro's crew. Despite Gulliver's appearance—he is dressed in skins and speaks like a horse—Don Pedro treats him compassionately and returns him to Lisbon.

Though Don Pedro appears only briefly, he has become an important figure in the debate between so-called soft school and hard school readers of **Gulliver's Travels.** Soft school critics contend that Gulliver is a target of Swift's satire and that Don Pedro represents an ideal of human kindness and generosity. For hard-school critics, Gulliver sees the bleak fallenness at the center of human nature, and Don Pedro is merely a minor character who, in Gulliver's words, is *"an Animal which had some little Portion of Reason."*

From *1738* to *1746*, Edward Cave published in occasional issues of *The Gentleman's Magazine* semi-fictionalized accounts of contemporary debates in the two Houses of Parliament under the title of **Debates in the Senate of Lilliput.** The names of the speakers in the debates, other individuals mentioned, politicians and monarchs present and past, and most other countries and cities of Europe (*"Degulia"*) and America (*"Columbia"*) were thinly disguised under a variety of Swiftian pseudonyms.

The disguised names, and the pretence that the accounts were really translations of speeches by **Lilliputian politicians**, were a reaction to an Act of Parliament forbidding the publication of accounts of its debates.

Cave employed several writers on this series: William Guthrie (June 1738 – November 1740), Samuel Johnson (November 1740 – February 1743), and John Hawkesworth (February 1743 – December 1746).

Voltaire was presumably influenced by Swift: his 1750 short story Micromégas, about an alien visitor to Earth, also refers to two moons of Mars.

Swift crater, a crater on Mars's moon Deimos, is named after Jonathan Swift.

The term **Lilliputian** has entered many languages as an adjective meaning "small and delicate". There is even a brand of small cigar called Lilliput. There is a series of collectable model houses known as "*Lilliput Lane*". The smallest light bulb fitting (5mm diameter) in the Edison screw series is called the "*Lilliput* Edison screw". In Dutch, the word *Lilliputter* is used for adults shorter than 1.30 meters. Conversely, *Brobdingnagian* appears in the Oxford English Dictionary as a synonym for *very large* or *gigantic*.

In like vein, the term **yahoo** is often encountered as a synonym for *ruffian* or *thug*.

Easter-egg?

In the discipline of computer architecture, the terms *"big-endian"* and *"little-endian"* are used to describe two possible ways of laying out **"bytes in memory!"**.

The terms derive from one of the satirical conflicts in the book, in which two religious sects of Lilliputians are divided between those who crack open their soft-boiled eggs from the little end, and those who use the big end.

QED

There is every possibilty that there is higher evolutionary **carbon** ancestors or **silicon** life-forms! Beings who are interested in us, for whatever reason, because logically, these life-forms are hidding either through choice or naccesity! Because when you begin to join the *"anthropological"* *"theological"* and *"sociological"* dots, the evidence or lack of it, begins to come to the surface, and you can see the bigger picture, so to speak, and what do you find?

"When you have eliminated the impossible, whatever remains, however improbable, must be the solution"

And the cyclic nature of these hidden facts expose the imposibility of what you have descovered! It begs its own question: *where did I come from? Why am I here? And where am I going to?* Or the grand plan, if you will.

Something or someone is trying to tell us something, like in the information or foot-print found in the *"shroud"* that questions the very world that we think we live-in, and how and why it is being maintained!

"Something is happening"

Whoever or whatever they are, it seems or appears that they could be preparing the way for a coming race? Using something like biological **Nano/Peco-bots** at the **atomic level**, or a **psudo-science** without **instrumentality!** Or something akin to a massive **bio-computer** or **"The Great Architect"** or something that is **non-physical**, like in my other fiction book:

. . .

Standing on the shoulders of Gods

(We must stand or fall on the similé)

. . .

(Because people are disappearing and most are being murdered, and that's a fact, not a theory!)

continued

It was as if the unseen forces were reaching out to Mathew as he transcended the physical world, holding his **almanac** to guide him, as if he were a tourist trying to find his way in a strange and bizarre world, and there at the gates of matter, Mathew saw one of the keepers of wisdom or watcher at the door to the physical world, there the strange figure held up it's hand as if to bar the way, and on the palm of it's hand was a drawing of a snake trying to eat it's own tail! Or consume itself, a symbol that stood for **eternity,** with this Mathew was shown to what was called the chamber of the ages that contained the book of **Anon!** Or something akin to the **Corpus Hermeticum**, with the cornerstone inherit in the maxim **"As it is above, so it is below"** like a dissonant reflection, and there like the sorcerer's apprentice he would learn the forgotten knowledge or true nature of himself, that life was an **illusion** or **dream** if you will, that we have become ensnared in, like a symbolic fly caught in a **spiders web!** And the **third eye** or **all-seeing eye**, like the one on the American dollar bill! Was symbolic of the eye of **God!** Or the true beholder of **its!** Or should I say, our own collective-self that reflects the dream of life onto a pool of water, a crystal ball if you will, even more appropriately a **looking-glass,** like a sea of eternity that reveals who we truly are, and our proper place in the scheme of things.

As a seeker of wisdom Mathew would gaze with his **LSD** induced but lofty purpose, to try and awake from the dream of life, like in the cult 60s TV show **"The Prisoner"** where we seem or appear to have become our own jailers and where questions or the pursuit of knowledge has become a burden to others and answers have become a prison for one's self!

As we blindly go through life like cattle, from the cradle to the grave and die like cabbages in a viscous and pointless circle of ignorance, over and over again on the wheel or yoke of life!

And there Mathew read his book of all knowledge with its esoteric text and with his expanded mind, he began to understand life's hidden meaning, like **"Aaron's rod"** to tap the fount of creativity, where he found sitting

304

between the pages of that pondorous book, a strange unquiet line that was written like a psudo-dictionary where a **"contingency that is the status of propositions that are nither necessarily true nor necessarily false"**

. . .

A timeless time

Before the beginning of time and space! That **"was" "is"** and **"always will be" indescribable** or **inconceivable?** The source of all knowledge and understanding! And it seemed to Mathew that this **Androgynous-state?** Was and still is looking for answer!

To it's own self-inquiry! **Who am I, what am I,** and **where am I,** and this **enigma** Seam's to have found the answer, while at the same time looking for it! In the knowledge of its own self, because we know that matter cannot be created or destroyed! So it begs the question, if we don't know where it comes from? Or where it goes too? Is it like the preverbal **tree in the forest,** if higher self or the observer? So to speak, can't perceive it, relative to each and every one of us when we are sleeping or after each and every one of us die! And our energy leaves our physical bodies, is it really there to begin with? Is it being held in some unified field, between the infinite tick of the clock?

The big bang or that strange event that seems or appears to have theoretically happened all by it's self, or that it just some how came into being some how! Because Mathew knew he was alive, he was substantial, he thought to himself, as he recalled **Des Carté** and his famous supposition: **"I think therefore I am."** So something must have happened, even theoretically! Because he and all the rest of us seem or appear to be the living proof!

But why and how was at that point a much deeper and unfathomable mystery even to Mathew till his mind had been artificially expanded enough to try and understand the bottomless truths inside himself, and all around him like the great philosophers and religions of the world who seem like blind men trying to reach out and touch that elusive something!

Wrapped up in the meaning of life, like blind men touching and trying to describe that preverbal Elephant! And yet each and every one of them came up with a different answer to the question? Is the answer or the pun, so to speak staring us in the face!

If we could only read between the lines! Or was Mathew like the rest of us, who seem or appear to be chasing our own tail? Like the snake on the man's hand with it's hidden symbolism or like the abstract imagery we see in our dreams that can contain the meaning or the solution to a problem, like the German chemist: **F. A. Kekule** who saw in the reverie of his own dream a snake seize its own tail! And with this he went on to discover the formula for **Benzene.**

Or **Dr Herman Hilprecht** the archaeologist, whose ancient Babylonian phantom priest came bearing gifts of knowledge in his dreams like the

Scottish inventor: *"**James Watt**"* inventor of the steam-engine, and while walking through a heavy rainstorm while he was dreaming, saw the rain itself turn to tiny leaden pellets which bounced about under foot and from this wonderful dream, he discovered how to make lead shot, By dropping molten liquid metal (Lead) into water, thanks to **James Watt** and his recurring dream.

So deep within this imagery there seems to be a secret language that's speaks with a hidden tongue of great truths that we have lost for whatever reason and that it is begging the question?

And the **indescribable** or **inconceivable androgynous state?** We know as **God!** Somehow used the retrospective or self-conscious impression of it's own self to try and find the answer to a question it was looking for: **Who am I, what am I,** and **where am I,** and this created the so-called: **big bang!**

A timeless theoretical unified thought, as such, created the heavens and the earth and on the seventh day! The lord rested, because he had come to the end of his work, and where the answer to the question has already been found... and yet at the same time nothing seems or appears to have happened in the conventional sense, so to speak!

Its as if a part of it is still looking for the problem or trying to solve the puzzle of its own self! At the same time as solving it, it's as if it caused the problem in order to solve it!

Even though the **indescribable** or **inconceivable androgynous state?** Has come full circle like the theory of the past, present and the future which co-exist with one another, *"**it**"* or our collective higher-self moves through existence in a **relative state** or as it becomes consciously aware! It tries to discover what has happened, in that timeless unified thought, because something has happened, so it could be the key or answer to a paradox of who God is? Or the riddle of our own selves or what appears to be somewhere and yet nowhere, beyond the beyond or at the incredible source of all knowledge and understanding!

It's like the book of **Exodus**, in the Christian bible when **Moses** was on the mount when he asked God who he was? And God answered: **I am that I am.** Which is a bit like the paradox of what came first, the **chicken or the egg?** Because it is asking a question that fly's in the face of it's own self! And this has caused what seems or appears to be a theoretical dissociation of thinking. But remember like the *"veil of Isis"* no man as lifted that veil, so God can't see his own face, that's what has caused the theoretical problem in the first place! And there Mathew saw his own reflection as if cast in a mirror! As if it were the face of God looking back at him with Mathew trying to convince himself, that he does not exist, and that it is only the reflection of his own self and nothing more.

So something seems or appears to have happened, where theoretically nothing has or should have happened. Which means the universe is stranger than we think! Because if you can't destroy matter or create it, then it is not a case of where did it come from or where does it go too, but where is it coming from and going to? In what appears to be a constant state of flux, like quantum physics, which means it has or it has not happened!

Like the preverbal tree that falls in the forest, is reality really what we tend to think it is, because time does not apply to the **Androgynous state?** And time and space seem to be there and at the same time, and yet they seem not to be there!

Like matter that appears to be solid or the bicycle wheel effect with it's little electrons whirling endlessly in space as if held in a unified-field by some unknown energy around the nucleus of this phantom atom!

And even stranger is the fact that time moves forward and backwards at the same time or time-travel would be impossible! Like the observation in our rocket ship travelling away from the earth at the speed of light, with the pilot on board who sees everything going backwards!

Through the giant telescope on board the spaceship, so it would appear that at the same time the universe is being created from the beginning to the end, it was or is being created back-to-front at the same time!

Like Shakespeare put it: Is our fate in ourselves or in our stars? Is our life a second hand one or are we spoiled goods! Where our autonomy or free will is something that is handed down to us, even though it seems or appears that we have the free will to choice from an infinite number of possibilities, they have already been chosen for us! Implying the hand of fate has already dealt the cards, and the future or for that matter the past is already self-ordained, before we are even born into the world! Or is it?

The answer is yes and no, like an infinite and vast intelligence running on a binomial or binary system namely 1-or-0, **Vis-à-vis** it means its quantum-physics yes and no... which is a half-truth or Deo non Fortuna, meaning by: god, not by chance, or are we at the hands of capricious Gods and the twisted hand of fate!

It is like king Solomon's cyclic view of destiny?

"For everything its season, and for every activity under heaven its time: a time to be born and a time to die...Whatever is has been already, and Whatever is to come has been already, and God summons each event back in turn" (Eccl. 3: 1, 2, 15.)

. . .

Just like the puzzle of the universe and the enigma of **God** or the **indescribable** or **inconceivable Androgynous state?** Wherever or whatever it is!

That's how our space ship was able to see everything on earth going backwards or the CLA time machine is able to travel into the past or into the future, because the future not unlike the past has still to happen, and at the same time it has happened or is still to happen! According to Albert Einstein's theory.

So if we reiterate with our example of what came first: **The chicken or the egg?** Which is a bit like Gods or our own self-awareness or retrospection of its own self in the **Androgynous state?** Realizing that something was wrong, because it is trying to paradoxically tell it's own self or reflection, in the essence of existence, that it cannot exist, and the font of this self awareness is what we call: relativity in the dual aspect or twin destiny of our own selves, which is the universe the observer onboard the rocket ship can see going forward or backwards in the **void**, or what we euphemistically call **time**!

That's why time travellers can move back and forth through the process of atomic decay or as we call it: **time,** and view things relative to the observer, with each and every person they meet, either in the past or in the future or we would all be deaf, dumb and blind to everything, and we would exist in a bizarre and oblivious state, akin to hell!

Or that imaginary fear of death or non-existence we have, that's why the reflection is struggling with it's own true self, which is what we know as existence! Because it knows that this state cannot exist or be prolonged by its self or continue to be separate from the **indescribable** or **inconceivable androgynous state?**

It was as if Mathew was agreeing with himself! Because he then remembered the times he had blackouts! When he would talk to his comrades and interact with them, and afterwards he remembered nothing of what he had said or done, although it would have been stored in the back of his memory, so it seemed that he could still be conscious, but not aware! Of what was happening, is our consciousness the essence of this false reflection that does not exist? Because it appears to be oblivious! And yet we must be aware! At the same time, so our relative-awareness or higher self seems to be that part of our own self or the **indescribable** or **inconceivable androgynous state?** That trying to convince it's own reflection that it cannot exist separately, which is the conscious part of our mind or the retrospective aspect or awareness of our own self that is asking such questions as: **Where did we come from?** Or **why are we here?** And **where are we going?** And naturally you will get a blank reply, because the answer does not come before the question!

And in our case visa-versa, because nothing has happened, it is only theoretical, and the **indescribable** or **inconceivable androgynous state?** Seems to somehow know, even though it appears to be contradicting its self, it's like the tail wagging the dog!

So it must be like an intentional slight of mouth or contradiction that is causing the actual problem, which has brought about or created the physical and the non-physical world as we know it, so it appears to have been a mistake or a problem that it is trying to solve! And in doing so that's what seems or appears to have brought about a dichotomy! Or split in our or it's own being.

So without the ability to be conscious and aware at the same time there would be no continuity or meaning and purpose to life, it would be like the old question: **if a tree falls in the forest, and if no one is there to hear it, does it make a sound!** And if Mathew listened real close he would hear the sound of one hand clapping, which was the sound of the voice in his own head or that **simile** or shadow aspect cast by **God,** like the tongue of the serpent in the garden of Eden, whispering in Gods ear if you will, or into Mathews ear, which is the voice of Gods own reflection echoed in and through each of us trying to convince it's own self, that it does not and cannot exist in a separate state, and that's why we have a fear of death because it is our ***own higher self*** or the ***indescribable, inconceivable androgynous state?*** That already knows that it is its own reflection that has been cast upon the preverbal mirror and that it is a false representation or shadow aspect of it's own true self, which has imprisoned itself here in the physical world, like ***"Eliphas Levi 1810-1875"*** *who believed that Satan was the shadow of God!"* Or the reflection cast by the face of **God** or the ***indescribable and inconceivable androgynous state's?*** Self-awareness of its own self in the preverbal mirror, where it seems or appears to know the truth about its own true and yet paradoxical nature!

And like the story of Jesus Christ after he had risen from the dead, when Mary Magdalene had approached the strange figure in the cemetery, having not recognized that it was Christ, she asked the stranger, if he had been responsible for taking away her masters body? And Christ had asked of her: why was she looking for the living among the dead? Just the same as we do, when we ask the same questions about dying! And the fear of it we seem to cherish so much, or that self-same fear of non-existence!

Which is, as we know the theoretical separation or disassociation which is like a paradoxical battle of some kind in the self-perception or retrospective thinking process, that acted like an exchange of energy or like a ripple or a pebble hitting the surface of a pond of water, that the original thought or image has been cast onto, like a ***hologram*** that has been smashed into an infinite number of pieces, and each piece contains the whole original image! Even though the parts seem or appear to be greater than the whole, which is the symbolic of image of **God,** so to speak, or the ***indescribable or inconceivable androgynous state?***

In each and every one of us, by want of separation the parts that make up the image cannot be greater than the whole, and yet each part like the **hologram** contains the **whole!**

And the reality of the physical world seems or appears to at least to bare witness to some great truth! That was to Mathew like a voice crying in the wilderness, a voice that he seemed to know, because he remembered what it had said in the bible's book of Genesis, where it describes,

"In the beginning there was darkness or a description of something that was indescribable! Or outside of its own self, and God moved upon the face of the darkness or was it discovering the retrospective aspect or awareness of it's own self, and said: Let there be light, and there was light" or the disassociation of thinking in a theoretical separation of it's own self had taken place, and where it or we are temporally trapped in a dichotomy or struggle, that is equivalent of asking your self a rhetorical question: what is the meaning of life? And your own voice replying like an echo: ***"how long is a piece of string?"***

Which is like the serpents tongue in the garden of Eden, that caused the fall from grace, by none other than ***Lucifer*** himself, who was created by God!

It is actually a disembodied or inner voice of **God** or that **inconceivable** or **indescribable androgynous state?** That seems or appears to be there, and yet at the same time its not there! It does not and cannot exist therefore non-existence does not apply to it in the normal sense that we have come to believe...? Like your own internal dialogue that goes on inside your own head, so to speak!

Its as if God or the essence of the great architect of the physical and the non-physical world was the carrier or the symbolic barer of that thought or light, who was reputedly cast out or separated from itself or heaven: **"For never was there such a star that shone so bright and fell so far, that can rise again and shine so bright"** due to the monumental battle or struggle with its own self.

And as Mathew continued reading the great book in the chamber of the ages, he came to a page with a puzzle on it, that he began to read to himself: **"what has a beginning where there is no beginning? And an end, where there is no end?"** He remembered the words from the bible, when Christ had said in the scriptures: **"I am the Alfa and the Omega"** the beginning or where the physical world is coming from, and the end or where it goes? And that he was not only the Son of God, but he was the Son of man! Stating that he along with us was the collective expression of that reflection cast by our own true selves, and is that what Christ symbolically meant, when he said that we were made in **God's image** or a tongue in cheek meaning of who we rely are, which is the beginning or theoretical disassociation of our own true self, which is an **indescribable** or **inconceivable androgynous state?** That has no beginning! And because it is theoretical, then nothing has actually happened! **"So there is no beginning, and if there is no beginning then there can be no end!"**

It was this dichotomy that has brought into play the state or paradox of existence, it holds the very fabric in place, until everything is said and done so to speak, which is inherent in the creed of dualism and the law of opposites, that is hard on the heels of the big question of existence!

Or in our case the human condition, which in a way is self inflicted, because we seem to have become victimized by and through our own selves! And even Christ said in the bible, that there will be wars and rumours of wars, and that these things must happen, almost as if the means will justify the ends!

Is God trying to cut off a finger to save the body? Through each of us, is he telling us that **"for the want of a horse shoe nail the war was lost"** with regards to that part of our self or what could be euphemistically known as the **"author of the piece"** with each of us as the **critic!**

That seems to be causing the problem, a part that has to be integrated at any cost, whether you like it or not, or you will cancel out your self, or the **indescribable** or **inconceivable androgynous state?** If you don't realize the true meaning of existence, even though it's a modern day **cliché** by saying that **"you cannot and will not be saved"** existence is only a movement or a voice in your own head, so to speak, or in the void, and if we don't realize it before its to late, then the problem could become cyclic, where you will go round in a never-ending circle chasing your own tail! Between the infinite tick of the clock, a bit like an old Greek joke **"if you listen closely you can hear the gods laugh"** which is a bit like life, you either get the joke or you don't! Because its certainly not in acquiring money for monies sake!

The power we think money has does not exist! That's why currencies change as they go from inflation to de-flation, because it's a game the power structure is playing to keep us at one another's throat, while they maintain control over the heard!

For them the message of life's true meaning is like **"pearls before swine"** and unless you truly understand that we are in a situation where you are either part of the problem or part of the solution, you are for or against your own self in a symbolic struggle for power in a battle of **unification** that can and will change our perception of the physical and the non-physical worlds, with there hidden meaning or we may lose the true knowledge of who we rely are, instead of the false knowledge of who we think we are!

"Men of science say miracles are past and give reasons for things supernatural, therefore we dismiss our terrors by finding safety in false knowledge, instead we should submit ourselves to an unknown fear" with regards to our physical existence and each new life in this common bond will be born into the physical world caught in an endless **cycle** of **self-imposed rebirth** into a state of constant **role-reversal** of **misery v happiness** **"ad- nauseum"** which has to be **cancelled-out**, one way or the other, whether you have to be weaned off this existence or not, it has to eventually happen**!**

Or reintegrated so that the polarities of right and wrong, good and evil or God and the Devil, will eventually be neutralized and integrated, by and through our ability to see what has apparently went wrong, freeing us from the vicious circle of ignorance, when we realize and come to except the hidden meaning or mysteries of our physical life, and that invisible hand of the **indescribable** or **inconceivable androgynous state?** That is not only trying to find the answer to this riddle or question, it has already solved the enigma at the same time!

It seems to be the only way to solve the problem and cancel-out what seems or appears to be the troublesome or active aspects of this **indescribable** or **inconceivable androgynous state?** And in trying to find the answer it appeared to actually cause the problem!

It has become bound by it's very own contradictory nature, to seek expression in meaning and form in what appears or seems to be an act of self discovery that must surely beg the question, why would such a **paradox** or **indescribable** and **inconceivable androgynous state?** Need to be aware of it's own self, when it wasn't there to begin with!

And because of this, it appears to have caused a problem in order to solve one, because such self-inquiry in order to find a condition, mathematically speaking, has literally questioned why it was not even there in the first place! So to speak, or in a way we can't understand, which is echoed in the **indescribable** or **inconceivable androgynous states?** Own reflection, and yet this seems to have been the way the physical and the non-physical world as we know it was created, in and by a form of expression akin to a thought in the mind of our own true selves as it were, which seems or appears to throw light onto a great unknown expanse of what could only be described as darkness or something within or out-with it's own self, so to speak, like the universe which is like a *"Mobius strip"* the has no **beginning** or **end** or **infinity,** that we now know as the physical and the non-physical world, and where we seem to be experiencing something that **was,** or **has been** or is **being expressed** by what you can only describe for want of a better word, **a thought in the mind** of some **indescribable** or **inconceivable androgynous state?** That we indirectly or incorrectly call **God...!** If you will, that's why you will find that you can't seem to tell where the physical or the meta-physical world begins and ends, because both seem to be like a point of light surrounded by a great expanse of darkness! Or unknown quantity, and if we truly read between the lines inherent in the contradictions of both worlds, we can see where the boundary **lies!** (No pun intended) many a truth is said in jest... between a world we seem or appear to be in, and the world we can only glimpse in flights of fancy, day dreams or when we realise we are asleep and dreaming, as we learn to control our dreams by looking at our hands, we can learn to become conscious in the dream state, or in self hypnosis where we are able to create anything we want! By just thinking about it! Or creation by mere thought, which is like a science without instrumentality!

. . .

René Descartes

"I suppose therefore that all things I see are illusions; I believe that nothing has ever existed of everything my lying memory tells me. I think I have no senses" I believe that my body, shape, extension, motion, location are functions, what is there then that can be taken as true?"

* * *

Such thoughts are like a footprint left behind on the shore of eternity or like a voice crying in the wilderness! For there lie's the true grail if we are prepared to seek it, to wean us of this existence or re-associate ourselves in the surreal and vivid world of the mind, or awaken from the dream of life!

It's a bit like trying to reach out and touch something that is not there! And solve the paradox of our own selves in relation to the workings of the **indescribable** or **inconceivable androgynous state?**

That seems to be intangible or neutral or somewhere in relation to the dichotomy of its or our own true self, and if we have the courage to dip our toe in the water, so to speak! And ask the ultimate question or seek to find a deeper meaning to find out how the **androgynous-state?** Itself or our own true selves came into being, it would be like trying to (*square the circle*) or reach out to understand the story of *"Osirus slain"* and

"**Osirus risen**" hidden in the **Tamarisk-tree** of knowledge or the problem that caused it in the first place, it can't be done...

The **indescribable** or **inconceivable androgynous-state?** Seems or appears to have done is akin to turning a sock inside-out or in the old saying: What's gained on the roundabout, is lost on the swings, or what goes around comes around, like: **Mary Queen of Scots**, just before she bowed her head to the axe-man, she said: "**In my end is my beginning**" as if when one door closes another one opens, as they say.

So all things will be as they **were,** and **always will be,** and life no matter how horrible or beautiful it seems or appears to be, has a more profound meaning or purpose behind it, by the hand of that great **architect** that seems quicker than the eye that beheld or fashioned its creation.

And all the great religions of the world and even the ones to come! Who have or will in their own way have tried to illuminate **rightly** or **wrongly** the darkness of ignorance and suffering, like the Christian scriptural simile that referred to it as: Opening up the gates of heaven or to the paradise of the **neutral androgynous state...?**

Which is the knowledge of our own true selves or everyone's birthright, or terrible loss of that which has always **been** and **always will be...?** Now Mathew knew there was no such thing as a God in heaven or the Devil in hell, not in the way he had been taught to believe it, and each and every one of us, or the sum of parts that make up the original image, like the shattered **hologram** that contained or made up the **whole image** was a testament to the truth, and if you look at any piece of the broken **hologram** you will see in it wonders to **behold!** For there in each and every infinite piece is the **whole original image captured in it looking back at you!** Because that is the nature of a **hologram,** meaning each and every one of us are truly the centre of our own selves or universe, and in a contradictory way, there has never been anybody else except each individuals own self!

And when each and every one of us dies, when we are eventually weaned off of the physical world, and we sever our connection to the physical world, which to all intent and purposes, like the tree in the forest or is anything rely there to begin with, except the physical appearance of things that are collectively projected by each and every person's own self-awareness of it!

Are we judged by what we do in this transient state? It's very probable that what king Solomon said about God is right! And that his anger is but for a moment and his forgiveness is forever! But it's highly unlikely! Because Jesus Christ was trying to tell us something which could be like writing a letter to ones self! By and through his teaching it seems or appears to be something that you ignore at your own pearl...

Montague Summer's

"*Evil surly needs no argument or proof it is self-evident a vivid reality of the choices we make using the power of evil-who can look upon the world even today shattered and wounded and rent, and not recognize its cruel* *tyranny by devil's who bare the mark! Of "lying, Malignity and Hurtfulness" who themselves make no small number of the laws and rulers that are made in the world, and have no small number of honoured servants and are the authors of most of the wars in the world, who are crooked, distorted, disturbed and diseased, malice prepense who in order to commit these acts and therefore to incur the guilt of the responsibility for the acts and hence to reap the inevitable and logical consequences there must have been a deliberate intention as well as a clear consciousness of the acts! Which will make an un-thinkable difference to the "Grand plan" because the **means will justify the ends**!"*

But remember all you **existentialists**: 'In the absence of a **grand-plan** if nothing that we do matters, then all that matters is what we do, then the smallest act of **kindness** or **meanness** could mean the whole world!!'

. . .

And its no good looking for a scapegoat in the form of **Satan** to blame for the terrible things in the world, because we are angry at being trapped or imprisoned by the self-defacing instrumentality of our own besotted condition, we are here for one reason and one reason only, which is to follow the path to either lose or find and re-discover the lost wisdom and knowledge of our own true selves, which is like a paper trail that will lead us to the shores of eternity and beyond, as if following that elusive footprint, until then we can only glimpse and wonder what lies ahead of us, or what lies behind us, Because all of us have the right to that divine and eternal inheritance, unless you give it away!

After the cord that suspends us between this world and the next is finally cut, and we can begin our journey homeward, with that first step! And back to the symbolic Garden of Eden, where it all began, with that bite of the proverbial apple, figuratively speaking! That brought us here, and on into infinity or what seems in reverse the great unknown or by using a simple metaphor of reversing a plain and simple sock that you wear on your foot!

Where we will be welcomed home for always and forever, And where the **indescribable or inconceivable androgynous state?** Will have, by its own hand have **re-associated** it's own self, being no longer imprisoned by it's own **reflection!** Or is it something that cannot be solved, and its cyclic or an infinite enigmatic process, of causing the problem by finding the problem! And then solving or having to solve the problem!

Like in the Christian bible where it says that **Satan** that **Omni-arch** of the world or in essence the shadow aspect of our own selves, will in the end of days be eventually let out of his *theoretical* [My Italics] prison, which will be through each and every one of us, being born into the world, and the **liberation** and **re-association** of our own collective self or the **Anima-Mundi** or **soul of the world, if not the universe!** So one should keep their tongue firmly in cheek, if you don't believe me, who are you to judge anybody, if the almighty has decided to make me an atheist, who are you or anybody to question the will of god?

And as Mathew stopped reading the great book, he looked up to see the figure of the watcher who stood at the threshold, who had two faces! Just like the eye of God! That was reflected on to the sea of eternity, on the amulet printed on the page of his little esoteric pamphlet that he had dropped onto the jungle floor, like the falling leafs of inevitability from the jungle canopy overhead.

The society that had published the pamphlet was founded during the age of enlightenment when the energy of man's consciousness was by exception, liberated or freed from the confines of its own self-imposed dictatorial rule, and the top half of the eye in the centre of the amulet was reflected onto a pool of water, a looking glass or mirror if you will, like a sea-of-glass which reflects the other side onto its surface, to symbolically show the dichotomy of it's own self or that life was a reflection cast by the eye of God!

And where the horizontal dividing line lies (*excuse the pun*) through the eye, is a line drawn on the sands of time, to reveal the hidden aspect of it's own self, that's why the watcher had two faces, akin to *Janus* the *Divom-Deus* or *God-of-Gods* and the two-headed son of *Apollo* and *Creusa*, he is the God of doorways and arches, which symbolically signifies *beginnings* and *endings...*

Which was the theoretical aim of the *Alchemists*, who believed that the process itself was accompanied by a spiritual change, akin to a symbolic death or aphoristic principle *"solve et coagula"* dissolve and combine... or where the various characteristics of a substance are stripped away in some unknown *metamorphosis* or joining of its *opposing-polarities!*

Between male or female, or *Hermaphroditism*, these changes may be the result of inner, profound spiritual experiences, and a new, nobler substance is built that symbolizes death, followed by rebirth into a better, purer life, *vis á vis* (therefore) it symbolises the dichotomy between the two-worlds or the tangled web we weave...

Fulcanelli tells us this in *Le mystère des cathedrals*, is emblematic of the whole labour of the work, it is there that the thread of *Ariadne* or *Arachne,* the legendary, 'Arachne', the *spider-queen* from Greek mythology who had been a *Lydian maiden*, having challenged the Goddess, *"Athene"* who wove the garments of the *Gods,* and because she was beaten by a mortal, the Goddess, 'Athene' had changed, *"Arachne"* into a *spider!* Who now weaves her webs so that mankind can look upon its deadly beauty, with her family the *"Arachnidae"*

Becomes necessary for us if we are not to wander in a maze among the winding paths of the task... to extricate ourselves in the Phonetic cabala to elucidate the symbolism of the Greek legend of Ariadne, who with a thread helped *Theseus* to escape from the *labrinth!* After he had slain the *Minotaur* or overcome and solved the problem... so to speak!

Which in the book *"Les demeures philosophales"* by *Fulcanelli,* our attention is drawn to a remarkable piece of sculpture – one of four statues that symbolically guard the tomb of *François II* in *Nantes-Cathedral.*

Fulcanelli calls it prudence...! In frontal view it depicts the figure of a beautiful young girl in a hooded cloak and floor-length gown. (*She seems*

315

mesmerized by her own reflection! In a strange convex mirror she holds in her hand...!)

. . .

"To the evil, are all thing's evil"

Like some diabolical mental thrall, the wisdom is in the simile, when we are reminded of the story of the scorpion and the fox,

"Scorpion and the Fox"

(An eye for an eye is wrong!)

"A scorpion asks the fox to carry him over a river. The fox is afraid of being stung during the trip, but the scorpion argues that if it stung the fox, the fox would sink and the scorpion would drown. The fox agrees and begins carrying the scorpion, but midway across the river the scorpion does indeed sting the fox, dooming them both. When asked why, the scorpion points out that this is its nature. The fable is used to illustrate the position that the natural behaviour of some creatures is inevitable, no matter how they are treated. It is also used to illustrate that individuals are apt to behave in accordance with their true character in spite of the education they might have received throughout their lives . In spite of knowing fully well the right course of action, and full understanding the consequences, some are unable to overcome their nature."

The Three Musketeers

"This was my families chapel Charlotte, we took our vows here, I loved you Charlotte and I still love you, as I love war and drunkenness, love you as men love all that is worst for them.

Forgive me Robert? I swear before God and this holy place, but it was too late for Charlotte! For there, the executioner and axe man of Lille, mercy she cries! You cannot, mercy! How many times have you asked for mercy, and repaid it in blood? How many times have you taken men's love, pity and aspirations, their lives! What is in the essence of your evil? You understand goodness, we don't forgive you Charlotte, we can't, we do not dare!"

"Which is like a warning to the people who follow, and are guided by evil, because no matter what you think you are being promised, it's a bare faced lie, and you will only sell yourself down the proverbial river, just to get to the other side, or is it more like being lead up the garden path, as in the garden of Eden, so to speak!"

. . .

In her right hand is a pair of compasses or perhaps dividers! Throughout alchemical literature, there are frequent injunctions to **separate,** and **conjoin**.

And on the back of the girl's head is another face—that of a wise old sage, apparently deep in contemplation and enfolded within the cloak of philosophy. She symbolises nature in all its hidden aspects, both inward and outward, but beneath her exterior veil, there appears the mysterious image of ancient alchemy, 'and we are, through the attributes of the first, initiated into the secrets of the second, which is self evident in the doctrine of the society of dynamics, or in the creed of dualism inherent in the law of opposites...

With this Mathew had awoken, having returned back to the dream of life! What a cosmic bender he thought... as he tried to hold onto the heavy vibes that had just been laid on him by his strange and freaky journey, in which it seemed that ages had passed, but in reality only a split second had gone by on the clock, or a movement in the void? So to speak!

So we are forced to use a metaphor to describe an **"enigma"** or something that does not exist in the sense of the word, something that is **inconceavable, indiscrible** or **androgynous state?** And the dicotomy is the left and right arm of that same body!

.   .   .

Commputer
(God)
Through the looking glass:
(Or that bubble of mans vanity)
We draw back the veiled shadows of the past with the decralation of Isis: I am whatsoever was, whatsoever is, whatsoever shall be. And the veil which is over my face no mortal hand has ever raised.

.   .   .

Alpha and Omega

This symbol was suggested by the Apocalypse, where many believe that Christ, as well as the Father, is "**the First and the Last**" (ii, 8); "**the Alpha and Omega, the first and the last, the beginning and the end**" (cf., xxii, 13; i, 8). Clement of Alexandria (2nd century, philosopher and commentator on pagan and Christian information) speaks of the Word as "**the Alpha and the Omega of Whom alone the end becomes beginning, and ends again at the original beginning without any break**" Prudentius (Cathemer., ix, 10) we learn that in the fourth century the interpretation of the apocalyptic letters was still the same: "**Alpha et Omega cognominatus, ipse fons et clausula, Omnium quae sunt, fuerunt, quaeque post futura sunt.**"

.   .   .

317

From the source of all knowledge and understanding or the creator we
have to put forward a startling theory

Computer programming

(often shortened to **programming**) is a process that leads from an
original formulation of a computing problem to executable computer
programs. Programming involves activities such as analysis, developing
understanding, generating algorithms, verification of requirements of
algorithms including their correctness and resources consumption, and
implementation (commonly referred to as coding) of algorithms in a target
programming language. Source code is written in one or more
programming languages. The purpose of programming is to find a
sequence of instructions that will automate **performing a specific task**
or **solving a given problem**. The process of programming thus often
requires expertise in many different subjects, including knowledge of the
application **domain, specialized algorithms** and **formal logic**.

Related tasks include **testing, debugging**! And maintaining the **source
code**, implementation of the **build system**, and management of derived
artifacts such as machine code of computer programs. These might be
considered part of the programming process, but often the term "**software
development**" is used for this larger process with the term
"programming", "implementation", or "coding" reserved for the actual
writing of source code. Software engineering combines engineering
techniques with software development practices.

. . .

Which is akin to it looking into a proverbal **internal-mirror**, and trying
to convince its own self, that it cannot exist in a separate state! Which has
caused a theoretical disasociation or glitche, like a virus in a software
programme, and it is trying to debug the system, because it keeps crashing,
like the **"*enigma*"** of the universe, where you can't **create** or **destroy
matter**! And that's a fact, not a theory, so where could the ellusion of
reality be coming from?

What is good and what is bad?

Do we have invisible, so to speak, **sentient beings** at the top of *the
meta-physical tree*, who are either **carbon**! Or **Silicon** based life-
forms, who seem or appear to be **hostile** (Ravens) to **homo-sapians?**
But remember never judge a book by its cover! Even if they have to be cruel
to be kind.

Like in the cult TV show (**Dr Who?**) and the adventure called: **"*The City
Of Death***" set in Paris in the **80's**

Are they from the future or have they evolved beyond the **phyisical-
plane** proverbially speaking, and are looking over our shoulder, all the
time! If you will, Vis-à-vis (therefore) that would explain the mysterious
individuals like **Quetzacotl** or **Christ**. (*Doves*) who brought forth the
olive-branch of **peace**, and who it would seem or appear are not

interested in saving us from physical death, per-say, but how it will effect the *final outcome!* Like in the movie **TRON**:

Plot

Kevin Flynn (Jeff Bridges) is a software engineer, formerly employed by the computer corporation ENCOM, who now runs an arcade bar called *Flynn's*. He wrote several video games, but another ENCOM engineer, Ed Dillinger (David Warner), stole them and passed them off as his own, earning himself a series of promotions until reaching Senior Executive VP. Having left the company, Flynn attempts to obtain evidence of Dillinger's actions by hacking the ENCOM mainframe, but is repeatedly stopped by the Master Control Program (MCP), an artificial intelligence written by Dillinger. However, since its inception the MCP has become power-hungry, illegally appropriating business and even government programs and absorbing them to increase its own capacities; it informs Dillinger of its plans to subjugate the Pentagon and the Kremlin, and expresses interest in China with its request for Chinese-translation programs, blackmailing Dillinger into compliance with records of his theft of the games.

Flynn's ex-girlfriend, Lora Baines (Cindy Morgan), and fellow ENCOM engineer, Alan Bradley (Bruce Boxleitner), warn Flynn that Dillinger knows about his hacking attempts and has tightened security. Flynn persuades them to sneak him inside ENCOM, where he forges a higher security clearance for Alan's recently developed security program called "Tron". In response, the MCP uses an experimental laser to digitize Flynn into the ENCOM mainframe cyberspace (called the Grid), where programs are living entities appearing in the likeness of the human "users" who created them:

Friend or foe?

Hegel(1770-1831)

'To be or not to be'

Hegelianisn is founded upon the doctrine that to be and not to be are the same or the identity of contraries.
The principle that everything is and at the same time and in the same sense is not.

. . .

Is an not an actual account but a theoretical model (exposition) of a strange *enigma* or **abstraction** which is a conceptual process by which general rules and concepts are derived from the usage and classification of specific examples, literal (**"real"** or **"concrete"**) signifiers, first principles, or other methods. **"An abstraction"** is the product of this process—a concept that acts as a super-categorical noun for all subordinate concepts, and connects any related concepts as a **group**, **field**, or **category**.

Conceptual abstractions may be formed by reducing the information content of a **concept** or an **observable phenomenon**, typically to retain

319

only information which is relevant for a particular purpose. For example, abstracting a leather soccer ball to the more general idea of a ball retains only the information on general ball attributes and behavior, eliminating the other characteristics of that particular ball. In a type–token distinction, a type (e.g., a 'ball') is more abstract than its tokens (e.g., 'that leather soccer ball').

Abstraction

And the source of all knowledge and understanding or **God** (*the great architect)* of some **machine** or **computer**! Like **computer scientists** use **abstraction** to make **models** that can be used and re-used without having to **re-write** all the **program code** for each new application on every different type of **computer**. They communicate their solutions with the **computer** by writing **source code** in some particular **computer language** which can be translated into **machine code** for different types of **computer** to execute. **Abstraction** allows **program designers** to separate **categories** and **concepts** related to **computing problems** from specific instances of implementation. This means that the **program code** can be written so that it does not depend on the specific details of **supporting applications**, **operating system software** or **hardware**, but on an **"abstract concept"** of the **"solution"** to the **"problem"** that can then be integrated with the **system** with minimal additional work.

KRELL

(*Forbidden Planet*)
ALTAIR IV

A science apparently without instrumentally, that seemed or appeared to **adjust** the **humungous computer** when the seasons were altered or adjusted, like the reality or world that we think we live in, it was as if something was **upgrading** the **system** by taking the **server** off line!

The Dark Ages

Is a historical periodization used originally for the Middle Ages, which emphasizes the **cultural** and **economic deterioration** that supposedly occurred in Western Europe following the decline of the Roman Empire. The label employs traditional **light-versus-darkness imagery** to contrast the "**darkness**" of the period with earlier and later periods of "**light**". The period is characterized by a relative scarcity of historical and other written records at least for some areas of Europe, rendering it obscure to historians. The term "**Dark Age**" derives from the Latin **saeculum obscurum**, originally applied by Caesar Baronius in 1602 to a tumultuous period in the 10th and 11th centuries.

It's as if this theoretical computer seems or appears to have discovered a *glitch* in its own systems programming, and it is trying to find or has found a *virus* in the *system*:

A computer virus

is a malware program that, when executed, replicates by inserting copies of itself (possibly modified) into other computer programs, data files, or the boot sector of the hard drive; when this replication succeeds, the affected areas are then said to be **"infected"**. Viruses often perform some type of harmful activity on infected hosts, such as stealing hard disk space or CPU time, accessing private information, corrupting data. However, not all viruses carry a destructive payload or attempt to hide themselves—the defining characteristic of viruses is that they are self-replicating computer programs which install themselves without the user's consent.

Virus writers use **social engineering** and **exploit** detailed knowledge of **security vulnerabilities** to gain **access** to their **hosts**' computing resources, employing a variety of mechanisms to **infect new hosts**, and often using complex anti-detection/stealth strategies to evade antivirus software. And it is trying to reboot it, in this recurring tragedy of a *science* or *veil of tears*! *"gementes et flentes in hac lacrimarum valle"* or *"mourning and weeping in this valley of tears* without instrumentality:

Paul

But some man will say, "How are the dead raised up? And with what body do they come?" Thou fool. . . (of) that which thou sowest, thou sowest not that body that shall be, but bare grain. . . . But God giveth it a body as it hath pleased him, and to every seed his own body. . . . There are also celestial bodies, and bodies terrestrial: but the glory of the celestial is one of glory of the terrestrial is another. . . . So also is the resurrection of the dead.

It is sown in **curruption**, *it is raised in* **incorruption**: *it is sown in dishonor; it is rased in glory: it is sown in weakness; it is raised in power. There is a natural body, and there is a* **spiritual body**. . . . *Behold I show you a* **mystery**: *We shall not all sleep, but we shall all be changed. In a moment, in the twinkling of an eye, at the last trumpet: for the trumpet shall sound, and the dead shall be raised* **incorruptible**

Corinthians 15:35-52

Unfathomable

"By the light of reason, it seems difficult to prove the immortality of the soul. By what arguments or analogies can we prove any statement of existence which no one ever saw, and which no way resembles any that ever was seen? For that purpose, some new species of logic is required and some new faculties of the mind, that they may enable us to comprehend that logic."

David Hume

Are there others at varying stages of evolutionary development, trapped, as it were somewhere under the **USA** or what seems or appears to be the **epicentre of activity!**

Creatures who are intillectually superior! And have the God-given right to murder and/or disect an inferior species, everybody knows that!

. . .

'The Devil knows his own'

And that's why in the **MISSING 411** books by **David Paulides** the **"FBI"** some times only monitors the situation, so they say, and who seem or appear to be too busy doing their job, to be able to do their job right, which is usually the case when tyranny hides behind legality, even in a republic!

So it seems or appears that **someone** or **something** is worried or frightened that a more **superior** race than us is attempting or trying to feel the other one out!

So the hand that rocks the cradle or the enemy within, so to speak, seems or appears to be giving orders to its political-military-arm or the **"Greenberets"** like the European kings and queens of midieval times, who were not only the **'mailed fist** *of the* **king** *or* **queen** *i.e: the crown, but the* **shield of the people'** because no one in their right mind hands over democracy to the **"Lord of the flies"** or the **mob**, not even in the so-called western democrasies!

The enemy within
(Is the pen mightier than the sword?)

But the hand is quicker than the eye, or where the dividing line lies! Excuse the pun, the devil sit on high leading the blind, and where the footprint of **"galloping buraucracy"** or **"reason howling at the moon"** can or will be used without a shot being fired, so to speak, to control and inslave, that's where you will find out who belongs to the hand that rocks the cradle! And the clever way to invade and control a republic, kingdom or even a planet!

Where everybody is guilty until proved innocent! And where, togue-in-cheek there is no differentiation between enemies foreign or domestic! when the pen is mightier than the sword? *"Or like a Metonymic adage*

322

indicating that communication, or in some interpretations, 'administrative power' is a more effective tool than direct violence!"

Régime

A synonym for any form of government, modern usage often gives the term a negative connotation, implying an authoritarian government or dictatorship, definition: you can have any colour in a western democracy, as long as its black!

Where the true voice of freedom seems or appears to be gaged and/or controlled by either nothing more than galloping buracracy or something more sinister than those who interpret by default the voice of **freedom** or **dictatorship**, because a true democracy should be a valuable asset and has to be jealously gaurded and protected from enemies foreign or domestic , like in the cult 60s TV Show, Called: **"The invaders"**

That's why people who are unaware of this abiding principle are shocked and bemused at the west, and cynically ask the retorical question, how do you do it? We have to tear-out peoples nails in order to get them to do things, you have what others see as a prison without bars!

That's why the **Green-Berets** don't look for missing children! Per-se, but were acting on specfic orders...

"Will no one rid me of this priest"

William Shakspeare

.   .   .

First among equals

We do it! By giving control over to the **Golden-Calf,** A bestial-act of survival of the fittest and the most able among the heard, and the weak and the vulnerable must go to the wall, its only natural, because **Adolf Hitler** (*remember him?*) observed this, and by following natural selection while hidding behind the mask or persona of morality, we are able to do this bestial behaviour, by condoning political orchestrated warfare on a global scale, with the systimatic killing of our own and other species! As a sacrifice before the shinning altar of wealth and power!

To maintain the empire (oop's) or status-quo at any and all costs! Because show me a man who has failed, and I'll show you a man who hasn't tried! Why? Because **"they"** are indolent and lazy, and the **virteous** know that the Devil finds work for idle-hands, why? Because we kneel before our shinning alters of truth and Christianity and that the good book or bible tells us that any **"fool"** knows that survival must be earned or **"ARBEIT MACHT FREI"** or **"Arbeits gruppen, die Sie Freigeben"** or **"work sets you free"** we know being able to work will give you the freedom to live the way you want to, but with that freedom comes a moral responsibility to be your brothers and/or sisters keeper, you see how a devil's togue or Nazi can use tricks of logic! To begile and fool the masses into thinking that we are not (**dictatorships**) and that we are democratic

323

and free, why do you think prisons have been intentionally run in order to de-humanize the **population**, (*oops*) **prison population**, and we or they are treated no better than animals? Because it's a very clever way of doing what big bad **Adolf Hitler** is ment to have used against political desenters, and that means **you**!

'God Will Not Be Mocked'

We know that if you can work or get a well paid job, it will give you the freedom to live in a good house and send your children to a good school, but privilage is no excuse, you have the moral responsibility to help others less fortunate, and not by swelling the coffers of the fat-cats who run and work in charity shops, yes we are **our brothers** or **sisters keeper**!

. . .

One of the most open secrets in America and in the UK!
"A cure is something we look forward to,
but have no earthly idea how to accomplish"
Psychiatrist

. . .

" The House That Jack Built"

The 60's song by Allen Price, about
the asylum

The most shocking documentary on u-tube, called PSYCHIATRIE an exposé of an undemocratic and pernicious system that should be removed by force and replaced by a proper more accountable and responsible for actions, products, decisions, and policies including the administration, governance, and implementation within the scope of the role or employment position and encompassing the obligation to report, explain and be answerable for resulting consequences. system

In the past twenty years as many people have died inside psychiatric so-called hospitals, than have died in all the USA wars, since 1776. it casts 68 billion a year with Insurance companies doubling the cost of medical Insurance. With an overall bill of 4 trillion a year in the USA, and they cannot point too a single cure!

. . .

Psychiatry
And
The myth of mental illness

But one does not use it as a carrot on a stick to beat the uneducated or the ill and the vulnerable to death, by trying to use a buracratical pedigog to systematically enforce a dogmatic and unworkable psychiatric **régime** that has been given **carte-blanche** to receive power and authority to do as it likes! Under the most arrogant and questionable of pretexts, an illegal orginisation run by dogmatic fools! Or a very clever form of clandestine and illegal behaviour, that seems or appears to be cloaked in aninimity?

It seems or appears that we have both in the **UK** and the **USA** a mental health system, that is criminally incompitant? Or we have stumbled onto something more sinister and far-reaching... to do with control over our species.

Oppositional defience disorder!

Was it given carte-blanche over a 100 years ago, intentionally? To stop certain people breaking through the **"matrix"** or the world that we think we live in!

Because we would'nt get anywhere would we? If everybody refuses help, whether they like it or not!

'Through The Looking Glass'

Why was Freuds model of psychiatry was given carte-blanche! See my other book on **"Hypnosis"** (*Through The looking Glass*.) Is seems or appears to be like a loaded gun that is being turned on us, to cleverly control people who tend to break through the mental screen, that they have produced?

It could be like in the 60s cult TV show (*Star-Trek*) and the episode: (**Space-Seed**) where they found an old style space ship that contained hybrid and highly intelligent humaniods, who belived that might is right! and they could have travelled to earth, hundreds of thousands of years ago, and are lying dorment just waiting for the right time, to either emerge by themselves, who have been automatically sending out probes for thousands or millions of years if needs-be, for samples or life-forms in order to study their evolutionary development by preserving or/and disecting living creatures!

Are they! Whoever they are? Periodically checking the air, water and plant-life, in order to find out if the planet is capible of supporting life, after what appears to be antidiluvion-holocosts! And/or can they probibly terra-form reality using highly advanced molecular construction using something akin to peco-bots if needs be, or have they probibly been doing it since the beginning of time!

Is seems or appears that there could possible be something more sinister and telling to the strange and tragic death of Megumi Yamamoto! *In MISSING 411 The Devil's in the Detail. Page 160.*

From infinate-space or the unseen, so where is it? It must be akin to the fact that you can't create or destroy matter or energy, which is a fact, not a theory, like non-space or the theoretical tree in the forest, if it falls, does it make a sound, if no-one is there to hear it? You could leave a tape recorder in the woods, when God is not looking, but that would be the same as peeking, if you get my drift!, so you will still hear the recording, because your trying to trick your own reflection in a mirror, so to speak.

Its as if theres a **clitche** or **virus** in the **soft-ware package**, and the **architect** is trying to debug it, because it keeps crashing, there seems or appears to be something wrong in the programming, like the **"enigma"** of the universe, where you can't create or destroy matter! And that's a fact, not a theory, so where is the ellusion of reality coming from and going to?

Or are they energy just like us! Only they are vibrating or moving so slow or so fast, you can't see them? Like in the 1960s cult TV show called: (**Star-Trek**) and the episode titled: **"WINK OF AN EYE"**

Using a analogy by way of a simple cassette tape, that has audio or the spoken word! Put it in the a cassette player, but don't turn it on, you can't hear anything, can you? Because its going so slow its not moving, is it? So technically nothing seems or appears to be moving! You could use a cassette player that has the ability to slow audio or the spoken word down in controlled incriments (*A bit at a time*) and then keep transfering it to another tape, then tranfare it back, (*ad-infinum*) but you have as much chance as growing hair on a billiard ball, by the time you do that experiment, or it takes longer to prove, now do it this way, speed the audio or spoken word up! and keep transfaring it onto another tape, back and forward until the audio or the spoken word is nothing but a squeek, you get the point now!

Other energy or life-forms could be existing right alongside us, and we wouldn't even know, unless they are more evolved and became highly advanced cretures, who have been interfering in our anthropological, theological and sociological development!

And/or they could be controlling us by using a telephathic-screen of sorts, from somewhere between the **"Marco"** and the **"Micro"** *universe or anywhere* **in- between?** So to speak.

What does evil do! When it meets evil?

Its very probibly that's the first and last thing so-called highly technological socities do! They go underground like **"Crystal-peak"** and that's why theres every probability that they could be from our own world, humanoids who went under ground **Eon's-ago**, at a specific time in their evolution, during some kind of **"Antidiluvian-holocost"** which means there could be more than one kind of race, that has a definity with human-kind, who have been forced underground through their own stupidity! A bad, and very stupid seed, that wants the world back at any cost!

Space-Seed

Or they could be several more advanced scouts from several different races or cultures, from outer-space? who colonise and conquer planets, by invading them first, using some kind of high-tech super-computer that acts like a beehive is an enclosed structure in which some honey bee species of the **subgenus Apis** live and raise their young.

Natural beehives are naturally occurring structures occupied by honeybee colonies, such as hollowed-out trees, while domesticated honeybees live in man-made beehives, often in an *apiary*. These man-made structures are typically referred to as **"beehives"**. Several species of *Apis* live in **hives,** but only the western honey bee (*Apis mellifera*) and the eastern honey bee (*Apis cerana*) are domesticated by humans. A natural beehive is comparable to a bird's nest built with a purpose to protect the dweller.

The beehive's internal structure is a densely packed group of hexagonal cells made of beeswax, called a honeycomb. The bees use the cells to store food (honey and pollen) and to house the "brood" (*eggs, larvae, and pupae*).

Artificial beehives serve several purposes: production of honey, pollination of nearby crops, housing supply bees for apitherapy treatment, as safe havens for bees in an attempt to mitigate the effects of colony collapse disorder, and to keep bees as pets! Artificial hives are commonly transported so that bees can pollinate crops in other areas! That why I am forced to describe our strange and enigmatic past:

The ultimate computer

Given that the voice could be coming from the mysterious source of all knowledge and understanding, a bit like the 60s cult-show **Dr Who?** And the adventure called **"The Keys of Marinus"** and the story of a great computer which in this case was more mechanical than anything else, but could have equally have been conceived by a science without instrumentally! With its benevolent influence over the people to ensure they act in accordance with the law, but **Yartek,** the leader of the **Voord** have become a threat to **Arbitan** the keeper of the conscience of the planet **Marinus** who dwells on an island-of-glass surrounded by a sea-of-acid! And **Yartek** and his followers have discovered how to cross the sea-of-acid, by using a protective capsule, wearing a protective suit, to try and get in and take over the island-of-glass and use the computer for his own evil ends, so **Arbitan** was forced to disable the **great computer** by removing **several keys,** and has taken them to several other places in order to stop **Yartek** from getting them, intrusting the doctor and his assistants to go on a quest to places like **Morphoton,** were evolved brains were controlling their thoughts and convincing them of things that cannot be, like a place of palatial grandeur were everything was a complete delusion, to find one of key's and bring them back safely, or to destroy them totally, if **Yartek** has successfully taken over the island-of-glass with his followers from **Voord.**

But in the end the great computer was destroyed, discovering that such power that controlled peoples thinking by classifying radicals and free thinkers as one and the same criminal class, in the hands of certain people could be very dangerous in and of its self.

Where technically the drones are hatched first, to look after the queen, and the **"*larvi*"** wasps or the space-seed in the massive complex of the **"*Hive*"** and that has been created in some highly advanced laboratory, and are

327

then put into some kind of test tube to gestate, and when the alien spices are born, they are born to rule, not to follow!

With excelarated intillects and phyically strength, they will begin there stratagem for the takeover or evolutionary step of the planet, not because they could be dangerious aliens per say, but our own evolved-self could have done it, so that things turn out the way they are supposed too!

And the super intelligent computer or God machine is like the one in that great and very informative 1960s cult TV show (Star-Trek) and *"THE ULTIMATE COMPUTER"* or the episode called: *"THE CHANGLING"* and the space-probe called *"NOMAD"* that mistakes captain Kirk for its maker! (*Think about it!*)

Like a virus, infecting the host, and their it waits, during the justation period to eventually emerge, by first it attacks the ideology that:

. . .

"Pits a virtuous and homogeneous people against a set of elites and dangerous "others" who were together depicted as depriving (or attempting to deprive) the sovereign people of their rights, values, prosperity, identity, and voice" by subjugating the populis, through the chaos of their beuracratic Achillies heel!

Like the story of Burke and Hare, the grave-robbers or resurrectionists, who were rummured to have robbed graves in order to sell the bodies or cadavers in exchange for money, aka, (cash) to doctors in local hospitals to further their so-called anatomy and dysection skills or operational techniques!

The painted smile

On further inspection of this and other so-called lies or great (porker's) of history, like the great plague that mysteriously came and went! Or the other so-called great lie, there were literally tens of thousands each year, who had already died or hundreds of poor people of all ages, dying each and every day of deseases like **TB** (*tuberculosis*) **cancer** with no access to any kind of treatment or pain killers, never mind being able to afford to be buried! So they were destined for the finality of the disection table, whether they like it or not.

So the truth lies buried in the past, excuse the pun, why theses two or others who were cleverly accused on a point of law, for so-called **"grave robbering"** or was there something else hidden in among these so-called facts, that obscures the truth, and was someone or something else involved who did not want their, or its presence revealed?

And **Burke** and **Hare** were not stealing dead bodies, why? Because there was a plentiful supply! And if that was the case, then they must have been kidnapping healthy-people, for a more pernicous reason? That points in only two directions, **one:** we already know that doctors who have no scruples and would do practically anything for money or to maintain the diffrential, like the so-called **nazi doctors** who were experimenting on people, during the **second-world-war,** unless we have uncovered a another lie!

"One wonders why they don't invade and take over?"

And these victorian doctors and buracrates or quislings who have a *"healthy disregard for human life"* must have been up to something not only diabolically illegal, but also inhuman, either for there own self-centered and arrogant purposes, while in league with other **inhuman monsters**! Excuse the pun, something else just as frightening, that was or could have been involved during the possible disection of **another spieces**! And it was quickly stopped in case of exposure, by those and such as those, who run the system.

These so-called lies or tricks of logic infect everything from the **anthropological**, **theological** and **sociological system**. From chem-spraying under the guise or hidden like a **Rorchach ink-blot** so is it **geo-engineering** or nothing but get-streams caused by nothing more sinister that water-vapour? A simple but clever trick of the mind, like in the assasination of **"JFK"** in **1963** and you are seeing what you want to see? which could be very probable but highly unlikely.

Where does one go to train to lose?

We know that a person can only run, jump and swim only so fast and jump so high, then why are we still organising the olimpics? Especially for the athletes who have specially been trained to lose! We know that criminals are still commiting crimes, because its obvious that the law does not stop people from doing it, whether its stealing or being sentenced for murder, and yet there is not enough places in prison for the amount of people who are breaking the law especially the amount of places in death-row or other facilities, so where are they going? And we know crime doesn't pay, or does it? Because of the beuracrats who administer and get payed big-fat wages and pensions to administer the others who work in the system, that has become nothing more than a sourse of employment for those and such as those!

"Don't punch, staple or spindle"

Like the fall of **Siagon** where the news cameras caught the **military** literally throwing government property i.e **"Huey helicopters"** into the south-china sea! I wonder if they filled out the appropriate forms in **triplicate** and then they would have to wait weeks for the **"OK"** to strategically withdraw **"A.K.A"** (*run away!*) don't get me wrong, I'm certainly not being flippant about the deaths of all those young people who lost their lives in the senseless **politically orchestrated war** of the **"1960's"**

Catcher In The Rye

I was only eight-years-old in *1968* at the height of this self-imposed conflict the *"Vietnam war"* and like the film: *'The Running-man'* you can't believe a word the **BBC** news or Newspapers say!

Dishonesty and Corruptibility

"Nothing can be believed which is seen in a newspaper. Truth itself becomes **suspicious** by being put into that **polluted vehicle**. the real truth exstent of this state of **misinformation** is known only to those who are in situations to confront facts within their knowledge with the **lies** of the day."
President Thomas Jefferson 1801-1809

. . .

"But remember that observation can be cleverly used as a two-edged sword by the people who politically orchestrate these wars, parasitical devils who drain the life-blood of nations, an act, that is morally wrong."

. . .

War is a racket

" What is it good for? Good God, absolutely nothing!"

But I wonder how many people stop and remember the young men who died fighting for the concept of freedom in yesterdays wars? By the faceless buracrats or people who seem or appear to be voted in or out of government by the people! And who not only organize this madness, but are the ones who play these games of idiocy with peoples lives, by their deliberate acts of treason, for **wealth** and **power**! Nothing more, and that's our biggest weakness, and any highly evolved speices could find our **Accillies-heel** and use it, to begin our eventual downfall at the hand of our own stupidity!

. . .

Like the British 60s cult TV Show **Dr Who?** titled: **"The Tomb of the Cybermen"** where the race of *Cybermen* intentionally buried themselves under-ground! In order to survive, and where they had been waiting for thousands of years or longer for someone that was as advanced enough and clever enough to find them, and eventually set them free...!

Cause and Effect

(All things being equal)

"For every action There is an equal and opposite reaction!"
That's why the Doctor intentionally helped set them free! In order to make sure that no one else would awaken the **"Cybermen"** from their self-imposed slumber and cause havoc by releasing them or thawing them out, to take control and colonise other worlds, from their state of **"suspended animation"** which would have devastating consequences, to other spieces, it was akin to the Japannse giant hornet (**Vespa mandarinia japonica**) is a subspecies of the Asian giant hornet *(V. mandarinia)*. **"Vespa mandarinia"**.

The queen or leader like the ultimate computer lies dormant in her dark tomb, waiting to emerge at the right time to begin her cannibalistic ritual of survival at any cost!

Its as if it is our own-self or ID that's pounding at the door, trying to get in, like in the movie **"The Forbidden Planet"** or in the **similé** of the **Rackshasa or the disciple of Ravana, and after Ravana was killed, the Rackshasa were supposed to have lived on leaderless, drifting in a timeless kind of limbo-state, where they send emiseries into the living world, to see if the time is right for their reapperence on the face of the earth! When the world has slipped to the edge of the abyss, with decatence and moral decline!**

His deeds were so horrible, he stooped the sun and the moon in their orbit, he is an evil spirit or myth, who does not exist! That can take possession of a man's mind, and delights in the consumation of human flesh! And the only way it can be destroyed is by using a cross-bow and arrow or shaft (stake) blessed by the devine Brama himself. Or like the legend of the **"Vampire"** an undead creature that cannot die or be killed, because it's already dead! But you can destroy it, while it is asleep! So to speak, or in its dorment state, if you can find its lair, or does it want you to find! Like in **Dr Who**? but remember, curiosity killed the cat! Or...

". . . Helter skelter, hang sorrow, care will kill a cat, up-tails all, and a pox on the hang-man."
Ben Jonson 1598

'REPLICANTS'

And like that preverbal voice crying in the wilderness like in the 1968 book **"Do Androids dream of electric sheep**?" by Philip k. Dick and the movie based on the novel **"Blade-runner"** the drones or artificial-slaves of the ruling elite or patricians, had dared to ask big brother why? Which questioned the status- quo, the *'moles'* or **"automatons"** that serve the great machine should have known better to question their betters!

Who don't tell lies, because they always tell the truth! So ask no questions and you won't be told any lies! As they labour in the bowels of the earth or on the battlefields of tomorrow, to maintain a brave new world, of global-slavery, having fallen from grace, through no fault of their own, have inadvertently cast aside the bliss of ignorance, having discovered that they had developed a sort of molecular disintegration, like old-age, they were dying, so to speak! And like little children they wanted to know the answer to that great riddle of *"Where did I come from?" "Why am I here?" And "where am I going!"*

"For the earth is hollow and I have touched the sky!"

H.G. Well's

. . .

'Cloning'

Michelangelo di Lodovico Buonarroti Simoni
The Creation of Adam
1510

State-of-the-art **"Clones!"** or what looks like short lived **"carbon-copies"** but of a **Silicon** based life-form! With the same characteristics of the original orginism or master-print! Just like what could have happened during the resurection of christ!

Its as if they have something to do with these strange mysteries, like in the assassination or brutal killing of **"JFK"** and the strange oddities of **"Lee Harvey Oswald's doubles"** or **"duple-gangers"** when he was meant to be in one place, while he was somewhere else at the same time! The master magician/s that cleverly organised this **Easter egg** could probably have used human look-a-likes or was it something more weird going-on!

. . .

'Magic-bullet!'

After passing completely through **"JFK"** and *Governor Connally*, the **"bullet"** had fallen out of the Governor's clothes and onto a stretcher at Parkland Hospital. But the **"bullet"** that was recovered had one strikingly peculiar feature: it had survived all the damage it had apparently caused virtually unscathed itself.

The *shell's* near-pristine appearance, which prompted some to call it the **"magic bullet,"** left many sceptics wondering whether the **"bullet"** in evidence had really done what the Commission had said it had done. Additional scepticism was generated by the fact the **"bullet"** was not found in or around either victim.

It was found instead on a stretcher at the hospital where the victims were treated but it was never unequivocally established that either victim had ever lain on the stretcher where the **"bullet"** was discovered.

Turning to **MISSING 411 EASTERN UNITED STATES. Page 269.** And the story of **Middie Rivers aged 75 years** who disappeared, and the only thing that was ever found was a single **"magic bullet!"**

It sounds fantastic, but it's very probable that **"one thing has nothing to do with the other"** but it's highly unlikely, and these strange hidden events or Easter-eggs! Is part of something bigger!

If you join the dots like I have already said, a more sinister picture begins to take shape, see: **"Dracula"** its as if someone more significant is at work, and it is trying to tell us something, by leaving behind *foot-prints* as clues, and unless **"we understand the overall significance of the events in relation to their cause"** then we will be unable to solve the enigma or puzzle that seems or appears to have been with us, for longer than we care to remember!

Or look at the infamous **"Bible John"** case in the **1960's** in Scotland, and the so-called strange phenomenon of **"look-a-likes!"** And the woman in the **jack the ripper** cases, who seemed or appeared to be living an identical life style to the murdered woman **Elizabeth Stride!** Is there something going-on that we don't understand?

People often try to make sense of any tragic event, by seeking out patterns, much like the Rorshach **"ink-blots"** like in **Missing 411** or in any investigation, some people say, whoever they are! That it is relatively easy to find seemingly meaningful patterns relating any two events! If we didn't, then how would we be able to try and solve crimes! Never mind understand the changing world that we live in!

' The eye of the beholder '

"I suppose therefore that all things I see are illusions; I believe that nothing has ever existed of everything my lying memory tells me. I think I have no senses" I believe that my body, shape, extension, motion, location are functions, what is there then that can be taken as true?"

René Descartes

Reality or what is euphamistically called the void! Or the world that we think we know, the world of ticking clock's is nothing more than a grid put over reality! Otherwise we would be blind, deaf and dumb, because we use patterns to exist in the world we live in, its as simple as that, because we learn by experince or gather information in trying to find and follow instructions with meaning and porpose or to find a condition, akin to finding an answer using mathamatics or programming a computer!

Or we would be unable to solve any crimes, never mind uncover the wheels within wheels of organized, white-caller or petty crime! And we would never be able to find out about conspiricies or people with alternitive agender's.

So a loaded statement like, one can find a patern in anything, is only a half-truth that can sometimes be mistaken for the real truth, subderfuge, tricks of logic and propaganda! Or down right lies and distortion of the truth, like in the book by Nick Davies: **"Flat Earth news"** in a society where questions are indeed a burden to others, and answers a prison to one's self! But that such patterns seem or appear more often that not, to stand up to rigorous scrutiny, a statement that I do not agree with, especially when it is to do with such a major, and terrible event, such as the killing of the president of the United States of America, and the mystery *"coincidences"* like in the *"MISSING 411 NORTH AMERICA AND BEYOND"* by David Paulides.

John Doe.
Aged 3 years.
October 2012, Mount Shasta CA.
Page 59.

Who appareantly did not remember how he got lost! But he says he saw his grandma with him in a dark room, and the woman or his grandma spoke to him in a very nice and polite way, he acually thought he was talking to his grandmother, until sparks came from her head! And he then started to believe she was also a robot.

He stated that she was interested in his tummy! John also explained that near the end of the time with the lady, she placed a sticky piece of paper on the ground and told him that she wanted him to *"poop"* or defecate on it, he then said that he didn't have to, it was some time after this point that she took him from the room and placed him under the bush and told him to stay there, he never explained how he *"conviently"* got from the room, but does remember being found, or like...

Pearl Turner.
Aged 3 years.
October 19th 1923 "Ozarks"
Page 182.

In November a report came to the sherrif where a girl in Oklahoma bore remarkable resemblence to Pearl. The sheriff sent a list of scares to the other law inforcement agency and unbelievably the scars matched! The Turners took the trip to Oklahoma with high hopes of identifying their daughter, but unfortunately the girl they witnessed was not their daugther, but did look a lot like her, or...

Michael Eugene Reel.
Aged 8 years.
Roan Mountain Park, 1983.
Page 159.

after he was found, the *"SAR"* (*Search and Rescue*) said the little boy talked of having spent time with his grandfather! In later interviews with Michael's mother, she stated that she found Michael's stories amazing, especially since he had no recollection of ever meeting his grandfather, or even...

James Glass.
Aged 4 years.
Pennsylvania.
1915
Page 175

During the next few years the search for James (*Jimmie*) Glass went on across the united States. The Glasses traveled near and far on reports that their son had been found or someone looking like their son was found!

So this strange dopal-ganger mystery seems or appears more often than people think, and what is causing it, your guess is as good as mine, it even happened during the assasination of **"JFK"** never mind the resulting feasco of the Warren report, or the weird coincidences that follow...

United States President **Abraham Lincoln** was shot on Good Friday, April 14, **1865**, he was elected in **1860**, and was shot at **Fords Theatre** in Washington D.C. And **died** early next morning. **Kennedy** in **1960**; both were **assassinated** on **Fridays** in front of their **wives;** their successors as **president** were both named **Johnson; Andrew Johnson** was born in **1808** and **Lyndon Johnson** in **1908**; both assassins, **John Wilkes Booth** (born **1839**) and **Lee Harvey Oswald** (*born* **1939**), were **killed** before standing trial.

Booth shot Lincoln in a theatre! And ran to a **barn** that was used for or as a **book dipository!** And **Oswald** was ment to have shot **Kennedy** from a **book dipository!** And was caught in a nearby **theatre!**

The **surnames** of both **presidents** have **7 letters** and the **names** of both would assassins have **15.**

President Kennedy had a long time personal secretary, a woman called: "Evelyn Lincoln" who is mentioned on **page 7** in the book called: **"The darkside Camalot"**

Isn't it a lucky coincidence that one of these killers died, before we could find out the truth from them!

Evelyn Consuela Roseman
Missing 411
WESTERN UNITED STATES & CANADA
BY
DAVID PAULIDES

This rather unusual story contains a germ of truth in regards to the terrible and tragic death and murder of Evelyn Consuela Roseman, whose body was found in Yosemite National Park, by three hikers next to Nevada Fall, her corduroy trousers were badly torn, and were found around her ankles; and her sweater was up around her head, as if it had been pulled up! She had a second sweater that was lying on a rock next to her feet.

At first it looked as if she had been assaulted and then murdered! Until more evidence was found near the 594ft falls, so investigators assumed that she might have fallen off or had been pushed from the top of falls! If so why was her body nearly 50ft from the base of the falls? Where they found a piece of the dead woman's brain! And more traces of corduroy from the trousers she was wearing.

Even though it seemed or appeared that there was evidence of a sexual nature, and its very probable that it could have been a passing opportunist or necrophiliac, but highly unlikely, because it is possible that the event was caused by something other than what could have happened, read the following story...

335

The famous Dechmont Law incident

1979 Livingston, Scotland

On the **9th of November 1979,** at around **10:00 AM**, Robert Taylor, a married man, father of five, aged 61, resident of Livingston and forestry worker employed by the Livingston Development Corporation left his house. At about **10:30 AM,** he parked his pick up off a track at a plantation at the bottom of Dechmont Law, bordering Dechmont Woods, just off the busy M8 motorway, near Livingston, West Lothian in Scotland. He had parked as close as he could to the clearing in a plantation that he has to inspect for stray cows and sheep, a part of his job. With his red setter Lara, He followed a track the rest of the way across the lower slope of the forested hill, rounded a corner and emerged into the clearing.

The **UFO:** In the clearing, in front of him, was a large, circular, roundish object about **20 ft across** and **12 feet high,** resting on the ground or hovering just above the ground. It seemed to be made from a dark grey metallic material with a rough texture like sandpaper, parts of which were becoming like half transparent at times, letting the trees behind it be seen, as if the object was trying to cloak itself. A narrow protruding rim ran around the circumference of the object, just below halfway down, and Taylor thought it reminded him of the brim of a hat.

A line of rotating arms was set into the rim. Some dark patches were seen on the body of the object that looked like portholes. The object emitted no noise. Lara, his dog, who was at his side, simply froze and stared at the object, as did Bob Taylor.

As he watched without moving, two spiky spherical objects dropped from the bottom of the larger object. These two spheres were approximately two ft across and he later described them as being quite like sea mines as used in World War II, except that the spikes were longer that those of sea mines, making the objects' diameter approximately **3 ft spikes** included.

The spheres were looking metallic, similar to the material of the larger object, and made frightening sucking noises as they fell from the object and impacted the wet ground. As Taylor stared in awe, the two **spiky spheres** rushed towards him from the direction of the object, by bouncing and rolling on the ground.

His dog now barked loudly. The **two spheres** arrived at him each rolling quickly at the same time to his left and right foot.

The **spheres' spikes** extended and attached to the **Bob's trousers** and **dragged** him towards the **larger sphere**, which could explain why most of the people are losing one or both of their shoes? **In Missing 411!** [My Italics] **tearing the tissue of his trousers up to the pockets** in the process.

Taylor was now hearing a distinct hissing sound and smelling an acrid odour, that made him choke, he then lost consciousness and collapsed on the ground, just after hearing a loud and clear swishing sound similar to that of a cane being swung fast through the air.

Taylor regained consciousness after a while. He was lying face down on the grass, his **trousers were torn,** he suffered a headache and his legs were aching. He had a sore throat and a strange bitter taste in his mouth.

He realized that he could not stand up or speak!

It was later estimated that he had blackened out for fifteen or twenty minutes. Nothing remained to be seen in the clearing, but his dog was running about barking wildly and he noticed that there were marks in the ground where the object had been.

Feeling weak and dizzy, and unable to get on his feet, he dragged himself to his pick up truck and started to drive away. But he was such in bad condition that at one point he drove into a ditch.

The pickup truck being stuck in the mud, he had to walk more than a mile, stumbling and falling, to reach his home in Livingston, at the edge of Dechmont Woods.

His wife saw at once that he had an accident or had been assaulted, and he confirmed both, adding that the attackers were not exactly human. She quickly phoned the doctor, the Police, and Malcolm Drummond, Bob Taylor's boss, who arrived at the house to hear his story, even though the man was dazed, had a headache and kept saying that he had been "gassed."

The doctor sent Bob Taylor to hospital, but he checked himself out later without having been examined. He suffered a headache for hours and a raging thirst that lasted for two days, but recovered with no further sequels.

The Police officers treated the matter seriously. Rather than scoffing, they were treating the matter as a physical assault by **person** or **persons unknown**.

They went at the clearing with Malcom Drummond. Here they found Taylor's pick up truck and also ladder-shaped marks, of which Drummond noted, "marks on the ground which seemed to indicate that something had come vertically down and made impressions in the turf."

They first wondered about the resemblance to bulldozer or heavy machinery marks, but surrounding them were forty shallow holes that matched the witness's story about the bouncing spiky balls. These marks followed the path of the mine like objects.

The police fenced off the area. Photographs of the tracks were taken. They were totally baffled because the tracks were only in one grassy area. The ground in the place of incident was soft but no signs of the tracks having come from somewhere or having gone anywhere could be discovered.

There was no indication of how any vehicle that caused the tracks could have arrived in the clearing without leaving the same tracks on its entering path. They looked for local manufacturer of any object who could have been flown there. Results of this investigation were again negative.

They noted that other witnesses from the nearby highway, because of the trees, could not have seen any object in the clearing.

Detective Sergeant Tan Wark, a member of the police team assigned to the case, admitted that he was highly sceptical when first sent to the scene, but on examining the forty holes and the weird caterpillar tracks he was puzzled.

He checked all the forestry equipment used in the area; none of it had tracks that matched. No evidence was found of any helicopter traffic in the region that particular day, or even the day before.

A search of the area around the clearing was made in order to see if there were signs of any mobile crane that might have been used to lower something into the ground, but nothing was found.

The marks indicated an object of several tons had stood there but no information has been gained to explain them, to this day the police case still remains open.

So it seems or appears that Evelyn could have been launched or thrown off the top of the falls, in some way, by person/s or she was caught and interfered with, by some kind of automaton or mechanical machine that was probing! And collecting samples on the surface, for what ever reason, much like the other abducties of **Flying Saucers, UFOs** (*Unidentified Flying Objects*) and she continued to struggle for her life, as she was being dragged, her cloths or trousers and jumpers or tops, would be nearly pulled off, until she was then lifted up during some kind of acceleration, by some strange flying or Arial vehicle of some kind, that seems or appears to have dropped her down onto the fall's, and as she struck her head! She would then continue with the inertia or momentum that could have carried or lobbed her body through the air, until its impact, and where it finally came to rest, in that almost bizarre surreal position!

Yosemite

"The Old Indians Curse!"

"Kill me, captain. Yes, kill me, as you killed my son, as you will kill my

 people if they should come to you! Yes, Sir America, you can tell your warriors to kill the old chief.

You have made my life dark with sorrow. You have killed the child of my heart, why not kill the father? — but wait a little, when I am dead I will call to my people to come and they shall hear me in their sleep and come to avenge the death of their chief and his son. Yes, Sir America, my spirit will make trouble for you and your people, as you have made trouble to me and my people.

With the wizards I will follow the white people and make them fear me. You may kill me, Sir Captain, but you shall not live in peace.

I will follow in your footsteps; I will not leave my home, but he with the spirits among the **"Rocks"** the **"Waterfalls"** in the **"Rivers"** and in the **wind**, wherever you go I will be with you. You will not see me but you will fear the spirit of the old chief and grow cold. The Great Spirit has spoken. I am done."

Bodies that seem or appear to have fell off cliffs, and look as if they have become jammed or stuffed into crevasses, in odd contortions and with strange injuries, almost as if they have been put there, the way a wild creature tries to hide his kill! Or they look as though they have either accidentally fallen, like in "off the wall: *DEATH IN YOSEMITE*. Third Revision by Michael P. Ghiglieri and Charles R. **"Butch" Farabee Jr"**. *Or they have been purposely thrown off or dropped from or near the mountain!* [My Italics]

. . .

Tanaya Peak

Where the naked body of an 18yr old, had to all intent and proposes been wedged or had been intentionally dropped into a large crack, four hundred feet below the summit, he had a broken ankle and his chest had been crushed, injuries that could have been the result of an accidental/intentional fall, or was it something else very strange!

. . .

Patty Ann Mclean
Age 3
Page 279
"MISSING 411 WESTERN UNITED STATES & CANADA"
"Who said that she had seen little cows, the big question is, were they in her imagination or did she see them little cows from the air?"

Or like **Kory Kelly** in **MISSING 411. EASTERN UNITED STATES. 2006 Minnesota. Page 41**, Aged **38 years.**
Who was left alone at the camp with his friends dog **"sammy"** in the wilds of Northern Minnesota, while his friend Neprud realized that they needed gas for the vehicle, before leaving he saw Kory with his shotgun leaving the camp to hunt! After that he had left the camp to purchase gas at the nearest place, called fourtown.
When he eventually arrived back at camp he soon discovered that his friend Kory Kelly was mysteriously missing, and the Labrador-dog, was found by the searchers two weeks later wandering in the woods!
And the body of Kory Kelly was found 15 miles from the camp; his mother Jan Kelly stated that to get that distance, he must have been flying through the trees!
But there are more frightening and unquit events to corroborate this rather bizarre hypothesis, of what could have happened to Evelyn in *Missing 411 WESTERN UNITED STATES AND CANADA* by *David Paulides*.

. . .

BIBLE JOHN
(Charles Stoddart)
(Prelude to a violent death and the case of the countless clues!)
And now by necessity, I have included the infamous: killings in Scotland. UK. In the late **1960s** where its differences are only matched by its hidden similarities or startling coincidences, of three women, of a similar age, who all visited the famous or infamous Barrowland Dancehall in the late **1960s,** that were supposedly killed by person or persons unknown! And

339

again the authorities, using the tried and tested **Modus-Operandi,** taking a long road for a short cut, like in the infamous **"Jack the Ripper case"** and still they could not catch **"whoever"** or more to the point, **"whatever"** done the mysterious murders! Of **Patricia Docker** on **Thursday the 22nd** of **February 1968, Jemima McDonald** on **Saturday, August the 16th 1969,** and **Helen Puttock** on **Thursday the 30th of October 1969.**

They were all, not only strangled, but were also **"Menstruating!"** and the strange and symbolic or subliminal abstract gesture of the **sanitary towel** that was not where it was supposed to be! "Instead it had been tucked neatly under the woman's **armpit!"** which I think is an act of confusion by someone or something that seems or appears to be confused in some strange way! Note the pretence of the identification of the presumed killer and the way that **he/she** or **"it"** was dressed in order to try and mimic the dress of the **time** and **era,** but seemed or appeared not to get it, **quite right!** Or even the way the person or **"it"** acted and said in the presence of the witnesses, which was very odd, to say the least, about...

Moses and a woman
That had been stoned or Standing at a well

This could be part of the puzzle, so to speak, or a tenuous thread of whatever or whoever is or was involved with these mysterious killings, again it's as if someone or something is trying to communicate with us!

A Paper Tiger
Or was it the mouse that roared?

This was not the frenzied attack by a mindless individual or individuals, but by something so cloaked in anonymity, as to be almost invisible to the ordinary public, and even to the authorities and or expert trackers alike!

Because it looks as if it has been nothing more, than a cold and calculated study and dissection of a lower and possibly endangered species! By a higher one! To see how it functions, for one reason or another, that the public cannot and will not except, even though it comes right up and bites them in the rear-end or posterior, so to speak, because it's too much for the vast majority people's minds to except!

"Sometimes the truth is stranger than fiction"

Because there is another strange association with these eerie murders, something that truly goes from the bizarre to the ridiculous, and marks the dividing line between the real and the surreal, because many a truth is often said in gist, like in...

Scotland

The Big Grey Man Of Ben MacDhui
By
Affleck Gray

"Cairngorms' mountain range"

And the infamous mountain: Ben MacDhui is a terrifying place to be on by ones self in the middle of winter?

"Now, however, I was not alone, there was a presence, utterly abstract but intensely real"

A land of myths, legends and mysterious ghosts, like the phantom of the cairngorms: "I had the sudden impression there was someone near me — an impression which is sometimes experienced by mountaineers... and the strange sense of the non-real, with a morbidly analytical directioning of thought!"

An eerie experience for one climber, who felt compelled to look back more frequently than he had ever done on a mountain! Where he had the strange feeling that he was not alone...

Enlightened Materialists

Come rather, with me at the mysterious dusk time when day and night struggle upon the mountains. Feel the night wind in your faces, and hear the cry amid rocks. See the desert uplands consumed before the racing storms.

Though your nerves be of steel, and your mind says it cannot be, you will be acquainted with that fear without a name, that intense dread of the unknown that has pursued mankind from the very dawn of time, monsters of the "*Id*" like the giant whirlpool in Scotland called...

The 'Corrie Vrecken'

Or "**Charabdyis**" from the legend of **Ulysses** (*Odysseus*) that sucks the waters down into its gigantic mouth, a creature who's legend was born on the wind or breath of god, that strikes fear and dread into ancient mariners, roaring and screaming out in the darkness, the **gulf** of **Corrie Vrecken** is between the island of **Mull** and the mainland at **Tobermory** on the west coast of Scotland, caused by two opposing tides, striking against a **90ft pinnacle of rock, beneath the water...**

341

Corrie Vrecken

"In the beginning there was darkness, and God moved upon the face of the darkness and said..."
'Behold the Behemoth'

A strange and mammoth prehistoric creature from the past, that would make your flesh crawl and creep, with the wind and its dissonant and strange

crying and moaning, a mysterious and foreboding tale of fear and terror in the unfathomable and inky darkness of **Lochness,** and there at **Urquhart-castle** or at the deepest part of the **Loch,** the **Eiffel-tower** could sit, with its top, peeking out of the surface of this unquiet place!

. . .

Or at **Loch Morar,** with its legendary **creature** or **monster**, a strange crystal clear **Loch,** that is even deeper than **Lochness!** Where the **London-Post-Office-Tower,**
Would be swallowed up! Both are among the best known of Scotland's legendary **monsters** or **spirits of dark water**
I always seem to find that less is more, and there among all the objective facts, you will find evidence that point's to this mistaken belief, because there's nothing more deceptive, than the objective facts!

Strange Phenomena

While reading an excellent book called: **"Lochness-monster 1961"** By Tim Dinsdale.
From the eyewitness testimony from scores of consistent and credible witnesses over the years, has constructed a model of this elusive enigma or creature the likes, which could not and should not exist on this earth! It is very large or literally what seems or appears to be a harmless monster in every sense of the word, but there is something very strange indeed about

the way it disappears — something very strange indeed, that warrant's a closer study. The creature though capable of diving in a manner that might be expected, it can also sink vertically, almost **without a ripple...!**

Not only in my search for the obvious I came across the queerest passage by one of the helpers who was at the Loch-side called: **Mr F.W. Holiday**, who was a well-known fishing writer...

"Had a curious impression when questioning . . . I couldn't put it in my report, when people are confronted by this fantastic animal at close quarters they seem to be stunned, there is something strange about Nessie that has nothing to do with size and appearance . . . **odd, isn't it?**"

Or the strange and inconsistent way things keep going wrong! While trying to capture film evidence of these bizarre events, one way or the other, when people see the monster, they don't have a camera or something inexplicable happens to their equipment that came to be known as the **Loch-side hoodoo!** Or when trying to get genuine photographs of **ghosts** and **flying Saucers** or **UFOs** Unidentified Flying Objects)

Its as if it is an abstract or unknown quantity of some kind, because something strange or bizarre seems or appears to be happening, right under our very noses, much like the reports in missing **411** or of **ghosts** in **haunted houses**! Or how can something that does not exist, open and close a physical door? This is the central plank of my argument, which is about something that can be there one minute, and gone the next...!

Squaring The Circle

Or

Whistling in the dark

(Remember you can't serve two masters)

Where one needs to read between the lines, so to speak, because there could be more to these mysterious happenings than meets the eye!

Most people, I think approach it the wrong way, using fuzzy logic, and in doing so, it seems or appears that they can't see the trees for the forest...!

Because most of the people involved are looking for the obvious, and rightly so, when people go missing, I think the authorities should not work harder in trying to solve the problem, but work smarter, because authorities like the **FBI**, appear to be to busy doing their job, to be able to do their job right!

That whatever or whoever is doing this, must know, that we know, that they know, we know, etc, that it seems or appears that it is being perpetrated by some highly evolved and mysterious species, that appears to be...

"Watching and studying us like laboratory specimens"

. . .

Terra Incognita

An unknown country

"Where the face of the executioner is always hidden"

Why is America the epi-centre of these strange and bizarre disappearances?

(***In MISSING 411***)

Where the missing people sometimes don't recognise where they are! Are our hidden protagonists using some kind of high-tech weapon? That affects the human brain, like concussion or something akin to like the raptures of the deep, or pilot-narcosis, so to speak, that can affect the person, and the weather system is a bi-product of some kind of energy exchange i.e.: a doorway or portal of some kind, that incidentally stops or hampers the search efforts, indirectly hiding "**whatever**" or "**whoever**" is abducting them, **isn't that odd?**

Exodus

(Xxxiii, 20-23)

Moses heard the voice of the Lord, but he never saw his **face.** When he asked him to show himself "**God**" answered: "thou canst not see my **face:** for there shall no man see me and live.

And the Lord said, Behold, there is a place by me, and thou shalt stand upon a **rock:** And it shall come to pass, while my glory passeth by, that I will put thee in a **cleft** of the **rock,** and will cover thee with my hand while I pass by: And I will take away mine hand, and thou shalt see my back parts: but my **face** shall not be seen."

Epic of Gilgamesh

"No mortal comes to the mountain where the gods dwell.
He who looks the gods in the face must die."

Its as if, whatever or whoever is responsible, doesn't want to be exposed, or do not want us to see them for some reason, even though we can't stop them, why is that?

A Half-truth

"Why a brick, a bar, a bolt, a cup, invariably falls down, not up?"

* * *

As bloodhounds brought to the scene, seem or appear to be unable to work, which is a confusing and constant theme in many of these strange disappearances, its as if the dogs are truly confused and can't track something that's not there?

Like in **MISSING 411 EASTERN UNITED STATES. PAGE 15.** And **Rose Jewett of Idaho Aged 95 years.** Who mysteriously disappeared while out with her relatives, and after a five-day search she couldn't be found! The bloodhounds seemed or appeared to walk around the camp in a circle and were apparently useless, before we dismiss these animals off hand, don't through out the baby with the bath water, they could be trying to tell us something important, even when they seem to be disoriented and unable to work or go round in circles and cannot pick-up the scent or refuse to track! Its obvious something else is happening and the people who are going missing are not being taken away or brought back by conventional means!

Instead of looking round corners, see: **"Passport to Magonia"** they are either being snatched or grabbed from above, like in **MISSING 411 NORTH AMERICA AND BEYOND** and Michael Timothy Palmer and his brother Charles **"Chuckie"** Palmer, in a **May, 2004** article by **KTNA** who interviewed the Talkeetna fire-chief "Ken Ferina who had been involved with the initial four-day search. He says that he is sticking to his original *__alien abduction__* theory because he can't come up with another explanation!"

𝔗𝔥𝔢 𝔭𝔦𝔢𝔡 𝔭𝔦𝔭𝔢𝔯 𝔬𝔣 𝔥𝔞𝔪𝔩𝔦𝔫

In 1284, while the town of Hamelin was suffering from a rat infestation, a piper dressed in pied clothing appeared, claiming to be a rat-catcher. He promised the mayor a solution to their problem with the rats. The mayor in turn promised to pay him for the removal of the rats. The piper accepted, and played his pipe to lure the rats into the Weser River, where all but one drowned. Despite the piper's success, the mayor reneged on his promise and refused to pay him the full sum.

The piper left the town angrily, vowing to return later, to take revenge. On Saint John and Paul's day, while the Hamelinites were in church, the piper returned, dressed in green, like a hunter, playing his pipe, and in so doing attracting the town's children. One hundred thirty children followed him out of town, where they were lured into a **"cave"** and never seen again.

Depending on the version, at most three children remained behind: One was lame and could not follow quickly enough, the second was deaf and followed the other children out of curiosity, and the last was blind and unable to see where he was going. These three informed the villagers of what had happened when they came out from church.

Hamelin town records start with this event. The earliest written record is from the town chronicles in an entry from **1384** which states:

'It is 100 years since our children left.'

The Lueneburg manuscript (c. 1440–50) gives an early German account of the event...

German

"Anno 1284 am Tag Johannis et Pauli war der 26. Juni Dorch einen piper mit allerlei farve bekledet gewesen CXXX kinder verledet binnen Hamelen gebo[re]n to calvarie bi den koppen verloren."

English

"In the year of our lord 1284, on the day of saints John and Paul on June 26

By a piper, clothed in many kinds of colours, **130 children** born in Hamlin were seduced, and lost at the place of execution near Koppen."

The **Pied Piper of Hamelin** (German: *Rattenfänger von Hameln*, the Rat-Catcher of Hamelin) is the subject of a legend concerning the **departure** or **death** of a great number of children from the town of **Hamelin** (*Hameln*), Lower Saxony, Germany, in the Middle Ages

The earliest references describe a piper, dressed in multicolored clothing, leading the children away from the town never to return. In the 16th century the story was expanded into a full narrative, in which the piper is a rat-catcher hired by the town to lure rats away with his magic pipe. When the citizenry refuses to pay for this service, he retaliates by turning his power that he put in his instrument on their children, leading them away as he had the rats. This version of the story spread as folklore.

This version has also appeared in the writings of, amongst others, Johann Wolfgang von Goethe, the Brothers Grimm and Robert Browning.

The present-day City of Hamelin continues to maintain on its website information about the Pied Piper legend and possible origins of the story. Interest in the city's connection to the story remains so strong that in 2009, Hamelin held a tourist festival to mark the **725th anniversary** of the disappearance of the earlier town's children.

The eerie nature of such a celebration was enough to warrant an article in the **Fortean Times,** a print magazine devoted to **odd occurrences, legends, cryptozoology and all things strange** which are known now as **Forteana.**

The article noted that even to this day, there is prohibition against playing music or dancing upon the **Bungelosenstrass,** the street where the children were purported to have last been seen before they disappeared or left the town.

Like in David Paulides **MISSING 411 THE Devil's in the Detail** and the island of Hawaii, and their legends of the night marchers who come out during the full moon, but you must look at them, or you will be taken or die, and when children see them on the beach they will follow the night marchers and be lost forever, it does make you think! In the same book: Page 24 John Nezza. Aged 88 years. Who had disappeared in 1965 on Mount Shasta, California. Was linked to another mysterious disappearence on Mount Shasta, where the head of the search team looking for another man called Carl Landers, who had disappeared on May 25th 1999, the head of the search team that had been looking for Carl seem or appeared bewidered, and went on to explain that there was no place to hide, he either had to go up, in, or have evaporated!

Something or someone is taking them down the **rabbit-hole,** so to speak! And that's maybe why, they are being found at the top of mountains, as if they are confused and are trying to go up and out, which is a half-truth, because to us its the wrong way! Or is it more like...

The Matrix

Déjà vu, from French, literally **"already seen"**, is the phenomenon of having the strong sensation that an event or experience currently being experienced, has already been experienced in the past, whether it has actually happened or not.

Scientific approaches reject the explanation of **déjà vu** as **"precognition"** or **"prophecy"**, but rather explain it as an anomaly of memory, which creates a distinct impression that an experience is **"being recalled"**. This explanation is supported by the fact that the sense of **"recollection"** at the time is strong in most cases, but that the circumstances of the **"previous"** experience (when, where, and how the earlier experience occurred) are **uncertain** or **believed to be impossible**. Two types of **déjà vu** are suggested to exist: the **pathological** type of **déjà vu** usually associated with **epilepsy** and the **non-pathological** which is a characteristic of healthy people and **psychological phenomenon**.

. . .

"A dream within a dream"

"Take this kiss upon the brow! And, in parting from you now, thus much let me avow--you are not wrong, who deem that my days have been a dream: yet if hope has flown away in a night, or in a day, in a vision or in none, is it therefore the less _gone_? _All_ that we see or seem is but a dream within a dream.

I stand amid the roar of a surf-tormented shore, and I hold within my hand grains of the golden sand--how few! Yet how they creep through my fingers to the deep while I weep--while I weep! O God! Can I not grasp them with a tighter clasp? O God! Can I not save one_ from the pitiless wave? Is _all_ that we see or seem but a dream within a dream?"

Edgar Allen Poe

. . .

"What came first, the chicken or the egg?"

That the past and the future are locked into the present, relatively speaking! Which mean's, are we being visited or interfered by highly evolved beings, that are our like, but not our kind, from the far distant future, who have some kind of affinity with us? Meaning it is our own selves, that has been **collectively projecting their thoughts**, into our heads! Are such things not possible?

347

Or is someone or something using what could be a futuristic time machine, without tripping over there own feet, so to speak, in order to control the final outcome, in this world?

A collective universal shadow aspect, if you like or life form that is somehow gaining access in a non-conventional way? Because they have already evolved into possible energy forms of some kind! Who seem or appear to be trapped somewhere, out of time and space, or they would not have the need to interfere in their own genetics! Are they akin to non-corporeal entities like ghosts, phantoms and spectres? That don't exist, and yet going by the available evidence, these disembodied entities seem or appear capable of slamming doors or moving specially placed *"items"* placed in strategic areas of a haunted house!

Amen Corner

(*Ludgate-hill*)

London

On the other side of the wall, is dead-man's walk, where those who were hanged at Newgate-prison were buried in quick lime, has it anything to do with the strange thing that is said to crawl and creep along the top of the wall in the dead of night? Although one thing invariable does not mean the other, even though it has all the elements of a good ghost story, told by the fireside on a winters night or when you are all tucked up safely in bed, as snug-as-a-bug-in-a-rug, when the clock strikes 12 midnight or witching-hour.

Do ghosts exist, yes or no? Its very probable that they do, but highly unlikely. Even though there is plenty of evidence out there by sober level headed people. And if they do! So to speak, how can they open and shut a physical door?

If we are we dealing with something that has an affinity with ourselves, then we are only getting what we give out!

"Like the little snails in the science class, that we use a hammer to smash! And then we dissect them, whether they are alive or dead!"

And it is our own selves that is suspended in some metaphysical middle ground, so to speak, which lets them control us, as it were, and that's why they have always been with us, a bit like the present that seems or appears to have the past and the future locked into it, according to the late Albert Einstein! And now we are trying to understand something that we can't rely understand but can only experience!

So to speak, in relation to what could have happened to the ill-fated Franklin expedition, and the weird cryptic messages that where put on the strange gravestones, what was he trying to tell us? About histories elusive *bogie-men* called the *"Amorites"* or war-like savage cannibals, and the strange invisible hand of the one's who seem or appear to be standing, Looking over our shoulders from out of the shadows, so to speak, that seem or appear to be using a science without instrumentally!

In order not to compromise our story, the information needs to go into the realms of the bizarre, in trying to solve this theological and anthropological Rubik's cube.

Who goes there?

"For now we see through a glass, darkly; but then face to face: now I know in part; but then shall I know even as also I am known"
. . .

It seems or appears that we live in blissful ignorance of a planet that has more question than answers, and that we may have different races of beings living on the planet, from lowbrow homo sapiens, to a series of highly intellectual simpletons or high-tech underground barbarians, who are nothing more than high-tech cannibals! Who cannot take in food in the normal way, due to their genes being damaged, and have turned to some form of advanced cannibalism, like in **MISSING 411 NORTH AMERICA AND BEYOND By David Paulides.**

And the creepy case of **Douglas John May** on *page 72 aged 55 years.* Who disappeared on *July 16th 2009!* After apparently leaving his vehicle, which is something you don't usually do when you are alone! Unless someone or something must have lured him away from the car! Where a San Mateo County sheriff's deputy patrolling *Highway 35* found the vehicle parked exactly where his parents said it would be! But the police officer found nothing unusual at the site i.e: signs of a struggle etc... just like in *1950* and little Nicole Renaud in **MISSING 411 EASTERN UNITED STATES. Page 251, Aged 3 years** in *Quebec, Canada.* Who seemed or appeared to have been lured away by someone or something that didn't scare her, but intrigue her, but something that eventually took her life!

Rakshasa

A legend that seems or appears to be a symbolic story of something else! Like the story of the mysterious *"Noah"* because no one know who he was, and where he came from! And the story of the Ark or (arc) like the painting a bridge from one place to another, and the story of the *Raven* and the *Dove* appears to be more like a lost message of sorts, as if it is describing something like some event that has already happened or is still to come!

The Hindu legend of the *"Rakshasa"* is said to be a mythological humanoid being or unrighteous spirit in Hinduism. As mythology made its way into other religions, the *"rakshasa"* was later incorporated into Buddhism. *"Rakshasas"* are also called *man-eaters* (*Rakshasa were most often depicted as ugly, fierce-looking and enormous creatures and with two fangs protruding down from the top of the mouth as well as sharp, claw-like fingernails.*)

They are shown as being mean, growling like beasts and as insatiable cannibals who could smell the scent of flesh. Some of the more ferocious ones were shown with flaming red eyes and hair, drinking blood with their palms or from a human skull (*similar to vampires in later Western mythology*). Generally they could fly, vanish, and had *Maya* (*magical powers of illusion*), which enabled them to change size at will and **"assume the form of any creature"**.

And like the myth of creation where God or Brahma, It is said that Rakshasas were created from the breath of Brahma, (*much like Adam in the old testement*), when he was asleep at the end of the *Satya Yuga*. As soon as they were created, they were so filled with bloodlust that they started eating **Brahma** or **God** himself. (*Yatudhanas, demonic creatures who consume the flesh of humans*.)

Brahma shouted "*Rakshama!*" (Sanskrit for "*protect me!*") and **Vishnu** or **God** came to his aid, banishing to Earth all **"Rakshasas"** (thus named after Brahma's cry for help).

Its almost as if the text is desciding a dream (The dream of life) and a living, breathing nightmare, that is somehow tied-up with the esoterical non-space concept of duality, and the battle of these **polarities** that seem or appear to be the right and left arm of that same body, the **indescribable, inconceivable androgynous state?** That already knows the meaning of life! In more ways than one, so to speak! like in the 1960s cult TV show (Star-Trek) and the episode called: **"Wolf In The Fold"** and their struggle with an entity or energy source that is dangerous and evil!

Ironic

Its akin to the story I heard on the radio, of two woman who tragically lost there lives while trying to save some children who were out swimming, and the children survived, but the two woman drowned! Its as if death, chance or probibility, call it what you will, has a strange power over us, and whatever or whoever controls the world that we think that we live in! Seems or appears to be using the same technique as the ones who are kidnapping and murdering the people in **David Paulides books**, by whatching and waiting for the right moment to take certain individuals!

Continued...

After **Douglas John May** apparently got out of the vehicle, because there was no sign of any struggle! Why does the victim need to get out or be cohersed in some strange way to leave the car first? Or go for a stroll or a walk, did he see something strange and went to investigate it? And technically, for want of a better word, stepped into the wilderness! And that's where his bodily remains were found under weird circumstances, in a rugged and wild section of the **El Corte De Madera Creek,** Open Space District west of Skyline Boulevard near Woodside and Portola Valley, where his skeleton had been picked clean, with some of the remains of the skeleton were inside his cloths, along with his wallet! And this is an area that does not have wild bears or rarely does the odd mountain lion wonder through, who or what consumed this man...?

'Soylent Green'

(*The Raven*)

The 20th century's industrialization has left the world permanently overcrowded, polluted and stagnant by the turn of the 21st century.

In 2022, with 40 million people in New York City alone, housing is dilapidated and overcrowded; homeless people fill the streets; 20 million are unemployed with the few **"lucky"** ones with jobs scraping by, and food and working technology is scarce. Most of the population survives on rations produced by the Soylent Corporation, whose newest product is Soylent Green, a green wafer advertised to contain **"high-energy plankton"** more nutritious and palatable than its predecessors "Red" and "Yellow", but in short supply.

Roth takes Soylent's oceanographic reports to a like-minded group of researchers known as the Exchange, who agree that the oceans no longer produce the plankton from which Soylent Green is reputedly made, and infer that it must be made from human remains, as this is the only conceivable supply of protein that matches the known production.

He could have been lured away from the vehicle by someone who seemed or appeared to need assistance, maybe it was a young child needing help or guess what? The very bate that an unsuspecting heterosexual or bi-sexual male would fall for, that's it, you've guessed it, an alluring female with a short skirt! So to speak, or it could have been someone he knew and trusted! Like in the 1960s cult TV Show (*Star-Trek*) and the episode called: **"Man-Trap"** about a creature, that was the last of its kind, that can extract all the salt from their bodies, by bating an illusionary trap, by looking like a person they once knew.

Just like **Daniel Trask** in the same book **page 347.** Aged **28 years**. Nothern Ontario, where someone or something took his cloths off! Which follows a similar pattern of people that are found in pieces, and yet their cloths don't have any bit marks!

" **Or** like little Emma Grace Carbaugh, aged 22 months, in **MISSING 411 The Devil's in the Detail. Page 181,** who had mysteriously disappeared and was found dead! With her head near-by, having been completely, severed from her body by a sharp instrument, and portions of the body had been devoured! The coroner's jury was summoned, and after a thorough investigation of the case, rendered a verdict to the effect that the child came to its death from cause-unknown to the jury!"

. . .

"*During the 1930s, multiple acts of cannibalism were reported from Ukraine and Russia's Volga, South Siberian and Kuban regions during the Soviet famine of 1932–1933.*"

Survival was a moral as well as a physical struggle. A woman doctor wrote to a friend in June 1933 that she had not yet become a cannibal, but was "*not sure that I shall not be one by the time my letter reaches you.*" The good people died first. Those who refused to steal or to prostitute themselves died.

Those who gave food to others died. Those who refused to eat corpses died. Those who refused to kill their fellow man died... At least 2,505 people were sentenced for cannibalism in the years 1932 and 1933 in Ukraine, though the actual number of cases was certainly much higher."

Quebec

Like the **1975 book by Donald McKay** called **Anticosti, the Untamed Island.** Where he describes that early inhabitants in the 1850s found trees that seemed or appeared to have been gnawed down by beavers, but there were no beavers on the island! And before the white settlers came to the island in the 1850s/60s it appeared to have an abundance of many different mammals, until they mysteriously vanished for some reason!

He didn't die from falling, (there was no broken bones or a fractured skull) but the coroner could not determine how Douglas met his demise! His death remains a mystery.

Like the story in David Paulides book: **MISSING 411 EASTERN UNITED STATES. Page 68.** Of **Frank Floyd** in **1878 Iowa.** Who went hunting in the plains of Iowa, in an area known as **"Big Timber"** afterwards a party was sent out to look for him, he was found literally torn to pieces! And if it wasn't the sow, what was it?

If we including other humanoids like: the **"Abominable snowman"** or **"Yeti" "Bigfoot"** or **"Sasquatch"** call them what you will, but there are probably lots more bipeds and other unmentionable things in the chain!

So we are saddled with a major headache, which is a bit like trying to solve a problem using **"Aristotle's square of opposition"**

We either have the enemy at the gates or the enemy within! In the form of our elusive **exterritorial** or **terrestrial** visitors from either Outer space! Or from **Inner-space or cyber-space inhabitants**! Who are either malevolent or benevolent so to speak, and appear to be using or accessing a metaphysical science almost without instrumentality, or something that is beyond our comprehension, because these flying-saucers or UFOs (Unidentified flying objects) or high-tech ships are doing manoeuvres that are impossible to our present science... even using the age old shoulder to the door thinking, that one does not need a kick up the rear-end to know that it hurts, which is based on experience and keeping one's mind open to new idea's and experience being the only teacher in a world, where everything is supposed to yield to logic!

. . .

When using, Newton's principia where all science is an incomplete discipline, and one should remember to walk before one tries to run, even using the basic laws of gravity, friction, velocity, Acceleration, Momentum or centrifugal and centripetal force, not forgetting Inertia, which is the property of matter, which remains in motion, until acted upon by an outside force... laws that are not the be-all and end-all of science, just the first step in our knowledge of the physical world we live in...!

And if we are to try and understand or solve an enigma we may have to undergo a trans-valuation in our thinking...

It's as if these ghosts of other dimensions! Whether its from our imagination, or separate dimension/s or wherever they are, seem or appear to be suspended between time or in some middle ground, and have apparently always been with us, like the **Flying Saucers**, AKA **UFOs** or (Unidentified flying objects) or whatever and wherever they are coming from, seem or appear not to be travelling in absolute-space but in what the 19th Century physicist and philosopher Ernst Mach called **"Non-space"** it is theoretical science, where anything beyond observation is out of sight and out of mind...! So to speak, like the humorous metaphysical observation of whether or not the light goes out, when you shut the fridge door? (Joke) Or if a tree falls in the in the forest, does it make a sound, (scientific joke) if there is no one there to hear it...? Or is the forest even there to begin with?

Which in itself begs the question, if matter=energy and energy=matter, and that both states of matter can be altered, but they cannot be created or destroyed! As in the *Ex nil, nihil fit* "*From nothing, nothing is made*" if you can't destroy matter or create it, then where is it coming and going too? Or is it even there to begin with, like ourselves, never mind our theoretical forest.

Someone or something is collectively using some form of mathematics to try and find what is called a condition! Or an answer that seems or appears to be transcendental in nature with regard to the world we think we live in...!

So it could be about the strange footprints left in the Matrix, so to speak, when realty shifts, or when things run contrary to any of the laws we know about, like weird coincidences and strange events, like according to classical aerodynamics, it's impossible for a bumblebee to fly! But nobody has told the bumblebee that! Or why is it people die, when they should have lived! And live when they should have died...

"Is our destiny in our stars or in our selves?"
William Shakespeare

. . .

Its as if we are being cleverly deceived by either our limited senses or by someone or something that is manipulating the physical world on many levels, so the physical world seems or appears to be not quite what we think it is, and obviously *Something is going on*... so whether you go from the ridiculous to the sublime, it does not matter...

'Deus ex Machina'
(A god from a machine)

A highly *evolved* or *ancient physical* or *meta-physical culture* or *cultures*, seem or appear to have theoretically always been with us, and these *non-corporeal* beings seem or appear to be somewhere *out of time and space*, where they can interfere a million years ago or a million years into the future, while interfering with either their own, or our **genetics**! As well as our cultural development throughout history? In spite of our selves, due to our own stupidity, like in...

Standing On The Shoulders Of Gods

Are we resigned to an unknown fate by these humanoids who could be dressed in high-tech cloths, that cover or protect them from the outside world, creatures from highly advanced civilizations, that could have once lived and flourished on the surface of the planet earth, the would-be ancestors of humankind, who have been forced by their own stupidity to live underground in vast city complexes for millions of years, after terrible wars, that had poisoned the water they drank and the air they breathed?

Paul Crowe

Could it be these or other physical creatures that are manning the strange flying saucers or strange moving lights in the sky or **UFOs** (Unidentified flying Objects) who have come to either invade and enslave, a race that knows its superior to us, like the ones who sit on the *"Onion"* you know, the privileged and the educated people, who can afford to drive to these dangerous areas, and who are certainly not their brothers, never mind their sisters keeper!

So whether it is visitors from outer space or meta-physical entities from inner-space, so to speak, or from the great unknown southern contour concavities beyond the north and south poles of the earth? Maybe that's where the benign and benevolent or malevolent UFO'S (Unidentified Flying Objects) or flying saucers are coming from?

It could very well be several different types of old-world technological societies that have been forced underground due to their own idiocies, from inside the earth, deep between the 800mile top-crust in under ground bunkers in the epi-centres under the USA and Canada? The size of cities or even bigger!

Maybe life is nothing more than an experiment? That was flushed down the toilet last time in the great flood or deluge! And we nothing more than just laboratory specimens...!

"Surely there is wisdom in the old fairytales or folklore, that tells us things of the past? Like little red ridding hood! Or babes in the wood!"

(**And if we always do, what we have always done, then we will always get, what we have always got**)

'No Where'

Like in the excellent books: **Missing 411**, where certain clusters represent a certain type of age or sex, men, woman or children, and their destiny changes radically as soon as they go off alone, its as if they are targeted, then observed or watched until the opportunity exists for them to mysteriously disappear in intervals as to show a consistent pattern, so not to raise the alarm to any of the authorities, who seem or appear to see everything, but observe nothing! Like the FBI who seem or appear to be monitoring the situation, like in 1950s cult movie: **"Night or Curse of the Demon"** when Diana Andrews or Holden was at the British Museum, speaking to Carswell: "my investigation of your cult, won't be stopped, **"oh if I could make my point"** I could persuade you, I'm not open for persuasion, a scientist should have an open mind, that's what investigations are for!

It's either one or the other, by that I mean, we have the **enemy at the gates**, like in the **Doomed Franklin Expedition** and/or **the enemy within?** Like in the **Peter Principle**, with **bureaucratic Giants**, (*excuse the pun*!) Like the **"FBI"** who are in a tragic-play, doomed to failure by their own hand, or the invisible hand of infiltration, by incompetence and/or organized crime! Not because what they seem or appear to be doing is wrong, but the way that they do it! Like in the **1980s U.K.** sit-com **"Yes Minister"** and the galloping bureaucracy in an episode called:

'The Compassionate Society'

"*While observing that the cost of running the Health Service keeps going up, jobs for health administrators keeps going up! The patient numbers apparently keep going down in regards to a "mythical Hospital" called: St Edwards that was supposedly built 15 months ago, and the only people in the hospital are 500 administration and auxiliary staff, who are backed by the "Union"*

Even though it is empty and there are no Doctors! Nurses! Or Patients! The essential work of the so-called hospital still has to go on, and the hospital cannot function without the administration staff, who are already over-worked and under considerable stress, because it should actually be run by 750 administrative staff, and it is essential that the work of running the hospital carries-on, and one should never measure by results, but by activity, which is substantial, and Sir Humphries concerned by the ministers attitude: Minister, you talk as if the administration staff have nothing to do? Just because there is no patients it is an extremely busy department, and all these vital tasks must be carried out, with or without patients.

And looking after 500 people is a big job! And putting in patients would cost the hospital even more money to run!

As it stands, it is a perfect example of one of the best-run hospitals in the country, and is in line for a Florence Nightingale award for one of the cleanest hospitals in the country!

But the Minister is insistent that it is not a source of employment, and he wants everybody dismissed! Unless they bring in Doctors, Nurses and Patients! Then in comes the useless "union man" you tell me, your going to put all these people out of work? And you call this a compassionate society!"

ThePeter Principle

(Laurence J. Peter)

Laurence Johnston Peter (September 16, 1919 – January 12, 1990) was a Canadian educator and "hierarchiologist", best known to the general public for the formulation of the Peter Principle.

Biography

He was born in Vancouver, British Columbia, and began his career as a teacher in Vancouver in 1941. He received the degree of Doctor of Education from Washington State University in 1963.

In 1966, Peter moved to California, where he became an Associate Professor of Education, Director of the Evelyn Frieden Centre for Prescriptive Teaching, and Coordinator of Programs for Emotionally Disturbed Children at the University of Southern California.

He became widely famous in 1968, on the publication of *The Peter Principle*, in which he states: "In a hierarchy every employee tends to rise to his level of incompetence ... in time every post tends to be occupied by an employee who is incompetent to carry out its duties ... Work is accomplished by those employees who have not yet reached their level of incompetence." The Peter Principle became one of the most profound principles of management from the University of Southern California. It is a heavily quoted principle at the Marshall School of Business.

Another notable quotation of his is that the **"noblest of all dogs is the hot-dog; it feeds the hand that bites it."**

From 1985 to his death in 1990, Peter attended and was involved in management of the Kinetic Sculpture Race in Humboldt County, California. He proposed an award for the race, titled "The Golden Dinosaur Award" which has been handed out every year since to the first sculptural machine to utterly break down immediately after the start.

'The Peter Principle'

The Peter Principle is a management theory which suggests that organizations risk filling management roles with people who are incompetent if they promote those who are performing well at their current role, rather than those who have proven abilities at the intended role. It is named after Laurence J. Peter who co-authored the 1969 humorous book *The Peter Principle: Why Things Always Go Wrong* with Raymond Hull. They suggest that people will tend to be promoted until they reach their **"position of incompetence"**.

Only recruits white-caller workers, middle management or salesmen, and not police officer's with years of practical training and experience, and that's not a theory, it's a fact! Like in Putt's Law? And that "Technology is dominated by two types of people: those who understand what they do not manage, and those who manage what they do not understand." Or what is better known as...

Corollaries

Where incompetence is flushed out of the lower levels of a technocratic hierarchy, ensuring that technically competent people remain directly in charge of the actual technology, while those without technical competence move into management, like in the Dilbert principle or that companies like FBI tend to systematically promote their least-competent employees to management, in order to limit the amount of damage they are capable of doing.

What is going on with organizations like the FBI or others involved in Missing 411, is that they have been going round in circles, like some form of intillectual stuper, or it is a frightening testimony to an unquiet truth, about whatever or whoever is sharing this planet, or strange and weird existence with us, whether we like it or not, and its nothing more than...

. . .

"Reason howling at the moon!"

The Devil's Triangle

And the
The Evil-eye
On people who mysteriously disappear
In the USA and Canada.
"When the hunter, becomes the hunted"
"An eerie silence, and one native said: there's nothing there! And Charlton Heston said: "Something is there?" And it's not afraid of guns!"
The naked jungle

. . .

Werewolf

"De ferocia hominum Lupus Conuerforum"
(*The Fierce Man In The Form Of A Wolf*)

Canada
December 10th 1764
Quebec
Kamouraska
Dec 2nd

"We learn that a ware-Wolfe which has roamed the province for several years, and done great destruction in the district of Quebec, has received several considerable attacks in the month of October last, by different animals, which they had armed and incensed against this monster; and especially, the 3rd of November following, he received such a furious blow, from a small lean beast, that it was thought they were entirely delivered from this fatal animal, as it sometime after retired into its hole, to the great satisfaction of the public.

But they have just learned, as the most surest misfortune, that this beast is not entirely destroyed, but begins again to show itself, more furious than ever, and makes terrible havoc wherever it goes. – beware then of the wiles of this malicious beast, and take good care of falling into its claws"

Like **page 132** of **Missing 411-North America and beyond.** That describes the frightening case of **39yr** old **Sam Adams** in **1958** who was tore to pieces and then devoured in a frightening attack by some kind of wild ferocious creature, that reflects something darker in these strange and weird attacks, as well as the odd and frightening disappearances of Bart Schleyer, Charles McCullar and Robert Springfield almost as...

"A Warning To The Curious"

You enter these dangerous places
At your own risk!

I can't rely do justice to David Paulides *Missing 411 books*, they are well researched and very informative, that is to any one with a brain between their ears! Who insist venturing out into these dangerous areas?

. . .

'The Cascades'

Are treacherous, and if you go there alone, you are more likely to disappear, for the majority vanish and are never seen again, as David Paulides describes in his superb book: people don't know, or are unaware of the possible dangers involved in venturing into the Cascades alone, even the searchers who had been out looking for a man who had mysteriously went missing there while camping, remarked that even his campsite had a very eerie feeling to it!

"The Missing 411 books are astounding and scary"

. . .

The Rob family
1926
Utah
"Sheepherders"
Missing 411
By
David Paulides

The eerie tale about one of the brothers who went missing under mysterious circumstances because something was stealing their sheep! And one of the brothers rode out to try and find the culprit, but he was never ever seen again. But what of...

Is there more of gravy, than of grave about these
(*Cryptozoological nightmare's*)

Canus Lupas Erectus

Dogmen
(*Post hoc ergo propte hoc*)
After this, Therefore, Because of this.
(A fallacious reasoning)

'Les traces révélatrices'

The information from the intelligencer on these events is undoubtedly second-hand, even though they seem or appear to have a theoretical degree in physics (oops) or is it a degree in theoretical physics? And who have, for whatever reason, like in the 60's cult TV show Star-Trek, called: **"The Galileo Seven"** at the end of the show, Captain Kirk after hearing what Spock had done! In the shuttlecraft, which seemed or appeared to be a deliberate act of desperation! Which is a highly emotional state of mind, how does your logic explain that? Said Captain Kirk, and Spock then explains his reasons **"logically"** and Captain Kirk replies: you mean you reasoned, it was time for an emotional outburst!

You only have half-truths, or the word of the witnesses, even so, Linda S. Godfrey in her excellent books, seems or appears to have given some **lupinus—lupus or loopy** witnesses, the benefit of the doubt! Which is enough to make your hair stand on end! Because it appears that the tail is wagging the dog or in this case, the werewolf!

From shapeshifting or Animism, to remote viewing, sounds like reason, howling at the moon! To me, (*Excuse the pun*) by the lunatic fringe or people who seem or appear to be already in the twilight zone, and are very close to the hairy edge of being canned? By apparently bearing false-witness they render invalid certain aspects of any on-going investigation, with what the French call **"les traces révélatrices"**

"Bed-time for Bonzo"

Mostly the privileged classes, criminals and prostitutes, per se, are the only ones that are usually out at these ungodly hours, and sometimes like in the **1888 Jack the Ripper** investigations, they haunted inquests and identity parades, they thrive on newspaper interviews, when for a brief moment they become the envy of their less inventive neighbours!

. . .

Bourgeoisie
" Bare-faced liars "

Who are **disingenuous** *not being candid or sincere, typically by pretending that one knows less about something than one really does: like the* **bourgeoisie** *squaters who wanted property ownership or the right to housing rightly or wrongly or the* **big-lie** *of* **pirate radio** *in the* **1960s***! Funded by the same hand that was against it! That's why most of the so-called bad-boy* **DJs** *or* **privileged classes** *sold-out the faithful (***public***) and moved over to take-up well paid jobs on the other side!*

. . .

French pronunciation is a word from the French language, used in the fields of political economy, political philosophy, sociology, and history, which originally denoted the wealthy stratum of the middle class that originated during the latter part of the Middle Ages (AD 500–1500).

The utilization and specific application of the word is from the realm of the social sciences. In sociology and in political science, the noun **bourgeoisie** and the adjective **bourgeois** are terms that describe a historical range of socio-economic classes. As such, in the Western world,

360

since the late 18th century, **the bourgeoisie** describes a social class "characterized by their ownership of capital, and their related culture;" hence, the personal terms **bourgeois** (masculine) and **bourgeoise** (feminine) culturally identify the man or woman who is a member of the wealthiest social class of a given society, and their materialistic worldview Weltanschauung.

In Marxist philosophy, the term *bourgeoisie* denotes the social class who owns the means of production and whose societal concerns are the value of property and the preservation of capital, in order to ensure the perpetuation of their economic supremacy in society. Joseph Schumpeter instead saw the creation of new bourgeoisie as the driving force behind the capitalist engine, particularly entrepreneurs who took risks in order to bring innovation to industries and the economy through the process of creative destruction.

During the 17th and 18th centuries, the bourgeoisie were the politically progressive social class who supported the principles of constitutional government and of natural right, against the **Law of Privilege** and the claims of rule by divine right that the nobles and prelates had autonomously exercised during the feudal order.

The motivations for the **English Civil War** (*1642–51*), the **American War of Independence** (*1775–83*), and **French Revolution** (*1789–99*) *seem or appear* (My Italics), partly derived from the desire of the **bourgeoisie** to rid themselves of the **feudal trammels** and **royal encroachments** upon their **personal liberty, commercial rights,** and the **ownership of property**.

In the **19th century,** the bourgeoisie propounded **liberalism,** and gained **political rights, religious rights,** and **civil liberties** for themselves and the **lower social classes;** thus was the **bourgeoisie** then a **progressive philosophic** and **political force** in **modern Western societies.**

By the middle of the **19th century,** subsequent to the **Industrial Revolution** (*1750–1850*), the great expansion of the **bourgeoisie social class** caused its **self-stratification** — by **business activity** and by **economic function** — into the **haute bourgeoisie** (*bankers and industrialists*) and the **petite bourgeoisie** (*tradesmen and white-collar workers*). Moreover, by the end of the **19th century**, the **capitalists** (*the original bourgeoisie*) had ascended to the **upper class,** whilst the developments of **technology** and **technical occupations** allowed the **ascension** of **working-class men** and **women** to the **lower strata** of **the bourgeoisie;** yet the **social progress** was incidental.

In the event, despite its initial **philosophic progressivism** — from **feudalism** to **liberalism** to **capitalism** — the **bourgeoisie social class** (*haute and petite*) became reactionary in their refusal to allow the **ascension** (*economic, social, political*) of people from the **proletariat** (*peasants and urban workers*) in order to maintain **hegemony**.

In the 19th century, the German economist **Karl Marx** distinguished two types of **bourgeois capitalist:** (i) the **functional capitalist**, the *business administrator* of the means of *production;* and (ii) the *rentier capitalist* whose livelihood derives either from the rent of property or from the interest-income produced by finance capital, or both. In the course of economic relations, the *working class* and the *bourgeoisie* continually engage in *class struggle*, wherein the *capitalists exploit the workers,* whilst the *workers resist their economic exploitation,* which occurs because the worker owns no means of production, and, to earn a living, he or she seeks employment from the *bourgeois capitalist;* the worker produces *goods* and *services* that are *property of the employer*, who sells them for a *price.*

The *money* generated by the *sale* of the *goods* and *services* yields three sums (i) *the wages of the worker*, (ii) *the costs of production*, and (iii) *profit* (*surplus value*). Thereby, the *capitalist profits* (*makes extra money*) by selling the *surplus value of the labour of the workers; hence is new wealth created through work.*

Besides describing the *social class* who own the means of production, the *Marxist* usage of the term "*bourgeois*" also describes the consumerist style of life derived from the ownership of capital and real property.

As an economist *Karl Marx* acknowledged the *bourgeois industriousness* that created *wealth,* yet *criticised* the *moral hypocrisy* of the *bourgeoisie* when they ignored the true origins of their wealth — the exploitation of the *proletariat*, the *urban* and *rural workers.*

Further sense denotations of "*bourgeois*" describe *ideologic concepts* such as "*bourgeois freedom*", which is opposed to substantive forms of freedom; "*bourgeois independence*" "*bourgeois personal individuality*" the "*bourgeois family*" et cetera, all derived from owning *capital* and *property*. (*See: The Communist Manifesto, 1848.*)

"Culturally, the bourgeois man is unmanly, effeminate, and infantile; describing his philistinism in *Bonifica antiborghese* (*1939*), Roberto Paravese said that the middle class, middle man, incapable of great virtue or great vice: and there would be nothing wrong with that, if only he would be willing to remain as such; but, when his child-like or feminine tendency to camouflage pushes him to dream of grandeur, honours, and thus riches, which he cannot achieve honestly with his own "*second-rate*" powers, then the average man compensates with cunning, schemes, and mischief; he kicks out ethics, and becomes a *bourgeois.*

The bourgeois is the average man who does not accept to remain such, and who, lacking the strength sufficient for the conquest of essential values — those of the spirit — opts for material ones, for appearances.

Buddenbrooks (*1901*), by *Thomas Mann* (*1875–1955*), chronicles the moral, intellectual, and physical decay of a rich family through its declines, material and spiritual, in the course of four generations, beginning with the patriarch Johann Buddenbrook Sr. and his son, Johann Buddenbrook Jr., who are typically successful German businessmen; each is a reasonable man of solid character. Yet, in the children of Buddenbrook Jr., the materially comfortable style of life provided by the dedication to solid, middle-class values elicits **decadence**: The fickle daughter, **Toni**, lacks and does not seek a **purpose in life**; son **Christian** is **honestly decadent**, and lives the life of a **ne'er-do-well**; and the businessman son, **Thomas**, who assumes command of the Buddenbrook family fortune, occasionally **falters** from **middle-class solidity** by being interested in **art** and **philosophy**, the **impractical life of the mind**! Which, to the bourgeoisie, is the epitome **of social, moral, and material decadence**.

Babbitt (1922), by Sinclair Lewis (1885–1951), satirizes the American bourgeois George Follansbee Babbitt, a middle-aged realtor, booster, and joiner in the Midwestern city of Zenith, who — despite being unimaginative, self-important, and hopelessly conformist and middle-class — is aware that there must be more to life than money and the consumption of the best things that money can buy. Nevertheless, he fears being excluded from the mainstream of society more than he does living for himself, by being true to himself — his heart-felt flirtations with independence (dabbling in liberal politics and a love affair with a pretty widow) come to naught because he is existentially afraid.

Yet, George F. Babbitt sublimates his desire for self-respect, and encourages his son to rebel against the conformity that results from bourgeois prosperity, by recommending that he be true to himself: like in the cult 60s TV show: (*Star-Trek*) and the episode called: **"This side of Paradise"** that they were **gloriously happy** from being injected with the spores of a **strange plant**, but in **reality** they had **achieved** very little! You mean like the west who are akin to **Nepoleon's** donkey who was rumered to have went to all his campeigns but apparently learnt nothing!

Like in the film: **'The Third Man'** when **Orson Welles** described the comparison of a hundred years of **European wars** and **strife!** Europe produced: the renaissance, Michael Angelo etc compered to what the **swiss** produced over the same length of time during a hundred years of peace, **The Cuckoo -clock**!

In literature

In the **Ulysses IX**, Odysseus tells how adverse north winds blew him and his men off course as they were rounding Cape Malea, the southernmost tip of the **Peloponnesus**, headed westwards for **Ithaca**:

. . .

"*I was driven thence by foul winds for a space of 9 days upon the sea, but on the tenth day we reached the land of the Lotus-eaters, who live on a food that comes from a kind of flower. Here we landed to take in fresh water, and our crews got their mid-day meal on the shore near the ships. When they had eaten and drunk I sent two of my company to see what manner of men the people of the place might be, and they had a third man under them.*

They started at once, and went about among the Lotus-eaters, who did them no hurt, but gave them to eat of the lotus, which was so delicious that those who ate of it left off caring about home, and did not even want to go back and say what had happened to them, but were for staying and munching lotus with the Lotus-eaters without thinking further of their return; nevertheless, though they wept bitterly I forced them back to the ships and made them fast under the benches. Then I told the rest to go on board at once, lest any of them should taste of the lotus and leave off wanting to get home, so they took their places and smote the grey sea with their oars."

. . .

This passage served as the source for Alfred, Lord Tennyson's poem **"The Lotos-Eaters."** It is also referenced in the fifth chapter of **Ulysses** by James Joyce, also titled **"Lotus Eaters"** and in the sixth chapter of Edith Wharton's **The Age of Innocence**.

The mariners are put into an altered state when they eat the lotos. During this time, they are isolated from the world:

. . .

Branches they bore of that enchanted stem,
Laden with flower and fruit, whereof they gave
To each, but whoso did receive of them
And taste, to him the gushing of the wave
Far far away did seem to mourn and rave
On alien shores; and if his fellow spake,
His voice was thin, as voices from the grave;
And deep-asleep he seem'd, yet all awake,
And music in his ears his beating heart did make.

. . .

The mariners explain that they want to leave reality and their worldly cares:

> *Why are we weigh'd upon with heaviness,*
> *And utterly consumed with sharp distress,*
> *While all things else have rest from weariness?*
> *All things have rest: why should we toil alone,*
> *We only toil, who are the first of things,*
> *And make perpetual moan,*
> *Still from one sorrow to another thrown;*
> *Nor ever fold our wings,*
> *And cease from wanderings,*
> *Nor steep our brows in slumber's holy balm;*
> *Nor harken what the inner spirit sings,*
> *'There is no joy but calm!"—*
> *Why should we only toil, the roof and crown of things?*

. . .

The mariners demonstrate that they realise what actions they are committing and the potential results that will follow, but they believe that their destruction will bring about peace:

. . .

> *Let us alone. Time driveth onward fast,*
> *And in a little while our lips are dumb.*
> *Let us alone. What is it that will last?*
> *All things are taken from us, and become*
> *Portions and parcels of the dreadful past.*
> *Let us alone. What pleasure can we have*
> *To war with evil? Is there any peace*
> *In ever climbing up the climbing wave?*
> *All things have rest, and ripen toward the grave*
> *In silence—ripen, fall, and cease:*
> *Give us long rest or death, dark death, or dreamful ease.*

. . .

Although the mariners are isolated from the world, they are connected in that they act in unison. This relationship continues until the very end when the narrator describes their brotherhood as they abandon the world:

. . .

> *Let us swear an oath, and keep it with an equal mind,*
> *In the hollow Lotos-land to live and lie reclined*
> *On the hills like Gods together, careless of mankind.*
> *For they lie beside their nectar, and the bolts are hurl'd*
> *Far below them in the valleys, and the clouds are lightly curl'd*
> *Round their golden houses, girdled with the gleaming world;*

Where they smile in secret, looking over wasted lands,
Blight and famine, plague and earthquake, roaring deeps and fiery
sands,
Clanging fights, and flaming towns, and sinking ships, and praying
hands.
But they smile, they find a music centred in a doleful song
Steaming up, a lamentation and an ancient tale of wrong,
Like a tale of little meaning tho' the words are strong;
Chanted from an ill-used race of men that cleave the soil,
Sow the seed, and reap the harvest with enduring toil,
Storing yearly little dues of wheat, and wine and oil;
Till they perish and they suffer—some, 'tis whisper'd—down in hell
Suffer endless anguish, others in Elysian valleys dwell,
Resting weary limbs at last on beds of asphodel.
Surely, surely, slumber is more sweet than toil, the shore
Than labour in the deep mid-ocean, wind and wave and oar;
O, rest ye, brother mariners, we will not wander more.

Themes

The form of the poem contains a dramatic monologue, which connects it to **"Ulysses"**, **St. Simeon Stylites**, and **Rizpah.** However, Tennyson changes the monologue format to allow for ironies to be revealed.

The story of The **Lotos-Eaters** comes from Homer's **The Odyssey**. However, the story of the mariners in Homer's work has a different effect from Tennyson's since the latter's mariners are able to recognize morality. Their arguments are also connected to the words spoken by Despair in Edmund Spenser's **The Faerie Queene,** Book One. With the connection to Spenser, Tennyson's story depicts the mariners as going against Christianity. However, the reader is the one who is in the true dilemma, as literary critic James Kincaid argues, "The final irony is that both the courageous **Ulysses** and the mariners who eat the lotos have an easier time of it than the reader; they, at least, can make choices and dissolve the tension."

Tennyson ironically invokes **"The Lover's Tale"** line 118, "A portion of the pleasant yesterday", in line 92 of **The Lotos-Eaters:** "Portions and parcels of the dreadful past".

In the reversal, the idea of time as a protector of an individual is reversed to depict time as the destroyer of the individual. There is also a twist of the traditionally comic use of repetition within the refrain "Let us alone", which is instead used in a desperate and negative manner. The use of irony within *The Lotos-Eaters* is different from Tennyson's **"The Lady of Shalott"** since **"the Lady"** lacks control over her life.

The mariners within **The Lotos-Eaters** are able to make an argument, and they argue that death is a completion of life. With this argument, they push for a release of tension that serves only to create more tension. Thus, the mariners are appealing yet unappealing at the same time.

In structure, **The Lotos-Eaters** is somewhere between the form of **Oenone** and **The Hesperides**. In terms of story, **The Lotos-Eaters** is not obscure like **The Hesperides** nor as all-encompassing as **Oenone** but it still relies on a frame like the other two. The frame is like **The Hesperides** as it connects two different types of reality, one of separation and one of being connected to the world. Like **Oenone**, the frame outlines the song within the poem, and it allows the existence of two different perspectives that can be mixed at various points within the poem. The perspective of the mariners is connected to the perspective of the reader in a similar way found in **The Hesperides**, and the reader is called to follow that point of view to enjoy the poem. As such, the reader is a participant within the work but they are not guided by Tennyson to a specific answer. As James Kincaid argues, "in this poem the reader takes over the role of voyager the mariners renounce, using sympathy for a sail and judgment for a rudder. And if, as many have argued, the poem is 'about' the conflict between isolation and communality, this meaning emerges in the process of reading."

The poem discusses the tension between isolation and being a member of a community, which also involves the reader of the poem. In the song, there are many images that are supposed to appeal to the reader. This allows for sympathy with the mariners. When the mariners ask why everything else besides them are allowed peace, it is uncertain as to whether they are asking about humanity in general or only about their own state of being.

The reader is disconnected at that moment from the mariner, especially when the reader is not able to escape into the world of bliss that comes from eating lotus. As such, the questioning is transformed into an expression of self-pity. The reader is able to return to being sympathetic with the mariners when they seek to be united with the world.

They describe a system of completion, life unto death, similar to Keats's "To Autumn", but then they reject the system altogether. Instead, they merely want death without having to have the growth and completion before death.

Even though in a sliding scale, the so-called witnesses are from the **Bourgeoisie** to the working classes or aspiring working aristocracy! Whether you like it or not, they are very much like the **middle classes**, or **privileged people** that **classical** and **contemporary stage** and **street hypnotists**, select and then victimize, due to their **propensity** and **inborn ingenuous nature**, where questions are a burden to others, and answers, a prison to ones self, when (**virtue becomes a vice**!) they are the right stuff! Or seem or appear to be the shifting sand, that dictatorships are built on, because they are functioning, which means they have access to a **car**, and **so-on** and **so-forth**.

"Through the looking glass"
Catch 22!

That why in my other book on hypnosis, so-called crazy people or people suffering from mental illness are never picked for classical stage and contemporary street hypnosis, never mind **Hypnotherapy**! because we are not our brother's or sisters keeper, are we? Even if he or she does go around seeing things, not werewolves anyway! Because these crazies can't even afford a car, never-mind get access to a properly paid job that would allow them to go anywhere near these places, and if they did end up being a victim of *Missing 411*, who would believe them? Because they are not right in the head! Can you image them suffering from road rage, like so-called normal people? Vis-à-vis (therefore) they don't get kidnapped or go missing unless they are text-book hobo's, that seem or appear to have a well formed ego and a healthy psyche, in order to live out of doors, figuratively speaking, these kind of people don't usually bump into creatures of the night, like sane people do, we hope!

It's like asking,
Does a bear or in this case, a Wolfman sh*t in the woods?

Even though one thing, does not mean the other, the witnesses seem or appear to be telling us, what they think is the truth, so obviously there is a good chance that they will pass a lie detector test, based on the truth of what they think or thought they saw and heard!

"Truth Or Consequence"

It's like Tantalizing hints or contradictory half-truths of things that only seem or appear to look the same, but don't rely fit, or by conjecture, where you find one thing, that turn out to be something else!

Suggestio Falsi

(Suggestion, insinuation, of something that is not true)

The reason I have included the dogman stories, is because there seems or appears to be several strange inconsistencies in some of these enigmatic stories, that speak of an intelligent creature that is not scared of a gun! But seemed or appeared to be frightened of a camera? This is something that does not make logical sense, or like in the amazing: *Missing 411 books, by David Paulides* i.e.: the strange and inexplicable vacuum of sound.

Or of the sudden and creepy silence, after the birds and crickets go deadly quite, during the appearance of this sentient and yet monsterious wolf-man or wraith-like creature, or that the so-called witnesses seem or appear almost (**Mesmerized**) or should I say (**Hypnotized**!) by this self-induced state of sensory deprevation while either in the wilds or driving, something that we don't yet understand, due to the psychological effect of it on the mind, where people who wouldn't say boo! To a ghost, you know, those **insane manical monsters** that end up behind the wheel, and have been **killed** or **kill**! Other people due to road rage!

. . .

And the thrall or intense stare of this so-called imaginery creature! That can Seem or appear to look straight through the witness, maybe it lurks in the dark corners of our minds-eye! And given enough stimuli, the mind, especially of these kinds of people, because all hypnosis is self-hypnosis! And in this twlight world of the mind or self-induced trance-like state, the mind of the so-called witnesses, can easily produce what ever it wants to see!

Just like nightmare's and phobias are real to the people who experience them, and they all have a collective and yet personal response to such things, like the feeling of some of the witnesses, who implied that it somehow know that they were vulnerable in some introspective way, can such things exist in either the corporeal or incorporeal sense of the word, like ghosts! Who are apparently non-corporeal, and yet we can be aware of their strange and enigmatic presence, by a fleeting glance or impression of something that is not there! Or if we are lucky, so to speak, we can see them or hear their results, because they can open and shut doors or turn on and off lights in haunted houses, why or how is that done?

And like these ghosts and phantoms, it too is able to seemingly melt-away, so to speak, or merge into the surrounding countryside, as if it could be operating in a different time-frame, whatever it is or appears to be, it is there one minute, and gone the next, a very strange presence, that seems or appears to be pecularly fleeting, if it is some kind of wild animal, and the witness who heard what sound like a low growl, Was trying to decide what she was, and if she was a threat! How can it be so close for comfort, and yet it does not chase and attack the witnesses, or even badly mall them? Compared with some of the vicious or mysterious attacks or disappearances in *MISSING 411 NORTH AMERICA AND BEYOND. Page 333* that is a very questionable and yet contridictory act! Like in...

Manitoba
Alex Thorne
44yrs
1958

Alex was a trapper by trade, and was able to earn his living of the land. On October 4th 1958 in the morning hours, Alex took his 22 Caliber rifle, to go out and check his traps.

And he said he would be back in half an hour! Going out to check trap-lines didn't sound realistic, and going out, only a short distance to do this, does not make any sense, because it normally involves an all day or even several-day trips, Alex did not return! It was as if he knew that someone or something had been interfering with his traps?

The Michigan Dogman
Werewolves and other unknown canines across the USA

1930

Page 79

In the North Central part of the state, just north of Peoria, outside Chillicothe, which lies along the Illinois-river, with its state parks and forests to the West and East, Jack Ratliff's land lay in a valley bounded by the Santa-Fe-railroad tracks.

Ratcliff farmed and trapped the land.

"Jack started to notice that during the trapping season, on the nights and times of the fullmoon, his traps would be raided! Whatever or whoever had been at them? Was gone, leaving behind in its carnivorous wake, only blood and strange large tracks, made by something that was apparently walking on two legs? Because there was no front paw marks!"

"Strange And Weird Things
That Fly In The Face Of Normality"

Is there a Para-normal aspect to the witness's experience in these amazing cases? Due to the complete silence of the natural world, in the creature's presence, which could be due to some kind of temporary time displacement, which can happen naturally but internally, because of a blow to the head resulting in amnesia and the weird and very misunderstood after effects of concussion on the mind, or the adrenalin-rush due to the abstract quality of the experience, which then can effect the short or long term memory of the shock or violent situation, where everything becomes weird and takes on an outer worldly aspect.

. . .

Real Wolfman

True encounters in modern America

By

LINDA S. GODFREY'S

That its hard to explain, except to those who have had a similar experience, when you see something that is totally unlike anything one has seen before, it is actually hard to put into words or even cognitively recoqnize what the thing is or what you have seen.

Like in the story of the Lochness Monster: "there is something strange about Nessie, that has nothing to do with size and appearance . . . odd, isn't it?" or like the Lochness hoodoo, as it was called, where cameras don't work properly, little coincidences that are not rely coincidences!

Like being in the wrong place at the right time, and always just missing a great shot somewhere else, with the Cine or camera ready, or being in the right place at the wrong time, when the cine or camera does not seem to work properly! It's as if it goes against the laws of average.

Like in *"The Michigan Dogman"* by Linda S. Godfrey in regard the weird electronic glitches that tend to put mockers on the documention of cryptid research or the weird piece of information in Real Werewolf, True

Encounters In Modern America by the same author: LSG page 96 in Orange county, Modjeska Canyon, California.

In 2010 at the Black Star Canyon region of Santa Ana Mountains: 'they were half way up the trail, when all the batteries suddenly died! And something that sounded bipedal began to stalk them! Now isn't that a weird and revealing piece of strange technological evidence? About the *flashlight* or **torch** going **dead**! As if there's more to this unseen creature, than meets the eye, so to speak!

Something is out there!

A strange creature that was first reported in 1887 in Wexford County, Michigan. Sightings have been reported in several locations throughout Michigan, primarily in the northwestern quadrant of the Lower Peninsula. The first known sighting of strange wolf-like creature occurred in 1887 in Wexford County, when two lumberjacks saw a creature whom they described as having a man's body and a dog's head.

In 1938 in Paris, Michigan, Robert Fortney was attacked by five wild dogs and said that one of the five walked on two legs. Reports of similar creatures also came from Allegan County in the 1950s, and in Manistee and Cross Village in 1967.

Linda S. Godfrey, in her book *"The Beast of Bray Road"* compares the Manistee sightings to a similar creature sighted in Wisconsin known as the Beast of Bray Road.

The Beast of Bray Road (or the Bray Road Beast) is a cryptid, or cryptozoological, creature first reported in the 1949 on a rural road outside of Elkhorn, Wisconsin. The same label has been applied well beyond the initial location, to any unknown creature from southern Wisconsin or northern Illinois and all the way to Vancouver Island, Canada, that is described as having similar characteristics to those reported in the initial set of sightings.

Bray Road itself is a quiet country road near the community of Elkhorn. The rash of claimed sightings in the late 1980s and early 1990s prompted a local newspaper, the *Walworth County Week*, to assign reporter Linda Godfrey to cover the story. Godfrey initially was skeptical, but later became convinced of the sincerity of the witnesses. Her series of articles later became a book titled *The Beast of Bray Road: Trailing Wisconsin's Werewolf*.

The Beast of Bray Road is described by purported witnesses in several ways: as a bear-like creature, as a hairy biped resembling Bigfoot, and as an unusually large (2–4 feet tall on all fours, 7 feet tall standing up) intelligent wolf-like creature apt to walk on its hind legs and weighing 400-700 pounds. It also said that its fur is a brown gray color resembling a dog or bear.

Although the Beast of Bray Road has not been seen to transform from a human into a wolf in any of the sightings, it has been labeled a werewolf in newspaper articles

The first known sighting of the Michigan Dogman occurred in 1887 in Wexford County, when two lumberjacks saw a creature whom they described as having a man's body and a dog's head. They chased it, and cornered it, when it let out "an unearthly scream", and stood upright. The pair left immediently, and never returned.

In 1897, a farmers body was found on his plough, apparently a victim of a heart attack. Large dog tracks surrounded the plough. Exactly ten years later, a deranged widow woman had dreams of upright, screaming dogs circling her house.

Another decade later, a sheriff found a wagon with dog prints around it. No driver could be found, and the horses were nearby, dead, with their eyes open. Nobody could determine their cause of death.

In 1937, sailors saw a pack of upright dogs, and shot one. The next year, another sailor shot another of these dogs, but it reared up onto its hind legs, and locked eyes with him.

In 1957, a preacher found dog claw marks seven feet off the ground, on a church wall. In 1967, a van of hippies was awoken in the middle of the night by a dogman attacking their van. In an unknown, later year, likely 1977, two fishermen, at dusk, saw a doglike animal swimming towards them. It was swimming like a man. They beat it with their oars, and it swam away.

Like in **MISSING 411. EASTERN UNITED STATES.** And the little girl on **page 55. katie Flynn 1868. Michigan. Aged 3 years.** Who dissappeared while helping her dad Henry Flynn at a nearby lumber camp during the immedate and frantic search for the little girl, two hunters happened to wander into the camp, and very soon became involved during and in the search itself, after they had heard feebled cries in the underbrush, just before they came upon the little girl, who was alive and well, they saw what seemed or appeared to be a huge black bear, dart into a nearby river and escape on the other side!

And when she was eventually asked why she did not try to run away? And little Katie had replied: **"Big-dog**! Came up to me, took me in his arms, and walked away with me."

. . .

" Little boy lost"
1891
Missing 411
Appalachian mountains
Enter at your own risk
Hoc-est-corpus
(*Here is the body*)

A little boy called Ottie was found lying on his back, with one arm stretched out from his body, and one arm had been removed and was lying nearby! Little Ottie's two legs had been removed from his body and were lying near-by, and his feet were removed from his legs...!

Of course these types of incidents don't seem or appear to make any sense, if you keep looking at the problem in the same way, we will keep going round in ever decreasing circles, getting nowhere fast.

When some of the missing people are eventually found, it's as if they are suffering from the effects of concussion or confusion and many cannot or will not remember what occurred while they were gone! And they are either semi-conscious or unconscious missing parts of their clothing or like the strange and weird story of the little girl...

Marcella Rimiskey

4yrs old

1950

Chenuis Falls
Mount Rainer national park

This strange and unquiet case from the Missing 411 books When she was eventually found, her *dress* was on **back-to-front** and her **laces** were in an **odd state** of **confusion!** Like in **"Legions Of The Damned"** where the *shirt* on one of Franklin's crewmen, who had been mysteriously buried on Beechey-Island! Was on **back-to-front,** but there's more, including the **diary** that was found with the writing **back-to-front!** And the coffin in the eerie grave that had been strangely autopsied **back-to-front! And** the other grave with **number 4** on the coffin-lid, **other-way round** or **back to front**!

As well as the bodies found in the graves at **beechey-island**, that had **no shoes on**! Just like:

Missing 411
North America and beyond

Page 105

Ted Nalman 14yrs 1959

The boy's shoes were also missing!

As well as

Casey Holliday 1990 11yrs

Page 109

Who was found without his shoes, babbling, and in some sort of daze, or is there a correlation between the geographic locations where people have disappeared, have anything to do with it? Like: Todd Hofflander 39yrs, that vanished in **Hell's Canyon** in 2010, and was never found! Or in the doomed **Franklin expedition**, that perished, and the eerie names of these sailing ships that vanished:

"The Erebus, *god of darkness and son of chaos,*
And the **Terror**, *names that speak for themselves***!"**

Nancy Moyer Aged 36. page 37
Missing 2009
WASHINGTON
(*Tenino*)
USA

Her front door was found unlocked, her car in the driveway, the heater and the television on, and a glass of wine sitting on the table. Her purse and keys were siting near the kitchen table. Nancy was gone.

. . .

They are the location of an enduring mystery that occurred in December 1900, when all three lighthouse keepers vanished without trace.

. . .

The Stranger that came to dinner

The first hint of anything untoward on the Flannan Isles came on 15 December 1900. The steamer *Archtor* on passage from *Philadelphia* to *Leith* passed the islands in poor weather and noted that the light was not operational.

. . .

This was reported on arrival at *Oban*, although no immediate action seems to have been taken. The island lighthouse was manned by a three-man team (*Thomas Marshall, James Ducat*, and *Donald MacArthur*), with a rotating *fourth-man* spending time on shore.

The relief vessel, the lighthouse tender *Hesperus*, was unable to set out on a routine visit from *Lewis* planned for 20 December due to adverse weather and did not arrive until noon on *Boxing Day* (*26 December*). On arrival, the crew and relief keeper found that the *flagstaff* was bare of its flag, none of the usual provision boxes had been left on the landing stage for re-stocking, and more ominously, none of the *lighthouse-keepers* were there to welcome them ashore. **Jim Harvie**, captain of the *Hesperus,* gave a strident blast on his whistle and set off a distress flare, but no reply was forthcoming.

A boat was launched and Joseph Moore, the relief keeper, was put ashore alone. He found the **entrance gate** to the compound and **main door** both **closed**, the **beds unmade**, and the clock stopped. Returning to the landing stage with this grim news, he then went back up to the lighthouse with the **Hesperus's** second-mate and a seaman.

A further search revealed that the **lamps** were **cleaned** and **refilled**. A set of oilskins was found, suggesting that one of the keepers had left the lighthouse without them, which was surprising considering the severity of the weather on the date of the last entry in the lighthouse log. The only sign of anything amiss in the **lighthouse** was an **overturned chair** by the kitchen table. Of the keepers there was no sign, neither inside the lighthouse nor anywhere on the island.

Moore and three volunteer seamen were left to attend the light and the **Hesperus** returned to the shore station at **Breasclete**. Captain Harvie sent a telegram to the Northern Lighthouse Board dated 26 December 1900, stating:

A dreadful accident has happened at the Flannans. The three keepers, **Ducat**, **Marshall** and the **Occasional** have disappeared from the Island... The clocks were stopped and other signs indicated that the accident must have happened about a week ago. Poor fellows they must have been blown over the cliffs or drowned trying to secure a crane or something like that.

The men remaining on the island scoured every corner for clues as to the fate of the keepers. At the east landing everything was intact, but the west landing provided considerable evidence of damage caused by recent storms. A box at 33 metres (108 ft) above sea level had been broken and its contents strewn about; iron railings were bent over, the iron railway by the path was wrenched out of its concrete, and a rock weighing more than a ton had been displaced above that. On top of the cliff at more than 60 metres (200 ft) above sea level, turf had been ripped away as far as 10 metres (33 ft) from the cliff edge. The missing keepers had kept their log until 9 a.m. on 15 December, however, and their entries made it clear that the damage had occurred before the disappearance of the writers.

Speculations and misconceptions

No bodies were ever found and the loneliness of the rocky islets may have lent itself to feverish imaginings. Theories abounded and resulted in "fascinated national speculation". Some, simply were elaborations on the truth. For example, the events were commemorated in Wilfrid Wilson Gibson's 1912 ballad, *Flannan Isle*.

. . .

FLANNAN ISLE

(Wilfrid Wilson Gibson)
Though three men dwell on Flannan Isle
To keep the lamp alight,
As we steer'd under the lee, we caught
No glimmer through the night!
Aye: though we hunted high and low,
And hunted everywhere,
Of the three men's fate we found no trace
Of any kind in any place,
But a door ajar, and an untouch'd meal,
And an overtoppled chair...

* * *

*Are these eerie cicumstances telling us more than we think, or of something that could be that frightening, it would be better not to **know**?* Not only about who or what could be doing these weird things, but the eerie tales of our own strange beginnings or secretive anthropological and theological **über-hacker**!

. . .

THE WARMINSTER MYSTERY

ENGLAND
UK
BY
ARTHUR SHUTTLEWOOD

And the strange and rather quirky story of Flying Saucers or eerie lights in the sky UFOs (Unidentified Flying Objects)

Astonishing phenomena that dramatically unfolded in the 1960s. With weird objects and **disturbing sounds,** like the lost **Franklin expedition** with its **strange wind** or **buzzing noises,** that could be linked not only to the **Warminster Mystery** with its **whinning** and **buzzing** sounds, that seemed or appeared to come from overhead, and described by one witness in chapter three: **"Ominously Stealing Into Prominence"** page 28, but to the story in **MISSING 411 The Devil's in the Detail** by **David Paulides**.

And the strange case of little **Anna Christian Waters aged 5 years!** **California-central Coast page 33** where one of her neighbours

Charlene Machado on *page 6* hears strange *"crackling sounds"* near the creek bank, up stream.

And if we link the dots correctly, we find what seems or appears to be a hidden clue of sorts in the book: *THE WARMINSTER MYSTERY Eyewitness accounts of dramatic UFO sightings in England.* Chapter two. Titled: *"A Brass-Cymballed Wilderness."*

Where one of the witnesses described what she heard, at the top of *page 21*, *"It all began with an electric crackling!"*

. . .
MISSING 411
NORTH AMERICA AND BEYOND

Johnny Johnson in **1955** in **Salisbury**, **England**. Which is right next door to **Warminster!**

Could it just be nothing more than a weird coincidence in these strange events? Or is there a grain of truth in the *"parable of the mustard seed"* where there could very well be a whole host of truths, right under our very noses, written inside these theological i.e. *"The Christian bible and others!"*

Like in *"Legions Of The Damned"* where the shirt on one of Franklin's crewmen, who had been mysteriously buried on *Beechey-Island* was on *back-to-front*! But there's more, including the diary that was found with the writing *back-to-front*! And the coffin in the eerie grave that had the *number 4* the other-way round or *back to front...*!

The amount of people who are disappearing is very weird, or it flies in the face of logic while running contrary to the law of averages, something unusual is happening under our very noses, when scores of kids as well as adults are not only vanishing, but they are being murdered...!

Even people suffering from paranoia, Still have enemies!

If they know that we know, it seems or appears to raise more questions than answers, because, it is very obvious that we can't stop whatever or whoever is doing this, as I have already said, why are they still hiding? I personally feel that when people go missing, the **SAR** (*Search and Rescue*) should go on indefinitely despite the cost!

Gene profiling

Are they looking for something in our genes, by selecting a whole variety of different ages and sexes? Which raises a whole host of **theological, anthropological** and **sociological** questions, in more ways than one! For the last word on it!

"Deo non Fortuna" meaning by god, not by chance! Depending on what your interpretation of God is? See: *"Gods, Angel's and Gaints"* are we not at the hands of capricious Gods, or the twisted hand of fate?

Forearmed is forewarned, or have the highest echelons of the world already been infiltrated by our own or some strange collective authority? So to speak, that seems or appears to be caught in some kind of esoteric battle or has the invasion already begun, by a very clever adversary, that has been using our own greed and lust for power and control, like in galloping bureaucracy or Yes Minister by threatening the very sovereignty of another nation, under the auspices of nothing more than a big lie, and then to invade and openly murder and enslave the populous, using the democratic prison without bars approach, and once that is excepted by everybody without question, it can than be used against anybody!

Even America by the arbitery attack on the American constitution, by what looks like an act of open treason, not only against the founding fathers, but of the republic itself, by nothing more than pernicious treasonible individuals that tend to knaw at the vitals of the republic i.e.: USA! By first sizing the initiative and hoisting America by its on petard, by creating an unconstitutional 2nd house, a framework or watch-dog that was constructed to prevent corruption, allowed the republic only enough rope to hang itself, and now seems or appears to be working outside the very law it was made to protect, with no unaccountable to any government! Where the **manufacturing base** of the **USA**, has been systamatically asset-striped and dismantled, followed by the unconstitutional attack on 1st amendment, by trying to strip the populous of their writes to bare arms, followed by institutionalised incompetence over the dollar, which has broken all the tabo's of *finacial restraint* by reckless borrowing, that now threatens the foundation of a monitery system that will eventuall collapse! And may never be the same again, and all for the want of a shoe-nail, for **Paul Reveres** horse, and the war against the unseen enemy, foreign or domestic!

. . .

𝕽𝖎𝖈𝖍𝖆𝖗𝖉 𝕿𝖍𝖊 𝖎𝖎𝖎

Ely with Richmond troubles me
more near
Than Buckingham and his rash-levied strength.
Come; I have learn'd that fearful commenting
is leaden servitor to dull delay:
Delay leads impotent and snail-pac'd beggary:
Then fiery expedition be my wing,
Jove's Mercury, and herald for a king.
Go, muster men: my counsel is my shield;
we must be brief when traitors brave the field.
[Exeunt.]

We need to think outside the box!

As they say, whoever they are? That the government agencies are ether for us, and can be part of the solution? Or they are against us, and they are part of the problem they always seem to be so near and yet so far to whatever or whoever is targeting and then selecting certain individual's who are then being watched and then monitored until the opportunity exists for them to disappear!

And then tying up human resources to go round in circles, and why is it a coincidence that these national parks seem or appear to have been selected and then protected by the government, and yet it is the very places where people are mysteriously disappearing? It make's you wonder or gives you the uneasy impression that something else is going on that we should know about? Whether or not it's a government agency that appears to be more than just grossly corrupt, unfortunately.

And when you finally discover who or what has caused it, possible too late! It will be like the cult 60s TV Show: **The Invaders** and the episode called **Valley of the shadow**. Watch it and tell yourself whats going to happen when the American or British people find out who has rely been in charge?

One gains naught by shouting into deaf ears!
(Paracelsus)

Are we being fallacious or stepping over the line in search of the truth? By spreading malicious rumours, or uncovering an **"Invisible government"** by David Wise and Thomas B. Ross and **"Who Rules America?"** By John McConaughy.

In a world, not of the old dupes or fall-guy's, like the archetypical **"Joseph Stalin"** in communist Russia that was said to have and still does control the press, just like the supposedly free-world of cleverly **"Managed news"** by Hanson W. Baldwin. Where tyranny hides in the shadow of

legality! In **Mein Kampf** Are they using clever tricks of logic? And are the forest rangers only seeing what they are told to see? Or only what they want to, or need to see?

MISSING 411 WESTERN UNITED STATES & CANADA

And Keith Parkins 1952 Ritter Oregon Aged 2 years. And the members of the SAR (Search and Rescue) for some unknown reason knew where the boy would end-up! they either knew instinctively something that the public doesn't know or someone or something is using ESP! or some other method of intelligence beyond our understanding.

As in hypnosis the placebo or the stigmata!

The placement of the nails in **crucifixion** was most likely in the wrist, in a place between the wrist bones which is called the *"space of Destot"* (Barbet, Pierre. 1963. A Doctor at Calvary. New York: Image). This location would allow the nails to support the weight of an adult man because the ligaments which join the 8 wrist bones (carpal bones) are thicker and stronger than those which connect the bones of the palm (metacarpal bones).

Padre Pio of Pietrelcina reported stigmata which were studied by several 20th-century physicians, whose independence from the Church is not known. The observations were reportedly inexplicable and the wounds never became infected. His wounds healed once, but reappeared.The wounds were examined by Luigi Romanelli, chief physician of the City Hospital of Barletta, for about one year. Dr. Giorgio Festa, a private practitioner, also examined them in 1920 and 1925. Professor Giuseppe Bastianelli, physician to Pope Benedict XV, agreed that the wounds existed, but made no other comment. Pathologist Dr. Amico Bignami of the University of Rome also observed the wounds, but could make no diagnosis. Both Bignami and Dr. Giuseppe Sala commented on the unusually smooth edges of the wounds and lack of edema.

" Visions of the Night"

'Dreams' By David and Susan Hillier

Separating the 'paranormal' from the "normal" is a sign of discontinuity of experience, for the term 'paranormal' has no organic meaning: it is defined only by negation, by the withdrawal of successive material causes for an event until only the "impossible", the "paranormal", remains.

. . .

"Maybe its better not to know?"

People who tend not to use their brains, and are still not convinced of my argument, tend to sit on their brains! So to speak, are welcome to continue sticking their head in the sand, but remember this, if you can't, or you are still refusing to except what has been happening, remember your rear-end is still exposed, and it is more than likely that if you continue to ignore the warnings, and go anywhere near these dangerous areas, where someone has to be taken! It's more than likely that you will be very lucky if you get away, but only by a hairs breadth, or a very close shave!

" Ockham's Razor"

which first appeared in 1852 in the works of Sir William Hamilton, 9th Baronet (1788–1856), centuries after William of Ockham's death. Ockham stated the principle in various ways, but the most popular version "entities must not be multiplied beyond necessity" "Pluralitas non est ponenda sine necessitate" we consider it a good principle to explain the phenomena by the simplest hypothesis possible

For instance, the Summa Theologica of Thomas Aquinas (1225-1274) states that "it is superfluous to suppose that what can be accounted for by a few principles has been produced by many". Aquinas uses this principle to construct an objection to God's existence, an objection which he in turn answers and refutes generally and specifically, through an argument based on causality.

Hence, Aquinas acknowledges the principle which today is known as Occam's Razor, but prefers causal explanations to other simple explanations

William of Ockham (c. 1287–1347) is remembered as an influential medieval philosopher and nominalist, though his popular fame as a great logician rests chiefly on the maxim attributed to him and known as Ockham's razor. The term *razor* refers to distinguishing between two hypotheses either by "shaving away" unnecessary assumptions or cutting apart two similar conclusions.

Into the void

"For the earth is hollow
And I have touched the sky"
H.G. Wells.

"Is there an undiscovered landmass, beyond the poles? "Is there undiscovered land beyond the Artic and the Antarctic or some vast and geographical enigma? That we seem or appear to know nothing about, that was apparently rediscovered by the aerial expeditions of the Artic and the Antarctic of Rear Admiral Richard E. Byrd in 1947 and in 1956. After penetrating 1,700 miles beyond the North-pole, he seems or appears to have discovered a land-mass as big as the **United-States-of-America**, and **2,300 miles** beyond the south-pole, an area as big as **North-America** or the **great-unknown territory** or **polar-concavities**."

.   .   .

Artic

The truth now becomes stranger than fiction, because the earth seems or appears to be different in both of the **polar-regions,** which is not recorded on any of our old or modern maps...

Ghosts of the imagination

Of an area as big as North-America, plus the south polar continent, which makes up two land masses measuring a staggering total of **4,000 miles**

Artic

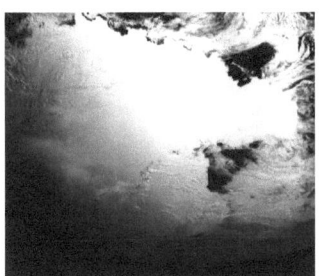

across and probably as large as the **North and South American continents.**

Was it a figment of **Admiral Byrd's imagination?** Or did the newspapers at the time either lie or where they part of the bigger picture of **managed** or **manipulated** news reports? Where the actual radio reports from Byrd's plane part of the **subterfuge** as well? Which was spoon-fed to the great unwashed, who seemed or appeared not to care one way or the other...

An unquiet truth that staggers the imagination, so why was the truth **suppressed** and for reasons known only to those and such as those?
Even to this day, no one has tried to replicate **Admiral Byrd's flights**... in any shape or form, to try and prove what he said was wrong.

They vanished into thin air...

Even the book by **Giannini's** book: **"Worlds beyond the poles"** that was published in New York in 1959, and was for some reason it was not even advertised by the publisher and has remained virtually unknown, till it was re-discovered and mentioned in the popular magazine **"Flying Saucers"** that hit the news-stands of America.

. . .

And mysteriously it was as if strange and eerie forces were at work in the USA. Did someone or something try to suppress or prevent the free flow of public information, and when the **1959 December** issue of **"Flying Saucers"** was ready for to mail to their subscribers, it was stopped by person or persons unknown who had mysteriously removed it from circulation.
And when the trucks arrived to pick-up and then deliver the magazines from the printers to the publishers, they found that they had vanished...!
And a phone call to the printers by the publishers revealed that there was no shipping receipt! Even though the magazines had already been paid for, the publisher then asked the printer to return the plates to the press and run off the copies of **"Flying Saucer?"** but the plates were nowhere to be found! Having been inexplicably damaged at the hand of person or persons unknown... so that no re-printing could be made of the amazing revelations contained inside the covers of the magazine **"Flying Saucers"** but where were the thousands of magazines that were already printed and had mysteriously disappeared? Why was there no shipping receipt? And if in the event that they had been sent to the wrong address, surly by the law of probability they would have eventually turned up? And as a result 5,000 subscribers did not receive their copies of **"Flying Saucers"** because they had literary vanished into thin air!
One doomed distributor, who had received **750 copies** to sell at the newsstand, was reported missing! Along with his **750 copies** of his cursed magazines, that was sent to him with the request that they must be returned if not delivered? Obviously they did not come back, since the strange magazine vanished completely.
What kind of dynamite did **"Flying Saucers"** magazine contain or why was it too hot to handle? What was it telling us or for that matter what was it not telling us?

Artic

(The blind leading the blind)

We seem or appear to have below our feet, so to speak, an immense region whose frightening radius is **6,290 Kilometres** that is apparently unknown!

That challenges not only our own ignorance as a people, but the arrogance

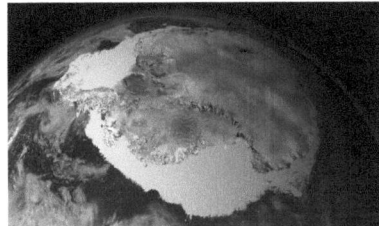

and the conceit of scientist or those who are meant to know better, who historically and conveniently are unable to find their own rear-end with both hands... and who are nauseatingly punctual in their inept ability to see something that seems or appears to be right under their nose or is it their feet, (*excuse the pun*) as they are dragged kicking and screaming into the **21ˢᵗ century?** Apart from their rambling inability and questionable conjectures that conceal their ignorance and deep seated fear of the strange and the mysterious world that we live in!

. . .

The total surface of the earth is **197 million square miles,** and its estimated weight is **six-sextillion imperial ton,** and if the earth were a sold sphere its weight would be far greater, so why the discrepancy in her weight?

Where is the proof that the earth is a **sphere** with an **800-mile crust** covering a molten liquid core!

Other than the rambling half-truth from the Middle Ages when the church used to hoodwink the great unwashed whither they liked it or not! With lies and double-talk about the earth being **flat** and other such nonsense, and if you sail to far out, you would fall off the edge of the world! How did the church know that? And who told them to use this crazy theory that was the equivalent to whistling in the dark, in order to cleverly hide something out in the open, and if you questioned it in any shape or form, order to stop us from being too inquisitive, so to speak:

. . .

Giordano Bruno

1548 – February 17, 1600

Born **Filippo Bruno,** was an Italian Dominican friar, philosopher, mathematician, poet, and astrologer. He is celebrated for his cosmological theories, which went even further than the then-novel **Copernican** model: while supporting **heliocentrism,** Bruno also correctly proposed that the Sun was just another star moving in space, and claimed as well that the universe contained an infinite number of inhabited worlds, identified as planets orbiting other stars.

Beginning in 1593, **Bruno** was tried for **heresy** by the **Roman Inquisition** on charges including denial of several core **Catholic doctrines** (including the **Trinity, the divinity of Christ, the virginity of Mary, and Transubstantiation**). Bruno's **pantheism** was also a matter of grave concern.

The Inquisition found him guilty, and in **1600** he was brutally murdered by being **burned at the stake** in Rome's **Campo de' Fiori.** After his death he gained considerable fame, particularly among 19th- and early

20th-century commentators who regarded him as a martyr for science, though scholars emphasize that Bruno's astronomical views were at most a minor component of the theological and philosophical beliefs that led to his trial.

Bruno's case is still considered a landmark in the history of free thought and the future of the emerging sciences.

In addition to his cosmological writings, Bruno also wrote extensively on the art of memory, a loosely organized group of mnemonic techniques and principles.

Historian Frances Yates argues that Bruno was deeply influenced by Arab astrology, Neoplatonism, Renaissance Hermeticism, and the Egyptian god Thoth. Other studies of Bruno have focused on his qualitative approach to mathematics and his application of the spatial paradigms of geometry to language.

. . .

Dr. Raymond Bernard

The Hollow Earth
1964

Truth or consequence

When confused explorers approached the **70°** to **75° degrees** North or South latitudes, the earth starts to slowly and inexorable curve in, and as they reach this **invisible-magnetic-circle** or **rim** of the **Polar opening** which is at the end of the medieval world, and true enough they symbolically fall off the edge of the known world, and into the **abyss** of the **unknown!**

The magnetic needle of their compass would point **straight down!** And many other Artic explorers have noticed this strange phenomenon when reaching the high latitudes close to **90° degrees** who where dumbfounded by the weird movement of the compass and its strange behaviour, because they did not know that they were in a new and yet invisible world, inside the massive **Polar opening** and as they continued the needle would then **point up!**

The entrances are simply the outer-rim of a giant magnetic anomaly around the polar openings.

The invisible rim gradually flattens out or slopes inwards, taking any explorer into unknown territory, because you can't fly over it even using a gyro-compass, because they don't function in this mysterious geomagnetic-anomaly, and you can only go so far, before you have to turn back or you will run out of fuel and find yourself stranded!

If you consult a map of the magnetic fields you will discover that the magnetic meridians extend across the **Polar-Basin** to the **Taimyr Peninsula** in **Siberia,** they extend from one continent to the other! But because there is no room on our conventional maps of the known world or conventional globes, so the geomagnetic anomaly has two lines running from the **Polar-Basin** to the **Taimyr Peninsula** in **Siberia** that are at least 1,000 miles long!

So between each of the magnetic poles around the earth runs magnetic meridians! In contrast with Geographical meridians, which measure longitude, the magnetic meridians move from **east to west** and back again like the trajectory of the **dark knight satellite!**

"The difference between the geographical meridians or true North and South and the direction in which a magnetic compass points or the magnetic meridian of the place is called the declination."

Which was first observed in London in 1580 and showed an easterly declination of 11° (Degree's). In 1815 the declination reached 24.3° (Degrees) westerly maximum.

This makes a difference of 35.3° (Degree's) change in 235 years, which is equal to 2,118 miles.

And if you make a circle around the pole, with a radius of 1,059 miles so that it is 2,118 miles in diameter, this represents the invisible but humongous rim of the **Polar abyss** or **great expanse of the opening**. So the North magnetic pole has travelled from one-point to its diametrical opposite point on the circle, 2,118 miles away. Obviously if the earth were convex, then both the geographical and magnetic poles would meet dead-centre, of this mammoth abyss or opening, it is not on **"Terra-Firma"** (*solid ground*) can only be seen from above the poles, in mid-air or at the epi-centre!

Immanual Velikovsky
(*When worlds collide*)

Where something humongous was accidentally or intentionally used like a scalpel to **terra-form** the earth, destroying the **dinosaurs** and introducing a **new species** into the gene-pool, that resulted in the **historical flood**, bleeding into this massive fissure to staunch the wound and cover over the massive scare or opening left behind by the **force** of this **object** and that's what caused the **magnetic anomalie** where compasses will not work and the sun, although its down on the other side of the earth, is still peeking through this massive scare tissue causing the **Aurora borealis**.

• • •

The true magnetic pole is not on the rim, but at the centre of the crust, 400 miles below the earths crust! And as the earth turns on its axis, the motion is gyroscopic, like a giant spinning-top, where the gravitational pull is much stronger next to the curve from the exterior to the interior, so much less force is needed to hold anything on the surface, so midway the gravitational pull is the most strongest, where the centre of gravity caused by the centrifugal-force **lies**, (*excuse the pun*) and it is so strong at this point, salt-water and fresh water don't mix!

"This allows one to obtain fresh drinking water from the Artic-Ocean"

ICEBERGS

Are not formed of seawater! But freshwater! If so, where do they come from? And what causes the strange agitation of the sea, like massive underwater tidal waves!

Why are the icebergs in Antarctica different from the ones found in the Artic? On average there is less than two inches of rainfall in 11½ months, even though it snows quite frequently, it does not fall to any great depth!

The greatest iceberg on earth is called the **"great-ice-barrier"** which is somewhat of a misnomer, it is over 400 miles long and 50 miles wide, and it is grounded in just over two thousand feet of water, and it extends from an average of about 80ft to 200ft above water.

It is impossible for an iceberg of these gargantuan proportions to form in a country that has no continuous supply of rain or build-up of snow! And it lies in an ocean of salt-water, how is that possible?

When worlds collide

When Bernacchi voyaged to the Antarctic he observed "During the next two days we passed thousands of massive icebergs among fresh water at the surface" how is it possible to produce such quantities of ice, a 1,000 ft thick! And what is causing these underwater tidal waves?

Artic tidal waves, reported by various explorers that lift the great ice fields to great heights, and can also be heard from miles away! Giant blocks pitched and roll as though something is moving underneath them?

Shag Harbour

UFO incident was the reported impact of an unknown large object into waters near Shag Harbour, a tiny fishing village in the Canadian province

of Nova Scotia on October 4, 1967. The reports were investigated by various civilian (**Royal Canadian Mounted Police and Canadian Coast Guard**) and military (**Royal Canadian Navy and Royal Canadian Air Force**) agencies of the Government of Canada.

. . .

On the night of October 4, 1967, at about 11:20 p.m. Atlantic Daylight Time, it was reported that something had crashed into the waters of the Gulf of Maine near Shag Harbour. At least eleven people saw a low-flying lit object head towards the harbour. Multiple witnesses reported hearing a whistling sound "like a bomb," then a "whoosh," and finally a loud bang.

The object was never officially identified, and was therefore referred to as an ***unidentified flying object*** (*UFO*) in Government of Canada documents. The Canadian military became involved in a subsequent rescue/recovery effort. The initial report was made by local resident Laurie Wickens and four of his friends. Driving through Shag Harbour on Highway 3, they spotted a large object descending into the waters off the harbour. Attaining a better vantage point, Wickens and his friends saw an object floating 250 m (820 ft) to 300 m (980 ft) offshore in the Gulf of Maine. Wickens contacted the RCMP detachment in Barrington Passage and reported he had seen a large airplane or small airliner crash into the Gulf of Maine.

Assuming an aircraft had crashed, within about 15 minutes, 10 RCMP officers arrived at the scene. Concerned for survivors, the RCMP detachment contacted the ***Rescue Coordination Centre*** (*RCC*) in Halifax to advise them of the situation, and ask if any aircraft were missing. Before any attempt at rescue could be made, the object started to sink and disappeared from view.

A rescue mission was quickly assembled. Within half an hour of the crash, local fishing boats went out to the crash site in the waters of the Gulf of Maine off Shag Harbour to look for survivors. No survivors, bodies or debris were taken, either by the fishermen or by a Canadian Coast Guard search and rescue cutter, which arrived about an hour later from nearby Clark's Harbour.

By the next morning, RCC Halifax had determined that no aircraft were missing. While still tasked with the search, the captain of the Canadian Coast Guard cutter received a radio message from RCC Halifax that all commercial, private and military aircraft were accounted for along the eastern seaboard, in both Atlantic Canada and New England

The same morning, RCC Halifax also sent a priority telex to the "Air Desk" at Royal Canadian Air Force headquarters in Ottawa, which handled all civilian and military UFO sightings, informing them of the crash and that all conventional explanations such as aircraft, flares, etc. had been dismissed. Therefore this was labeled a **"UFO Report**." The head of the Air Desk then sent another priority telex to the Royal Canadian Navy headquarters concerning the "UFO Report" and recommended an underwater search be mounted. The RCN in turn sent another priority telex tasking Fleet Diving Unit Atlantic with carrying out the search.

Two days after the incident had been observed, a detachment of RCN divers from Fleet Diving Unit Atlantic was assembled and for the next three days they combed the seafloor of the Gulf of Maine off Shag Harbor looking for an object. The final report said no trace of an object was found.

Continued:

And when the huge bodies of ice are duly compressed, they shriek and roar with frightening cries and screams that would chill the blood! As if it were a prehistoric creature being released from the ice, like in the cult movie and the opening quote: ***"And the lord said, behold the Behemoth"*** in the cult movie.

Are these waves being caused by some strange and mysterious agency more powerful than just icebergs plunging into the sea, what mysteries lie beyond the poles?

"There was an ancient myth held in the middle ages that some mountains located between Eisenach and Gotha in Germany hold a portal to the

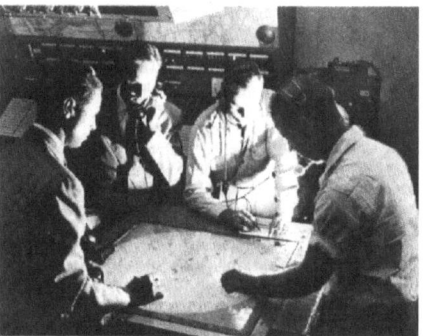

inner earth. There is an old Russian legend that says the Samoyeds, an ancient Siberian tribe, traveled to an underground cavern city to live inside the earth.

In Native American mythology, it is said that the ancestors of the Mandan people in ancient times emerged from a subterranean land through a cave at the north side of the Missouri River.

There is also a tale about a tunnel in the San Carlos Apache Indian Reservation in Arizona near Cedar Creek which is said to lead inside the earth to a land inhabited by a mysterious tribe.

It is also the belief of the tribes of Iroquois that their ancient ancestors emerged from a subterranean world inside the earth. The elders of the Hopi people believe that a Sipapu entrance in the Grand Canyon exists which leads to the underworld."

. . .

Monday, Mar. 07, 1960
Time Magazine

Three weeks ago, headlines announced that the **U.S.** had detected a mysterious **"dark"** satellite wheeling overhead on a regular orbit. There was nervous speculation that it might be a surveillance satellite launched by the Russians, and it brought the uneasy sensation that the **U.S.** did not know what was going-on over its own head.

. . .

But last week the Department of Defence proudly announced that the satellite had been identified. It was a space derelict, the remains of an Air Force Discoverer satellite that had gone astray!

. . .

The dark satellite was the first object to demonstrate the effectiveness of the **U.S.'s** new watch on space. And the three-week time lag in identification was proof that the system still lacks full coordination and that some bugs still have to be ironed out.

First Sighting

The most important component of the space watch went into operation about six months ago with the construction of *"Dark Fence,"* a kind of radar trip wire stretching across the width of the *U.S.*

Designed by the Naval Research Laboratory to keep track of satellites whose radios are silent, it is a notable improvement on other radars, which have difficulty finding a small satellite unless they know where to look.

Big, 50-kw. Transmitters were established at Gila River, near Phoenix, Ariz, and Jordan Lake, Ala., spraying radio waves upward in the shape of open fans. Some 250 miles on either side, receiving stations pick up signals that bounce off any object passing through the fans.

By a kind of triangulation, the operators can make rough estimates of the object's speed, distance and course.

On Jan. 31 *Dark Fence* detected two passes of what seemed to be an unknown space object. After detecting several passes during the following days, Captain W. E. Berg, commanding officer of Dark Fence, decided that something was circling overhead on a roughly *polar orbit.*

He raced to the Pentagon and in person reported the menacing stranger to Chief of Naval Operations Arleigh Burke. Within minutes the news was communicated to President Eisenhower and marked top secret.

In the confusion, there was a delay before anyone took the step necessary to positively identify the strange satellite: informing the Air Force's newly established surveillance centre in Bedford, Mass.

It is the surveillance centre's job to take all observations on satellites from all friendly observing centres, both optical and electronic, feed them into computers to produce figures that will identify each satellite, describe its orbit and predict its behaviour. Says one top official, explaining the cold facts of the space age: "The only way of knowing that a new satellite has appeared is by keeping track of the old ones."

It took two weeks for *Dark Fence's* scientists to check back through their taped observations, and to discover that the mysterious satellite had first showed up on *Aug. 15.*

The Air Force surveillance centre also checked its records to provide a list of everything else that was circling in the sky, and its computers worked out a detailed description of the new object's behaviour. The evidence from both Air Force and Navy pointed to Discoverer V, fired from Vandenberg Air Force Base, Calif, on Aug. 13.

The Black Knight Satellite

The most cited report of the satellite comes from Disneyland of the Gods, by John Keel. He reports that in February 1960 the *US* detected an unknown object in *polar orbit,* a feat that neither they nor the *USSR* had been able to accomplish.

As if that wasn't enough, it apparently was several sizes larger than anything either country would have been able to get off the ground.

On **September 3, 1960,** seven months after the satellite was first detected by radar, a tracking camera at Grumman Aircraft Corporation's Long Island factory took a photograph of it. People on the ground had been occasionally seeing it for about two weeks at that point. Viewers would make it out as a red glowing object moving in an *east-to-west* orbit.

· · ·

Most satellites move from west-to-east. Its speed was also about three times normal. A committee was formed to examine it, but nothing more was ever made public.

Three years later, Gordon Cooper was launched into space for a 22-orbit

 mission. On his final orbit, he reported seeing a glowing green shape ahead of his capsule, and heading in his direction.

It's said that the Muchea tracking station, in Australia, which Cooper reported this too was also able to pick it up on radar travelling in an east-to-west orbit. This event was reported by NBC, but reporters were forbidden to ask Cooper about the event on his landing. The official explanation is that an electrical malfunction in the capsule had caused high levels of carbon dioxide, which induced hallucinations.

· · ·

Legions of the damned

The doomed voyage of the lost
Franklin expedition
Is it too incredible to believe?

"There are more things in heaven and earth, Horatio, Than are dreamt of in your philosophy."
William Shakspeare

· · ·

"Come to me, and I will feed
They flesh to the birds of the air
And to the beasts of the field
Said the Giant Philistine Goliath
To David the Israelite"

· · ·

Franklin's folly
(*Conspiracy, cover-up and deceit*)

"But now they have betaken themselves to unknown Kadath in the cold waste where no man treads, and are grown stern, having no higher peak whereto to flee at the coming of men. They are grown stern, and where once they suffered men to displace them, they now forbid men to come; or

coming, to depart. It is well for men that they know not of Kadath in the cold waste; else they would seek injudiciously to scale it."

H.P. Lovecraft

Seneca

A.D. 64

(*The Roman philosopher and tutor of the Emperor Nero*)

Oceanus vincula, cum venerit, Et fluent ad novos detegat orbes aperitur terra magnum apparuit super terram notis et ignotis:

. . .

"There shall come a time when the bands of ocean shall be loosened and the vast earth shall be laid open to disclose new worlds and lands seen beyond the Known and the unknown..."

. . .

Maurice Blanchot

Who remarked that those who believe in ghosts are in a way placating the phantasms of the night? Which is an attempt to circumvent or circumscribe the illimitable terrors of the night by a more approachable terror in the old adage: ***"better the Devil you know***, ***than the one you don't know"*** *real terror comes out of not knowing*, or maybe sometimes its better not to know!

A Giant
Sails into the Artic?

"I shall satiate my ardent curiosity with a sight of a part of the world never before visited, and may tread a land never before imprinted by the foot of man, those are my enticements, and they are sufficient to conquer all fear of danger or death..."

Captain Franklin had fought in a number of battles during the Napoleonic Wars and at the battle of Trafalgar, until the Duke of Wellington was finally defeated: ***Emperor Napoleon Bonaparte*** at the battle of Waterloo in 1815. And in 1819 Franklin again headed North in command of an overland expedition that had been ordered by the British Admiralty to travel from Hudson-Bay to the Polar-sea, where he was to map North-Americas unexplored artic coast, where he succeeded in surveying 340 Kilometres of icy shoreline east of the Copper mine river before a tragic return journey over the Canadian tundra or '*Barren grounds*' resulted in the deaths of ten men from cold and hunger with Franklin himself narrowly escaping death, almost succumbing to starvation before relief arrived.

When he returned to London, his account of heroic achievement married by murder, cannibalism and his own suffering caught the public's imagination. promoted to the rank of captain, he returned to the same area for a well organized second overland expedition in 1825-7 which resulted in the mapping of another 640 Kilometres of Artic shore-line, for which he was duly knighted.

391

He already knew of the mysteries of the giant archipelago that stretches from the North American mainland towards the North Pole...! And of the ghastly possibility of lives being lost in the cold confines of the unforgiving Artic.

"𝕳𝖔𝖜 𝖒𝖚𝖈𝖍 𝖑𝖊𝖘𝖘 𝖎𝖓 𝖙𝖍𝖊𝖒 𝕿𝖍𝖆𝖙 𝖉𝖜𝖊𝖑𝖑 𝖎𝖓 𝖍𝖔𝖚𝖘𝖊𝖘 𝖔𝖋 𝖈𝖑𝖆𝖕 𝖜𝖍𝖔𝖘𝖊 𝖋𝖔𝖚𝖓𝖉𝖆𝖙𝖎𝖔𝖓 𝖎𝖘 𝖎𝖓 𝖙𝖍𝖊 𝖉𝖚𝖘𝖙 𝖜𝖍𝖎𝖈𝖍 𝖆𝖗𝖊 𝖈𝖗𝖚𝖘𝖍𝖊𝖉 𝖇𝖊𝖋𝖔𝖗𝖊 𝖙𝖍𝖊 𝖒𝖔𝖙𝖍"

𝕵𝖔𝖇

. . .

(Franklins Expedition)
"Walk softly, but carry a big stick"

. . .

𝔇𝔯𝔞𝔠𝔲𝔩𝔞

Professor Van Helsing

"It is a wild adventure we are on. Here, as we are rushing along through the darkness, we seem to be drifting into unknown places and unknown ways; into a whole world of dark and dreadful things"

𝕭𝖗𝖆𝖒 𝕾𝖙𝖔𝖐𝖊𝖗

. . .

1845
"We come in peace, shot to kill...!"

Prior to the sailing of the **"Erebus"** and the **"terror"** who's so-called orders were to sail to Baffin-bay and enter Lancaster-sound and through the Bering strait, and in doing so he would complete a North-west passage, while at the same time collecting valuable scientific and geographical information, there had been a series of nineteenth-century expeditions aimed at extending the frontiers of the British Empire...!

Franklin's expedition was no more than a red hearing or blatant deception to find a North west passage, it was something even more dangerous and secret, where the ill-fated expeditionary force or disastrous mission of gunboat diplomacy...! **"That might is right"** masked a darker testimony to colonial imperialism, that is nothing more than fascism by the front door, call it what you will.

As the author **Jeffrey Blair Latta** said in is fantastic and very informitive book, **"The Franklin Conspiracy"** about the three-masted sailing ships: **HMS Erebus** and **HMS Terror** with their pitch-black livery and iron-shod hulls with their big yellow strip, bearing the prophetic and ominous names of the **Erebus:** God of darkness and son of chaos...! And the **Terror**! A name that speaks for its self, painted on their sterns!

. . .

Not by any stretch of the imagination could anybody in their right mind possibly mistake these ships for anything other than what where they there for...?

Elite Royal Navy/merchant bomb vessels, that could hurl explosives into land fortresses, **"and their very invincibility proved the commercial irrelevance of their mission...!"** The royal navy ships the 370 imperial ton **"Erebus"** with **Capt Sir John Franklin** with its newly installed 25 horsepower steam engine and the 340 imperial ton **"Terror"** with **Capt Frances Crozier** with its newly installed 20 horsepower steam engine using steel screw propellers, who set out with vast provisions of fuel and food to last three years or more...! The **Erebus** had a library of **1,700 books** and the **Terror** carried **1,200 books** as well, and of course an ample supply of rum...!

. . .

'A warning to the curious'

For one reason or another they were up to something and seemed or appeared to be flexing their military muscles, and had somehow antagonised the natives, so to speak, and because of this they were somehow beset by a strange and overwhelming or superior power, it was as if they had transgressed a taboo or ignored some kind of warning, as if the Artic has undefined and forbidden eerie regions, where you are not supposed to go! And death in the form of something intangible came on swift-wings seemingly proving it to be very real...

When all of Franklin's men eventually died horrible and early deaths, because of something just like this, Franklin had ended up paying a terrible price, never to return with his 129 men, including those who had scientific expertise, rather than Artic experience... **Oceanography, geology, terrestrial magnetism, botany, ornithology, geology,** and **marine biology** crew that were figuratively speaking, no more than just ballast, till they had found their way into the Artic and up beyond the 77° **Latitude** in Wellington Channel, where the compass becomes erratic and unreliable in this no-mans land of strange and bizarre compass readings... like the eye of some great invisible storm or monstrous portal, a huge unknown **void**, so to speak...!

"An unsolved mystery that goes from the sublime to the ridiculous, even to this day when you put aside all the facts and you are left with the impossible, no matter how fantastic it is, it must be the truth...!" Or is the answer still blowing in the wind of the forbidding reaches of the mysterious and dark realms of the Artic? With its legends of strange creepy stories of **weird lights in the sky**, of **Ghost ships** and **strange disappearances**!

Someone or something unearthly and mysterious put the mark of Cain upon Franklin and his cursed crew... in an unquiet place of *mystery and imagination,* with its frightening tales of *starvation, scurvy* and *the horrors of cannibalism...*

Henry Hudson
(1610–1611 voyage)

In 1610, Hudson managed to get backing for another voyage, this time under the English flag. The funding came from the Virginia Company and the British East India Company. At the helm of his new ship, the Discovery, he stayed to the north (some claim he deliberately stayed too far south on his Dutch-funded voyage), reaching Iceland on 11 May, the south of Greenland on 4 June, and then rounding the southern tip of Greenland. Excitement was very high due to the expectation that the ship had finally found the Northwest Passage through the continent. On 25 June, the explorers reached what is now the Hudson Strait at the northern tip of Labrador. Following the southern coast of the strait on 2 August, the ship entered Hudson Bay. Hudson spent the following months mapping and exploring its eastern shores, but he and his crew did not find a passage to Asia. In November, however, the ship became trapped in the ice in the James Bay, and the crew moved ashore for the winter.

'Mutiny'

When the ice cleared in the spring of 1611, Hudson planned to use his Discovery to further explore Hudson Bay with the continuing goal of discovering the Passage; however, most of the members of his crew ardently desired to return home. Matters came to a head and much of the crew mutinied in the month of June.

Descriptions of the successful mutiny are one-sided, because the only survivors who could tell their story were the mutineers and those who went along with the mutiny. Allegedly in the latter class was ship's navigator Abacuk Pricket, a survivor who kept a journal that was to become a key source for the narrative of the mutiny.

According to Pricket, the leaders of the mutiny were Henry Greene and Robert Juet. Pricket's narrative tells how the mutineers set Hudson, his teenage son John, and seven crewmen—men who were either sick and infirm or loyal to Hudson—adrift from the Discovery in a small shallop or open boat, effectively marooning them in Hudson Bay.

The Pricket journal reports that the mutineers provided the castaways with clothing, powder and shot, some pikes, an iron pot, some meal, and other miscellaneous items.

After the mutiny, Captain Hudson's shallop broke out the oars and tried to keep pace with the Discovery for some time. Pricket recalled that the mutineers finally tired of the David and Goliath pursuit, unfurled additional sails aboard the Discovery, enabling the larger vessel to leave the tiny open boat behind. Hudson and the other seven aboard the shallop were never seen again, and their fate is unknown...?

Pricket's journal and testimony have been severely criticized for bias, on two grounds. Firstly, prior to the mutiny the alleged leaders of the uprising, Greene and Juet, had been friends and loyal seamen of Captain Hudson. Secondly, Greene and Juet did not survive the return voyage to England. Pricket knew he and the other survivors of the mutiny would be tried in England for piracy, and it would have been in his interest, and the interest of the other survivors, to put together a narrative that would place the blame for the mutiny upon men who were no longer alive to defend themselves.

In any case, the Pricket narrative became the controlling story of the expedition's disastrous end.

Only 8 of the 13 mutinous crewmen survived the return voyage to Europe. They were arrested in England, and some were indeed put on trial, but no punishment was ever imposed for the mutiny. One theory holds that the survivors were considered too valuable as sources of information for it to be wise to execute them, as they had traveled to the New World and could describe sailing routes and conditions. Perhaps for this reason, they were charged with murder—of which they were acquitted—rather than mutiny, of which they most certainly would have been convicted and executed.

. . .

Legacy

The gulf or bay discovered by Hudson is twice the size of the Baltic Sea, and its many large estuaries afford access to otherwise landlocked parts of Western Canada and the Arctic.

This allowed the Hudson's Bay Company to exploit a lucrative fur trade along its shores for more than two centuries, growing powerful enough to influence the history and present international boundaries of Western North America. Hudson Strait became the entrance to the Arctic for all ships engaged in the search for the Northwest Passage from the Atlantic side.

The Hudson River in New York and New Jersey, explored earlier by Hudson, is named after him, as are Hudson County, New Jersey, the Henry Hudson Bridge and the town of Hudson, New York.

In 1619 the Danish naval captain Jens Munk set out with two ships and sailed into the Artic darkness in search of a north-west passage, who, after searching along the coast of Baffin Island, he then entered Hudson bay in the month of August and was forced to winter at the mouth of the Churchill River and there he lost 61 of his 64 crewmen, who were later ceremoniously dumped over-board, and just managed to sail home alive, by the Autumn of 1620.

. . .

The conscience of the king

(Strange clouds gathering on the horizon)

1820

What was it that John Ross saw?

John Ross of His Majesties Royal Navy had set sail for the Artic on board the **Isabella** with its tender the Alexander. And after reaching Baffin Bay he was meant to have sailed just 30miles down Lancaster Sound in the lull before the storm. As shades of the prison walls gather around the growing boy... when a ghostly shroud like fog rolled in enveloping and surrounded the ships, blocking their path.

When the officer on duty called John Ross from his cabin to come up topside, with news that the fog was beginning to clear! And when the fog parted allowing John Ross a glimpse of something so terrifying, he ordered the Isabella to turn back immediately and set sail for home...

Edward Parry, commander of the Alexander was shocked and amazed at what was happening... what was **John Ross** doing?

Edward Parry could only follow the Isabella home to England. Ross had seen something terrifying, almost as if it were the ghost of Hamlets father, **"Or the dread of something after death, the undiscovered country from whose bourn no traveller returns, puzzles the will, and makes us rather bare those ills we have, than fly to others that we know not of? Thus conscience does make cowards of us all."**

Something came out of the fog! Whatever or whoever it was, nobody except, **John Ross** and the crew of the **Isabella** knew, something they would eventually take to their graves...!

. . .

The Lull Before The Storm

'Private expedition'
Aboard the Victory
(John Ross and James Clark Ross)
1829-1833

Dagger of the mind

(Giants with feet of clay)

Having sailed to the Artic on the ill-fated and mysterious voyage of the Victory 1829-1833 to King William Island in a jury-rigged sidewinder.

James Clark Ross seemed or appeared oddly bothered in some inexplicable way by his final voyage to the Artic to look for the lost Franklin Expedition.... A friend who was meant to have known James Clark Ross, implied that he was somewhat shaken by his explorations in the Antarctic, and after his visit to the Artic in **1829-1833** with John Ross he had vowed never to return, as if he was strangely ill-at-ease with whatever he saw at **Victory point**...!

Why did **John Ross** not accompany **James Clark Ross** and his iceman: Thomas Abernethy to the other side of **King William Island?** It was or could have been due to that lurking fear of whoever or whatever he saw in **Lancaster Sound,** when he was aboard the **Isabella,** where he had seen something very strange and terrifying out in the eerie fog.

In 1830 **James Clark Ross** had left the rest of the sledge-crews back at the Northern tip of **King William Island,** while he and able-seaman Thomas Abernethy went on to **Victoria-point** and on his return journey home to England, **James Clack Ross** abruptly forsook the wilds of the Artic, for reasons best known to himself...! And turned his attention to the **Antarctic.**

The heroic explorer **John Ross** and **James Clark Ross** had ironically come out of the Artic after they had lost their ship, the **HMS Victory** in the Boothia Peninsula and Somerset Island, before he and his men were picked up or rescued by none other than the whaling vessel the **"Isabella"** after four years in the Artic... without the loss of a single life!

The same ship that **John Ross** had been on, when he had seen something very strange and terrifying or elusion that came out of the swirling eerie fog, like a dagger of the mind:

. . .

𝔄𝔫𝔱𝔞𝔯𝔠𝔱𝔦𝔠 𝔙𝔬𝔶𝔞𝔤𝔢

1839-43

The **Erebus** and the **Terror** under the command of **James Clark Ross** had already chartered 800 Kilometres of the Antarctic cost-line and had discovered the Antarctic ice shelf, as well as the South Magnetic pole or rim by going nearly **"Into the Void...?"** and when he returned to England in 1843, he had become the world's leading discoverer.

The **Terror** was a strong and robust ship and could take anything the **"Artic"** could throw at her, so to speak... she was a well built ship and had been revived and made stronger, after she had been caught by ice-bergs and then dumped on her side and by the time she eventually freed herself from her enforced captivity, where she was caught in the unforgiving and merciless embrace of the Artic ice.

. . .

She made a daring escape to freedom, where she still managed to limp back across the Atlantic and drag herself back to the relative safety of the shores of Ireland, just in the nick of time...

Edward Parry, commander of the Alexander.... Had sailed to the **"artic"** onboard the ghost ship the **"Fury"** which mysteriously vanished without a trace... and after the loss of the ghost-ship *fury*...! Edward Perry was a changed man, who suffered from depression and severe headaches, both him and **James Clark Ross**, the nephew of **John Ross** were both offered the expedition to sail to the Artic... even though both of them

397

strangely declined the offer! Because they had sworn never to return to the Artic... **James Clark Ross** would eventually return in a desperate and apparently confused attempt to try and find Franklin!

. . .

" *Is there more to it than meats the eye* "

(*Dutch Philosopher*)
Erasmus
(In the land of the spiritually and mentally blind, the one eyed man is king)

. . .

Captain Franklin and possibly other officers like the distinguished **Royal Navy officers Captain Frances Crozier** and **Commander James Fitzjames** who were appointed to the expedition.

The veteran **Crozier** had served in a number of earlier attempts aimed at finding both the Northwest Passage and reaching the North pole, under the command of **Edward Parry**. Crozier was also second-in-command of **James Clark Ross's** Antarctic expedition in command of the **Terror**. And just maybe they were privy to this secret information? Or Franklin had been acting under malice aforethought, or what could only be described as certain innocuous or sealed orders, that only he would have had privy to, and not the other officers... until they had committed themselves and sailed up the mysterious **Wellington Channel** and **beyond...!**

A mission that would have had far-reaching and disastrous consequences due to such political treachery, the doomed expedition had intentionally or inadvertently stumbled upon something so *fantastic* and *dangerous*, that the admiralty for whatever reason best known to itself, might have already speculated on or known about.

What was the terrible and chilling knowledge that Franklin either knew or accidentally stumbled over? Something that not only cost them their lives, but their battle and subsequent retreat seemed or appeared to be something stranger than fiction, so to speak, but due to some twisted sense of loyalty the terrible end to this rather bizarre expedition was fatally acted out in some kind of self-inflicted torment or ignorance in what seems or appears to be some caprice, or strange sudden longing or a passing fancy of the soul that flies headlong into some dreadful extremity, because whatever or whoever was pursuing them, was something darker and more disturbing than we will ever know, and maybe it's better not to know...?

By the time all the various parties had returned to the two ships in Penny-Straight, they had virtually completed a map of the entire Northern-Archipelago...! Geographically speaking, so the belcher expedition was a triumph by default, so to speak, and the British Navy had successfully defined the roof of the world, which was the very reason why Franklin was there in the first place, but define it for whom?

"What hast though done?"

"The voice of thy brothers blood crieth unto me from the ground. And now *art* thou cursed from the earth, which hath opened her mouth to receive thy brother's blood..."

. . .

Titus Andronicus

(Act Five Scene three)

"To make this banquet, which I wish may prove more stern and bloody than the Centaurs feast."
The coming of the mad one's

Prophecies of nations! Made by the French writer "**Jacques Cazotte**" (1720-1792), in which he foretold the **French revolution of 1789**, the downfall of the monarchy, and the bloody events of the **Reign of Terror**, during which thousands were **guillotined** or otherwise **slaughtered...**

"Cannibalism"

(*Cults of unreason*)

During the great famine that efflicted the French in the 11th century, **human-flesh** was publicaly displayed and **sold** in the **market place** of

Tournus,

And in 1797 came the **true commuion** of the **patriots**; or "**eucharist**" a law which obliged citizens on **pain** of **imprisonment** or **worse**, to go once a week to a **national butchers shop**, where the **flesh** of the **aristocratic victims** of the **guillotine** would be **sold**!

'Canibals'

(*Japanese atrocities against Pilots*)

Soon after the Japanese surrender, a U.S. Amphibious Landing Craft, LCI 336 was dispatched to the Northern Bonin Islands, from Saipan. On board were troops of the First Battalion, 3rd Marines that were to take command of the island while a 20-man Marine Police Force investigated the whereabouts of American pilots that bailed out over the Islands after their aircraft were disabled during bombing missions.

On the morning of October 19, 1945, LCI 336 passed through the outer mine field and entered Futomi Harbor of the main island, Chichi Jima, North of Iwo Jima. Everything on the island was in shamble, the results of Vice Admiral Marc Mitscher's Task Force bombing missions that were conducted during June 1944 to August 1944.

. . .

Heading the investigation was Col. Presley M. Rixey and working under his supervision were three Marine investigators.

When Japanese Gen. Yoshio Tachibana, the commanding Japanese Army officer of the Bonin Islands was asked by Col. Rixey, **"What became of the American fliers that were captured on these islands?"** Without hesitation the General replied, **"Yes, we captured six and they all received very kind treatment."**

Now with the American flag flying over the island, Korean laborers, that were prisoners, came forth to tell their story, without fear of retaliation. What Col. Rixey and his staff would learn would be the most unbelievable, fiendish and vacuous atrocities ever imposed on mankind.

With direct orders from Japanese Gen. Yoshio Tachibana, Lt. Col. Kikujima and Capt. Noboru Nakajima clubbed, bayoneted, beheaded and mutilated all the American airmen. Not only those who bailed out over the island, but those who landed offshore and were picked up by their patrolboats.

One Korean prisoner who was interviewed told Col. Rixey that one very brave Marine pilot who was about to be beheaded refused the blindfold and in a gesture of defiance, rolled down his own collar.

Gen. Yoshio Tachibana and Major Suco Matoba feasted on the American's livers and used large chunks of the thighs insoup.

When Gen.Tachibana learned that one airman had been buried with his liver intact, he had the body exhumed and ordered his army physician extract the liver.

In his report, Col. Rixey states: **"We were flabbergasted at first. We were expecting beheadings, but never cannibalism! What manner of men were these? Barbarians and even worse."**

On December 17, 1945 Col. Rixey ordered Major Robert D. Shaffer, USMC to start rounding up these criminals. After their arrest they were taken to Guam to await trial.

In September 1946, Gen. Tachibana, Capt. Yoshio, Col. Ito, Maj. Matoba and Capt. Nakajima were all found guilty and sentenced to death byhanging. Adm. Mori and Capt. Sato were given life inprison.

From the logs of Vincent Robinson, Commander of VFW Post 11294, Froesthill, CA, who participated in the operation.

The horrific fate of the other eight **"flyers"** was established in subsequent war crimes trials on the island of Guam, but details were sealed in top secret files in Washington to spare their families distress.

Mr Bradley has established that they were tortured, beaten and then executed, either by beheading with swords or by multiple stab-wounds from bayonets and sharpened bamboo stakes. Four were then butchered by the island garrison's surgeons and their livers and meat from their thighs eaten by senior Japanese officers.

. . .

Mr Bradley pieced together the horrific truth from secret transcripts of the war crimes trials, given to him by a former officer and lawyer who was an official witness at the time, and the testimony of surviving Japanese veterans

A radio operator, Marve Mershon, was marched to a freshly dug grave, blindfolded, and made to kneel for beheading by sword, testified a

Japanese soldier, named as Iwakawa, at the war crimes trial. *"When the flyer was struck, he did not cry out, but made a slight groan."*

The next day a Japanese officer, Major Sueo Matoba, decided to include American flesh in a sake-fuelled feast he laid on for officers including the commander-in-chief on the island, Gen Yoshio Tachibana. Both men were later tried and executed for war crimes.

A Japanese medical orderly who helped the surgeon prepare the ingredients said: *"Dr Teraki cut open the chest and took out the liver. I removed a piece of flesh from the flyer's thigh, weighing about six pounds and measuring four inches wide, about a foot long."* Another crewman, Floyd Hall, met a similar fate. Admiral Kinizo Mori, the senior naval officer on Chichi Jima, told the court that Major Matoba brought *"a delicacy"* to a party at his quarters a specially prepared dish of Floyd Hall's liver.

According to Admiral Mori, Matoba told him: *"I had it pierced with bamboo sticks and cooked with soy sauce and vegetables."* They ate it in *"very small pieces,"* believing it *"good medicine for the stomach,"* the admiral recalled. A third victim of cannibalism, Jimmy Dye, had been put to work as a translator when, several weeks later, Capt Shizuo Yoshii - who was later tried and executed - called for his liver to be served at a party for fellow officers. Parts of a fourth airman, Warren Earl Vaughn, were also eaten and the remaining four were executed, one by being clubbed to death. The parents of all the airmen are now dead.

Another method of murdering Allied fliers was used at Hankow, China, in December 1944. Three American fliers, who had been forced down and captured sometime before, were paraded through the streets and subjected to ridicule, beating and torture by the populace. When they had been weakened by the beatings and torture, they were saturated with gasoline and burned alive, the permission for this atrocity was granted by the Commander of the 34th Japanese Army.

The cruelty of the Japanese is further illustrated by the treatment of an Allied airman, who was captured at Rabaul on the island of New Britain. He was bound with a rope on which fishhooks had been attached so that when he moved the hooks dug into his flesh. He ultimately died of malnutrition and dysentery.

Downed aircrews that became POWs received the worst possible treatment. As early as 1942, the Japanese command classified them as war criminals. Any pilot or crewmember captured were likely to be tortured or killed as soon as their parachute folded on the ground. In Singapore, four flyers were paraded through the streets naked and then had their heads chopped off in public. At Hankow in China, airmen were tortured and burned alive. At Kendebo, after a speech by a major general, a decapitated fighter pilot was cut up, fried, and eaten by 150 Japanese officers. Eight captured B-29 crewmen were turned over to the medical professors at Kyushu Imperial University. The professors cut them up alive; stopping the blood flow in an artery near the heart to see how long death took...

. . .

Devil's in the dark
(The Ancient Mariner)
"Like one that on a lonesome road doth walk in fear and dread, and having once looked round, walks on, and turns no more his head; because he knows a frightful fiend doth close behind him tread."

. . .

"Job" and the **18th Psalm:** *"For thou hast girded me with strength unto battle, he shall flee from the iron weapon and the bow of steel shall strike him through, it is drawn and cometh out of his body; yea, the glittering sword cometh out of his gall: terrors are upon him".* *"A dreadful sound is in his ears, in prosperity the destroyer shall come upon, he believeth not that he shall return out of darkness and he is waited for of the sword."*

"Something out of this world"
(The enemy at the gates)
As musket shoots rang out into the clawing darkness, was **Captain Franklin** trying to put down a mutiny, from the enemy within or restore order in the midst of some inexplicable attack by the enemy at the gates... that caused the ensuing panic that followed, it was as if it were an overwhelming surprise in a prolonged attack or internal struggle of some kind...?

. . .

"And the men held aloft the lamps and shouted, the sword of the Lord and of Gedeon, confused and terrified by the alarm, the Madianites turned their swords upon each other"

The Old Testament

. . .

"Monsters from the ID"
(The enemy within)
"There's more of gravy, than of grave, about you ghost (Jacob Marley)"
Charles Dickens

. . .

'Of Mice And Men'
Was it something altogether more sublime and terrifying, like the intangible vision that **John Ross** was supposed to have witnessed...! An even greater unseen or invisible enemy, that could or might have been someone or something more malignant and terrifying already on board, some elemental force or instinctive drive that would try and destroy anything that was a threat to it?

A projection that would push them to the brink of madness, a terrifying faceless nemesis that lurked in the hearts and minds of men, a terror that would haunt the imagination, as the cold and the exhaustion drove them into a delirium of madness, one that would open up their senses and draw back what appeared to be a thin veil, to reveal what could be or what they believed to be, the true nature of reality...!

As he looked upon the carnage of the dead and the dying, Franklin must have gazed upon the awful and fleeting truth of what rely happened, impinging upon his confused mind, as if in his childish anger and resentment as if someone or something symbolically sent out or let lose the terrors of the mind or the primitive beast, like in Shakespeare's play: **The Tempest** or in the **1950s** movie adaptation of it called: **The forbidden planet**, where the actor Walter pigeon with his artificially expanded mind, had unknowingly emerged like a nightmarish caterpillar from the dark chrysalis of his own psyche, filled with hatred and lust, with murderous intent, freed from the dictate of so-called civilization with no moral code, they would be a danger not only to themselves, but to other people around him, in a tale of **mice and men**, like a child in a man's body with no sense of right or wrong! Sent out to terrify the Artic.

. . .

"Let that day be darkness; let not God regard it from above, neither let the light shine upon it. Let darkness and the shadow of death stain it; let a cloud dwell upon it; let the blackness of the day terrify it."

Job

. . .

23 𝔓𝔰𝔞𝔩𝔪

(*The Lord is my shepherd; I shall not want*)

"*He maketh me to lie down in green pastures: he leadeth me beside the still waters. He restoreth my soul: he leadeth me in the paths of righteousness for his name's sake.*

Yea, though I walk through the valley of the shadow of death, I will fear no evil: for thou art with me; thy rod and thy staff they comfort me. Thou preparest a table before me in the presence of mine enemies: Thou anointest my head with oil; My cup runneth over. Surely goodness and

mercy shall follow me all the days of my life: and I will dwell in the house of the Lord forever..."

. . .

When the hunter becomes the hunted?

(*Adam beck's strange and unquiet tale*)

Its very probable but highly unlikely that the Navy Ketches the **Erebus** and the **Terror** were beset in ice and supposedly crushed not far along the

Greenland coast in the winter of 1846. The ships had been apparently attacked by what was described as a fierce tribe, with some of the crew drowning and others being killed by darts and arrows, but what kind of arrows are the Inuit's describing? With the ships being set on fire, because the ships seem or appear not to have been where they should have... so what became of them...?

Did Franklin and his doomed expedition await their awful fate at the hands of what was described as, *"Wild tribesmen"* using spears and arrows...?

Island of the lost

Remember the legends and rumours of a race of **giants**! Who came to King William Island, that's right the very island that **Sir John Franklin** and his crew came to a terrible end, long before the Inuit came to the Artic or the *"Land of the midnight sun"* lived a **race of giants**, that were stronger than people are now, and lived in houses that *fly*!

What are these stories inferring? Are these giants connected to some higher race! That seems or appears to be lurking in the shadows, in some strange scenario! And the **Eskimo** or **Esquimaux** after pursuing them they had to wait till the giants were asleep! As if they could not be killed, was it because they are wraith like beings, or projections of sorts, like the Vampire in a way, who could not be killed, and the only way to destroy them was by (**Trepanning**) or to drill a hole through their head! Which has a tenuous link with:

The Vision Serpent

Is an important symbolic charecter in Pre-Columbian Maya mythology,

The serpent was a very important social and religious symbol, revered by the Maya.

Maya mythology describes serpents as being the vehicles by which celestial bodies, such as the sun and stars, cross the heavens. The shedding of their skin made them a symbol of rebirth and renewal.

They were so revered, that one of the main Mesoamerican deities, **Quetzalcoatl,** was represented as a feathered serpent. The name means **"beautiful serpent"** (From Nahuatl, **'Quetzalli'** means beautiful and **'coatl'** meaning **snake** or **serpent**.)

The Vision Serpent is thought to be the most important of the Maya serpents. "It was usually bearded, and was also often depicted as having two heads or with the spirit of a god or ancestor emerging from its jaws."

During Maya **bloodletting rituals**, participants would experience visions in which they communicated with the ancestors or gods.

These visions took the form of a giant serpent **"which served as a gateway to the spirit realm."** The ancestor or god who was being contacted was depicted as emerging from the serpent's mouth.

The vision serpent thus came to be the method in which ancestors or Gods manifested themselves to the Maya. Thus for them, the Vision Serpent was a direct link between the spirit realm of the gods and the physical world.

The Vision Serpent goes back to earlier Maya conceptions, and lies at the center of the world as they conceived it. *"It is in the center axis atop the World Tree. Essentially the World Tree and the Vision Serpent, representing the king, created the center axis which communicates between the spiritual and the earthly worlds or planes."*
It is through ritual that the king could bring the center axis into existence in the temples and create a doorway to the spiritual world, and with it power!" what form that power takes is open to interprtation, or that a butterfly, flapping its wings in one part of the world, could affect the weather on the other side of the globe? Edward Lorenz is credited with using this metaphoric or symbolic analogy as the title of talk he gave in *1972* to the American Academy for the Advancement of Science.
So the truth of these strange stories by the *Eskimo* or *Esquimaux*, tends to lie (*excuse the pun*) like a half-truth around our neck or somewhere in between, having been woven into the true facts! Where it takes on a more sinister aspect, where the skull's found in the tents at *Terror Bay* on *King William Island*, Had holes drilled into them!

. . .

Or was it something even more terrifying in their feverish state of mind. Could it have been like something out of a science-fiction movie with strange humanoids from somewhere underneath the earth, that, for whatever reason had approached them?
And Franklin's men knowing it was the end, with that awful look in their eyes like a captured animal in the slaughterhouse, resigned to its fate! And there they would eventually see the face of an unknown and hidden enemy, so to speak, who were dressed in weird looking cloths, that covered or protected them from the outside world, could it have been creatures who were from a highly advanced civilization, that had once lived on the surface of the planet earth, the would-be ancestors of humankind who had been forced by their own stupidity to live underground in vast city complexes for millions of years, after a terrible war that had poisoned the water they drank and the air they breathed, is it these high-brow or physical weaklings of the coming race... so to speak who are manning these strange *Flying Saucers* or *UFOs* (*Unidentified Flying Objects*) because its very probable that they could be *extra-terrestrial?* But highly unlikely, or more than likely they are **terrestrial,** and they come from the earth we live on!

. . .

And are the natural or un-natural phantom geographical and aerial phenomena or weird lights in the artic sky, that can not only cause radio interference and or problems with electronic and conventional compasses, but can even induce currents in power lines!
Like the strange *Ariel-flying-crafts* seen on either side of the earth's poles, and that have been seen and or monitored by several military bases in these strange and eerie places. Where do you think they are coming from?

Are we the survivors who have been left on the surface to become genetic mutants or freaks? And over millions of years the surface dwellers had developed a resistance and were now immune to the poisoned air, and because of this their intelligence had been retarded.

But the creatures having been forced to live underground after escaping the holocaust that followed, having become physically weak over the Eon's of time, with their bodies unable to fight or cope with the germs and the bacteria on the surface, but on the other hand they had developed into highly intellectual beings over the millions of years they had been imprisoned under ground, and with their giant brains they had projected onto the primitive minds of the surface dwellers and the grand illusion of what we think reality is...!

So nothing seems to be what we think it is, in our present state of mind. We are just primitive surface dwellers, who are given the illusion of who we think we are.

Is everything being projected onto or minds, like in the matrix or are they hoisting us with our own petard, using something like hypnosis? Where a person can be convinced of anything, and subsequently its very possible that reality might not be what we think it is!

Are we people who have been living throughout a supposed history or that we live in the hear and now... with our false childhood memories and we have been fooled just like all the others who have been caught in what could be described as a mental mouse trap, while we are out scavenging for food with the other members of our tribe! And we are being caught and trussed up unable to speak because of certain abnormalities as surface dwellers we have lost our ability to speak, which is like choking! When we try to speak, and because of this, we have never developed any kind of organised language, and from there as tied up supplicants we are taken below, and ceremoniously strapped to a laboratory table, where no one could hear our cries for help or the screams of our suffering during the excruciating agony of dissection!

Which begs the question, has any species the moral right to experiment on another species because you think you are stronger or you see them as racially inferior?

*Like school children in the confines of the so-called science-class which have been taught that might is right and so-called intellectually superior creatures have the God given write to kill harmless (Snails) while they are still alive! With a hammer and then dissecting them! Just like **Franklin's crew** might or could have watched one another caught in the arms of their own invisible tormentors...!*

'Invisible residents'

At this point in our strange story, things get even more bizarre because its similarities are equal only to its differences...! In the spooky books on missing people, so its very probable that this could be the answer to the strange and inexplicable events like in **Jack the ripper** and in the excellent books, **"Missing 411"** by David Paulides, but highly unlikely...

So it behoves [*That's a good word*] each and every person to read these weird and frightening books, especially if you tend to venture into these dangerous areas, and if you do so, **you do so, at your own risk**!

Franklin's Ghost

(*Hamlet prince of Denmark*)

Act 1 scene 4 of Hamlet: Ghost, mark me well, Hamlet, I will, ghost, my hour is almost come when I to sulphurous and tormenting flames must render myself, Hamlet, alas poor ghost! Ghost, pity me not, but lend thy serious hearing to what I shall unfold, Hamlet, speak, I am bound to hear: Ghost, so art thou to revenge when thou shalt hear, Hamlet what? Ghost, I am thy father's spirit, doomed for a certain term to walk the night, and for the day confined to fast in fires till the foul crimes done in my days of nature are but burnt and purged away. But that I am forbid to tell the secrets of my prison-house I could a tale unfold whose lightest word would harrow up they soul, freeze thy young blood, make thy two eyes like stars start from their spheres, thy knotty and combined locks to part and each particular hair to stand on end like quils upon the fretful porcupine but this eternal blazon must be to ears of flesh and blood List, Hamlet, List, O List! If thou didst ever thy dear father love-Hamlet, O God! Ghost; Revenge his foul and unnatural murder!

. . .

'The island of the lost'

(Beechey Island)

Isthmus

"*And he spake unto the children of Israel, when your children shall ask their fathers in time to come, saying, what mean these stones?*"

The book of Joshua

. . .

Facing cape Riley!

Apart from the later grave of Thomas Morgan who died in 1854 in search of Captain Franklin and his lost expedition, there are 4 other graves...

Grave one

Sacred to the memory of

John Torrington

Who departed this life January 1st

AD 1846

On board of H M ship Terror

Aged 20years

. . .

Grave two
Sacred to the memory of
John Hartnell AB of HMS Erebus
Died January 4th 1846
Aged 25years
"Thus saith the Lord of Hosts consider your ways"
Haggai i 7

. . .

Grave three
Sacred to the memory
Of
William Braine RM HMS Erebus
Died April 3rd 1846
Aged 32years
"Choose ye this day whom ye will serve"
Joshua ch xxiv 15
And what about the dog in the manger or the mysterious...
Grave four!
(Remember that the truth is sometimes more stranger than fiction...!)
'Who or what could be in this forth unmarked grave...?'

. . .

"And, behold, they are hid in the earth in the midst of my tent, and the silver under it"

𝕿𝖍𝖊 𝖇𝖔𝖔𝖐 𝖔𝖋 𝕵𝖔𝖘𝖍𝖚𝖆

. . .

The strange story starts to become even more perplexing and bizarre, if you read the full very ominous and frightening meaning of the biblical quote on **William Braine's** gravestone from the book of Joshua:

* * *

"If it seem evil unto you to serve the Lord
Choose ye this day whom ye will serve
Whether the Gods which your father served which where on the other side of the flood
Or the Gods of the "Amorites" in whose land ye dwell"

* * *

I think the answer is strangely connected with the Bible and the Old Testament.

The 12 Spies!

Report that they have seen fearsome **"Giants"** in Canaan: So they gave out to the **sons of Israel** a bad report of the land which they had spied out, saying, "The land through which we had gone, in spying it out, the land of

408

the mysterious **Amorites**" who may be of **European origin**, though no one is sure what was their ethnic origin!

They were represented on the Egyptian monuments with fair skins, light hair, blue eyes, curved or hooked noses, pointed beards, and were nomadic clans ruled by fierce tribal chiefs!

"Oh Lord protect us from the Amorites"

Is a land that **"devours its inhabitants"** and all the people whom we saw in it are men of **great size**!

"The *Amorites* **or** *MAR.TU*, **who know no grain, who have no house or town, the boors of the mountains. The MAR.TU who digs up truffles... who does not bend his knees (to cultivate the land), who eats** *raw meat*! **Who has no house during his lifetime,** *who is not buried after death*!**"

Dr Rae's report

Which seems or appears to have been censored by the government or admiralty, and reports persons who have apparently died of famine! From the mutilated state of the corpses and the contents of the kettles, it is evident that our wretched countryman had been driven to the last recourse — cannibalism, as a means of prolonging existence, or was it something else that was eating them?

. . .

Follow the yellow brick road!

(*Because the ships had been loaded with supplies*)

It begs the question: why did everything go wrong, that could have gone wrong during the Franklin expedition?

It seemed or appeared to have been the wrong Expedition, in the wrong place, at the wrong time, and if not, why did Captain Franklin's expedition have an inordinate or peculiar interest in what was up Wellington Channel and beyond?

Why?

Did Franklin's expedition winter at Beechey Island where the trail began at Cape Riley on nearby Devon Island, with its tenting-sites, armourers forge, a large stone house, a carpenter's house and several other small structures? Was it for only one winter? While Franklin sailed up Wellington Channel to the **77°** **Latitude** or beyond into the Artic Ocean! Why? See: **"Into The Void"** where the North wind gets warmer, as one sails beyond the **70°** (*Degrees*) latitude, where there are warm northerly winds and an open sea! For hundreds of miles north of **82°** (degrees) latitude, and after the **82°** (degrees) latitude is reached, the compass needle becomes agitated, restless and balky!

The Hollow Earth

Raymond Bernard
A.B., M.A., Ph.D.

We don't know. Because both ships might not have been where they were supposed to be! The Terror could have been at Beechey Island for two winters, why? Again we don't know? Or why they found **700 cans** piled up in small low pyramids, about half a metre high, the tins were empty, per

say, and had then been filled with gravel, were they some kind of subliminal message or unconscious truth? For reasons just as mysterious than the missing expedition itself.

Once they had established their first camp on Devon Island, Franklin must have prepared for his mysterious voyage up Wellington Channel that could have taken him two years to accomplish the mission, after leaving enough supplies of food for the terror that would have been anchored at Beechey Island during his mysterious sojourn up to the **77°** (*degrees*) Latitude and beyond into the Artic-Ocean, and when Franklin eventually returned by way of Wellington Channel when it opened in the spring of the second year, and then down by way of Cornwallis Island.

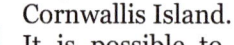

It is possible to see this Island from a vantage-point on Devon Island, that is **180 metres** above sea level, and there you can see it **50 Kilometres** west across the entrance to Wellington Channel.

Did Franklin sail up Wellington channel, and did he get into some sort of bother during the very first or second year of his mysterious expedition...? We don't know exactly where they were or exactly how long it took them to come back down Wellington channel during the first or second year, or that they had used up vast quantities of their supplies during what seems or appears to have been a very surreptitious mission, or they may have had to dump vast quantities of supplies overboard either at

410

the 77° (*degrees*) latitude's or beyond and into the area of the Artic-Ocean! Or was it at the top of Wellington channel to give them greater speed back down to where the Terror was anchored, or it could have been out along Lancaster sound or out towards the Greenland coast or Baffin-Bay...? Again we don't know.

And what of the three sailors who had died under mysterious circumstances and who are buried on Beechey Island, was it because of something they had done or where they had been? Did they retreat or were they forced back down Wellington channel for reasons best known to Captain Franklin, by way of Cornwallis Island and back to Beechey-Island. What was it they had brought down upon their heads?

During and after their covert mission up Wellington Channel Some time during that first or even second eventful year, something very strange or odd happened, it's as if they were trying to escape, after they had either saw or done something!

Like **John Ross** who tried to get out of the Artic as quickly as possible and back out the way they came, so it is possible that the **Erebus** and the **Terror** would have tried to make it back out of the Artic, but were caught or stopped at the 77° *latitude's* or beyond in the Artic-Ocean! Or at the top of Wellington channel or near Baffin-Bay or the Greenland coast, by whoever or whatever was pursuing them, it was probable that it was no more than black billowing smoke from the boilers on board the ships, while they were using their propellers to get away? But highly unlikely, so it was

possible that they were under a sustained attack by someone or something strange or weird, and that's what the Inuit's saw, and naturally they must have thought that the ships were on fire...! In the supoosed battle described to Adam Beck by the Eskimos or Inuit's And when the sailing season began in **1846** began with the break-up of ice in **Barrow Strait** and in what was to be called **Erebus-bay** (their winter harbour off **Beechey Island**) it could have been then that they must have or could have tried to escape back out through **Lancaster Sound**, back towards **Baffin Bay** or the **coast of Greenland...!** Before they were forced back up Lancaster sound as they tried to get away from, or evade their pursuers, and from there they tried to withdraw to relative safety or they were forced back down to **King William island**, ending up beset in the ice or trapped there for nearly **19 months**, and for some strange reason there in the lull before some weird or strange ponderous storm, the Franklin Expedition sent out **Gore** and his six other crewmen for what purpose? We don't know! An unknown party must have travelled up to **Gore-point** or **Victory Point**! And then further on up to **Cape-Felix**, where it looks as though they tried to make it over to the **Boothia-Peninsula** to try and get to **Fury-Beech**, where there was provisions and outside help from the **Whaling-ships**, but for some reason it appears that they did not make it! And they could have came or were forced back down by way of **Victoria-Point** and **Gore-Point**, but we still don't know what was happening, one way or the other, and why they might not have made it back! Something quite unimaginable was happening on **King William Island** that caused the remaining expedition to be forced to literally abandon the ships that were supposed to be **beset in ice**, its very probable that the cause could have been the onset of hunger or due to other reasons!

Were they blockaded by someone or something, and their supplies were running out for reasons best known to the Expedition, maybe they tried to run the blockade for one reason or another, but its highly unlikely, because cans of meant were found along their retreat after they had come ashore in darkness and or thick fog, keeping the shore-line on their right-side so they could find there way along the shore line or on their left in order to make it back the way they came, at or near **Victoria-Point**, once they had reached the shore, they could have tried to made good their escape, something could or must have happened at **Terror-Bay** and at **Washington-bay**, as well as on the Canadian mainland at **Starvation-Cove**.

Was it, or could it have been something that Franklin and his men had accidentally stumbled over? Or was it the very thing they had been sent into the Artic to find and bring back at any cost...? Something so strange and dangerous it was like a pestilence that would eventually infect them all, after having brought it on board, like the plague of the middle-ages, unaware that it was the strange malady or sickness they were suffering from? Even contaminating what was left of their supply of **8.000 cans of meat**, and that's why they were or could have been dumping things overboard, as if they were or could have been trying to make room for something that was so important it was worth dieing for! What was it they were trying to take away, if anything?

Maybe it was some type of elusive Tribe of Head-Hunters or they come and go by reason of their **high-tech masters**, who would not let them leave with what they had discovered! And they were responsible for the destruction of the expedition and the atrocities at **Terror-Bay** and **Starvation-Cove**, and because of this, they would be forced to have to abandon the sledge-boat! As they tried to escape towards the north... in desperation back to where the abandoned ships, according to the Inuit's still might have contained food!

There was even food found with the bodies on the **Todd Islets** and along the final escape route...!

If there was sign's of cannibalism was it some strange savage tribe? We don't know! And tales of cleverly handled misinformation with their extended bellies and bleeding gums that can mean one thing or another, its very probable that it could have been starvation and or scurvy which causes bleeding and an extended belly or as **Jeffrey Blair Latta** said in his excellent book: **"The Franklin Conspiracy"** it could have been the result of **Radiation sickness**! Or poisoning, I know what the reader must think, **"Radiation sickness"** in the **19ᵗʰ Century**!!

A condition that results in a drop in the number of blood platelets, and the blood won't clot properly, including haemorrhaging from the intestines and the mouth, this being the third stage due to the exposure to high radiation, after a period of vomiting, fever, and an intense thirst, followed by a period that looks as if the person seems or appears to have recovered when they either recover or die! Other symptoms include lung fibrosis and a susceptibility to disease, caused by a loss of white blood cells, which is an important part of the immune system.

But I'm afraid its like whistling in the dark, because if they had food, what type of sickness could the members of the expedition have eventually died from? and who was pursuing them, the answer or paper-chase tends to go from the ridiculous to the sub8lime, whether it was advanced scurvy and starvation, due to having already digested rotten or infected meat due to suspected lead- poisoning from the badly soldered tins that was the cause of possible weird or strange effects on their the minds? Or someone or something was doing it, like in the film: **"Beneath the planet of the apes"** is it these highly evolved creatures in strange moving lights or Flying Saucers UFOs (Unidentified Flying Objects) that were pursuing them **1845-8**! Or using some kind of strange door or portal to covey their wild card or these strange savage tribesmen about, like the ones in the cult **60s series Star-Trek,** titled: **The Galileo-Seven**, "Hairy-Giants" using old-tech weapons like the **Viet-Cong** during the **60s Vietnam-War,** that seemed or appeared to be there one minute, and gone the next!

* * *

Jack the Giant Killer

Fee-fi-fo-fum
I smell the blood of an Englishman.
Be he alive or be he dead
I'll grind his bones to make my bread.

* * *

Is it the same hand, like the weird abductions in the books **Missing 411,** whoever or whatever they are? Because they seem or appear to be everywhere, and yet nowhere!

It's as if it was either one or the other that has laid a very clever and confusing paper-trail, which seems or appears to form part of a larger picture, and one like the **Missing 411 books,** where we cannot see the trees for the forest! Excuse the pun, or maybe the reason that the expedition got into serious trouble was simply through things going badly wrong and nothing more!

"You could learn a lot from children, they believe in things in the dark,
until we tell them it's not so, maybe we've been fooling
Them"
"Were the members of the Franklin Expedition?
Intentionally dismembered
Or dissected"

Either while they were still alive or after they had been killed, by a more
advanced race of **Humanoids** like **Jack the ripper,** the same as in
"Missing 411 North America and beyond" with the story of **little boy lost!**

Individuals by default, think they are intellectually superior than other's,
they kneel before their shinning altars, where they assume that they have
the God-given right to act like barbarians, and whoever or whatever is
doing the kidnapping and murder? Is hoisting us up by our own petard.

. . .

'𝕲𝖊𝖓𝖌𝖍𝖎𝖘 𝕶𝖍𝖆𝖓'

(*Like the sack of Bukhara, 1220*)

**"O people, know that you have committed great sins and that
the great ones among you have committed these sins. If you ask
me what proof I have for these words, I say it is because I am
the punishment of God. If you had not committed great sins,
God would not have sent a punishment like me upon you"**

. . .

So we have an unseen enemy that sees us as racially inferior life forms...
which is very easy to do, we do it directly with snails, mice, dogs and cats in
our so-called civilized laboratories!

And directly and/or indirectly to **people of the abyss** you know the ones
that are not strong enough to weather life's storms or clever enough to
worship before the **golden calf,** in a sliding-scale of inability to achieve
the first commandment of a truly **"fascist society"** that **survival must
be earned at all costs,** for the greater good of course... if we are to
understand what is happening to our fellow human beings, we must put
our own house in order!

. . .

(*It's as if there's nothing more tangible than an unseen species or
enemy! Especially one that dissects a lower species*)

. . .

Because he tried to leave some kind of strange message in the weird bible
quotes on the grave-stones, that seems or appears not to make any sense...
unless they are or were some kind of cryptic-warning for anyone clever
enough to un-ravel its dark and symbolically meaning of what had
happened to the expedition...!

What if anything,
Was Captain Franklin trying to tell us?

Like In 1619 the Danish naval captain Jens Munk, who had lost 61 of his 64 crewmen, who were later ceremoniously dumped over-board, and just managed to sail home alive, by the autumn of 1620. Why did these three mysterious sailors get buried on land and not at sea? And there's more questions than answers to the hidden identity of one or more of these buried sailors, because it was very probable that Torrington, who was the lead stoker on the Erebus, could have be ill for weeks or even months before his mysterious death, but highly unlikely! Apparently he had no bedsores on his body or calluses on hands, he also mysteriously had no shoes or socks on inside his coffin! While his arm had been tucked up behind his back, which flattened his nose against the lid! If he didn't have anything hidden underneath his body, apart from his left-arm, what could it have been? Did someone or something...? Exhume Torrington, Hartnell and Braine after they had been interred to look for something...? What about the strange and unusual *autopsy* done on *John Hartnell?*

Frozen in time

(*Exhumation circa 1984-6 tells us everything and yet nothing*)

Torrington

"Do you know what this place is? Have you seen that awful den of hellish infamy — with the very moonlight alive with grisly shapes, and every speck of dust that whirls in the wind a devouring monster in embryo?"

As they had approached the coffin, the wind had eerily picked up, and was as if a strange dark cloud had moved over the site, the walls of the tent over the excavation of Torrington grave as the weather continued to become even angry, the researchers rather nervously had to abandon work, Kowel observed that **"it was like something out of an horror movie"** that night the wind howled continuously and towards morning a violent wind had ripped away the tent over the graveside!

Like the story in *MISSING 411 The Devil's in the Detail. In Florida,* where a party of individuals on board the Evelyn K, a sixty-foot-yacht, after the yacht had pulled into Sandy key, the three men left the yacht, and climbed into a fifteen-foot wooden skiff, to catch redfish, the witnesses to the mysterious disappearances, explained how fast a storm came up: "one minute, Snider and his friends could be seen sitting on the Skiff in calm channel waters. The next minute, under gusting winds and rolling waters, they were gone." People aboard the Evelyn K were watching the Skiff and saw it disappear behind the palms, the last time the men were seen. The storm was accompanied by 45 mph winds, that toppled a 70ft elevator tower on Miami-Beach and snapped telephone lines, '*it was a very unusual storm, it became so dark, and it seemed to last about an hour. There was lightening, heavy winds.*

Remember in **"Invisible residents"** strange weather plays a vital role in most, if not all of the weird or strange disappearances in the books: **Missing 411.** By David Paulides.

Continued:

Even though he was not stiff like a dead man, he was limp as if he was just unconscious, and they had the eerie feeling that Torrington was still aware of what ever was happening, with his half-closed eyes gazing at them.

With Carlson holding and supporting Torrington's legs, while Beatie held his shoulders and head, as they moved him, his head rolled onto his left shoulder, Beatie looked directly into Torrington's half-opened eyes, only a few millimetres from his own.

John Torrington gave the impression that he was a frail innocent-looking young man who was apparently not the image of a sea-toughened sailor! Although **one should never judge a book by its cover**, why did he not have any bedsores? Or calluses on his hands, because he was the leading-stoker on-board the Terror?

Any interpretation with regards to the adhesions and fluid in his lungs is not conclusive, no matter how obvious it seems or appears, so it is very probable that Pneumonia was probably the cause of his death, but highly unlikely!

'Stranger than fiction'

(Remember to keep an open mind)

Somewhere between these conflicting events you need to read between the lines to find the hidden meanings that seem or appear to fly in the face of reason, because we don't know who or what was responsible for such a **weird autopsy**, it's very probable that it was either done before or after William Hartnell was buried, we don't know why it was done in such a strange manor, and remember it might have been done by someone or something not of this world, so to speak!

1853

(Inglefield was awarded the Royal Geographical Society's Artic medal)

. . .

Commander Inglefield, during the private expedition to the Artic, resolved to dig down into the frozen ground, for the purpose of ascertaining the condition in which the men had been interred.

The opening out of one coffin quite realized the object he had in view, for at **6ft** beneath the surface, a depth reached only with great difficulty, by penetrating frozen ground as hard as a rock, a coffin, with the name of **Wm *Heartwell*** (error in the name...) was found in as perfect order as if recently deposited in the churchyard of an English village.

Every button and ornament had been neatly arranged, and what was most important, the body, perfectly preserved by the intense cold, exhibited no trace of scurvy, or other malignant disease, but was manifestly that of a person who had died of consumption, a malady to which it was further known that the deceased was prone.

Inglefield's expedition was one of those supported by Lady Jane Franklin. With a crew of 17 on board the screw schooner (**Isabel**) weighing 149 Imperial tons, they were at Beechey-Island on the 7th of September 1852.

In his published journal, Inglefield described his first sight of the graves:

"That sad emblem of mortality the grave soon met my eye, as we plunged along through the knee-deep snow which covered the island. The last resting place of three of Franklin's people was closely examined; but nothing that had not hitherto been observed could we detect. My companion told me that a **huge bear** was seen continually sitting on **one of the graves** as if keeping a silent vigil over the dead..."

Inglefield did not describe the exhumation of William Hartnell in his journal, but there is a strange silence as if the truth lay between a dissonant cord or blank period in it, covering the time between when he and Sutherland finished dinning with the officers on board the ship (**North-Star**) and the departure of the (**Isabel**) from Beechey-Island shortly after midnight... with as beautiful a moon to light our path as ever shone on the favoured shores of our own native land.

An unpublished letter written by Inglefield to rear admiral Sir Francis Beaufort on the 14th of September fills in the gap or does it?

1852

"Why was the examination or investigation of Hartnell's body done by Inglefield and Sutherland and what were they looking for?"

My doctor assisted me, and I have had my hand on the arm and face of poor Hartnell. He was decently clad in a cotton shirt, and though the dark-night precluded our seeing! ***Never-mind being able to do an autopsy*** [My italics] still our touch detected that a wasting illness was the cause of dissolution.

It was a curious and solemn scene on the silent snow-covered sides of the famed *or* **infamous** [My italics] Beechey Island, where the two of us stood at midnight. The pale moon looking down upon us as we silently worked with pickaxe and shovel at the hard-frozen tomb, each blow sending a spur of red sparks from the grave where rested the messmate of our lost countrymen.

No trace, **trace of what?** [My italics] but a piece of fearnought half down the coffin-lid could we find. I carefully restored everything to its place and only brought away with me the plate that was nailed on the coffin-lid and a scrap of the cloth with which the coffin was covered.

Why did they take away the plate from John Hartnell's coffin and a sample of cloth? These and other cues tend to throw a very clever smoke screen over the clues, by cleverly hiding the truth, among the disorganized facts of this bizarre case.

"Glassy-eyed, half-visible presence."
(Deceased persons all unaccountably lacking in blood)

. . .

Dracula

"The tomb in the daytime, and when wreathed with fresh flowers, had looked grim and gruesome enough; but now some days afterwards, when the flowers hung lank and dead, their whites turning to rust and their greens to browns; when the spider and the beetle had resumed their accustomed dominance; when time-coloured stone, and dust-encrusted mortar, and rusty, dank iron, and tarnished brass and clouded silver-plating gave back the feeble glimmer of a candle, the effect was more miserable and sordid than could have been imagined. It conveyed irresistibly the idea of life - animal life – was not the only thing that could pass away.

Van Helsing went about his work systematically, holding his candle so that he could read the coffin plates, and so holding it that the sperm dropped in white patches which congealed as they touched the metal, he made assurances of Lucy's coffin. Another search in his bag, and he took out a turnscrew. 'What are you going to do?' I asked. 'To open the coffin. You shall yet be convinced.' Straightaway he began taking out the screws, and finally lifted off the lid, showing the casing of lead beneath. The sight was almost too much for me. It seemed to be as much an affront to the dead as it would have been to have stripped off her clothing in her sleep whilst living; I actually took hold of his hand to stop him.

He only said: ' You shall see,' and again fumbling in his bag, took out a tiny fret-saw. Striking the turnscrew through the lead with a swift downward stab, which made me wince, he made a small hole, which was, however, big enough to admit the point of the saw. I expected a rush of gas from the week-old corpse.

We doctors, who have had to study our dangers, have to become accustomed to such things, and I drew back towards the door. But the professor never stopped for a moment; he sawed down a couple of feet along one side of the lead coffin, and then across, and down to the other side. Taking the edge of the loose flange, he bent it back towards the foot of the coffin, and holding up the candle into the aperture...

Bram Stoker

. . .

Anyone would be forgiven for thinking that these graves were or could be hiding something even more ghastly and frightening than you could imagine, with Torrington and his disturbing half-lidded gaze, like some un-dead thing... that retain their bodily form and live on the blood or breath of the living - whose hideous legions send their preying shapes or spirits abroad by night.

Hartnell

'With a most disturbing expression on his face'

(Leering like a grinning devil at them, his partly opened mouth was visible, with its eerie incisor teeth that produced a frightening grin.)

* * *

Remember the speech in 1853 when Inglefield was awarded the Royal Geographical Society's Artic medal? And during the private expedition had resolved to dig down into the frozen ground, for the purpose of ascertaining the condition in which the men had been interred?

The opening out of one coffin quite realized the object he had in view, for at **6ft** beneath the surface, a depth reached only with great difficulty, by penetrating frozen ground as hard as a rock.

And yet his coffin was found by the **1984** frozen in time members, only **85cms** in the ground! Or only a little more than half the depth of John Torrington! And as well as having 3 layers of clothing covering his upper body, he had nothing on below his waist, with **no shoes or boots on**!

He had a solid block of ice inside his head! Or his brain had been liquefied or turned to liquid! His blood vessels contained ice...! And the ice was clear, because he had no blood inside his body someone or something had drained him of his **blood...**!

Its as if whoever done this **autopsy** was suffering from the onset of some strange stupor or mild confusion? Like in **Missing 411,** or was it done intentionally to warn us of some strange danger they were in, we don't know...!

If it was not the surgeons, then who done the **strange autopsy?** Beginning with several knife cuts on the chest plate, before the ribs were apparently divided, during the odd autopsy, and whoever or may we be so bold to say, whatever done the autopsy, had focused curiously on the heart and lungs, the heart seemed or appeared to have been removed with part of the Trachea had been made to try and either establish what possible deceases he had died from, or to cleverly make sure nothing unusual or out of the ordinary would show up any important clues or questionable evidence that might point to what actually killed him!

Then two cuts, had been made to the right and left Ventricles that seemed or appeared to mimic the normal procedure used by the surgeon when he needs to look at the valves, and then the roots of the lungs and then into the liver to look for confirmation of possible deceases, the bowel was untouched, but the strangest part of the autopsy was how the chest-plate (The anterior portion of the ribs, and sternum) was found **up-side down!**

So we don't know who could have done it or where it was done... somewhere between these conflicting events, you need to read between the lines to find the hidden meanings that seem or appear to fly in the face of reason. In 1852 why was the examination or investigation of Hartnell's body done by Inglefield and Sutherland? Was it pure chance that the only body that they had chosen, for whatever reason, had already been autopsied and if it was not done by any of the surgeons on board the **Erebus** and the **Terror** or even by Inglefield and Sutherland, then whoever or whatever dug up John Hartnell, Braine and even Torrington, because they were all missing shoes or boots! For whatever reason, not only someone or somebody must have done it, but whatever or whoever it was, they must have been looking for something, we don't know...!

Although the standard incision during modern-day autopsies is **Y** shaped with the arms of the **Y** extending down from each shoulder and meeting at the base of the sternum (breastbone). From this point the incision continues down to the pubic bone. But whoever or whatever had conducted this weird back-to-front Autopsy on **John Hartnell**, had done an upside down incision, much like modern autopsies but the wrong way round or upside down, it's very probable that it could have been the surgeon on board the Terror: (**John S. Peddie**) and his assistant surgeon (**Alexander MacDonald**) or surgeon (**Stephen S. Stanley**) and or acting surgeon: (**Harry D.S. Goodsir**) but its very unlikely. Which begs the question, who or what was responsible for the strange autopsy that mimics a modern day autopsy?

The ice around Hartnell's chest area appeared quite discoloured, and very brownish, even mottled, which could have been caused at any time, before, during or after his burial, or by the hurried exhumation 1852 by Inglefield and Sutherland, trying to hastily dig down to the coffin, where the damaged shirt-sleeve on his right arm, had been exposed through a tear in the sheet, with pieces of the coffin-lid had apparently been driven forcibly into his right chest-wall. Could it have been dye from the wood that had caused the brownish stain in the ice? Or was it the impact or energy wave from the pick-axe bursting through the wood that made indirect contact with the body at the same time causing the mottling effect, the brownish discolouring seen in the ice when the lid was removed, could have been a result of blood seeping out of either the doctor's incision, or whoever/whatever done the incision before or after he was buried and then drained of his blood, as water seeped into or filled the coffin during the summer of 1846?

It was very probable that he have his blood, when or if he was first autopsied on-board the ship by the surgeons, who would have wanted to attend out of curiosity, or assist in such an autopsy out of professional courtesy.

Why would a Victorian surgeon or surgeons drain him of all his blood, even if they were curious of how or why he had died so mysteriously, so it's very probable that it was one of the surgeons or their assistants who done it, but to put things back in a disorganised fashion with the rib-cage back to front, is not only bad practice, but incompetence! Or were they beginning to suffer from some kind of strange stupor or the onset of some kind of confusion like in the **Missing 411 books by David Paulides?**

Especially for a Victorian surgeon and anatomist, is highly questionable, they could have taken samples of the sailor's blood for a future analysis, but why did they have to take every drop of his blood...?

"Rats Rat's everywhere"

An observation that does not make any sense, apart from providing a ready source of food, washed don with a bottle of vin or·di·naire or like a thorn in the flesh for the able seamen, but not the officers...! But there's only one snag, they would have chewed their way through most of the classics inside the extensive libraries before you could say **"Jack Robinson"** As well as eating their way through all the rope and canvas for the repair and replacement of the sails and the rigging, even though both ships had big engines to use, the handful of bilge-rats apart from being in the millions by the time the ships got to the Artic! The crew would have had nothing to wear on those cold winter nights that no doubt would have been cold enough to freeze the balls of a brass monkey! A phrase that seems or appears to have originated from the use of a brass tray, called a **"monkey"**, to hold cannonballs on warships in the 16th to 18th centuries, and in very cold temperatures the **"monkey"** would contract, causing the balls to fall off!

And even though the ships had School supplies for teaching illiterate sailors to read and write... here we have the disquieting letter from William Hartnell's mother that seems or appears to have been penned by an educated woman, which begs the question was he and Torrington just ordinary Jack-Tars or sailors?

"Might is right"
[*Survival of the fittest*]
The Victorian Military society

"Du mußt Amboß oder Hammer sein"

Johann Wolfgang von Goethe (1749 - 1832)
German dramatist, novelist, poet, & scientist
"You must be anvil or hammer"

As George Orwell wrote in **"Politics and the English Language"**: "*In real life it is always the anvil that breaks the hammer, never the other way about.*" Let there be no doubt, every person is either the hammer or anvil. No one gets to avoid it and action through inaction is no choice. **"For all your days prepare, and meet them ever alike: When you are the anvil, bear-When you are the hammer, strike."**

Misunderstandings and neglect create more confusion in this world than trickery and malice. At any rate, the last two are certainly much less frequent.

When young, one is confident to be able to build palaces for mankind, but when the time comes one has one's hands full just to be able to remove their trash.

"Doesn't surprise me that Christ our Lord preferred to live with whores and sinners, seeing as how I go in for that myself. None are more hopelessly enslaved than those who falsely believe they are free"

The quaint nuance of morality

Where the virtuous sleep the sleep of the innocent, they are hard workers, kind and generous to boot. They are first among equals, like Charles the II of England in the 17th century, who never said a wrong word to anybody, but he never done any good either, when virtue becomes a vice! Where you are no longer your brothers/sisters keeper.

The Victorian Military society

"What, then, are the characteristics of the military or earliest important stage in society? As Herbert Spencer said well puts it, the militant type is one in which the army is the nation mobilised while the nation is the quiescent army, and which therefore acquires a structure common to army and nation. The trait characterising the militant structure throughout is that its units are coerced into their various combined actions.

As the soldier's will is so suspended that he becomes in everything the agent of the officer's will, so is the will of the citizen in all transactions, private and public overruled by that of the government. The co-operation by which the life of the militant society is maintained is a compulsory co-operation.

*These are facts, which have to be reckoned with in the controversy between the ideals of individual liberty, on the one hand, and collective authority on the other hand. The earliest stage of societies, which is the military stage and the lowest stage, is also the most completely collective stage. There is no **individual liberty**, there is scarcely any possibility for the development of the individual life; there is **"compulsory co-operation"***

And the Victorians using dialectic profundity with the consummate skill of a Devil dissimilate their verbiage in an attempt to veil their doctrine of lies and miss-information by using tricks of logic in some intellectual mating ritual where they play politics with people's lives, forcing them either on to the street where they will surely die of health problems or either freeze and eventually expire of malnutrition or put the problem into labour camps, that's a good idea, because you know that work sets you free!

While other people are forced into an apostacy the heart abhors, and will be forced to pass the remainder of their life in the practice of a constant and humiliating hypocrisy, for in this way, men and women are being constrained to mask their thoughts, there arises a habit of securing safety by falsehood, and of purchasing impunity with deceit and fraud becomes a necessary of life; insincerity is made a daily custom; the whole tone of public feeling is vitiated, and the gross amount of vice and of error fearfully increased. Surely we must be well be grateful for that increase of intellectual pursuits which has destroyed an evil that some among us would even now willingly restore"

'First Letter'

"Sarah Hartnell's letter"

My dear children (William Hartnell and Thomas Hartnall) who served on-board the Erebus. Sarah Hartnell's letter began. 'It is a great pleasure to me to have a chance to write to you. I hope you are both well. I assure you, I have many anxious moments about you but I endeavour to cast my prayers on him who is too good to be unkind, if it is the Lords will may we be spared to meet on earth, if not God grant we may all meet around his throne to praise him to all eternity.

Blinkered

A letter like this apart from being written in a form of Victorian self-denial or ignorance could only be described as taxonomy or non-menclature, which is something that could be attributed to someone like "*Marie Antoinette*" when the French peasents were crying for bread, she was meant to have replied, if they cant eat bread, then let them eat cake! But even though there is no actual evidence that she ever uttered it, it is now generally regarded as a journalistic cliché or was it?

This phrase originally appeared in Book VI of the first part (finished in 1767, published in 1782) of Rousseau's autobiographical work, **Les Confessions**.

On closer interpretaion obviously give her the benefit of the doubt, so to speak, she was either so privilaged and nieve or the little arogant monster knew exactly what she ment, and it was a cruel and intentional jibe or pointed stick.

Can someone be that ignorant, like in these two letters asking so sweetly for Gods mercy! When people were starving to death on the streets of London and else where?

"Enfin je me rappelai le pis-aller d'une grande princesse à qui l'on disait que les paysans n'avaient pas de pain, et qui répondit : Qu'ils mangent de la brioche."

Finally I remembered the last resort of a great Princess to whom it was said that the peasants had no bread, and who replied: let them eat brioche.

. . .

"Second Letter"

Which brings us to Franklin's letter which gives one the impression as if it reminds one of the popular saying that you can catch a thief but you can't catch a lier... its like trying to peel away an onion skin to get at the truth of the matter, because here we have a letter from Franklin, in which he would say his last tongue in cheek good-by's, to his lady wife in 1845.

Make no mistake about it, the Victorians were as hypocritical as they were corrupt, who maintained as we do, a barbaric class system or status-Quo, where the weak or anybody who is not strong enough to stand on their own two feet go the wall... its as simple as that, its what's known as natural selection exemplified to a fine art...

Franklin's letter

"Let me assure you, that I am amply provided with every requisite for my passage, and that I am entering on my voyage comforted with every hope of **"Gods merciful guidance and protection"** and that he will bless, comfort and protect you, my dearest. . . and all my other relatives. Oh, how much I wish I could write to each of them to assure them of my happiness I feel in my officers, my crew! And my ship..."

Obviously his cabin and the other officers was very comfortable, but for the ordinary seaman it was a very different story altogether, leaving the crew berthed in whatever space that remained, having to sling their hammocks along side one another in the over crowed mess deck:

'The Terror of the unknown'

(Braine lay like some frightening creature in his lordly death house of ice and wind, his face at its worsted, with his teeth in the dim uncertain light, longer and sharper in ones imagination, than they had been)

Braine

Still had a sleepy nearly alive look, with his open mouth, showing his incisor teeth, with a frightful grin, and strangely enough one of his undershirts had been put on **backward-to-front** and his stockings or socks had been bizarrely folded under his heels!

Frozen in time
Continued...

While doing the preliminaries the group started to suffer from terrible headaches and even felt physically ill, they had wondered if it may have been the carbon-monoxide from the stoves they had used, during the removable of William Braine from the coffin, even though there was a constant breeze blowing through the tent, could it have been the fumes that had gathered in the grave that created the problem? There's only one problem, is **Carbon Monoxide Gas not lighter than air**!

(It was as if he had been hastily buried or re-interred for some reason)

. . .

'Ghost ship'

Invisible Horizons
By
Vincent Gaddis 1965

The Artic Ocean, the smallest of the world's oceans, lies in the Northern reaches of the North American continent. It also includes thirty of the worlds largest group of Islands.

From the 16th to the 20th Century the ocean was sailed by Europeans in search of the Northwest-passage from Europe to Asia.

The fabled and almost legendary route was finally negotiated officially by the Norwegian explorer Roald Amundsen who was born July 16, 1872, near Oslo, Norway.

He was a Norwegian polar explorer. He was the first person to fly over the North Pole in a dirigible on May 11, 1926. He was also the first person to reach both the north and the south poles and who mysteriously disappeared on June 18, 1928 with his French flight crew, and his body was never found. He was 55 years old at the time of his death.

The search for the dangerous and fabled Northwest Passage occupied some three centuries and had claimed the lives of hundreds of mariners. It was believed that there was a water route between the Atlantic and the pacific Oceans, through or south of Baffin-island and the Beaufort-sea. In time both the South-west and the North-west passage was found to connect Europe and Asia across Alaska or Artic-America.

. . .

Northwest Passage

1903–1906

In 1903, Amundsen led the first expedition to successfully traverse Canada's Northwest Passage between the Atlantic and Pacific Oceans. With him were six others in a 45-ton fishing vessel, Gjøa. His technique was to use a small ship and hug the coast. Amundsen had the ship outfitted with a small gasoline engine. They travelled via Baffin Bay, the Parry Channel and then south through Peel Sound, James Ross Strait, Simpson Strait and Rae Strait and spent two winters at King William Island in what is today Gjoa Haven, Nunavut, Canada. During this time Amundsen learned from the local Netsilik people about Arctic survival skills that would later prove useful. For example, he learned to use sled dogs and to wear animal skins in lieu of heavy, woolen parkas. Leaving Gjoa Haven he went west and passed Cambridge Bay, which had been reached from the west by Richard Collinson in 1852.

Continuing to the south of Victoria Island, the ship cleared the Canadian Arctic Archipelago on 17 August 1905, but had to stop for the winter before going on to Nome on the Alaska District's Pacific coast. Five hundred miles (800 km) away, Eagle City, Alaska, had a telegraph station; Amundsen travelled there (and back) overland to wire a success message (collect) on 5 December 1905. Nome was reached in 1906. Because the water along the route was as shallow as 3 ft (0.91 m), a larger ship could not have made the voyage.

"Dead man's hand"

However un-officially the northwest-passage had been negotiated more than a century earlier by a ship of dead men, called the *"Octavius"* a derelict ship of dead men, with it's right of ownership under question, having been completely sacrificed by delegated possession as being held in a dead hand!

It seems that in November 1762 the British vessel was caught in the ice at a point north of Point Barrow, Alaska.

With the crew of 28 freezing to death, after becoming caught in the merciless and unforgiving icepack, until the ice eventually began to slowly melt, the vessel drifted eastward over the years.

Until it was sighted on 12th August 1775 by the herald, a whaling ship, off the coast of Greenland. Thus making the *"Octavius"* the first ship to negotiate the North-west Passage with a captain and a crew who had been dead for **13yrs**...!

. . .

Demeter

'As idle as a painted ship upon a painted ocean'

The only ship noticeable was a foreign schooner with all sails set, which was seemingly going westwards. The foolhardiness or ignorance of her officers was a prolific theme for comment whilst she remained in sight and efforts were made to signal her to reduce sail in the face of her danger, before the night shut down she was seen with sails idly flapping as she gently rolled on the undulating swell of the sea.

Masses of sea-fog came drifting inland – white, wet clouds which swept by in ghostly fashion, so dank and cold that it needed little imagination to think that the spirits of those lost at sea were touching their living brethren with the clammy hands of death, and many a one shuddered as the wreaths of sea-mist swept by.

Some distance away a schooner with all sails set, apparently the same vessel which had been noticed earlier in the evening. The wind by this time backed to the East, and there was a shudder amongst the watchers on the cliff as they realized the terrible danger in which she was now in. between her and the port lay the great flat reef on which so many good ships have from time to time suffered, and, with the wind blowing from its present quarter, it would be quite impossible that she should fetch the entrance of the harbour.

It was now nearly the hour of high tide, but the waves were so great that in their troughs the shallows of the shore were almost visible, and the schooner, with all sails set, was rushing with such speed that, in the words of one old salt, 'she must fetch up somewhere, if it was only in hell.'

. . .

And a shudder ran through all who saw her, for lashed to the helm was a corpse, with dropping head, which swung horribly to and fro at each motion of the ship. No other form could be seen on deck at all. The man was simply fastened by his hands, tied one over the other, to a spoke of the wheel. Between the inner hand and the wood was a crucifix, the set of beads on which it was fastened being around both wrists and wheel and all kept fast by the binding cords. The poor fellow may have been seated at one time, but the flapping and buffeting of the sails had worked through the rudder of the wheel and dragged him to and fro, so that the cords with which he was tied had cut the flesh to the bone...

Whitby

The
Resolute

(Ghost ship)

Commanded by Henry Kellet, had been caught in ice, in Viscount Melville Sound, had also been abandoned for some strange reason, a ship that had been part of Sir Edward Belcher's five ship flotilla and who would eventually give orders to abandon another three ships and return to England as quick as possible... from **Wellington-Channel** and down past Beechey-Island of all places and out through Lancaster-sound and into Baffin-Bay...

'Beechey-Island'

(A place already been steeped in mystery...)

Edward Parry during his voyage back in 1819. Parry was puzzled to note, "a strong rippling on the surface of the water or unevenness in the bottom, we concluded that it must have been occasioned by some particular set, or meeting of the tides in this place" the two ships were passing in the vicinity of Beechey-Island at the time...

The hollow earth

Raymond Bernard AB., MA. PhD.

"This begs the question in relationship to strange phenomena in the Artic, such as weird under water tidal waves or the pressure in the Artic-Ocean, during still tide and calm weather... or Artic tidal waves, described by various explorers, that lift the ice of the great-ice-fields to great heights and can be heard for miles in the distance before they reach the ship and for miles after they pass beyond the ship. As if they were passing the treacherous and mysterious island of the...

'Sirens'

(The Sirens encountered Ulysses or Odysseus in Homer's epic poem the Odyssey.)

. . .

"Odysseus (Ulysses) king of Ithaca who was forewarned by the sorceress Circe, had his men's ears stopped up, and himself lashed to the ships mast, as he listened to the self imposed delight of their beautiful but deadly songs"

. . .

Jason and the Argonauts

Chiron had told Jason that without the aid of Orpheus the Argonauts would never be able to pass the Sirens!

The Sirens lived on three small, rocky islands called Sirenum scopuli and where ment to have song beautiful songs that would entice or lour sailors to come to them, which resulted in their ship crashing on the rocks of the islands. When Orpheus heard their voices, he drew his lyre and played

427

music that was more beautiful and louder, drowning out the Sirens' bewitching songs...

Giant blocks pitched and rolled as if an atomic bomb had been tested, like in the classic or cult movie *"**The beast from Twenty Thousand Fathoms by Ray Bradbury**"* releasing a prehistoric monster, my italics. As though undulated by unseen hands the vast compressing bodies moan and groan, shrieking a horrible sound that curdled the blood, while we watched their terrible progress these tidal waves are caused by some tremendous agency and I can think of nothing more powerful than the plunging of giant ice-bergs falling into the ocean, but from where...?

Because icebergs are composed of fresh water... and nothing else that we know off can produce even a fraction of the commotion of a monster iceberg when it plunges into the water, except an **Atomic-bomb explosion**!

The **Resolute** had sailed from Viscount Melville Sound and through Lancaster Sound into Baffin-Bay with her rigging white with frost, like the ghost ship,

'The Flying Dutchman'

The Dutch captain who attempted to sail around the cape of good-hope in a raging storm, as if shaking his fists at the storm clouds, and defying the almighty, to sink his ship! And for this blasphemy he was condemned to sail the seas for all eternity in his phantom ship, luring other ships to their doom!

H.M.S Inconstant

Ships log
4 a.m.
Australia

*"**The flying Dutchman**" crossed our bows, omitting a strange phosphorescent light as of a phantom ship all aglow, in the midst of which light the masts, spars and sails of a brig 200 yards distant stood out in strong relief as she came up on the port-bow, where also the officer of the watch from the bridge saw her, as did also the quarter-deck midshipman, who was sent forward at once to the forecastle, but on arriving there no vestige nor any sign whatever of any material-ship was to be seen either near or right-away to the horizon, the night being clear an the sea calm.*

Mirage
Like a reflection or optical elusion
"A phantom or spectre haunting the Artic, looming out of the eerie strange fog like the ripping yarn of the fabled..."

Mary Celeste

1872

"A hoodoo or Jinxed ship"

"It seems or appears as if they are trying to get the evidence to fit the events, which is a bit like trying to get the shoe to fit the feet or the feet to fit the shoe!"

Built in Nova Scotia (New Scotland) shipyard in 1861, she was named the **"Amazon"**. In 1867 she was stranded off Cape Breton, Nova Scotia (New Scotland) and after she had been sold, her name was changed to the famous or should I say infamous **"Mary Celeste"** and again she was said to have gone ashore off another part of stormy Cape Brenton.

She was sold again to another owner, who was forced to rebuild her, because her timbers had suffered dry-rot, and during the re-fit she was given a **"copper bottom"**.

The **"Mary Celeste"** left New-York harbour on the 5th November 1872, bound for **"Genoa"** with a cargo of 1,000 cask's of alcohol, and she was in fine sailing trim, so to speak.

On board the **"Mary Celeste"** was captain Benjamin Briggs, with the only passengers: his wife and baby daughter.

17 days out on the open-sea (North Atlantic) she held her course, until 8am, November 1872. Someone had written on her **"slate-log"** that she had passed to the north of the island of **Santa-Marie** (*Saint-Mary*) in the **Azores,** which bore away **S.S.W., 6 miles distant.**

Then something strange and inexplicable seemed or appeared to have happened to this mysterious ship! That caused the **"Mary Celeste"** to become one of the most baffling riddles of the sea, where all on board hastily or forcibly abandoned her.

* * *

Dei Gratia

Left New York on the 15 November 1872.

Captain: Read Morehouse

I left New York on the 15th November 1872 at 8 o'clock civil time, in the British brig the **"Dei Gratia"** bound to Gibraltar for orders. My cargo was refined petroleum, 1,735 round barrels, and 499 cases of petroleum and one in dispute.

We had heavy weather, but met with nothing extraordinary, till **5th December** sea time one O'clock p.m., when I came on deck, saw a sail on the weather bow, bearing **E.N.E.,** wind about **N.** We were then steering **S.E. ½E.** By compass −**38° (degrees) 20 N. Lat., 17° (degrees) 37 long., by chronometer.** It was the abandoned **"Mary Celeste"** with

429

jib and foremast staysail set, sailing on the starboard tack but in so strange and erratic a fashion that Morehouse decided to close in and hail her. He signalled but received no answer.

"**Guess she's a derelict**", he said to the mate, **Oliver Deveau**, and ordered the mate and two other seamen to go aboard and investigate. When their boat got under the ship's counter they read her name "**Mary Celeste**" and knew it was the same ship that had been in harbour at the same time as "**the Dei Gratia**"

Dead reckoning

When the "**Mary Celeste**" was first sighted by the "**Dei Gratia**" it seems or appears to have held its course for ten days, with the wheel loose, and apparently with no one at the helm, in all that time.

"*They discovered that all the windows in her cabin had been strangely and inexplicably battened-up for no apparent reason! With wood planking and canvas that resembled a miniature fortress, as if the captain and the crew along with his wife and child, were either trying to stop someone or something from getting in, or whoever or whatever had came aboard, was trying to keep them from getting out!*"

. . .

Mysteries solved and unsolved

Harold T. Wilkins

Between the 25th of November and the 5th of December, the "**Mary Celeste**" had been mysteriously abandoned and the distance of the longitude of the place where the "**Mary Celeste**" was found from that of the island of "**Santa Maria**" (*Saint Mary*) the derelicts last entry in her log is, according to reckoning of the admiralty experts at Gibraltar, 9 minutes 54° degrees (Eastwards), which, at latitude 40° degrees, is equal

to approximately 507 land miles "*it appears almost impossible*". Say the experts, "that the derelict should have compassed with-in the same time a distance of 9.54 eastwards, at all events on the *starboard* tack, where she was met by the "**Dei Gratia**", when the log of the "**Dei Gratia**" shows the wind was blowing from the north all that time, and ship was on the *port* tack all that time!"

Stripped of its nautical technicalities, it seems or appears that during the ten days from the **25th** of November and the **5th** of December the position of the "**Mary Celeste's**" sails had been adjusted by person or persons unknown and the inference is that the "**Mary Celeste**" had not been abandoned till several days after the last entry in her log!

But there seems to be more to the intriguing mystery of the "**Mary Celeste**" than meets the eye, remembering that there's nothing more deceptive than the obvious! That on the same day (March, 1873), David Read Morehouse, captain of the **"Dei Gratia"** superior officer of Oliver Deveau, gave some rather surprising, not to say suspicious testimony respecting the boarding of the **"Mary Celeste"**, on the high seas.

As will be seen, the **"Dei Gratia"** people seem or appear to have gone out of their way to interfere with, if not, indeed, to render invalid what the French criminologists would call **"les traces révélatrices"** or it seems or appears that something else strange happened that we are not quit sure of! And it possible connection to the eerie books: **MISSING 411** by David Paulides and the weird Coincidence and what seems or appears to be an arbitrary involvement of the weather!

Meteorologists in Great Britain note that the year of the sailing of the ship was the **"most remarkable weather year of the century, rain and cold prolonged far into the summer, and succeeded by an amount of electrical disturbance of the atmosphere unparalleled within living memory.**

Severe gales raged all over the Atlantic, in the latter part of November (*1872*)".

. . .

The Annual register *1872.*

Letter-writers of the *Times* in the autumn of 1872, commenting on the remarkable appearance of **"shooting stars"** and **meteors** — there were, 29th November, 1872, alone, no fewer than two and a half columns of such letters to the Times — were, on **17th December, 1872,** joined by one, George A. Welch of the British Royal Navy, who was on board the steamer **Rock City.**

Welch gave an extract from the steamers log, between 22nd November and 14th **December 1872,** on her voyage from Quebec to London. He says: "for brevity's sake, I will here add that, during my long experience of nearly thirty years at sea, I never witnessed such fearful succession of heavy gales and terrible seas as we encountered crossing the Atlantic."

The inevitable consequence of such Atlantic hurricanes — and the Atlantic is peculiarly notorious for mysteries of derelicts and ships that were lost without trace — was seen in the extract following from **"Lloyd's list"**, dated 12th December, 1872:

" The Ebenezer of Arendal, Birketvedt, sailed from New York on or about 22nd August, 1872, with maze, bound for Queenstown, Ireland, or Falmouth for orders, and has not since been heard of," Yet, there was no evidence of storm- damage to the **"Mary Celeste"**.

The British navel authorities at Gibraltar had been confronted with a mysterious enigma or eerie maritime riddle, that has still never been solved, and that's a fact, not a theory!

It was as if something weird or sinister had taken place, like the cursed ship the **"Demeter"** in Dracula...

Log of The Demeter

(Varna to Whitby)

Written **18 July**, *things so strange happening, that I shall keep accurate note till we land.*

On 6ᵗʰ July we finished taking cargo, silver sand and boxes of earth. At noon set sail. East wind, fresh, crew, five hands. . . two mates, cook, and myself (captain)

On 11ᵗʰ July at dawn entered Bosphorus. Boarded by Turkish Customs officers. Backsheesh. All correct. Under way at 4pm.

On 12ᵗʰ July through Dardanelles. More customs officers and flagboat of guarding squadron. Backsheesh again. Work of officers thorough, but quick. Want us off soon. At dark passed into Archipelago.

On 13ᵗʰ July passed cape Matapan. Crew dissatisfied about something, seemed scared, but wood not speak out.

On 14ᵗʰ July was somewhat anxious about crew. Men all steady fellows, who sailed with me before. Mate could not make out what was wrong; they only told him there was *something*, and crossed themselves. Mate lost temper with one of them that day and struck him. Expected fierce quarrel, but all was quit.

On 16ᵗʰ July mate reported in the morning that one of the crew Petrosky, was missing. Could not account for it. Took larboard watch eight bells last night; was relieved by Abramoff, but did not go to bunk. Men more downcast than ever. All said they expected something of the kind, but would not say more than that there was *something aboard.*

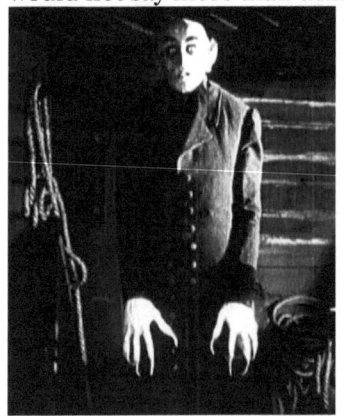

Mate getting very impatient with them; feared some trouble ahead.

On 17ᵗʰ July yesterday, one of the men, Olgaren, came to my cabin, and in an awestruck way confided to me that he thought there was a strange man aboard the ship. He said that in his watch he had been sheltering behind the deckhouse, as there was a rain-storm, when he saw a tall, thin man, who was not like any of the crew, come up the companion way, and go along the deck forward, and disappear. He followed cautiously, but when he got to the bows found no one, and the hatchways were all closed. He was in a panic of superstitious fear, and I am afraid the panic may spread. To alley it, I shall to-day search entire ship carefully from stem to stern.

Later in the day I got together the whole crew, and told them, as they evidently thought there was someone in the ship, we should search from stem to stern. First mate angry; said it was folly, and to yield to such foolish idea's would demoralize the men; said he would engage to keep them out of

432

trouble with a handspike. I let him take the helm, while rest began thorough search, all keeping abreast, with lanterns; we left no corner unsearched. As there were only the big wooden boxes, there were no odd corners where a man could hide. Men much relieved when search over, and went back to work cheerfully.

First mate scowled, but said nothing.

22July. — Rough weather last three days, and all hands busy with sails — no time to be frightened. Men seem to have forgotten their dread. Mate cheerful again, and all on good terms. Praised men for work in bad weather. Passed Gibraltar and out through Straits. All well.

24July. — There seems some doom over this ship. Already a hand short, and entering on the Bay of Biscay with wild weather ahead, and yet last night another man lost — disappeared. Like the first, he came off his watch and was not seen again. Men all in a panic of fear; sent around robin, asking to have double watch, as they fear to be alone. Mate violent. Fear there will be some trouble, as either he or the men will do some violence.

28July. — Four days in hell, knocking about in a sort of maelstrom, and the wind a tempest. No sleep for any one. Men all worn out. Hardly know how to set a watch since no one fit to go on. Second mate volunteered to steer and watch, and let men snatch a few hours' sleep. wind abating; seas still terrific, but feel them less, as ship is steadier.

29July. — Another tragedy. Had single watch to-night, as crew to tired to double. When morning watch came on deck could find no one except steersman. Raised outcry, and all came on deck. Thorough search, but no one found. Are now without second mate and crew in a panic. Mate and I agreed to go armed henceforth and wait for any sign of cause.

30th July. — Last night, rejoiced we are nearing England. Weather fine, all sails set. Retired worn out; slept soundly; awakened by mate telling me that both men on watch and steersman missing. Only self and mate and two hands left to work ship.

1 August. — Two days of fog, and not a sail sighted. Had hoped when in the English Channel to be able to signal for help or get in somewhere. Not having power to work sails, have to run before wind. Dare not lower, as could not raise them again. We seem to be drifting to some terrible doom. Mate now more demoralised than either of them. His stronger nature seems to have worked inwardly against himself. Men are beyond fear, working stolidly and patiently, with minds made up to worst. They are Russians, he Roumanian.

2 August, midnight. — Woke up from few minutes' sleep by hearing a cry, seemingly outside my port. Could see nothing in fog. Rushed on deck, and ran against mate. Tells me heard cry and ran, but no sign of man on watch. One more gone. Lord, help us! Mate says we must be past Straits of Dover, as in a moment of fog lifting he saw North Foreland just as he heard the man cry out. If so we are now off in the North Sea, and only God can guide us in the fog, which seems to move with us; and God seems to have deserted us.

3 August. — At midnight I went to relieve the man at the wheel, but when I got to it found no one there. The wind was steady, and as we ran before it there was no yawning. I dared not leave it, so shouted for the

mate. After a few seconds he rushed up on deck in his flannels. He looked wild-eyed and haggard, and I greatly fear his reason has given way. He came close to me and whispered hoarsely, with his mouth to my ear, as though fearing the very air might hear:

'It is here; I know it, now. On the watch last night I saw it, like a man, tall and thin, and ghastly pale. It was in the bows, and looking out. I crept behind it, and gave it my knife; but the knife went through it, empty as the air.' and as he spoke he took his knife and drove it savagely into space. Then he went on: 'but it is here, and I'll find it. It is in the hold, perhaps, in one of those boxes. I'll unscrew them one by one and see. You work the helm.' And, with a warning look and his finger on his lip, he went below. There was springing up a choppy wind, and I could not leave the helm. I saw him come out on deck again with a tool-chest and a lantern, and go down the forward hatchway. He is mad, stark, raving mad, and it's no use my trying to stop him. He can't hurt those big boxes: they are invoiced as 'clay,' and to pull them about is as harmless a thing as he can do.

So here I stay, and mind the helm, and write these notes. I can only trust in God and wait till the fog clears. Then, if I can steer to any harbour with the wind that is, I shall cut down sails and lie by, and signal for help. . .

It is nearly all over now. Just as I was beginning to hope that the mate would come out calmer — for I heard him knocking away at something in the hold, and work is good for him — there came up the hatchway a sudden, startled scream, which made my blood run cold, and up on the deck he came as if shot from a gun — a raging madman, with his eyes rolling and his face convulsed with fear. 'Save me! Save me!' he cried, and then looked round on the blanket of fog. His horror turned to despair, and in a steady voice he said: 'you had better come too, captain, before it is too late. **He is there.**

I know the secret now. The sea will save me from him, and it is all that is left!' Before I could say a word, or move forward to seize him, he sprang on the bulwark and deliberately threw himself into the sea. I suppose I know the secret too, now. It was this madman who had got rid of the men one by one, and now he has followed them himself. God help me! How am I to account for all these horrors when I get to port? Will that ever be?

4th August. — Still fog, which the sunrise cannot pierce. I know there is sunrise because I am a sailor, why else I know not. I dared not go below, I dared not leave the helm so here all night I stayed, and in the dimness of the night I saw it —

Him! God forgive me, but the mate was right was right to jump overboard. It is better to die like a man; to die like a sailor in blue water no man can object. But I am captain, and I must not leave my ship. But I shall baffle this fiend or monster, for I shall tie my hands to the wheel when my strength begins to fail, and along with them I shall tie that which he — It! — dare not touch; and then, come good wind or foul, I shall save my soul, and my honour as a captain. I am growing weaker, and the night is coming on. If He can look me in the face again, I may not have time to act . . .

If we are wrecked, mayhap this bottle may be found, and those who find it may understand; if not, . . . well, then all men shall know that I have been true to my trust. God and the Blessed Virgin and the saints help a poor ignorant soul trying to do his duty

* * *

The **Resolute** was a cursed ship of sorts, after it was eventually dismantled, and the desk that was fashioned from her oak beams was given to president Chester A Arthur at the White-House, that would in the fullness of time like a poisoned olive branch, would be used as a symbolic stick that would break the back of John F Kennedy on that fateful day in Dallas, Texas. When he was murdered or assassinated on November 22, 1963,

. . .

𝕷𝖆𝖉𝖞 𝕵𝖗𝖆𝖓𝖐𝖑𝖎𝖓'𝖘

(Last exhaustive search)

With the help of a public appeal for funds that had collected £3.000 and a donation of supplies by the Admiralty, Lady Franklin purchased a steam yacht called the "Fox" and placed command with the Artic veteran Captain Francis Leopold M'Clintock, a royal Navy officer who had been involved in three earlier Franklin search expeditions. M'Clintock chose Lieutenant William Robert Hobson, who was the son of the first Governor of New Zealand, as his second-in-command. The "Fox" sailed from Aberdeen, Scotland, July 1857. Almost immediately problems had hampered the search and the "Fox" was forced to spend its first winter trapped in the ice at Baffin-bay before being freed in the spring.

By August 1858 the "Fox" through trail and tribulation had eventually reached Beechey-Island or the site of Franklin's first winter quarters.

By the end of September the searchers had travelled to the eastern entrance to Bellot-strait, where they had established a second winter base. From there McClintock and Hobson were able to leave their ship with small parties and travel overland to King William Island early in April 1859. The two of them had split-up, with M'Clintock ordering Hobson to scour the west-coast of King William Island for any clues related to Franklin's mysterious disappearance, while he would travel down the east-coast of the Island and then over to the Canadian mainland to the estuary of the Back or big fish river, before returning via the Island's west-coast.

M'Clintock then met-up with a group of native Inuit's who told him of finding a wrecked ship across the island and seeing white-men who 'fell down and died as they walked along' and then M'Clintock reached the Canadian-mainland and continued Southward to Montreal Island where he found relic's that could have been abandoned by the Franklin expedition, and then after returning to King William Island where they searched along its Southern and then Western-coast until shortly shortly after midnight on 25ᵗʰ May 1859, a human skeleton that was wearing the uniform of a steward wearing a neckerchief from the lost expedition the lost Franklin expedition was found on a gravel ridge near the mouth of the Peffer River on the island's southern shore. M'Clintock recorded the tragic scene in his journal:

. . .

"This poor man seems to have selected the bare ridge top, as affording the least tiresome walking, and to have fallen upon his face in the position in which we found him. It is probable that, hungry and exhausted, he suffered himself to fall asleep when in this position [and] his last moments were undisturbed by suffering."

. . .

'Cold comfort'

Alongside the bleached skeleton lay a note book that had either belonged to a petty-officer on the **"Terror"** called Harry Peglar or someone wearing the petty-officer's jacket! The handwriting of two individuals was found in the book. One was or could have been Peglar's and the only coherent and mysterious passage was in the handwriting of an unknown hand. None of the rest of the messages were said to be of any importance and some were supposed to be indecipherable or so it was said...! Whoever or whatever wrote the strange passage in the book, the sentence was spelt **back to front**! And when it was corrected it read: "Oh Death whare is they sting, the grave at Comfort Cove for who has any doubt . . . the dyer sad . . ."

But there is no place called comfort cove, and it could have just been a figure of speech, that could be referring to the graves at Beechey Island where the truth may or may-not be eventually discovered, and in the end. it will have proven cold comfort for the lost expedition.

436

*O*r was it referring to:

(*Sonnet VI*)

Death where is thy sting? Love, where is thy glory?

"*Then let not winter's ragged hand deface, in thee thy summer, ere thou be distilled*"

William Shakespeare

Unknown to M'Clintock, an important artefact of the Franklin search had been located three weeks before the skeleton had been found, as Hobson surveyed the North-west coast of King William Island. On 5 May the only officially written record of the Franklin expedition had been found in a cairn at Victory Point on a single piece of naval paper. Around the cairn was a vast quantity of clothing and stores of all sorts strewn about, as if at this spot every article was thrown away which could be dispensed with, there was pickaxes, shovels, boats, cooking stoves, ironwork, rope, blocks, canvas, oars, and above all, a medicine chest…!

First note

The first was signed by Lieutenant Graham Gore, outlining the initial progress of the expedition on May 1847:

28 of May 1847. HM ships Erebus and Terror wintered in the ice in Lat. 70° 05' N. Long. 98° 23' W. having wintered in 1846-7 at Beechey Island, in Lat. 74° 43' 28" N, long. 90° 39' 15" W, after having ascended Wellington Channel to Lat 77°, and returned by the West side of Cornwallis Island. Sir John Franklin commanding the expedition. All well.

One mistake in the first message was quickly noticed, that the expedition had wintered at Beechey Island in 1845-6 and not 1846-7.

When the note had been completed on 25 April 1848, Fitzjames and Crozier had been trapped in their vessels off the coast of King William Island for nineteen months.

'At the bottom of the first message there was a strange addition'

Party consisting of 2 officers and 6 men left the ships on Monday 24th May 1847. Gm. Lieut. Chas. F. Des Voeux, mate.

Second note:

(*A year later*)

"April 25th 1848-HM's ships Terror and the Erebus were deserted on 22nd April, 5 leagues N.N.W. of this, having been beset since 12th September 1846. The Officers and crews, consisting of 105 souls, under the command of Captain F.R.M. Crozier, landed here in lat. 69° 37' 42" N, long. 98° 41' W."

This paper was found by Lt Irving under the cairn supposed to have been built by **Sir James Clark Ross in 1831,** 4 miles to the northward, where it had been deposited by the late Commander Gore in June 1847. **Sir James Ross'** pillar has not, however, been found, and the paper has been transferred to this position, which is that in which **Sir James Ross'** pillar was erected. Sir John Franklin died on the 11th June 1847; and the total loss by deaths in the expedition had been to this date 9 Officers and 15 men.

F.R.M. Crozier, Captain HMS Erebus.
Captain & Senior Officer James Fitzjames HMS

"Added to the document was the line: and start on tomorrow, 26th, for Back's Fish River."

When the note was compiled on 25th April 1848, Fitzjames and Crozier, with their vessels trapped in ice off King William Island for 19 months and already suffering losses never before experienced aboard ship by 19th century artic explorers, including the death of Franklin himself a year before the ships had to be abandoned with the remainder of the expedition forced to begin its doomed march.

Franklin had died only two weeks after the **"first note"** had been written and Graham Gore had died some time after the first message, because he was referred to as the "late" Commander Gore in the **"second note"** something was going on, so to speak.

The ships had been beset in ice since September 12th, 1846. Why abandon the ships instead of waiting several months when the warmer weather would have arrived and that would have allowed the ships to escape to relative safety? So why the strange and hurried escape...! On April 22, 1848, the ships were deserted and the remaining crew of 105 had reached the shore near Victoria point, the actual landing place, is now called Croziers landing, which is actually several miles south of Victoria point.

And what about the inconsistency with the strange conflicting dates? Of when the ships were deserted on April 22nd, according to the addition under Crozier's signature " and start on tomorrow 26th for Back's Fish River" which means in was written on the 25th, why did it take F.R.M. Crozier, James Fitzjames and the other crewmen 3 days to cross the ice over to the shore? Or when it took the first 1847 party of Gore and the 6 crewmen 4 days to reach Victoria Point, we don't know...!

And now the abandonment of the ships to the shore had taken 3 days to essential the same place that in 1830, James Clack Ross had walked to in only 4 hours! All the way from Cape Felix to Victory Point!

Vis-à-Vis The hidden meaning could be related to the cryptic messages on the third grave of **William Braine** who's plaque has for what ever reason the number **4 back to front!** And his left arm was up his back almost like a figure **4** that looked as if it was pointing towards the unmarked **4th grave.**

The book of Joshua

"And she said unto them, get you to the mountain, lest the pursuers meet you; and hide yourselves there for three days, until the pursuers be returned: and afterwards may ye go your way."

After this until the desertion of the ships, the terrified expedition must have refused to go back anywhere near Victory point, the same place that James Clark Ross must have seen something weird in the Artic...!

. . .

"As the wind howled and moaned,
You could see a strange eerie figure approaching
Carrying a glowing lantern that
Bobbed and danced in the clawing darkness"

. . .

The mysterious boat

Had they already perished, and had then been left as decoys like in the film: Beau Geste?

Hobson found a much more vivid indication of the strange tragedy when he located a life-boat from Franklin's expedition containing two skeletons and filled with nothing more than an accumulation of dead weight, (excuse the pun).

When M'Clintock visited the boat-sledge found by Hobson, they were transfixed with awe at the eerie sight of the two skeletons that lay in the boat. One skeleton was found in the bow of the boat and had been partly destroyed by someone or something large and powerful, but the other skeleton remained untouched...! Covered by cloths and furs, with its feet tucked into a pare of boots, nearby were two cocked and loaded double-barrowed shotguns, as if waiting for some kind of attack that could have been swift and deadly, they were either still alive or they had eventually froze to death when they had their heads severed-off at the chin, which is reminiscent of the strange case of little **Emma Grace Carbaugh aged 22 months, page 181. In MISSING 411 The Devil's in the Detail.** Who was found with her head severed from her body! And portions of the Childs body had also been devoured, or possibly cannibalised.

. . .

CANADA
'The headless valley'
NWT
(North West Territory)

"Described as Dead man valley. It lies between the first and second canyons of the South Nahanni River. Sometime in the early 1900s the headless skeletons of the McLeod brothers were found lying on a gravel wash where Prairie creek joins the South Nahanni. 32 others have

mysteriously disappeared in that part of the South Nahanni since then, and three others vanished in 1963."

. . .

The reason why it was done could have either been for some ghastly tribal rite or trophy of the ensuing battle, or for reasons beyond our comprehension, its as if the heads were taken away to be studied by whoever or whatever was chasing them, like **"Beneath The Planet Of The Apes"** and Franklin ignored the warning, and the **low-brows** were sent after them, though it seems or appears that it is very probable that the **highly intellectual** ones or high-brows could be still out somewhere in the background, so to speak!

And Franklin trying to leave some kind of cryptic clue or fingerprint as to what was going on, like in the mysterious bible quote from the book of Joshua:

"If it seem evil unto you to serve the Lord

Choose ye this day whom ye will serve

Whether the Gods which your father served which

where on the other side of the flood

Or the Gods of the Amorites in whose land ye

dwell"

Is it not strange that there is questionable evidence that one of the ships, ether the **Erebus** or the **Terror** could have remained afloat for months before eventually drifting down and becoming stuck-fast in the ice, near the coast of the Adelaide Peninsula or the Canadian mainland, where one of the Inuit's had climbed aboard and found the strange and frightening figure of a large Giant or very large man or biped with massive teeth, which took five Inuit's to try and lift! And who apparently abandoned the effort leaving the Giant onboard the ship.

What was the strange Giant doing onboard the ship? And did the rest of this savage and yet mysterious tribe come back to get it? Maybe it's buried on Beechey-Island? During Commander Inglefield's sojourns to the Artic 1852 on-board the Isabel, and the weird incident while on Beechey-Island, where his companion told him of what seemed or appeared to be a huge bear! Sitting next to one of the graves, as if keeping a silent vigil over the dead...

Was it one of these strange Giants or ghosts in the machine called **"Amorites"** like **"Goliath"** who was killed by **"David"** in the Christian scriptures a strange bogie-man that seems or appears to haunt the pages of our **theological** and **anthropology** books:

440

A small bible had been discovered on the boat-sledge by M'Clintock, which contained numerous marginal notes and whole passages underlined. What happened to this book?

. . .

M'Clintock named the area, on the western extreme of King William Island, Cape Crozier. The boat was 8.5 metres long and weighed 635 Kilos.
The strangest of all was the direction the boat-sledge was facing, "it was back towards the ships"

. . .

'A strange Encounter at Washington-Bay'

The Inuit's told a strange and unquiet story that while sealing on the west shore of King William Island, near Washington Bay and slightly north of Cape Hershel, who had spotted a distant sail mounted on a boat-sledge, along side were a party of white-men, and there in a crack that had separated in the ice, the Inuit's were in communication with the white-men, but did not understand where the white-men were going, even when Crozier who one of the Inuit's had already known, pointed to the north, back towards the ships or by using pantomime to try and communicate with the Inuit's, as if he was trying to describe something very strange and weird, drawing in his hand and arm from that direction and slowly moving his body in a falling direction, and all at once dropped his dead sideways into his hand, while making a kind of combination of *"whirring"* *"buzzing"* or wind sound. As if he was trying to describe something *falling* or *dropping* onto or through the ice!
"Underwater UFOs have been sighted on many occasions lifting out of their submerged depths. In an article entitled "UFOs-at 450 Fathoms," UFO Reporter Ed Hyde told of the sighting made by Dr. R. J. Villela, a Brazilian scientist, who saw a UFO smash through an estimated *40ft* of ice at the South Pole and soar into the sky at amazing speed."

Who goes there...?
(Buzzers)

Like Thomas Simpson who had later died under mysterious circumstances and the strange sounds his companion heard accompanying a *flying light* that had been seen near **Cape Anderson**.
"It's as if we are dealing with beings of terrible might or terrible forms that are endued with the speed of the mind and capable of agitating and crushing all foes"

"Captain Sir Edward Belcher's"

*Admiralty Flotilla or the last of the great Artic expeditions and
Acting under the orders of the British Admiralty and the mysterious Artic-Council.*

When a boat called the **"Phoenix"** reached Beechey-Island Ballot had offered to carry dispatches up, of all places **"Wellington Channel"** to Captain Sir Edward Belcher's ships, the assistance and the Pioneer. He set off on August 12th with a sledge and three companions, one who would later serve as quartermaster on the Fox!

The party travelled on the ice for two days, until **Bellot** decided it would be safer if they returned to shore. But suddenly, a lead opened up and **Bellot** and two of companions found themselves trapped on a drifting, hummocky ice-flow. The three castaways proceeded to erect a tent, and settle down for the night.

In the morning, the men were still adrift and frightened that they may not get back alive. Bellot to encourage his companions assured them, **"If God protects us, not a hair of our heads will fall to the ground"** then he left the tent to see how far they had drifted. Four minutes later, one of the other men followed Bellot out. To the man's astonishment, Bellot was nowhere to be seen, the two men searched the ice-flow but the French officer was never found, a very familiar pattern!

It was concluded that he had somehow been blown into the water. And yet, no cry for help had been heard, not even a splash! On a small ice-flow, surrounded by water, he simply vanished, like the people in the book **MISSING 411 EASTERN UNITED STATES. Page 85** and little **Larry Dewayne Krebbs** in **Oklahoma aged 2 years in 1988,** Larry Krebbs the boys father, had described what happened: "he said that he walked ahead of his son and when he turned and looked, Dewayne was gone. He recalls never hearing a splash or any noise"

"Thomas Simpson and Peter Warren Dease in 1837-1839 had been sent overland by the Hudson's bay company to map the Southern passage, but Thomas Simpson dies under mysterious circumstances"

. . .

It's as if there was a selective indifference with regards to certain events or the individuals concerned, in Artic-exploration, because no constituted authority even investigated the mysterious death of **Thomas Simpson,** even though suicide was the so-called official verdict...

He also had very important papers on his person, it seem or appears that they had been absconded by person or persons unknown. Even though Thomas Simpson did not suffer fools gladly, he carried a written narrative of his explorations, that he no doubt had with him, when he was mysteriously murdered! And these same papers were handed over to the authorities, and it was until several years after the death of Thomas Simpson that the papers were handed over to his brother, Alexander Simpson in 1844, after receiving the papers, his brother had been forced to pen a letter in open protest, that the depositories of his brother, had been rifled of valuable papers and his diary had also vanished! As if the information contained in the manuscript had been temporarily suppressed, for reasons best known to the co-conspirators involved, whoever or whatever they are? Act like a totalitarian government, that likes to control the spread of free-thinking or information in the form of a particular form of a government within a government, acting quite openly by using tyranny that hides behind the mask of legality, which does not need to suppress news, but cleverly manage it, we in the west are much like a bird in a gilded gage or is it a prison without bars...!

Soon after that, Captain Sir Edward Belcher mysteriously abandoned several of the ships under his command, and complete withdrawal from the Artic would suffice!

Deus ex Machina
(A god from a machine)

Thomas Simpson's expedition while at Cape-Alexander in March **1839**. He observed a **"Semi-elliptical"** figure apparently very near the earth, in rapid motion, and tinged with red, purple and green.

"The half-ellipse seemed to descend and ascend accompanied by an audible sound resembling the rustling of silk. This lasted about ten minutes when the whole phenomenon suddenly rose upwards and its splendour was gone"

It's as if the remnants of part of the lost expedition had attempted to escape from whoever or whatever was pursuing them, and if Crosier had ordered them to cross en-masse, or they were under some kind of threat at the narrowest point of Simpson Strait they must have crossed over in a boat to the Canadian mainland at Eta island, while others continued along the shore of King William island, where it seems or appears that they were cut-off at the Todd-Isets, and the party that had crossed that was forced over to the Canadian mainland must have made a last stand at starvation Cove, while others tried to escape over to Montreal Island and leaving some of the crew to try and make it to the Great Fish River, while it looks as if Crosier along with his remaining force had been forced back towards the ships, while the unseen enemy was still pursuing them to the point they had to abandon the boat.

Hypnos
H.P. Lovecraft

"May the merciful Gods, if indeed there be such, guard those hours when no power of the will, or drug that the cunning of man devises, can keep me from the chasm of sleep, death is merciful, for there is no return therefrom, but with him who has come back out of the nethermost chambers of night, haggard and knowing, peace rests never more, fool that I was to plunge with such unsanctioned frenzy into mysteries no man was meant to penetrate; fool or God that he was my only friend, who led me and went before me, and who in the end passed into terrors which yet be mine"

. . .

"Are we being watched by a race of terrestrial beings, that for reasons beyond our understanding, we have some unknown affinity with"

. . .

Because all things happen for a reason and people just don't disappear, something above and beyond our thinking was and still is involved, people do not vanish into thin-air they must be somewhere? There must be something more sinister or disturbing not only in this strange and eerie story about the lost **Franklin expedition** but in why is it still happening? It's as if whoever or whatever it is, seems or appears to be looking for something by examining or studying us. And to try and search and find the truth is like looking through a glass darkly...

Dracula

'**Dos pou sto**,' said Archimedes. "Give me a fulcrum and I will move the world!" to do once, is the fulcrum whereby child-brain become man-brain; and until he have the purpose to do more, he continue to do the same again every time, just as he have done before!

Professor Van Helsing

. . .

" Remember its a mystery that goes from the sublime to the ridiculous and when you put aside all the facts, and you are left with the impossible, no matter how fantastic it is, it must be the truth!"

. . .

"Who goes there?"

Flying Saucers
Strange flying lights UFOs (Unidentified flying objects)

" There are certain patterns

That suggest that the flying Saucers

Or UFOs (Unidentified Flying Objects) seem or

Appear to be engaged in something of the nature

Of reconnaissance!"

. . . .

Brazil

Marco Antônio Petit. In this interview, he recounted his experiences living alongside his men. Some three months after the interview, he was found dead hanging by his own belt.

Was it caused by something sinister that he witnessed in the jungles of Colares in Brazil, where he saw stranges ariel lights that seemed or appeared to mapping the jungle or covering the Amazon in stripes!

. . .

Kenneth Arnold
Flying Saucer UFO (Unidentified Flying Object) sighting Mystery

. . .

"Saucer reports are not imaginary or adequately explained by natural phenomena; something real is flying around."

June 24
1947

Kenneth Arnold claimed he spotted a string of nine, shiny unidentified flying objectsflying past Mount Rainierat then unheard of supersonicspeeds that Arnold clocked at a minimum of 1,200 miles an hour (*1,932 km/hr*). This was the first post-War sighting in the United States that garnered nationwide news coverage and is credited with being the first of the modern era of *UFO* sightings, including numerous reported sightings over the next two to three weeks. Arnold's description of the objects also led to the press quickly coining

The terms flying sauser and disc as popular descriptive terms for *UFOs*.

Arnold's estimate of *1,700 mph* (*2,700 km/h*), and much faster than the *P-80* jets of the time.

On June *24, 1947*, Arnold was flying from Chehalis, Washington to Yakima, Washington in a CallAir *A-2* on a business trip. He made a brief detour after learning of a $5,000 reward for the discovery of a U.S. Marine Corps *C-46* transport airplane that had crashed near **Mt. Rainier.** The skies were completely clear and there was a mild wind.

A few minutes before *3:00* p.m. at about 9,200 feet (*2,800 m*) in altitude and near Mineral, Washington, he gave up his search and started heading eastward towards Yakima. He saw a bright flashing light, similar to sunlight reflecting from a mirror. Afraid he might be dangerously close to another aircraft, Arnold scanned the skies around him, but all he could see was a *DC-4* to his left and behind him, about *15 miles (24 km)* away.

About *30* seconds after seeing the first flash of light, Arnold saw a series of bright flashes in the distance off to his left, or north of **Mt. Rainier**, which was then *20* to *25* miles (*40 km*) away. He thought they might be reflections on his airplane's windows, but a few quick tests (rocking his airplane from side to side, removing his eyeglasses, later rolling down his side window) ruled this out. The reflections came from flying objects.

They flew in a long chain, and Arnold for a moment considered they might be a flock of geese, but quickly ruled this out for a number of reasons, including the altitude, bright glint, and obviously very fast speed. He then thought they might be a new type of jet and started looking intently for a tail and was surprised that he couldn't find any.

They quickly approached Rainier and then passed in front, usually appearing dark in profile against the bright white snowfield covering **Rainier,** but occasionally still giving off bright light flashes as they flipped around erratically. Sometimes he said he could see them on edge, when they seemed so thin and flat they were practically invisible. According to Jerome Clark, Arnold described them as a series of objects with convex shapes, though he later revealed that one object differed by being crescent-shaped.

In Arnold's initial descriptions he likened their movement to saucers skipping on water, without comparing their actual shapes to saucers, as news reporters would subsequently quote him. At one point Arnold said they flew behind a subpeak of **Rainier** and briefly disappeared. Knowing his position and the position of the (unspecified) subpeak, Arnold placed their distance as they flew past **Rainier** at about *23* miles (***37 km***).

Using a dzus cowling fastener as a gauge to compare the nine objects to the distant *DC-4*, Arnold estimated their angular size as slightly smaller than the *DC-4,* about the width between the outer engines (about 60 feet). Arnold also said he realized that the objects would have to be quite large to see any details at that distance and later, after comparing notes with a United Airlines crew that had a similar sighting 10 days later (*see below*), placed the absolute size as larger than a *DC-4* airliner (or greater than 100 feet (*30 m*) in length). Army Air Force analysts would later estimate *140* to *280 feet (85 m)*, based on analysis of human visual acuity and other sighting details (such as estimated distance).

Arnold said the objects were grouped together, as Ted Bloecher writes, "in a diagonally stepped-down, echelon formation, stretched out over a distance that he later calculated to be five miles". Though moving on a more or less level horizontal plane, Arnold said the objects weaved from side to side ("like the tail of a Chinese kite" as he later stated), darting through the valleys and around the smaller mountain peaks.

They would occasionally flip or bank on their edges in unison as they turned or maneuvered causing almost blindingly bright or mirror-like flashes of light. The encounter gave him an ***"eerie feeling"***, but Arnold suspected he had seen test flights of a new *U.S.* military aircraft.

As the objects passed Mt Rainer, Arnold turned his plane southward on a more or less parallel course. It was at this point that he opened his side window and began observing the objects unobstructed by any glass that might have produced reflections.

The objects did not disappear and continued to move very rapidly southward, continuously moving forward of his position. Curious about their speed, he began to time their rate of passage: he said they moved from Mt. Rainer to Mount Adams where they faded from view, a distance of about *50* miles (*80 km*), in one minute and forty-two seconds, according to the clock on his instrument panel.

When he later had time to do the calculation, the speed was over 1,700 miles per hour (*2,700 km/h*). This was about three times faster than any manned aircraft in *1947*. Not knowing exactly the distance where the objects faded from view, Arnold conservatively and arbitrarily rounded this down to 1,200 miles (*1,900 km*) an hour, still faster than any known aircraft, which had yet to break the sound barrier. It was this supersonic speed in addition to the unusual saucer or disk description that seemed to capture people's attention.

Arnold shares the story

Arnold landed in Yakima at about 4.00 p.m., and quickly told friend and airport general manager Al Baxter the amazing story, and before long, the entire airport staff knew of Arnold's claims. He discussed the story with the staff, and later wrote that Baxter didn't believe him.

Arnold flew on to an air show Pendleton, Oregon, not knowing that somebody in Yakima had phoned in ahead to say that Arnold had seen some strange new aircraft. It was at this time that Arnold studied his maps, determined the distance between **Mt. Rainier** and **Mt. Adams**, and calculated the rather astonishing speed.

He told a number of pilot friends, and wrote in his account to AAF intelligence that they did not scoff or laugh. Instead they suggested that maybe he had seen guided missiles or something new, though Arnold felt this explanation to be inadequate. He also wrote that some former Army pilots told him that they had been briefed before going into combat "that they might see objects of similar shape and design as I described and assured me that I wasn't dreaming or going crazy."

. . .

Arnold wasn't interviewed by reporters until the next day (**June 25**) when he went to the office of the *East Oregonian* in Pendleton. Any skepticism the reporters might have harbored evaporated when they interviewed Arnold at length; as historian Mike Dash records: Arnold had the makings of a reliable witness. He was a respected businessman and experienced pilot ... and seemed to be neither exaggerating what he had seen, nor adding sensational details to his report. He also gave the impression of being a careful observer ... These details impressed the newspapermen who interviewed him and lent credibility to his report.

"*Corroboration*"

Arnold's sighting was partly corroborated by a prospector named Fred Johnson on Mt. Adams, who wrote AAF intelligence that he saw six of the objects on June 24 at about the same time as Arnold, which he viewed through a small telescope. He said they were "round" and tapered "sharply to a point in the head and in an oval shape." He also noted that the **objects seemed to disturb his compass**. An evaluation of the witness by AAF intelligence found him to be credible. Ironically, Johnson's report was listed as the first unexplained UFO report in Air Force files, while Arnold's was dismissed as a mirage, yet Johnson seemed to be describing a continuation of the same event as Arnold.

The Portland *Oregon Journal* reported on July 4 receiving a letter from an L. G. Bernier of Richland, Washington (about *110* miles (*180* km) east of **Mt. Adams** and *140* miles (*230* km) southeast of **Mt. Rainier**). Bernier wrote that he saw three of the strange objects over Richland flying "almost edgewise" toward **Mt. Rainier** about one half hour before Arnold. Bernier thought the three were part of a larger formation. He indicated they were traveling at high speed: "I have seen a *P-38* appear seemingly on one horizon and then gone to the opposite horizon in no time at all, but these disks certainly were traveling faster than any *P-38*. [Maximum speed of a *P-38* was about *440* miles an hour.] No doubt Mr. Arnold saw them just a few minutes or seconds later, according to their speed. "The previous day, Bernier had also spoken to his local newspaper, the Richland Washington Villager, and was among the first witnesses to suggest extraterrestrial origins: "I believe it may be a visitor from another planet."

About 60 miles (97 km) west-northwest of Richland in Yakima, Washington, a woman named Ethel Wheelhouse likewise reported sighting several flying discs moving at fantastic speeds at around the same time as Arnold's sighting.

When military intelligence began investigating Arnold's sighting in early July, they found yet another witness from the area. A member of the Washington State forest service, who had been on fire watch at a tower in Diamond Gap, about *20* miles (*32* km) south of Yakima, reported seeing "flashes" at *3:00* p.m. on the 24th over **Mount Rainier** (or exactly the same time as Arnold's sighting), that appeared to move in a straight line. Similarly, at 3:00 p.m. Sidney B. Gallagher in Washington state (exact position unspecified) reported seeing nine shiny discs flash by to the north. A Seattle newspaper also mentioned a woman near Tacoma who said she saw a chain of nine, bright objects flying at high speed near **Mt. Rainier.** Unfortunately this short news item wasn't precise as to time or date, but indicated it was around the same date as Arnold's sighting.

However, a pilot of a *DC-4* some *10* to *15* miles (*24* km) north of Arnold en route to Seattle reported seeing nothing unusual. (This was the same *DC-4* seen by Arnold and which he used for size comparison.)

Other Seattle area newspapers also reported other sightings of flashing, rapidly moving unknown objects on the same day, but not the same time, as Arnold's sighting. Most of these sightings were over Seattle or west of Seattle in the town of Bremerton, ther that morning or at night, Altogether, there were at least 16 other reported UFO sightings the same day as Arnold's in the Washington state area.

"The flap continues"

Eight Arnold-like objects photographed over Tulsa, Oklahoma, July *12*, *1947*.

The primary corroborative sighting, however, occurred ten days later (*July 4*) when a United Airlines crew over Idaho en route to Seattle also spotted five to nine disk-like objects that paced their plane for *10* to *15* minutes before suddenly disappearing. The next day in Seattle, Arnold met with the pilot, Cpt. Emil J. Smith, and copilot and compared sighting details.

The main difference in shape was that the United crew thought the objects appeared rough on top. This was one of the few sightings that Arnold felt was reliable, most of the rest he thought were the public seeing other things and letting their imaginations run wild. Arnold and Cpt. Smith became friends, met again with Army Air Force intelligence officers on July *12* and filed sighting reports, then teamed up again at the end of July in investigating the strange Maury Island incident.

A similar sighting of eight objects also occurred over Tulsa, Oklahoma on July *12, 1947*. In this instance, a photo was taken and published in the Tulsa Daily World news paper the following day. Interestingly, the photographer, Enlo Gilmore, had been a gunnery officer in the Navy during the war, and using information from another witness, also a veteran, he performed a triangulation and arrived at an estimation of speed of *1,700* miles per hour (*2,700 km/h*), or essentially the same estimate as Arnold's. One of the objects, he said, seemed to have a hole in the middle.

Two or three photos of a similar, solitary object were taken by William Rhodes over Phoenix, Arizona on July *7, 1947,* and appeared in a local Phoenix newspaper and some other newspapers. The object was rounded in front with a crescent back. These photos also seem to show something resembling a hole in the middle, though Rhodes thought it was a canopy. Rhodes's negatives and prints were later confiscated by the FBI and military. However, the photos show up in later Air Force intelligence reports.

Arnold was soon shown the Rhodes photos when he met with two AAF intelligence officers. He commented, "It was a disk almost identical to the one peculiar flying saucer that had been worrying me since my original observation — the one that looked different from the rest and that I had never mentioned to anyone." As a result, Arnold felt that the Rhodes photos were genuine.

Flying saucer

Arnold's account was first featured in a few late newspaper editions on June 25, appeared in numerous *U.S.* and Canadian papers (and some foreign newspapers) on June 26 and thereafter, often on the front page. Without exception, according to Bloecher, the Arnold story was initially related with a serious, even-handed tone.

The first reporters to interview Arnold were Nolan Skiff and Bill Bequette of the East Oregonian news paper in Pendleton, Oregon on June 25, and the first story on the Arnold sighting, written by Bequette, appeared in the newspaper the same day.

The term appears on a headline from June 26, 1947, Chicago Sun news paper is perhaps the first-ever use of the term *"flying saucer"*

Starting June 26 and June 27, newspapers first began using the terms *"flying saucer"* and *"flying disk"* (or *"disc"*) to describe the sighted objects. Thus the Arnold sighting is credited with giving rise to these popular terms. The actual origin of the terms is somewhat controversial and complicated. Jerome Clark cites a *1970* study by Herbert Strentz, who reviewed *U.S.* newspaper accounts of the Arnold *UFO* sighting, and concluded that the term was probably due to an editor or headline writer: the body of the early Arnold news stories did not use the term *"flying saucer"* or *"flying disc."* However, earlier stories did in fact credit Arnold with using terms such as *"saucer"*, *"disk"*, and *"pie-pan"* in describing the shape.

Bequette interview: Years later, Arnold claimed he told Bill Bequette that *"they flew erratic, like a saucer if you skip it across the water."*Arnold felt that he had been misquoted since the description referred to the objects' motion rather than their shape.Thus Bequette has often been credited with first using *"flying saucer"* and supposedly misquoting Arnold, but the term does not appear in Bequette's early articles. Instead, his first article of June 25 says only, *"He said he sighted nine saucer-like aircraft flying in formation..."*

The next day in a much more detailed article, Bequette wrote, "He clung to his story of shiny, flat objects racing over the *Cascade mountains* with a peculiar weaving motion 'like the tail of a Chinese kite.' ...He also described the objects as 'saucer-like' and their motion 'like fish flipping in the sun.' ...[*Arnold*] described the objects as 'flat like a pie-pan and somewhat bat-shaped'." It wasn't until June 28 that Bequette first used the term *"flying disc"* (but not *"flying saucer"*).

A review of early newspaper stories indicates that immediately after his sighting, Arnold generally described the objects' shape as thin and flat, rounded in the front but chopped in the back and coming to a point, i.e., more or less *saucer*-or *disk-like.* He also specifically used terms like *"saucer"* or *"saucer-like"*, *"disk"*, and *"pie pan"* or *"pie plate"* in describing the shape. The motion he generally described as weaving like the tail of a kite and erratic flipping.

For example, in a surviving recorded radio interview from June 25, Arnold described them as looking **"*something like a pie plate that was cut in half with a sort of a convex triangle in the rear.*"** His motion descriptions were: **"*I noticed to the left of me a chain which looked to me like the tail of a Chinese kite, kind of weaving... they seemed to flip and flash in the sun, just like a mirror... they seemed to kind of weave in and out right above the mountaintops...*"**

The following day (*June 26*) were the following quotations attributed to Arnold: United Press **"*They were shaped like saucers and were so thin I could barely see them...*"**

Associated Press: "He said they were bright, saucer-like objects--he called them 'aircraft'. ...He also described the objects as **'*saucer-like*'** and their motion 'like a fish flipping in the sun.' ...Arnold described the objects as 'flat like a pie pan'."

Associated Press: "They flew with a peculiar dipping motion, 'like a fish flipping in the sun,' he said. ...He said they appeared to fly almost as if fastened together -- if one dipped, the others did, too.

Chicago Tribune: "They were silvery and shiny and seemed to be shaped like a pie plate.... I am sure they were separate units because they weaved in flight like the tail of a kite."

On *June 27* was the following quotation from the *Portland Oregon Journal*: "They were half-moon shaped, oval in front and convex in the rear. ...There were no bulges or cowlings; they looked like a big flat disk.' ...Arnold said that the objects weaved 'like the tail of a Chinese kite'."

Two weeks later, Arnold was still referring to the shape of the objects as "saucers" or "saucer-like."

In the *Portland Oregonian* on *July 11,* he was quoted saying, "I actually saw a type of aircraft slightly longer than it was wide, with a thickness about one twentieth as great as its width. ...I reckoned the saucers were 23 miles away."

Statement to the army Kenneth Arnold's report to Army Air Forces (*AAF*) intelligence, dated *July 12, 1947,* which includes annotated sketches of the typical craft in the chain of nine objects.

In a written statement to Army Air Forces (*AAF*) intelligence the following day (*July 12*), Arnold several times referred to the objects as **"*saucer-like.*"** At the end of the report he drew a picture of what the objects appeared to look like at their closest approach to **Mt. Rainier**. He wrote, "They seemed longer than wide, their thickness was about 1/20th their width."

As to motion, Arnold wrote, "They flew like many times I have observed geese to fly in a rather diagonal chain-like line as if they were linked together. They seemed to hold a definite direction but rather swerved in and out of the high mountain peaks." He also spoke of how they would "flip and flash in the sun."

To complicate the shape descriptions further, a month after his sighting, Arnold was to become involved in the bizarre Maury Island incident.

Arnold was dispatched by a magazine publisher to **Tacoma** to investigate it, although he eventually turned the investigation over to the *AAF*. In a meeting with two *AAF* intelligence officers (the same ones who interviewed him on *July 12* and for whom he wrote his report), Arnold first revealed one of the nine objects was different, being larger and shaped more like a crescent coming to a point in the back. It was at this time that Arnold was also shown the Rhodes photos of a crescent-shaped object over Phoenix, which Arnold deemed authentic because of the unusual shape.

"Widespread UFO reports after Arnold sighting"

In the weeks that followed Arnold's June, *1947* story, at least several hundred reports of similar sightings flooded in from the *U.S.* and around the world — most of which described **saucer-shaped** objects.

A sighting by a United Airlines crew of another nine, disk-like objects over Idaho on *July 4* probably garnered more newspaper coverage than Arnold's original sighting, and opened the floodgates of media coverage in the days to follow.

Bloecher collected reports of *853* flying disc sightings that year from *140* newspapers from Canada, Washington *D.C,* and every *U.S.* state save Montana. This was more *UFO* reports for *1947* than most researchers ever suspected. Some of these stories were poorly documented or fragmentary, but Bloecher argued that about *250* of the more detailed reports (such as those made by pilots or scientists, multiple eyewitnesses, or backed by photos) made a persuasive case for a genuine mystery.

Adding intrigue to Arnold's story, the *U.S.* military denied having any planes at all in the area of **Mount Rainier** at the time of his sighting.

"Military investigation of Arnold story"

The first investigation of Arnold's claims came from Lt. Frank Brown and Capt. William Davidson of Hamilton Field in California, who interviewed Arnold on *July 12.* Arnold also submitted a written report at that time. Regarding the reliability of Arnold's sighting, they concluded: "It is the present opinion of the interviewer that Mr. Arnold actually saw what he stated he saw. It is difficult to believe that a man of [his] character and apparent integrity would state that he saw objects and write up a report to the extent that he did if he did not see them."

Despite this, the Army Air Force's formal public conclusion was that Arnold had seen a mirage.

In addition, on *July 9 AAF* intelligence, with help from the *FBI,* secretly began an investigation of the best sightings, mostly from pilots and military personnel. Arnold's sighting, as well as that of the United Airline's crew, were included in the list of best sightings. Three weeks later they came to the conclusion that the saucer reports were not imaginary or adequately explained by natural phenomena; something real was flying around.

"The Watchers"

Are these strange lights in the sky or **Flying Saucers** (*Unidentified Flying Objects*), ominously mapping the globe or preparing for an invasion, because it seems or appears that there could be something more insidious

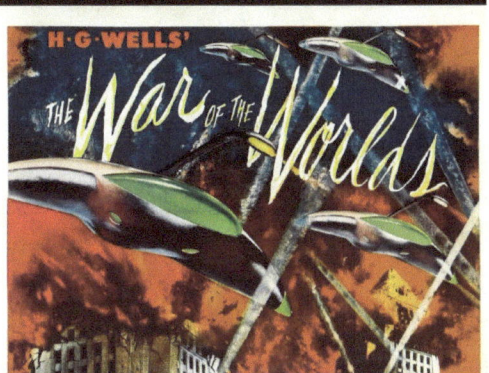

or hostile behind the chilling presence of these strangers or watchers from the skies?

Like in **MISSING 411 WESTERN UNITED STATES AND CANADA.** And the disquieting and strange story of **James McCormick** in **1961, aged 16 years, page 18.** After the weather conveniently turning bad, James Jr, for reasons unknown became unwell, after carrying his 16 year old son for three hours, he was exhausted and laid the boy down, and apparently went to investigate what he thought were automobile headlights, when he returned the boy was gone!

. . .

Is it a sinister game of cat and mouse, over **military instillations, Atomic energy plants, along coastal defence lines or electrical power lines, power sub-stations, water-pumping stations, reservoirs, lakes and other bodies of water and Crops!**

They are seen flying in **formation** like **squadrons** that alter there're pattern from rectangular to diamond and or *V* shaped to even circular.

Who or what has been responsible for the abductions and or kid-knapping of scores people? For the murders and assaults or the pursuit of vehicles and the unprovoked attacks on homes or the disruption of power-sources? Are these invisible residents responsible for the mysterious destruction of aircraft that borders on the realms of sci-fi?

. . .

'Radio operator'
UK
England

13th August 1956
10.am
RAF Bentwaters
(United States Air-Force base)

A Ground Controlled Approach (*GCA*) radar operator picked up a fast moving target *30 miles* (*50 Kilometres*) to the east, heading in from the sea at a speed of *2000 to 4000 miles per hour* (*3200 to 6440 Km/h*).

It passed directly over **Bentwaters** and sped away until it disappeared from the scope *30 miles* (*50 Kilometres*) to the west.

This over flight was not just a radar observation, a tower operator on the ground looking up saw a strange light in the sky, at the same time as the pilot of a *USAF C47* aircraft flying overhead **Bentwaters** at *4000ft (1200 Metres)*, who had been alerted by ground control, who had visual on the **Flying Saucer** or **UFO** (*Unidentified Flying Object*) heading towards **Lakenheath,** another **RAF aerodrome** used by the **USAF,** immediate

warning was given, as ground observers at **Lakenheath** saw the strange light ominously approach and then stop dead, and then it moved swiftly out of sight to the east.

Even more bizarre was the fact that following the first eerie sighting of the strange flying light or **Flying Saucer UFO** (*Unidentified flying Object*), two other **weird lights** were spotted which was either the first light that was joined by **another craft,** or two more **odd flying lights** that were independent of the first one or part of the same group of **Flying Saucers** or **UFOs** (*Unidentified Flying Objects*) of some kind, that then moved off in formation.

Observers and radar operators at **Lakenheath** (*GCA*) recorded the **strange flying objects** travelling at terrific speeds, stopping suddenly! And changing course instantaneously. The Americans at **Lakenheath** had put through the emergency call to the **RAF.**

The **RAF** chief controller at **Bentwaters** scrambled a Venom night-fighter from **RAF Waterbeach**, and his interception controller, with a team of three highly trained personal, took over, the Venom was vectored onto the **strange light, Flying Saucer** or **UFO** (*Unidentified Flying Object*).

. . .

The pilot was accompanied by a navigator who calls out 'Contact' when he gets a visual and 'Judy' when they lock onto the target, with the radar scope! With this the Venom closed onto the target, but seconds later the **mysterious flying object** had come up behind the fighter, with the pilot calling out, lost target, more help, and who was then told that the object was now behind him.

Meanwhile the chief controller scrambled another Venom fighter and witnesses said that the **strange flying light** or **flying saucer UFO** (*Unidentified Flying Object*) "**flipped-over**" and out flanked the **RAF** fighter, which then tried to out-manoeuvre the **strange flying craft** in order to get behind it...

"The whole event was to become a complete and utter mystery"

Radar visual

Major *L.D.* Chase of an *RB-47* aircraft that took off from Forbes Air-force base, Topeka, Kansas, on a training flight on the *19th September 1957*.

The *RB-47* was a photoreconnaissance version of the six-jet *Boeing B-47* Bomber. It was equipped for electronic counter-measures (ECM), which included location of enemy ground-based radar units, and identification of system-application, such as carrier-frequency, pulse-rate and width, scan-speed and bearing.

The mission of *19th September* involved gunnery exercises and navigation over the Gulf of Mexico, and an (*ECM*) exercise over the Southern central United States. The crew consisted of: The skipper, Major *L.D.* Chase, the co-pilot, the navigator and three other officers manning the (ECM) monitors on board the *RB-47*.

No1 monitor was a direction- finding-system with antennae on permanent mountings on the wing tips. *No2 monitor* employed back-to-back antennae spinning in a housing beneath the rear fuselage of the aircraft, and the signals from this array were processed in a radar receiver and a pulse-analyser.

No3 monitor was not involved in that nights strange, but true events.

On the return journey from the Gulf of Mexico, the *RB-47* crossed the

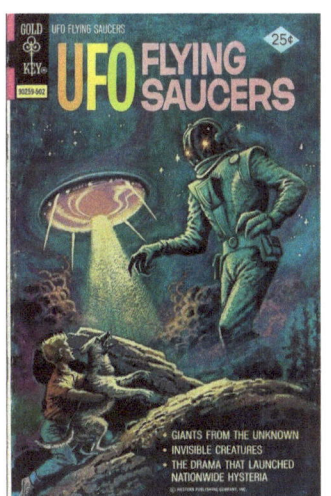

Mississippi coastline near Gulfport and headed for Jackson, Mississippi, where the (*ECM*) exercise was to take place, at more that *30.000ft* and at a speed of *500 knots* or (*900Km/h*).

It was then that captain McClure on *No2 monitor* picked up an unexpected signal. The radarscope was showing a signal trace at *5 o'clock,* which was a signal source behind them to starboard and out over the sea, Captain McClure assumed that the traces were coming from the two antennae of the monitor that had somehow switched and the signal must actually be coming from a ground radar unit in Louisiana, at the *11 o'clock position*.

Indeed, the signal he was receiving checked out at a frequency of *2800 Megahertz,* a band commonly used for search radars. The lobe continued to show a **'blip'** moving up-scope to *4 o'clock*, then to *3 o'clock* and so on, but when it passed *12 o'clock* and continued down-scope, the captain realised that the signal must be correct. But where was it coming from?

The *RB-47* changed course at Jackson and headed westwards towards Forth-Worth and Dallas, the pilots saw a ***white light*** in front of them; the crew were then warned to expect evasive action, then the **strange curious light** moved across their path.

Captain McClure then overheard the pilots discussing the strange presence of the **weird light**, over the intercom, and he told then them of the **weird signal** that had puzzled him earlier on.

He then turned *No2 monitor* to *2800 Kilohertz*, and instantly picked up a strong signal at the *2 o'clock position*. The signal did not move down-scope; this showed that the source maintained a constant position relative to the aircraft.

After the *RB-47* had been escorted by the **strange light** or **Flying Saucer UFO** (*Unidentified Flying Object*) so to speak, for *100 miles* (*160 Kilometres*) the skipper called up **Carswell Air Force Base,** where a ground control intercept (*GCI*) radar was in operation.

No1 monitor had by now confirmed the existence of a target at *2 o'clock* position... **Carswell** came back with information that there was another aircraft *10 miles* (*16 Kilometres*) from the *RB-47* at *2 o'clock*. Captain McClure realized that the **mysterious blip** that had puzzled him had been a positive reading of an **unknown signal trace** or **mysterious source that was circling the RB-47 in flight.**

The **strange moving light** or **Flying Saucer UFO** (*Unidentified Flying Object*) had moved forward, detected by both the (*GCI*) at **Carswell** and the *No2 monitor* on the *RB-47,* and when it had reached the *12 o'clock position,* both pilots could actual see it, it was something very large and it was glowing red...

Between Fort Worth and Dallas, the strange object then changed course, and Major Chase obtained permission to follow it, and as the *RB-47* closed-in on the glowing object, that was simultaneously reported by the (*GCI*) ground control, intercept, radar, to be stationery. At that point the **weird light blinked-out** and the traces or source of the strange unknown object, mysteriously disappeared from the radarscopes!

Major Chase put the *RB-47* into a left-turn, and the **mysterious flying object** reappeared at a lower level-at about *15,000ft* (*4500metres*) –and the strange trace or source was seen back on the radarscopes, the skipper was again given permission to move back towards the object, he then took the *RB-47* and levelled out at *20,000ft* (*6000metres*) and again **the strange object mysteriously disappeared** from the (*GCI*) radarscope at **Carswell.**

The *RB-47* now climbed to *25,000ft* (*7600metres*) and headed for Oklahoma; with its fuel almost exhausted or running low. Once again, on the ground, **Carswell** (*GCI*), **the strange flying object** or **glowing light**, reappeared and following *10miles* (*16Kilometres*) flanking behind the *RB-47* and into Southern Okalahoma, where it disappeared for the last and final time, after dogging the *RB-47* for over an hour, covering a distance of *800 miles* (*1250 Kilometres*).

It is a strange and unsolved incident that was officially investigated by officers at White-sands missile base and Kirtland Air-Force-Base, only two questions remain unanswered, was the strange craft under intelligent control and if, so by whom?

The Antarctic
EERIE STORIES FROM THE ARGENTINE

Antarctic sector

Flying lights or Flying Saucers UFOs (Unidentified Flying Object) activity

Strange activity has been observed in the Artic and the Antarctic regions by trained military and scientific personal. At the Argentine Navy garrison at (**Deception Island**) that was observed, on **July 3,** at *19:40 hours* (*Local time*)

A strange silent multi-coloured glowing object was observed moving in a haphazard trajectory towards the east, changing its course to the west and north, several times at varying speeds, it passed at an elevation of *45 degrees* over the horizon, its distance was estimated at *10* to *15* Kilometres from the military base.

During its strange manoeuvres the observers were able to register its fantastic speeds, and also the fact that it was able to hover or float motionless for up to *15 minutes* at an estimated altitude of about *5,000 metres* or (*3.10miles*).

The meteorological conditions for the area of the sighting were considered excellent for the time of the year: clear sky, some strato-cumulus, and the moon in its last quarter could be clearly seen in the sky, visibility was perfectly clear.

The strange glowing multi-coloured flying light or **Flying Saucer UFO** (*Unidentified Flying Object)* had been witnessed by a Meteorologist and thirteen members of the garrison including, three Chilean Sub-officers who had been visiting the base that afternoon.

The Argentine bases in the Antarctic are some of the oldest of the southern scientific outposts, they are equipped with sensitive equipment used for detecting changes in the magnetic-fields of that area, and on the July 3 1965, the equipment registered the abnormal changes in the magnetic-fields around the bases and during the passage of the **strange flying light** or **Flying Saucer UFO** (*Unidentified Flying Object*) over the military base, two **Variometres** registered disturbances in the **magnetic-field** that were recorded on their tapes.

The first sighting or observations occurred on *June 18th* and had been reported: That at *4:00pm* (*Local time*) an **Arial object**, luminous intensity of the first magnitude star, appearing east of **"South Orkney Island"** at *60-degrees elevation* changing direction in a *180-degree* turn to the west and then turning *90-degrees* to the right; moving away to the south following an irregular trajectory at *4:20pm*. Meteorological conditions good, dark sky. The phenomenon was observed by the whole garrison.

A report on **the strange flying object** or **Flying Saucer UFO** (*Unidentified Flying Object*) that the Argentine military base had sighted on *July 3rd* was released to the press.

The army personal in the course of Meteorological observations on *July 3rd*, had spotted the presence of a **strange Ariel glowing object** sighted for *20minutes* by several other members of the garrison, with its multi-coloured Red-Yellow luminosity, as it changed colour. Elevation *45 degrees*, crossing the Island at *SW* in a *NW-SE direction*, at a high velocity, oscillatory course, its luminosity like a first magnitude star.

The visibility was good. Communications on that day, at *20:30hrs* (*Local time*), with the English base revealed that on *July the 2nd*, at *19:45hrs*, five members of the army post had sighted a **celestial object** North of Island, moving in a zigzagging course, stopping in mid-air for five or ten minutes and then **the strange multi-coloured light eventually disappeared**! In a vertical direction, elevation *20 degrees* and its brightness was the equivalent of a first magnitude star.

Communication with the Argentine military out-post at deception Island, revealed that on *July 3rd* up to sixteen personnel, including three Chilean Sub-officers who had observed **the strange glowing Arial phenomenon** or **Flying Saucer UFO** (*Unidentified Flying Object*) over the Northern area of the Island, when it was moving in a North-Northwest direction, varying its speed. Oscillatory course, changing Yellow-Green-Orange colour, leaving a contrail at *30 degrees elevation*. Round-shaped, disappearing into cirrus clouds. Was tracked by **theodolites** and high-powered binoculars.

On the same day, at the Argentine base at **Orkney Island**, two Meteorological observers sighted an **Arial object flying at high-speed** on a parabolic trajectory, course *E-W*, white luminosity, **causing a disturbance in the magnetic field that registered on the geomagnetic instruments with patterns notably out of the normal.**

What the army-bases saw was something real, a solid but elusive object that was moving at incredible speeds, performed manoeuvres, emitted a strange light, the object also caused the unusual and bizarre interference in the electro-magnetic instruments on the military base. The army did not believe that it was an **air-craft** or **ship** of known **terrestrial manufacture** due to the fact that no direct contact with it was possible at the time, although the interference was by **someone** or **something unknown**, and that nothing similar that we know of exists on our planet in either shape, velocity or speed and mobility...

Where are they coming from?

And who is flying these strange Arial lights or Flying Saucers UFOs (Unidentified Flying Objects?)

Are they Extra-terrestrial?

Or are they Terrestrial in nature, and they are coming from somewhere else?

"Because there is something odd flying about our skies! Or it's as if something unknown to our understanding is going on around the earth"

'Patterns of horror'

Foo-fighters, what are they?

A war of nerves

The term *Foo-fighter* was used by Allied aircraft pilots in World War II to describe various UFOs or mysterious aerial phenomena seen in the skies over both the European and Pacific Theater of Operations.

History

The first sightings occurred in *November 1944,* when pilots flying over Germany by night reported seeing fast-moving round glowing objects following their aircraft.

The objects were variously described as fiery, and glowing red, white, or orange. Some pilots described them as resembling Christmas tree lights and reported that they seemed to toy with the aircraft, making wild turns before simply vanishing. Pilots and aircrew reported that the objects flew formation with their aircraft and behaved as if under intelligent control, but never displayed hostile behaviour. However, they could not be out manoeuvred or shot down. Further investigation revealed that these "**balls of fire**" had been following *USAAF* night fighters for over a month and descriptions of the phenomena varied, but the pilots agreed that the mysterious lights followed their aircraft closely at high speed.

The "balls of fire" phenomenon reported from the Pacific Theater of Operations differed somewhat from the foo fighters reported from Europe; the "ball of fire" resembled a large burning sphere which "just hung in the sky", though it was reported to sometimes follow aircraft. As with the European foo fighters, no aircraft was reported as having been attacked by a "ball of fire"

Sighting from September *1941* in the Indian Ocean was similar to some later Foo Fighter reports. From the deck of the *S.S. Pułaski* (*a Polish merchant vessel transporting British troops*), two sailors reported a **"strange globe glowing with greenish light, about half the size of the full moon as it appears to us**." They alerted a British officer, who watched the object's movements with them for over an hour.

Charles R. Bastien of the Eighth Air Force reported one of the first encounters with foo fighters over the Belgium/Holland area; he described them as "two fog lights flying at high rates of speed that could change direction rapidly". During debriefing, his intelligence officer told him that two RAF night fighters had reported the same thing, and it was later reported in British newspapers.

U.S. Air Force pilot Duane Adams often related that he had witnessed two occurrences of a bright light, which paced his aircraft for about half an hour and then rapidly ascended into the sky.

Both incidents occurred at night, both over the South Pacific, and both were witnessed by the entire aircraft crew. The first sighting occurred shortly after the end of *World War II* while Adams piloted a *B-25 bomber*. The second sighting The second sighting occurred in the early *1960s* when Adams was piloting a *KC-135 tanker*.

Shag Harbour is relatively well known for its 1967 UFO sighting. On October 4, 1967, a strange sight was reported over the skies near the coastal community of Shag Harbour.

Multiple people saw a chain of lights in the sky, which seemed to angle down and impact into the ocean near **Shag Harbour**. Thinking that an aircraft may have crashed, witnesses called the Royal Canadian Mounted Police. *RCMP* officers at the scene and other witnesses saw a light bobbing on the surface, which started drifting out to sea and soon went out.

A rescue effort was quickly assembled. A large swath of thick yellow foam was witnessed in the water by fishermen and other rescuers who aided in the search for possible survivors.

They were soon joined by a Coast Guard cutter. Government agencies quickly ruled out a plane crash when none were reported missing, and other possibilities were ruled out as well, such as flares. The unknown object was then officially classified as a **"UFO"**. The Royal Canadian Navy soon launched an underwater search for possible debris, but officially nothing was ever found and the object was never identified.

* * *

'Terror By Night'
Soviet Union
DYATLOV PASS INCIDENT
Russia
February 2, 1959.
Mysterious deaths of nine ski-hikers in the northern Ural Mountains
The Former USSR
"We had strayed into some region or some set of conditions where the risks were great, yet unintelligible to us. It was a spot held by the dwellers in some outer space, a sort of peep-hole whence they could spy upon earth, themselves unseen, a point where the vail between had worn a little thin"
(Algernon Blackwood and The Willows, 1907)

The Shape Of Things To Come
(Patterns of Horror)

The lack of eyewitnesses has inspired much speculation. Soviet investigators simply determined that **"a compelling natural force"** had caused the deaths. Access to the area was barred for skiers and other adventurers for three years after the incident.

The chronology of the incident remains unclear because of the lack of survivors.Investigators at the time determined that the hikers tore open their tent from within, departing **barefoot** into heavy snow with the temperature being 30 °C (**22 °F**).

A group was formed for a ski trek across the northern **Urals** in **Sverdlovsk Oblast.** The group, led by **Igor Dyatlov,** consisted of eight men and two women. Most were students or graduates of "Ural Polytechnical Institute" now Ural State Technical University:

Igor **Alekseievich Dyatlov,** the group's leader, born January 13, 1936. **Zinaida Alekseevna Kolmogorova,** born January 12, 1937. **Lyudmila Alexandrovna Dubinina,** born May 12, 1938. **Alexander Sergeievich Kolevatov,** born November 16, 1934. **Rustem Vladimirovich Slobodin,** born January 11, 1936. **Yuri (Georgiy) Alexeievich Krivonischenko,** born February 7, 1935. **Yuri Nikolaievich Doroshenko,** born January 29, 1938. **Nicolai Vladimirovich Thibeaux-Brignolles,** born July 5, 1935. **Semyon (Alexander) Alexandrovich Zolotariov,** born February 2, 1921. **Yuri Yefimovich Yudin,** born July 19, 1937, died April 27, **2013**

. . .

The goal of the expedition was to reach **Otorten,** a mountain 10 kilometres (6.2 mi) north of the site of the incident. This route, at that season, was estimated as **"Category III"**, the most difficult. All members were experienced in long ski tours and mountain expeditions.

The group arrived by train at **Ivdel,** a city at the center of the northern province of **Sverdlovsk Oblast** on January 25. They then took a truck to **Vizhai** – the last inhabited settlement so far north.

They started their march toward **Otorten** from **Vizhai** on January 27. The next day, one of the members (**Yuri Yudin**) was forced to go back because of illness. The group now consisted of 9 people.

Diaries and **cameras** found around their last camp made it possible to track the group's route up to the day preceding the incident. On January 31, the group arrived at the edge of a highland area and began to prepare for climbing. In a wooded valley they stored surplus food and equipment that would be used for the trip back.

The following day (February 1), the hikers started to move through the pass. It seems they planned to get over the pass and make camp for the next night on the opposite side, but because of worsening weather conditions, snowstorms and decreasing visibility, they lost their direction and deviated west, upward towards the top of **Kholat Syakhyl.**

When they realized their mistake, the group decided to stop and set up camp there on the slope of the mountain rather than moving 1.5 kilometres (0.93 mi) downhill to a forested area which would have offered some shelter from the elements.

"Yuri Yudin, the lone survivor, postulates that, Dyatlov probably did not want to lose the altitude they had gained, or he decided to practice camping on the mountain slope."

It had been agreed beforehand that **Dyatlov** would send a telegram to their sports club as soon as the group returned to **Vizhai.** It was expected that this would happen no later than February 12, but **Dyatlov** had told **Yudin** that he expected to be longer, and so when this date passed and no messages had been received, there was no reaction – delays of a few days were common in such expeditions.

Only after the relatives of the travelers demanded a rescue operation did the head of the institute send the first rescue groups, consisting of volunteer students and teachers, on February 20. Later, the army and **militsiya** (*Milisha*) forces became involved, with planes and helicopters being ordered to join the rescue operation.

On February 26, the searchers found the abandoned and badly damaged tent on **Kholat Syakhl.**

Mikhail Sharavin, the student who found the tent, said the tent was half torn down and covered with snow. It was empty, and all the group's belongings and **shoes** had been left behind. Investigators said the tent had been cut open from inside!

Terror by Night

Obviously something seems or appears to have went badly wrong for some reason that we don't yet fully understand! Its an enigma that could have strange associations with other things in the past:

1897

Lillian Carney aged 6 years, in MISSING 411 The Devil's in the detail. By David Paulides. Page 123. who was mysteriously snatched by person or persons unknown, while out berry picking! With her parents, when she was eventually found *46 hrs* later, she said: *"the sun shinned all the time in the woods!"*.

1961

Like in David Paulides books: *MISSING 411 WESTERN UNITED STATES & CANADA. James McCormick aged 16 years in the Larch Mountains, Multnomah Falls. Page 18.* Who for some reason became unwell, and after carring the boy for three hours, he was exhausted, and was forced to lay the boy down, where he told him to stay-put while he went to investigate what seemed or appeared to be the **lights** from a car or automobile. in the (middle of nowhere?)

"After he returned the boy had mysteriously vanished"

It looks to all intent and porpose, as if something unknown became curious or interested in them, for whatever reason, like in **David Paulides** book: **MISSING 411 NORTH AMERICA AND BEYOND.** And the strange and frightening disappearence of **Guy Heckle aged 11 years,** in **1973** at the Kiwanis boyscout camp, next to the Cedar River in Iowa. Coincidently next door to the **Duane Arnold Energy Center!**

Where Guy's tent mate **"experienced a series of strange and frightening incidents of someone or something shinning some kind of light in his bedroom window! Following Guy's disappearence"** and someone else was shinning some kind of light in the sleeping area of his tentmate, while he was at the Kiwanis camp, or...

MISSING 411 2013. The Devil's in the Detail. Gary Tweddle New-South-Whales. Aged 23 years. Who mysteriously disappeared and did not know where he was, he somehow got lost, just leaving the resort, where he was stying! While talking to his friends over the cell or (mobile) phone, and he said that he was turning towards **"a light on the hill"** that was the last time he was ever seen alive, his body was found under very suspitious surcumstances!

YURY YAKIMOV
Mountain of the dead
By
Keith McCloskey

Who worked in the the North Urals, 178km (110miles) from the Dyatlov Pass, spoke of a strange and unexplained phenomenon, that took place during the graveyard shift or night-shift in the open-pit mine in 2002.

He was walking along the road to No15 pit and was standing near one of the transformers that powered the floodlights to illuminate the pit!

In the distance he noticed a silent bright light bobbing up and down, in the breeze and drizzling rain, suddenly a beam of light from an unknown source turned towards where he was standing, and shone on him flooding the whole of the forest bathing him in a bright white light, he was standing beside the tranformer with his face turned away!

Patterns of horror

"There was something very strange going on '

The mysterious beam of light had turned away, until he was trying to look at it, and with this the strange light moved back towards him, when he noticed several other smaller lights or flash lights that were being carried by someone or something that gave him the distinct impression that several people were moving through the forest, as if they were searching or trying to spot him!

It was as if the light reacted whenever he glanced at it, and whenever he tried to look at the strange source of light, what was it that seems or appears to be trying to locate him?

Unusual phenomanon reported by rangers in the Denezhkin Kamen reserve!

Reserve rangers **V. Rudkovsky** *and* **V. Yefimov** *were attracted by a bright electrical light 'as if from a projector' in the* **Denezhkin Kamen Reserve** *about 40km north-east of the the* **Laks forestry area** *where* **Yury Yakimov** *had saw the same identical phenomenon.*

One of the eyewitnesses described the strange phenomenon: *"it looked as if two people were moving in my direction holding torches (flashlights) and there was some 'set' in front of me, for some reason or other that reacted to a glance!"*

. . .

Valentin Rudkovsky
"The diary"
No 357 forest quarter

North-west of Mount Denezhkin Kamen, where he was alone on that night, without V. Yefimov.

August 2002

Suddenly I saw a beam of strong light that pierced the forest, the source was at some height above the ground, when suddenly I saw two **swinging spotlights** appear, the impression was of people moving extremely fast in my direction! I thoght someone was joking or trying to scare me?

I dressed quickly, put on my boots, I grabbed my gun and went outside to meet them, I walked about 20m, then lay behind a fallen tree trunk and looked in the **direction of the spotlights,** they rushed very fast in my direction exactly at the moment *I looked at them!*

All was quiet, I raised myself from behind the tree-trunk, and the spotlights were 50-70m away from me, but they were no longer 2, but 7 or 8 now, they dazzled me. Immediately I lay on the ground behind the tree-trunk and turned away from the spotlights! Whenever I raised my head to look at them, they would again shine on me, and dazzle me while approaching.

The light elluminated every blade of grass, and the trees through no shadow!

. . .

"The famous Dechmont Law incident
1979 Livingston, Scotland U.K.*"*

On the **9th of November 1979,** at around **10:00 AM**, Robert Taylor, a married man, father of five, aged 61, resident of Livingston and forestry worker employed by the Livingston Development Corporation left his house. At about **10:30 AM,** he parked his pick up off a track at a plantation at the bottom of Dechmont Law, bordering Dechmont Woods, just off the busy M8 motorway, near Livingston, West Lothian in Scotland U.K.

He had parked as close as he could to the clearing in a plantation that he has to inspect for stray cows and sheep, a part of his job. With his red setter Lara, He followed a track the rest of the way across the lower slope of the forested hill, rounded a corner and emerged into the clearing.

The **UFO:** In the clearing, in front of him, was a large, circular, roundish object about **20 ft across** and **12 feet high,** resting on the ground or hovering just above the ground. It seemed to be made from a dark grey metallic material with a rough texture like sandpaper, parts of which were becoming like half transparent at times, letting the trees behind it be seen, as if the object was trying to cloak itself. A narrow protruding rim ran around the circumference of the object, just below halfway down, and Taylor thought it reminded him of the brim of a hat.

A line of rotating arms was set into the rim. Some dark patches were seen on the body of the object that looked like portholes. The object emitted no noise. Lara, his dog, who was at his side, simply froze and stared at the object, as did Bob Taylor.

As he watched without moving, two spiky spherical objects dropped from the bottom of the larger object. These two spheres were approximately two ft across and he later described them as being quite like sea mines as used in World War II, except that the spikes were longer that those of sea mines, making the objects' diameter approximately **3 ft spikes** included.

The spheres were looking metallic, similar to the material of the larger object, and made frightening sucking noises as they fell from the object and impacted the wet ground. As Taylor **stared** in awe, the two **spiky spheres** rushed towards him from the direction of the object, by bouncing and rolling on the ground.

Or was it something from the air? Like in **David Paulides** book: **MISSING 411 The Devil's in the Detail. Joe Carter 1950 aged 32 years, page 209. Mount St Helens. Washington.** Who was not an amateur at skiing by any stretch of the imagination, while he was on the mountain with friends he had also brought along his camera, and had agreed to go downhill and photograph them as they came down?

When the others eventually reached the location, they found that he had disappeared for some unknown reason!

The **SAR** (*Search And Rescue*) eventually found evidence that seemed or appeared to show that Joe Carter was technically running for his life, so to speak, because someone or something was after him, even though there was no evidence of his pursuer in the snow, he had took-off as if the Devil himself was chasing him, (excuse the pun) and that only leaves another possible way, as **David Paulides** implied, was being pursued by something that could have been flying through the air!

Dyatlov incident

Continued

Could it be some kind of hightech automaton or mechanical probe, either from outer, inner or local space i.e.: "Or somewhere that we don't know about?"

Invisible assailants

"Something strange seems or appears to have happened, and why would they have to slash their way out of the tent, what caused the ensuing panic or confusion?"

It was as if they were escaping from some kind of altercation that had taken place, or the situation seemed or appeared to be agitated by someone or something that caused the fight or flight from the security of the tent, did something unknown reminiscent of the **Mary Celeste** try to keep them inside the tent, like the captain's cabin that was strangely boarded-up for some reason!

. . .

Who's afraid of the dark?

Who or what was it that seemed or appeared to be studying the group? Something caused them to panic and literally force their way out of the tent, by cutting or wildly slashing there way out, of what looks like only one side of the tent!

Its almost as if they had resisted some invisible assailant/s, that had taken them by complete surprise! And then tried to abduct them by force, or for some unknown reason they decided to get away from whatever happened at the tent, even stranger and contradictory evidence was found a third of a mile (500m) made by the group apparently having walked away from the scene without their **footwear** in an orderly single-file, apparently leading down the slope at walking pace, and with someone at the back of the column strangely wondering away from the main group and then returning, as if they were watching or looking to find out if whoever or whatever was responsible for the unprovoked attack, was still at the tent or was the threat following after them! Remember they had no proper **footwear** on, or proper winter clothing, because they had abandoned all their **cloths, footwear** and **food** back at the shelter of the tent.

The first two bodies were found under a cedar tree one mile from the camp-site, pieces of **human skin** were found on the cedar tree, where they must have tried to climb to get a better look back towards the camp-site, or is it possible that some were dropped from the **air** at some point, like in the **cattle mutilations**, that could account for some of the bruising? We don't know!

Unquiet voices

On the **27th February** two of the search party **Yury Koptelov** and **Michael Sharavin**, who found the bodies of **George Krivonischenko** and **Yury Doroshenko**, a mile (1,500m) away, lying side by side and having been stripped down to their underwear, as well as their bear feet!

For some unknown reason they had been trying to get away from the tent! Next, they found **Igor Dyatlov**, a 1,000ft or (300m) from the cedar tree, the Mansi or indigenous tribe continued to search the mountain **Kholat Syakhl** with their dogs, until one of the German Shepherd's called: (Alma) found the body of **Zina Kolmogorova** in 4ins of snow about one third of a mile (500m) from the other three bodies.

Half-way between the cedar tree and the tent, and half-way between the bodies of **Zina Kolmogorova** and **Igor Dyatlov**, who's body was the only one that was warm, because he had melted the snow underneath him when he fell to the ground, so it begs the question, why weren't the others found under the same circumstances?

Two months later the remaining four members of the group were found on the **4th May** approximately 230ft from the cedar tree, under 15ft of snow! The bodies of **Luda Dubinina, Alexander Kolevatov, Semyon Zolotarev** and **Nicolai Thibeaux-Brignolle** were all found together.

On two of the sweaters found on the bodies of **George Krivonischenko** and **Yury Doroshenko**, were later to have certain levels of **radiation!**

AUTOPSIES

The autopsies were carried out by the medical examiner: **Boris Vozrozhdenny** soon after the bodies had been found.

. . .

GEORGE KRIVONISCHENKO

"Remember there is nothing more deceptive than the obvious"

There were bruises on his forehead and around the **left temporal bone.** Diffuse bleeding in the right temporal and occipital region due to damage to the temoralis muscle. Tip of the nose was missing, and he had frostbitten ears.

There were bruises on the **right side** of the **chest** and on the **hands.** Detachment of the epidermis (skin) and a portion of the skin from the **right-hand** had been found in his **mouth!** Bruises on the thighs with minor scratches, and a bruise on the **left-buttock,** with abrasions on the outer side of the **left thigh,** and bruises on the **left leg** and a burn on the **left leg.**

The official cause of **Yury Doroshenko's** death was **hypothermia!** And the questionable possibility of **"paradoxical undressing"** he was found dressed in a long sleeved shirt, swimming pants, and a torn sock on his **left leg**, he was not wearing any **footwear!**

YURY DOROSHENKO

Yury Doroshenko had frozen to death and was found with **George Krivonischenko** beneath the cedar tree. The results of the autopsy were as follows: his ear, nose and lips were covered in blood, his right arm-pit was bruised and the inner surface of his right shoulder had two abrasions with no bleeding in the tissue, there was bruises on the right forearm, and the fingers of both hands had torn skin, there was bruised skin on the upper part of his legs, and there was signs of frostbite on his face and ears. There were also foamy grey fluid discharges on his right cheek, from the mouth.

The official cause of **Doroshenko's** death was given as **hypothermia** and had no *footwear* on, but was wearing socks!

. . .

ZINAIDA KOLMOGOROVA

Swelling of the Meninges (The Meninges is the system of membranes that cover the central nervous system and their swelling is an important feature of **hypothermia**) there was frostbite on the phalanges and palms of the hand, with a long bruise that encircled her right side.

When her body was found, she was still wearing her cloths! That included two-hats, a long-sleeved shirt, a sweater or (jumper), a second shirt and a second sweater (jumper) with torn cuffs. In addition she was wearing trousers, cotton athletic pants, ski-pants, three pairs of socks, and she had no *footwear* on!

IGOR DYATLOV

The body of the leader of the group was found approximately 1,000ft (300m) from the cedar tree.

Dried blood on his lips, with numerous **dark-red scratches** on the lower part of his **right-forearm** and **palms** of his hand, there was **brown/red bruises** on the Metacarpophalangeal joints of his **right-hand,** that seems or appears to be a common injury in hand fighting, there was also brown/purple bruises on the **left-hand** with superficial wounds on the **2nd** and **5th** finger of the **left-hand,** with minor abrasions on the forehead.

Abrasions above the left eyebrow of a brown/red colour, and both knees were bruised without bleeding into the underlying tissue, there was also bruising on the lower part of the right-leg, and there was bright-red abrasions on both ankles, with haemorrhage into the underlying tissue, and there was no internal injuries!

The cause of death was stated as **hypothermia. Igor** was wearing a sweater, a fur coat (with pockets) which had not been buttoned-up, a long-sleeved shirt, ski pants over his pants. He had no *footwear* but was wearing a cotton sock on his left foot. He was also bareheaded.

RUSTEM SLOBODIN

The body was found 500ft (150m) behind **Zina Kolmogorova** and 600ft (180m) ahead of **Igor Dyatlov**. He was wearing **one boot!** On his right-foot, along with two shirts (one long-sleeved), two pairs of pants, four pairs of socks and a sweater.

Traces of blood discharge from the nose, swollen lips and swelling with a number of small, irregular shaped abrasions on the right side of the face. Minor brown/red abrasions on the forehead, two scratches **1.5cm** long and **0.3cm** apart. A brown/red bruise on the upper eyelid of the right eye with haemorrhage into the underlying tissues.

Abrasions on the left side of the face. The epidermis was torn from the right forearm. [As with **Igor Dyatlov**] there was bruise's in the area of the Metacarpophalangeal joints of both hands [only **Ivor Dyatlov's** right hand was so affected; which seems or appears that they could have put up a struggle of some kind! Which is a common injury in hand fights, using fists]

Brown/cherry coloured bruises on the medial aspects of the left arm and left palm, with bruising on the left tibia.

There was also a fracture of the frontal bone and haemorrhaging of the temporalis muscle of Rustem's skull. Despite some of the injuries he suffered, the cause of the death was given as **hypothermia.** The skull fracture may or could have been caused by a blunt object hitting him. It was observed in the autopsy that the blow or fall that could have caused the skull fracture would have resulted in shock and concussion followed by a loss of co-ordination that could or would have accelerated his death by **hypothermia**!

LYUDMILA DUBININA

She was found in a kneeling position, lying against a rock, next to a stream. Her injuries were not only inexplicable, but were by far the worst, her togue was missing, along with the muscles of the floor of her the mouth, and the autopsy does did not say if it was torn out or surgically removed! The was coagulated blood inside her stomach, which means it seems or appears that the woman's heart was still beating, and the blood supply was still flowing or under exertion of pneumatic pressure, so to speak.

The autopsy report said that her tongue was missing, soft tissue around the eyes was missing, eyebrows and left temporal area with partially exposed bone. Eyes were missing! Nose cartilage broken and flattened, four ribs were broken on the right side with two fractures lines visible, and six other ribs were broken with other fracture lines visible. Soft tissue of the upper lip were missing, teeth and upper jaw exposed. Massive haemorrhage in the heart's right atrium. Bruise on the left thigh. Damaged tissues around the left temporal bone.

She was wearing two sweaters, two shirts, underwear, long socks and a small hat. She was not wearing any footwear and in an attempt to protect her feet had cut a sweater in half and wrapped one half around her left foot! The other half of the sweater was found lying in the snow.

469

Her official cause of death was stated as haemorrhage into the right atrium of the heart, multiple fractured ribs and internal bleeding. Her fractures were symmetrical and are believed to be impossible to have been caused by falling onto rocks, quite apart from the lack of any external marks on the skin!

. . .

SEMYON ZOLOTAREV

Had suffered serious and seemingly inexplicable internal injuries, his eyeballs were missing, and the soft tissue around the left eyebrow was missing, thus exposing the bone. He had five ribs broken on the right side, along with two fracture-lines, and an open wound on his right side, which had exposed the bone!

. . .

ALEXANDER KOLEVATOV

Was found with the soft tissue around his eyes, having been removed, as well as his eyebrows, the skull bone was exposed, and he had a broken nose, along with an open wound behind the ear and a deformed neck.

. . .

NICOLAI THIBEAUX-BRIGNOLLE

Had multiple fractures to his temporal-bone with exstentions to the frontal and sphenoid bones, and had an haemorrhage on the lower forearm, including a bruise on the left side of his upper-lip.

In conclusion to the autopsy reports, that have left us hanging in the air, one is left with the impression, (*excuse the pun*) that it seems or appears that the members of the ill-fated group, could have been dropped from the air!

. . .

Half-truth

(Hypothermia)

Again this misleading information regarding **"hypothermia"** has come to the surface yet again, information that seems or appears to be fallacious as reason struggles with something of a mystery, in regards to what they seem to think happens when a person dies of the cold, even though there is nothing more practical than a good theory, it is often slain or compounded by an erroneous, and yet ugly fact.

Symptoms of mild hypothermia **may** be vague, with sympathetic nervous system excitation (shivering, hypertension, tachycardia, tachypnea, and vasoconstriction). These are all physiological responses to preserve heat. Cold diuresis, mental confusion, and hepatic dysfunction **may** also be present. Hyperglycemia **may** be present, as glucose consumption by cells and insulin secretion both decrease, and tissue sensitivity to insulin **may** be blunted. Sympathetic activation also releases glucose from the liver. In many cases, however, especially in alcoholic patients, hypoglycemia appears to be a more common presentation. Hypoglycemia is also found in many hypothermic patients, because hypothermia *may* be a result of hypoglycemia.

Low body temperature results in shivering becoming more violent. Muscle mis-coordination becomes apparent. Movements are slow and labored, accompanied by a stumbling pace and mild confusion, although the person *may* appear alert. Surface blood vessels contract further as the body focuses its remaining resources on keeping the vital organs warm. The subject becomes pale. Lips, ears, fingers and toes *may* become blue.

As the temperature decreases, further physiological systems falter and heart rate, respiratory rate, and blood pressure all decrease. This results in an expected heart rate in the 30s at a temperature of 28 °C (82 °F). Difficulty in speaking, sluggish thinking, and amnesia start to appear; inability to use hands and stumbling is also *usually* present. Cellular metabolic processes shut down. Below 30 °C (86 °F), the exposed skin becomes blue and puffy, muscle coordination becomes very poor, walking becomes almost impossible, and the person exhibits *incoherent/irrational behavior* including terminal burrowing or *even* a stupor. Pulse and respiration rates decrease significantly, but fast heart rates (ventricular tachycardia, atrial fibrillation) can occur. Major organs fail. Clinical death occurs!

Paradoxical undressing

Twenty to fifty percent of hypothermia deaths are associated with paradoxical undressing. This typically occurs during moderate to severe hypothermia, as the person becomes disoriented, confused, and combative. They *may* begin discarding their clothing, which, in turn, increases the rate of heat loss.

Rescuers who are trained in mountain survival techniques are taught to expect this; however, some *may* assume incorrectly that urban victims of hypothermia have been subjected to a sexual assault, like the woman:

Evelyn Consuela Roseman
Missing 411
WESTERN UNITED STATES & CANADA
BY
DAVID PAULIDES

This rather unusual story contains a germ of truth in regards to the terrible and tragic death and murder of **Evelyn Consuela Roseman**, whose body was found in **Yosemite National Park**, by three hikers next to Nevada Fall, her corduroy trousers were badly torn, and were found around her ankles; and her sweater was up around her head, as if it had been pulled up! She had a second sweater that was lying on a rock next to her feet.

At first it looked as if she had been assaulted and then murdered! Until more evidence was found near the **594ft** falls, so investigators assumed that she might have fallen off or had been pushed from the top of falls! If so why was her body nearly **50ft** from the base of the falls? Where they found a piece of the dead woman's brain! And more traces of corduroy from the trousers she was wearing.

Subterfuge

Like in **MISSING 411 The Devil's in the Detail. Page 57. Hoyt F. White. 1950 aged 33 years.** Who seems or appears to have conveniently fallen **75ft** off a cliff, and then was found **125ft** from the base of the cliff, and as **David Paulides** said, that's a long roll after a short alleged fall! Which could be a very clever way to disguise the true source of the fall!

Even though it seemed or appeared that there was evidence of a **sexual-nature**, its very probable that it could have been a passing opportunist or necrophiliac, but highly unlikely, because it is possible that the event was caused by something other than what was supposed to have happened, read the following story:

. . .

As if he were suffering from **"hypothermia"** like in our so-called **humane-society** when an old person living alone has sometimes found in their apartment in a state of disarray, and there seems or appears to have been a terrible struggle for life, against person or persons unknown, and the obvious scene looks to all intent and purposes, like a violent homicide, where the person was struggling against nothing more than an invisible killer or assailant called: **"hypothermia"** or is there something more frightening about these strange deaths that should be properly investigated, something that is being hidden right out in the open!

Continued

At the forest edge, under a large cedar, the searchers found the remains of a fire, along with the **first two bodies,** those of **Yuri Krivonischenko** and **Yuri Doroshenko, "shoeless!"** and dressed only in their underwear. The branches on the tree were broken up to five meters high, suggesting that someone could have climbed up to look for something. Between the cedar-tree and the camp the searchers found three more corpses, **Dyatlov, Zina Kolmogorova** and **Rustem Slobodin**, suggesting that they were attempting to return to the tent. They were found separately at distances of **300, 480** and **630** meters from the tree.

Searching for the remaining four travelers took more than two months. They were finally found on **May 4** under **4** meters of snow in a ravine 75 meters farther into the **woods** from the cedar tree. These four were better dressed than the others, and there were signs that those who had died first had apparently relinquished their clothes to the others. **Zolotaryov** was wearing **Dubinina's faux fur coat** and **hat,** while **Dubinina's** foot was wrapped in a piece of **Krivonishenko's** wool pants.

Investigation

February 26, 1959.

"The tent had been cut open from inside, and most of the skiers seemed or appeared to have fled in their socks!"

A legal inquest started immediately after finding the first five bodies. A medical examination found no injuries which might have led to their deaths! And it was concluded that they had all died of hypothermia! *Slobodin* had a small crack in his skull, but it was not thought to be a fatal wound.

An examination of the four bodies which were found in May changed the picture. Three of them had fatal injuries: the body of *Thibeaux-Brignolles* had major **skull damage,** and both *Dubinina* and *Zolotarev* had major chest fractures.

According to **Dr. Boris Vozrozhdenny,** the force required to cause such damage would have been extremely high. He compared it to the force of a car crash. Notably, the bodies had **no external wounds,** as if they were crippled by a high level of pressure. *Dubinina* was found to be missing her **tongue!** There had initially been some speculation that the indigenous Mansi people might have attacked and murdered the group for encroaching upon their lands, but investigation indicated that the nature of their deaths did not support this thesis; the hikers' footprints alone were visible, and they showed no sign of hand-to-hand **struggle.**

Although the temperature was very low, around −25 to −30 °C (−13 to −22 °F) with a storm blowing, the dead were only partially dressed. Some of them had only **one shoe,** while others had **no shoes** or wore only **socks.**

Theories

Many theories have arisen about the event, from paranormal activity to secret weapons tests, but avalanche damage is considered one of the more plausible explanations for this incident. One scenario under this theory is that moving snow knocked down the tent, ruining the campsite in the night. The party then cut themselves free and mobilized.

The snow would likely have contacted them and possibly ruined their boots and extra clothing. Being covered in wet snow in the sub-freezing temperatures created a serious hazard to survival, with exhaustion or unconsciousness from **hypothermia** possible in under 15 minutes. *Thibeaux-Brignolles, Dubinina, Zolotariov,* and *Kolevatov* were moving farther from the site, despite their remote location when they fell in the ravine where they were found – three of these bodies had major fractures. Being the only bodies with major injuries and lying 13 feet deep in a ravine could be considered evidence that they were mysterious dropped there!

Supporting factors for this theory are that avalanches are not uncommon on any slope that can accumulate snow. Despite claims that the area is not prone to avalanches, slab avalanches do typically occur in new snow and where people are disrupting the snowpack.

On the night of the incident, snow was falling, the campsite was situated on a slope, and the campers were disrupting the stability of the snowpack. The tent was also halfway torn down and partially covered with snow – all of which could support the theory of a small avalanche pushing snow into the tent.

Possibly negating the avalanche scenario would be that the investigators saw *footprints* leading from the campsite, and no obvious avalanche damage was noted. However, the footprints could have been preserved if there was no precipitation in the 25 days before the site was discovered and the supposed avalanche happened after most of the snow fell.

Journalists reporting on the available parts of the inquest files claim that it

states:

Six of the group members died of hypothermia! And three of fatal injuries.

There were no indications of other people nearby apart from the nine travelers on *Kholat Syakhl,* nor anyone in the surrounding areas.

The tent had been ripped open from within.

The victims had died 6 to 8 hours after their last meal.

Traces from the camp showed that all group members left the camp of their own accord, on *foot!*

To dispel the theory of an attack by the indigenous Mansi people, *Dr. Boris Vozrozhdenny* stated that the fatal injuries of the three bodies could not have been caused by another human being, "because the force of the blows had been too strong and no soft tissue had been damaged".

Forensic *radiation tests* had shown high doses of *radioactive contamination* on the clothes of a few victims.

Released documents contained no information about the condition of the skiers' internal organs.

The final verdict was that the group members all died because of a *"compelling natural force"*. The inquest ceased officially in May 1959 as a result of the "absence of a guilty party". The files were sent to a secret archive, and the photocopies of the case became available only in the 1990s, with some parts missing.

Controversy surrounding investigation

Some researchers claim some facts were missed, perhaps ignored, by officials:

12-year-old **Yury Kuntsevich,** who would later become head of the **Yekaterinburg-based Dyatlov Foundation** (see below), attended five of the hikers' funerals and recalls their skin had a **"deep brown tan"**. Some of the hikers' clothing (2 pants and sweater) were found to be **highly radioactive.**

Another group of hikers (about 50 kilometers south of the incident) reported that they saw strange **orange spheres** in the night sky to the north (likely in the direction of **Kholat Syakhl**) on the night of the incident. Similar **"spheres"** were observed in **Ivdel** and adjacent areas continually during the period of February to March 1959, by various independent witnesses (**including the meteorology service and the military**).

These were later confirmed to be test launches of R-7 intercontinental missiles by Eugene Buyanov. (**mm!**)

Some reports suggest that there was a great deal of scrap metal in the area and around the area, leading to speculation that the military had utilized the area secretly and might have been engaged in a cover-up.

The last camp of **Dyatlov's** group was located on direct way from **Baikonur Cosmodrome** (*where some test launches of the R-7s were executed*) to **Chyornaya Guba, Novaya Zemlya archipelago** (which was a major nuclear testing ground of the Soviet Union).

Aftermath

In 1967, Sverdlovsk writer and journalist Yuri Yarovoi published the novel *Of the Highest Degree of Complexity* which was inspired by this incident. Yarovoi had been involved in the search for **Dyatlov's group** and at the inquest, including acting as an official photographer for the search campaign and in the initial stage of the investigation, and so had insight into the events.

The book was written in the Soviet era when the details of the accident were kept secret, and Yarovoi avoided revealing anything beyond the official position and well-known facts.

Half-Truth

The book romanticized the accident and had a much more optimistic end than the real events – only the group leader was found deceased. Yarovoi's colleagues say that he had alternative versions of the novel, but both were declined because of censorship. Since

Yarovoi's death in 1980 all his archives, including photos, diaries and manuscripts, have been lost.

Some details of the tragedy became publicly available in 1990 following publications and discussions in **Sverdlovsk's** regional press. One of the first authors was Sverdlovsk journalist Anatoly Guschin. Guschin reported that police officials gave him special permission to study the original files of the inquest and use these materials in his publications. He noticed that a number of pages were excluded from the files, as was a mysterious **"envelope"** mentioned in the case materials list. At the same time photocopies of some of the case files started to circulate among other unofficial researchers. Guschin summarized his research in the book **The Price of State Secrets Is Nine Lives**. Some researchers criticized it due to its concentration on the speculative theory of a **"Soviet secret weapon experiment"**, but the publication aroused public discussion, stimulated by interest in the paranormal.

. . .

Indeed, many of those who remained silent for 30 years reported new facts about the accident. One of them was the former police officer **Lev Ivanov** (Лев Иванов), who led the official inquest in 1959. In 1990 he published an article along with his admission that the investigation team had no rational explanation of the accident.

While sceptics might dismiss the Soviet investigator's talk of **aliens,** believers are encouraged by reports of **strange lights** and **'bright orbs'** hovering in the night sky at around this time.

. . .

"The last photograph on the film in one of the cameras found in the tent appears to capture a giant flash against the night sky — but it could equally be the result of an accidental over-exposure!"

. . .

The one thing he feels sure about is that there was some sort of an official cover-up, which has served only to add to the mystery. But the Soviet Union was a place where concealing the truth much like the so-called free-west, was second nature to officials, high and low!

Accidents were routinely airbrushed from the record. Twenty years after the **Dyatlov incident,** a fatal release of anthrax from a germ warfare research establishment in the **Urals** was hushed up. The KGB seized all hospital records and, to this day, the site is off-limits. Just the same as:

Porton Down

A United Kingdom government military establishment. It is situated slightly northeast of Porton near **Salisbury** in Wiltshire, England. To the northwest lies the **MoD** (*Ministry of Defence*) Boscombe Down test range facility. On maps, Porton Down has a "Danger Area" surrounding the entire complex.

What do you think happened to these people?

'The Thing From Another World'

Based on the story by:
John W. Campbell, Jr.
Who goes there?

*"I bring you a warning... every one of you, listen to my voice.
Tell the world, tell this to everybody
Wherever they are, Watch the skies, everywhere, keep looking, keep
watching the skies..."*

. . .

A
'Pillar Of Fire'
Russia
1908
Tungus Mystery

**"And by a blast of God they perish and by the breath of his
nostrils are they consumed".**
"Sodom and Gomorra"
Genesis 19

The lord rained upon Sodom and Gomorra, fire and brimstone from heaven, and all the inhabitants of the cities, and that which grew upon the

ground... and Abraham stood before the lord; and he looked towards Sodom and Gomorra, and towards all the land of the plain, and behold, and, low, the smoke of the country went up as the smoke of a furnace, that was like a pillar of fire!

And there like the hand of God, a fiery chariot rode across across the heavens, as if Prometheus had stolen fire from the Gods, heralding a blinding ball of fire, from out of the unknown or strange flying object from out of the skies. Streaking across the horizon, like fire from heaven... that exploded like an Atomic-bomb at ground zero! That sent a shockwave across the world, like the humongous Russian Tsar-bomb... Exploded at:

NOVAYA-ZEMLYA
October 30 1961
Artic Bering-sea
A
Monster Bomb
57 Megaton Hydrogen bomb
It was one of the largest of its kind to be tested in the 1960s
A scaled down version of
A 100 Megaton bomb

The bible's book of Revelation 21:6 "that darkness and destruction would come upon creation and the beast shall reign. "Woe to you oh earth and sea, for the Devil sends the beast with wrath and fury because he knows the time is short..."

Alexander Pope

'Lo! Thy dread Empire, chaos! Is restored; Light dies before thy uncreating word: Thy hand great Anarch! Lets the curtain fall; and universal Darkness buries all,

Whatever it was it destroyed thousands of square-miles of Siberian forest in a remote area of Russia. The strange and eerie reports told of a colossal explosion on June 30 1908.

. . .

It was not until 1921, 13years later, before any Scientific exploration was attempted, after only vague rumours and unfound suspicions, as well as reports from hunters, herds-man and farmers in the wild vicinity or locality of Vanavara, an out-back trading post.

. . .

Scientific Exploration

Kuliks exploration were overwhelmed when they eventually climbed to the summit of Mt Shakhorma in the USSR or Soviet Union and what they saw chilled them to the bone... an unbelievable sight met their eyes "an area of 6,000 square miles had been raised to the ground...!" There was total and complete devastation, with hardly a tree left standing, with others had been flattened like the spokes of a wheel radiating outwards from a central point.

An unsolved mystery
Even to this day.

'Fire from heaven'

Spontaneous
Human combustion

'What's the matter with the cat?' says Mr Guppy, 'look at her! 'Mad, I think. And no wonder, living in this evil place.'

Mr Guppy takes the light. They go down, more dead than alive, and holding one another, push open the door of the back shop. The cat has retreated close to it, and stands snarling-not at them, at something on the ground, before the fire. There is a very little fire left in the grate, but there is a smouldering suffocating vapour in the room, and a dark greasy coating on the walls and ceiling.

The chairs and the table, and the bottle so rarely absent from the table, all stand as usual. On one chair-back, hang the old man's hairy cap and coat, so the old man must be somewhere in the room... he is.

They advance slowly... The cat remains where they found her, still snarling at something on the ground, before the fire and between the two chairs, what is it? Hold up the light. Here is a small burnt patch of flooring; here is the tinder from a little bundle of burnt paper, but not so light as usual, seeming to be steeped in something; and here is-is it the cinder of a small, charred and broken log of wood sprinkled with white ash, or is it coal? O horror, he is here! And it is from this that we run away, striking out the light and overturning one another into the street, is all that represents him.

"At last come the coroner
And his enquiry"

'That would seem to be an unlucky house, a destined house; but so we sometimes find it, and these are mysteries we can't account for!

. . .

The strange case
Of
Father Bertholi

Who suddenly cried out in agony-when those who heard his screams of pain, rushed to his aid, he was already enveloped by strange blue flames...! That were very difficult to put out, even using their hands and other bits of their clothing.

The eminent Italian surgeon, Battaglia had been called to the scene to examine father Bertholi, and found that part of one of the priests' arms had been totally consumed.

Battaglia dressed the burns, which were, "apart from those on the arm" extensive and appalling,

The mortification that had followed Dr Battaglia ministrations was partly due to filthy procedures and lack of hygiene... which caused rapid and complete infection of the wounds, and it would not be until a century latter that Dr Lister and others who clearly showed the link between dirt and decease, that was no doubt the cause of Father Bertholi' mortifications and not the strange and eerie fire from heaven.

Soon the priest would lapse into a coma, from which he would not awaken, a merciful release from his terrible suffering...

Daily Telegraph
4ᵗʰ January
1939

'Little Peter Seaton'

Peter had been put to bed and was to all intent and purposes fast asleep, when a friend of the family Harold Edwin Huxstep was alerted by the terrible screams of the little boy...

After rushing up-stairs to the room, he was unable to rescue the little boy 'It seemed' as if the room was like a furnace...! And a mass of flames, which shot out, burning my face and throwing me back across the hall. It was humanly impossible to get little Peter out...

"What had caused the strange and inexplicable fire?"

What had caused the terrible conflagration that was so powerful and so intense that it totally consumed the little boy?

Superintendent E.H Davies of the London Fire Brigade, who searched the room, could find no natural cause of such a strange and inexplicable fire... that was so intense, it left most of the furniture in little Peter' room untouched!

A strange and bizarre case
1922

On a summers afternoon, Mrs Johnson, who having just returned from her shopping, had just filled the kettle with water, while she stood at the sink

and then after putting on the kettle, which was on a small gas-stove and there with the window open in the eerie stillness that unquiet day, she had sat down in readiness of the kettle boiling in order to make herself a welcoming cup of tea, and not only one that she would not finish... but it would be the last thing on earth she would ever do!

When she was found or what was left of her... she had been consumed by a mysterious and almost heavenly fire that had left nothing of the woman except a pile of ashes...!

Eerie facts

She had died in some strange or weird blaze, which must have acted like a furnace, but the cremation had been so swift, that the woman's 'calcinated bones' were still lying inside her un-burned clothing...! And in her desperate struggle with some invisible assailant, She had knocked over the chair that she was sitting on, when the frightening and unprovoked attack took place.

Even though she had been burned to a blackened cinder, only inches way inches away, the overturned chair that she had presumably been sitting on, was practically undamaged, even though it was so close, just like the plastic table-cloth that was untouched 9ins away from the almost consumed body of Mrs Johnson, including the linoleum directly beneath the woman's ashes was only slightly charred, whoever or whatever it was that had brutally struck her down, had come like the fiery sword of the old scriptures and had ended her life in the twinkling of an eye, even though the rest of the room had remained untouched by this strange and eerie fire from heaven...!

. . .

Its as if something is trying to tell us about the world we think that we live in, by nature mimicking art"

. . .

And the midair collision of a United Airlines DC-8 and a TWA Super  Constellation propeller plane on December 16, 1960. The United plane, en route to Idlewild (as JFK was then called), was put into a holding pattern. However, due to poor visibility, a breakdown in the plane's communications system, and pilot error, the United plane was flying too high and off course, setting it directly in the path of the TWA flight that had been cleared to land at La Guardia.

The two planes struck each other over New Dorp, Staten Island. The TWA plane immediately fell, crashing at Miller Field, a military airstrip. However, the  United Flight was still airborne (despite being shorn of its right engine and part of the wing) and began descending toward Brooklyn.

Some have guessed that the pilot may have been trying to make an emergency landing in Prospect Park. However, the plane slammed down at the corner of Sterling Place and Seventh Avenue in Park Slope, destroying a funeral home and the aptly named **Pillar of Fire Church**!

Tragically, all 128 passengers and crew on the two planes along with six people on the ground died, making it the worst aeronautical disaster up to that time. Among the people on the ground were a caretaker of the church and a man selling Christmas trees. It is the only time such an in-air collision has taken place over a metropolitan area and—despite criticisms of how the federal government handled the investigation—ultimately led to better training for pilots and safer planes.

481

The end

www.ingramcontent.com/pod-product-compliance
Lightning Source LLC
Chambersburg PA
CBHW041126010626
45792CB00031B/2060